Contents

INTRODUCTION	4
FUNCTIONAL REQUIREMENTS	7
DETAILING PRINCIPLES	26
MATERIALS	40
FOUNDATIONS	58
MASONRY CONSTRUCTION	64
FOUNDATION & FLOOR DETAILS	79
WALL DETAILS	109
ROOF DETAILS	143
TIMBER FRAME CONSTRUCTION	172
FOUNDATION & FLOOR DETAILS	179
WALL DETAILS	195
ROOF DETAILS	221
STEEL FRAME CONSTRUCTION	236
STEEL FRAME DETAILS	239
STRUCTURAL INSULATED PANELS (SIPS)	258
SIP DETAILS	261
INSULATED CONCRETE FORMWORK (ICF)	284
GREEN ROOF	298
BIBLIOGRAPHY / FURTHER READING	310
INDEX	312

A SPECIAL THANK YOU TO
JOHN BRADLEY & JOHNATHON CLOUS
FOR THEIR CONTRIBUTIONS TO THE BOOK

The information contained in this ebook is for educational purposes only.

All rights reserved. No part of this publication may be reproduced, distributed, or transmitted in any form or by any means, including photocopying, recording, or other electronic or mechanical methods, without the prior written permission from the author.

Users of this guide are advised to use their own due diligence when working up construction details. Whilst we believe that the contents reflect current Building Regulation requirements it is the architect, contractor or project manager overall responsibility to ensure compliance and to seek approval from Buidling Control Officers or other certifiers, as no warranty is given or should be implied as to the accuracy of the information for any specific application.

It should be noted that only one of many permutations of thermal insulation type and positioning is shown in each example. Insulation requirements, performance, positioning, installation all vary according to manufacturer.

Under no circumstances should any of the contents of this book be used as construction drawings. Drawings must always be checked and verified by a fully qualified architect or associated professional. The entire contents of this book and associated digital files are for educational purposes only.

To read the full terms of use follow this link: http://www.firstinarchitecture.co.uk/about/terms-of-use/

Copyright © 2017 by Emma Walshaw
First In Architecture
ISBN 978-1-9163343-0-4

INTRODUCTION

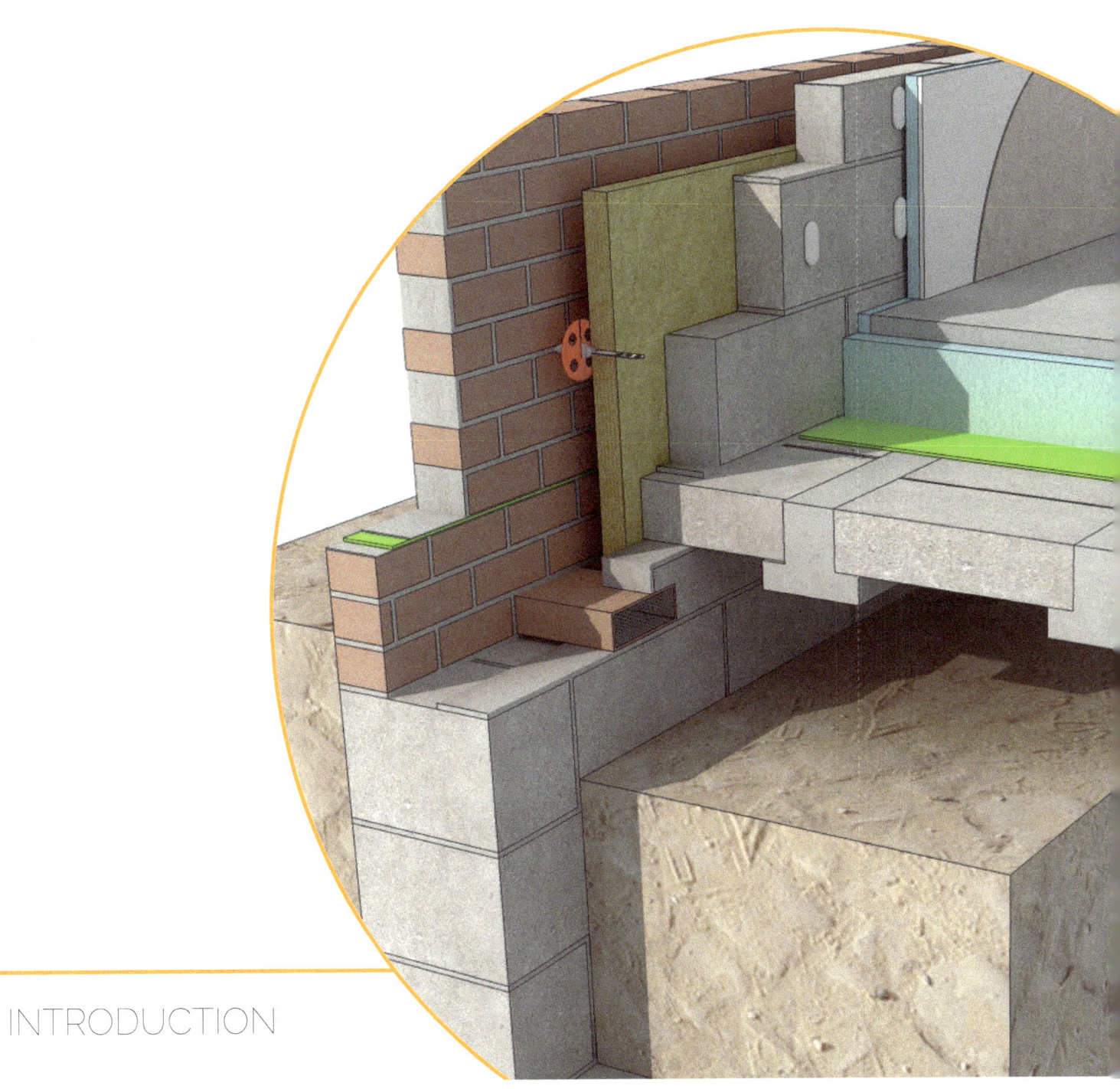

INTRODUCTION

INTRODUCTION

This book is the third edition of the popular book Understanding Architectural Details, the first in the construction detailing series.

I originally developed this series after realising that architectural and construction details are difficult to learn. Throughout my university experience I always felt I was lacking in both knowledge and understanding of construction details, and as much as I tried to learn, I found it hard to find literature that encompassed all of my queries and knowledge gaps. When I did find information on detailing, I found it difficult to absorb the black and white images with an abundance of labels, arrows and lines which seemed to just blur into one on the page.

While working in practice I still felt my knowledge was lacking, but as I was working on feasibility and planning schemes I was short of the opportunity to develop my knowledge with construction drawings.

I decided to take things into my own hands and develop a manual of architectural and construction details that would build my knowledge base, and while compiling the information solidify my understanding. I soon got the opportunity to work in more construction project stages and used this experience to develop my collection further. As I developed my manual, I realised just how useful it could be to students and professionals in the architecture and construction field that could benefit from breaking down the elements of construction and absorbing the information in a visual way.

I have purposefully included both 2D and 3D colour details to help the reader really grasp the elements of construction and understand how the building is put together. I hope that being able to compare a 2D detail with a 3D colour detail will give far more of an explanation than a 2D detail alone.

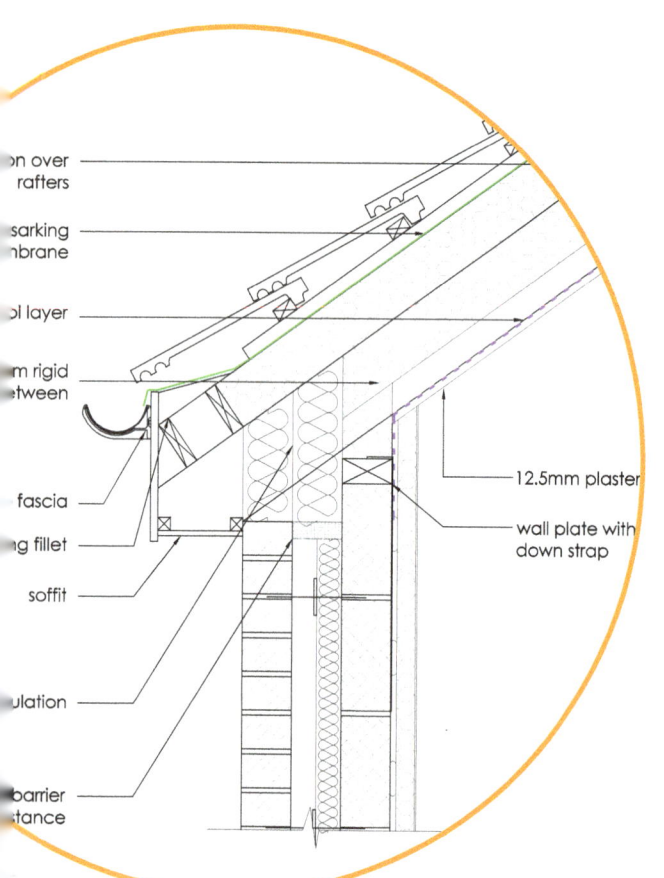

I am not an expert, I do not know everything there is to know about construction detailing. These drawings have been produced for educational and instructional purposes only. Some information has been removed or omitted for clarity in description/information. Under no circumstances should these drawings be used as building regulation/construction drawings. They are a guide, and should only be used as such.

These details are not here to provide ready made solutions but to inform, and be used as an instructional tool.

I invite you to study the details, and decide for yourself whether you can find a better solution to the problems we face in construction - air leakage, water ingress (and so on). Question every aspect of the detail presented to you, in order for you to gain a full understanding. Be aware that often there are many solutions to one problem, and here we are only able to demonstrate a fraction of the solutions that are available to us.

I hope that you find this book useful, and that it helps you to improve your knowledge and understanding of basic architectural detailing.

Emma
First In Architecture

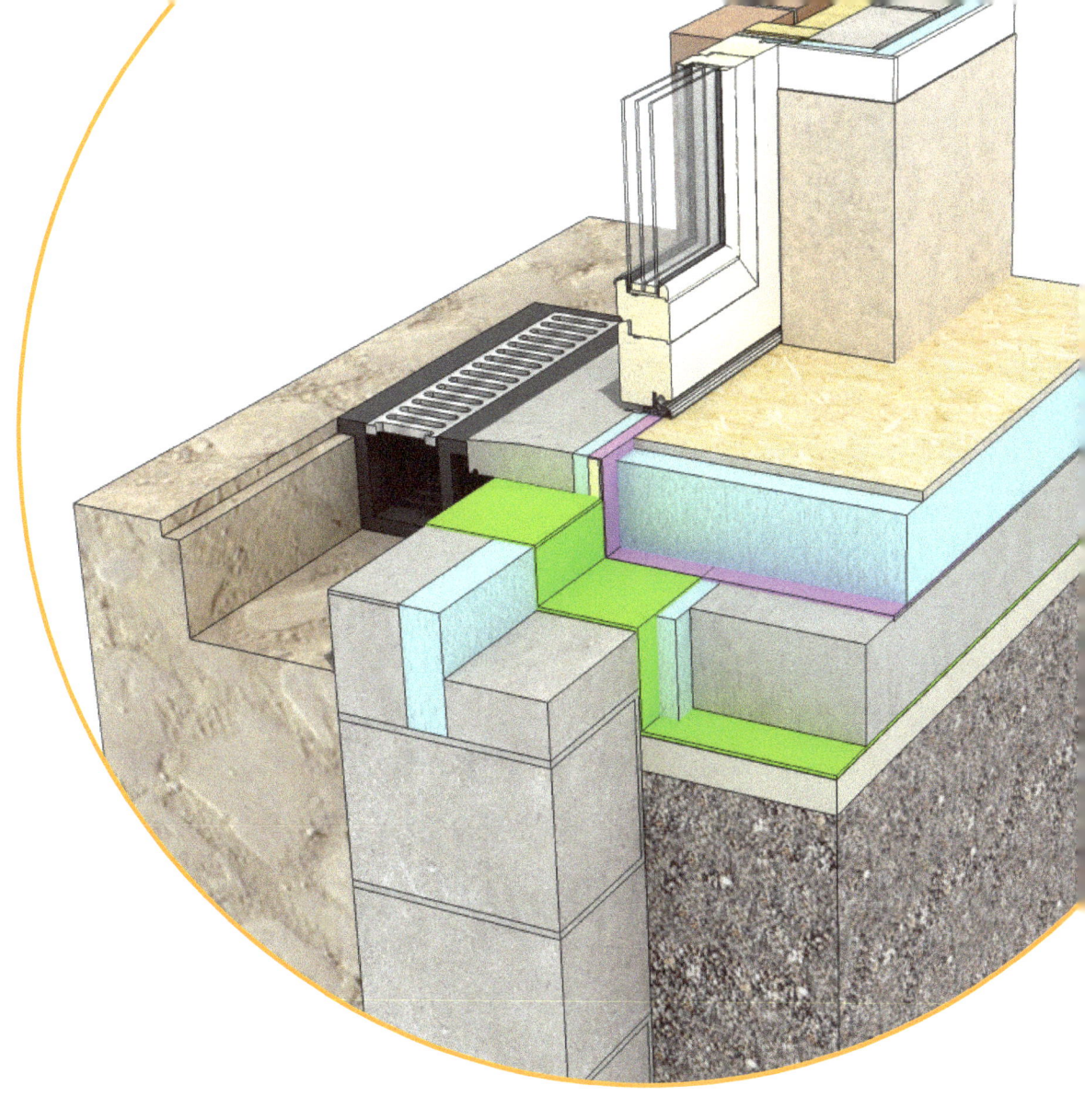

FUNCTIONAL REQUIREMENTS

In this section we look at the key requirements of a building. Much of the best work in the area of the principles underlying architectural detailing has been done in a north American context, by authors such as Edward Allen, and John Sraube and Joseph Lstiburek at the Building Science corporation. Construction methods and climate in the UK differ from north America and this section draws on the work of these authors but applies it to the UK context.

It is estimated that we now spend on average 90% of our time in buildings - much more than in the past. Buildings are structures that enclose human activities, and their primary function could be thought of as enabling people to carry out their activities of daily life in comfort.

The building fabric and building services should be designed so as to separate the external environment from the internal environment in order to produce a comfortable internal environment, by ensuring that the transfer of water, air, heat, light and sound is appropriately regulated. Of course, buildings cannot carry out that purpose unless they are sound and safe structures, in other words that they are strong and stable structures that do not pose a hazard to people in and around them.

The requirements we are placing on buildings are changing. The scope of the regulatory framework has come to embrace a wider range of requirements; for example as well as keeping weather out, we now require buildings to be more air tight than in the past. This can have an effect on occupants' health and comfort and we need to take this into account in considering the impact of changing building requirements.

The Building Regulations define the functional requirements of buildings, through the individual Parts and the associated Approved Documents provide guidance on how these requirements can be met. There are 14 Parts to the Building Regulations, and this section covers the requirements relating to the following:

- 1 - Strength and stability
- 2 - Environmental protection
- 3 - Conservation of heat and power
- 4 - Airflow and ventilation
- 5 - Light
- 6 - Acoustics
- 7 - Fire

1 - STRENGTH AND STABILITY

Approved Document A: Structure covers this requirement.

"Strength is the ability of a structure to resist a force (e.g. wind, load or gravity) and is a function of the tensile and compressive strength of most of the commonly used materials."

"Stability is the ability of a structure to remain in or return to a stable, balanced position when forces act on it."

Approved Document Part A stipulates that a building should be constructed so that the combined dead, imposed and wind loads are sustained and transmitted by it to the ground safely and without causing such deflection or deformation of any part of the building, or such movement of the ground, as will impair the stability of any part of another building. The building must be constructed so that in the event of accident the building will not suffer collapse to an extent disproportionate to the cause.

So that buildings do not deflect, deform or collapse they must be strong and stable. A structure's ability to withstand a load depends on its overall strength. Failure of building structures is caused either by material failure (governed by material strength) or by structural instability (governed by geometry and size).

To ensure that low-rise residential building is stable under likely imposed and wind loading conditions:

- The internal and external walls should form a robust three-dimensional box structure.
- The internal and external walls should be adequately connected by masonry bonding or mechanical connections.
- The roof and any intermediate floors should provide local support to the walls and transfer wind forces to buttressing elements.

2 - ENVIRONMENTAL PROTECTION

The building envelope or enclosure effectively separates the external environment from the internal environment. Approved Document Part C requires that the building enclosure should:

- Resist the passage of moisture from the ground to the inside of the building
- Not be damaged by moisture from the ground and not carry moisture from the ground to any part which would be damaged by it
- Resist the penetration of precipitation to components of the structure that might be damaged by moisture
- Resist the penetration of precipitation to the inside of the building
- Be designed and constructed so that their structural and thermal performance are not adversely affected by interstitial condensation
- Not promote surface condensation or mould growth

2.1 EXTERNAL ENVIRONMENT

The building envelope must be designed to cope with temperature variation, wind, rain and snow. These forces can act in combination to produce severe effects, for example, wind-driven rain. The effect of the external environment on a building depends on its altitude, latitude and longitude. Figure 1.1 shows the considerations that will influence the impact of the external environment:

- number of storeys
- building's exposure
- way in which architectural features provide shelter
- complexity of the building envelope

Figure 1.1 - Factors influencing the impact of the external environment

2.2 WATER

It has been estimated that 75% of building failures are due to water. These occur mainly through rain water penetration, but also interstitial condensation that occurs within the building fabric and surface condensation affects building finishes.

Water also affects the performance of the building in other ways, particularly in terms of thermal performance and the effect on human health. For example, damp external walls exhibit considerably lower thermal resistance, while surface condensation on the inside of houses causes moulds, which are not good for human health.

Water is attracted to hygroscopic materials (which have capillary pores) in both the liquid and vapour state. Liquid water is sucked into very small tubes, capillaries which are present in porous materials. The sucking, or wicking, of interconnected capillaries is what causes water to be drawn up into a brick for example, or into the end grain of timber. Hydrophobic materials, such as glass, steel and plastics, repel water, which causes water to bead, for example, rain on oil soaked concrete.

Liquid water tends to exist in large clusters, because of molecular attraction. When liquid water evaporates as its temperature increases, the clusters break up into their individual vapour molecules. The size difference between liquid water molecule clumps and lone water vapour molecules explains how materials such as Gore-Tex and breather membranes such as Nilvent, Spirtech and Tyvek can simultaneously be watertight and vapour permeable.

All buildings are made of relatively small components. Each joint between materials is a potential leak, and moisture has many ways to move through any gap in the structure:

- Gravity: water will naturally move downwards
- Surface tension: causes water to cling to underside of a surface where it can run through into an opening
- Capillary action: water can also move upwards - cracks or holes with smooth sides may act as capillaries and by mechanisms of surface tension, draw in water
- Momentum: wind-driven rain possesses momentum that can move it through an opening
- Pressure differential: water will move from areas of higher pressure to areas of lower pressure

Deflection is the first line of defence against moisture ingress. Driving rain can be minimised by good siting, plantings, landscaping and choice of building height. The shape of the roof and overhangs is important; by shadowing and redirecting airflow, as shown in Figure 1.4 hipped roofs provide the opportunity to shelter walls from rain on all four sides.

Figure 1.2 shows the forces leading to moisture ingress and Figure 1.3 how they can be neutralised (adapted from Lstiburek).

Forces	Neutralised by
Gravity	Wash and overlap
Surface tension	Overhang and drip
Capillary action	Capillary break
Absorption	Drain and weep
Momentum	Labrynth
Air pressure differentials	Rainscreen assembly

Figure 1.2 - Forces leading to moisture ingress

Wash	A slope on a horizontal surface to drain water away from vulnerable areas of a building eg. window or door sill, sloping roof, slopes to drain, pitch to drain, ground slope away from building
Overlap	A higher surface extended over a lower surface so water moved by the force of gravity cannot run behind or beneath them. Cannot be used on a level surface e.g. roof slates, timber cladding.
Overhang and drip	Water running down wall can be kept away from openings by creating a projecting profile above the opening (overhang) and by creating a continuous groove in the underside of the projection (drip) so that gravity will pull the adhering water free of the overhang e.g. door and window sills
Capillary break	Water can be pulled by capillary action through a narrow crack; a capillary break is a crack/gap large enough so that a drop of water cannot bridge it e.g. cavity wall.
Drain and weep	Collect and conduct away water that may leak through the outer leaf e.g. cavity tray and weep hole
Labrynth	A joint in which a straight line cannot be constructed through it without passing through solid material
Rainscreen	A detail that blocks air currents passing through a joint to prevent water being pushed through by differential pressures e.g. ventilated cavity

Figure 1.3 - Neutralising moisture ingress

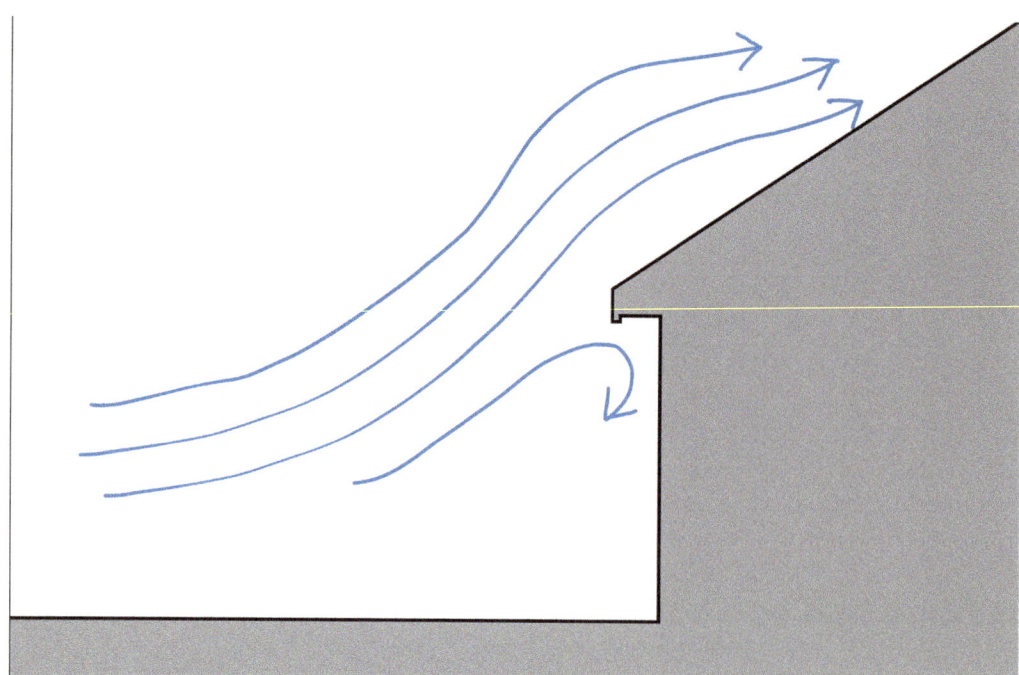

Figure 1.4 - Deflection of airflow with a pitched roof overhang

Once water is on the wall it will form a film and begin flowing downward under the force of gravity. Wind flowing over the surface will tend to deflect the flow from this path and may even force the water upward. Surface features such as trim (slopes and drip edges), surface texture and openings influence the flow paths, either concentrating or dispersing surface flows.

Siting, building shape and surface rainwater control rarely provide complete rain control therefore some strategy to deal with rainwater that penetrates the surface has to be used. There are three fundamental strategies, as outlined by Straube and Lstiburek:

- Mass walls: this requires the use of, for example solid masonry with enough storage mass and moisture tolerance to absorb all rainwater that is not drained or otherwise removed from the outer surface. This moisture is eventually removed by evaporative drying before it reaches the inner surface of the wall. A large mass of material is required to provide sufficient moisture storage. Examples include adobe, solid masonry.
- Perfect barriers: stop all water penetration at a single plane e.g. some window frames, some metal and glass curtain walling systems. Some systems use factory built wall elements that are perfect barriers. The joints between them may also be designed as perfect barriers e.g. a single line of caulking/sealant. These are not very effective.
- Screen-drained walls: this strategy assumes some rainwater will penetrate the outer surface and remove this water by designing an element that provides drainage within the wall e.g. cavity wall.

3 - CONSERVATION OF HEAT AND POWER

The requirement for buildings to be energy efficient is one of the key requirements imposed on designers and builders. The burning of fossil fuels to provide the energy to heat, cool and power buildings contributes nearly half the UK's CO_2 emissions. The Government is committed to reduce the UK's greenhouse gas emissions by 80% by 2050 and reducing emissions from buildings is a key way of achieving this. Approved Document Part L of the Building Regulations is the vehicle by which the Government seeks to improve energy efficiency by reducing heat loss from buildings.

3.1 - HEAT LOSS

Heat is lost from buildings in two ways. It is lost through the fabric of the building (the building envelope) by radiation, convection and conduction exchanges. This is known as **fabric heat loss**. Buildings are not completely airtight and heat is also lost by heated air leaving the building through gaps in the building fabric and being replaced by colder air that needs to be heated. This is known as **ventilation heat loss**.

Total Heat Loss (Q) = Fabric Heat Loss (Qf) + Ventilation Heat Loss (Qv)

3.1.1 - FABRIC HEAT LOSS

The amount of heat that is lost through this route (Qf) depends on three things:

- The difference between the inside design temperature and the outside temperature (ΔT)
- The area of the different building elements exposed to the temperature differential (A)
- The rate at which heat flows through the different building elements exposed to the temperature differential, known as the U-value (U)

This can be represented as the equation:

$Q_f = \Sigma (U.A.\Delta T)$ measured in Watts (Σ simply means 'the sum of')

The temperature differential and area of the building elements are straightforward, but the U-value is an important concept that needs further explanation.

3.1.2 - U-VALUES

A measure called a U-value, (also called the thermal transmittance coefficient) is the conventional way of expressing the rate at which heat flows through a building element such as an external wall, window, ground floor or roof. Its formal definition is:

"The rate at which heat flows, in Watts, through one square metre of a building element when the air temperature either side differs by one degree (K or °C)"

The units in which the measure is expressed are therefore:

W/m^2K

Watts per square metre per degree Kelvin (the formal SI unit of temperature: a change in temperature of 1K is the same as a change in temperature of 1°C).

The U-value is a measure of the rate at which a building element transmits heat. The higher the U-value, the more heat is transmitted, or lost, through the building element. From an energy conservation point of view therefore, **the lower the U-value of a building element the better**.

The Building Regulations specify maximum U-values that should not be exceeded for different building elements. Approved Document Part L 1A sets the 'reasonable limits' shown in Figure 1.5. In practice, compliance with the requirements of the Building Regulations to conserve heat and power mean that design U-values need to be much lower than these 'reasonable limits'. The notional dwelling specification shown in the table represents the U-values that designers should be aiming to achieve.

Element	Limiting U value (fabric elements of building) (W/m²K)	Notional dwelling specification U value (W/m²K)
Wall	0.30	0.18
Floor	0.25	0.13
Roof	0.20	0.13
Windows/Doors	2.00	1.40

Figure 1.5 - Table of U-values

3.1.3 - CALCULATING U-VALUES

A U-value is a measure of thermal transmittance. Heat flow through a material is usually expressed in terms of thermal resistance (R). Transmittance is the inverse of resistance and can therefore be expressed as the reciprocal of resistance:

$$\text{Thermal Transmittance (U-value)} = \frac{1}{\text{Thermal Resistance (R)}}$$

A building element is composed of a number of materials, each of which has a resistance to the flow of heat. The U-value of a building element can therefore be calculated by adding together the thermal resistances of the components of the building element (ΣR) and dividing the result into one (taking its reciprocal). The shorthand expression of that, and the formula for calculating a U-value (U) is:

$$U = \frac{1}{\Sigma R} \quad (\text{Units W/m2K})$$

3.1.4 - THERMAL RESISTANCE

The amount of resistance that a material offers to the heat flow through it depends on the thermal properties of the material and its thickness. It can be calculated from the following formula:

$$R = \frac{d}{\lambda}$$

R is the thermal resistance of a material (m²K/W)
d is the thickness of the material (in metres)
λ is the thermal conductivity of the material (W/mK)

3.1.5 - SURFACE AND AIRSPACE RESISTANCE

In a building element it is not only materials that provide a resistance to the transfer of heat; surfaces and airspaces or empty cavities also offer resistances that need to be taken into account in calculating U-values. These are usually standard values that can be found from tables such as those published by CIBSE.

3.1.6 - THERMAL CONDUCTIVITY

The thermal conductivity (λ) of a material is the heat flow in watts across a thickness of 1 square meter when the air temperature either side differs by one degree.

Materials which have a high thermal conductivity, such as copper, are good conductors of heat and therefore poor thermal insulators. Conversely, materials that have a low thermal conductivity, such as expanded polystyrene, are poor conductors of heat and therefore good thermal insulators. A table of the thermal conductivity of common construction materials is shown below.

Material	Thermal Conductivity (W/mK)
Aluminium	190.00
Steel (mild)	60.00
Concrete (medium density)	1.13
Tiles (clay)	1.00
Brickwork	0.77
Lightweight concrete block	0.57
Plaster (dense)	0.57
Plasterboard	0.21
Aircrete block	0.18
Timber	0.13
Glass fibre insulation	0.04

Figure 1.6 - Table of thermal conductivity of common construction materials

The thermal conductivity figures are based on measurements in controlled environments and make standard assumptions about, for example, moisture content. In practice, the moisture content of materials may be higher than assumed. If a material, such as mineral wool insulation, becomes wet then its thermal conductivity will be higher (because thermal conductivity of water is greater than that of air).

3.1.7 - CALCULATING A U-VALUE: WORKED EXAMPLE

Calculation of a U-value for an external cavity wall
The structure of the wall is shown in the diagram below along with information on the thermal conductivities of the materials and standard values for surface and air gap resistances. From this information, the thermal resistances of the components of the wall are calculated. These are then added to the resistances of the surfaces and air gap. The total resistance is then divided into one to determine the U-value.

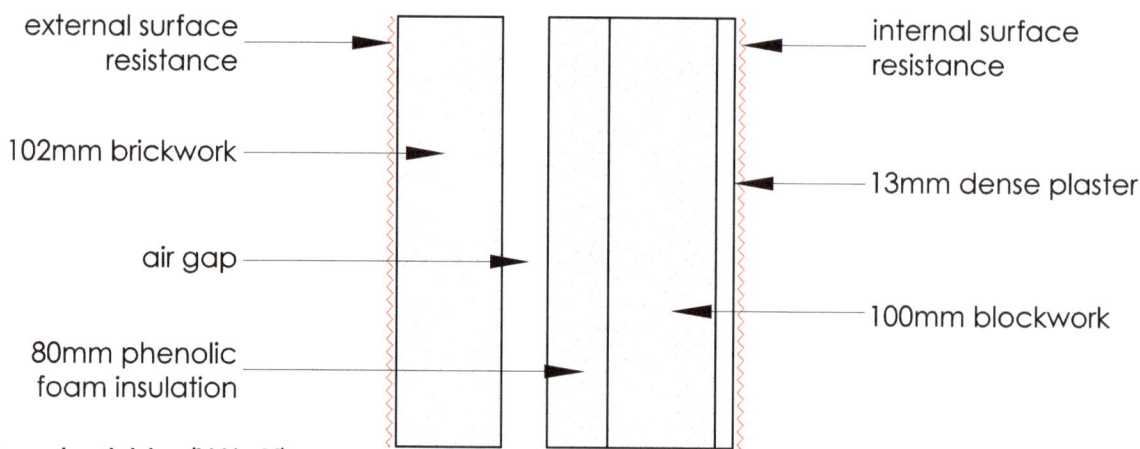

Thermal conductivities (W/mK)

Dense plaster	0.50
Lightweight blockwork	0.11
Brickwork	0.84
Phenolic foam insulation	0.02

Surface and air gap resistances (m²K/W)

Internal surface	0.12
External surface	0.06
Air gap	0.18

	Thickness (d)	Thermal Conductivity (λ)	Thermal Resistance R=d/λ
Internal Surface	-	-	0.120
Plaster	0.013	0.50	0.026
Blockwork	0.100	0.11	0.909
Insulation	0.080	0.02	4.000
Air gap	-	-	0.180
Brickwork	0.102	0.84	0.121
External Surface	-	-	0.060

Total Resistance (ΣR) = 5.416

U-value = 1/ΣR = 1/5.416 = 0.18 W/m²K

U-value = 0.18 W/m²K

SECTION 1 - FUNCTIONAL REQUIREMENTS

3.1.8 - THERMAL BRIDGING

Standard U-value calculations assume that the materials in the building element are homogeneous, in other words that the thermal resistance is constant in the plane of the material. In practice that is not always the case. There may be gaps in the layer of material, or the material may be 'bridged' in some way.

For example in a timber frame external wall construction, the timber studs interrupt, or bridge, the insulation layer in the framed wall. In a cold roof the ceiling joists interrupt the layer of insulation placed between the joists. In a cavity wall, a combined lintel bridges the cavity. These are all examples of thermal bridging.

A thermal bridge is created when materials that are poorer insulators than surrounding materials come in contact, allowing heat to flow through the path created. Thermal bridging has become a significant source of heat loss as insulation standards have improved and this has to be allowed for in estimating the heat loss from buildings.

3.2 - VENTILATION HEAT LOSS

Building fabric has improved over time to meet more stringent Building Regulation requirements, U-values have therefore declined and building fabric heat loss has decreased. There has been less regulatory concern with airtightness with the result that ventilation heat loss can now account for up to a third of total heat loss in a new dwelling.

The ventilation heat losses in a building are determined by:

- the volume of air passing through the building that requires heating to achieve the desired internal temperature (calculated by the number of air changes per hour multiplied by the volume of the building)
- the amount of heat energy required to raise the air temperature by one degree (the specific heat capacity of air)
- the difference between the temperature to which the inside of the building is designed to be heated and the temperature outside of the building

Ventilation heat loss can therefore be estimated using the following equation:

$$Qv = \frac{Cv.N.V.\Delta T}{3600}$$

Qv is the ventilation heat loss (Watts)

Cv is the specific heat capacity of air - usually given as 1210 J/m³K

N is the number of air changes per hour (ach): divided by 3600 gives air changes per second, which is the correct unit as Qv is measured in Watts, or Joules per second

V is the volume of the building that is conditioned, or heated

ΔT is the difference in temperature between the inside and outside of the building

The recommended ventilation requirements for UK dwellings are between 0.5ach and 1.0ach.

3.3 - HEAT LOSS: THEORY AND PRACTICE

The above equations are only an approximation of what is called 'steady state' heat transfer, in which variables such as temperature differential do not change. Such formulations cannot provide a dynamic picture of heat transfer over time, which would be necessary to assess for example, whether summer overheating is likely to occur. To do this, much more complicated dynamic models are required.

Furthermore, thermal models tend to seriously underestimate actual heat loss from a building. Research carried out by Leeds Beckett University has shown that a significant discrepancy exists between the energy performance of a dwelling as designed and that realised in practice, typically around 20% higher than predicted by modelling. The difference between measured and predicted performance can be accounted for by factors such as:

- Thermal bypasses. A thermal bypass is set up whenever air movement is able to take place in such a way as to reduce the effectiveness of an insulation layer, for example via the party wall cavity or if insulation boards in a cavity wall are not butted firmly up to the blockwork.
- Higher than predicted thermal bridging, for example as a result of the timber fraction in a timber frame wall being significantly higher than the nominal value.
- Real fabric U-values higher than nominal, for example installing windows who 'centre page' U-values equate to the design U-value but whose 'whole window' U-value is significantly higher. Another example would be where components such as insulation become damp, resulting in higher heat loss than predicted using manufacturer's data on thermal conductivity in laboratory conditions.
- As-built differing from design intent. This can happen in relation to the fabric in many ways, for example the omission of a perimeter insulation detail. It can also happen in relation to airtightness, for example service penetrations not being properly sealed.

4 - AIRFLOW AND VENTILATION

Ventilation is dealt with in Approved Document Part F of the Building Regulations. The requirement is that there should be adequate means of ventilation provided. The ventilation system should:

- extract water vapour from areas with high rates of generation (e.g. kitchens, utility rooms and bathrooms) before it can spread widely;
- extract hazardous pollutants from areas where they are produced in significant quantities, before they can spread widely;
- rapidly dilute pollutants and water vapour in habitable rooms, occupiable rooms and sanitary accommodation;
- provide a minimum supply of outdoor air for occupants and disperse residual pollutants and water vapour;
- perform in a way which is not detrimental to the health of people in the building;

The control of airflow is important for several reasons: to control moisture damage, reduce energy losses, and ensure occupier comfort and health.

- Moisture control: water vapour in the air can be deposited within the building envelope by condensation and cause health, durability and performance problems.
- Energy savings: warmed air leading out of a building is replaced by (usually) colder air which requires energy to heat it - about a third of space heating energy consumption is due to air leakage through the building enclosure.
- Comfort and health: cold draughts and excessively dry wintertime air that result from excessive air leakage directly affect human comfort, airborne sound transmission control requires good airflow control and external odours and gases can cause health and comfort problems.

Airflow across buildings is driven by wind pressures, stack effects, and mechanical air handling equipment such as fans, illustrated in Figure 1.7. A continuous, stiff, durable, air permeable barrier system is required between the external and internal space to control airflow driven by these forces. Uncontrolled air leakage through the building envelope is a major cause of building performance problems.

Increased airtightness must be matched by an appropriate ventilation system to dilute pollutants, provide fresh air and control humidity levels.

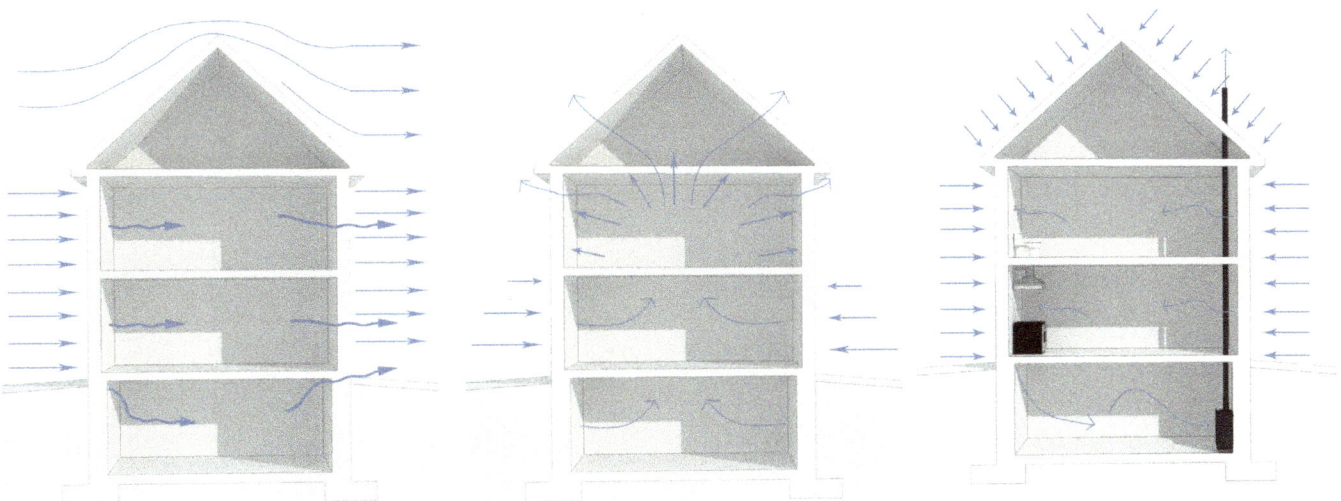

Wind effect   **Stack effect**   **Combustion and ventilation**

Figure 1.7 - Forces driving airflow through the building enclosure

Typical leakage paths through the building envelope are shown in Figure 1.8 below.

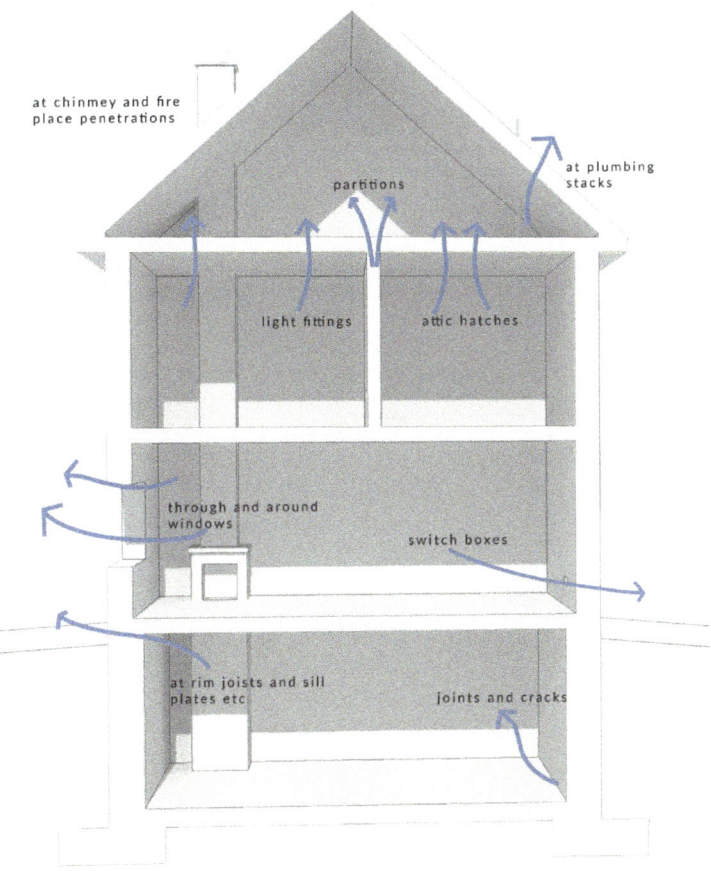

Figure 1.8 - Typical leakage paths

For airflow to occur there must be both:
- A pressure difference between two points, and
- A continuous flow path or opening connecting the points

The general approach taken to control airflow is to attempt to seal all openings at one plane in the building enclosure. The primary plane of airtightness is called the air barrier system: an assembly of materials including every joint, seam and penetration.

Winds pressure effects (see Figure 1.9 below). Low slope roofs tend to have mostly negative (uplift) pressures, especially on the leading edge. Roofs with slopes above 25° degrees experience positive pressures on the windward face and suctions on the leeward.

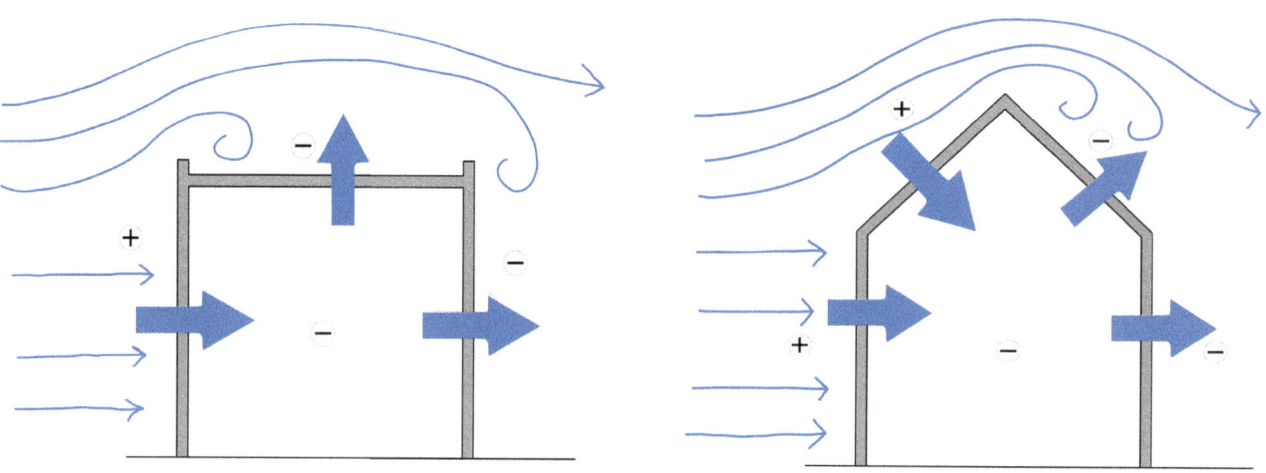

Figure 1.9- Wind pressure effects

Stack effect pressures (see Figure 1.10 below) are generated by variations in air density with temperature. The density of warm air is less than that of cold air. Therefore hot air rises and cold air sinks. In a building, during winter, as heated air rises it 'sucks in' colder air from outside.

Bathroom exhaust fans, clothes dryers, cooker hoods all exhaust air from a building. This creates a negative pressure inside the building that can cause inward air leakage through the building enclosure.

Figure 1.10- Stack effect pressures

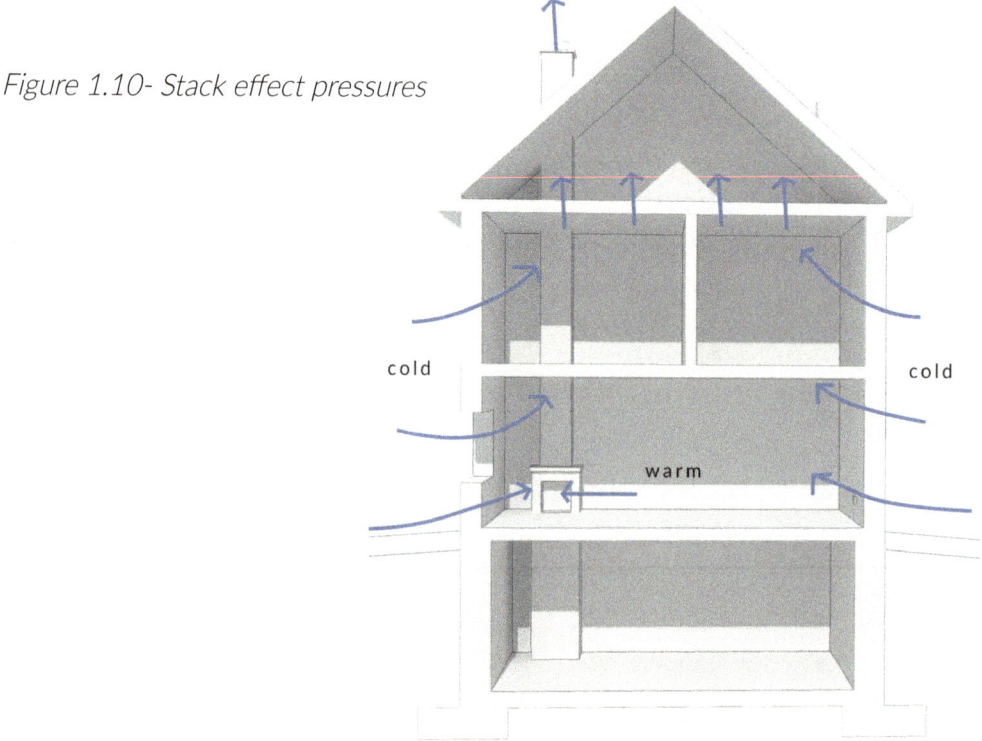

SECTION 1 - FUNCTIONAL REQUIREMENTS

It is generally accepted that pollutants, such as dust mites, pet allergens, pollen, moulds, fungi, bacteria and viruses are increasing in buildings and have an increasingly negative impact on human health, such as the prevalence of asthma. Some are introduced by occupants or are brought in from the outside. However, many are a result of the built environment itself, and in the main are due to environmental conditions of humidity and temperature that have only been experienced in buildings in the very recent past.

All these pollutants generally require very high levels of humidity to thrive. They cannot thrive, if relative humidity is kept between 40% and 60%. In addition, other chemical reactions such as those involving VOCs, are more dangerous to the human body as humidity levels rise, particularly at levels over 70% RH. At levels under 40% human mucus membranes become dry and more vulnerable to irritation from chemical pollutants and small particles. People become much more sensitive to odours at low RH levels, and people wearing contact lenses can suffer irritation. Under 35% RH the effect of static on the human body is considerable both internally and externally. For example external static shocks from walking on nylon carpets can be as high as 35,000 volts at low RH levels. Increasing RH to above 35% would automatically reduce the potential of static shock to 1,500 volts or less.

5 - ACOUSTICS

In addition to temperature and humidity, acoustic isolation is also important for comfort. As a result of the growing number of complaints about domestic noise disturbance and the potential litigation arising from these, Building Regulations have considerably improved acoustic insulation requirements since 2002.

There are a number of issues in relation to acoustics in buildings:
- sound insulation
- between dwellings
- between rooms in a building
- reverberation in rooms
- internal noise levels from building services
- outside noises
- noise emitted from the building

Approved Document Part E is intended to reduce the transmission of sound into, and between the rooms of residential buildings. The requirements are that dwellings, flats and rooms for residential purposes shall be designed and constructed in such a way that:

- they provide reasonable resistance to sound from other parts of the same building and from adjoining buildings; and
- that (a) internal walls between a bedroom or a room containing a WC, and other rooms; and (b) internal floors, provide reasonable resistance to sound

6 - LIGHT

Lighting in the indoor environment has three basic purposes: to enable the occupants to work and move about in safety; to enable tasks to be performed, and to make the interior look pleasant.

Buildings can be lit either naturally, by daylight received from the sky, or artificially - by electric lamps or other artificial light sources.

The quantity and quality of natural light in an interior depends on the external environment (site layout and planning) and the internal environment (size and positioning of windows, depth and shape of rooms). The primary reference in the UK for daylighting criteria is BS8206: Lighting for buildings: Part 2: Code of practice for daylighting, which treats daylight as two distinct sources of light:

- Sunlight - That part of solar radiation that reaches the earth's surface as parallel rays after selective attenuation by the atmosphere
- Skylight - That part of solar radiation that reaches the earth's surface as a result of scattering in the atmosphere.

Sunlight and skylight may therefore be considered as the direct and diffuse components of daylight.

Interior daylight is measured by the Daylight Factor (DF).

Daylight factor is defined as:

$$\text{Daylight Factor (\%)} = \frac{\text{Interior Illuminance}}{\text{Simultaneous horizontal unobstructed exterior illuminance}} \times 100$$

The Daylight Factor is a combination of three components:
- The sky component (SC) - the light received directly from the sky.
- The externally reflected component (ERC) - the light received directly by reflection from buildings and obstructions outside the room.
- The internally reflected component (IRC) - the light received from surfaces inside the room.

Estimates for the SC and ERC can be obtained from a number of sources, including: BRE Daylight Protractors, BRE Simplified Daylight Tables, Waldrum Diagrams, Fuller Moore Dot Charts. The IRC can be obtained from tabulated data.

Understanding artificial lighting requires the use of a number of terms:
- Luminous flux (F) - the amount of light emitted by a light source. Measured in lumens (lm).
- Luminous efficacy – a measure of how effectively a lamp transforms electricity into light or luminous flux: the luminous efficacy is the lamp light output in lumens per watt of electrical power consumption, (lm/W).
- Luminous intensity (I) - is the power of a light source, or illuminated surface, to emit light in a particular direction. Measured in candelas (cd).
- Illuminance (E) - the luminous flux density (spread of light) at a surface measured in lux (lx), where 1 lux = 1 lm/m2. A common minimum level for working is 200 lx, but in bright sunlight it can reach 50000lx.
- Luminance (L) - this is a measure of the ability of an area of light source, or reflecting surface, to produce the sensation of brightness.
- Colour rendering - this is the ability of a lamp to reveal the colour of a surface, compared to the colour of the surface viewed in daylight: a measure of how accurately the colour of surfaces appears under different light sources. It is expressed by a colour rendering index (Ra) of up to 100. An Ra of between 80-89 is considered very good, while one between 90-100 is regarded as excellent.
- Colour temperature - gives an indication of the appearance of the light. Lower colour temperatures mean a 'warmer' appearance. Early fluorescent lamps had a high colour temperature giving a very 'cold' appearance; but now a wide range of colour temperatures is available, including some that are similar to incandescent lamps.

7 - FIRE

Approved Document Part B1, Volume 1 - Dwellinghouses, defines the key aspects of fire safety in the construction of buildings. Some of these are:
- The building shall have a means of early warning and escape in the event of a fire.
- The internal spread of fire should be inhibited within the building by ensuring linings adequately resist the spread of flame over their surface.
- The building shall be designed and constructed so that its stability will be maintained for a reasonable period in the event of a fire.
- Walls common to two or more dwellings are to adequately resist spread of fire between those buildings.
- Unseen spread of fire and smoke within a concealed space within the structure must be inhibited.
- External walls and roofs of a building are able to resist spread of fire from one building to another.

7.1 STRUCTURAL ELEMENTS

Although it is preferable to build new structures with non combustible materials, that is not always feasible. Many of the structural elements are combustible in some way, but we have developed suitable understanding and methods to allow use of these materials in a safe and effective manner. Timber, for example is a combustible material, but if a structural element is specified with sufficient thickness the rate of combustion of any excess timber should provide sufficient time for the building to be evacuated in the event of a fire. Masonry construction materials tend to have a good fire resistance, due to their manufacturing process being at high temperatures. Concrete however, does suffer damage in a fire is natural aggregates are used.

Steel can demonstrate a loss of strength in temperatures over 500 degrees, and it is often treated with a fire retardant coating, or covered with a material that has good fire resistance in order to protect it from fire.

7.2 NON STRUCTURAL ELEMENTS

Internal and external finishes to a building also have an important bearing on fire resistance of an overall structure. It is key that any surfaces do not encourage the spread of fire and have a low rate of heat release or fire growth if ignited.

7.3 FIRE PROTECTION

7.3.1 EXTERNAL WALLS

The regulations state that external walls of a dwelling must provide suitable fire resistance for the building and retain its structural stability for a period to allow occupants to escape. It is recommended that dwellings with a top floor within 5m of ground level require 30mins fire resistance, while any houses above this level require 60mins fire resistance. Any wall to an adjoining property must have 60mins fire resistance, regardless of height.

7.3.2 FLOORS

Any floor must resist collapse for a sufficient period of time in order to allow occupants to escape in the event of a fire. The regulations state that floors within 5m of ground level have 30mins fire resistance, and any floors above 5m have 60mins fire resistance.

7.3.3 CAVITY BARRIERS

In order to restrict spread of fire or smoke in concealed places within the structure, the building regulations require any cavities in timber structures to be closed with a cavity barrier. A cavity barrier is capable of providing fire resistance of at least 30mins, and are generally a polythene sleeved mineral wool. The barriers are required at openings, roof verges and eaves and party wall lines.

Fire stops are also required at the junction of any separating wall, the external wall at the junction of separating wall and roof in any terraced or semi detached house. These are made of a non combustible material, usually a wire reinforced mineral wool quilt.

7.3.4 PROTECTING OPENINGS

Any openings should be protected by sealing or fire stopping in order to maintain the effectiveness of fire separating elements. Not only does fire stopping and sealing delay the passage of fire, it also can retard the spread of smoke.

Table A1, A2 and A8 demonstrate some of the requirements set out in Approved Document Part B Volume 1. Table A1 gives requirements for each element in terms of one or more of the following criteria:
- Resistance to collapse
- Resistance to fire penetration
- Resistance to the transfer of excessive heat

Table A2 sets out the minimum periods of fire resistance for elements of a structure.

Table A2 Minimum periods of fire resistance for dwellinghouses

Minimum periods (minutes) for elements of structure in a:

Basement storey [1] including floor over	Ground or upper storey	
	Height (m) of top floor above ground	
	Not more than 5	More than 5
30 [2]	30 [2]	60 [3]

Notes:

Modifications referred to in Table A2:

1. The floor over a basement (or if there is more than one basement, the floor over the topmost basement) should meet the provisions for the ground and upper storeys if that period is higher.
2. Increased to a minimum of 60 minutes for compartment walls separating buildings.
3. 30 minutes in the case of three storey dwellinghouses, increased to 60 minutes minimum for compartment walls separating buildings.
4. Refer to Table A1 for the specific provisions of test.

Figure 1.11- Table A2 from Approved Document Part B, Fire Safety, Volume 1 Dwellinghouses

Table A1 Specific provisions of test for fire resistance of elements of structure etc

Part of building	Minimum provisions when tested to the relevant part of BS 476 [1] (minutes)			Minimum provisions when tested to the relevant European standard (minutes) [9]	Method of exposure
	Loadbearing capacity [2]	Integrity	Insulation		
1. **Structural** frame, beam or column.	See Table A2	Not applicable	Not applicable	R see Table A2	Exposed faces
2. **Loadbearing wall** (which is not also a wall described in any of the following items).	See Table A2	Not applicable	Not applicable	R see Table A2	Each side separately
3. **Floor** [3]					
a. In upper storey of 2-storey dwellinghouse (but not over garage or basement);	30	15	15	R 30 and REI 15	From underside
b. Any other floor – including compartment floors.	See Table A2	See Table A2	See Table A2	REI see Table A2	From underside
4. **Roof** any part forming an escape route;	30	30	30	REI 30	From underside [4]
5. **External walls**					
a. any part less than 1000mm from any point on the relevant boundary;	See Table A2	See Table A2	See Table A2	REI see Table A2	Each side separately
b. any part 1000mm or more from the relevant boundary [5];	See Table A2	See Table A2	15	RE see Table A2 and REI 15	From inside the building
c. any part adjacent to an external escape route (see paragraph 2.10 and 2.15 and Diagram 7).	30	30	No provision [6][7]	RE 30	From inside the building
6. **Compartment walls** (other than in item 8)	See Table A2	See Table A2	See Table A2	REI see Table A2	Each side separately

SECTION 1 - FUNCTIONAL REQUIREMENTS

Table A1 continued

Part of building	Minimum provisions when tested to the relevant part of BS 476 [1] (minutes)			Minimum provisions when tested to the relevant European standard (minutes) [9]	Method of exposure
	Loadbearing capacity [2]	Integrity	Insulation		
7. **Enclosure** (which does not form part of a compartment wall or a protected shaft) to a:					
a. protected stairway;	30	30	30 [8]	REI 30 [8]	Each side separately
b. lift shaft.	30	30	30	REI 30	Each side separately
8. **Wall or floor** separating an attached or integral garage from a dwellinghouse	30	30	30 [8]	REI 30 [8]	From garage side
9. **Fire-resisting construction:** in dwellinghouses not described elsewhere	30	30	30 [8]	REI 30 [8]	
10. **Cavity barrier**	Not applicable	30	15	E 30 and EI 15	Each side separately
11. **Ceiling** described in paragraph 2.14, Diagram 6	Not applicable	30	30	EI 30	From underside
12. **Duct** described in paragraph 6.8e	Not applicable	30	No provision	E 30	From outside
13. **Casing** around a drainage system described in paragraph 7.8, Diagram 15	Not applicable	30	No provision	E 30	From outside
14. **Flue walls** described in paragraph 7.11, Diagram 16	Not applicable	Half the period specified in Table A2 for the compartment wall/floor	Half the period specified in Table A2 for the compartment wall/floor	EI half the period specified in Table A2 for the compartment wall/floor	From outside
15. **Construction** described in Note (a) to paragraph 10.9	Not applicable	30	30	EI 30	From underside
16. **Fire doors**		See Table B1		See Table B1	

Notes:
1. Part 21 for loadbearing elements, Part 22 for non-loadbearing elements, Part 23 for fire-protecting suspended ceilings, and Part 24 for ventilation ducts. BS 476-8 results are acceptable for items tested or assessed before 1 January 1988.
2. Applies to loadbearing elements only (see B3.ii and Appendix E).
3. Guidance on increasing the fire resistance of existing timber floors is given in BRE Digest 208 Increasing the fire resistance of existing timber floors (BRE 1988).
4. A suspended ceiling should only be relied on to contribute to the fire resistance of the floor if the ceiling meets the appropriate provisions given in Table A3.
5. The guidance in Section 9 allows such walls to contain areas which need not be fire-resisting (unprotected areas).
6. Unless needed as part of a wall in item 5a or 5b.
7. Except for any limitations on glazed elements given in Table A4.
8. See Table A4 for permitted extent of uninsulated glazed elements.
9. The National classifications do not automatically equate with the equivalent classifications in the European column, therefore products cannot typically assume a European class unless they have been tested accordingly.

    'R' is the European classification of the resistance to fire performance in respect of loadbearing capacity; 'E' is the European classification of the resistance to fire performance in respect of integrity; and 'I' is the European classification of the resistance to fire performance in respect of insulation.

Figure 1.12- Table A1 from Approved Document Part B, Fire Safety, Volume 1 Dwellinghouses

Table A8 Typical performance ratings of some generic materials and products

Rating	Material or product
Class 0 (National)	1. Any non-combustible material or material of limited combustibility. (composite products listed in Table A7 must meet test requirements given in Appendix A, paragraph 13(b)). 2. Brickwork, blockwork, concrete and ceramic tiles. 3. Plasterboard (painted or not with a PVC facing not more than 0.5mm thick) with or without an air gap or fibrous or cellular insulating material behind. 4. Woodwool cement slabs. 5. Mineral fibre tiles or sheets with cement or resin binding.
Class 3 (National)	6. Timber or plywood with a density more than 400kg/m^3, painted or unpainted. 7. Wood particle board or hardboard, either untreated or painted. 8. Standard glass reinforced polyesters.
Class A1 (European)	9. Any material that achieves this class or is defined as 'classified without further test' in a published Commission Decision.
Class A2-s3, d2 (European)	10. Any material that achieves this class or is defined as 'classified without further test' in a published Commission Decision.
Class B-s3, d2 (European)	11. Any material that achieves this class or is defined as 'classified without further test' in a published Commission Decision.
Class C-s3, d2 (European)	12. Any material that achieves this class or is defined as 'classified without further test' in a published Commission Decision.
Class D-s3, d2 (European)	13. Any material that achieves this class or is defined as 'classified without further test' in a published Commission Decision.

Notes (National):

1. Materials and products listed under Class 0 also meet Class 1.
2. Timber products listed under Class 3 can be brought up to Class 1 with appropriate proprietary treatments.
3. The following materials and products may achieve the ratings listed below. However, as the properties of different products with the same generic description vary, the ratings of these materials/products should be substantiated by test evidence.

   Class 0 – aluminium faced fibre insulating board, flame retardant decorative laminates on a calcium silicate board, thick polycarbonate sheet, phenolic sheet and UPVC.

   Class 1 – phenolic or melamine laminates on a calcium silicate substrate and flame-retardant decorative laminates on a combustible substrate.

Notes (European):

For the purposes of the Building Regulations:

1. Materials and products listed under Class A1 also meet Classes A2-s3, d2, B-s3, d2, C-s3, d2 and D-s3, d2.
2. Materials and products listed under Class A2-s3, d2 also meet Classes B-s3, d2, C-s3, d2 and D-s3, d2.
3. Materials and products listed under Class B-s3, d2 also meet Classes C-s3, d2 and D-s3, d2.
4. Materials and products listed under Class C-s3, d2 also meet Class D-s3, d2.
5. The performance of timber products listed under Class D-s3, d2 can be improved with appropriate proprietary treatments.
6. Materials covered by the CWFT process (classification without further testing) can be found by accessing the European Commission's website via the link on the CLG website www.communities.gov.uk
7. The national classifications do not automatically equate with the equivalent classifications in the European column, therefore products cannot typically assume a European class unless they have been tested accordingly.
8. When a classification includes 's3, d2', this means that there is no limit set for smoke production and/or flaming droplets/particles.

Figure 1.13- Table A8 from Approved Document Part B, Fire Safety, Volume 1 Dwellinghouses

DETAILING PRINCIPLES

SECTION 2

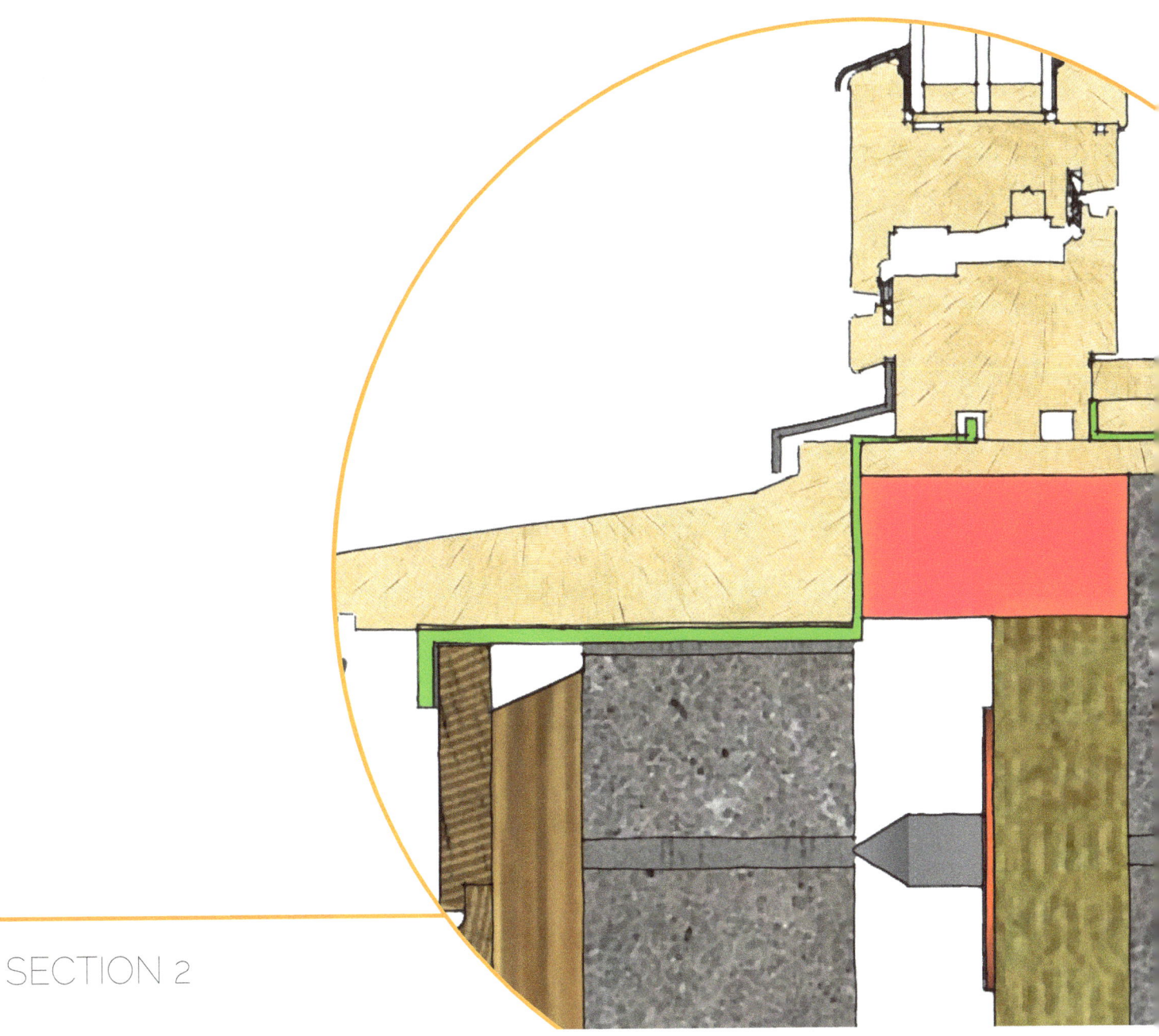

DETAILING PRINCIPLES

INTRODUCTION

There is not one book, resource, or website that will ever provide a one size fits all answer to our construction detailing requirements. Every project is different, and with that, the designer is faced with a multitude of choices that need to be assessed and decisions that must be made.

The designer must consider selection of materials and components, meeting client requirements, financial restraints and budgets, aesthetic aspirations amongst many other things. It is crucial that guidance documents are consulted, manufacturer information, regulations and standards in order to present the most effective solution to the problem.

Some key sources of information are described below.

- Building Regulations Approved Documents https://www.gov.uk/government/collections/approved-documents
- British Standards http://shop.bsigroup.com/Browse-by-Sector/Building--Construction/?t=r
- Building Research Establishment (BRE) publications http://www.bre.co.uk
- Trade Association publications
- Manufacturer technical guidance and literature
- Building Information Centres
- BBA - British Board of Agrement - http://www.bbacerts.co.uk

The details in this book are meant as a guide - a base point for your own development of construction details. They shouldn't be copied as a quick solution to any construction problem - but be used as a starting point. You should question the detail.

- Is it right for your scheme, how does it integrate with the rest of the design?
- What should I change, and why?
- What elements need to be implemented from building regulations or guidance documents?
- How would this detail work in my particular region of the country?

It is important to develop a critical approach, analyse the details and provide your own solution to each situation. Particular attention must be paid to junctions, due to the complexity of the geometry at these points, heat and moisture flow will not be straight through the fabric but influenced by both two and three dimensional effects. A junction is likely to contain structural elements that will have a higher thermal conductivity than the materials surrounding them. Junctions are also places where different materials meet, which can have differing properties, resulting in possibility of air gaps, movement and so on.

Beyond the guidance documents it is important to develop a key understanding of the detailing principles so that you are able to select strategies and solutions naturally, with a full understanding of the requirements and purpose of each construction detail or element. This next section looks at understanding the performance of the detail and what is required to address common functional requirements of a building.

WATER

Water can penetrate a building when there is an opening in the building assembly, there is water at the opening, and there is suitable force to push the water through the opening. This opening can be a crack around a window or door, a gap between a roof tile or a joint between two elements of cladding. In order to stop water penetrating a building we must try to reduce the openings in the building assembly, keep water away from the openings that do occur, and neutralise the forces that can move the water through the assembly.

Reducing gaps and openings in the building assembly is about finding ways to eliminate these openings. Sealants and gaskets are a form of doing this, however a building skin shouldn't rely on this alone as sealants and gaskets will leak over time. It is better to create an overall strategy that addresses all three elements to be sure of a watertight design.

Strategies to keep water away from the building include methods such as a wash, overhang and overlap amongst others. These will be addressed individually in this chapter.

The forces that can push water through a building assembly are:

- Gravity: water will naturally move downwards
- Surface tension: causes water to cling to underside of a surface where it can run through into an opening
- Capillary action: water can also move upwards - cracks or holes with smooth sides may act as capillary and by mechanisms of surface tension, draw in water
- Momentum: wind-blown rain possesses momentum that can move it through an opening
- Pressure differential: water will move from areas of higher pressure to areas of lower pressure

Forces	Neutralised by
Gravity	Wash and overlap
Surface tension	Overhang and drip
Capillary action	Capillary break
Absorption	Drain and weep
Momentum	Labrynth
Air pressure differentials	Rainscreen assembly

Figure 2.1 - Forces leading to moisture ingress

WASH

A wash is a slope given to a horizontal surface to drain water away from the building. A wash is used in door or window sills, sloping roof, slopes to drain, ground slopes away from a building. If the material is particularly porous it is important that the slope is steeper to allow for a faster removal of water.

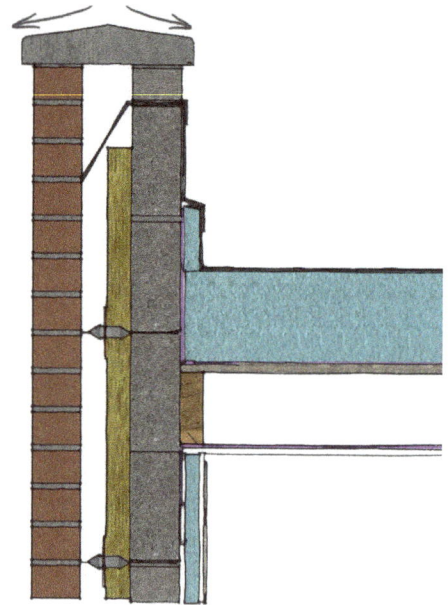

Figure 2.2 - Wash of a parapet coping stone

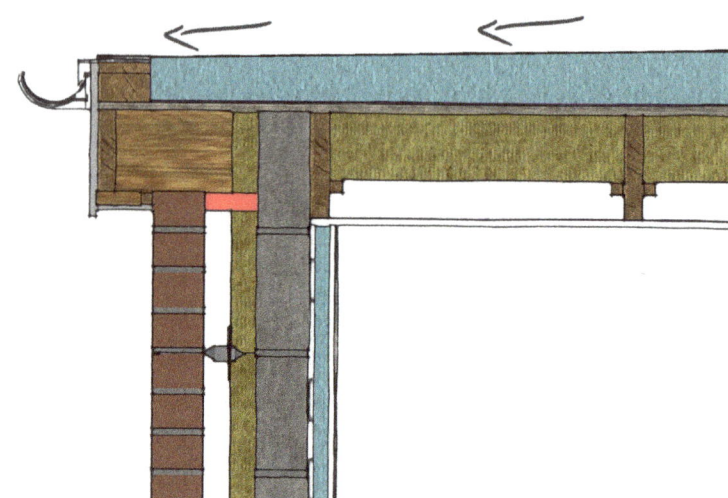

Figure 2.3 - Wash of a flat roof with insulation cut to falls

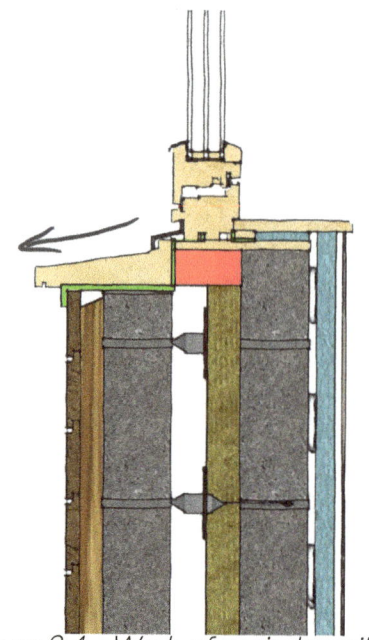

Figure 2.4 - Wash of a window sill

SECTION 2 - DETAILING PRINCIPLES

OVERLAP

Used on a sloped or vertical plane, an overlap is where a higher element is extended over the lower element with enough distance that water cannot run behind or beneath the element. Gravity pulls the water down the sloped or vertical plan away from the overlap. An obvious example of this would be tiles on a roof. If the material is particularly porous it is important that the slope is steeper to allow for a faster removal of water.

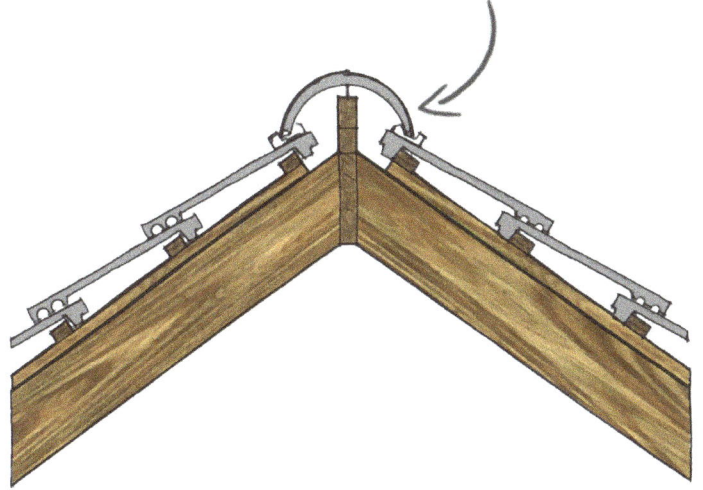

Figure 2.5 - Overlap of ridge tile

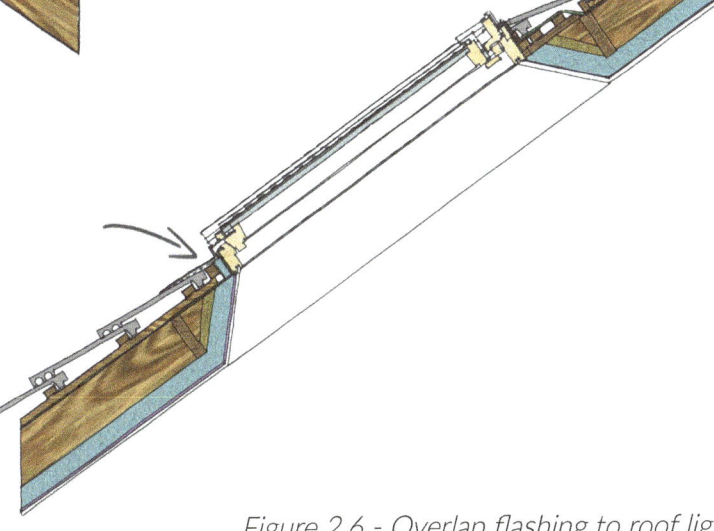

Figure 2.6 - Overlap flashing to roof light

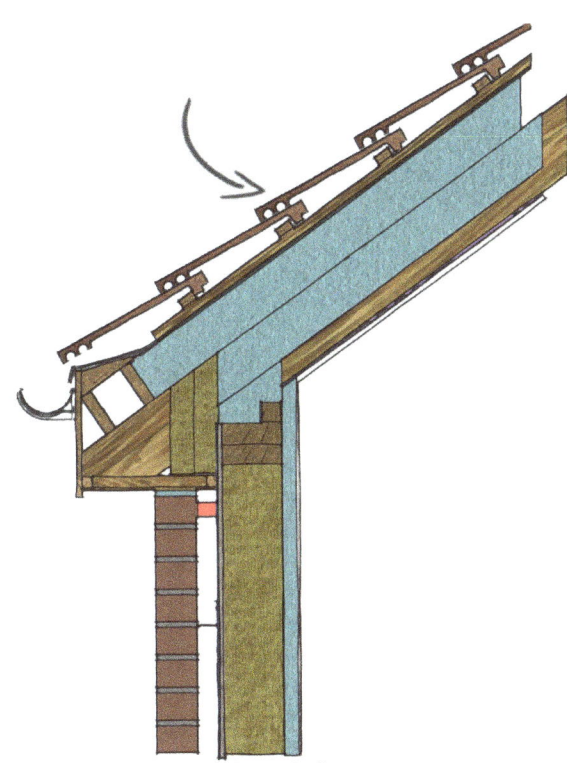

Figure 2.7 - Overlap of roof tiles

OVERHANG AND DRIP

Water running down a wall or element of the building assembly can be diverted from an opening by creating a projection above the opening - this is the overhang. The water is then forced by gravity to drip away from the overhang using a drip, often a groove on the underside of the overhang. An example of the overhang and drip can be seen on window sills, door sills, and coping.

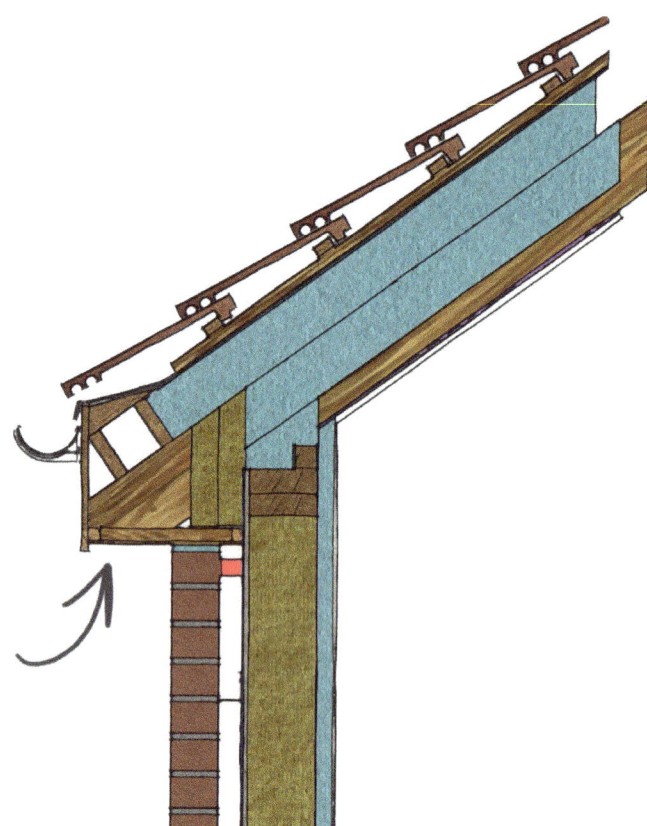

Figure 2.8 - Overhang and drip of roof eaves

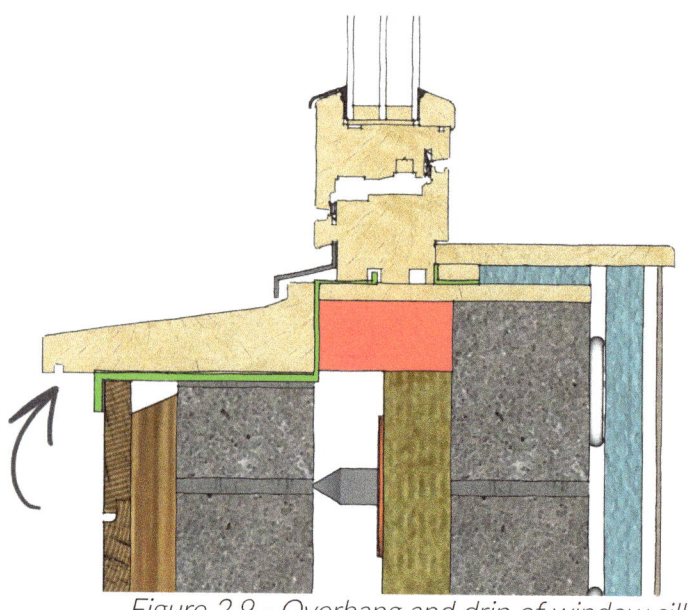

Figure 2.9 - Overhang and drip of window sill

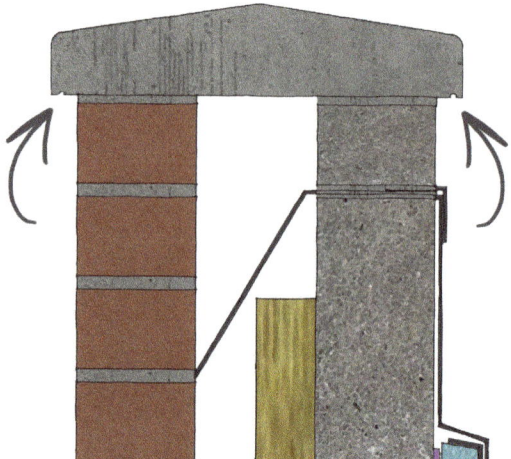

Figure 2.10 - Overhang and drip of parapet coping stone

SECTION 2 - DETAILING PRINCIPLES

CAPILLARY BREAK

Capillary action is the process in which water is able to pull itself upward or across a narrow crack. The crack has to be narrow for the water to be able to travel. In order to prevent capillary action, a break is provided so the water cannot bridge it.

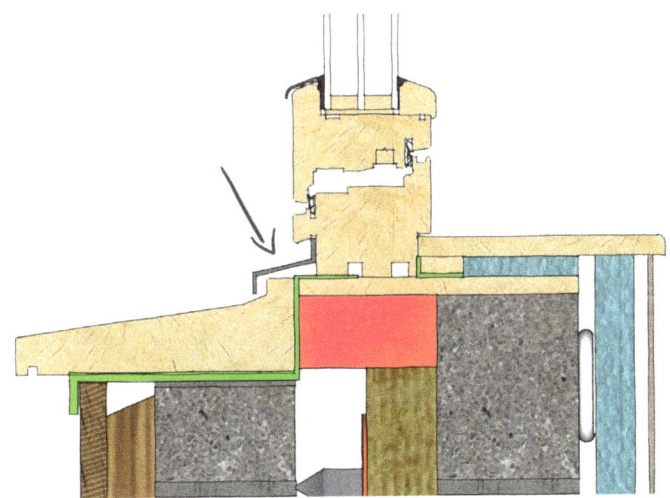

Figure 2.11 - Capillary break of a window flashing

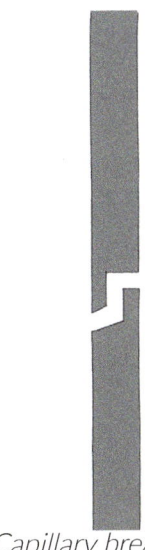

Figure 2.12 - Capillary break in a vertical panel joint

DRAIN AND WEEP

In some constructions we can anticipate that water will penetrate the assembly and in this case we can detail in suitable measures. A drain and weep allows water to be conducted away from a cavity for example, and allowed to drain out of weep holes within the assembly. It can also be a suitable system to control any condensation that has built up in the construction. The drain and weep is used in masonry cavity wall construction.

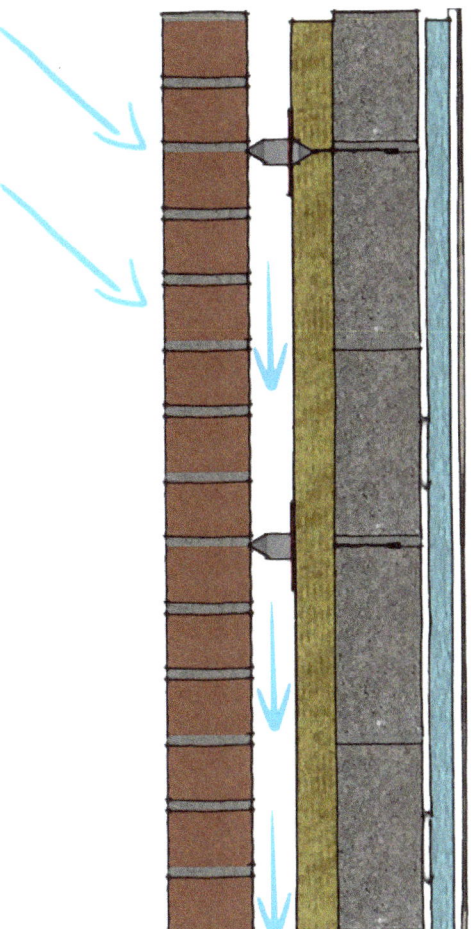

Figure 2.13 - Drain and weep of a cavity wall

LABYRINTH

A labyrinth is used in a joint to stop a raindrop passing through the joint. The labyrinth is designed so that there is no straight line through the joint for anything to pass through with its own momentum.

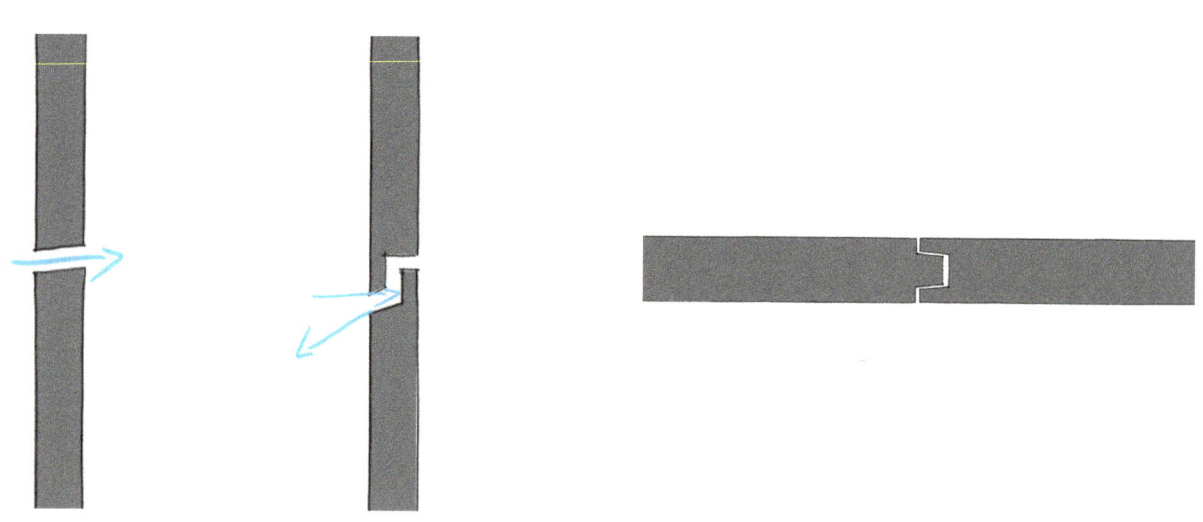

Figure 2.14 - Labyrinth in both vertical and horzontal joints between panels

WATER VAPOUR

Water vapour is always present in the air, however it can cause problems if it condenses on or within the building assembly. Condensation is caused when the moisture laden air comes into contact with a cold surface and the water vapour within the air is deposited as water onto the surface. Windows, solid walls on exposed parts of the house, cold water pipes and thermal bridges are all areas where condensation is most likely to occur. In turn, condensation is less likely to occur on double glazing or a well insulated wall because the internal temperature will be relatively high, above the dew point.

Interstitial condensation occurs when moist air permeates through elements of the building fabric. Typically, there will be a temperature difference across the building assembly, so as warm moist air passes through the structure towards the cooler air the temperature will drop. The dew point may be reached which is when the temperature is cool enough for the water vapour in the warm air to condense on the building fabric. This can cause many problems in the building assembly.

Water vapour is often produced by activities in the house such as bathing, cleaning, drying clothes, cooking. These activities lead to condensation.

General precautions and procedures to avoid condensation include:
- the prevention of excess moisture being generated - this is largely down to the occupants.
- removal of excess moisture - in the form of suitable ventilation

There are some detailing principles that should be adopted in order to avoid water vapour condensing on or within the building assembly:

High air and fabric temperature will reduce the risk of condensation by keeping the temperature of the structure above dew point. This is best achieved with suitable thermal insulation - seen later in this chapter.

Other principles adopted to avoid water vapour condensing include the use of a vapour control layer and breather membrane.

SECTION 2 - DETAILING PRINCIPLES

VAPOUR CONTROL LAYER

A vapour barrier or vapour control layer is usually placed on the warm side of the insulation in order to reduce the passage of water vapour and potential problems of interstitial condensation. The VCL is a thin sheet material which reduces the diffusion of water vapour and improves the airtightness of the building fabric which in turn limits uncontrolled ventilation and leakage of warm moist air into the building assembly.

In timber frame, or steel frame construction it is most common for the air and vapour control to be served by one membrane and air and vapour control layer (AVCL).

Figure 2.15 - Vapour control layer   *Figure 2.16 - Breather membrane*

BREATHER MEMBRANE

A breather membrane is a vapour permeable membrane, often positioned on the outside of a construction to protect vulnerable construction elements from rain during construction, and as a secondary protection throughout the life of the building. The breather membrane allows any trapped moist air within the construction to pass through and escape, while stopping any new moisture from penetrating the construction. It is typically seen on the outer face of a timber frame wall.

AIR

As we have mentioned in the previous chapter, leaking air can cause a number of problems to not only the structure but our occupants as well. An air leak within a building assembly can result in building performance problems such as:
- uncomfortable drafts
- wasted heated and cooled air which results in lost energy
- interstitial condensation resulting in damage to building fabric or reduced performance
- surface condensation resulting in mould growth, damage to finishes
- sound leaks
- transmission of heat or smoke in a fire from one part of the building to another

An air leak is an uncontrolled passage of air through an exterior wall of a building. Studies have shown that air leakage can contribute up to a third of total heat loss in a dwelling. For air leakage to occur there must be a pressure difference between the two points and a continuous flow path or opening connecting those two points.

AIR BARRIER SYSTEM

In order to reduce air leakage it is important to create an air barrier system that seals all openings at one plane in the building envelope. Great care needs to be taken when detailing junctions to ensure the air barrier remains constant.

In masonry construction the air barrier is often formed as part of the internal leaf of the cavity wall. If the inner leaf is well built with a coat of wet finish plaster properly applied with correct detailing, air tightness will be achieved. Dry-lining can also deliver air tightness, if detailed with appropriate sealing and taping, but often use of an airtight membrane is advised for improved performance in both cases.

In timber frame or steel frame construction the vapour control layer often serves as the airtightness barrier. The airtight layer is usually at or close to the inside of the building insulation envelope which also serves to prevent warm moist air from entering the building assembly.

Sealants, gaskets and weather strips are also used to ensure air tightness. Door and window openings utilise weather strips or gaskets to reduce possible air flow.

HEAT FLOW AND INSULATION

The excessive conduction of heat through a building can result in wasted energy, high heating and cooling costs, condensation leading to mould and general discomfort for the building occupants. Controlling this heat flow is crucial and this can be achieved by engaging a few detailing principles.

A thermal bridge, sometimes referred to as a cold bridge, is a weakness or discontinuity in the thermal envelope of a building. Most often seen at junctions, a thermal bridge occurs when the insulation is interrupted by a material more conductive. At these junctions heat can be lost as it is able to pass more easily through the building assembly. Thermal bridging can contribute quite significantly to overall heat losses in an otherwise well insulated dwelling. A thermal bridge can also result in condensation build up and mould growth which in turn has an effect on the building occupants. This occurs where the element that passes through the insulation layer creates a lower surface temperature and those locations, resulting in both surface and interstitial condensation.

When developing details, it is important to ensure the insulation layer remains consistent and unbroken to minimise thermal bridging. Insulation should be tightly fitted against and between construction elements to eliminate gaps and prevent slump or movement that could degrade performance.

THERMAL BREAKS AND ELIMINATING THERMAL BRIDGES

A thermal break is an insulation strip that is inserted into the building assembly where there is a risk of increased heat conduction. An example of this could be in a timber frame wall. The timber stud work will conduct heat more rapidly than the insulation between the studs. A layer of insulation is added to the inside or outside of the frame to improve the overall thermal resistance of the wall. The stud work of a timber frame wall can make up 15% of the wall, so it is worth countering this with the extra insulation. Another example of a practical use of thermal break would be in a steel frame wall, where metal conducts heat at a much higher rate.

The key design aim for any junction is to ensure that there are no single elements or combination of elements that will conduct heat more rapidly through the construction. A continuous layer of thermal insulation should be designed throughout the building envelope. Heat loss can be reduced by ensuring any junctions allow the insulation within different elements to abut and/or overlap.

To avoid condensation risk there are two methods that can be considered. The first is a vapour permeable construction where the vapour permeability on materials from the warm side to the cold side of construction are increased. This allows water vapour to pass through the construction to reach a ventilated zone where it can be dispersed. The second is to install a vapour control layer on the warm side of construction to prevent the water vapour from penetrating areas of the building assembly that can cause problems. This option should always be used if there is not suitable ventilation to disperse the water vapour.

It is also worth noting that the use of two different types of insulation can cause condensation. If a rigid insulation is used with a fibrous insulation, the rigid insulation must be positioned on the warm side. If positioned the other way around, the water vapour could pass through the fibrous insulation and become trapped when it meets the rigid insulation creating a potential build up of condensation.

It is possible to read more about the risk of surface condensation in the document BRE IP 1/06 "Assessing the effects of thermal bridging at junctions and around openings" and BS 5250:2011.

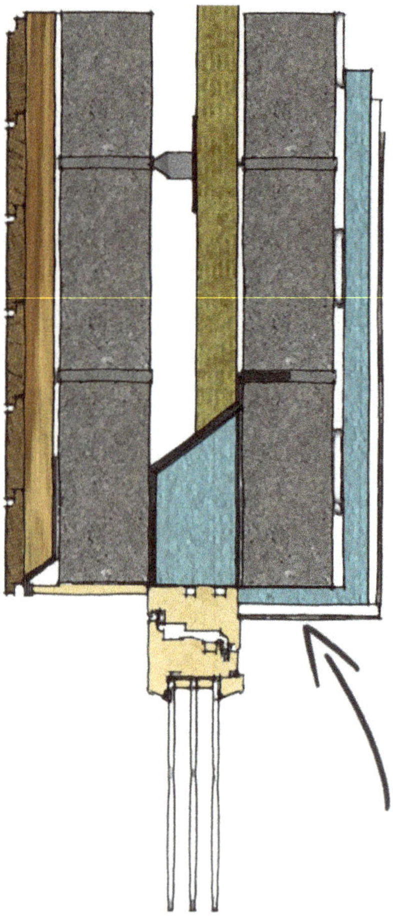

Figure 2.17- Insulated plasterboard reveal to window head

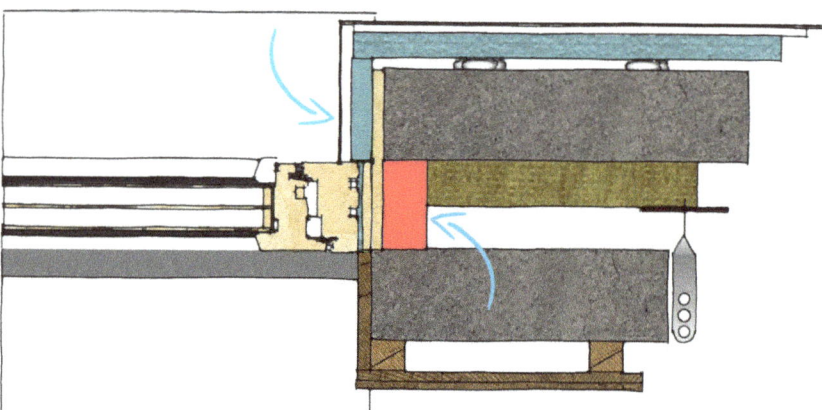

Figure 2.18- Insulated plasterboard reveal and PU/PIR insulated cavity closer to window jamb

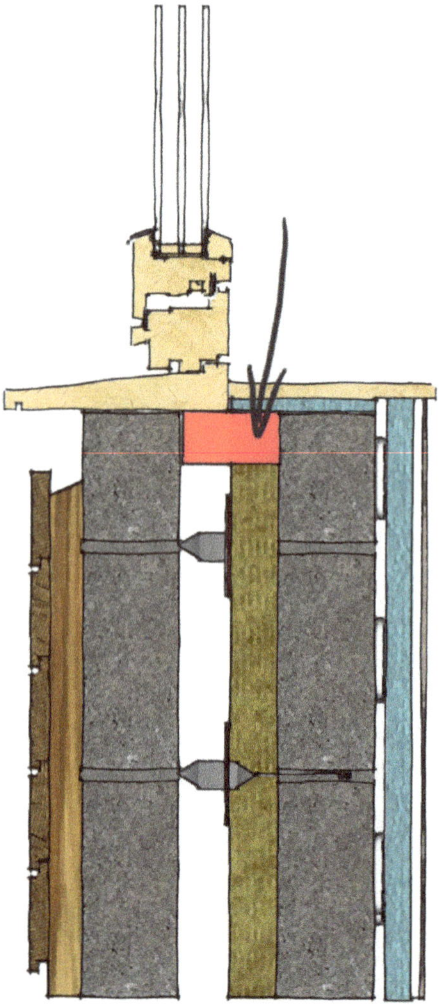

Figure 2.19- Cavity closer with PU/PIR insulation core, insulation under internal window sill

SECTION 2 - DETAILING PRINCIPLES

Figure 2.20- Increased eaves insulation

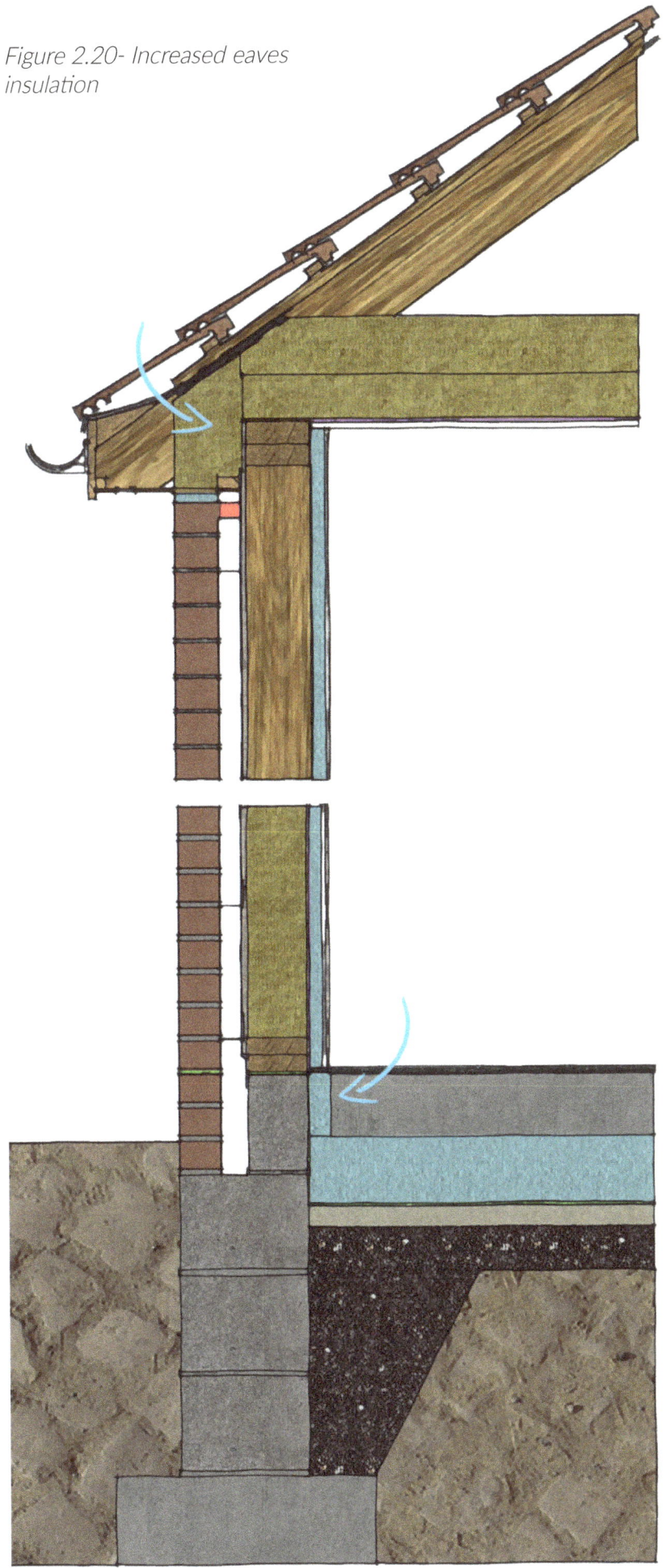

Figure 2.21- Perimeter insulation to concrete slab and lightweight blockwork to innerleaf

Figure 2.22- Additional insulation on inside face of a timber frame and steel frame construction

Blank Page

MATERIALS

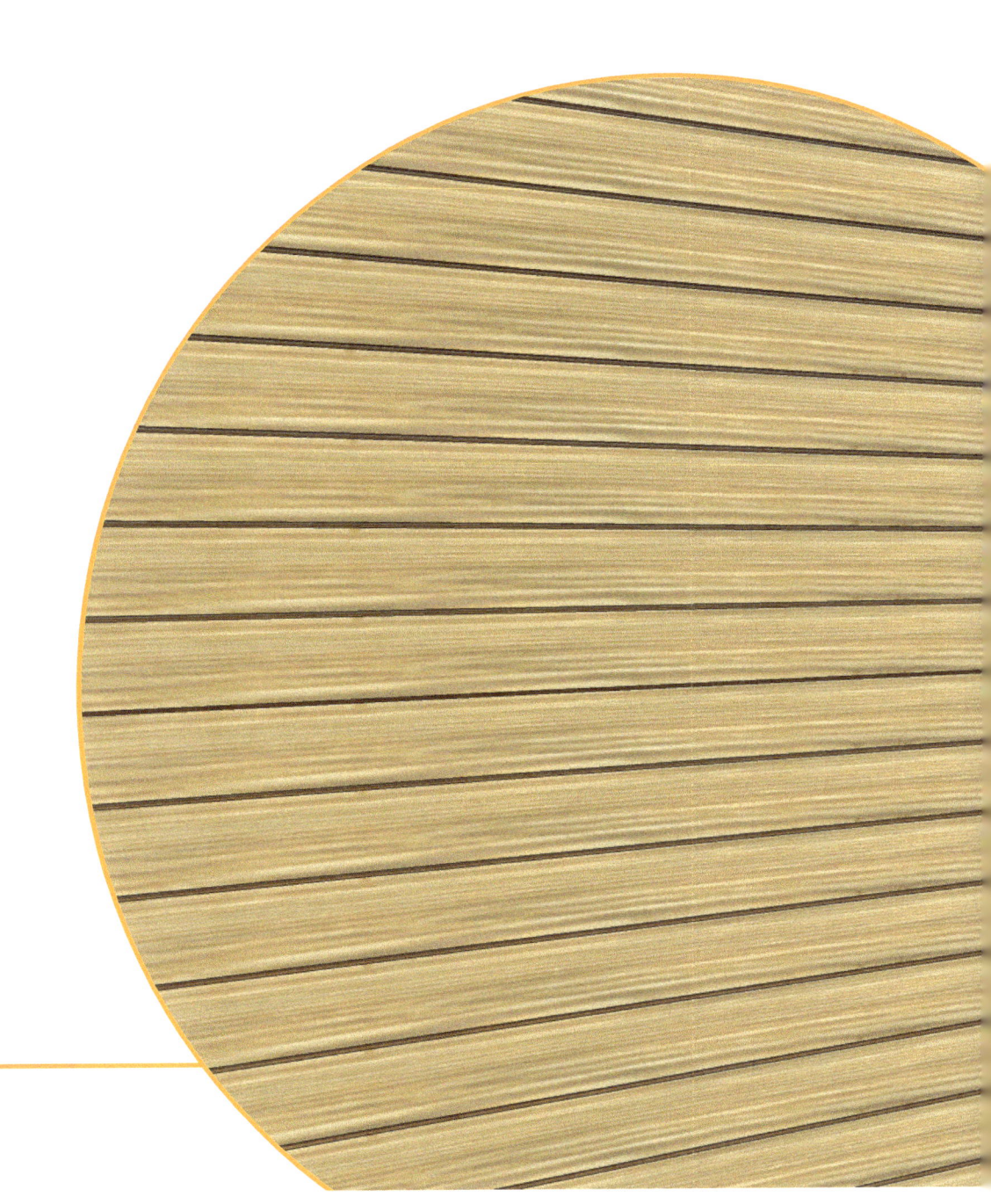

SECTION 3

MATERIALS

In this chapter we will briefly look at some of the more common materials used in domestic construction and their properties.

BRICK

CLASSIFICATIONS

Bricks are classified according to their use:

Common
These are used in situations where they may not be seen, they are able to carry the loads normally supported by brickwork, but have a dull texture or poor colour. They have acceptable general brick properties, but produced cheaply. They are often used on walls that will then be rendered or plastered.

Facing
Facing brick is also capable of carrying normal loads but have a better appearance and are produced in a range of colours and finishes, used in areas where they will be seen. They are more expensive to produce but have similar performance characteristics to the common brick.

Engineering Bricks
These bricks are made from selected clays and carefully produced to be able to carry heavier loads than a standard brick. They are mainly used for applications such as brick piers, engineering works, or works below ground.

Special Bricks
Special bricks are made for specific applications, such as copings, plinths, bullnose edges and so on.

SIZES

Standard metric brick dimensions are 215mm x 102.5mm x 65mm. These dimensions are sometimes known as working dimensions or nominal sizes. The coordinating dimensions which include the mortar required on one bed, one header face and one stretcher face - 225mm x 112.5mm x 75mm.

PROPERTIES

When specifying bricks, certain performance characteristics need to be considered.

Compressive Strength
Compressive strength of bricks is measured by crushing 12 bricks individually until they fail or crumble. The average strength of the brick is measured in newton per millimetre of surface area required to crush the brick. The resistance can vary from about 3.5 N/mm^2 for soft facing bricks up to 140N/mm^2 for engineering bricks. This is clearly quite a range.

Water Absorption
Absorption rates in bricks can vary between 1% and 35%. The amount of water a brick will absorb is a guide

to its density and therefore its strength. The level of water absorption is critical for bricks below dpc level or for dpcs. Water absorption should be a maximum of 4.5% for Class A engineering bricks or bricks used for damp proof courses, and a maximum of 7% for Class B engineering bricks. Absorption can cause problems in the bricklaying process whereby bricks with high suction rates absorb water rapidly from the mortar making repositioning difficult as work proceeds.

Thermal and moisture movement

Building materials expand and contract as a result of moisture or temperature changes. Allowance must be made for this in brickwork by using control joints. A brick wall will be constructed using movement joints at intervals according to current standards in order to allow for the movement in the material. Restrained walls should feature joints allowing 1mm of movement per 1m of brickwork, typically at 10 - 12m centres. Unrestrained walls should have movement joints at 7-8m centres. Manufacturers will offer guidance and current standards information for the positioning of movement joints. Building joints can be hidden using careful detailing and choosing suitable locations for structural forms to adjoin, abutments, returns, recesses, downpipes and so on.

Thermal Conductivity

Generally clay bricks have high thermal conductivity and therefore a poor thermal insulation value. The thermal conductivity value varies with the type and density of the brick along with moisture content. Thermal conductivity of a clay brick with 5% moisture content typically ranges from 0.65 to 1.95 W/mK.

Fire Resistance

The fire resistance of clay brickwork is generally good - it retains its stability, integrity and insulating properties since the bricks have been fired at a higher temperature than that which normally would occur in house fires.

Appearance

Bricks are available in a wide range of colours and textures. Choice can be influenced by neighbouring buildings, local authority requirements or personal choice.

Sound Insulation

The sound insulation of brickwork is directly proportional to the density of the wall. Brickwork is a good barrier to airborne sound provided there are no voids through the mortar for the passage of sound.

For further information on bricks visit:
Brick Development Association http://www.brick.org.uk

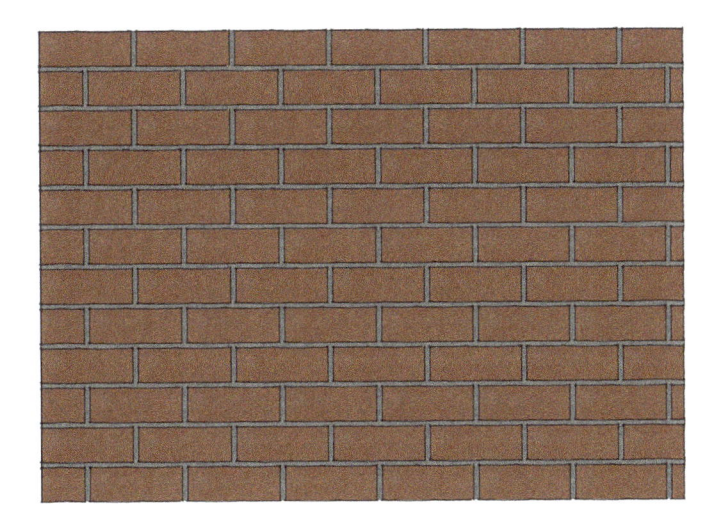

BLOCKS

Modern blocks in the UK are generally made from a form concrete. The blocks are larger in size than bricks and used extensively for both load bearing and non load bearing walls.

There are three general categories for concrete blocks - dense concrete, lightweight concrete and autoclaved aerated concrete (AAC). Blocks are manufactured from cement and either dense or lightweight aggregates as solid, cellular or hollow blocks. A solid block contains no formed holes or cavities. Cellular blocks contain one or more formed holes or cavities that do not completely pass through the block, whilst a hollow block has holes that pass completely through the block. Autoclaved aerated concrete blocks are made from a mixture of cement, sand or pulverised fuel ash admixtures to aerate the mix, and water. These blocks are extremely lightweight and have a density as low as 475kg/m^3 with high thermal resistance properties. They also have high water absorption characteristics.

The most common size for a concrete block is 440mm long by 215mm high. The height of the block coincides with three courses of brick in order to correspond with wall ties and bonding to brickwork. For cavity walls and internal load bearing walls 100mm thick blocks are used. 75mm thick lightweight aggregate blocks can be used for non load bearing walls.

PROPERTIES

Compressive Strength
The majority of concrete blocks have a compressive strength ranging from 2.8 to 30 N/mm^2. Aerated concrete blocks have strengths up to approximately 5.5N/mm^2

Water Absorption
Blocks have a higher water absorption than bricks due to their porous composition and they generally contain holes or cavities in their construction. Concrete blocks that contain dense aggregates are better for below ground level use. Aerated concrete blocks are especially porous and must be protected from moisture penetration prior to their installation.

Thermal and Moisture movement
Moisture movement can be a problem with concrete blocks, particularly aerated concrete blocks and can lead to cracking due to drying shrinkage if they have been allowed to get wet prior to installation.

Thermal conductivity
Blocks have relatively good thermal resistance, in part due to their cellular or hollow construction. Thermal conductivities for blocks range from 0.70 W/mK to 1.28W/mK for dense cellular blocks, 0.11W/mK-0.20W/mK for lightweight cellular blocks and autoclaved aerated blocks.

Fire resistance
Concrete blocks offer good fire resistance with a solid 90mm un-plastered block giving up to 60 minutes fire protection, while thicker blocks can achieve up to 360 minutes fire protection.

Sound insulation
Sound insulation of concrete blocks is lower than that of bricks as they have a lower density.

For more information visit:
Concrete Block Association https://www.cba-blocks.org.uk

CONCRETE

Concrete is a mixture of cement, aggregates and water, combined together to the correct proportions to give a strong, dense material ideal for structural components. When initially mixed, concrete is a plastic material which takes the shape of the mould or formwork. While the cement provides the setting and hardening element to the concrete, the water provides the chemical reaction with the cement allowing it to set and harden. The aggregates provide the bulk to the concrete and contribute to the overall strength. Concrete can be cast in situ (in the position it is meant to occupy in the building) or it can be cast in moulds away from its final position and moved into place when it has set. The moulds take the form of timber or steel formwork or shuttering.

CEMENT

Cements are manufactured in three main types - portland cements, super sulphated cements and high alumina cements. Portland cement is the most commonly used of the three types, it is available in many sub types but most common is OPC. OPC (Ordinary Portland Cement) has good setting time and strength development to suit most uses. Others include Rapid Hardening Portland Cement, which allows earlier striking of formwork, Sulphate Resisting Portland Cement which can resist sulphate salts attack which is present in some soils.

AGGREGATES

Aggregates form a major component of concrete - without aggregates concrete would be expensive and suffer from high amounts of drying shrinkage. Aggregates make up approximately 80% by weight of the concrete mix, with the shape and size of the particles being important factors that will influence workability and strength of the concrete. Aggregates fall into two main categories, fine aggregates made up of particles smaller than 5mm in diameter, and coarse, made up of particles larger than 5mm. They can also be classified according to their density, dense and lightweight aggregates.

Typically 20mm aggregate is used for most construction work. Lightweight aggregate concretes give a better fire resistance and thermal insulation value than concretes manufactured using a dense aggregate. However, lightweight aggregate concrete has a higher porosity and as a result does not perform so well with weather resistance and durability.

Aggregates are usually graded, ensuring that all voids between the particles are filled and that all particles are evenly coated with cement.

PROPERTIES

Strength
Concrete is strong in compression but the tensile strength of concrete is usually only 10% of the compressive strength. As a consequence steel reinforcement bars or a fabric mesh is often used as a reinforcing material. Strength is also influenced by the proportioning of the materials and the type of aggregate used.

Fire Resistance
Concrete has good fire resisting properties, with no significant loss of strength up to 250°C. The fire resistance can be increased by using specific aggregates such as blast furnace slag, crushed bricks or lightweight aggregates.

Weather resistance
The proportioning mix of the concrete will dictate the weather resistance of the concrete. Where concrete needs to be weather and frost resistance it is important that the porosity of the concrete is minimised.

Thermal insulation
Concrete made from lightweight aggregates has an improved thermal insulation performance due to these aggregates containing more air which is a good thermal insulator.

For more information visit:
Concrete Society http://www.concrete.org.uk
BRMCA http://www.brmca.org.uk
The Concrete Centre https://www.concretecentre.com

TIMBER

Timber is a very popular material in the construction industry due to its versatility, diversity, availability, and aesthetic properties. The material is relatively cheap, strong and can be easily converted into different shapes and sizes as required. Approximately 30% of the annual worldwide timber harvest is for use in construction with the rest going to paper production and fuel.

Commercial timber is classified into two main categories, hardwood and softwood. Hardwoods have a more complex cellular structure to softwoods and therefore present different characteristics and qualities.

Typical Hardwood	Typical Softwood
Imported:	*Imported:*
Afrormosia, Mahogany, Obeche, Sapele, Teak, Utile	Douglas Fir, Parana Pine, Pitch Pine, Redwoods, Wester Hemlock, Wester Red Cedar
Home produced:	*Home produced:*
Ash, Beech, Birch, Elm, Oak, Sycamore	European Spruce, Larch, Scots Pine, Yew

Figure 3.1 - Typical hardwoods and softwoods
(Information from Fundamental Building Technology - See References)

Softwoods are from conifers, generally with needle shaped leaves, evergreen and growing in the northern temperate forests. Softwood examples can be seen in Figure 3.1. Softwoods are characteristically fast growing, and therefore cheaper than hardwoods. Softwoods take up about 75% of timber used in the UK construction industry. They have a lower density than hardwoods, so they are not as structurally strong, they are also less durable and tend to require preservative treatment.

Hardwoods are broad leafed deciduous trees, although the tropical varieties are evergreen. Hardwoods are strong, durable and are often used for decorative purposes. Hardwoods are generally more expensive than softwoods depending on species and dimensions of timber required.

PROPERTIES

Strength
Timber has a high strength to weight ratio, with the strength increasing in direct proportion to its density. Timber is quite elastic and can retain its original shape after deforming under a load that has then been removed. Defects in the timber, such as knots, checks and splits can affect the strength of the wood.

Timber is graded into Strength Classes. Softwoods are divided into 12 strength classes, (C14 to C50) and hardwoods into 8 strength classes (D18 to D70). This grading allows designers to specify timber fit for purpose and not over specify resulting in an increased cost and waste of material unnecessarily. The most commonly used strength classes for softwood in residential construction are C16 and C24.

TRADA have produced span tables as a guide for specifiers designing structural elements in construction. These span tables cover floors, ceilings, rafters, and so on, allowing for accurate timber sizing according to project requirements.

Thermal and moisture movement
Wood is an anisotropic material, it can take up moisture in the surrounding atmosphere which will cause it to swell or shrink when it loses the moisture again. If a timber has a high moisture content during construction, which then dries when the building is heated, it can have quite significant effects such as gaps forming, damage to finishes, or in worst cases the timber can even split or crack.

Thermal insulation
Timber is a good thermal insulator in comparison to other structural components such as steel or concrete.

Fire Resistance
Timber is a combustable material, but it is possible to provide a level of fire resistance due to the predictability of the timber. Timber has a charring rate, meaning as it burns it results in a loss of section at a predictable speed, where just a few millimetres under the burning zone the temperature of the timber will be close to normal. It is therefore able to retain its strength unlike other structural elements such as steel. Timber can be treated with surface coatings to retard the spread of fire.

Durability
Timber has a good resistance to sunlight and frost, and can be submerged in water for periods of time. However, timber is susceptible to attack from fungi, insects and marine borers. Fungal attack can be avoided if moisture content is kept below 20%. Fungal issues such as dry rot and wet rot are both related to moisture content and can cause quite significant damage.

Timbers have a grading for durability classified into five groups:
- Class 1: Very durable
- Class 2: Durable
- Class 3: Moderately durable
- Class 4: Slightly durable
- Class 5: No durable

Timbers with low durability can be treated with preservatives to improve durability and reduce possibility of decay. Areas that would be particularly important are:
- where timber is in contact with ground
- where timber is used at or below the DPC level
- where the timber is encased in concrete or masonry
- where ventilation can not be provided
- where moisture content is likely to exceed 20%
- where low durability class timber is used in a high risk area
- where fungal or insect attack are high risk

Sustainability
There is a large emphasis on sustainability in timber production which has led to a number of schemes to ensure that timber is being used from sustainable sources. These schemes vary from country to country, but the UK has the FSC - the Forest Stewardship Council, and the Programme for the Endorsement of Forest Certification (PEFC). Specifiers are urged to use FSC timber wherever possible to ensure that it has come from well managed forests and is truly sustainable.

Timber has the highest sustainability credentials of all the construction materials, given that it takes up CO^2 from the air rather than produce it. It is also a great product for recycling and reclaiming, as well as being biodegradable. Chippings and sawdust from production can also be used in various boardings, such as particle board.

TIMBER PRODUCTS

There are a wide range of timber products manufactured from wood materials. Many products are manufactured from small timber sections or by-products. These include:
- Plywood
- Fibreboard
- Blackwood and laminboard
- Laminated timber
- Cross laminated timber
- Structural insulated panels

- Shingles
- Veneer

The main products we will look at are the boarding materials.

PLYWOOD

Plywood is made by laminating a series of thin timber layers or plies - they are bonded together using adhesive. The plies are crossed at 90° to each other around a central core ply. They are then cured in a hot press, sanded and trimmed to the standard dimensions - usually 1200mmx2400mm. Sheet thickness ranges from 4mm to 25mm for normal construction use.

Plywood is classed according to the adhesive used and suitability to given applications:
- Class1: Dry conditions (suitable for interior use)
- Class 2: Humid conditions (suitable for protected applications such as behind cladding or under roof coverings.)
- Class 3: Exterior conditions (exposed weather)

Plywood is used for a range of applications in the construction industry due to its strength and versatility. It is used for making structural beams such as box beams and I beams, as well as plywood panels, sheathing for timber frame, floor and roof decking, formwork amongst other things.

PARTICLEBOARD

Particle boards comprise of particles of wood, such as flakes, chips, shavings or sawdust, bonded tighter under pressure and heat to form a panel material. Particleboard can come in a range of qualities dependent on the resin used. Wood particle board is made with a resin, whereas cement particle board uses a cement binder. Wood particleboard (chipboard) is predominantly used in the furniture industry, veneered flat pack furniture is a perfect match to the qualities of chipboard. Flooring grade particle board is popular in residential construction, with heavy duty flooring and flat roof decking a structural grade moisture resistant panel would be specified.

The cement particleboards offer improved resistance to fire and water and is suitable for use both internally and externally.

OSB (ORIENTED STRAND BOARD)

OSB is manufactured from 0.5mm thick timber flakes or strands up to 75mm in width. They are formed into boards using adhesive and pressed and heated to set and form the board. OSB is similar in make up to particle board but similar in strength to plywood. OSB is used in large quantities for sheathing in timber frame housing, while the moisture resistant grade is suited to roof sarking, with the even higher grade used for flat roof decking. OSB can also be used in I Beams and heavy duty flooring. Its thickness can range from 6mm to 40mm. OSB is graded as follows:
OSB 1: General purpose, interior - dry conditions
OSB 2: Load-bearing - dry conditions
OSB 3: Load bearing - humid conditions
OSB 4: Heavy duty, load bearing - humid conditions

For more information visit:
Structural Timber Association http://www.structuraltimber.co.uk
TRADA https://www.trada.co.uk

METALS

Metals are categorised into ferrous and non ferrous. The term ferrous metal indicates a predominance of iron within the element. Examples of ferrous metals include steel and pig iron, and alloys of iron with other metals such as stainless steel.

Non-ferrous metals do not contain iron in appreciable amounts. Examples of non ferrous metals include aluminium, copper, lead, nickel, zinc.

A wide range of metals are used in the construction industry, ranging from structural uses, to fixings, to roof coverings and claddings. The most popular being iron, steel, aluminium, lead and zinc. Although metal has a relatively large energy input for production, this is often offset by its long life and recycling options.

Metal is a high density, high thermal conductivity material, which is generally prone to corrosion. Often alloys are used to reduce this effect.

STEEL

Structural Steel
Steel is a very common construction material. Structural steel is formed into profiles, with a specific cross section according to structural requirements and standards. The most common structural shapes in the UK are the I-Beam (an I shaped cross section) which includes the Universal Beam (UB) and the Universal Column (UC). Also the SHS structural hollow section which include square, rectangle and circular cross sections, are common structural steel shapes. Structural steel can be made by hot or cold rolling, or in some cases they can be made up of individual sections welded together.

PROPERTIES

Strength
Steel, unlike concrete, has good compressive strength as well as tensile strength - hence its consistent use in commercial and industrial construction.

Fire Resistance
Steel does not retain its strength and stiffness well when heated to high temperatures. As a result a number of fire protection measures are often taken to give suitable fire rating performance. These measures include intumescent coatings, sprayed coatings, boxing in or encasing the steel in masonry or concrete.

Corrosion
Steel can corrode after prolonged contact with water and as a result is often treated to provide water resistance. The fire resistant coatings often provide water resistance.

Steel frame construction
Light steel frame construction is an alternative to timber frame construction. The steel frame tends to be a galvanised steel channel section which is assembled off site and bolted together once in situ. Steel frame construction is covered later in this book.

Profiled Steel Sheeting
Steel sheeting, with varying profiles is often used in roof and wall cladding, particularly in a commercial and industrial setting.

Sheet Metal Coverings for Roofing
A sheet metal covering for a roof must be malleable, in order to adapt to the varying profiles of a roof. A great advantage of sheet metals for roofing and cladding is that they are durable, aesthetically pleasing and

recyclable. They are however a fairly expensive option. Sheet metals will tend to have more thermal movement than other roofing materials and therefore require joints that can accommodate this movement.

ALUMINIUM

Aluminium is popular due to its durability and is lightweight compared to steel. It is used for roofing, cladding, curtain walling, structural glazing, flashings, rainwater goods, and much more.

Aluminium has a natural extremely thin aluminium oxide film on its surface, that, once scratched will immediately be produced. This makes it a durable choice for many uses in construction.

Aluminium can receive various coatings to improve either appearance or durability. Surface textures can be achieved such as polished, matt, etched and pattern rolled.

Corrosion
Aluminium is susceptible to corrosion from the alkalinity of wet cement, concrete and mortar. Therefore, it is important during construction that any aluminium is protected. Aluminium can also be affected by preservatives used to treat timber which could cause problems in conditions of high humidity. It is also susceptible to corrosion from other metals, in particular copper, so rainwater from a copper roof must not come into contact with an aluminium cladding for example.

COPPER

Copper is used in construction for roofing, and in some cases wall cladding. Copper is well known for its patina, the development of the green colour which gradually spreads when exposed to environmental conditions. In typical settings, the green patina will develop over about ten years. On wall cladding, or vertical settings however, the copper will often retain its colour due to fast water run off.

Corrosion
Copper is resistant to corrosion although it can cause staining to other materials from rainwater run off. Zinc, galvanised steel and non anodised aluminium should not be used under copper.

LEAD

Lead is used in construction for roofing, cladding and flashings, along with gutter linings. In roofing, lead is installed in continuous smooth sheets, with the joints wood cored rolled, hollow rolled, or standing seams. In wall cladding the joints are similar to roofing, but in some cases a lead faced panel can be used and fixed to the support system.

Corrosion
Lead can cause some staining to surrounding materials, which can be avoided by the use of a patination oil after the lead has been installed. Lead is generally resistant to corrosion but care must be taken to avoid a build up of condensation underneath the lead.

ZINC

Zinc is often used in roofing and cladding in the construction industry. Roll cap and standing seam roofing systems are both used, usually installed over a timber deck. In cladding, zinc can be used as interlocking tiles, held in place with fixing clips. Zinc tarnishes in the air and produces a protective oxide film - this prevents further degradation. Zinc used in a roofing system would have an expected life span of 40 years, while in a wall cladding position could last up to 60 years.

Corrosion
As mentioned previously, zinc doesn't get along very well with copper, where rainwater draining from copper discharges onto zinc. Galvanised steel above zinc can cause staining. Similar to lead, condensation build up underneath the zinc will also cause corrosion.

FLAT ROOF MATERIALS

Flat roof materials that are used in residential construction consist of mastic asphalt, bitumen sheet built up roofing or single ply sheeting or membranes, along with metal sheeting which we have covered previously.

MASTIC ASPHALT

Mastic asphalt is a jointless, weather proof and impermeable material with a low softening point. It is delivered onto site in the form of blocks ready to be melted before applying to the roof. The hot material is then spread over the roof in two layers which then cools and forms a hard waterproof surface. The layers tend to come to 20mm with up stands of 150mm to any masonry, roof lights or pipes. The mastic asphalt is laid over a sheathing felt to prevent any effects from structural or thermal movement, and finished with 10mm of stone chippings to protect the surface from softening under sunlight. This also prolongs the life of the mastic asphalt. If there is no parapet wall the asphalt is designed to overhang and drain into gutters. A flashing is usually positioned to drain run off from the asphalt to the gutter.

Asphalt is considered to be a relatively cheap flat roofing option, and more durable than built up bitumen sheeting, with a life of around 20 years. Mastic asphalts is derived from crude oil, and is said to cause harm to the environment in its manufacturing process. However, it is reclaimable and possible to remove from the roof and reuse.

BITUMEN FELT ROOFING

Bitumen felt or sheet roofing consists of a mat of glass or synthetic fibres impregnated with a bitumen coating which creates a water resistant sheet.

The sheets are applied to the roof surface using a hot bonding bitumen, in three layers. The first layer is partially bonded to the roof, to allow for any movement. They are laid with side laps of 75mm, which is then staggered on the following layers to avoid excess side laps on top of one another. At eaves, the sheets are lapped over the fascia to an edge trim (usually aluminium) which drains into the gutter. Any upstands to parapets or walls will need to be 150mm high, and dressed into the masonry, with a protective flashing over the top. The final layer is finished with an aggregate topping, to protect the surface from sunlight, and extend the life of the roof. A glass fibre based sheet has an expected life span of 7-15 years, while a polyester based sheet will have an expected life span of 15-25 years - the cost of the two products reflects this.

Bitumen products are not considered to be an environmentally suitable choice as they are made from crude oil, and are non recyclable.

SINGLE PLY MEMBRANES

Single ply roofing systems are becoming increasingly popular and are now not just an option for commercial projects. They consist of a continuous layer between 1mm and 3mm thick that provides excellent weather protection.
They are fixed over a polyester fleece to prevent damage to the membrane, using a variety of fixing options, from bonding to mechanical fixings and in some cases loose laid. Single ply roofing systems require specialist installers as the quality of workmanship is key to the performance of the material.

The single ply systems are generally derived from petrochemicals and have poor sustainability credentials, and it is also not possible to reuse or recycle the membranes easily. The life expectancy of a single ply roofing system can be between 20-30 years.

PITCHED ROOF MATERIALS

The roof pitch is often determined by the material of the roof tile, and its style. Generally, residential constructions uses three main types of pitched roof tile material:
- Slate
- Clay
- Concrete

SLATE

Slates are derived from metamorphic rocks which are split into tiles of between 3mm to 10mm thickness. They tend to come from areas such as the Lake District, North Wales and Cornwall, although we now see imports from China, Brazil and Spain. Depending on the region of the slate the colour will vary from blues, greens, greys and plum. Slates have a relatively low embodied energy, however can be considered to be degrading to the landscape. Slates can be reclaimed for reuse but often require restorative work due to the damage that can be done when the tiles are stripped from a roof during demolition. The imports from China and Brazil are certainly cheaper but of course have a higher embodied energy due to their transportation.

A synthetic alternative to natural slate has been developed consisting of a mix of recycled slates, and various synthetic fibres. These are generally lighter in weight than natural tiles and are less expensive, but they are not as durable as natural slate.

Slates require a double lap system when installing and are nailed in place either at the head or centrally to the battens below. A minimum pitch for a slate roof is 20° under sheltered or moderate exposure, or 22.5° under more severe exposure. Generally the lap required is a minimum of 75mm or with a lower pitch it can be up to 100mm.

Roof pitches, laps and gauges should always be checked with the tile manufacturer.

CLAY TILES

Clay tiles have a relatively high embodied energy and can cause land degradation due to extraction, although reduced transportation costs due to the production being in this country. Clay tiles are suitable for reclamation and reuse due to their durability.

Plain
Plain clay tiles are either hand made or machine presses clay that is fired in a similar production process to bricks. Plain tiles have been used in Britain since the middle ages. They vary in colour and have a thickness of between 10-15mm, with nibs at the top to allow them to be hooked over the roof battens. They are nailed every fourth course due to the stability the nibs allow.

Clay is an absorbent material and therefore the roof pitch of a clay tile roof must be steep in order to allow for sufficient rain water run off. If the roof is not steep enough, water can build up and cause damage if it freezes during cold weather. Clay tiles have a double lap, in a 40° roof pitch the tile has a head lap of 65mm and a gauge of 100mm.

They are costly in both labour and materials, and as a result a concrete version was introduced which has become more popular than the clay alternative.

PANTILE

Pantiles have a waved profile, similar to an S, with overlapping side joints, which allows them to be single lapped. Pantiles were originally imported from Holland and only produced in Britain towards the eighteenth century. In modern construction the clay pantile has been superseded by a concrete alternative. The pantile was popular before the introduction of interlocking tiles.

ROMAN AND SPANISH TILES

Roman tiles are similar sized to pantiles with opposite chamfered corners, they can be either a single or double tile. Originally clay, these are now most commonly seen in their concrete alternative. Spanish tiles have an upper and a lower tile, convex and concave respectively.

CONCRETE TILES

A mix of cement and well graded sand make up the concrete tile. They are available in a wide range of colours and surface finishes, as plain tiles, pantiles, Roman tiles and interlocking.
The interlocking tile has grooves along its vertical edge that allows the tiles to lock into one another under and over the edge of the adjacent tile. This means that they are single lap tiles as the water can run down the grooves of the connecting tiles. They are available in a range of profiles including the pantiles and Roman style tiles. The pitch of an interlocking tile roof can be a minimum of around 20° right up to vertical. The lap is generally 75mm. Tiles can be fixed using both nails or clips.

Concrete tiles have a high embodied energy, along with land degradation due to extraction of materials. They are however, durable and have low transportation energy costs due to being produced in this country.

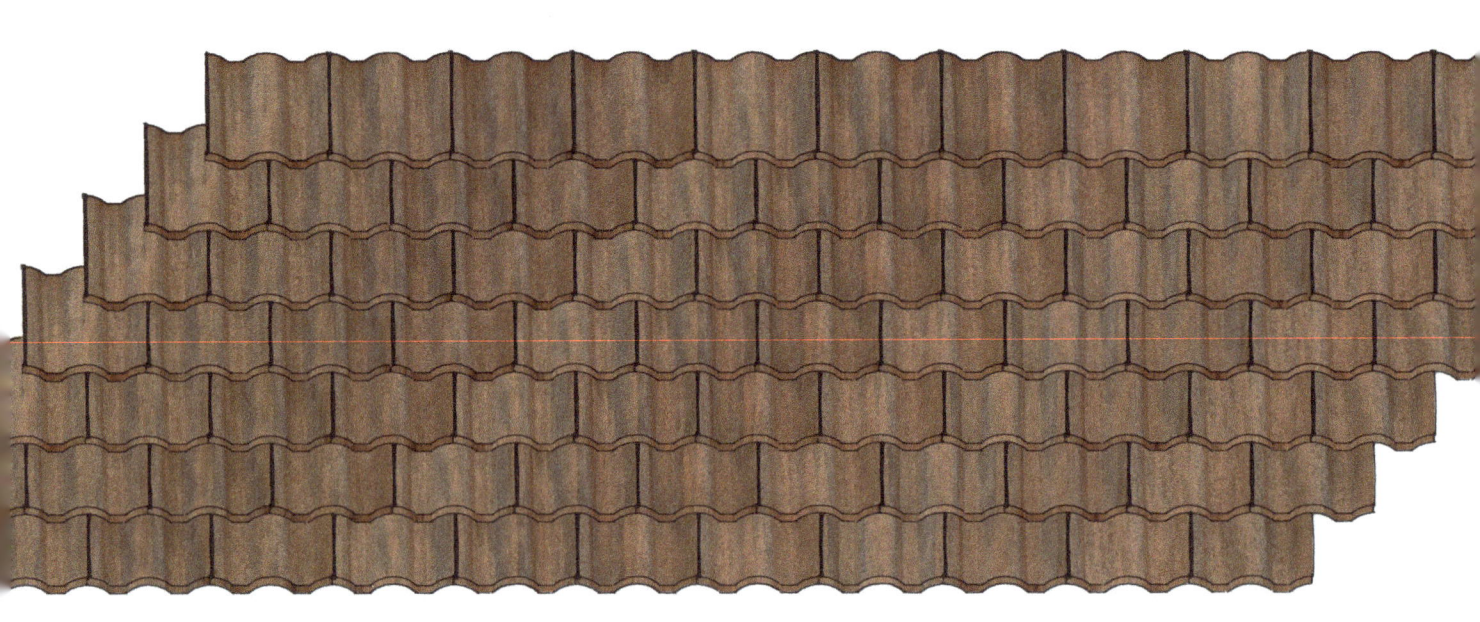

SECTION 3 - MATERIALS

PLASTER AND PLASTERBOARD

Plasters and plasterboards provide an internal finish to walls and ceilings. The benefits of using this method is to provide a smooth clean surface for decoration, whilst masking any background unevenness. The plaster or plasterboard can also provide an additional sound, thermal and fire resistance.

Lime plastering was bought to Britain by the Romans. Lime plastering is used in the renovation and conservation of older buildings but modern UK practice is based on gypsum plastering. Gypsum is a naturally occurring product that is mined and factory produced. The advantage of gypsum plasters is that they are less likely to crack due to their very slight expansion on setting.

Gypsum plasters are generally applied in two coats, an undercoat and finishing coat. The undercoat tends to contain coarser aggregates than the finishing coat, with variations to suit specific site requirements. A typical thickness for an undercoat is 11mm on a wall, and 8mm for ceilings.

The finishing coat will have a finer aggregate and gives a smoother even finish. The typical thickness for a finishing coat is 2-3mm.

The type of plaster specified and its application is determined by the background surface of the wall that will be plastered. A rough textured surface such as bricks or concrete blocks has a 'key' which will allow the plaster to adhere to the wall. With smooth surfaces or surfaces that absorb water a bonding agent is required. This can be in the form of PVA applied to the wall prior to plastering, or a polymer bonding agent.

PLASTERBOARD AND DRY LINING

In recent times, wet applied plaster systems have been replaced with dry finishes. The dry finish will consist of plasterboard fixed to the background, with the joints between the boards filled, ready to receive decoration. This method is referred to as dry lining. In some cases the plasterboard receives a skim plaster finish.

Plasterboard consists of a solid gypsum core encased in strong paper liners. Plasterboard is used for dry lining or as a background for plaster, in ceilings, stud partitions and so on. The boards come in standard sizes that coordinate with timber/metal framing systems - 1200mm and 900mm wide. The standard thickness of the plasterboard is 12.5mm, 15mm and 19mm. Boards are available in moisture resistant grades suitable for use in humid conditions such as bathrooms and kitchens. It is also possible to specify fire resistant boards, or sound insulation boards. Insulated plasterboards have also been developed to improve thermal insulation properties of the external wall.

Plasterboard can be fixed to its background by steel lath, nails or screws - to timber frame or steel frame systems. The boards will be fixed directly to solid walls using a bonding of dots of plaster or adhesive. The dot and dab system has raised concerns with regard to airtightness and is now regulated to ensure improved air tightness.

Wallboard is used for a variety of applications including dry lining walls and ceilings, and has tapered or square edges. The tapered edged boards are for direct decoration, as the tapered joint allows for taping, jointing and finishing. Avoiding a wet plaster finish can keep costs down, and prevents the need for skilled plasterers. The jointing can be done by hand or by machine, and consists of applying a jointing compound, to which a jointing tape is added. The compound is then applied over the tape and feathered out.

The square edged boards tend to be skim finished in plaster.

Wallboards are available with a vapour control membrane where interstitial condensation needs to be prevented.

Gypsum used for both plasterboard and plaster is mined which can cause landscape degradation. Energy is required in production, and large amounts of waste are created on site and sent to landfill. Plasterboard is manufactured using around 50% of recycled materials, and the lining papers are usually recycled. As plaster and plasterboard is produced in the UK transportation energy is low.

For more information visit:
British Gypsum http://www.british-gypsum.com

INSULATION

Insulation is playing an increasingly vital role in building design and construction following the growing energy conscious world and knowledge of the environmental impact of the construction industry. With that, occupant comfort is at higher demand than ever before. Buildings need to be sufficiently insulated to prevent excessive amounts of heat escaping from the structure to the outside, and also to prevent excessive heat or cold from affecting the internal environment. Over the years building regulations have substantially increased with regard to thermal performance and will no doubt continue to do so.

Air is an efficient thermal insulant, and therefore most insulating materials used in construction contain large amounts of air voids. When we consider the thermal performance of a material we look at the thermal conductivity W/mK, which measures the ability of a material to conduct heat. In terms of insulation, the the lower the figure, the better the performance of the insulant will be, as heat finds it more difficult to travel through the material.

As an example, a high performing new insulating material aerogel has a thermal conductivity of 0.018 W/mK while a sheet of glass can have a thermal conductivity of 1.05 W/mK.

The materials used in buildings as insulation can be grouped into organic and inorganic insulants.

INORGANIC INSULANTS

Inorganic insulants are made from naturally occurring materials, that are formed into fibre or cellular structures such as mineral wool, glass wool, exfoliated vermiculite and so on. These types of insulant are generally incombustible, they do not support the spread of flame. Inorganic insulants generally have a higher U-Value than organic insulants.

Wood wool slabs are made from wood fibres and cement. They have good load bearing properties and therefore are suitable for roof decking material. Mineral wool is manufactured from volcanic rock to create a fibrous roll or slab of insulation. It is available in a variety of forms to be used in different settings. It can be loose for blown cavity insulation, mats for insulating lofts, batts (slabs) for cavity fill in masonry, rigid slabs for pitched roofs, weather resistant boards and more. Thermal conductivity of mineral wool is typically between 0.031 and 0.036 W/mK. Mineral wool is also used for the manufacture of fire stops to prevent fire spreading through cavities due to its good fire performance.

Glass wool is also a non combustible product, and used in similar forms as mineral wool. It can be loose for blown cavity wall insulation, rolls for roofing, batts for cavity insulation and so on. It has a typical thermal conductivity range of 0.031 to 0.040 W/mK.

Aerogel is a lightweight material with a very low density. It can be used to fully fill thin panels, or glazing units to create a high performing product. It is an expensive material but has a thermal conductivity of 0.018 W/mK.

ORGANIC INSULANTS

Some organic materials are based on hydrocarbon polymers, creating materials such as extruded polystyrene and polyurethane. Organic insulation also includes products made from natural materials such as hemp and sheep's wool or newspaper.

Expanded polystyrene (EPS) is a closed cell product with a thermal conductivity ranging from 0.033 to 0.040 W/mK. It is a combustible product and produces noxious smoke when burning, but it can be treated with a flame retardant additive. Generally seen as boards, EPS is lightweight and used in cavity walls, floors and both pitched and flat roofs.

Extruded polystyrene (XPS) is denser than EPS and therefore stronger also used in cavity wall and pitched roof insulation. It also has a high resistance to water absorption so is suitable for flooring applications below concrete slab, and on inverted roofs. Thermal conductivity ranges from 0.025 to 0.027 W/mK

Polyisocyanurate foam (PIR) is used in roof insulation, cavity walls and floor insulation. PIR is combustible but can be treated to achieve a Class 0 rating. Thermal conductivity ranges from 0.023 to 0.025 W/mK.

Polyurethane foam (PUR) is a closed cell foam, made into boards or used as a foam. It is another combustible material produces high levels of noxious fumes and smoke in a fire, although a flame resistant material is available. It is used in roofing, as well as an insulator to profiled metal sheeting. It can be injected into cavity walls but this is typically as a remedial measure and not a new build situation. PUR is often used as a spray to fill gaps around service voids and for filling small inaccessible locations. Thermal conductivity ranges from 0.019 to 0.023 W/mK for the rigid boards.

Sheep's wool is a renewable resource and comes in the form of batts. It has a low conductivity and suitable for ventilated lofts, and in timber frame construction. Care must be taken with the installation of vapour permeable breather membranes to the cold side of construction. It cannot be used in wet applications. Thermal conductivity of 0.039W/mK, although it is a renewable source with a low embodied energy it is still more expensive than standard mineral wool.

Cellulose insulation is made from shredded recycled paper. It is treated to improve its fire rating and smouldering resistance. It can be used for internal floors and loft insulation, roof voids and breathing walls - it can also be damp sprayed in between wall studs before the wall is closed. Thermal conductivity of cellulose is between 0.035 and 0.040 W/mK depending on application.

Hemp fibre insulation is a response to the demand on sustainable materials along with flax and coconut fibre insulations. Similar to cellulose it is suitable for a breathing structure. The batts can be used in ceilings and walls, wile the rolls can be used in lofts, floor and walls. The fibres receive borax treatment for fire resistance. Thermal conductivity of flat fibre insulation is 0.037W/mK, while hemp ranges between 0.038 and 0.040 W/mK, and coconut fibre is 0.045 W/mK.

Material	Thermal conductivity (W/mK)
Aerogel	0.018
Phenolic foam	0.018-0.031
Polyurethane foam	0.019-0.025
Foil faced foam	0.020
Polyisocyanurate foam	0.023-0.025
Extruded polystyrene	0.025-0.027
Expanded PVC	0.030
Mineral wool	0.031-0.040
Glass wool	0.031-0.040
Expanded polystyrene	0.033-0.040
Cellulose	0.035-0.040
Flax	0.037
Sheep's wool	0.037-0.039
Rigid foamed glass	0.037-0.048
Urea-formaldehyde foam	0.038
Hemp wool	0.040
Corkboard	0.042
Coconut fibre boards	0.045
Fibre insulation board	0.050

Manufacturers products may vary, information from Materials for Architects -
see references

Figure 3.2- Typical thermal conductivity of insulation materials

Manufacturers products may vary, information from Materials for Architects (See References)

FOUNDATIONS

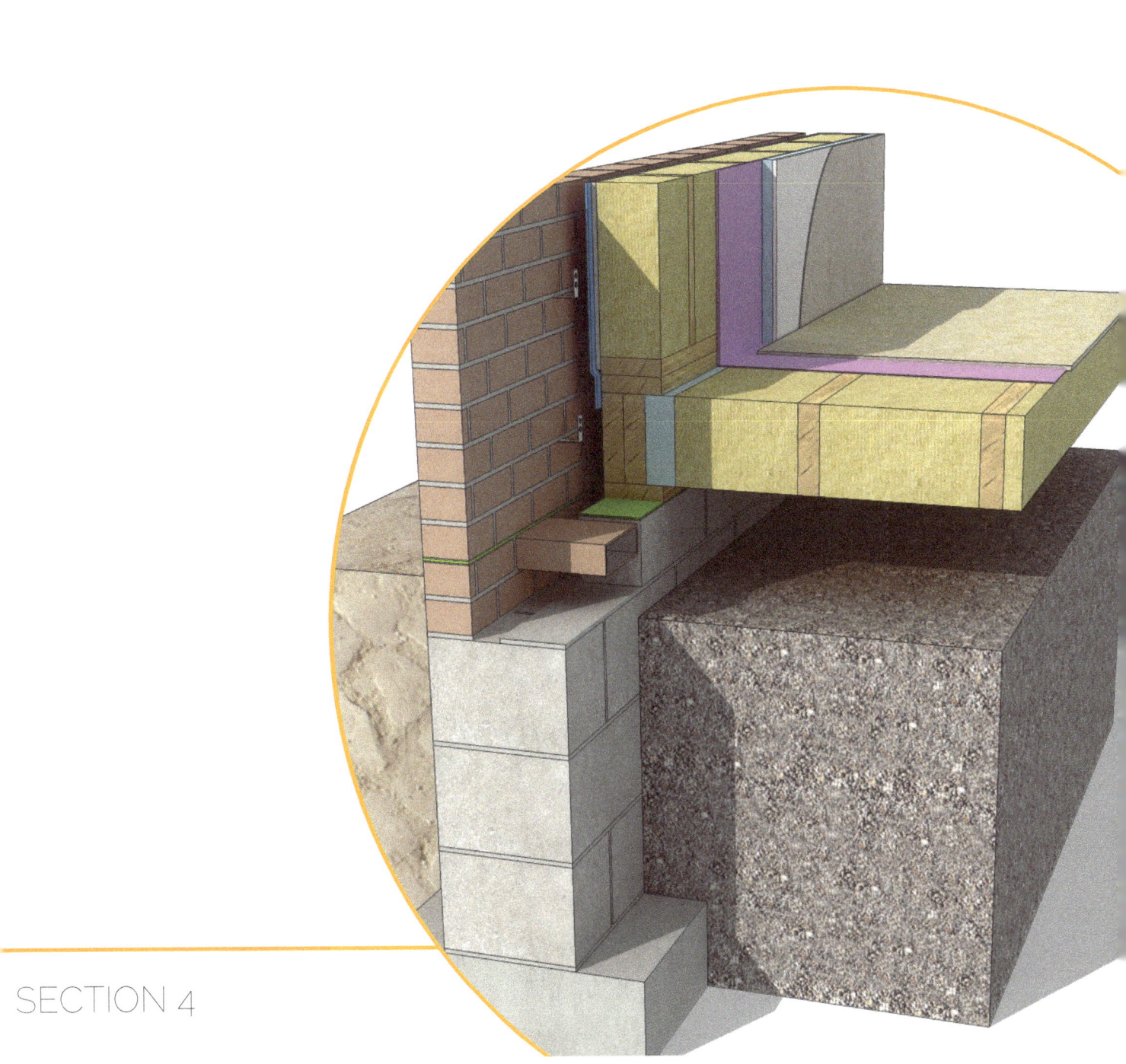

SECTION 4

INTRODUCTION TO FOUNDATION DESIGN

The main role of foundations is to structurally support the building by transferring the loads of the building through the walls into the surrounding soil. In terms of a timber frame structure, the foundations must also protect the timber from moisture ingress by lifting the members above the ground.

The foundation must transmit the combined, dead and imposed loads on a building to the ground safely. Building Regulations in the UK have led to standard forms of concrete foundations along with rigorous investigations into the bearing capacity of soils and bedrock.

IMPLICATIONS ON FOUNDATION DESIGN

The type of soil and bedrock on site will have a strong implication to the foundation design.
The size and depth of the foundation is determined by the size and scale of the structure it must support, along with the bearing capacity of the ground that surrounds it.

Soil
Top soil usually consists of a mixture of solid particles, water and air. It usually contains organic remains of decayed vegetation close to the surface. Top soil is unsuitable for supporting foundations, and should be stripped from the immediate site, and retained for landscaping the surrounding site.

Sub-Soil
Sub-soils range from rocks, such as granite or sandstone, all the way through to soft clay and silt. This subsoil sits below the top soil and supports the load of the building. Different types of sub-soil can require specialist foundation design due to their poor bearing capacity. The following table shows the types of sub-soil and its suitability to supporting house foundations.

Ground Type	Notes
Granite	
Limestone	
Sandstone	These sub-soils provide good support to foundations. They generally require pneumatic or hydraulic tools for excavation
Slate	
Hard chalk	
Compact sands	Sub-soils provide good support. They do not require special tools for excavation, only standard machinery
Gravels	
Firm and stiff clays	Wider foundations may be required than sands and gravels. Excavation can be done by hand or machine
Sandy clays	
Loose sand	
Soft silt	Easy to excavate but generally will require specially designed foundations
Soft clay	

Figure 4.1 - Soil types and suitability

Before detailed foundation design can begin various site and ground investigation studies need to be carried out in order to ensure accurate design.

Site investigations determine:
- The nature, past use and condition of the site
- Whether this has any implications for the proposed building and its foundations

Ground investigations can gather information on:
- The nature and thickness of top soil
- The nature, thickness and stratum depth of sub-soil
- Assessment of bearing pressure
- Ground water levels
- Presence of chemicals in the ground
- Any existing hazards in the ground

Approved Document Part A of the Building Regulations states that a building must be constructed so that any ground movement caused by shrinkage, swelling or freezing of the subsoil or any other landslip or subsidence, will not impair the stability of the building.

Frost Heave

If the water table is high, and close to the surface, some soils will expand when frozen. This is due to ice crystals forming in the soil and causing it to expand - creating frost heave. In the UK the ground is rarely frozen at depths of more than 600-700mm which should be sufficiently deep for most strip foundations in these types of soil.

Change in volume

Sub-soils than contain clay can often suffer shrinkage caused by drying and expansion on wetting, due to the changes in the season. These changes in volume can be further impacted by proximity to trees and shrubs. The more vigorous the growth of shrubs and trees in firm clay soils, the greater the depth below surface the volume change will occur. Likewise, when trees or shrubs are removed from site to enable building work, there can be movement in the clay soil for some years after clearance, as the clay recovers moisture previously taken up by the trees. The same can be said when planting new trees and shrubs in existing clay soils, as the trees will change the existing moisture in the clay which can result in shrinkage. In these types of scenarios, specialist foundations must be designed to ensure suitable resistance to the changes in the soil volumes.

TYPES OF FOUNDATION

There are four main types of foundations:

- Strip - the preferred and most common choice for low rise housing. Strip of concrete under all load bearing walls.
- Pile - Long concrete members take the load of the building through weak soils to load bearing strata.
- Pad - More commonly used under point loads, such as columns, but can be used under ground beams to transfer loads.
- Raft - Concrete raft which spreads the loads over the whole ground floor, used where building loads are high, or ground conditions poor.

STRIP FOUNDATIONS

Strip foundations are the common foundation design in residential construction. They consist of a strip of reinforced concrete formed centrally under a load bearing wall. The width of the concrete strip is determined by the structure it will be supporting, along with the bearing capacity of the soil in order for the load to be safely transmitted to the ground.

The greater the bearing capacity of the soil, the less the width of the foundation. The following table (based on Approved Document Part A) suggests recommended minimum width of concrete strip foundations.

Type of ground	20kN/m (equivalent of single storey dwelling)	40kN/m (equivalent of two storey dwelling)	60kN/m (equivalent of three storey dwelling)
Gravel or sand (medium dense)	min 250mm	min 400mm	min. 600mm
Firm clay, firm sandy clay	min. 300mm	min 450mm	min 750mm
Loose clay or sand	min. 400mm	Foundation to be specially designed to suit conditions and specific requirements	

Figure 4.2 - Minimum width of concrete strip foundations

Trenches are excavated to a level of undisturbed compacted soil, where the concrete strip will be spread. The width of the excavated trench must allow for the bricklayer to build the wall off the strip, usually a minimum of 600mm. A trench depth of 450mm is the minimum set out in the Building Regulation requirements, however, this is increased to 700mm if there is a danger of frost heave.

Given that most sands and gravels can support low rise housing with a concrete strip width of only 400-500mm a cost effective alternative option is a trench fill method. This avoids the need for working space and can be a more economic option. The trench fill is a deeper concrete fill bringing it closer to ground level, where the wall is then constructed.

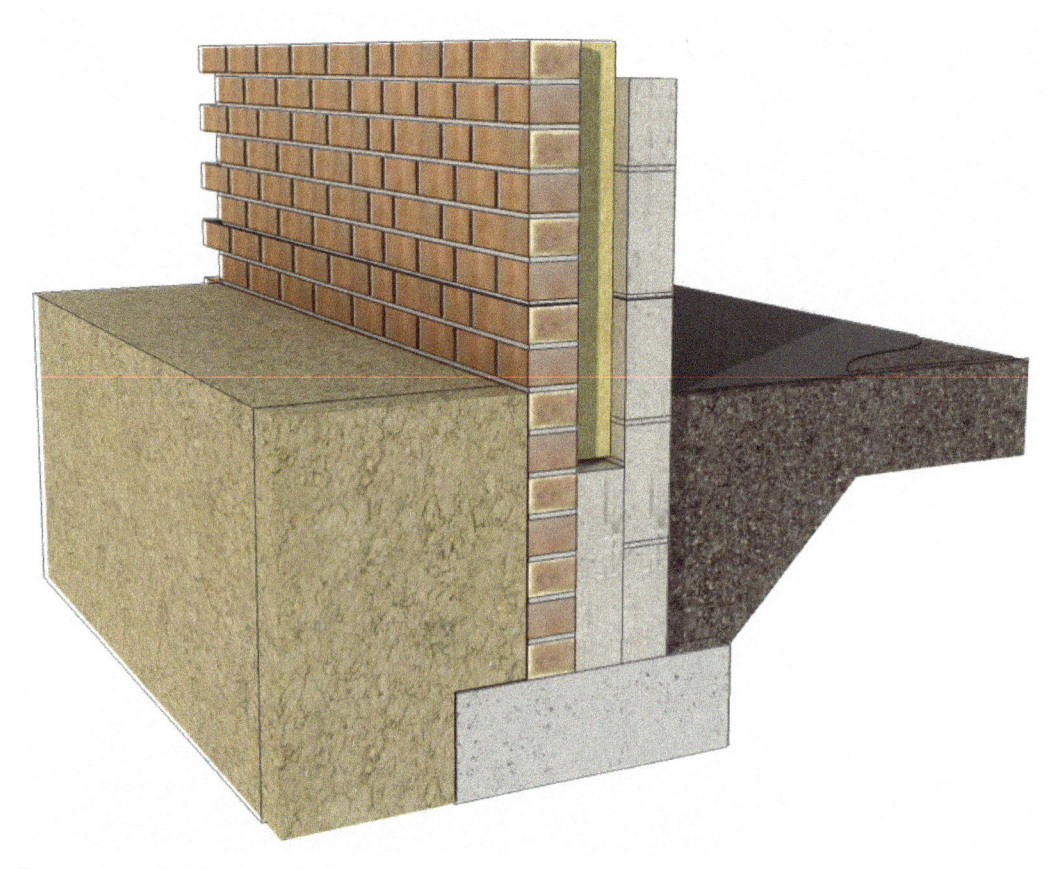

Figure 4.3 - Examples of strip foundation

SECTION 4 - FOUNDATIONS

PILE FOUNDATIONS

When strip foundations are not suitable, a pile foundation system can be used. Pile foundations can be seen where trees or shrubs are in close proximity to the proposed structure, or where a site has been cleared of existing trees and could be susceptible to volume changes. Pile foundations transfer the load of the building to a depth that is capable of supporting the full loads of the structure. It is an expensive process, due to the requirement of specialist subcontractors.

Once the piles have been driven into the ground in the correct position, the tops are cut to the required level in order to have a concrete beam cast over them forming the base for the walls. The beam spans from pile to pile, therefore not requiring support from the soil below.

PAD FOUNDATIONS

Pad foundations generally consist of a concrete square pad which supports ground beams onto which the structural walls can be built. Pad foundations differ from pile foundations as they do not extend to such depths as piles, and the width of the pad varies in order to distribute the loads to a greater area. Pits are excavated to the required depth, where the concrete is then cast. Brick or concrete piers are then built or cast on the pad foundations up to the underside of the concrete beams that support the walls.

RAFT FOUNDATION

Raft foundations may be used where soils consist of very soft clay, or other situations where strip, pad or pile foundations are not suitable. A reinforced concrete raft is designed to distribute the loads of the building over the whole area under the raft, which results in little if any settlement. Two main types of raft foundation, the flat slab raft and the wide toe raft.

The flat slab raft is used for smaller buildings where the loads are comparatively small. It is of uniform thickness, and consists of reinforcing to the top and bottom of the slab. Where loads on the foundations would require a thick slab, the wide toe raft is used. The wide toe has a reinforced stiffening edge beam, with a toe at the edge to provide a base for the outer leaf of a cavity wall.

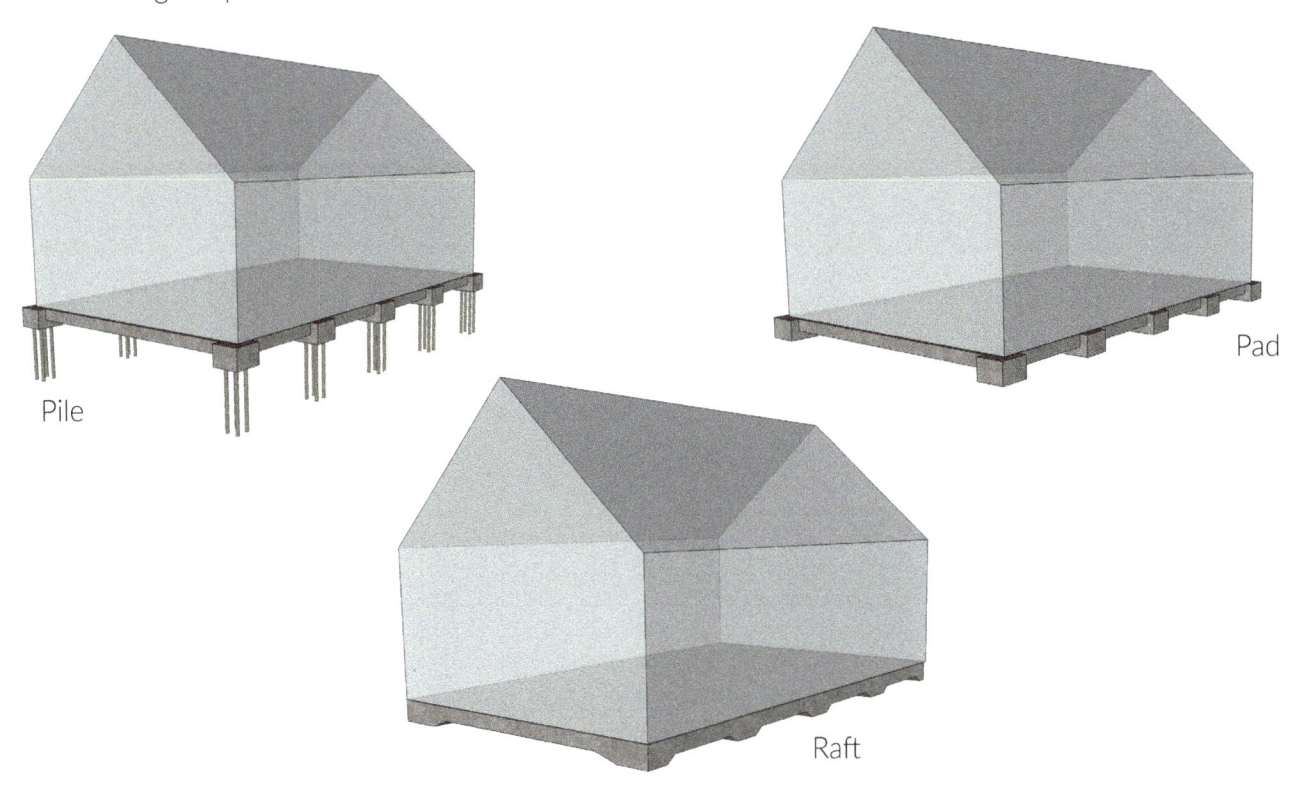

Figure 4.4 - Examples of pile, pad and raft foundations

Blank Page

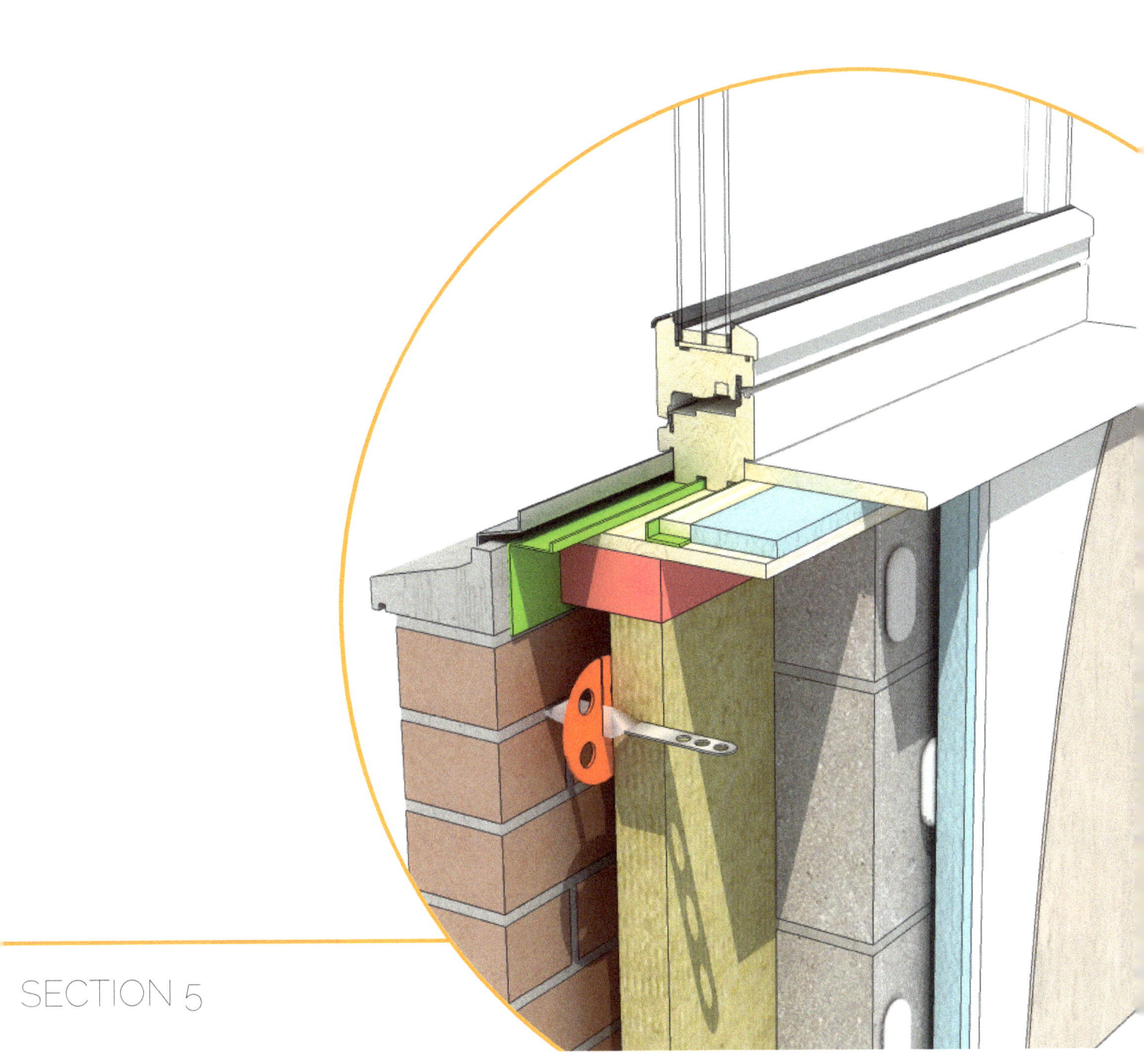

MASONRY CONSTRUCTION

SECTION 5

FLOORS

The most common materials used for the construction of ground and upper floors tend to be concrete or timber. Required span, resistance to passage of sound, and fire resistance will often be factors to consider when deciding which material to use in floor design.

FUNCTIONAL REQUIREMENTS

The functional requirements of a floor are:
- Strength and stability
- Resistance to weather and ground moisture
- Durability
- Fire safety
- Resistance to passage of heat
- Resistance to passage of sound

TYPES OF GROUND FLOORS

CONCRETE FLOORS

There are two types of concrete floor system commonly used in residential construction; ground bearing and suspended. Ground bearing floors, where the concrete slab is supported by the ground below. Suspended concrete floors do not rely on the ground below, but instead are supported by the external walls and therefore the foundations below. In this section we will look at both types of concrete floor.

Ground Bearing Concrete Floor

The ground bearing concrete floor slab is supported by the load bearing strata below. The slab abuts but is not tied to the external walls. The build up of this type of system can typically be:
- Hardcore fill to compacted to create suitable level (approx 200mm thick)
- Damp proof membrane (DPM), often laid over sand binding
- Rigid floor insulation (can be position above or below the concrete slab)
- Concrete floor cast in situ
- Floor screed if required, followed by floor finishes

There are many different options for positioning of damp proof membrane and insulation which can be seen in the following details in this section.

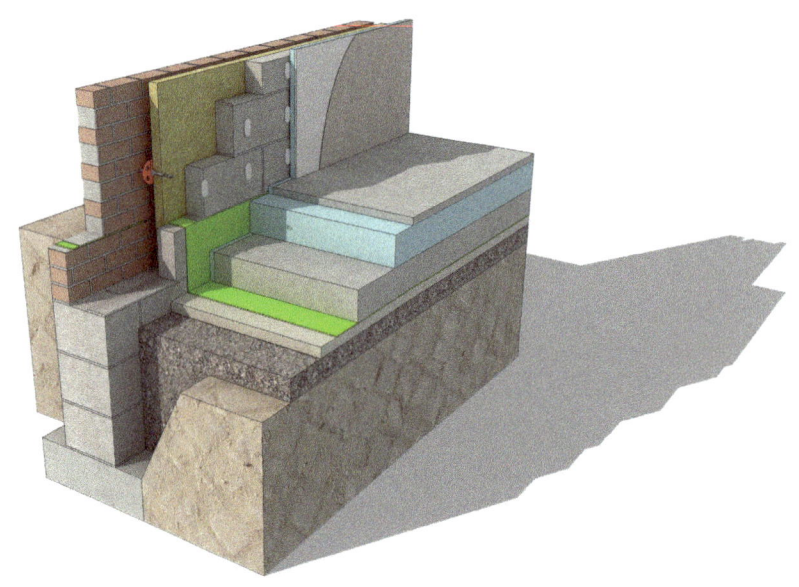

Figure 5.1 - Ground bearing concrete floor

Suspended Concrete Floor

Suspended concrete floors have become popular in UK house construction. They are typically used in situations such as sloping sites, the ground has poor bearing capacity, or there is likelihood of ground volume change. Suspended floors are also used when the water table is high, or when aggressive chemicals are present in the soil that may attack the concrete slab.

The ground floor is made up of suspended concrete slab or beam and block floor, supported by the external and internal load bearing walls, which transfer the loads to the foundations below. Both pre-cast concrete planks or slabs can be used, as well as cast in situ reinforced slabs along with beam and block systems.

Beam and block

These systems use concrete T beams that span between the walls, concrete infill blocks are then inserted between the beams to provide a solid base for the concrete topping or screed that is spread and levelled over the concrete units. Depth of the beams is between 130mm and 250mm and is determined by the span required, and the loads to be supported.

Figure 5.2 - Beam and block floor

Damp Proof Membrane (DPM)

Concrete is not impervious to water and it is therefore necessary to protect the floor with a water resistant barrier to prevent moisture penetrating the building from the ground. This barrier is a damp proof membrane usually in the form of a thin sheet of polythene or polyethylene, although bitumen in various forms can also be used.

The membrane position varies according to the type of floor construction selected. If the membrane is positioned below the concrete slab, it is placed over the hardcore on a sand blinding to protect it from damage. The edges of the membrane are turned up the sides of the external walls so that it overlaps the damp proof course. When using rigid, impermeable insulation, it is prudent to use a vapour control layer on the warm side of the insulation (or position DPM on warm side of insulation) to minimise the possibility of interstitial condensation. While concrete does offer a good level of natural resistance, poor workmanship can sometimes result in the passing of vapour through the structure. Likewise, if a timber floor is being used, it is important to install a vapour control layer under the timber floor.

Damp Proof Course (DPC)

A DPC acts as a barrier to the passage of moisture into the structure, be it upwards in wall foundations, downwards in a parapet or horizontally in a window jamb. Generally made from dense polythene, the DPC should not penetrate the cavity, unless weep holes are provided that can direct water away from the cavity. In a traditional masonry cavity wall the DPC is laid in two separate strips, one internal and one on the external leaf, 150mm minimum above external ground level. The DPC should be lapped with the DPM to provide a good joint and prevent moisture tracking between them.

TIMBER FLOORS

Although timber ground floor construction used to be a popular method, today it is not as common as the concrete alternatives. A suspended timber floor is constructed as a timber platform of boards nailed across timber joists supported on sleeper walls, and the external and internal load bearing walls surrounding them.

Ventilation must be provided throughout the underfloor void and through any sleeper walls with cross ventilation. Due to airtightness, acoustic and sometimes structural requirements of the Building Regulations, joist ends tend to be supported by joist hangers rather than being built into external or sleeper walls.

The floor is insulated in the form of rigid insulation between joists, or quilt between joists supported by netting. Floorboards are fixed over the floor joists and insulation, usually in the form of plywood, chipboard or OSB to required structural performance. These boards are then applied with a floor finish, such as carpet, vinyl and so on.

UPPER FLOORS

TIMBER UPPER FLOORS

Timber has traditionally been the material of choice for upper floor construction. Nowadays, there are suitable

Figure 5.3 - I beams and web joists

alternatives in steel and concrete, however, these are seen more in commercial buildings or residential flats. It is still most common to see timber upper floors in domestic house construction.

Upper floor construction tends to consist of a series of timber joists or beams covered with timber floorboards, or more commonly sheets of chipboard. The size of the joists depend on the span and expected loading. The joists are supported by the external walls on joist hangers or built into the internal leaf, and internal load bearing walls, but also act as a restraint for the external walls.

In order to prevent twisting or warping in the joists, it is sometimes common to find a line of strutting fixed at right angles to the joists. This strutting can reduce bounce in the floor.

More recent additions to timber floor construction are the timber I beams or metal web joists. These engineered joists can span greater distances than traditional timber cut joists and reduce the requirement of internal load bearing walls. The web joists also have the added benefit of not requiring notching or drilling for pipes and cables as they already have voids within the joist.

The Building Regulations require a minimum performance standard of acoustic insulation for floors to bedrooms, bathrooms and other rooms containing a WC. Likewise, upper floors over an unheated area of the dwelling, such as a garage, require the same insulation standard as that of a ground floor.

CONCRETE UPPER FLOORS

As mentioned previously, timber upper floors are still widely used in domestic construction today. However, in recent years some new build houses have been constructed using concrete upper floors, usually as beam and block or plank floors.

This form of concrete pre cast floor is very similar to the ground floor version mentioned earlier in this chapter. When the external walls have been built to the correct level, the pre-cast beams are lifted into position supported at either end by the internal skin of the cavity wall. As with the ground floor, once the beams are in position, the concrete blocks are placed between the beams to provide a base for the cast in situ concrete topping.

Pre-cast plank floors are also used in upper floor construction, and are also supported by the internal leaf of the cavity wall.

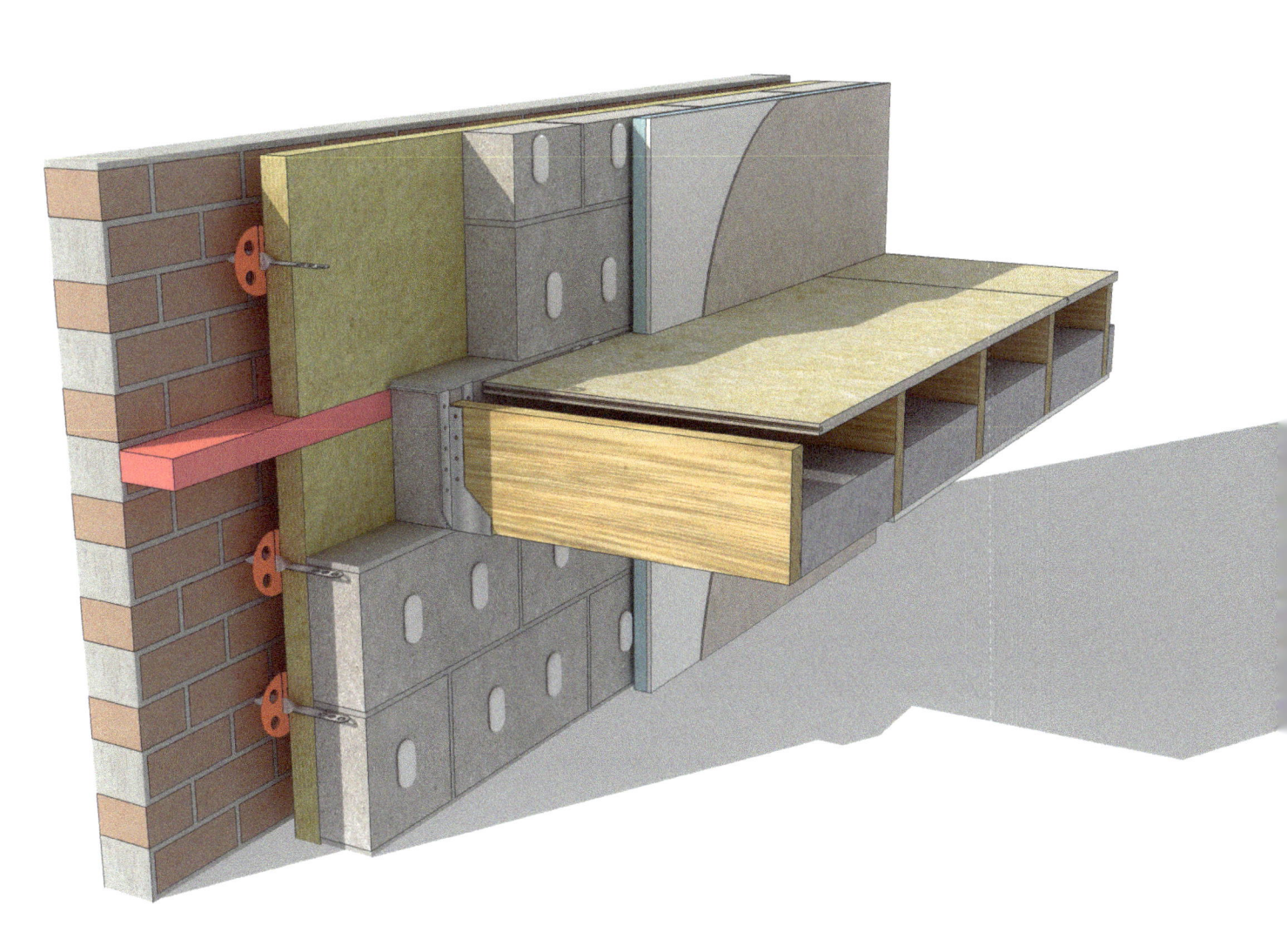

WALLS

The main function of an external wall is to provide shelter against the weather and fluctuations of outside temperature. The wall requires sufficient strength to support loads from upper floors and the roof. The majority of walls are constructed with load bearing masonry walls, or are a framed construction with timber, steel or concrete. On a domestic building, masonry and timber frame are most common and shall be the focus of this book.

FUNCTIONAL REQUIREMENTS

The functional requirements of the external wall are:
- Strength and stability
- Resistance to weather and ground moisture
- Durability
- Fire safety
- Resistance to the passage of heat
- Acoustic control
- Security
- Aesthetics

A standard cavity wall consists of an outer leaf of facing brickwork, a cavity (usually 100mm) with full or partial fill insulation, with an inner leaf of blockwork. There are of course many variations to this dependent on U-value requirements, internal and external finishes, structural loading and so on. The outer leaf and the cavity serve to resist the penetration of rain to the inside face, the inner leaf supports the floors and provides a solid internal wall surface.

The Building Regulations Approved Document Part A accepts a cavity of 50-100mm for cavity walls with leaves at least 90mm thick, built of coursed brickwork or blockwork with wall ties spaced at 450mm vertically and from 900 to 750mm horizontally.

WALL TIES

Wall ties do exactly as they say, they tie the wall together. They are positioned at intervals and can often be used as a fixing aid for insulation within the cavity. Early versions of the wall tie saw issues with moisture, where the ties provided a passage for water, and also a thermal bridge. Another issue with the wall tie is that they can collect mortar droppings as the outer leaf is being built which again cause issues with thermal bridging and moisture penetration. Now, wall ties usually have a twist or a drip, to prevent any moisture from reaching the inner leaf, and instead dripping down the cavity and out through weep holes. The ties are generally made from plastic or galvanised wire, and are as thin as possible to avoid collecting mortar droppings.

INSULATING THE WALL

Cavity insulation boards are generally rigid and fixed to the inner leaf of the cavity wall. They are fixed with plastic washers that are clipped to the wall ties. The cavity can be partially filled or completely filled by the insulation boards.

A partial fill cavity secures the insulation to the inner leaf, leaving a 50mm air gap between the insulation and the outer leaf of the cavity. The installations boards are secured in place by clips that fix onto the wall ties.

A full fill cavity is where the insulation is built in as the walls are constructed, and as it suggests, completely fills the cavity. Semi rigid batts or slabs are used to maintain a vertical layer within the cavity.

Additional insulation can be provided on the internal leaf of the wall in the form of insulated plasterboard, or insulation between battens.

SOUND INSULATION AND PARTY WALLS

The Building Regulations recommend minimum performance standards of walls between two dwellings, i.e. party walls. This can be achieved by using dense blocks or brickwork in either a 215mm solid wall or 250mm cavity wall. It is important to seal cavities in party walls in order to reduce flanking sand and reduce air circulation within the cavity. Cavity barriers are used not only for this purpose, but also to withhold the passage of smoke and fire. Party walls must also achieve a minimum U-value of 0.2W/m²K.

DAMP PROOF COURSE

The Building Regulations stipulate that the wall should adequately resist the passage of moisture to the inside of the building. Moisture may penetrate the wall by absorption of water from the ground and therefore it is key to use a damp proof course. The damp proof course will prevent water rising through the wall and floors. Moisture can also move downwards in parapets and chimneys or horizontally at junctions of openings like windows and doors.

It is important that the damp proof course laps with the damp proof membrane to ensure good continuity between the two and to avoid moisture penetration. The DPC must be at least 150mm above finished ground level.

OPENINGS

Approved Document Part A states that the number, size and position of openings should not impair the stability of a wall, it provides detailed requirements limiting the size of openings and recesses. When designing openings it is good practice to use cavity closers, or DPCs backed with insulation to avoid cold bridging at the reveal. Door and window frames are set in position to overlap the outer leaf with a resilient mastic pointing as a barrier to rain penetration between the frame and the jamb.

The function of the cill is to protect the wall below a window, so they are shaped to slope out and project beyond the external face of the wall in order to allow water to run off. It is good practice for the cill to project at least 45mm beyond the face of the wall below and have a drip on the underside of the projection.

At the head of an opening the brickwork or blockwork requires support by a lintel. Steel section lintels are often used, they are a galvanised strip that also act as a damp proof tray, or can be dressed with damp proofing material. The lintel is filled with EPS insulation to reduce thermal bridging. However, given the steel lintel spans between the inner and outer leaf of the cavity wall, there is still heat flow through the material. A more effective lintel arrangement that can further limit cold bridging is two independent concrete lintels.

CAVITY TRAYS

Some lintels have an integral cavity trays while others need a separate cavity tray which is usually formed using DPC materials on site. The cavity tray sits directly above the lintel, or sometimes a couple of courses above it. Any moisture trapped inside the cavity will be caught by the cavity tray and directed to the weep holes and out to the external face of the wall.

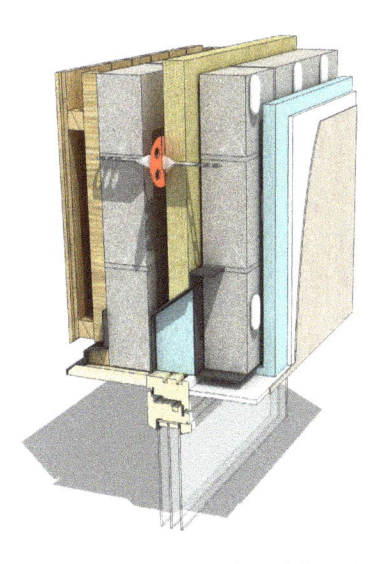

Figure 5.4 - Insulated lintel

ROOFS

The roof is a key element of the building structure, providing protection from the elements and has a vital role in reducing heat loss from the building. Roofs tend to be either pitched or flat, and typically in residential construction, timber is the most common material used.

FUNCTIONAL REQUIREMENTS

The functional requirements of the roof are:
- Strength and stability
- Protection from the weather
- Durability
- Resistance to passage of sound
- Thermal insulation
- Resistance to air leakage
- Fire safety
- Security
- Aesthetics

PITCHED ROOF

The majority of residential houses in the UK are constructed with pitched roofs. These pitched roofs are often constructed as a symmetrical roof with equal slopes that meet at a central ridge. Roof covering materials often determine the angle of the pitch, being the minimum slope that is necessary to prevent rain and snow ingress.

There are quite a few different types of pitch roof construction, some of which we will briefly explore in the next section.

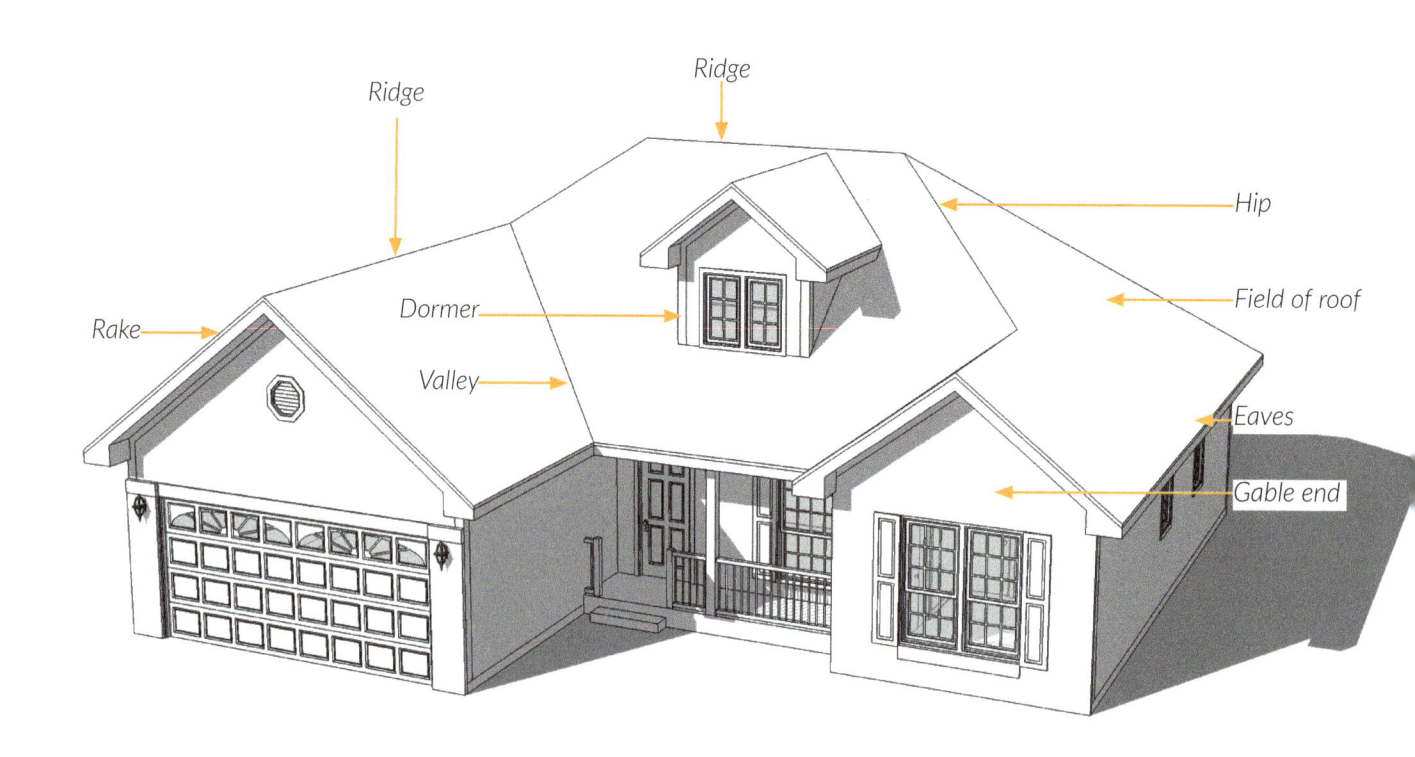

Figure 5.5 - Parts of a roof

SECTION 5 - MASONRY CONSTRUCTION

SINGLE PITCHED ROOFS

Mono Pitch Roof - the simplest form of pitched roof, sometimes referred to as the lean-to. The foot of the rafters generally sit on a timber wall plate, that is fixed to the top of supporting wall. The top of the rafters are supported on a timber plate that is fixed to the supporting wall. The mono pitched roof has a limited span, therefore the double pitched roof is a more popular option.

DOUBLE PITCHED ROOFS

Couple Roof - simple pitched roof structure, consisting of timber rafters pitched up from the walls that support them, to a central ridge. A central ridge board is used to fix the rafters each side. This form of roof is often seen in farm buildings, stores and more simple structures. The maximum span of this roof is 3.5m, wider spans than this can cause the foot of the rafters to push the supporting walls outwards. Rafters are spaced at 400-600mm intervals, sizes are calculated according to span and support required for the roof covering. The ridge board is a continuous softwood board, usually 32mm thick. The foot of each rafter is fixed to the timber wall plate, which is fixed to the top of the wall to provide a level fixing surface. The wall plate tends to be 100x75mm, it serves to spread the load of the rafters along the wall. A notch (or birds mouth) is cut into the rafters at the foot, so the rafter can fit tightly onto the wall plate.

Figure 5.6 - Couple roof and close couple roof

Close Couple Roof - construction very similar to the couple roof, but in this instance horizontal ceiling joists are nailed to the foot of each pair of rafters. This serves as a tie to resist the tendency for the rafters to push the walls outwards, but also serves as support for ceiling finishes. This type of roof is seen in small houses and bungalows. The ceiling joists can be 38-50mm thick, and a depth can range from 98mm to 220mm depending on span requirements and centres of the joists. These joists can provide roof space for services storage, such as water storage cisterns, along with general attic storage. The close couple roof tends to have a maximum span of 5.5m.

Collar Roof - similar to the close couple roof, rafters are framed by collars one third up the height of the roof. This opens up some of the roof to the first floor rooms, whilst providing support to the rafters. This system is often integrated with dormer window arrangements in order to maximise light penetration into the room. Providing support to the rafters a third of the way up the roof, is not as structurally effective as support at the foot of the rafters as described in the close couple roof. The collar roof tends to have a maximum span of 4.5m.

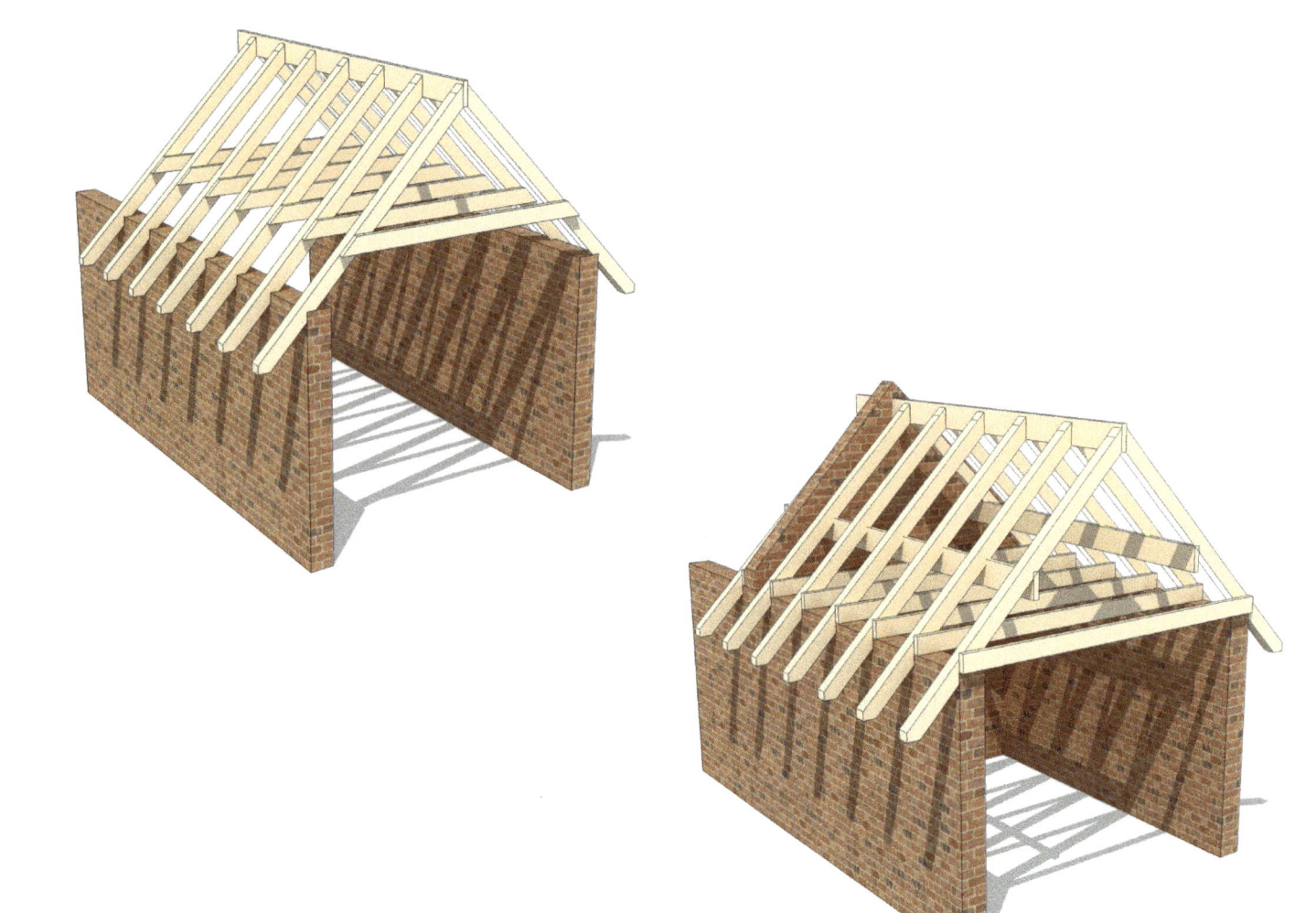

Figure 5.7 - Collar roof and purlin roof

Purlin Roof - Purlins are horizontal timbers that are supported by end walls or struts to internal load bearing walls, that offer support to the rafters, thus enabling a reduced rafter section. The overall clear span of the rafter is reduced by half, therefore making a large saving in required rafter size. Purlins supported by gable end walls sit on masonry corbels projecting from the wall, or on joist hangers. If there is no gable end support, the purlins can be supported by the internal load bearing walls, using support struts between the wall and the rafters.

Guidance of rafter spacing, spans and sizes can be found in the Building Regulations Approved Document Part A and also the TRADA document "Eurocode span tables for solid timber members in floors, ceilings and roofs for dwellings".

Truss Roof - a truss roof system is a prefabricated triangular frame of timbers tied together. As the trusses are prefabricated, predominantly mechanised, it results in a very accurate finish to the roof system. The trusses are delivered to site ready to be lifted into position. They are fixed to the timber wall plates. The Building Regulations Approved Document Part A provides specific requirements relating to stability of trusses roofs and associated bracing. Some domestic timber trusses can span up to 15m. The disadvantage of the truss roof system is the loss of attic space for storage or additional rooms which tends to be in demand these days. It is not possible to convert a truss roof into a usable loft space that has without major structural works, such as new purlins, floor beams and joists.

A pitched roof is usually covered with a roof tile, some of the most common types covered previously in Section 3 - Materials. Beneath the roof tiles, a secondary weather proof barrier is provided using a sarking membrane, usually in the form of a bituminous felt or sheet, or a proprietary reinforced plastic sheeting. The membrane is placed over the rafters with the tile battens nailed on top. At the eaves, the membrane is dressed into the gutter so that any moisture that has penetrated the tiles can run freely into the gutter.

EAVES

The eaves of a roof can be described as the lowest courses of tiles and the timber that supports them. The eaves of a pitched roof tend to extend around 150-300mm beyond the external face of the wall, to provide protection from rain. In some cases a closed or flush eaves can be designed, which stops the rafters and ceiling joists at the face of the external wall, where a fascia board is then fixed to the ends of the joists and the rafters.

A closed eaves provides soffit boards with ventilation gaps or channels to allow air into the roof space, to be expelled at ridge level.

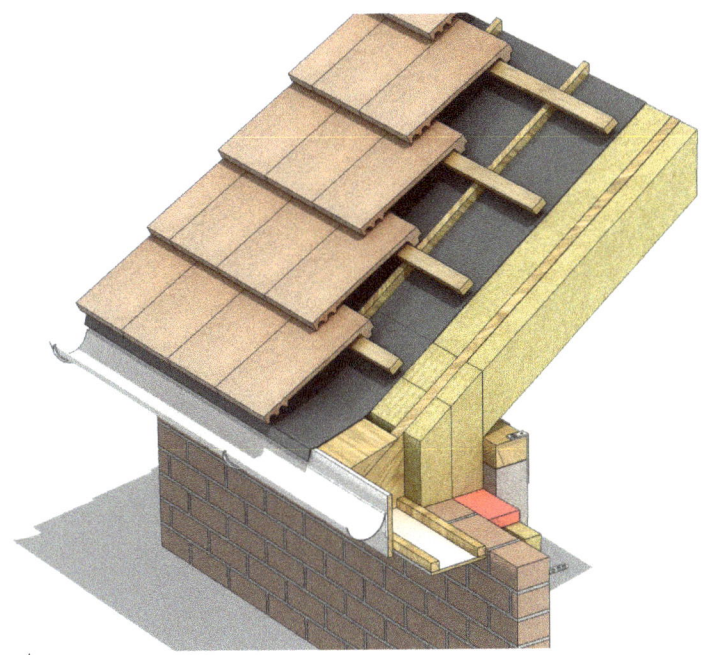

Figure 5.8 - Eaves example

INSULATING THE ROOF

Providing sufficient roof insulation design is key to minimising heat loss through the fabric of the building. The Building Regulations specify a minimum U-value for the insulation of roofs of dwellings to be 0.13W/m2K target notional, with a maximum 0.2W/m2K limiting fabric parameter.

Cold Roof
The roof can be insulated in a number of ways. Insulation can be fixed between or across the ceiling joists, an economical option as the area of the ceiling is less than the slopes of the pitched roof. This is defined as a cold roof. Any water carrying service pipes, water storage cisterns in the roof will need to be insulated to prevent damage from freezing, as the roof space itself is a cold unheated space. This type of roof system requires ventilation, in order to prevent a build up of condensation in the roof space.

Warm Roof

A warm roof construction is used when the roof space is used for storage or as part of the building itself. The insulation is fixed either between the rafters, or above or under the rafters in varying combinations. The advantage of this system is that the roof space will be warmed by heat rising from the rooms below.

Warm roof and cold roof construction is also seen in flat roofs, discussed later in this chapter.

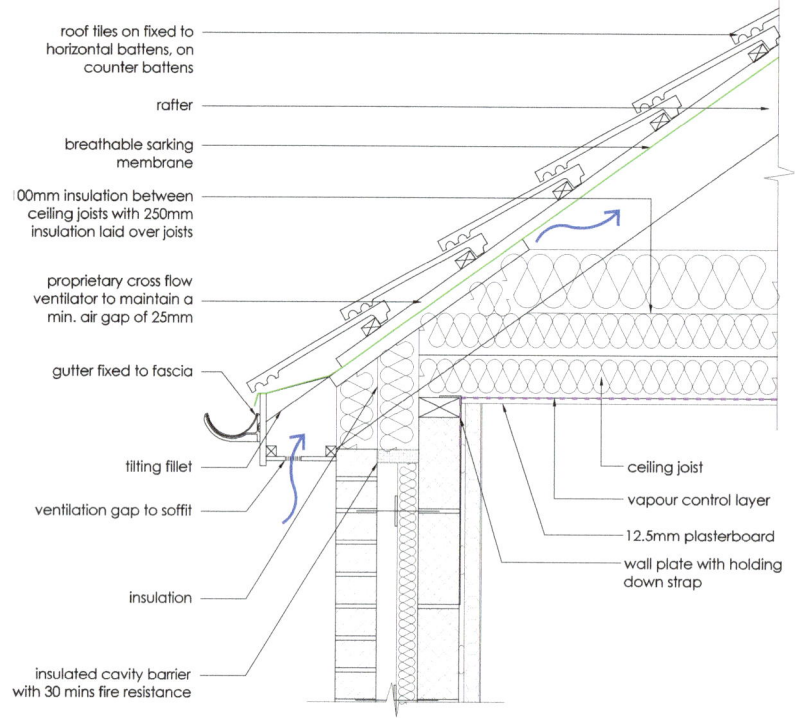

Figure 5.9 - Cold roof example

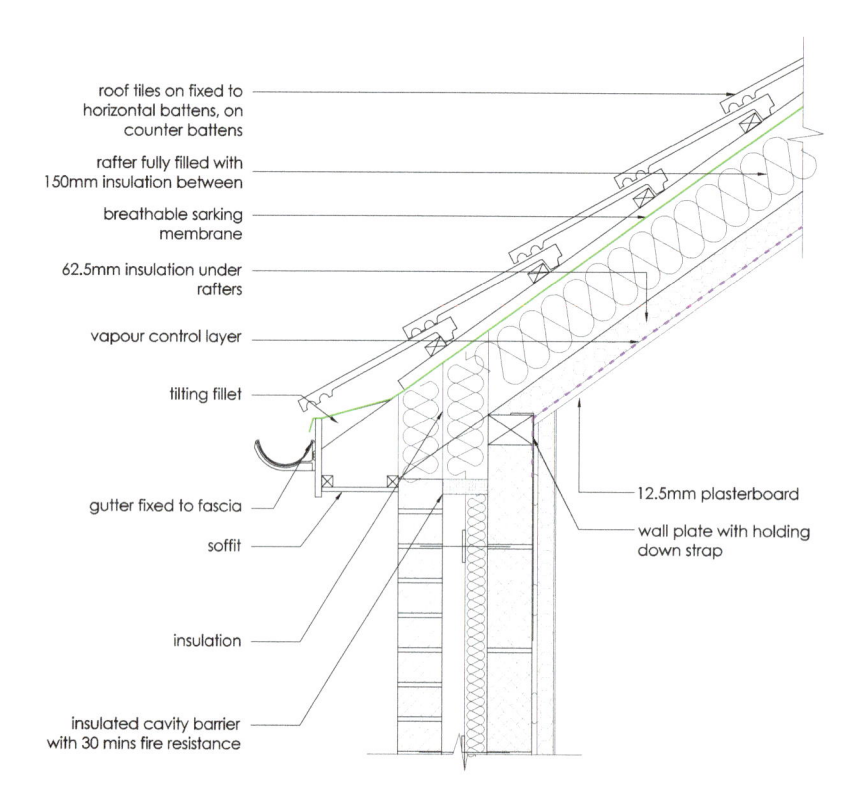

Figure 5.10 - Warm roof example

SECTION 5 - MASONRY CONSTRUCTION

MOISTURE CONTROL

The Building Regulation Approved Document Part C requires that the roof is designed, constructed and insulated in such a manner as to prevent the build up of condensation and growth of mould.

Condensation forms on surfaces within the structure when warm moist air from inside the building moves to the cold side of insulation. If water vapour is allow to penetrate cold areas of the building or structure the air will not be able to hold the moisture and condensation will form on the cold surfaces.

Condensation can be prevented by the use of roof ventilation, which removes the warm moist air. It is also best practice to install a vapour check (vapour barrier) immediately below the insulation, to prevent the flow of warm moist air.

The most effective ventilation method provides ventilation openings at the eaves, with ventilated ridges to allow the air to pass through. Building Regulations Approved Document Part C provides requirements for the design of ventilation in roof spaces to prevent the build up of condensation. It is important to provide a channel or tray over the insulation in order to allow the air to pass through from the eaves.

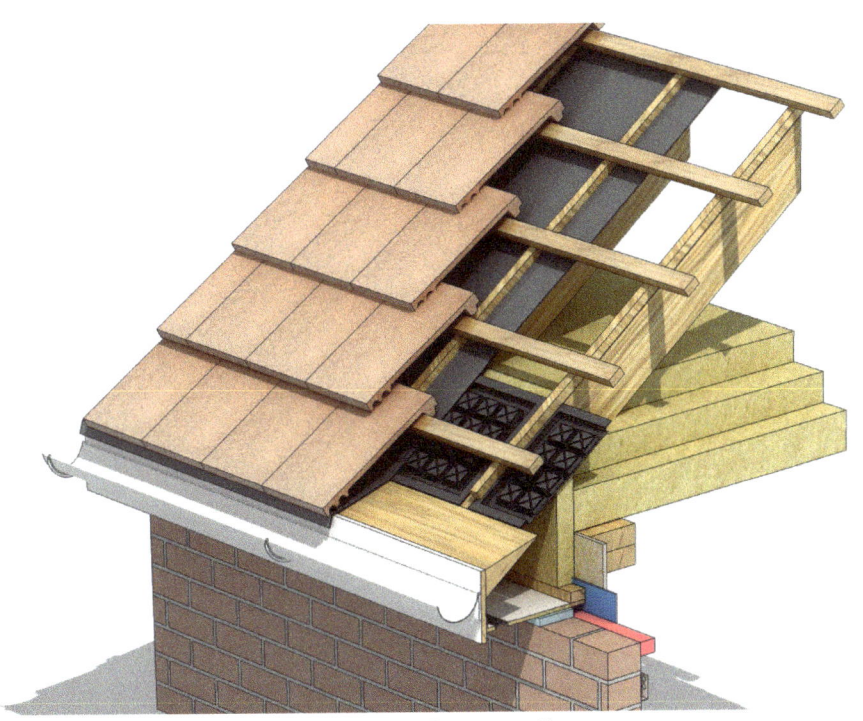

Figure 5.11 - Ventilation through the roof using cross flow ventilator

In a warm roof configuration, ventilation must be provided above the insulation, following the line of the rafters. A 50mm clear gap should be provided between the roofing felt and the top of insulation which leads to the ridge vent. If this is not implemented condensation can occur above the insulation on the roofing felt, and cause problems of rot, poor insulation performance and general damp issues.

However, breathable sarking membranes negate the need for ventilation directly above the insulation layer. They have a low vapour resistance which allows water vapour to escape through the breathable membrane to the outside of the building. Some of the following examples show the specification of such a breathable membrane.

A vapour control layer (vcl) should be installed at ceiling level underneath the insulation - this will help reduce the amount of moisture entering the roof space from the habitable rooms below. The vapour control layer cannot be used as a substitute to roof ventilation, but as an additional defence. It is worth noting that vcl's can have vulnerable areas of leakage, for example light fittings, joints and loft hatches to mention a few. Seals added to those weak points can help to reduce the amount of vapour that enters the roof space.

FLAT ROOF

A roof is considered to be flat when it is of a slope of 1-5° to the horizontal. Although flat roofs are cheaper to build than pitched roofs, they have a shorter life span.

A flat roof usually consists of the following:
- Waterproof membrane to prevent water penetrating the structure and interior of the building
- Roof deck, providing the base for the waterproof membrane, and in some cases the insulation
- Thermal insulation
- Load bearing or primary structure, usually constructed in timber in a residential construction.

The construction of the flat roof is similar to that of the timber upper floor. Joists are placed on edge, spaced at 400-600mm centres, supported by external and internal load bearing walls. TRADA and Approved Document Part A give guidance on sizes of joists for flat roofs relating to spans and loading. Strutting is fixed between the joists to provide lateral restraint.

Depending on the roof build up, a roof deck, is then fixed to the joists over firring strips, to provide the fall of the roof. The roof deck material is usually chipboard or plywood. The firring strips allow the roof to have the slope required to enable water run off to the rain water outlets. An alternative to this method sees insulation boards made into shallow wedge sections to provide the fall.

INSULATING A FLAT ROOF

Similar to the pitched roof, a flat roof can be insulated as a cold or a warm deck. The position of the insulation dictates which type it is.

Cold Roof/Deck
A cold roof system sees the insulation placed immediately above the ceiling between the joists, with ventilation space above the insulation. The disadvantage of this method is wasteful cutting of insulation to install between the joists, labour required to install the material and increased electrical cables required to prevent overheating, that run within the insulation. It is also difficult to provide suitable ventilation of the void above the insulation to prevent condensation. This roof system is rarely used these days.

Warm Roof/Deck (Sandwich roof)
Warm roof systems benefit from the insulation sitting above the deck. This enables the temperature of the structure and the deck to be kept close to the temperature of the inside of the building (hence warm). The insulation is tapered to provide a fall to the roof to enable water to run to the water outlets.

With the warm roof deck, there is less likelihood of condensation forming in the warm roof space, so ventilation is not required. A vapour control layer is still installed to minimise any moisture movement. This system is probably the most common arrangement for residential flat roofs.

The disadvantage of this roof system is that the insulation is directly under the roof covering, so the covering suffers considerable temperature fluctuations. An inverted roof system avoids this issue.

Inverted Roof
The inverted roof puts the insulation above the roof covering. The insulation is then protected with a layer of chippings or concrete paving. This system is often seen in more commercial projects.

Both of the warm roof options prevent wasteful cutting of insulation and decrease installation time, therefore labour costs.

PARAPET WALLS

External walls of a building can sometimes be raised above the roof level as a parapet wall. A parapet is exposed on both faces and are more susceptible to damage from driving rain, frost and wind than external walls below eaves level. Building Regulations Approved Document Part A sets guidance to the thickness and height of parapet walls.

It is important to adequately protect the top surface of the parapet wall with a cap or cover that can prevent rain saturating the wall. Natural stone is often used, which project about 50mm either side of the wall, with a drip edge on the underside. Coping stones, either natural or cast, are available in different sections to ensure good run off and protection. Metal flashings are also used as a capping to parapet walls.

The parapet wall has a DPC installed to prevent moisture in the exposed parapet penetrating the roof.

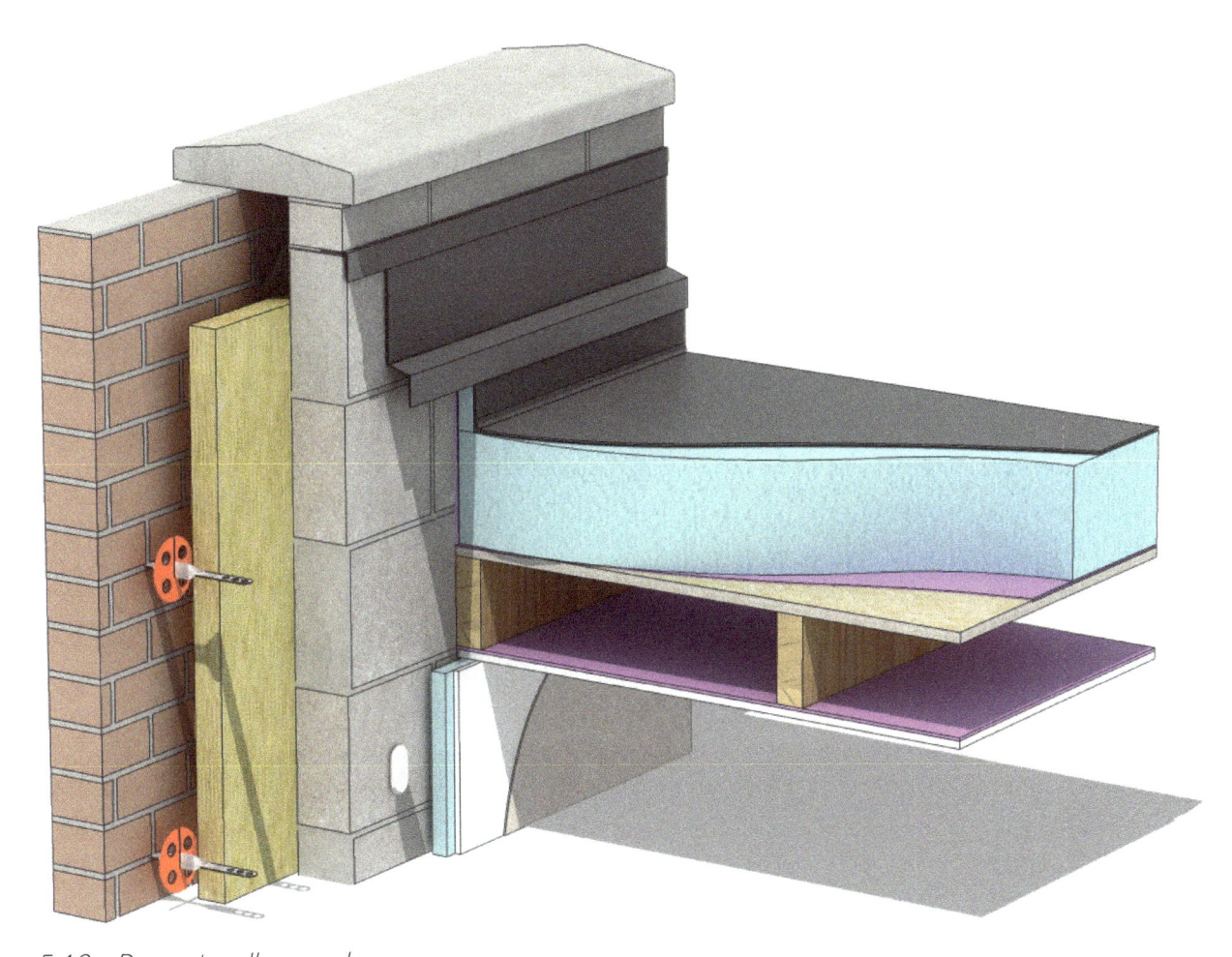

Figure 5.12 - Parapet wall example

FOUNDATION & FLOOR DETAILS

M-G1

EXTERNAL MASONRY CAVITY WALL, GROUND BEARING CONCRETE SLAB, INSULATION BELOW SLAB

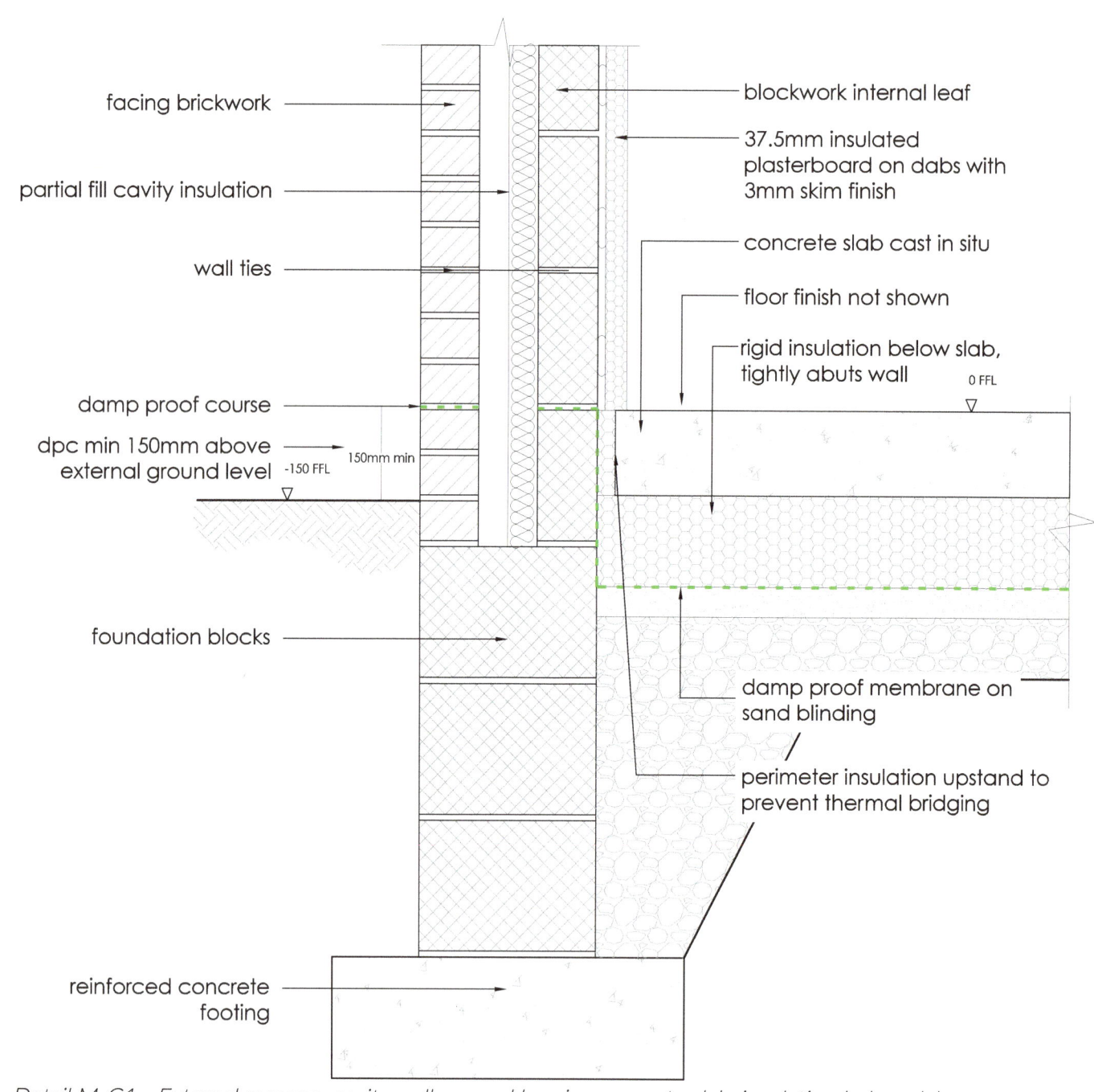

Labels (left side):
- facing brickwork
- partial fill cavity insulation
- wall ties
- damp proof course
- dpc min 150mm above external ground level (-150 FFL, 150mm min)
- foundation blocks
- reinforced concrete footing

Labels (right side):
- blockwork internal leaf
- 37.5mm insulated plasterboard on dabs with 3mm skim finish
- concrete slab cast in situ
- floor finish not shown
- rigid insulation below slab, tightly abuts wall (0 FFL)
- damp proof membrane on sand blinding
- perimeter insulation upstand to prevent thermal bridging

Detail M-G1 - External masonry cavity wall, ground bearing concrete slab, insulation below slab

NOTES:
U-value 0.13 Wm²K or better
Perimeter strip of insulation abuts concrete slab and blockwork wall. Concrete slab ready to receive floor finish. Base course to have weep holes at intervals.
Vapour control/seperation layer over insulation to prevent interstitial condensation and seeping of concrete into insulation board creacks - check with insulation manufacturer.

SECTION 5 - MASONRY CONSTRUCTION

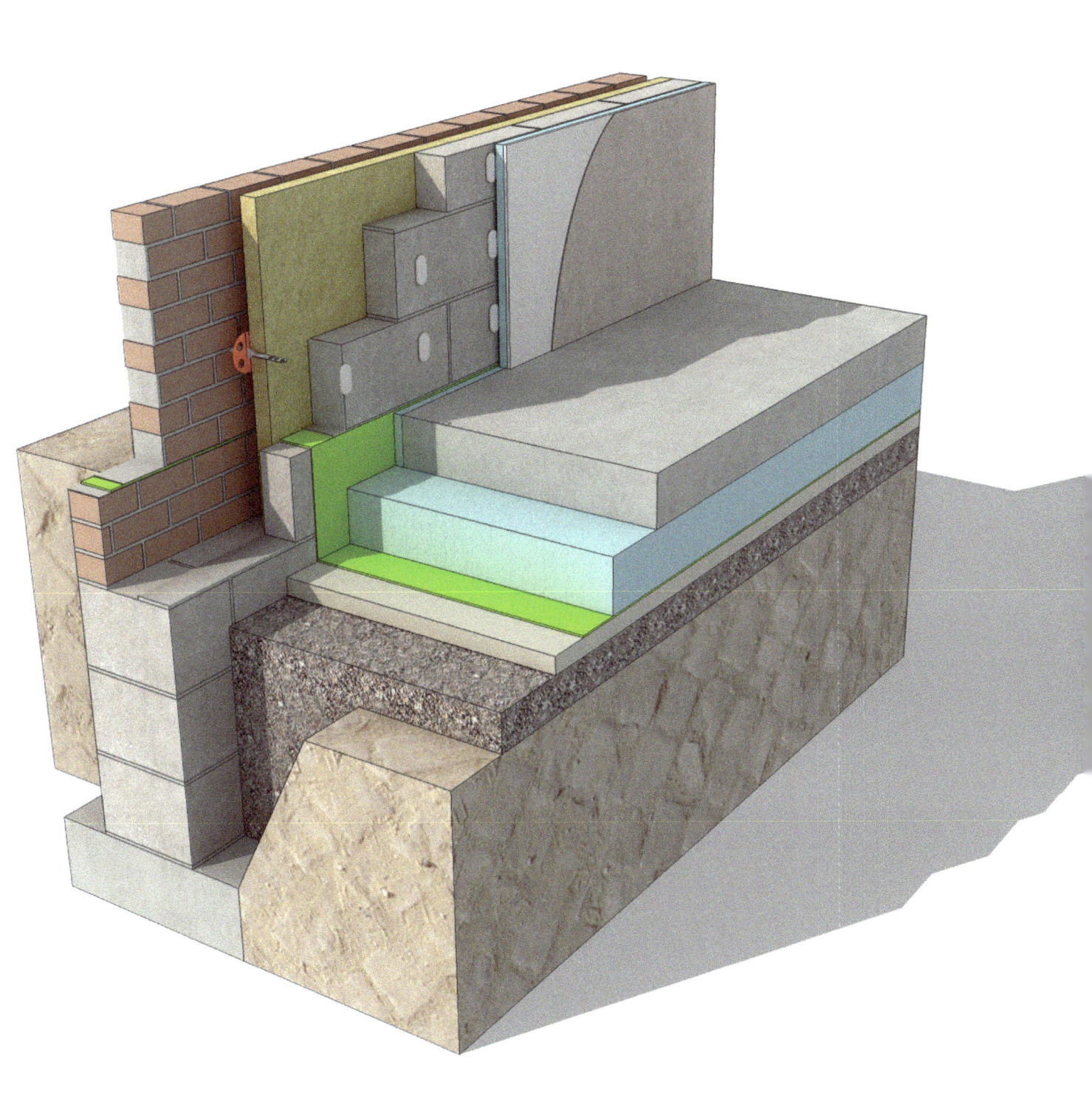

3D Detail M-G1 - External masonry cavity wall, ground bearing concrete slab, insulation below slab

M-G1A

EXTERNAL MASONRY CAVITY WALL, GROUND BEARING CONCRETE SLAB, INSULATION BELOW SLAB, CAVITY FOUNDATION WALL OPTION

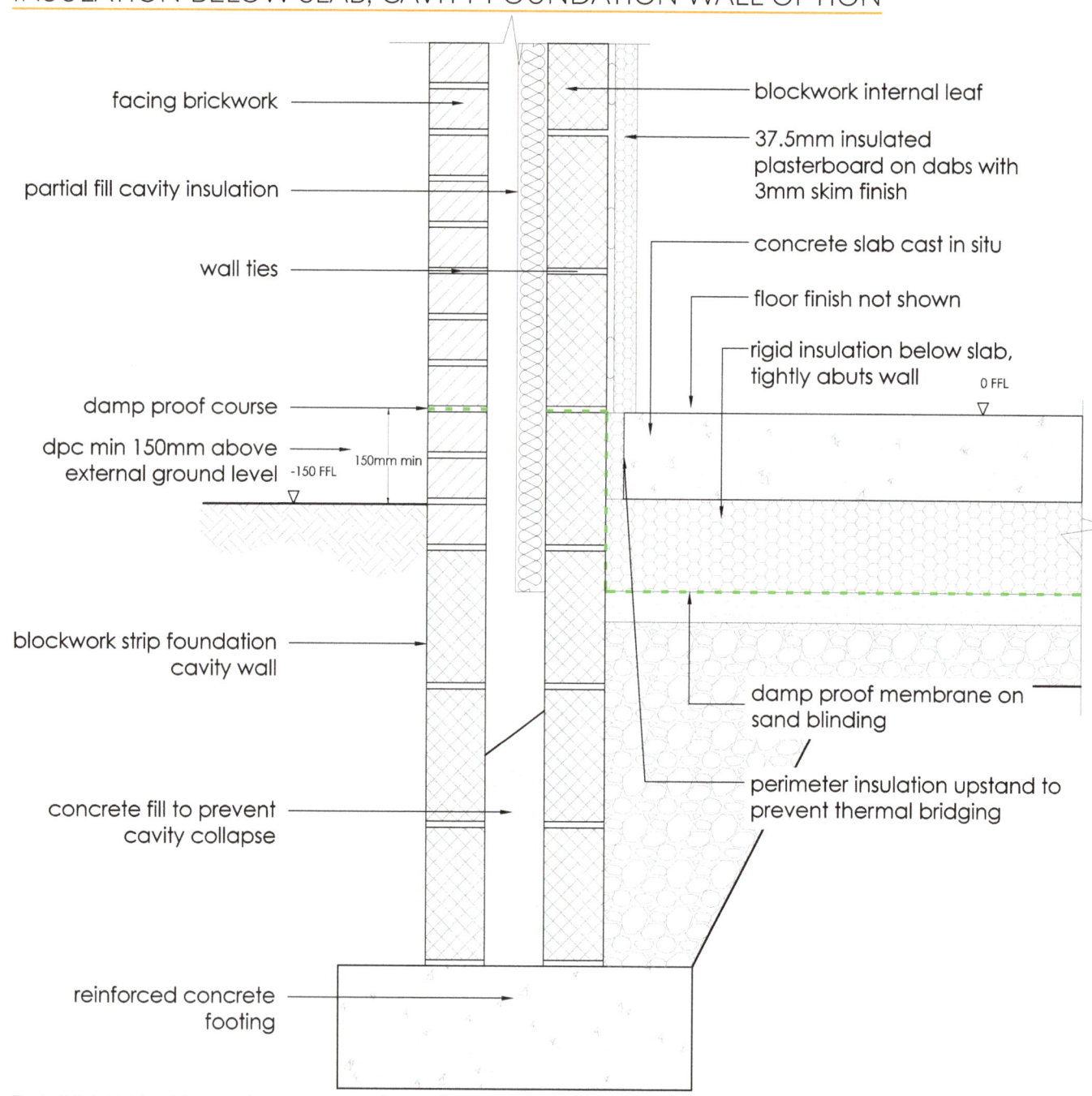

Labels (left side):
- facing brickwork
- partial fill cavity insulation
- wall ties
- damp proof course
- dpc min 150mm above external ground level (-150 FFL, 150mm min)
- blockwork strip foundation cavity wall
- concrete fill to prevent cavity collapse
- reinforced concrete footing

Labels (right side):
- blockwork internal leaf
- 37.5mm insulated plasterboard on dabs with 3mm skim finish
- concrete slab cast in situ
- floor finish not shown
- rigid insulation below slab, tightly abuts wall (0 FFL)
- damp proof membrane on sand blinding
- perimeter insulation upstand to prevent thermal bridging

Detail M-G1A- External masonry cavity wall, ground bearing concrete slab, insulation below slab, cavity foundation wall option

NOTES:

U-value 0.13 Wm²K or better

Perimeter strip of insulation abuts concrete slab and blockwork wall. Concrete slab ready to receive floor finish. Base course to have weep holes at intervals.

Vapour control/seperation layer over insulation to prevent interstitial condensation and seeping of concrete into insulation board creacks - check with insulation manufacturer.

SECTION 5 - MASONRY CONSTRUCTION

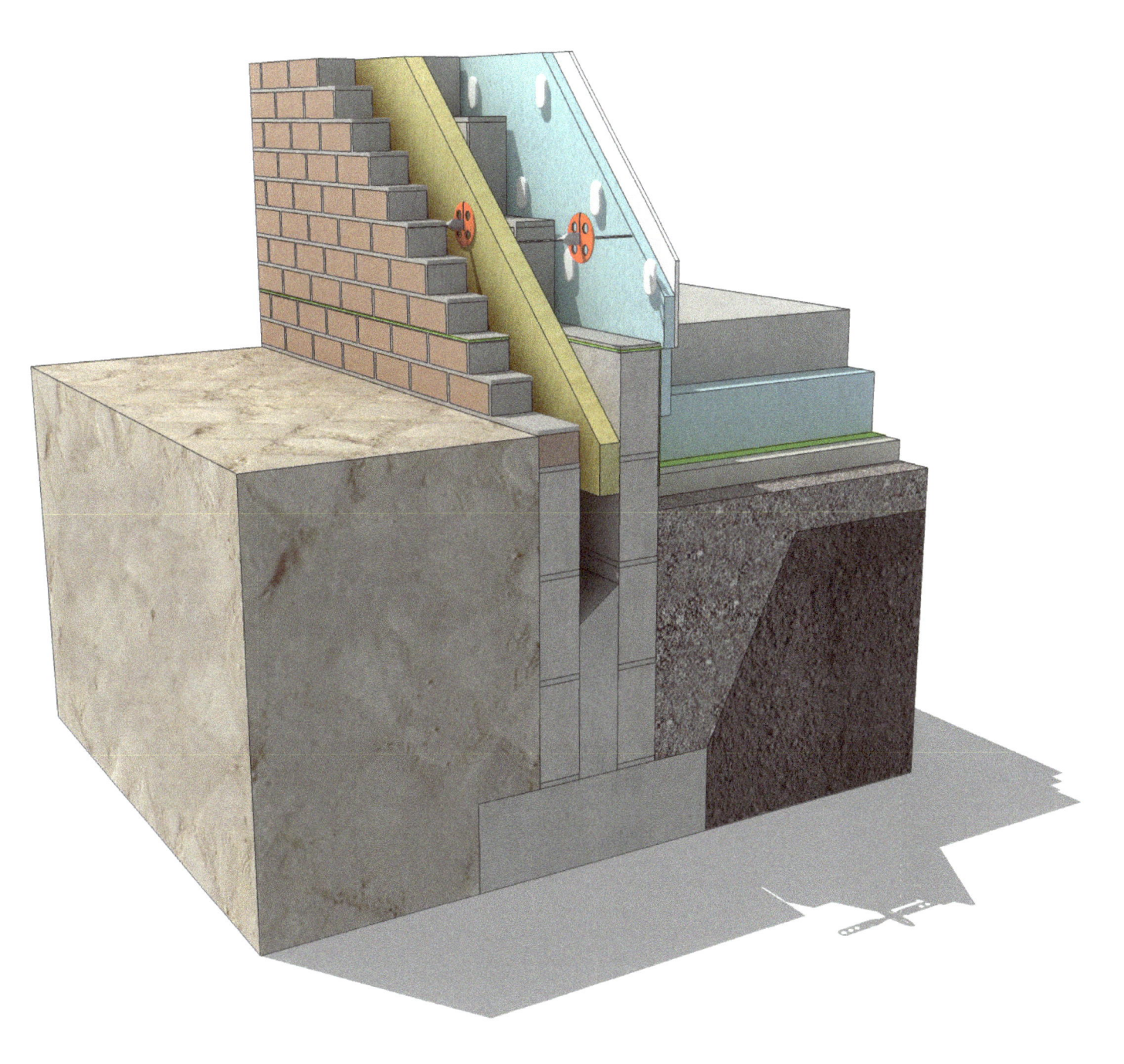

3D Detail M-G1A - External masonry cavity wall, ground bearing concrete slab, insulation below slab, cavity foundation wall option

M-G2

EXTERNAL MASONRY CAVITY WALL, GROUND BEARING CONCRETE SLAB, INSULATION ABOVE SLAB

Labels (left side):
- facing brickwork
- partial fill cavity insulation
- wall ties
- damp proof course
- dpc min 150mm above external ground level (150mm min, -150 FFL)
- foundation blocks
- reinforced concrete footing

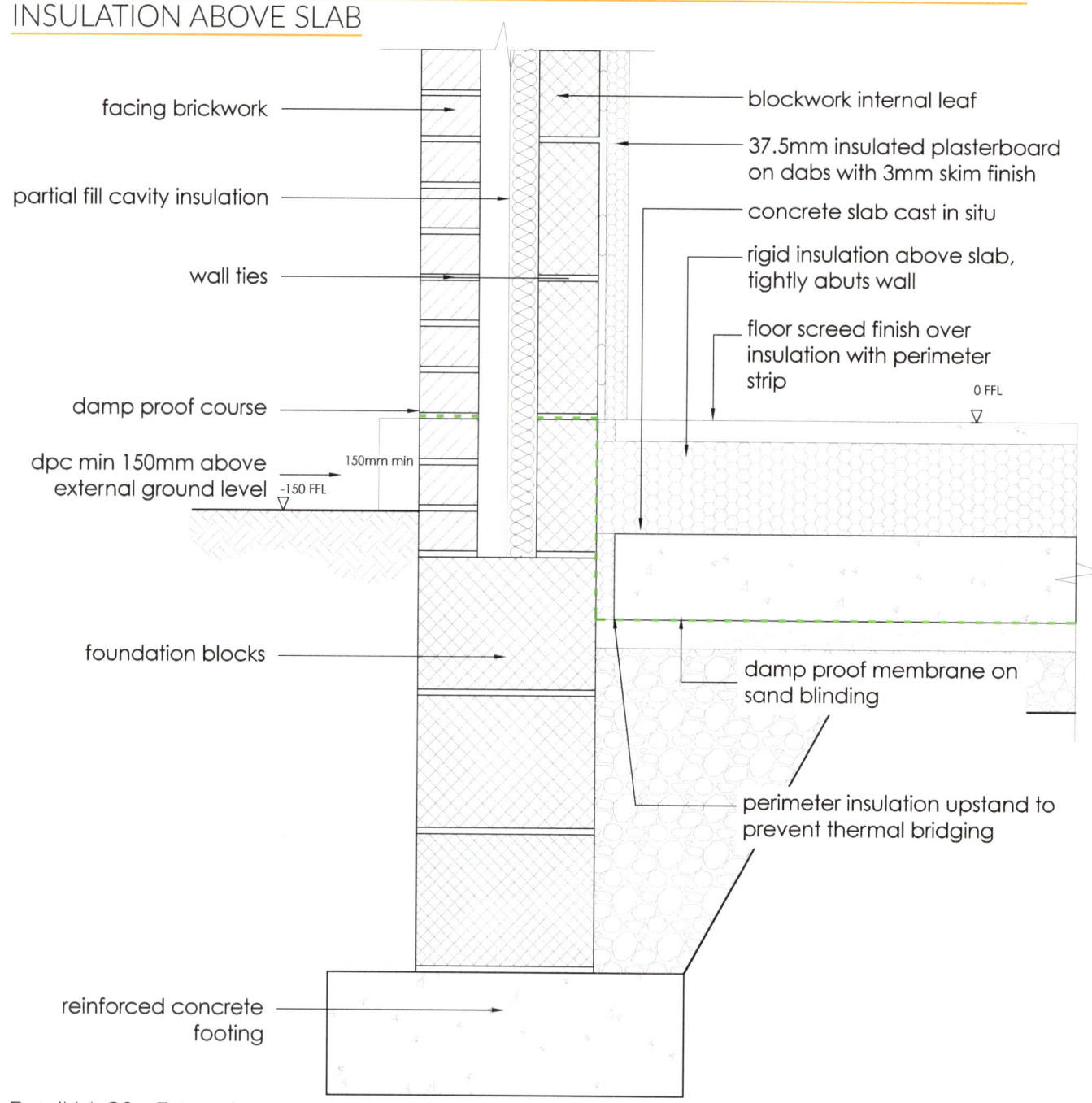

Labels (right side):
- blockwork internal leaf
- 37.5mm insulated plasterboard on dabs with 3mm skim finish
- concrete slab cast in situ
- rigid insulation above slab, tightly abuts wall
- floor screed finish over insulation with perimeter strip (0 FFL)
- damp proof membrane on sand blinding
- perimeter insulation upstand to prevent thermal bridging

Detail M-G2 - External masonry cavity wall, ground bearing concrete slab, insulation above slab

NOTES:

U-value 0.13 Wm²K or better
Perimeter strip of insulation abuts concrete slab and blockwork wall. Floor screed over insulation, minimum 65mm thick, or proprietary screed min 35mm thick. Perimeter strip of insulation to floor screed. Alternative floor finish over insulation between chipboard and insulation. Base course of external leaf to have weep holes at intervals.
If timber floor finish is used instead of screed, a vapour control layer will be required over insualtion to prevent interstitial condensation, check with insulation manufacturer.

SECTION 5 - MASONRY CONSTRUCTION

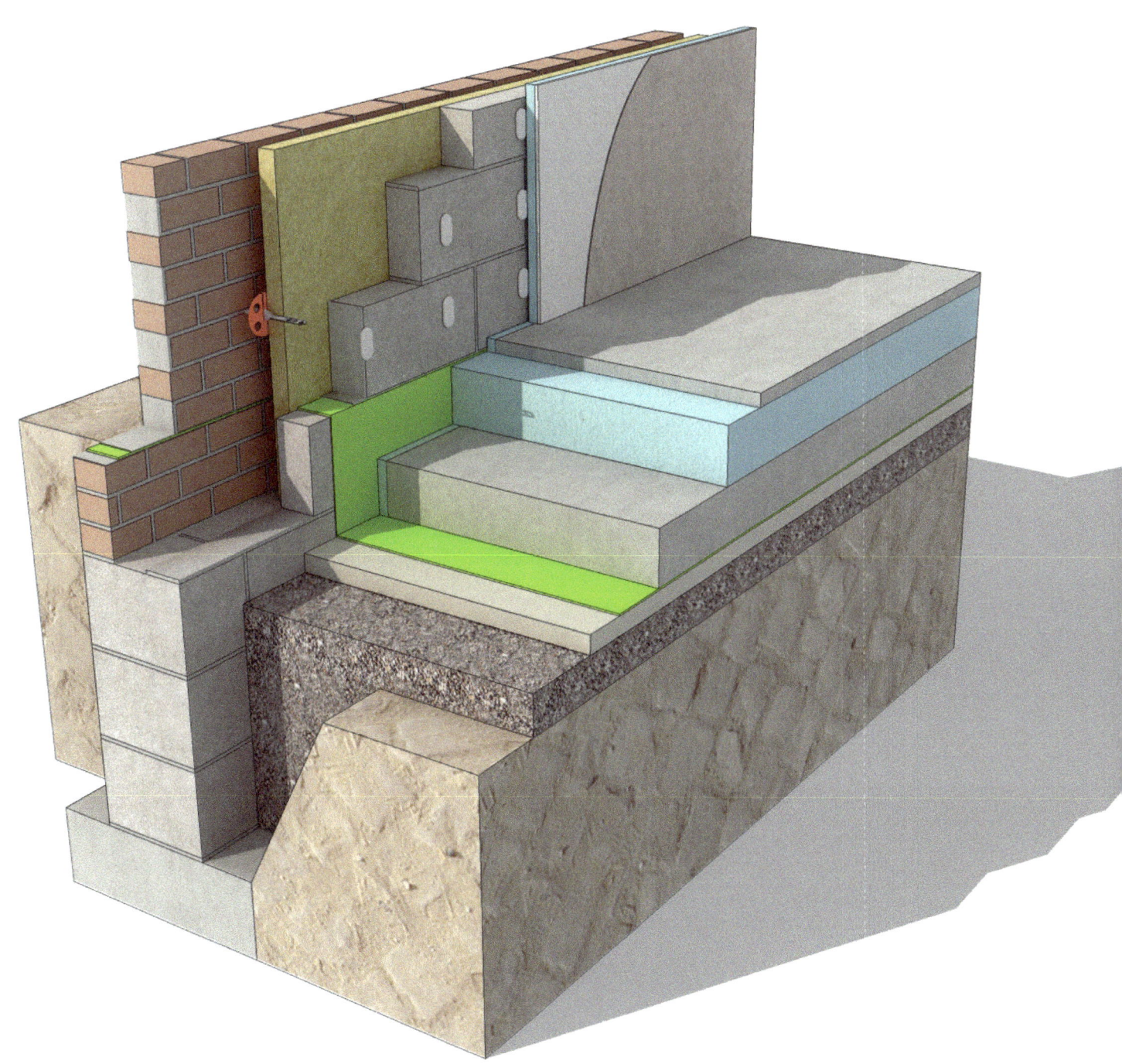

3D Detail M-G2 - External masonry cavity wall, ground bearing concrete slab, insulation above slab

M-G2A

EXTERNAL MASONRY CAVITY WALL, GROUND BEARING CONCRETE RAFT, INSULATION ABOVE SLAB

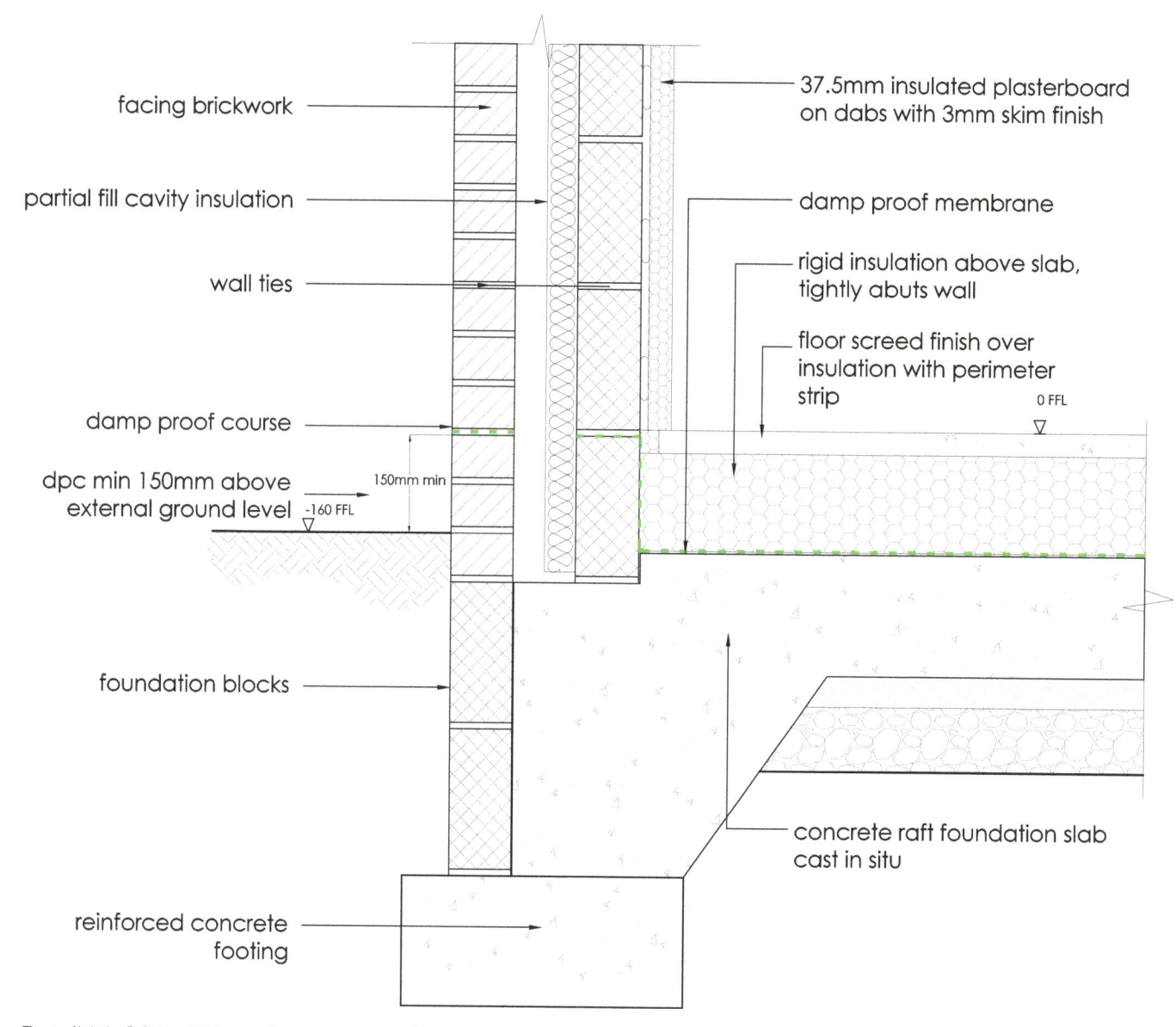

Labels on diagram (left side):
- facing brickwork
- partial fill cavity insulation
- wall ties
- damp proof course
- dpc min 150mm above external ground level -160 FFL
- foundation blocks
- reinforced concrete footing

Labels on diagram (right side):
- 37.5mm insulated plasterboard on dabs with 3mm skim finish
- damp proof membrane
- rigid insulation above slab, tightly abuts wall
- floor screed finish over insulation with perimeter strip   0 FFL
- concrete raft foundation slab cast in situ

150mm min

Detail M-G2A - External masonry cavity wall, ground bearing concrete raft, insulation above slab

NOTES:

U-value 0.13 Wm²K or better

Floor screed over insulation, minimum 65mm thick, or proprietary screed min 35mm thick. Perimeter strip of insulation to floor screed. Alternative floor finish over insulation between chipboard and insulation. Base course of external leaf to have weep holes at intervals.

If timber floor finish is used instead of screed, a vapour control layer will be required over insualtion to prevent interstitial condensation, check with insulation manufacturer.

SECTION 5 - MASONRY CONSTRUCTION

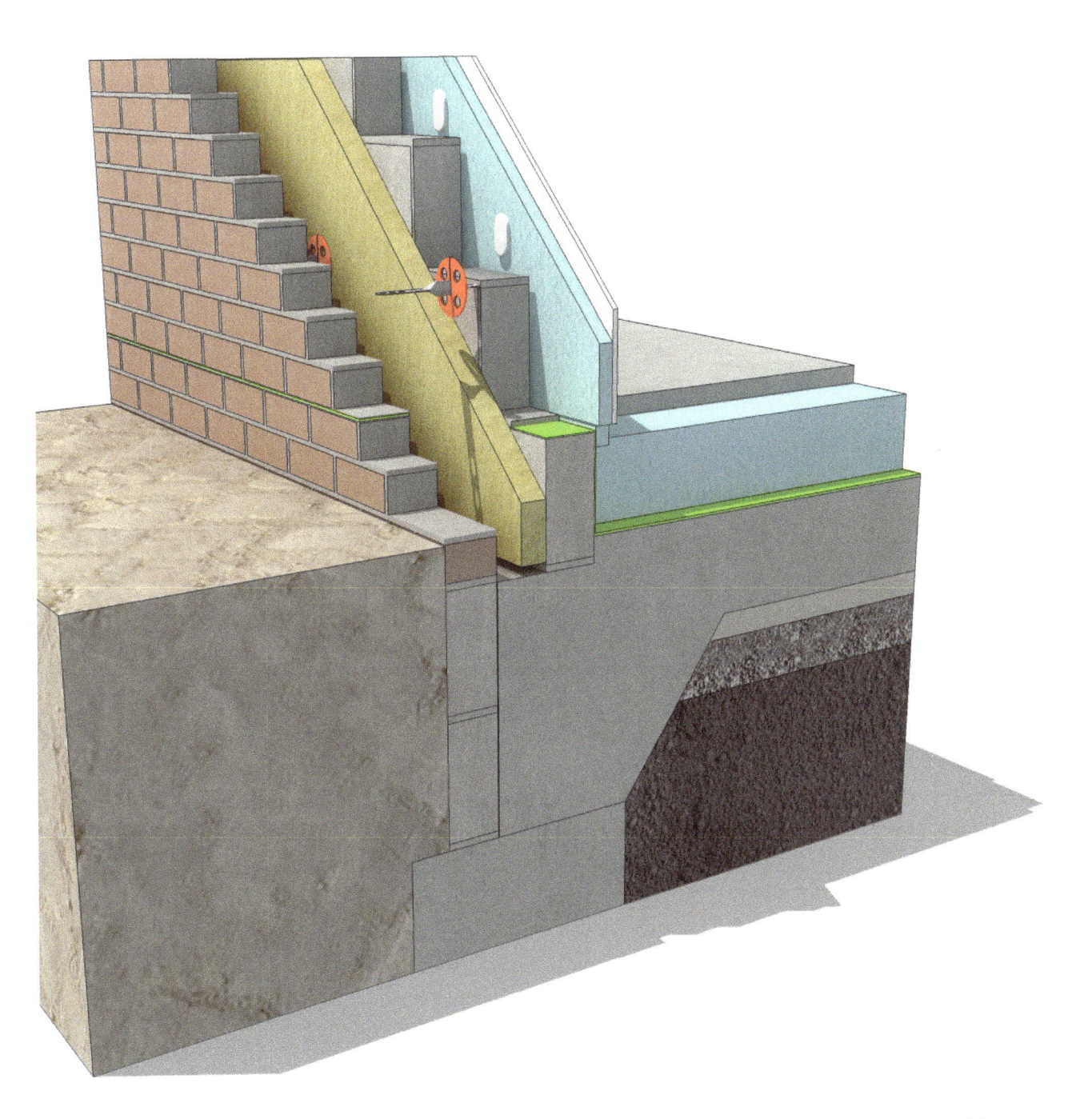

3D Detail M-G2A - External masonry cavity wall, ground bearing concrete raft, insulation above slab

M-G3

EXTERNAL MASONRY CAVITY WALL, SUSPENDED CONCRETE SLAB, INSULATION BELOW SLAB

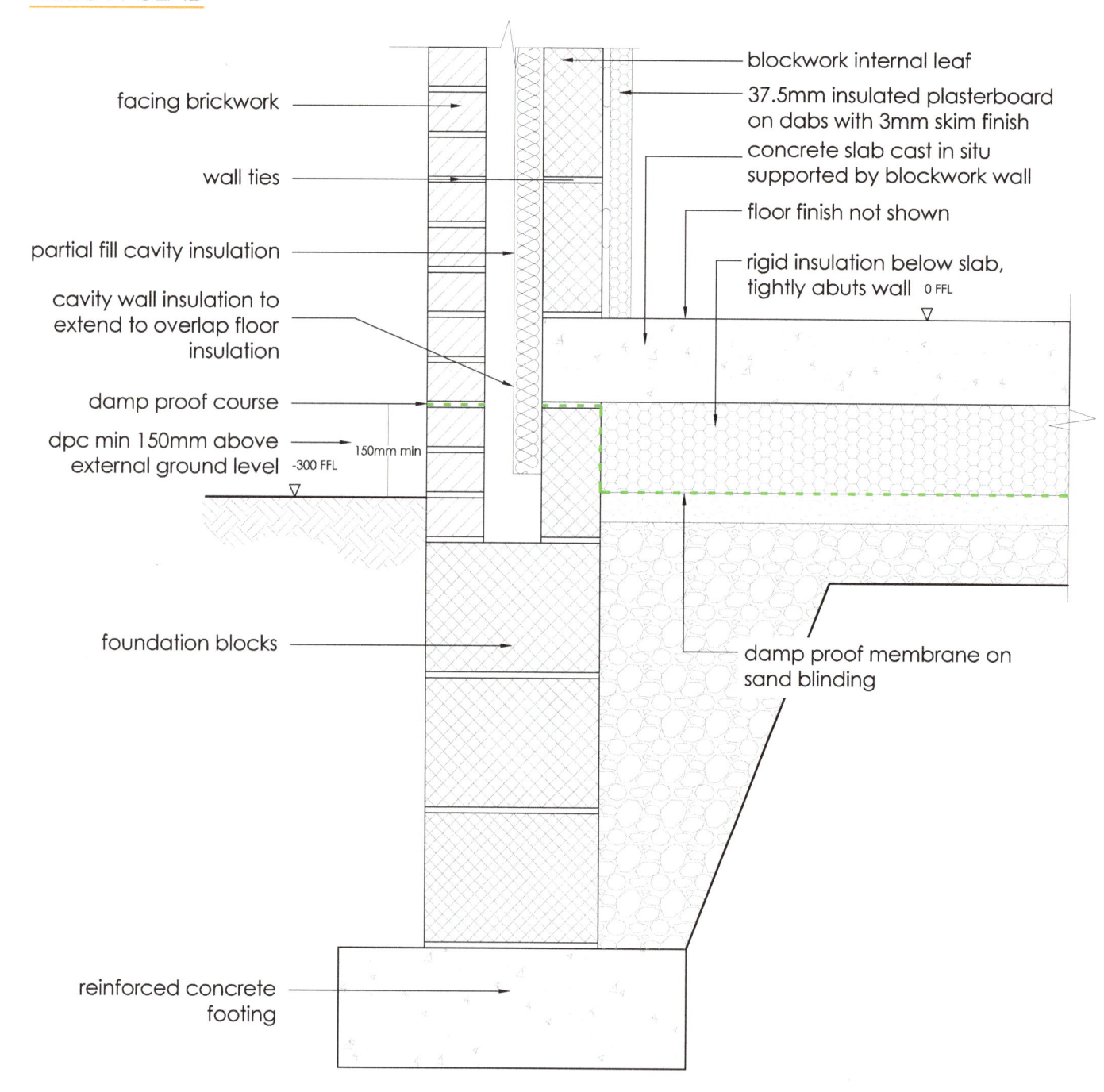

Labels (left side):
- facing brickwork
- wall ties
- partial fill cavity insulation
- cavity wall insulation to extend to overlap floor insulation
- damp proof course
- dpc min 150mm above external ground level
- foundation blocks
- reinforced concrete footing

Labels (right side):
- blockwork internal leaf
- 37.5mm insulated plasterboard on dabs with 3mm skim finish
- concrete slab cast in situ supported by blockwork wall
- floor finish not shown
- rigid insulation below slab, tightly abuts wall
- damp proof membrane on sand blinding

Dimensions: 150mm min; -300 FFL; 0 FFL

Detail M-G3 - External masonry cavity wall, suspended concrete slab, insulation below slab

NOTES:

U-value 0.13 Wm²K or better
If using timber floor, vapour control layer required between concrete slab and timber floor.
Base course of external leaf to have weep holes at intervals.
Vapour control/seperation layer over insulation to prevent interstitial condensation and seeping of concrete into insulation board creacks - check with insulation manufacturer.

SECTION 5 - MASONRY CONSTRUCTION

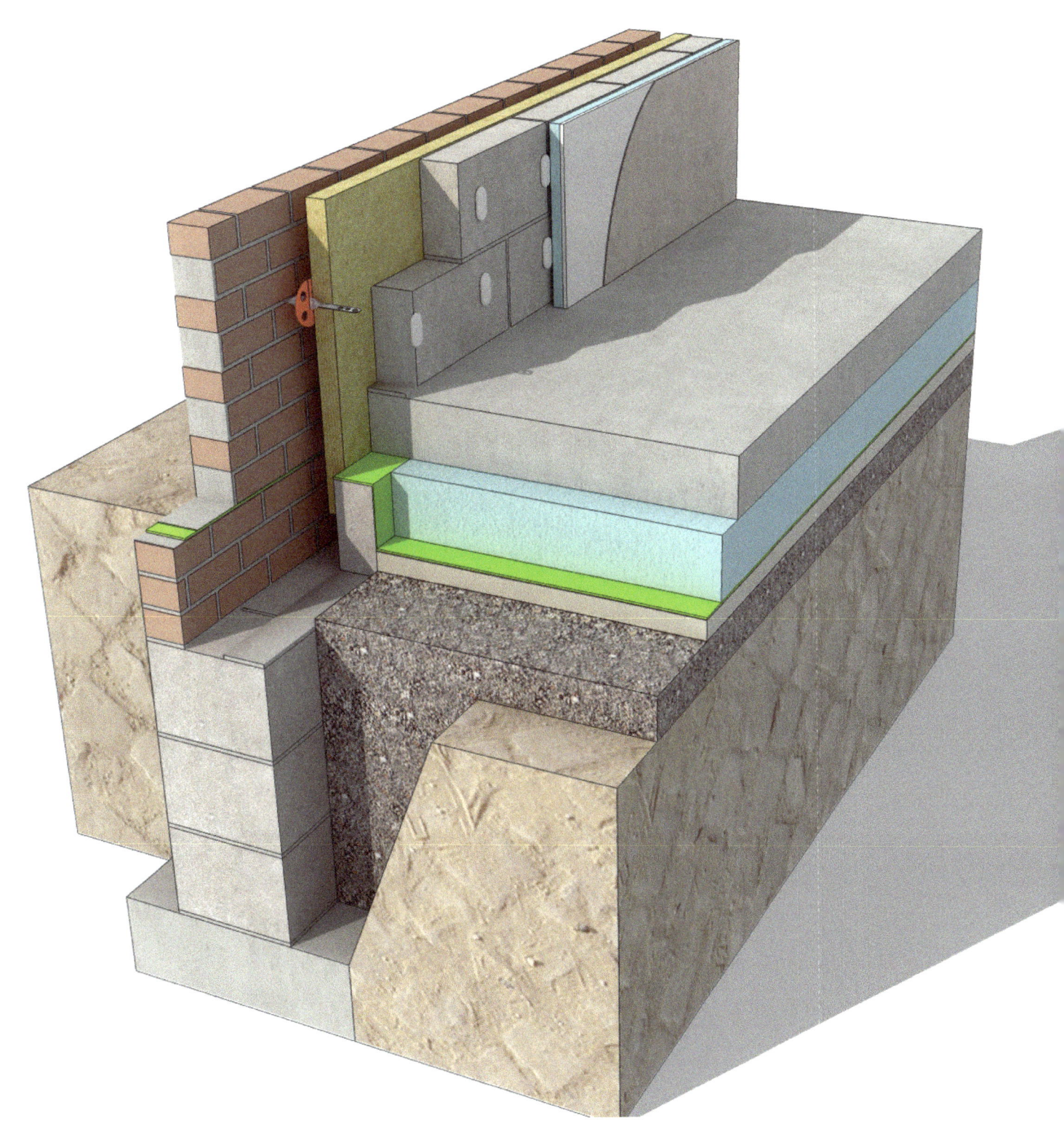

3D Detail M-G3 - External masonry cavity wall, suspended concrete slab, insulation below slab

M-G4

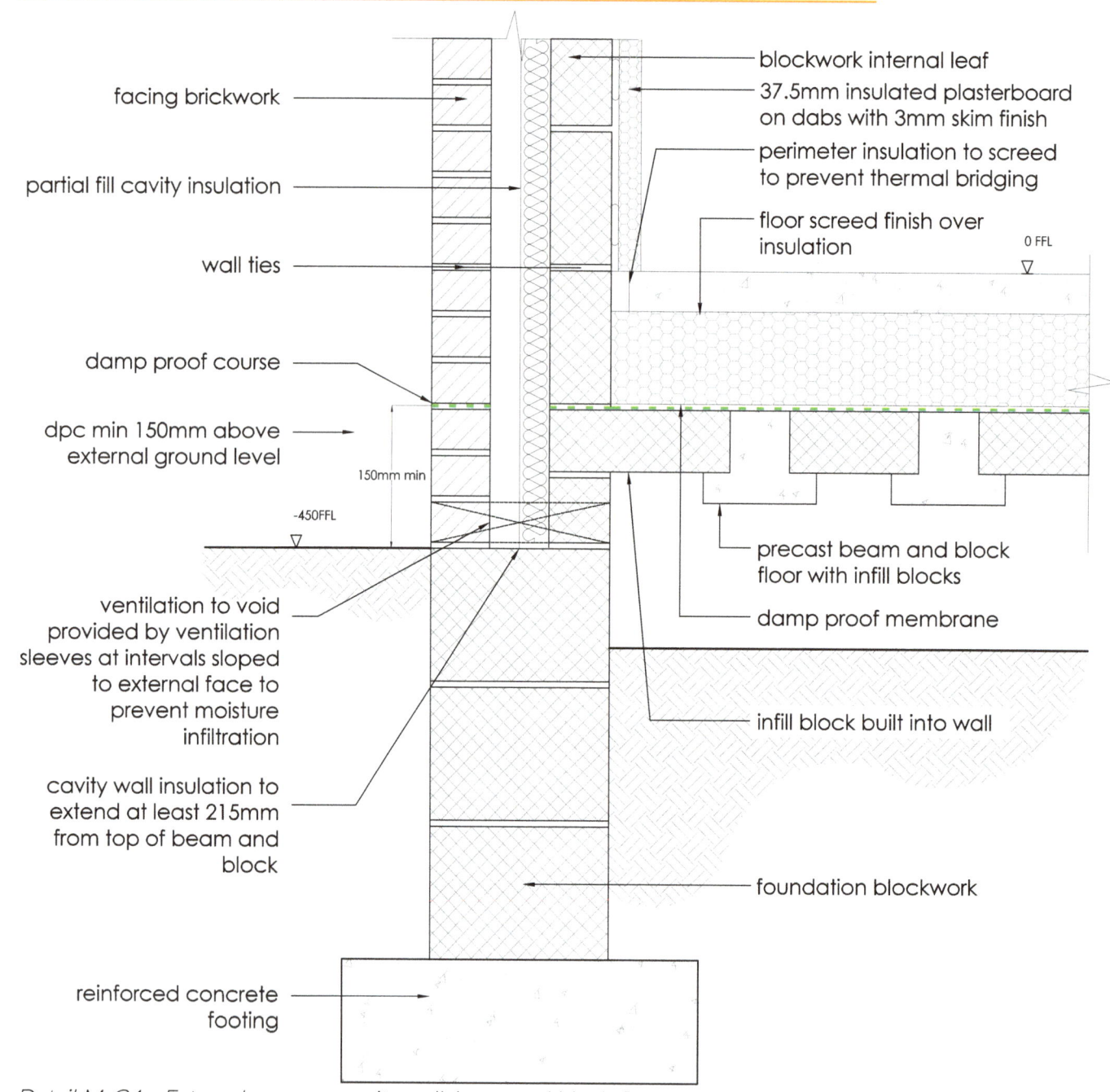

EXTERNAL MASONRY CAVITY WALL, BEAM AND BLOCK FLOOR

Labels (left side):
- facing brickwork
- partial fill cavity insulation
- wall ties
- damp proof course
- dpc min 150mm above external ground level
- ventilation to void provided by ventilation sleeves at intervals sloped to external face to prevent moisture infiltration
- cavity wall insulation to extend at least 215mm from top of beam and block
- reinforced concrete footing

Labels (right side):
- blockwork internal leaf
- 37.5mm insulated plasterboard on dabs with 3mm skim finish
- perimeter insulation to screed to prevent thermal bridging
- floor screed finish over insulation
- precast beam and block floor with infill blocks
- damp proof membrane
- infill block built into wall
- foundation blockwork

Levels: 0 FFL, -450 FFL, 150mm min

Detail M-G4 - External masonry cavity wall, beam and block floor

NOTES:

U-value 0.13 Wm²K or better

Perimeter strip of insulation abuts screed and blockwork wall. External wall insulation must overlap the insulation below beam and block floor to avoid thermal bridging. Floor screed over insulation, minimum of 65mm thick or proprietary screed min 35mm thick.

Alternative floor finish over insulation of chipboard or similar must include vapour control layer between chipboard and insulation.

Void below beam and block floor is ventilated using air bricks and connection sleeves at intervals.

SECTION 5 - MASONRY CONSTRUCTION

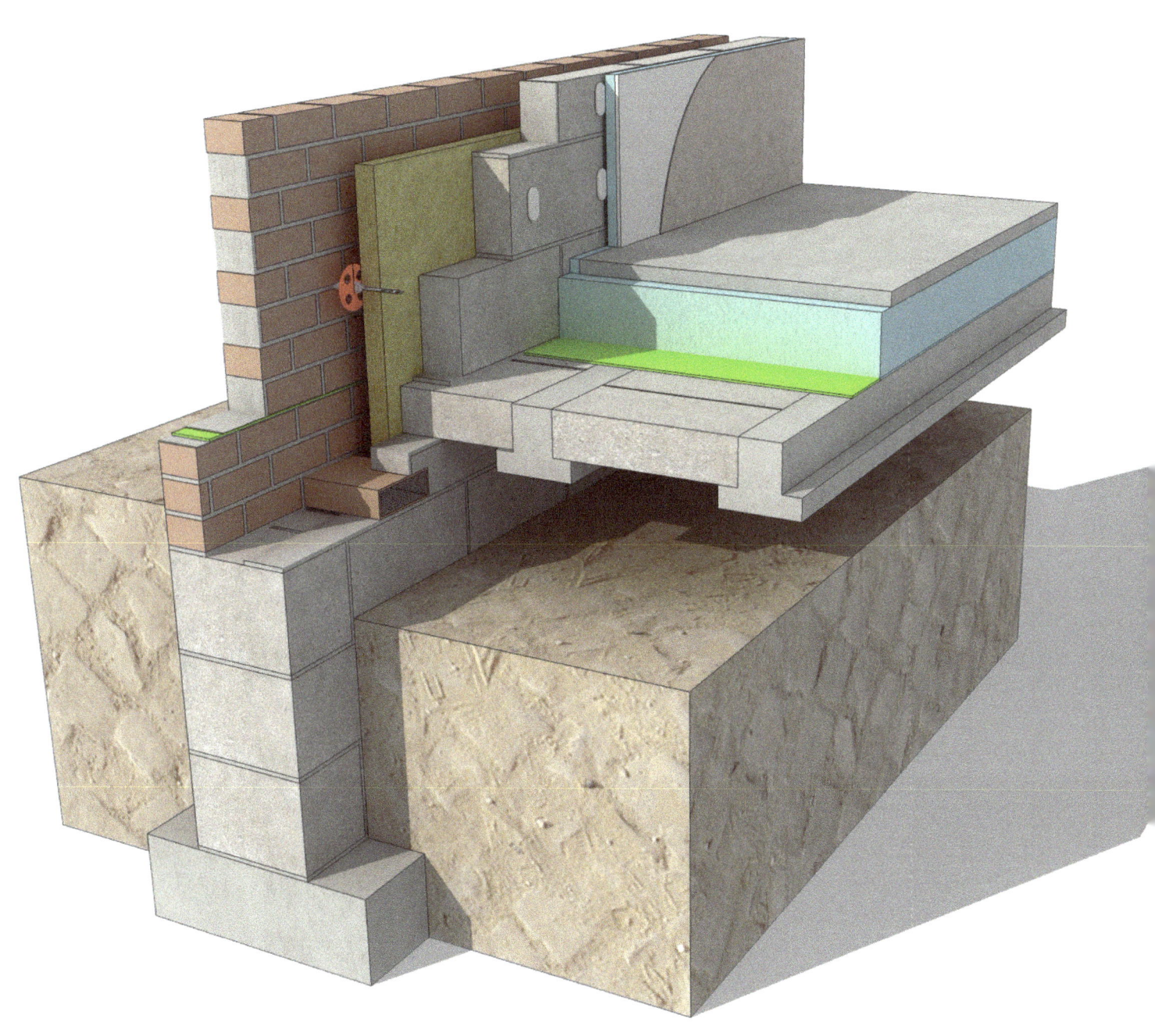

3D Detail M-G4 - External masonry cavity wall, beam and block floor

M-G5

EXTERNAL MASONRY CAVITY WALL, SUSPENDED TIMBER FLOOR

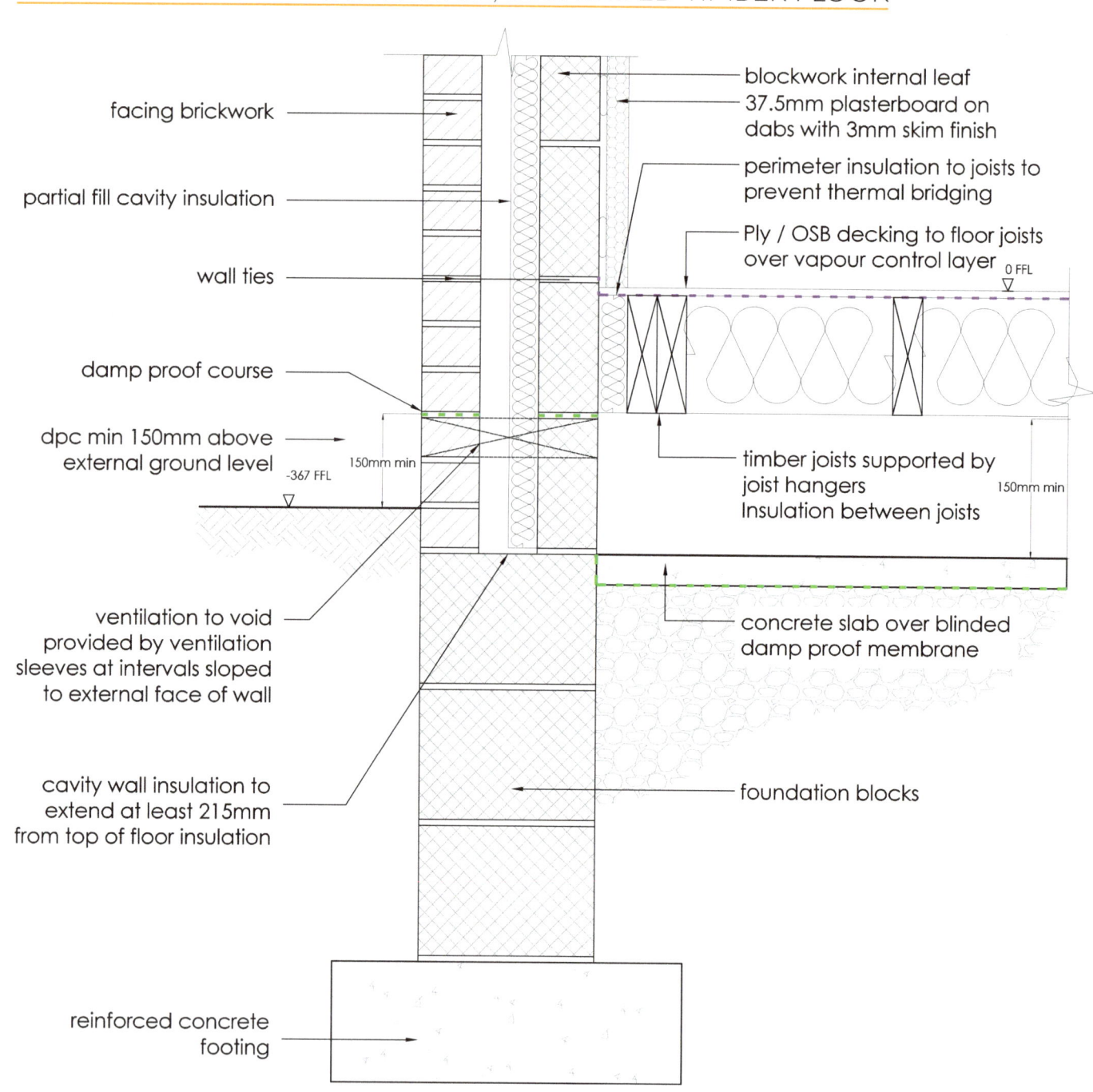

Labels (left side):
- facing brickwork
- partial fill cavity insulation
- wall ties
- damp proof course
- dpc min 150mm above external ground level
- ventilation to void provided by ventilation sleeves at intervals sloped to external face of wall
- cavity wall insulation to extend at least 215mm from top of floor insulation
- reinforced concrete footing

Labels (right side):
- blockwork internal leaf 37.5mm plasterboard on dabs with 3mm skim finish
- perimeter insulation to joists to prevent thermal bridging
- Ply / OSB decking to floor joists over vapour control layer
- timber joists supported by joist hangers Insulation between joists
- concrete slab over blinded damp proof membrane
- foundation blocks

Dimensions: 150mm min; 150mm min; 0 FFL; -367 FFL

Detail M-G5 - External masonry cavity wall, suspended timber floor

NOTES:

U-value 0.13 Wm²K or better
Perimeter strip of insulation abuts screed and blockwork wall. External wall insulation must extend below top of floor insulation to avoid thermal bridging. Void below suspended floor is ventilated using air bricks and connection sleeves at intervals. Minimum 150mm ventilation void area. Joists design according to individual project requirements - see TRADA span tables for guidance.

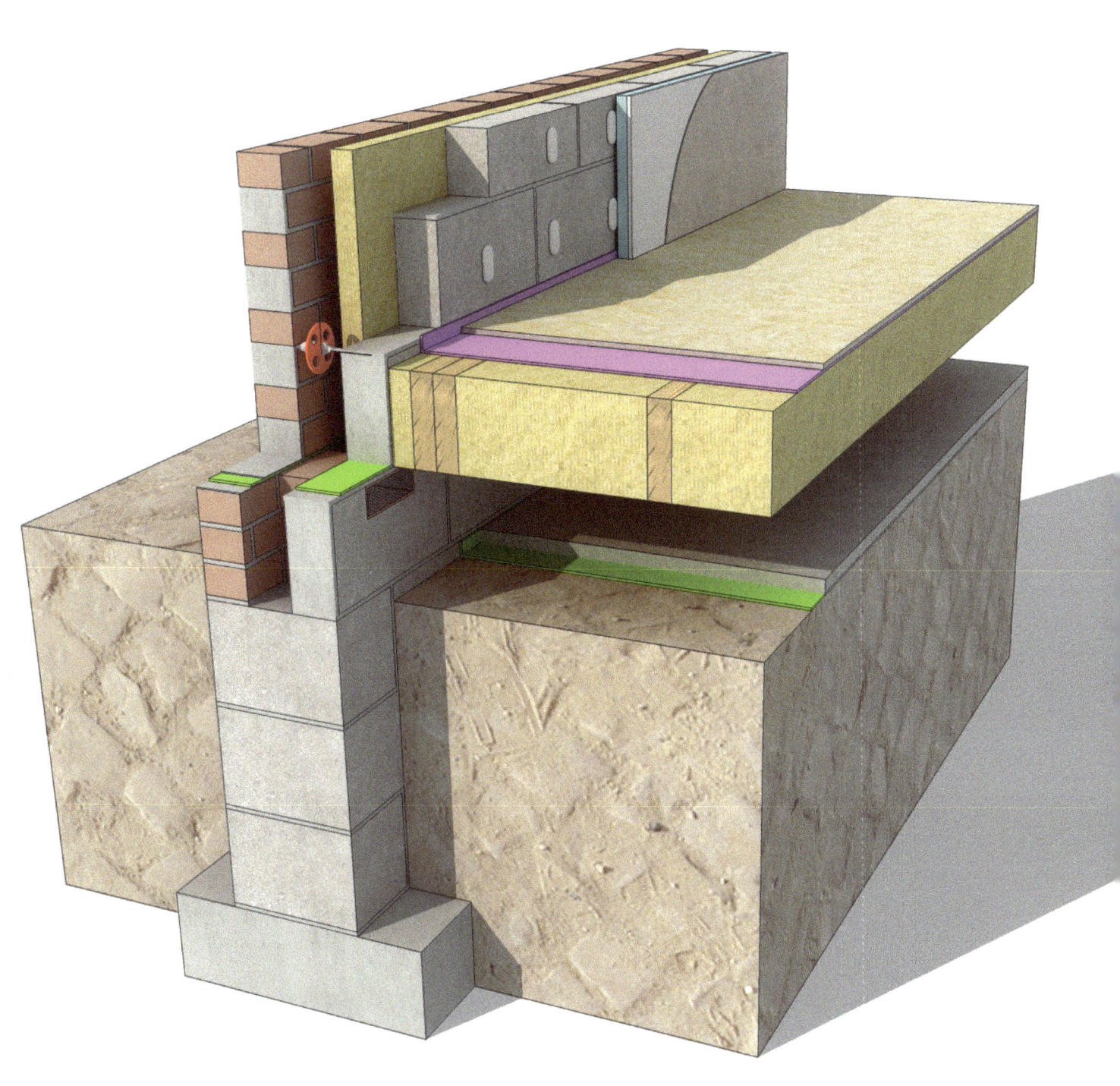

3D Detail M-G5 - External masonry cavity wall, suspended timber floor

M-G6

GROUND FLOOR BUILD UP OPTION - TIMBER FLOOR ON BATTENS

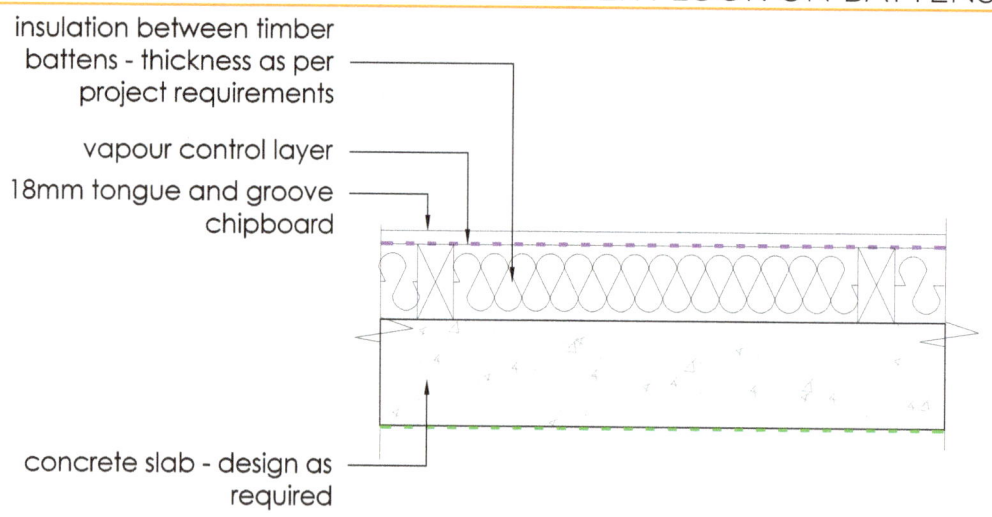

- insulation between timber battens - thickness as per project requirements
- vapour control layer
- 18mm tongue and groove chipboard
- concrete slab - design as required

Detail M-G6 - Ground floor build up option - timber floor on battens

NOTES:

Insulation levels and concrete designed according to project requirements

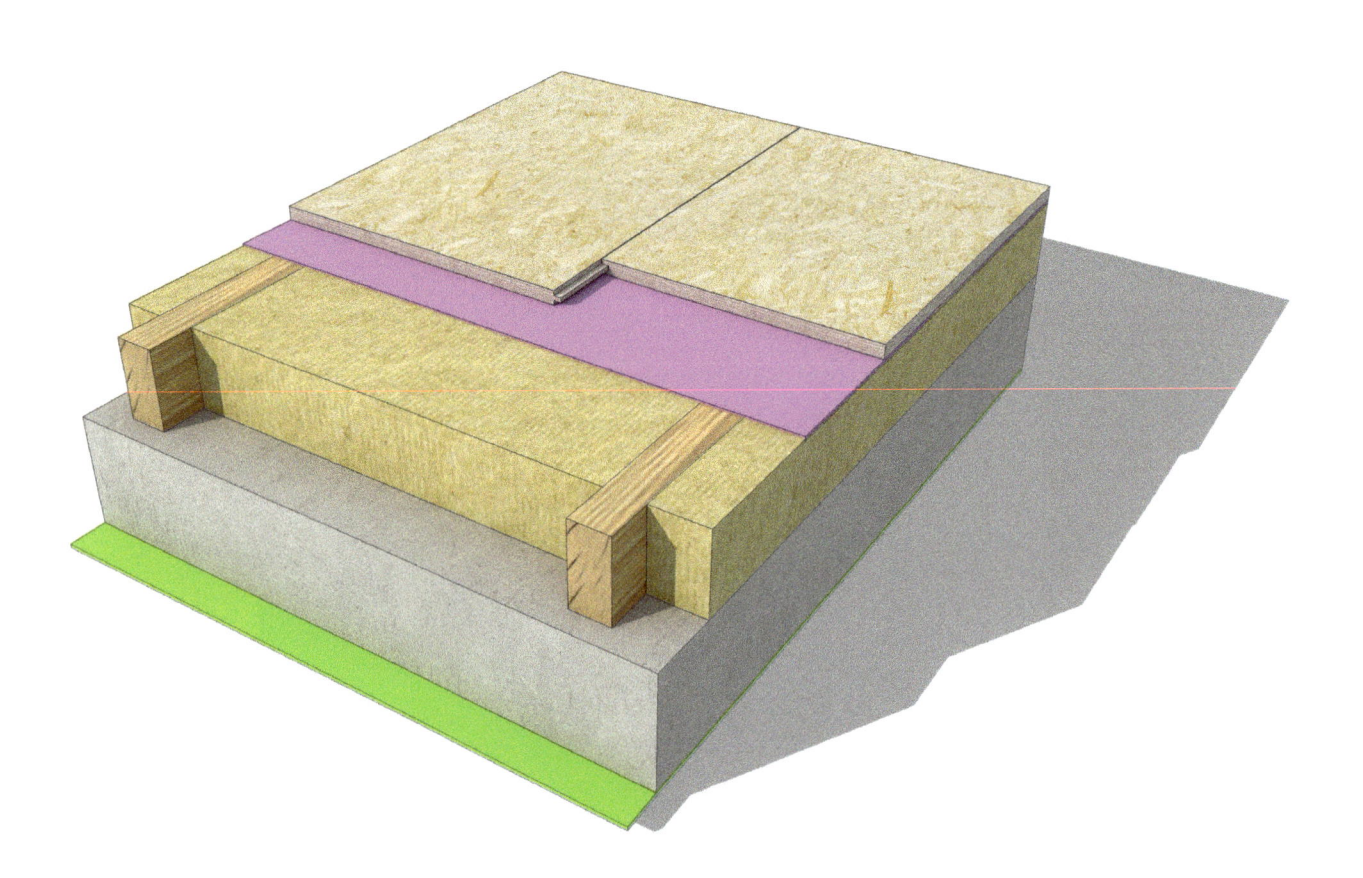

3D Detail M-G6 - Ground floor build up option - timber floor on battens

SECTION 5 - MASONRY CONSTRUCTION

M-G7

GROUND FLOOR BUILD UP OPTION - TIMBER FLOATING FLOOR

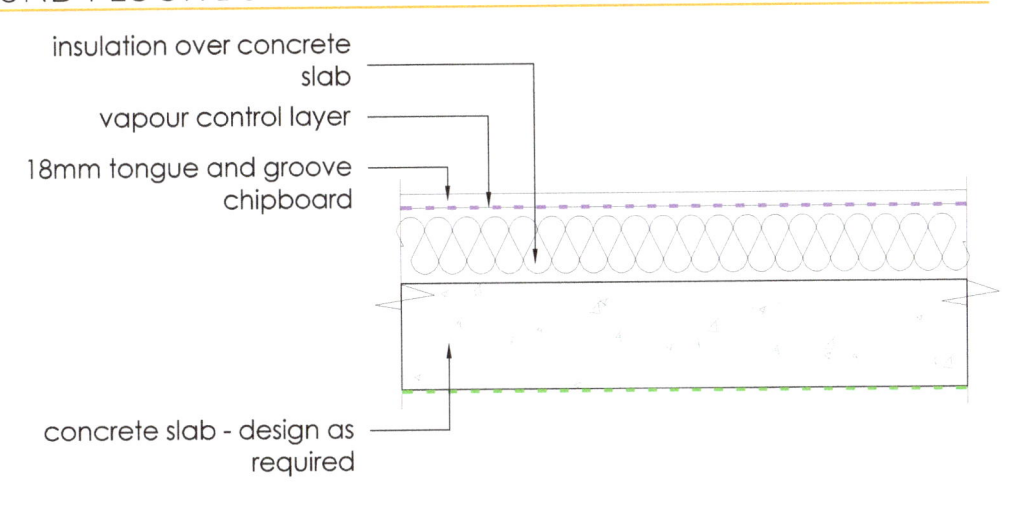

- insulation over concrete slab
- vapour control layer
- 18mm tongue and groove chipboard
- concrete slab - design as required

Detail M-G7 - Ground floor build up option - timber floating floor

NOTES:

Insulation levels and concrete designed according to project requirements

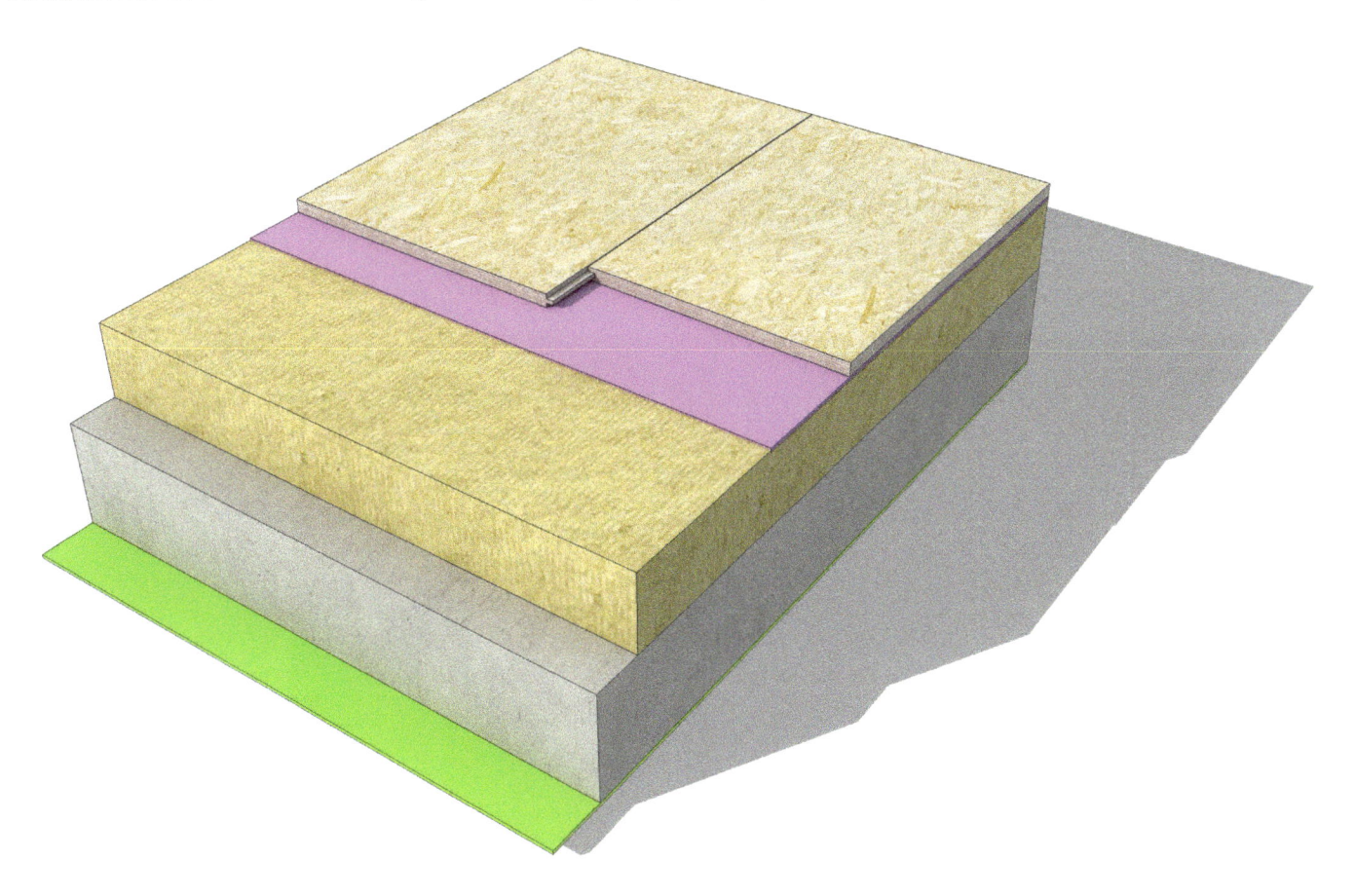

3D Detail M-G7 - Ground floor build up option - timber floating floor

M-G8

GROUND FLOOR BUILD UP OPTION - SCREED FINISH, INSULATION UNDER SLAB

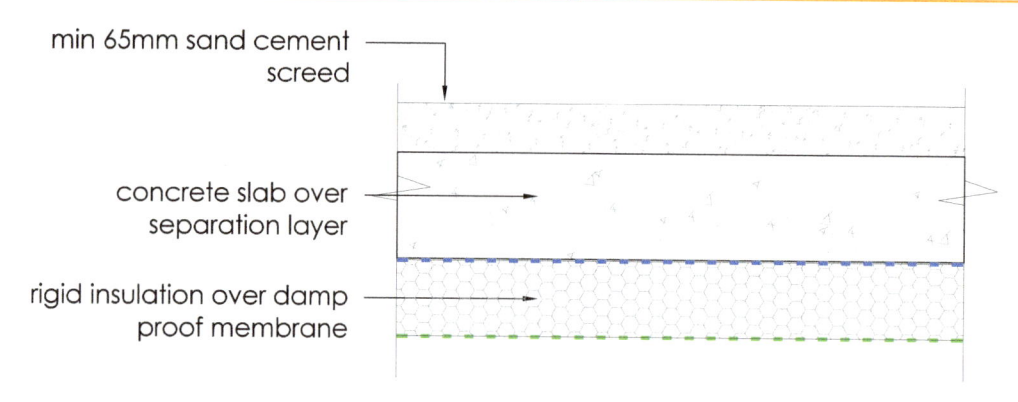

- min 65mm sand cement screed
- concrete slab over separation layer
- rigid insulation over damp proof membrane

Detail M-G8 - Ground floor build up option - screed finish, insulation under slab

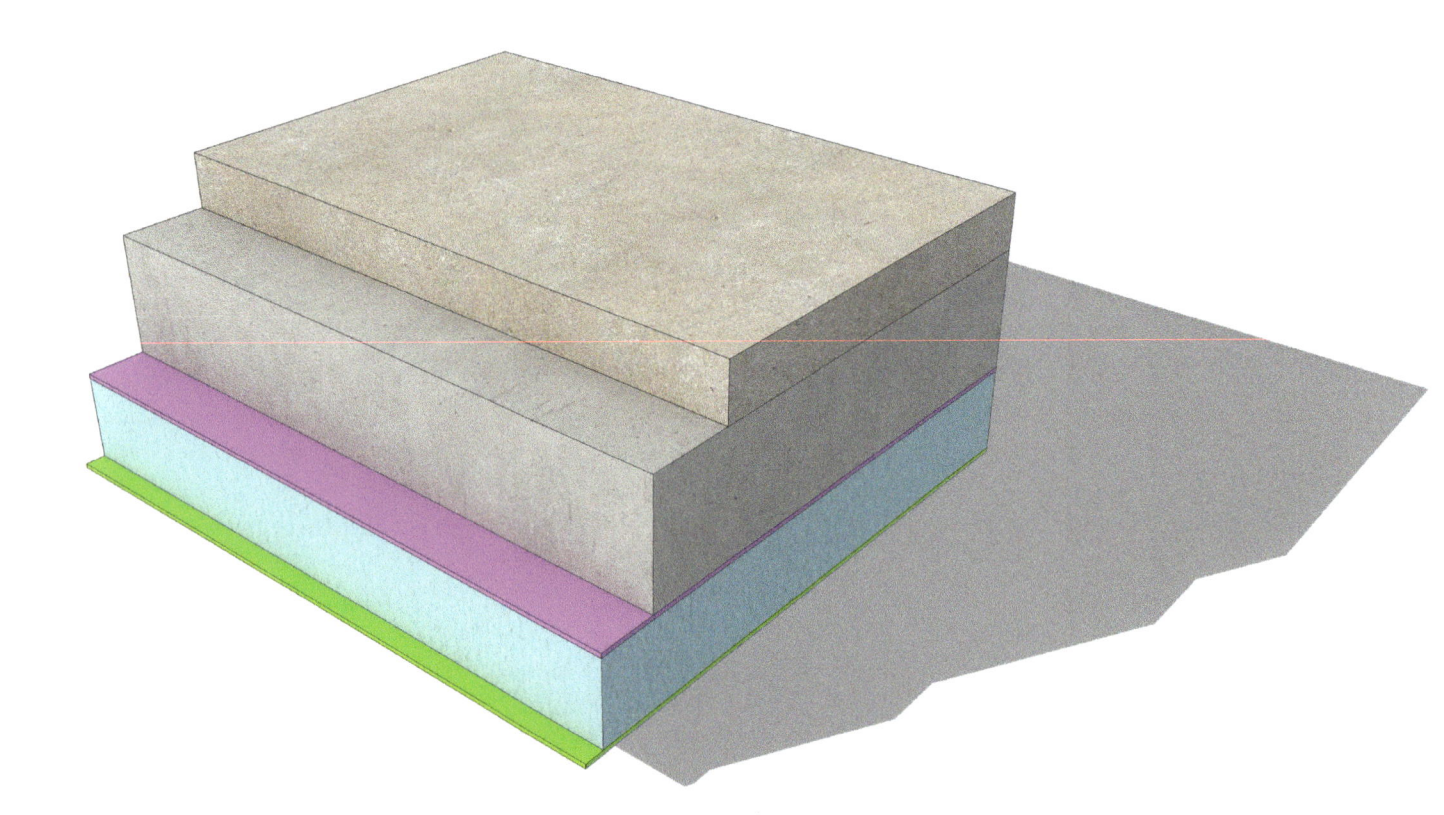

NOTES:

Insulation levels and concrete designed according to project requirements

3D Detail M-G8 - Ground floor build up option - screed finish, insulation under slab

SECTION 5 - MASONRY CONSTRUCTION

M-G9

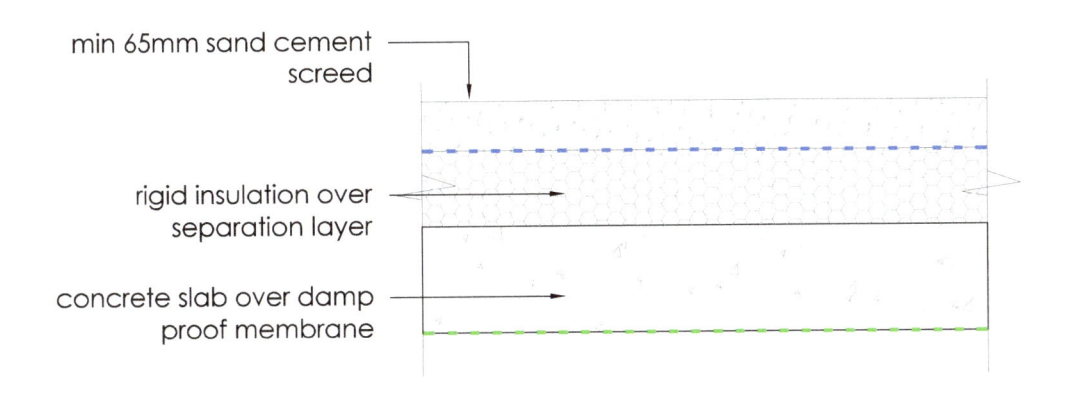

GROUND FLOOR BUILD UP OPTION - SCREED FINISH, INSULATION OVER SLAB

- min 65mm sand cement screed
- rigid insulation over separation layer
- concrete slab over damp proof membrane

Detail M-G9 - Ground floor build up option - screed finish, insulation over slab

NOTES:

Insulation levels and concrete designed according to project requirements

3D Detail M-G9 - Ground floor build up option - screed finish, insulation over slab

M-G10

UNDERFLOOR HEATING - SUSPENDED TIMBER FLOOR

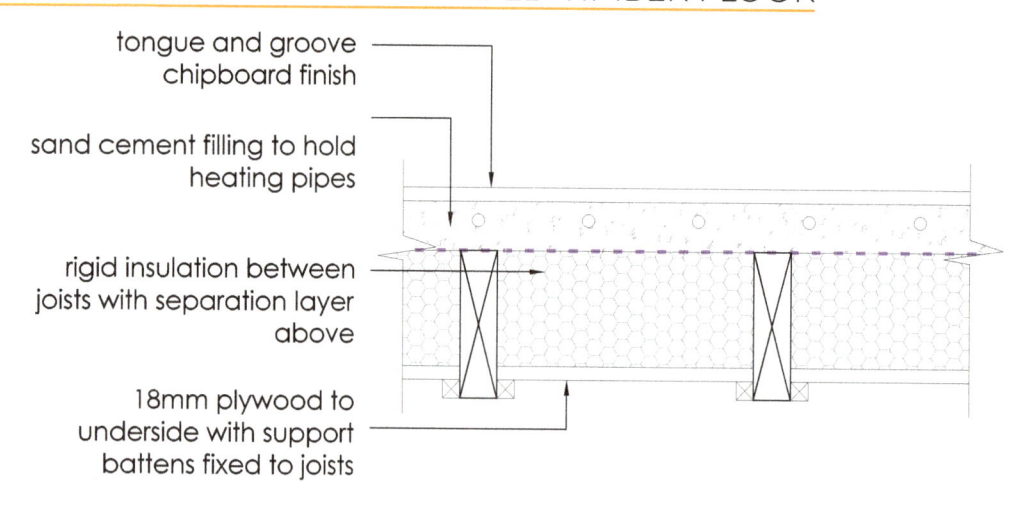

- tongue and groove chipboard finish
- sand cement filling to hold heating pipes
- rigid insulation between joists with separation layer above
- 18mm plywood to underside with support battens fixed to joists

Detail M-G10 - Underfloor heating - suspended timber floor

NOTES:

Underfloor heating design, layout and heating pipe specification according to project requirements and manufacturers recommendations

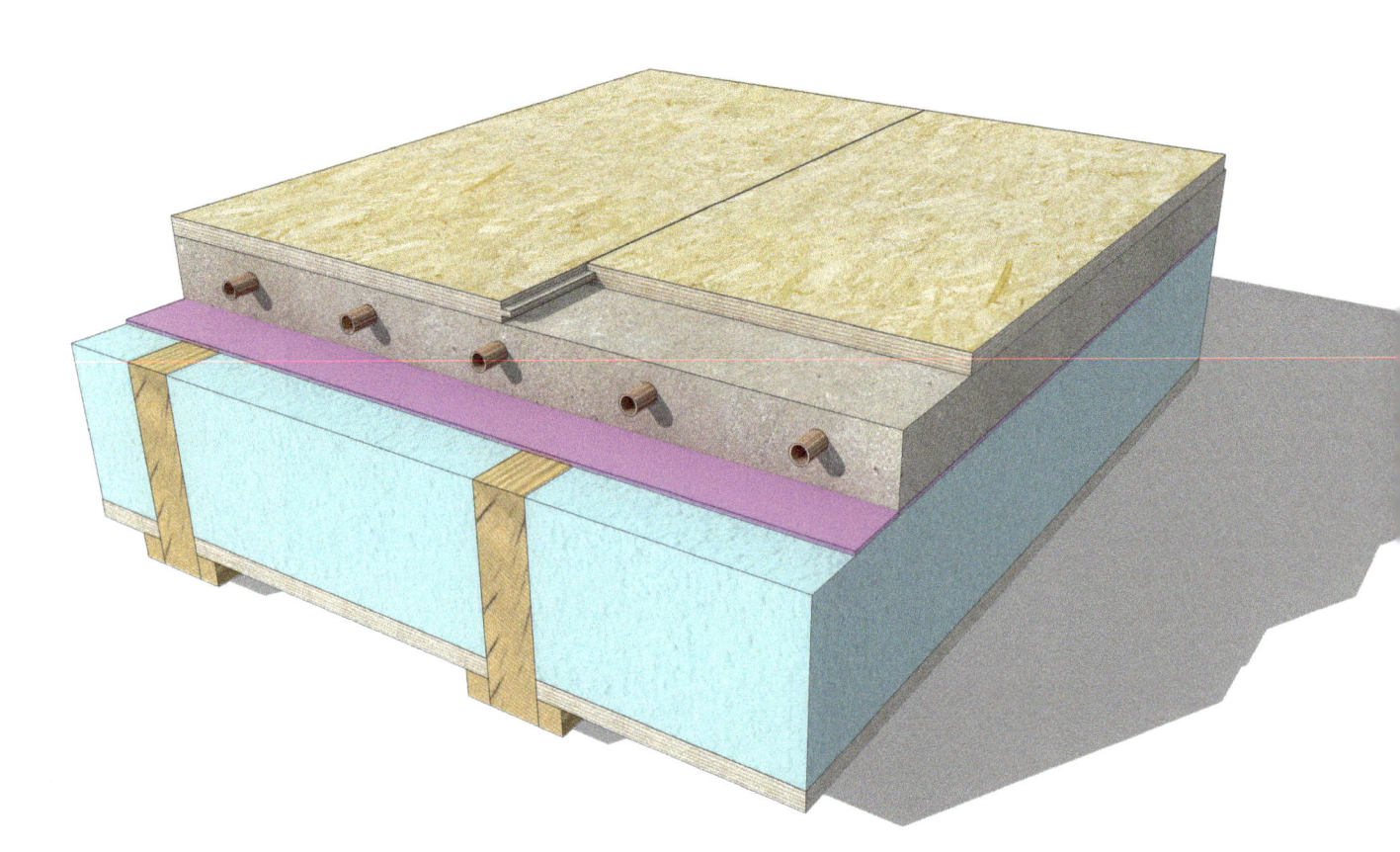

3D Detail M-G10 - Underfloor heating - suspended timber floor

SECTION 5 - MASONRY CONSTRUCTION

M-G11

UNDERFLOOR HEATING - TIMBER FLOOR ON BATTENS

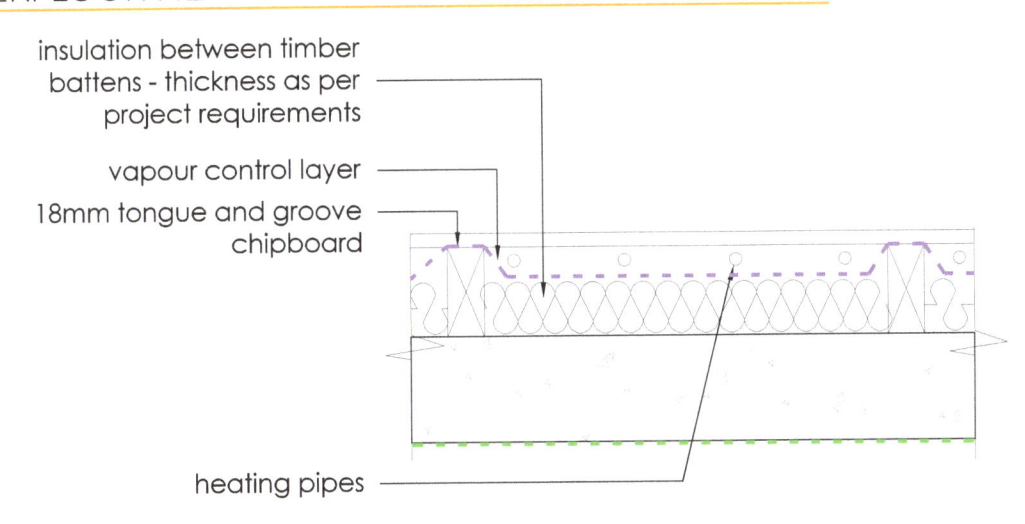

- insulation between timber battens - thickness as per project requirements
- vapour control layer
- 18mm tongue and groove chipboard
- heating pipes

Detail M-G11 - Underfloor heating - timber floor on battens

NOTES:

Underfloor heating design, layout and heating pipe specification according to project requirements and manufacturers recommendations

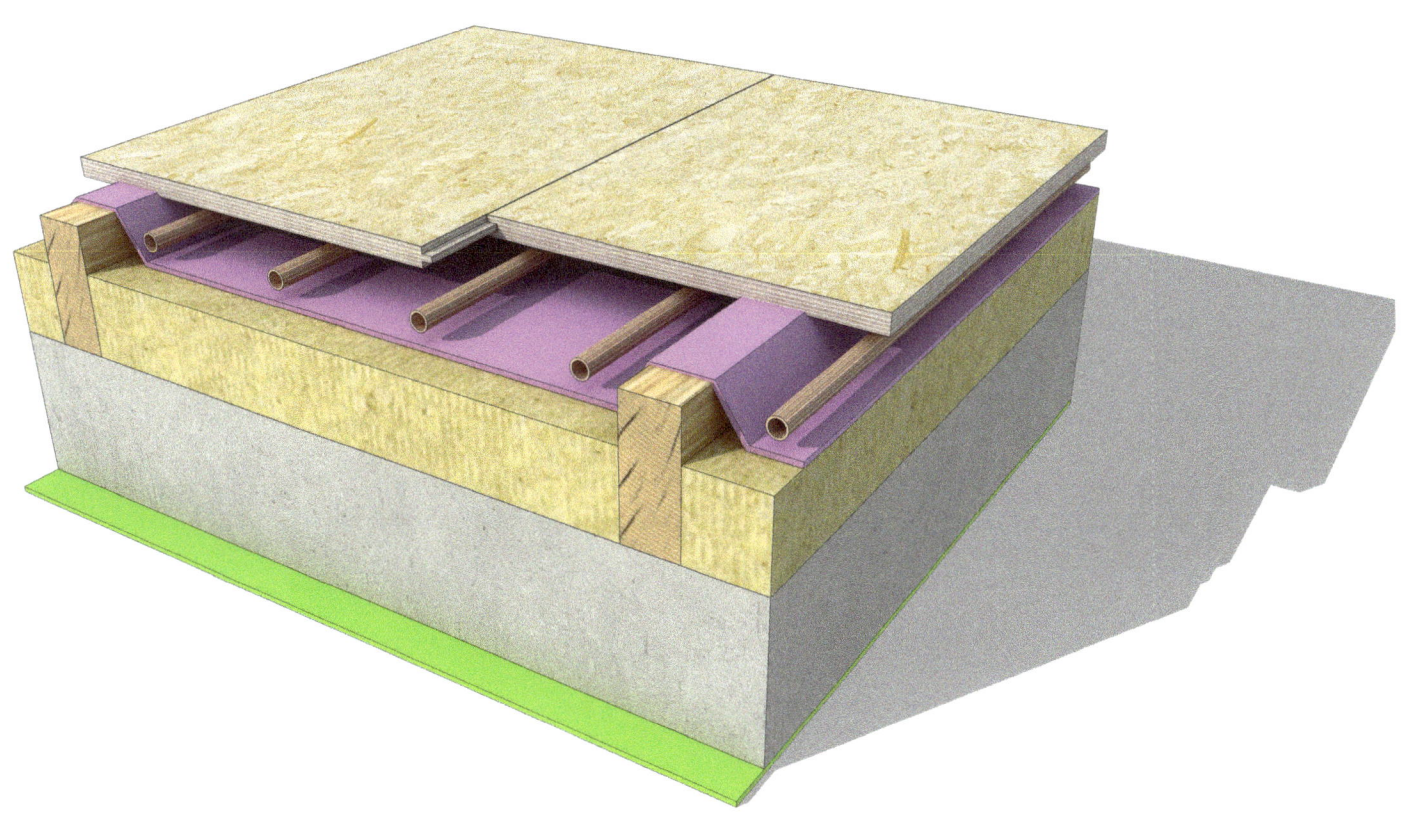

3D Detail M-G11 - Underfloor heating - timber floor on battens

M-G12

UNDERFLOOR HEATING - SCREED FINISH, INSULATION OVER SLAB

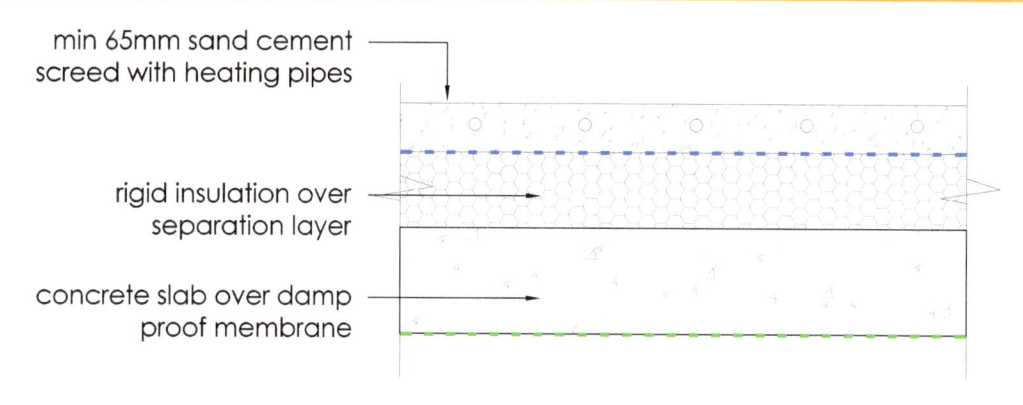

- min 65mm sand cement screed with heating pipes
- rigid insulation over separation layer
- concrete slab over damp proof membrane

Detail M-G12 - Underfloor heating - screed finish, insulation over slab

NOTES:

Underfloor heating design, layout and heating pipe specification according to project requirements and manufacturers recommendations

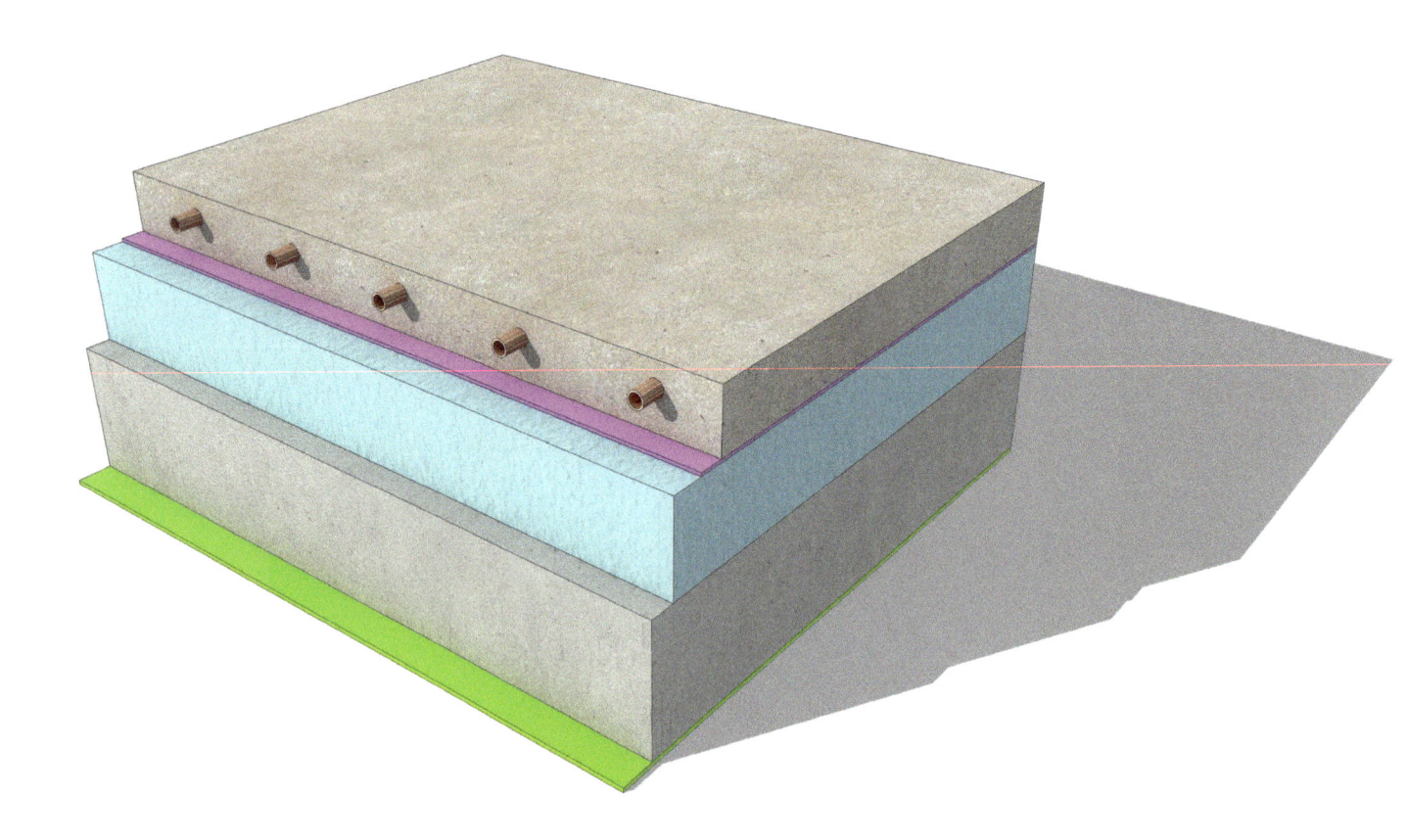

3D Detail M-G12 - Underfloor heating - screed finish, insulation over slab

SECTION 5 - MASONRY CONSTRUCTION

Blank Page

M-G13

EXTERNAL MASONRY CAVITY WALL, TIMBER INTERMEDIATE FLOOR

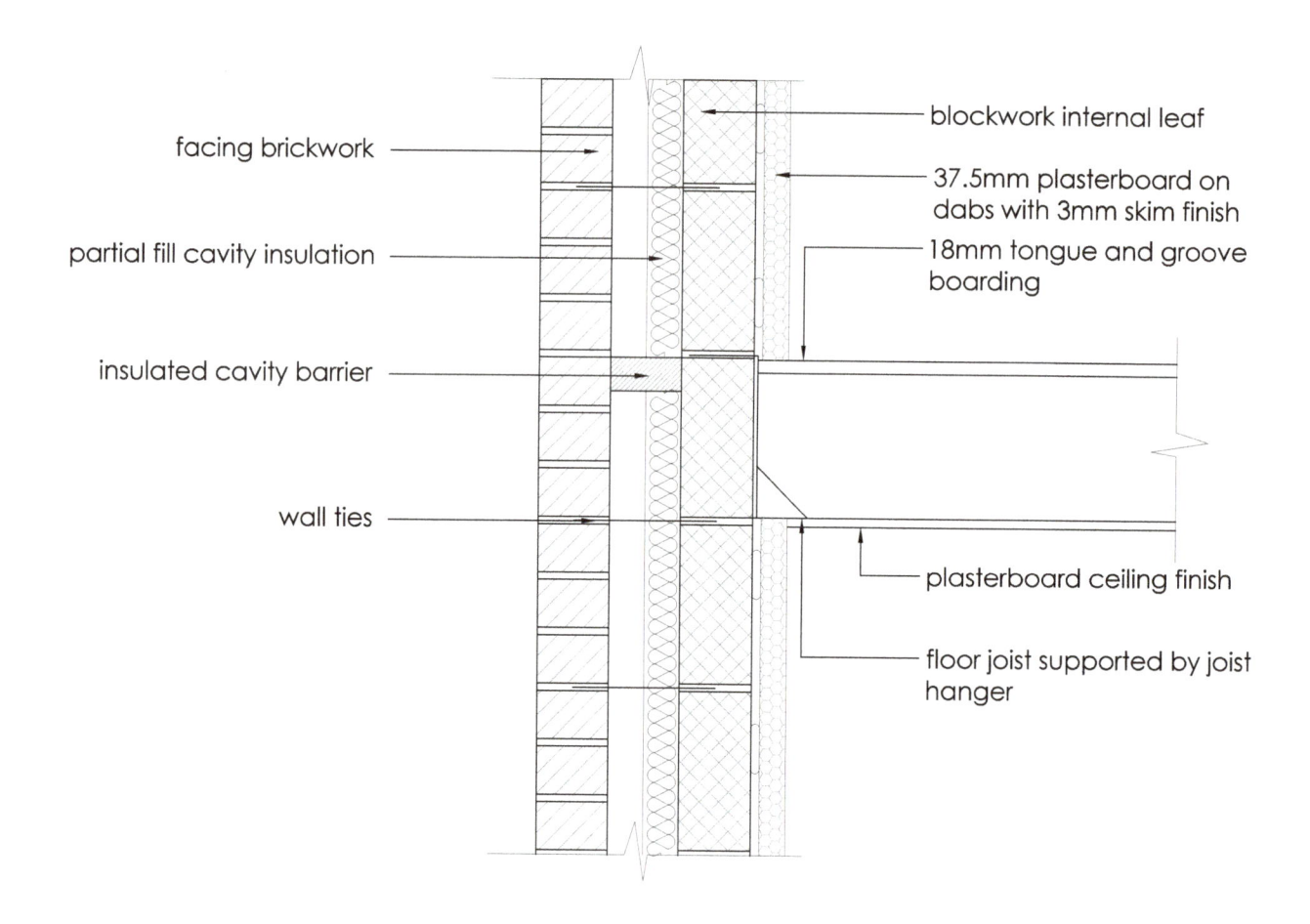

Labels (left side):
- facing brickwork
- partial fill cavity insulation
- insulated cavity barrier
- wall ties

Labels (right side):
- blockwork internal leaf
- 37.5mm plasterboard on dabs with 3mm skim finish
- 18mm tongue and groove boarding
- plasterboard ceiling finish
- floor joist supported by joist hanger

Detail M-G13 - External masonry cavity wall, timber intermediate floor

SECTION 5 - MASONRY CONSTRUCTION

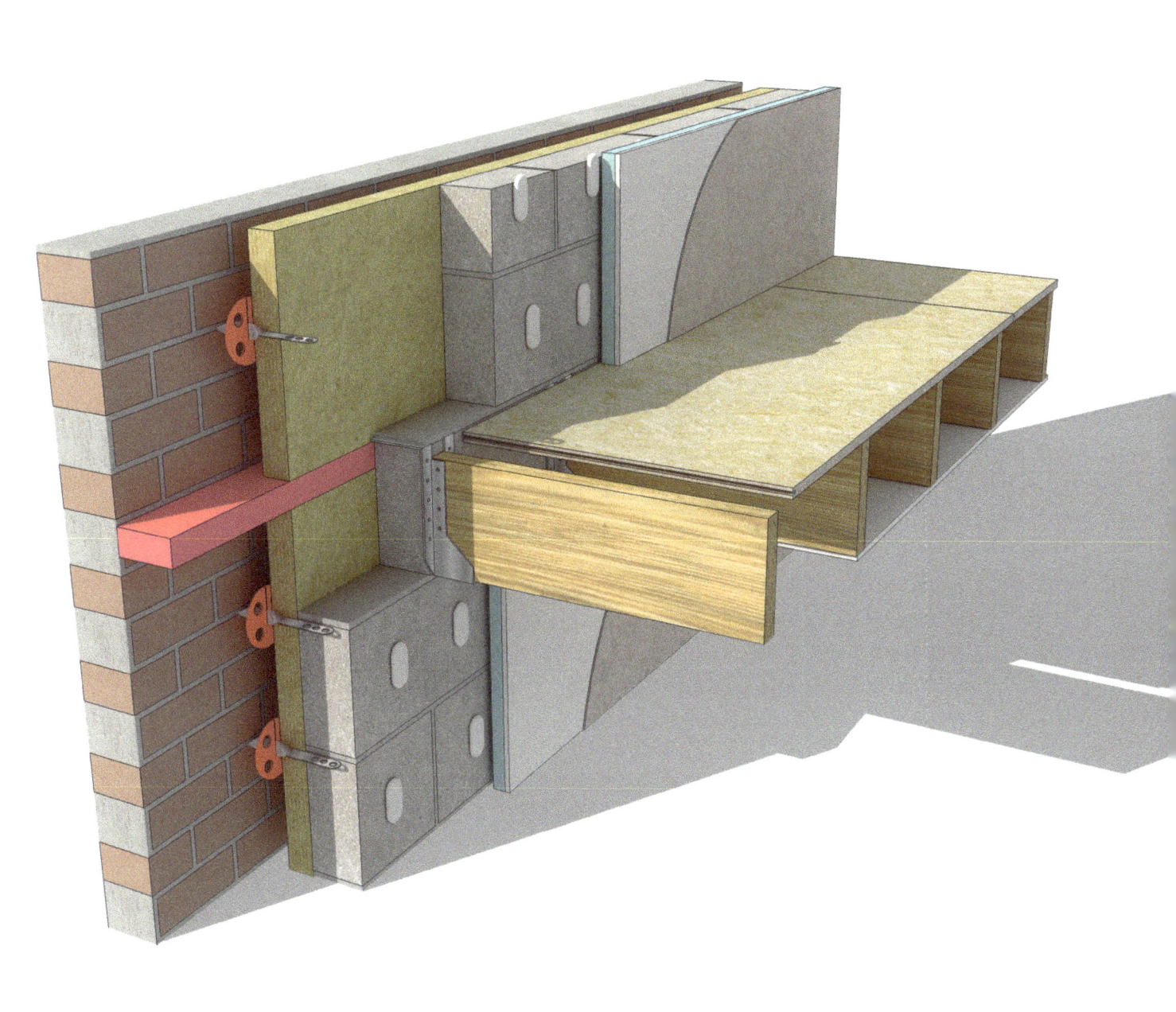

3D Detail M-G13 - External masonry cavity wall, timber intermediate floor

M-G14

EXTERNAL MASONRY CAVITY WALL, TIMBER INTERMEDIATE FLOOR WITH SOUND INSULATION

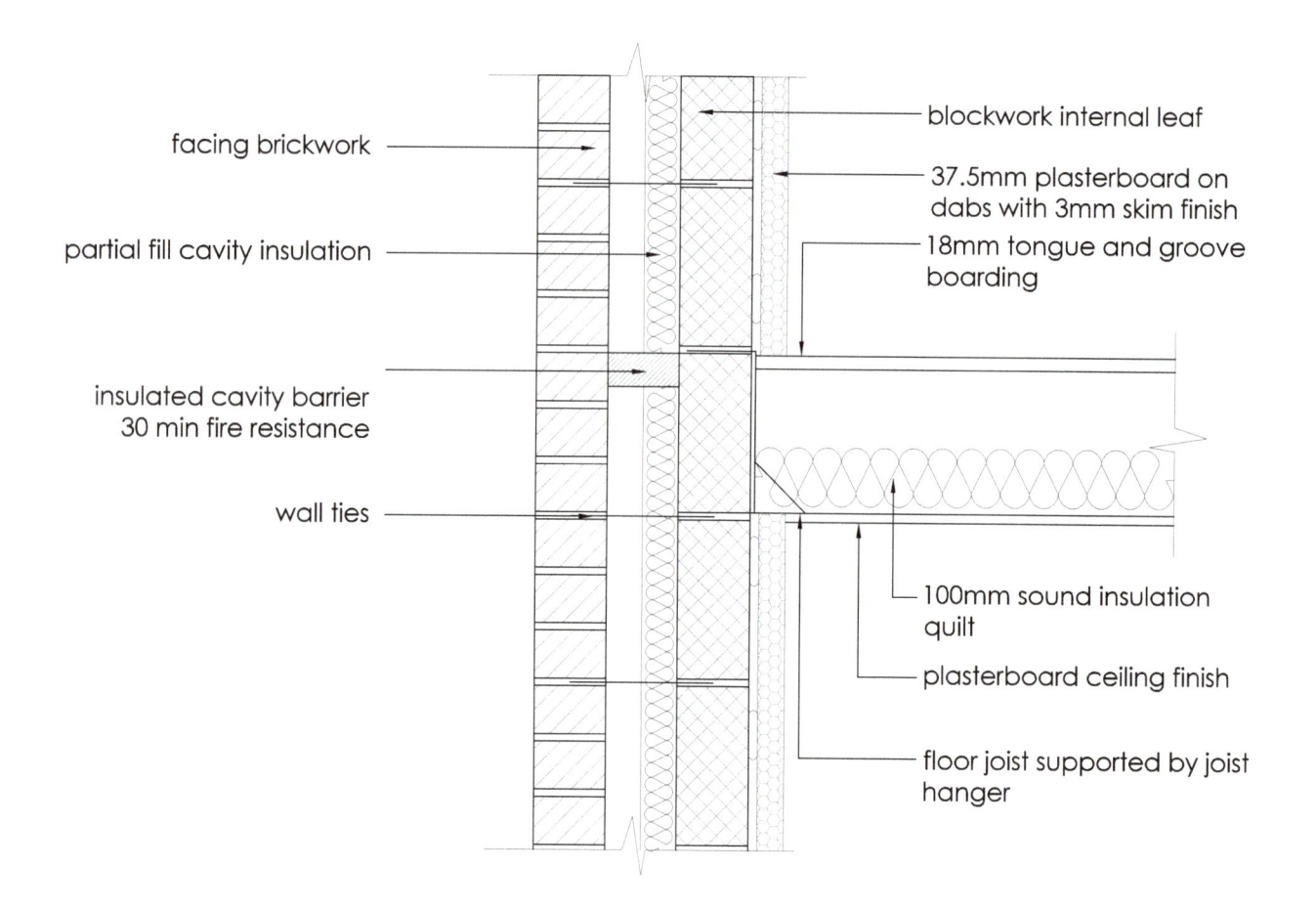

- facing brickwork
- partial fill cavity insulation
- insulated cavity barrier 30 min fire resistance
- wall ties
- blockwork internal leaf
- 37.5mm plasterboard on dabs with 3mm skim finish
- 18mm tongue and groove boarding
- 100mm sound insulation quilt
- plasterboard ceiling finish
- floor joist supported by joist hanger

Detail M-G14 - External masonry cavity wall, timber intermediate floor with sound insulation

NOTES:

For sound insulation between floors, resilient bars can also be used - fixed to underside of joists with plasterboard fitted to resilient bars.

SECTION 5 - MASONRY CONSTRUCTION

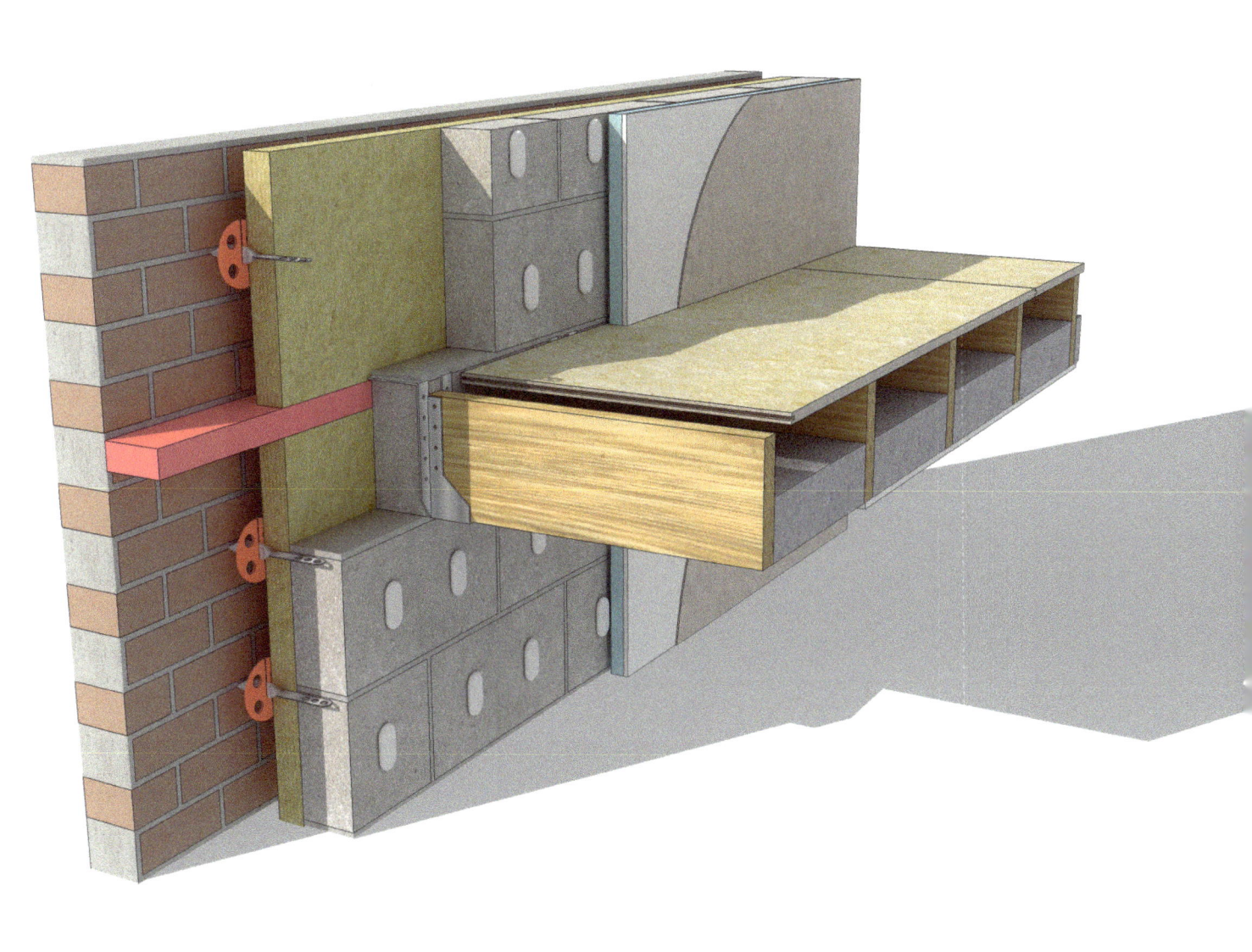

3D Detail M-G14 - External masonry cavity wall, timber intermediate floor with sound insulation

M-G15

EXTERNAL MASONRY CAVITY WALL, CONCRETE SEPARATING FLOOR

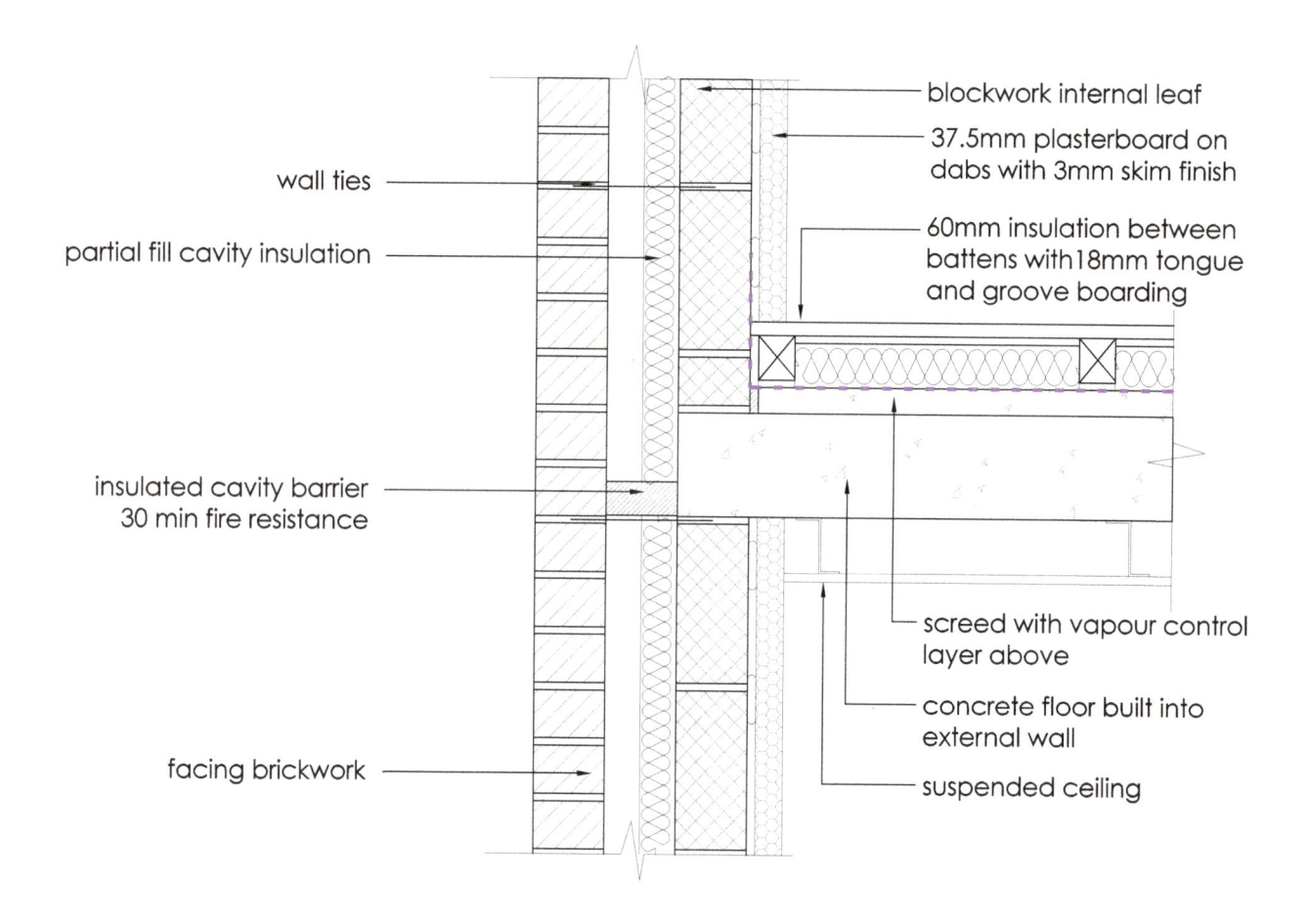

- wall ties
- partial fill cavity insulation
- insulated cavity barrier 30 min fire resistance
- facing brickwork
- blockwork internal leaf
- 37.5mm plasterboard on dabs with 3mm skim finish
- 60mm insulation between battens with 18mm tongue and groove boarding
- screed with vapour control layer above
- concrete floor built into external wall
- suspended ceiling

Detail M-G15 - External masonry cavity wall, concrete separating floor

SECTION 5 - MASONRY CONSTRUCTION

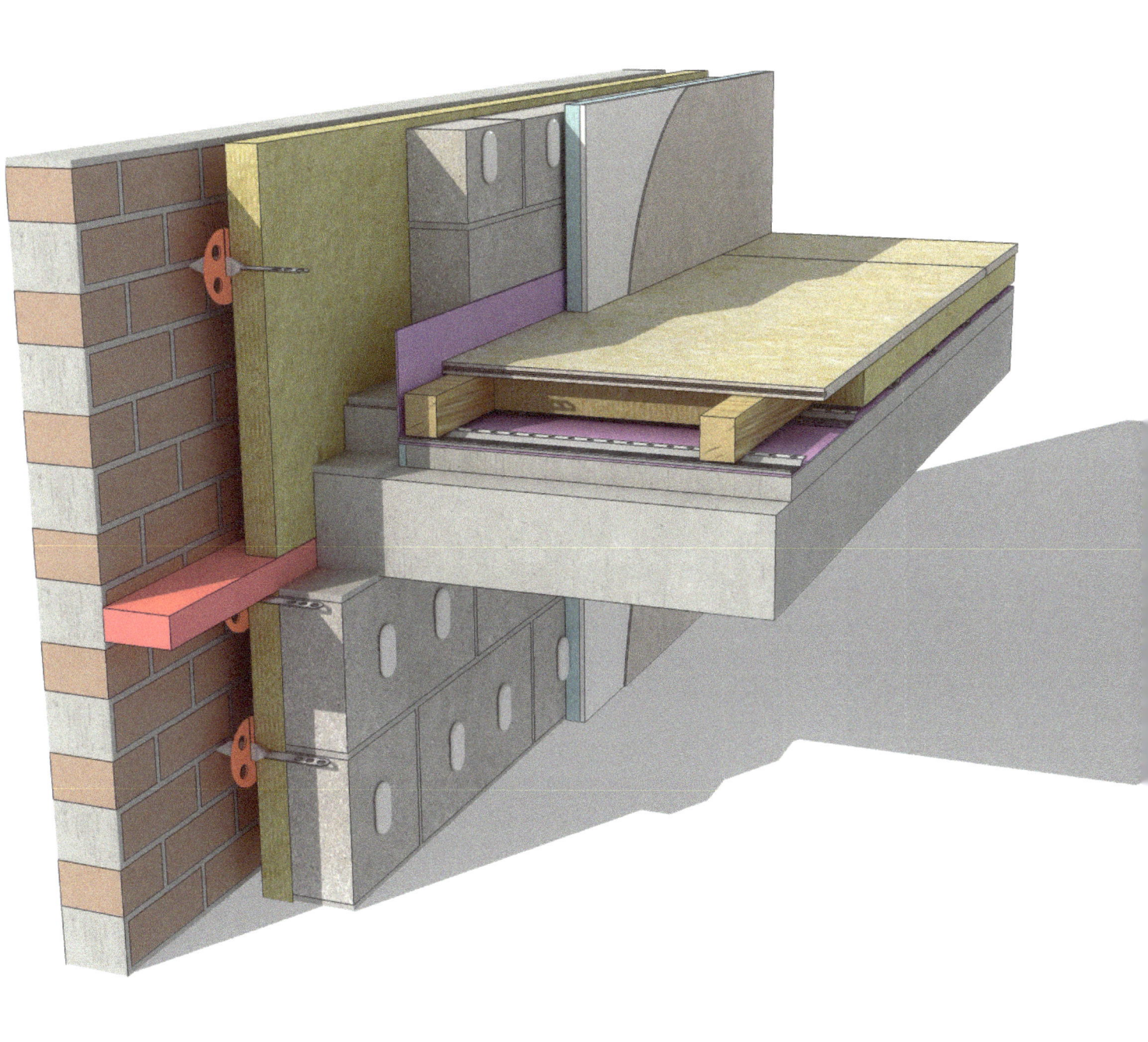

3D Detail M-G15 - External masonry cavity wall, concrete separating floor

NOTES ON THE REGS

The following information is a partial list of requirements from the **Building Regulations Approved Documents** - for full and detailed explanations and requirements please consult the full publications.

GENERAL REQUIREMENTS - FOUNDATIONS

The building shall be constructed so that:
- the combined dead, imposed and wind loads are sustained and transmitted by it to the ground, safely and without causing any building deflection/deformation or ground movement that will affect the stability of any part of the building.
- ground movement caused by swelling, shrinkage or freezing of the sub-soil, land slip or subsidence will not affect the stability of any part of the building.

(Approved Doc A)

The walls and floors of the building shall adequately protect the building and people who use the building from harmful effects caused by ground moisture, precipitation wind wind-driven spray, interstitial and surface condensation, and spillage of water from or associated with sanitary fittings or fixed appliances. All floors next to the ground, walls and roof shall not be damaged by moisture from the ground, rain or snow and shall not carry that moisture to any part of the building that it would damage.

(Approved Doc C2)

Site preparation and resistance to contaminants and water

- The ground to be covered by the building shall be reasonably free from any material that might damage the building or affect its stability, including vegetable matter, topsoil and pre-existing foundations.
- Reasonable precautions shall be taken to avoid danger to health and safety caused by contaminants on or in the ground covered, or to be covered, by the building and any land associated with the building.
- Adequate subsoil drainage shall be provided if it is needed to avoid: passage of ground moisture to the interior of the building; damage to the building, including damage through the transport of water-borne contaminants to the foundations of the building

(Approved Doc C1)

Rainwater drainage
Rainwater drainage systems shall ensure that rainwater soaking into the ground is distributed sufficiently so that it does not damage foundations of the proposed building or any adjacent structure.

(Approved Doc H3)

GENERAL NOTES:

Foundations - plain concrete
There should not be:
- non engineered fill or a wide variation in ground conditions within the loaded area
- weaker or more compressible ground at such a depth below the foundation as could impair the stability of the structure.

Foundations stepped on elevation should overlap by twice the height of the step, by the thickness of the foundation, or 300mm, whichever is greater.

Residential Buildings
The maximum height of the building measured from the lowest finished ground level to the highest point of any wall or roof should be less than 15m.
The height of the building should not exceed twice the least width of the building.

GENERAL REQUIREMENTS - FLOORS

Construction
The building shall be constructed so that the combined dead, imposed and wind loads area sustained and transmitted by it to the ground:
- safely
- without causing such deflection or deformation of any part of the building as will impair the

SECTION 5 - MASONRY CONSTRUCTION

stability of any part of another building.
(Approved Doc A1)

The building shall be constructed so that ground movement caused by:
- swelling, shrinkage or freezing of the subsoil
- landslip or subsidence
will not impair the stability of any part of the building

(Approved Doc A2)

Fire Precautions
As a fire precaution, the spread of flame over the internal linings of a building and the amount of heat released from internal linings shall be restricted;
- all load bearing elements of structure of the building shall be capable of withstanding the effects of fire for an appropriate period without loss of stability;
- ideally the building should be subdivided by elements of fire-resisting construction into compartments;
- all openings in fire-separating elements shall be suitably protected in order to maintain the integrity of the continuity of the fire separation;
- any hidden voids in the construction shall be sealed and subdivided to inhibit the unseens spread of fire and products of combustion, in order to reduce the risk of structural failure, and the spread of fire.

(Approved Doc B3)

Precautions against moisture
The floor son the building shall adequately protect the building and people who use the building from harmful effects caused by:
- ground moisture
- precipitation
- interstitial and surface condensation
- spillage of water from or associated with sanitary fittings or fixed appliances.

All floors next to the ground, walls and roof shall not be damaged by moisture from the ground, rain or snow and shall not carry that moisture to any part of the building that it would damage.

Airborne and Impact sound
Dwellings shall be designed so that the noise from domestic activity in an adjoining dwelling (or other parts of the building) is kept to a level that:
- does not affect the health of the occupants of the dwelling
- will allow them to sleep, rest and engage in their normal activities in satisfactory conditions

(Approved Doc E1)

Dwellings shall be designed so that any domestic noise that is generated internally does not interfere with the occupants ability to sleep, rest and engage in their normal activities in satisfactory conditions.
(Approved Doc E2)

Domestic buildings shall be designed and constructed so as to restrict the transmission of echoes.
(Approved Doc E3)

Ventilation
There shall be adequate means of ventilation provided for people in the building
(Approved Doc F)

Conservation of fuel and power
Reasonable provision shall be made for the conservation of fuel and power in buildings by:
- limiting heat gains and losses through thermal elements and other parts of the building fabric,
- from pipes ducts and vessels used for space heating, space cooling and hot water services.
- providing fixed building services which are energy efficient and have effective controls and are commissioned by testing and adjusting as necessary to ensure they use no more fuel and power than is reasonable in the circumstances.

(Approved Doc L)

GENERAL NOTES:
Suspended timber floors must:
- Ensure the ground is covered so as to resist moisture and prevent plant growth.
- Have a ventilated air space between he ground covering and the timber.
- Have a damp proof course between the timber and any material which can carry moisture from the ground

Floors that separate a dwelling from another dwelling shall resist the transmission of airborne sounds. Floors above a dwelling that separate it from another dwell shall resist:
- the transmission of impact sound (such as speech, music, loudspeakers and impact sources such as footsteps or furniture moving)
- the flow of sound energy through walls and floors
- the level of airborne sound

WALL DETAILS

M-W1

EXTERNAL MASONRY CAVITY WALL, RENDER FINISH

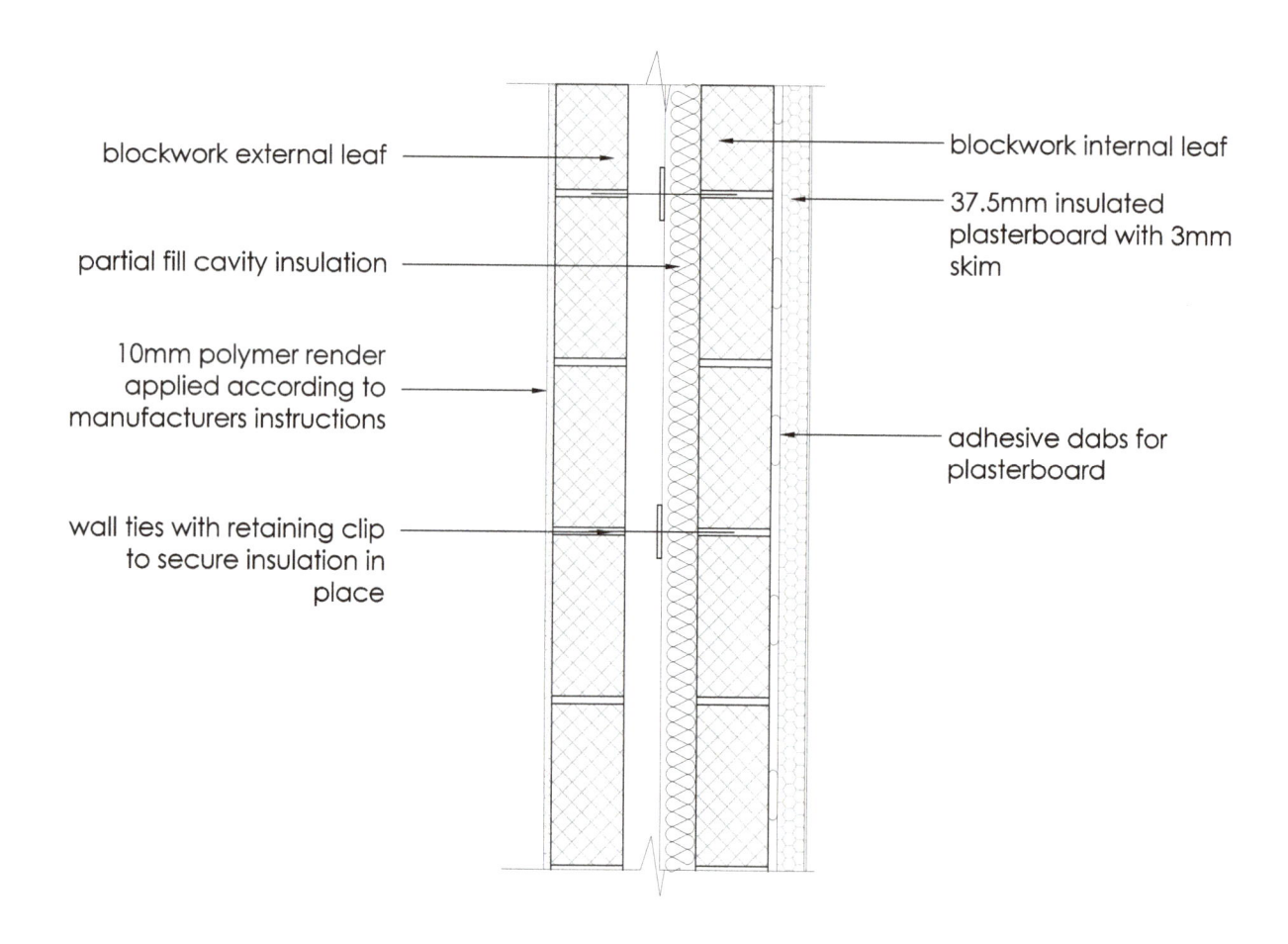

- blockwork external leaf
- partial fill cavity insulation
- 10mm polymer render applied according to manufacturers instructions
- wall ties with retaining clip to secure insulation in place
- blockwork internal leaf
- 37.5mm insulated plasterboard with 3mm skim
- adhesive dabs for plasterboard

Detail M-W1 - External masonry cavity wall, render finish

NOTES:
U-value 0.18 Wm²K or better

SECTION 5 - MASONRY CONSTRUCTION

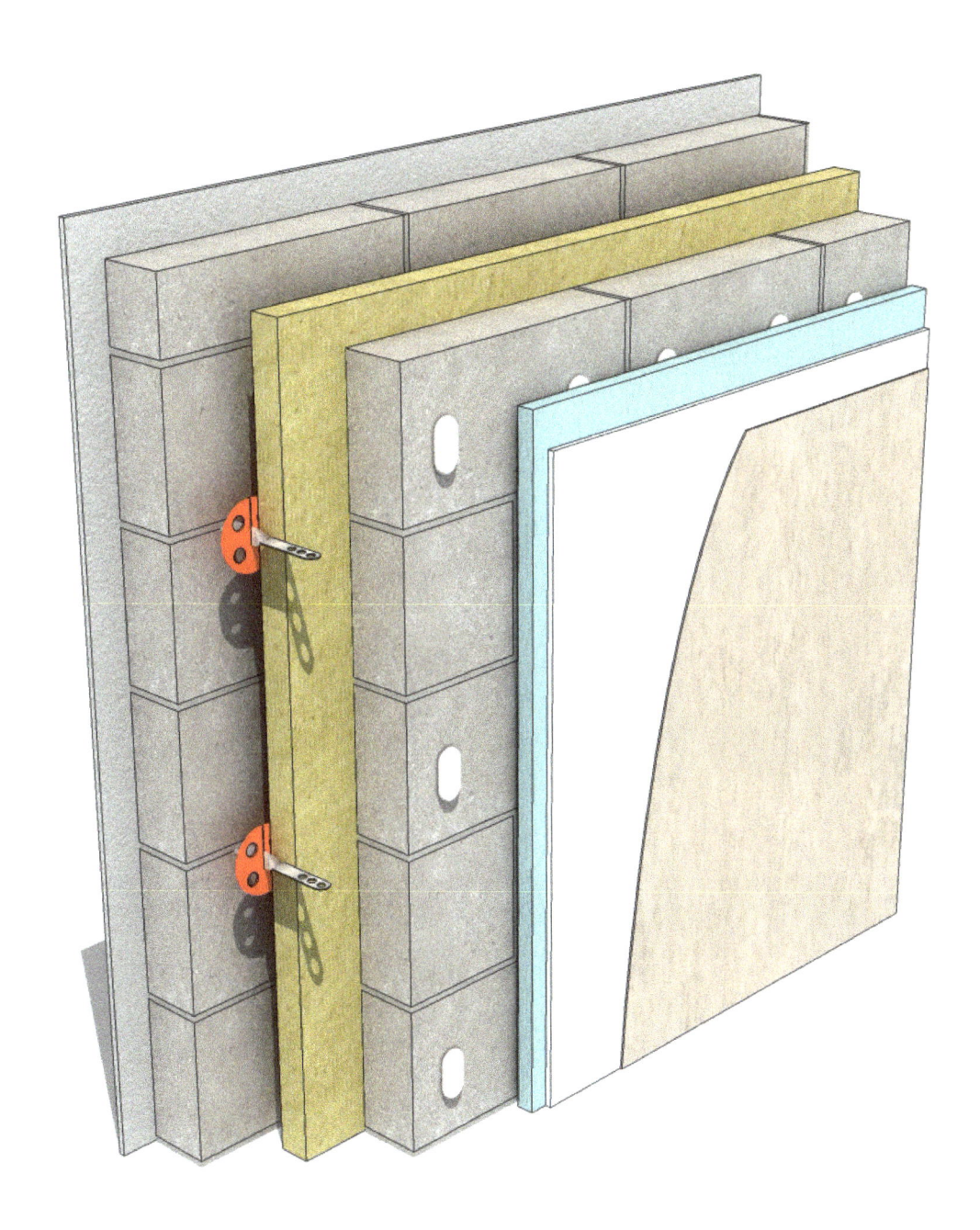

3D Detail M-W1 - External masonry cavity wall, render finish

M-W2

EXTERNAL MASONRY CAVITY WALL, INSULATED RENDER FINISH

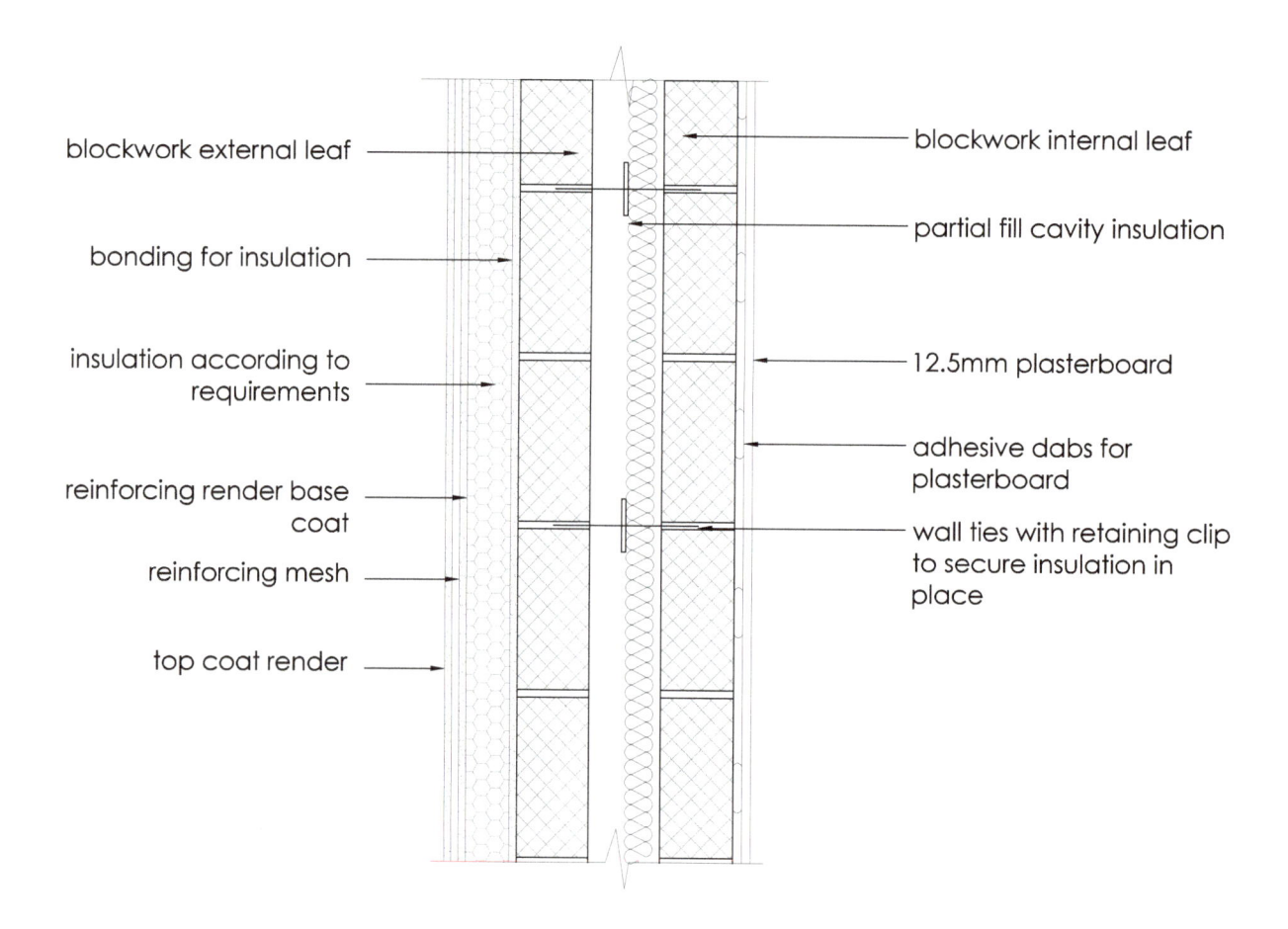

Labels (left side):
- blockwork external leaf
- bonding for insulation
- insulation according to requirements
- reinforcing render base coat
- reinforcing mesh
- top coat render

Labels (right side):
- blockwork internal leaf
- partial fill cavity insulation
- 12.5mm plasterboard
- adhesive dabs for plasterboard
- wall ties with retaining clip to secure insulation in place

Detail M-W2 - External masonry cavity wall, insulated render finish

NOTES:

U-value 0.18 Wm²K or better
External insulation can be bonded or rail fixed to external leaf of blockwork. Insulation thickness according to project requirements. Render design in accordance with manufacturers recommendations.

SECTION 5 - MASONRY CONSTRUCTION

3D Detail M-W2 - External masonry cavity wall, insulated render finish

M-W3

EXTERNAL MASONRY CAVITY WALL, HORIZONTAL TIMBER CLADDING

- blockwork external leaf
- partial fill cavity insulation
- 38mm vertical timber battens
- wall ties with retaining clip to secure insulation in place
- horizontal timber cladding fixed to timber battens

- blockwork internal leaf
- 37.5mm plasterboard with 3mm skim finish
- adhesive dabs for plasterboard

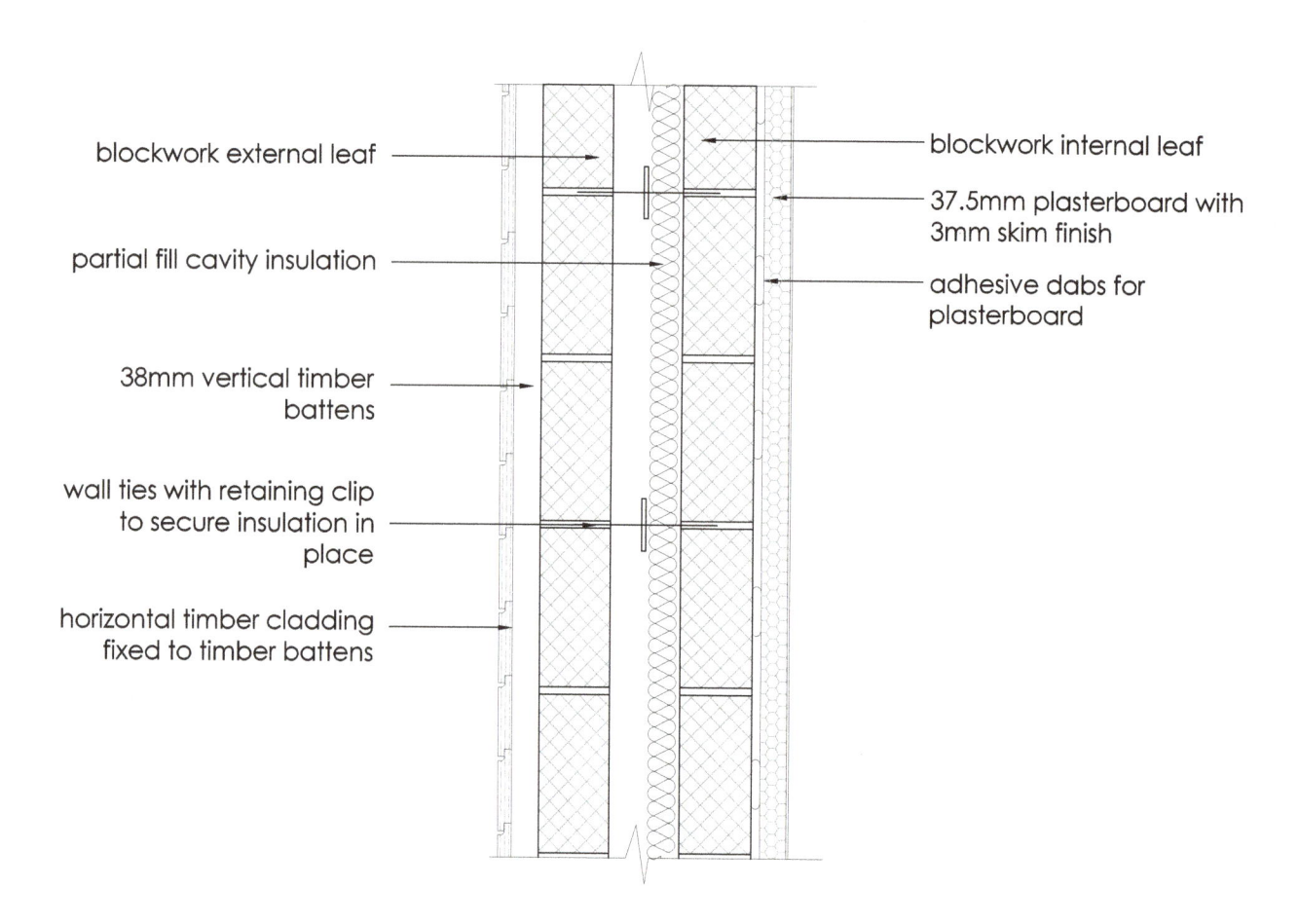

Detail M-W3 - External masonry cavity wall, horiztonal timber cladding

NOTES:

U-value 0.18 Wm²K or better
No breather membrane required behind cladding with masonry wall.

SECTION 5 - MASONRY CONSTRUCTION

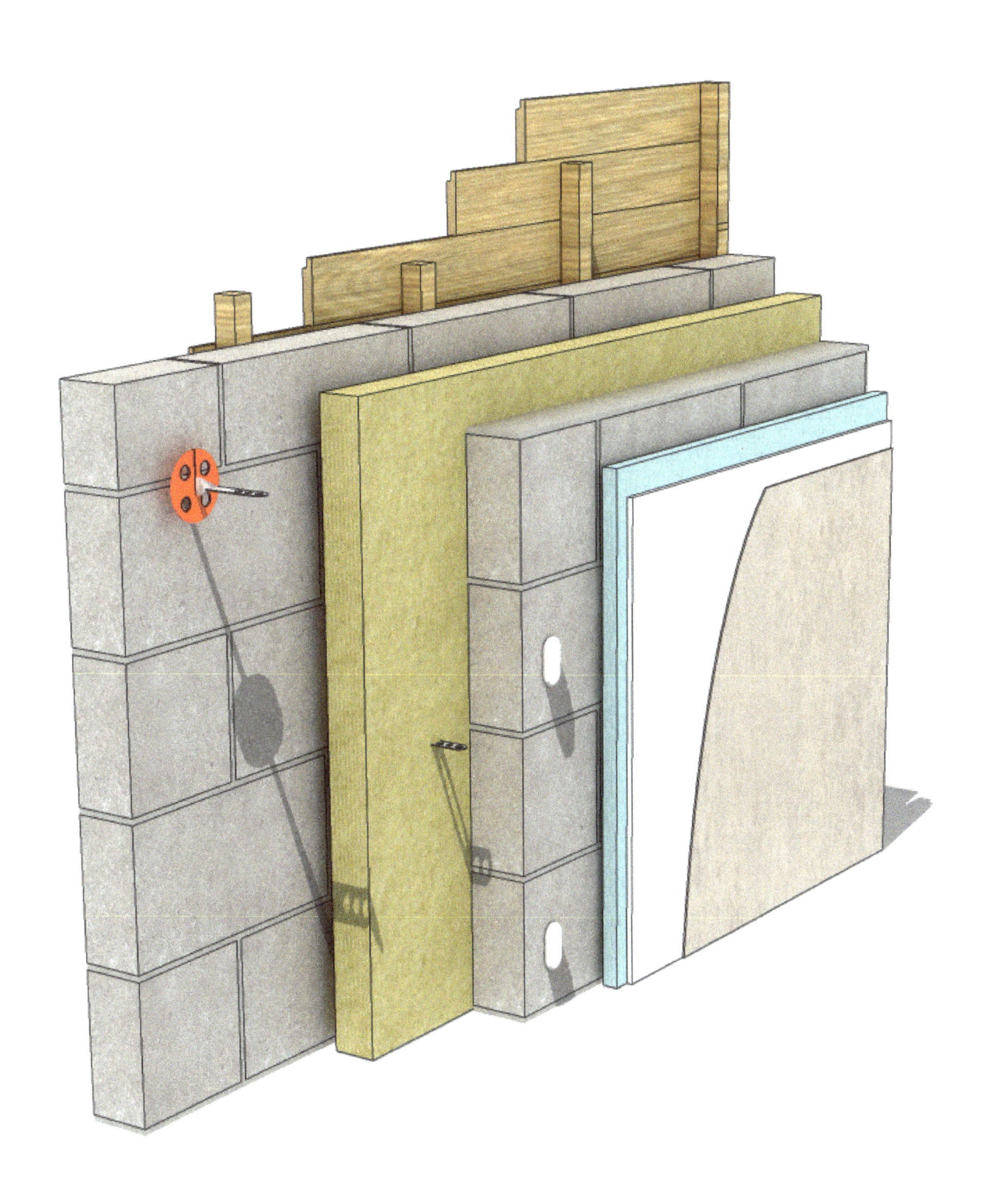

3D Detail M-W3 - External masonry cavity wall, horizontal timber cladding

M-W4

EXTERNAL MASONRY CAVITY WALL, VERTICAL TIMBER CLADDING

Labels (left side):
- blockwork external leaf
- partial fill cavity insulation
- 38mm vertical battens
- wall ties with retaining clip to secure insulation in place
- vertical timber cladding fixed to timber battens
- 38mm timber horizontal counter battens

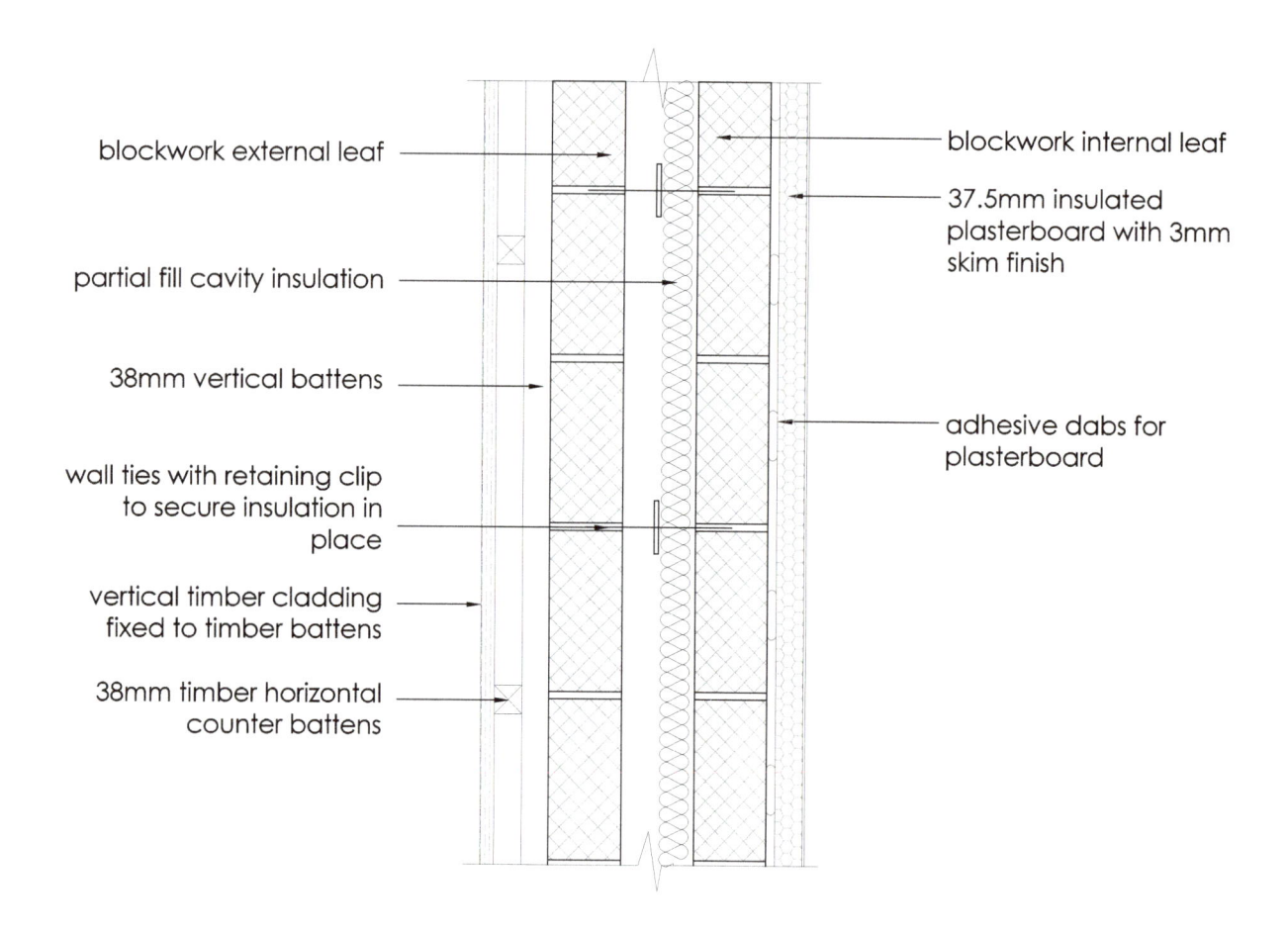

Labels (right side):
- blockwork internal leaf
- 37.5mm insulated plasterboard with 3mm skim finish
- adhesive dabs for plasterboard

Detail M-W4 - External masonry cavity wall, vertical timber cladding

NOTES:

U-value 0.18 Wm²K or better

No breather membrane required behind cladding with masonry wall. When using tongue and groove cladding vertical counter battens are required. The horizontal battens should be cut to fall in toward the cavity to shed water away from the cladding and into the cavity. If using a board on board system, or open jointed, vertical counter battens are not required, as there will be sufficient space for ventilation and drainage. In this case the horizontal battens must be cut to fall away from the structure toward the cladding.

SECTION 5 - MASONRY CONSTRUCTION

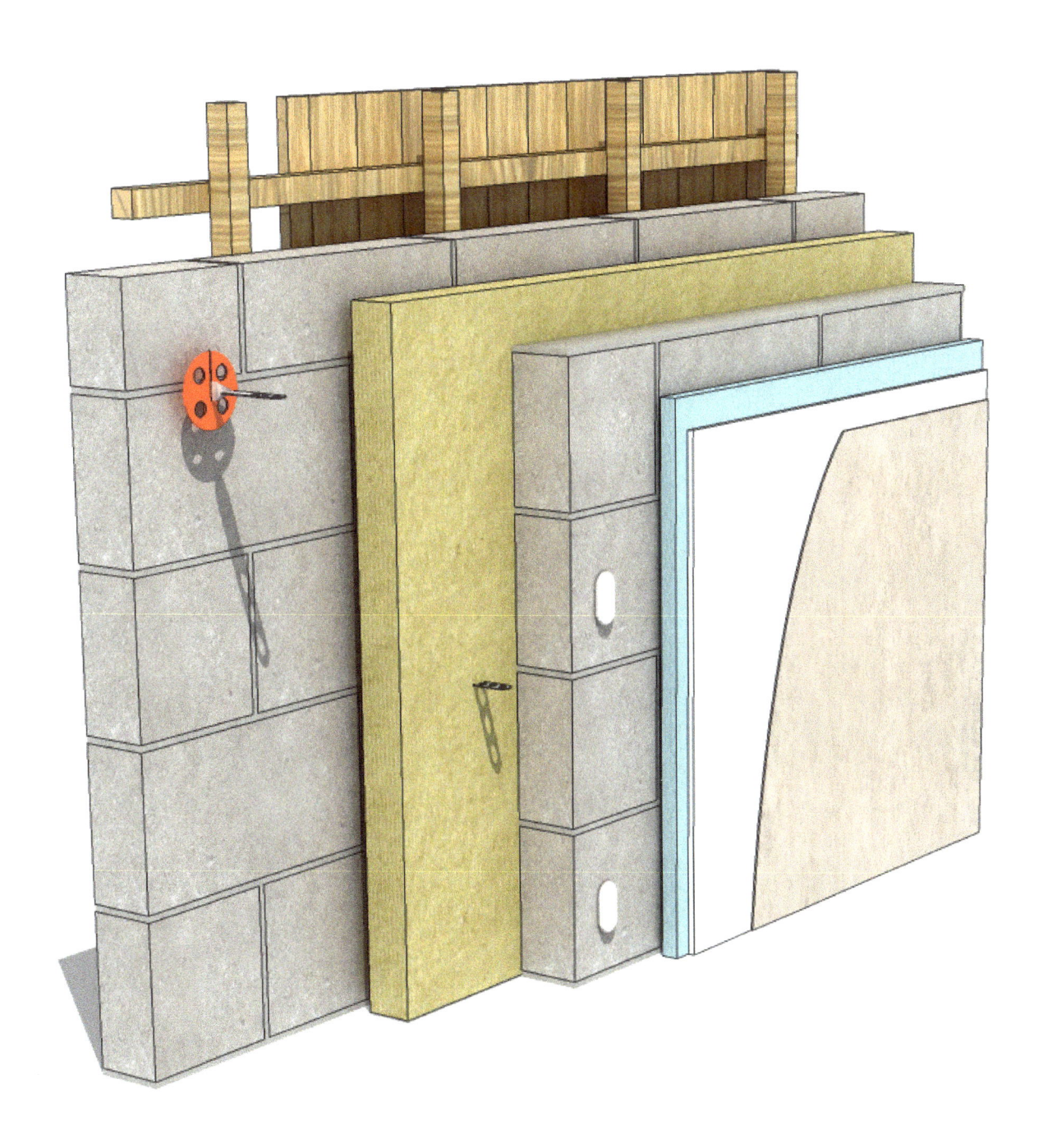

3D Detail M-W4 - External masonry cavity wall, vertical timber cladding

M-W5

EXTERNAL MASONRY CAVITY WALL, PARTIAL FILL, INSULATED PLASTERBOARD

- brickwork external leaf
- partial fill cavity insulation
- wall ties with retaining clip to hold partial fill insulation in place
- blockwork internal leaf
- 37.5mm insulated plasterboard on adhesive dabs
- 3mm skim to plasterboard

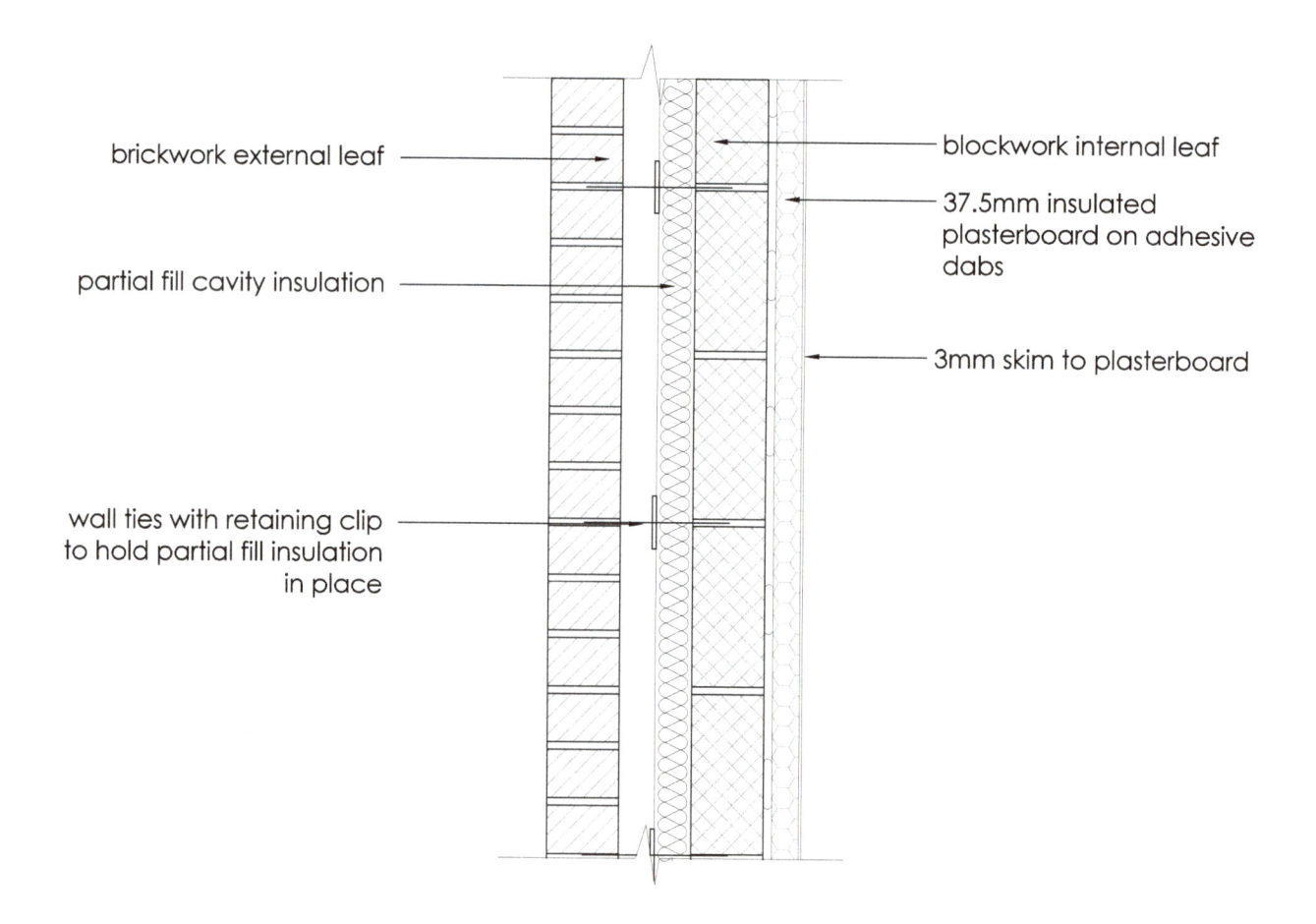

Detail M-W5 - External masonry cavity wall, patial fill, insulated plasterboard

NOTES:

U-value 0.18 Wm²K or better

SECTION 5 - MASONRY CONSTRUCTION

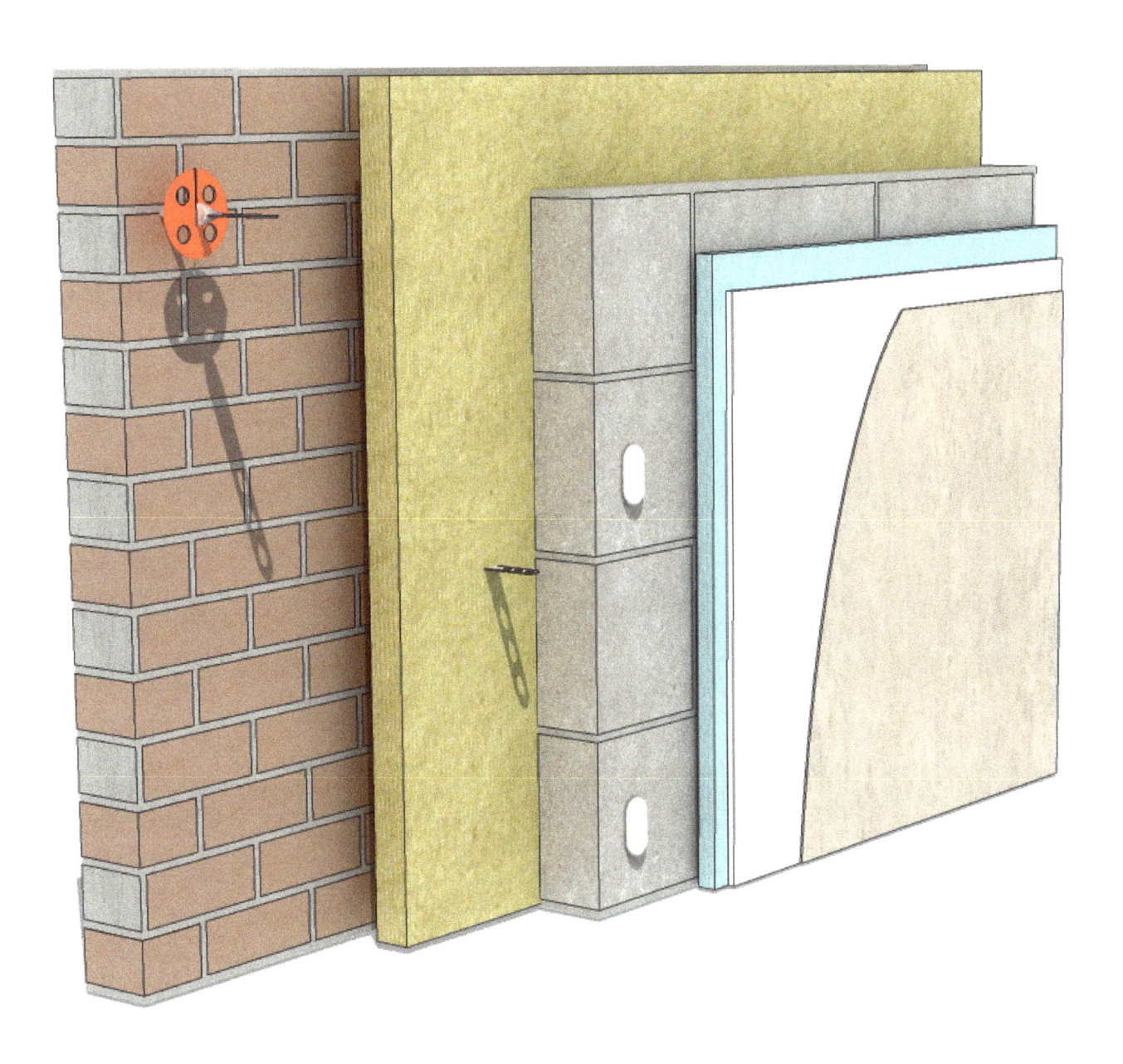

3D Detail M-W5 - External masonry cavity wall, partial fill, insulated plasterboard

M-W6

SOLID MASONRY WALL, EXTERNAL RENDER, INSULATED PLASTERBOARD

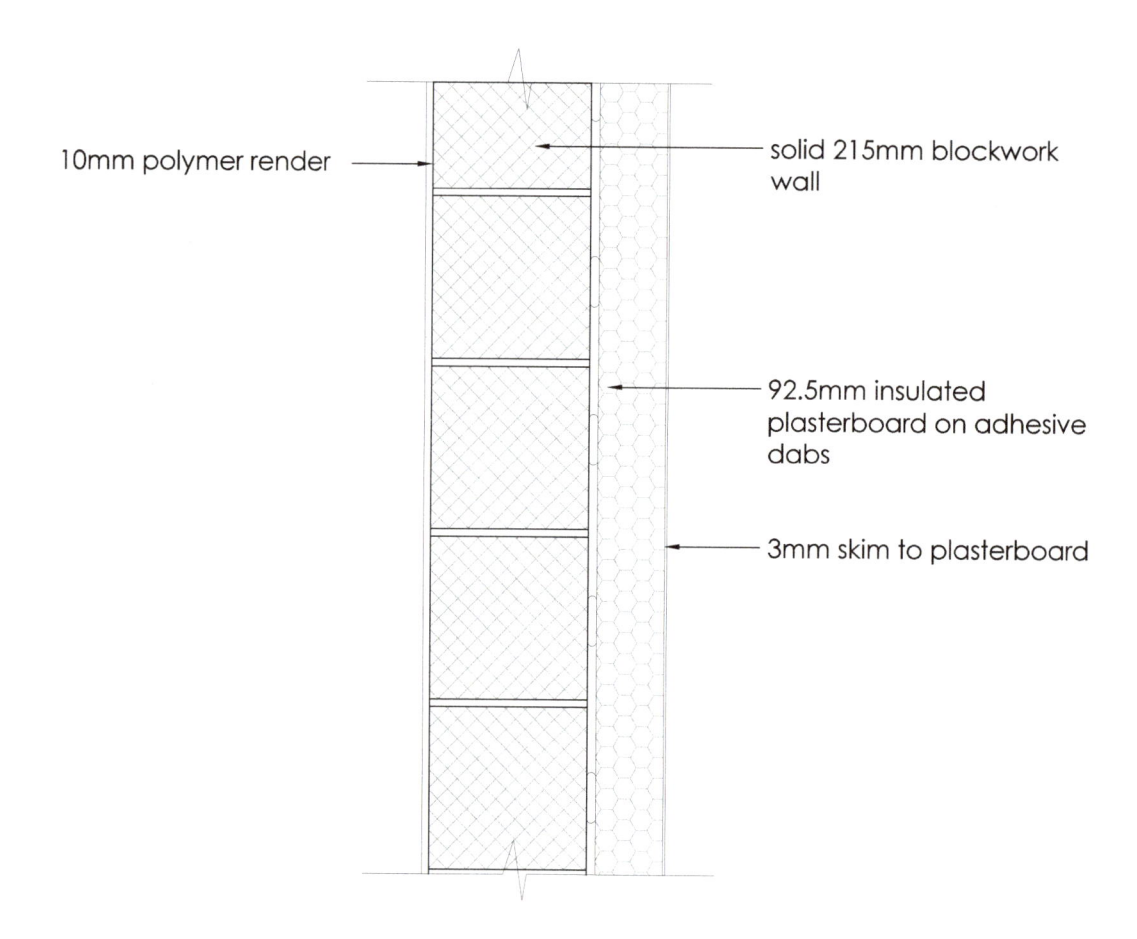

- 10mm polymer render
- solid 215mm blockwork wall
- 92.5mm insulated plasterboard on adhesive dabs
- 3mm skim to plasterboard

Detail M-W6 - Solid masonry wall, external render, insulated plasterboard

NOTES:

U-value 0.18 Wm²K or better
Insulated plasterboard cannot be used on non rendered masonry walls due to the risk of water ingress. Check manufacturers instructions.

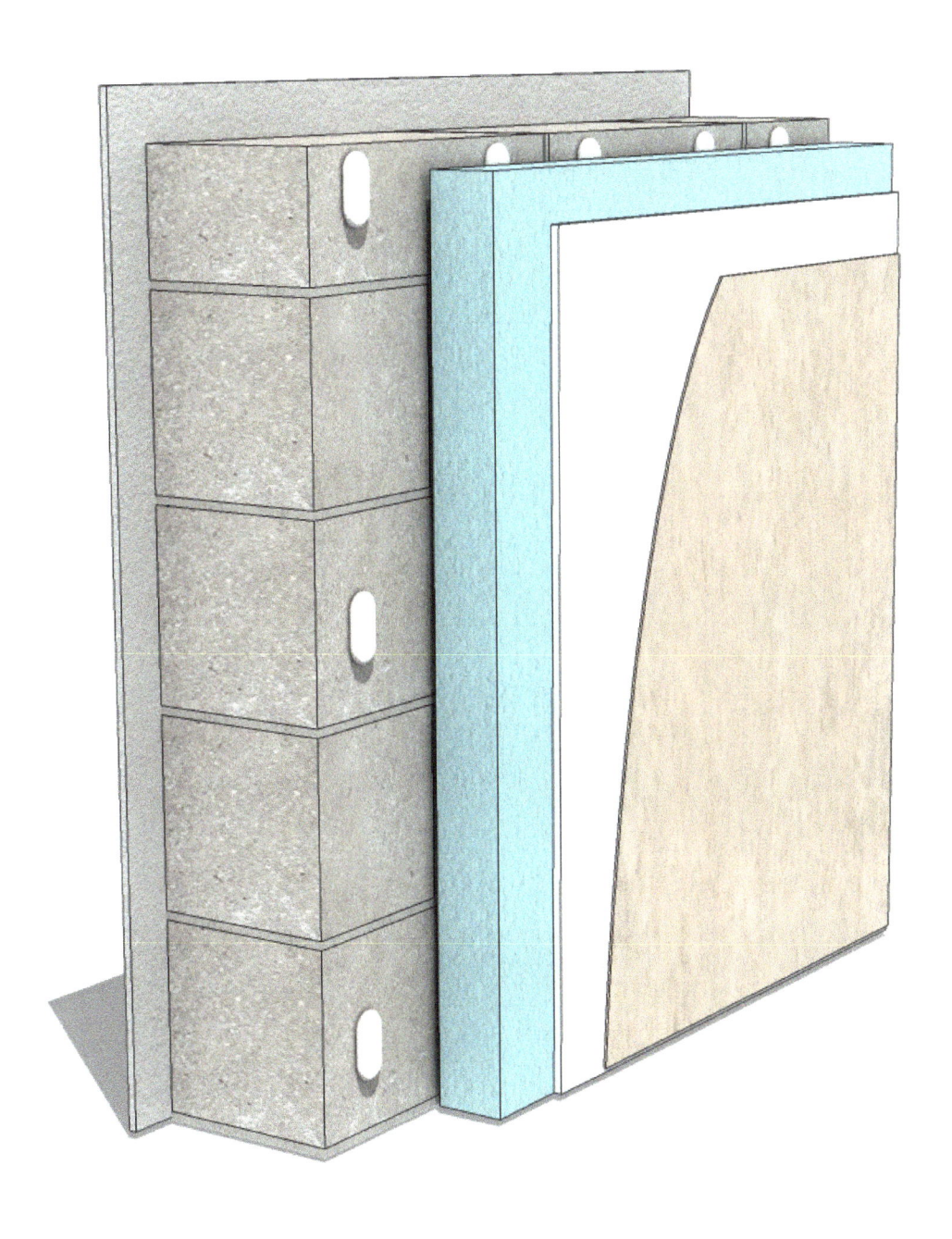

3D Detail M-W6 - Sold masonry wall, external render, insulated plasterboard

M-W7

PARTY WALL, TO ACHIEVE ZERO U VALUE (PLAN)

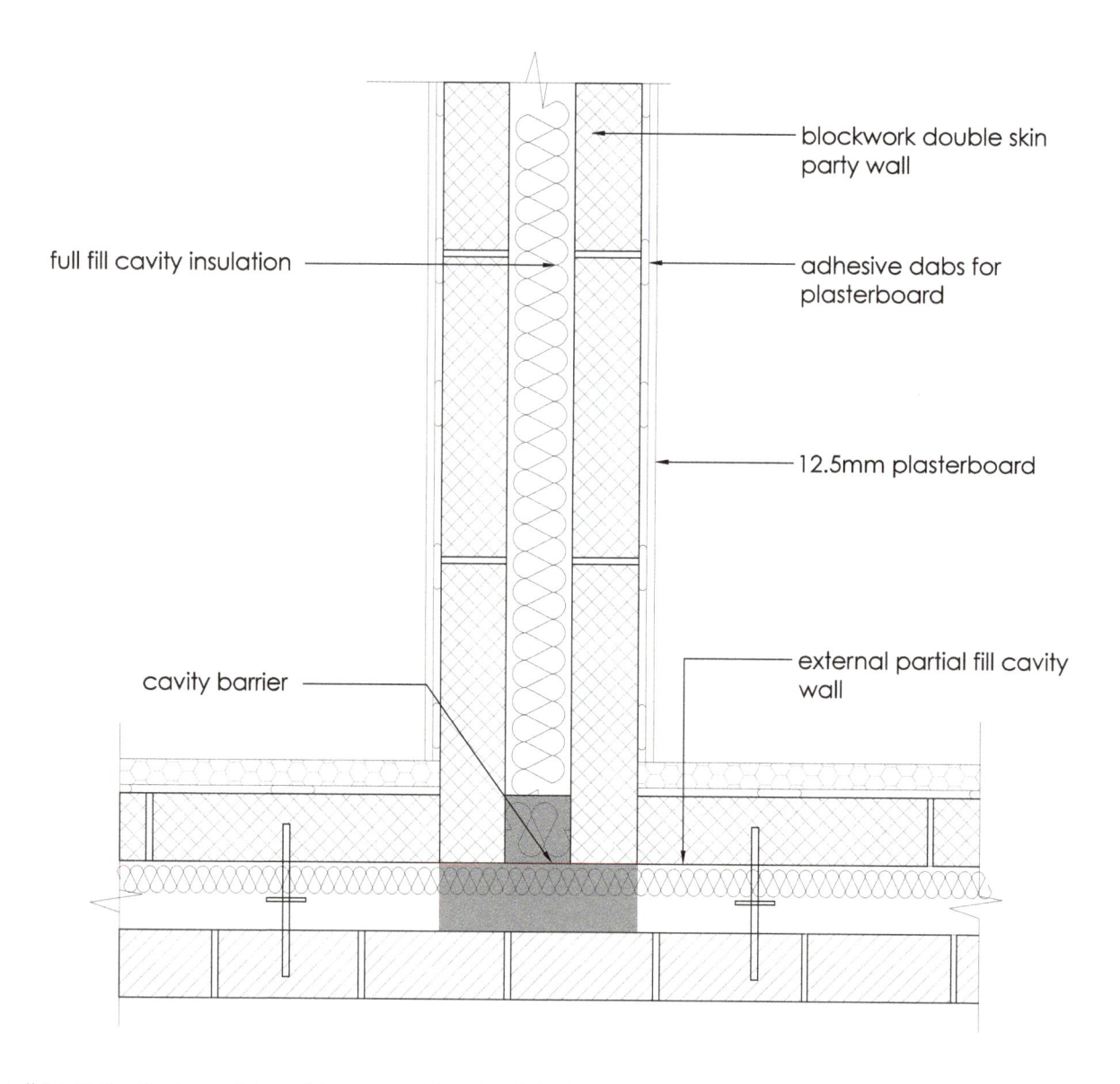

- blockwork double skin party wall
- full fill cavity insulation
- adhesive dabs for plasterboard
- 12.5mm plasterboard
- external partial fill cavity wall
- cavity barrier

Detail M-W7 - Party wall to achieve zero U-value (plan)

NOTES:

U-value 0.0 Wm²K
Cavity barrier reduces flanking sound and air circultation within the cavity. It is also required to withold the passage of smoke and fire. Cavity barriers need to be fitted tightly with no gaps.

SECTION 5 - MASONRY CONSTRUCTION

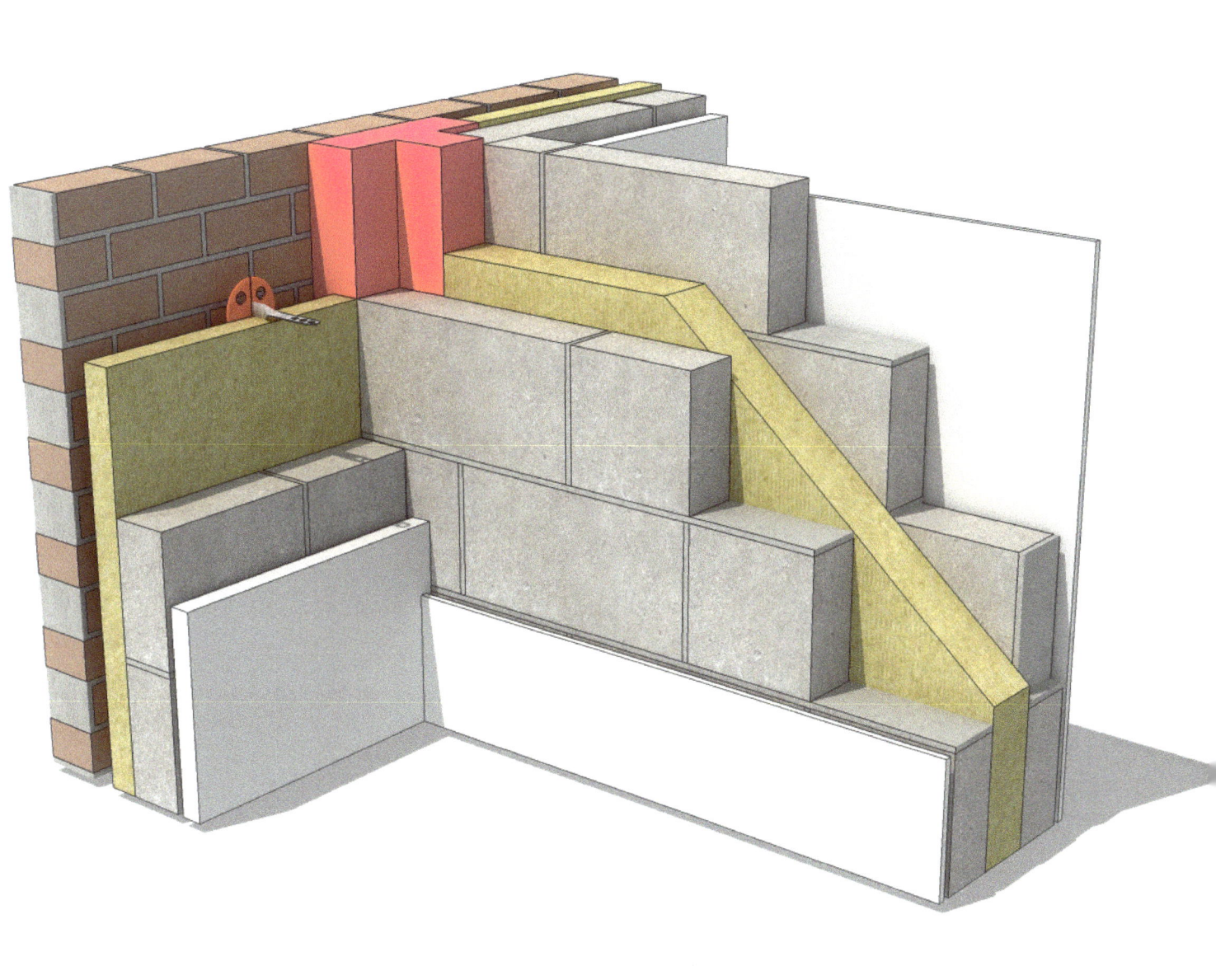

3D Detail M-W7 - Party wall to achieve zero U-value

M-W8

EXTERNAL MASONRY CAVITY WALL, WINDOW HEAD, SOLID TIMBER WINDOW

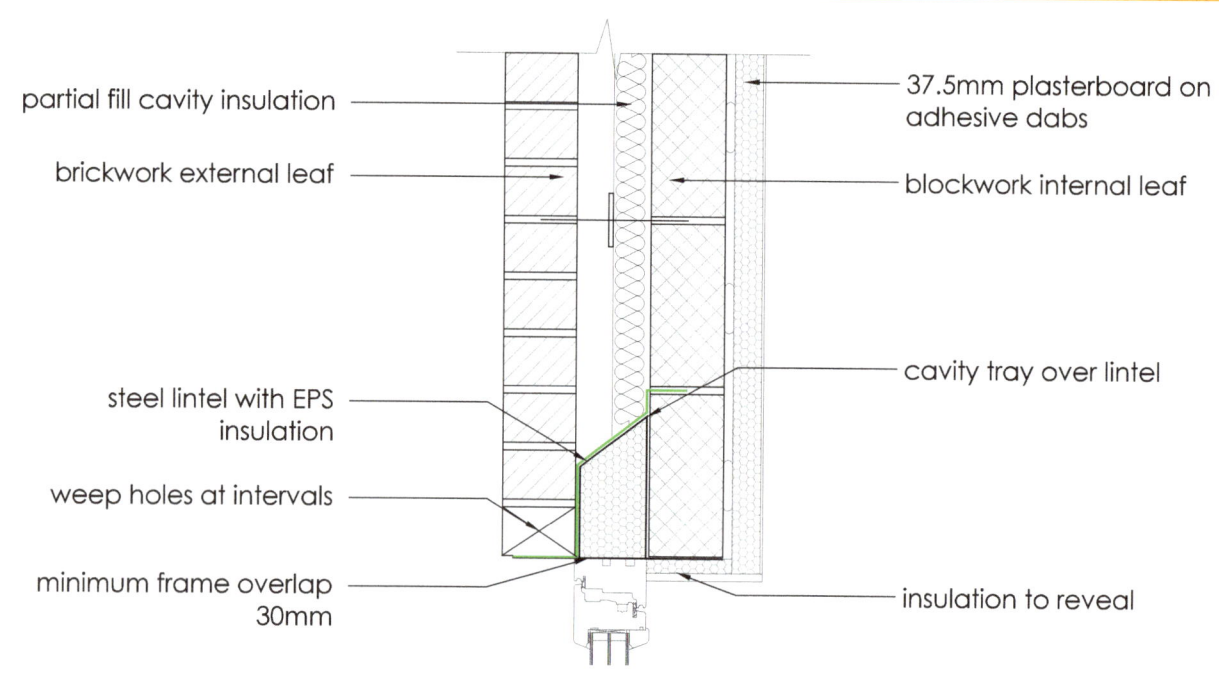

Labels (left):
- partial fill cavity insulation
- brickwork external leaf
- steel lintel with EPS insulation
- weep holes at intervals
- minimum frame overlap 30mm

Labels (right):
- 37.5mm plasterboard on adhesive dabs
- blockwork internal leaf
- cavity tray over lintel
- insulation to reveal

Detail M-W8 - External masonry cavity wall, window head, solid timber window

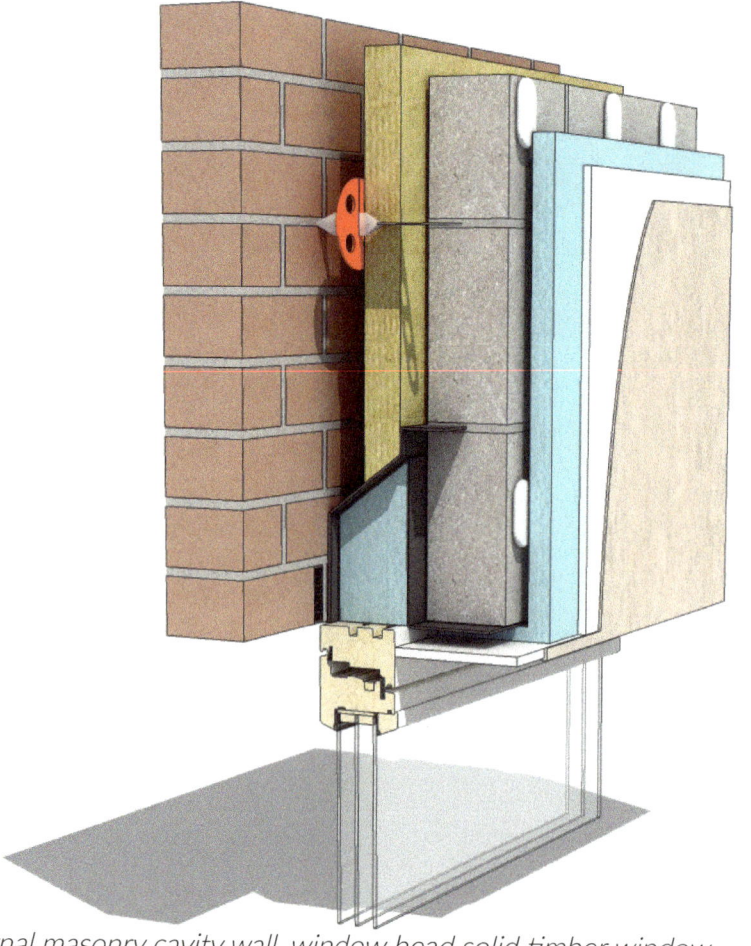

3D Detail M-W8 - External masonry cavity wall, window head solid timber window

SECTION 5 - MASONRY CONSTRUCTION

M-W9

EXTERNAL MASONRY CAVITY WALL, WINDOW SILL, SOLID TIMBER WINDOW

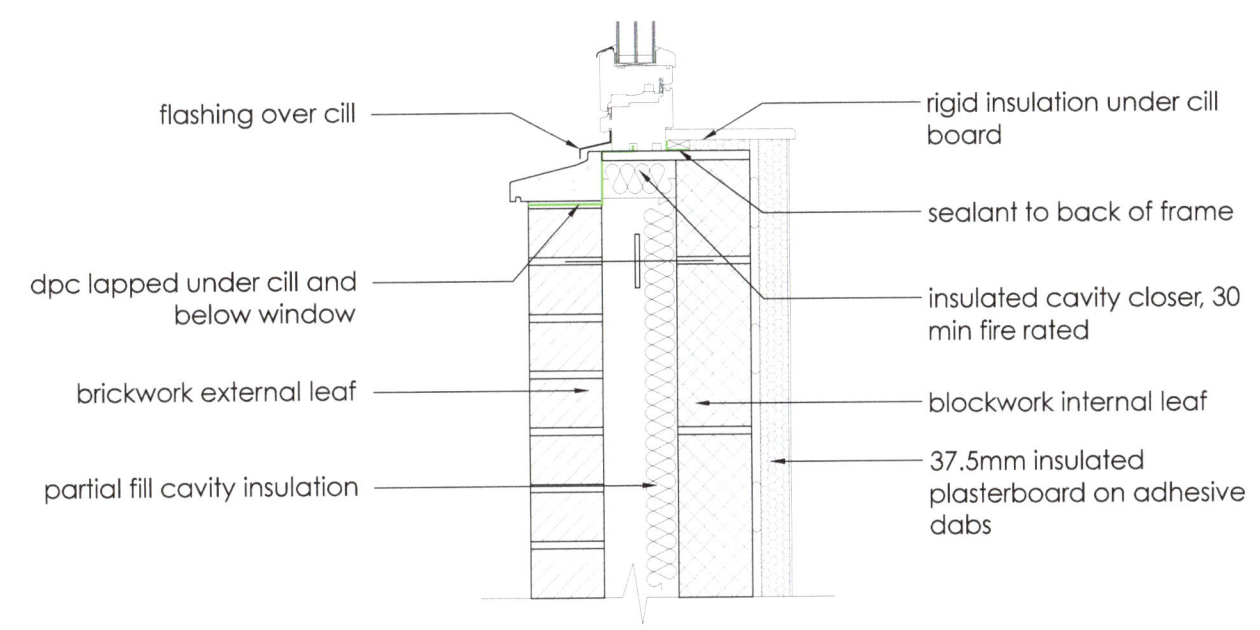

- flashing over cill
- dpc lapped under cill and below window
- brickwork external leaf
- partial fill cavity insulation
- rigid insulation under cill board
- sealant to back of frame
- insulated cavity closer, 30 min fire rated
- blockwork internal leaf
- 37.5mm insulated plasterboard on adhesive dabs

Detail M-W9 - External masonry cavity wall, window sill, solid timber window

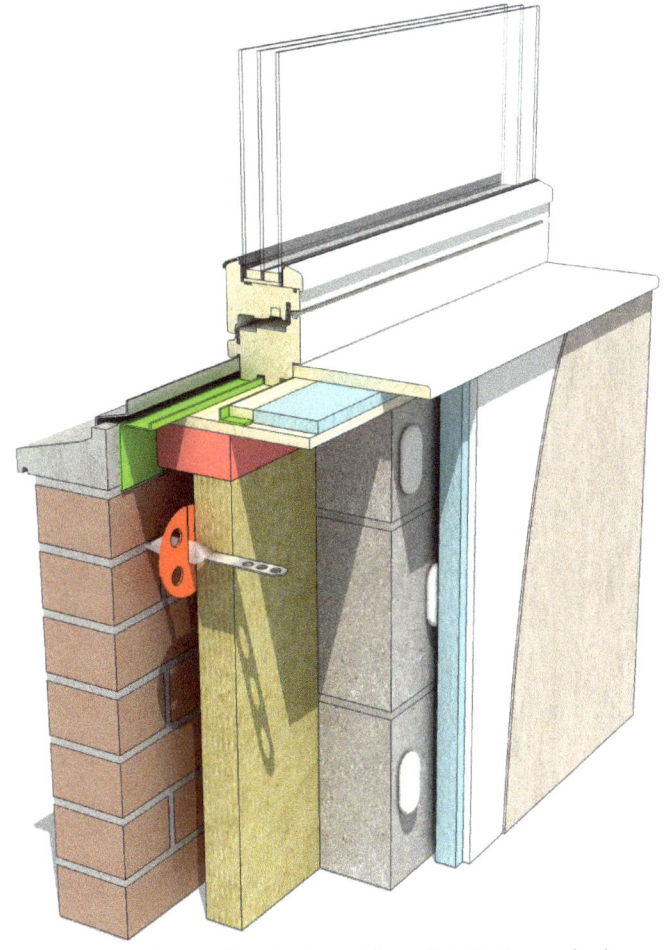

3D Detail M-W9 - External masonry cavity wall, window sill, solid timber window

M-W10

EXTERNAL MASONRY CAVITY WALL, WINDOW JAMB (PLAN)

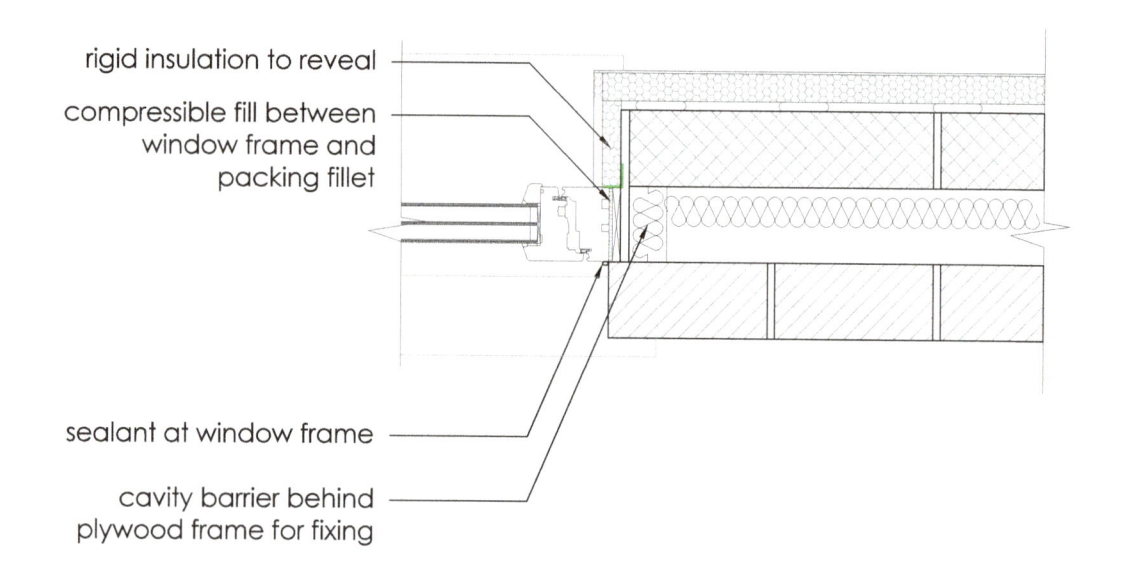

- rigid insulation to reveal
- compressible fill between window frame and packing fillet
- sealant at window frame
- cavity barrier behind plywood frame for fixing

Detail M-W10 - External masonry cavity wall, window jamb (plan)

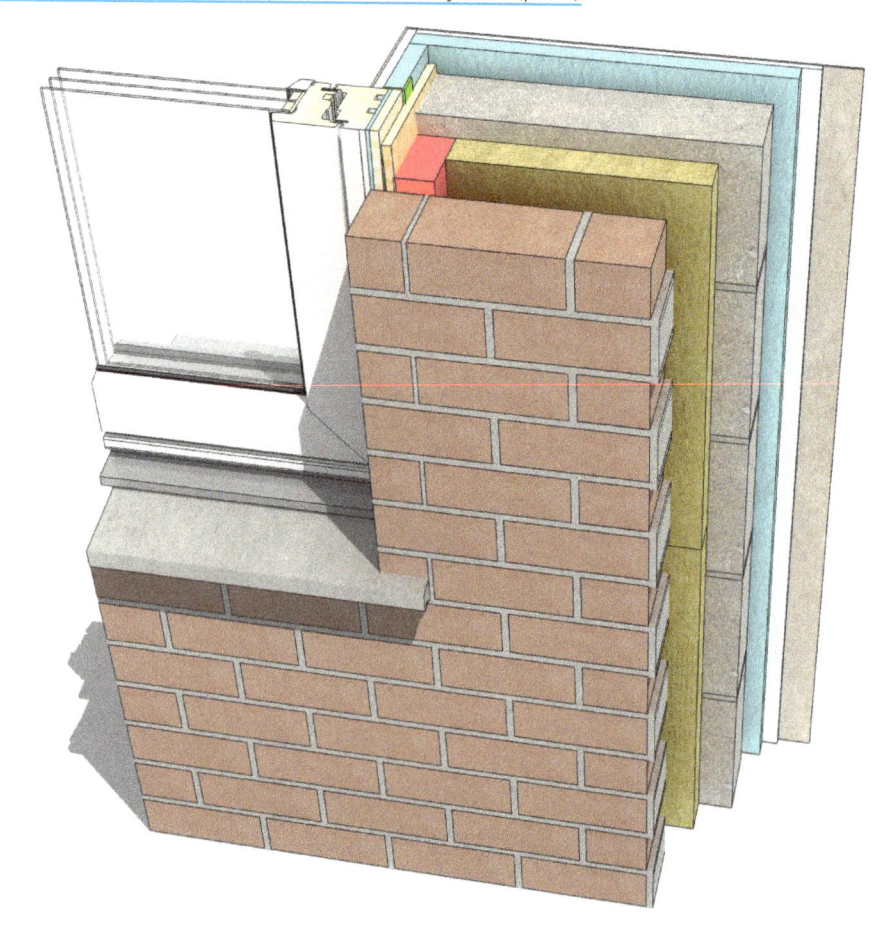

3D Detail M-W10 - External masonry cavity wall, window jamb

SECTION 5 - MASONRY CONSTRUCTION

M-W11

EXTERNAL MASONRY CAVITY WALL, RENDER FINISH, WINDOW HEAD

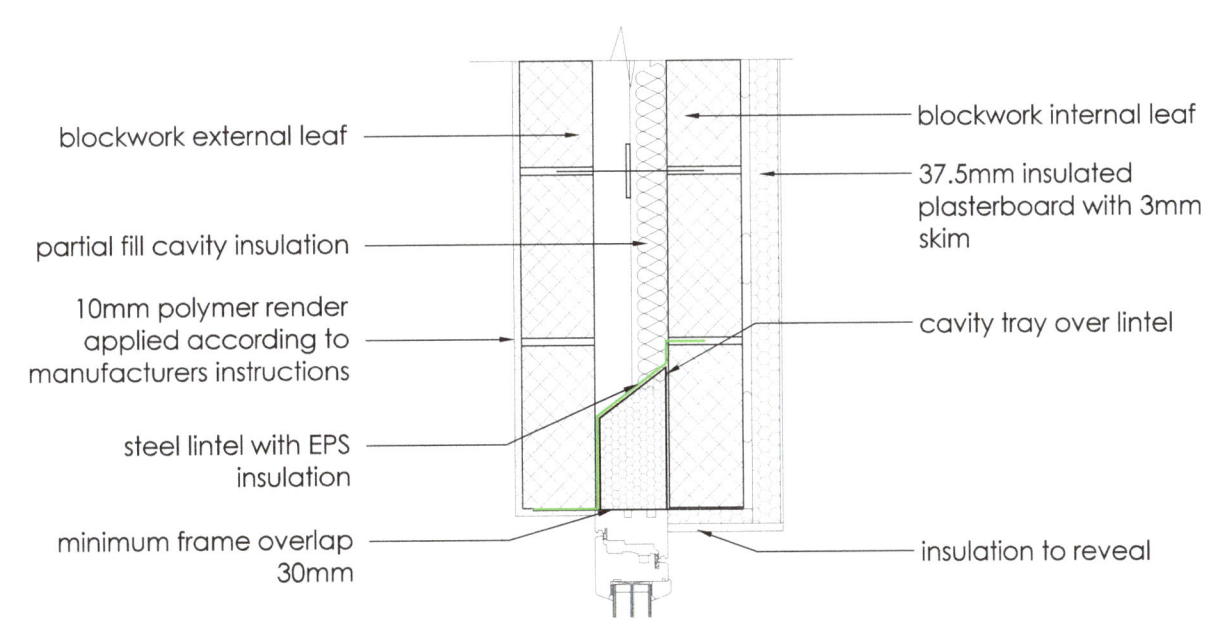

- blockwork external leaf
- partial fill cavity insulation
- 10mm polymer render applied according to manufacturers instructions
- steel lintel with EPS insulation
- minimum frame overlap 30mm
- blockwork internal leaf
- 37.5mm insulated plasterboard with 3mm skim
- cavity tray over lintel
- insulation to reveal

Detail M-W11 - External masonry cavity wall, render finish, window head

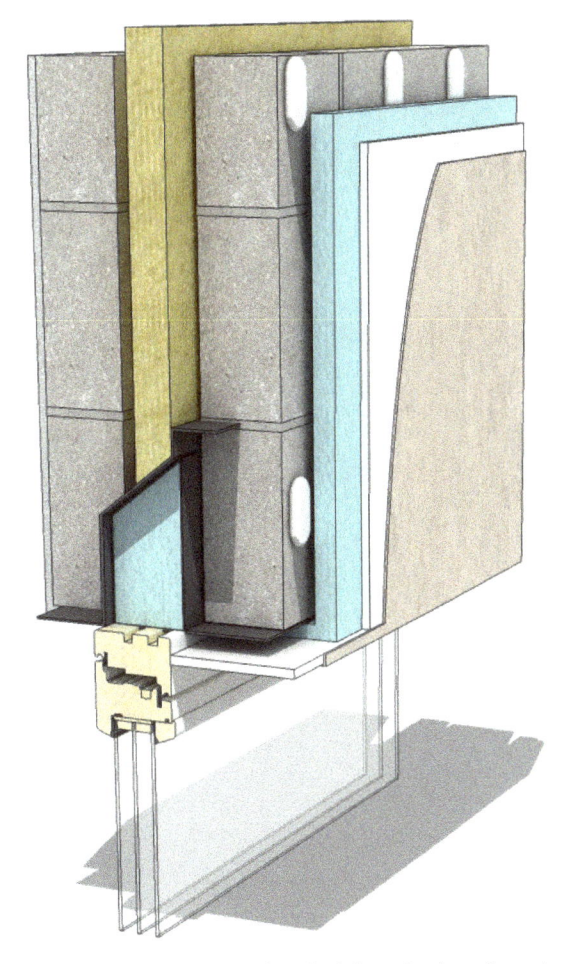

3D Detail M-W11 - External masonry cavity wall, render finish, window head

M-W12

EXTERNAL MASONRY CAVITY WALL, RENDER FINISH, WINDOW SILL

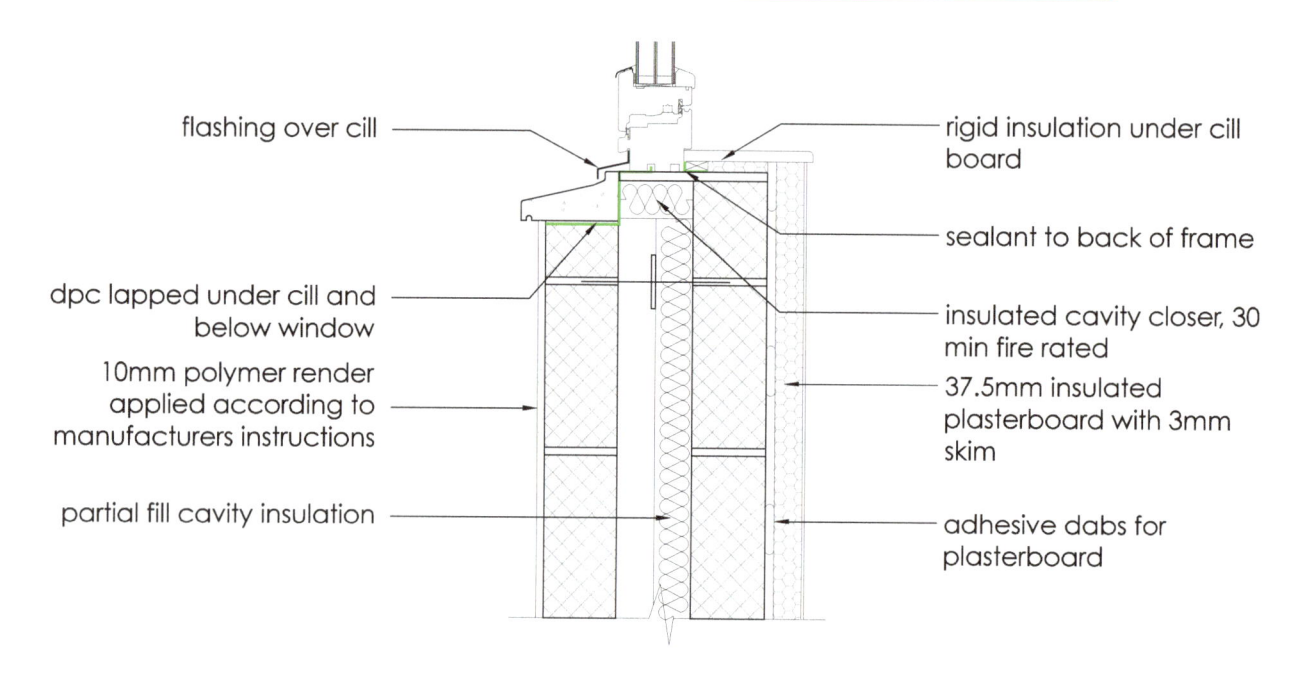

Labels (left):
- flashing over cill
- dpc lapped under cill and below window
- 10mm polymer render applied according to manufacturers instructions
- partial fill cavity insulation

Labels (right):
- rigid insulation under cill board
- sealant to back of frame
- insulated cavity closer, 30 min fire rated
- 37.5mm insulated plasterboard with 3mm skim
- adhesive dabs for plasterboard

Detail M-W12 - External masonry cavity wall, render finish, window sill

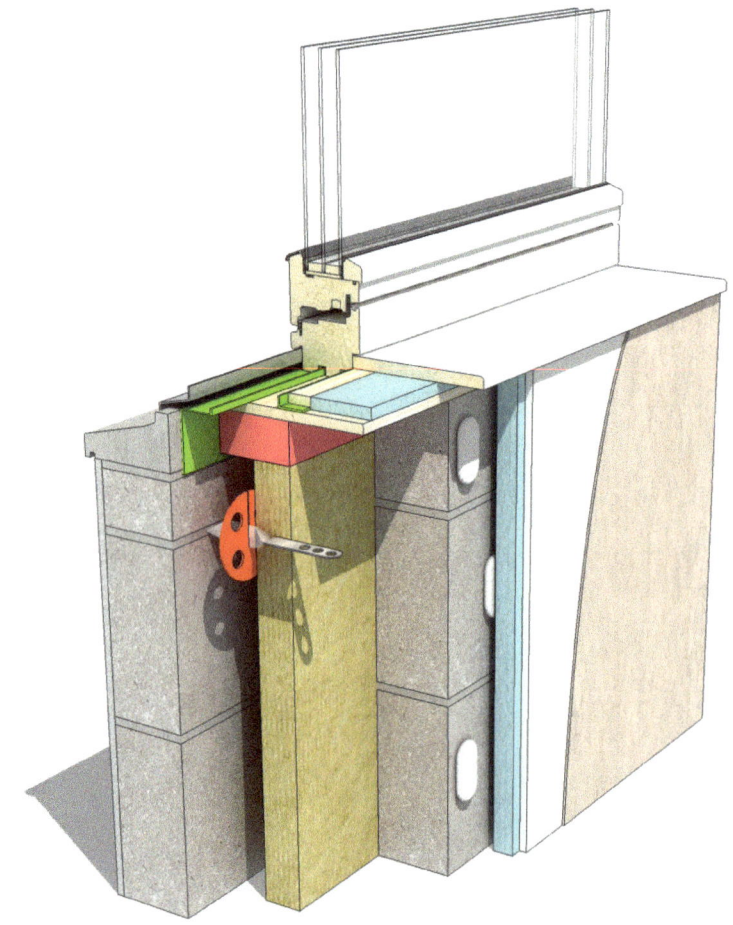

3D Detail M-W12 - External masonry cavity wall, render finish, window sill

SECTION 5 - MASONRY CONSTRUCTION

M-W13

EXTERNAL MASONRY CAVITY WALL, RENDER FINISH, WINDOW JAMB (PLAN)

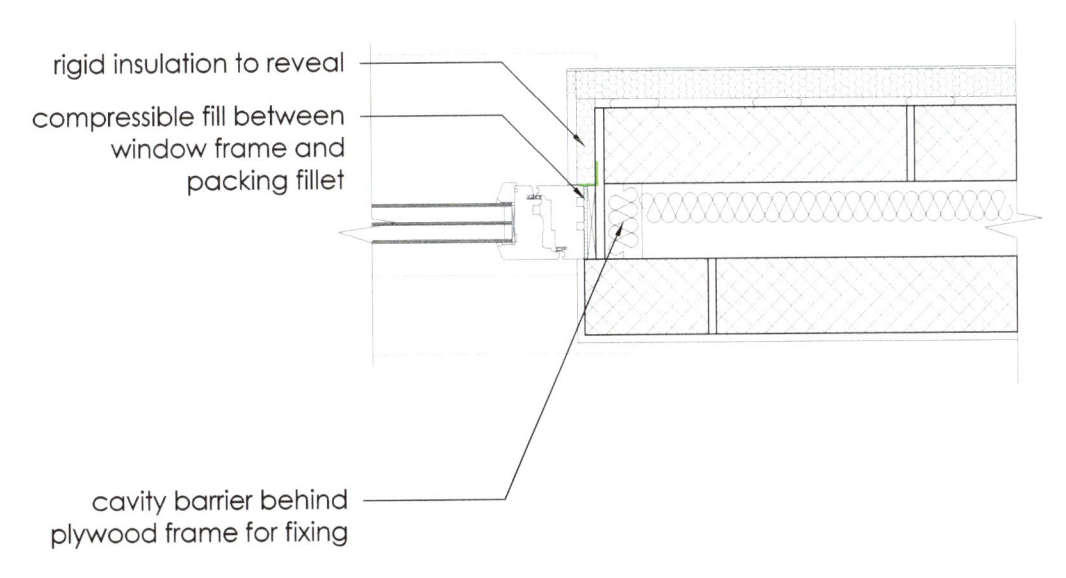

- rigid insulation to reveal
- compressible fill between window frame and packing fillet
- cavity barrier behind plywood frame for fixing

Detail M-W13 - External masonry cavity wall, render finish, window jamb (plan)

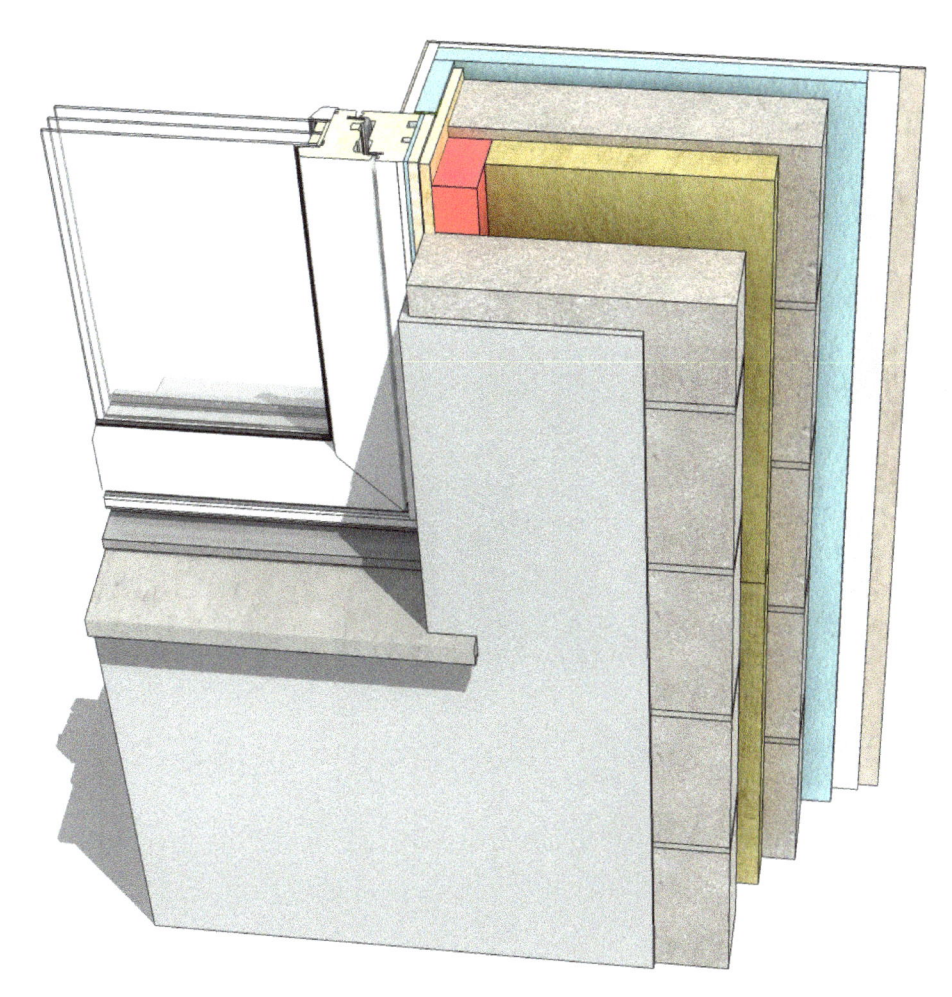

3D Detail M-W13 - External masonry cavity wall, render finish, window jamb

M-W14

EXTERNAL MASONRY CAVITY WALL, HORIZONTAL TIMBER CLADDING, WINDOW HEAD

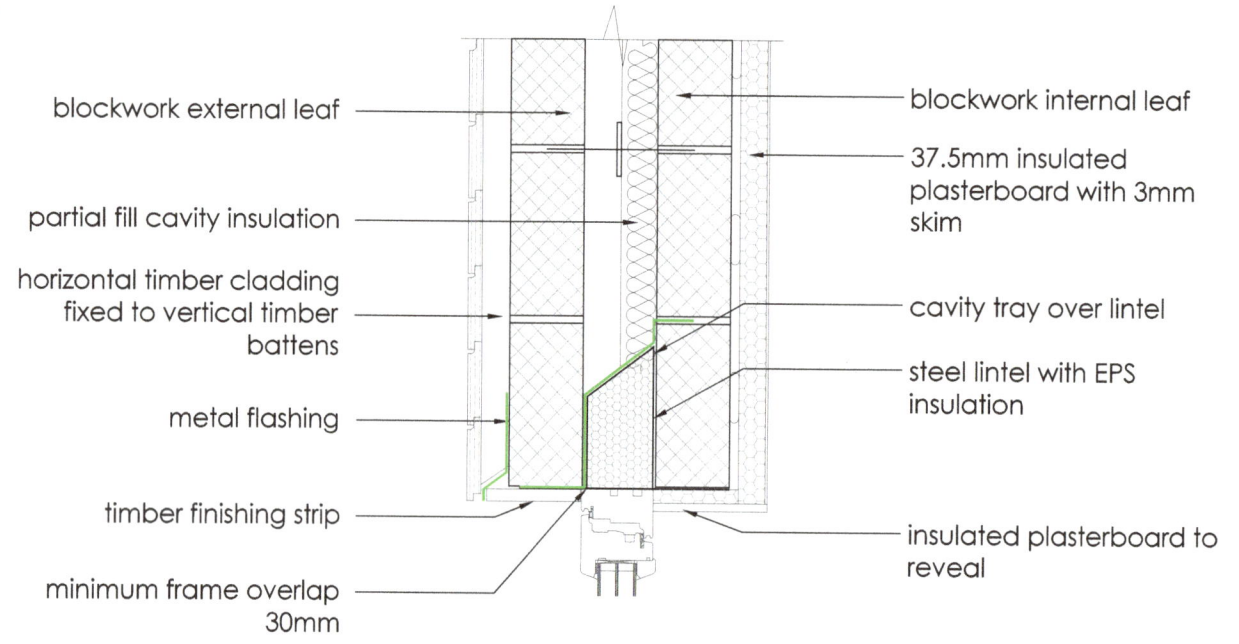

- blockwork external leaf
- partial fill cavity insulation
- horizontal timber cladding fixed to vertical timber battens
- metal flashing
- timber finishing strip
- minimum frame overlap 30mm
- blockwork internal leaf
- 37.5mm insulated plasterboard with 3mm skim
- cavity tray over lintel
- steel lintel with EPS insulation
- insulated plasterboard to reveal

Detail M-W14 - External masonry cavity wall, horizontal timber cladding, window head

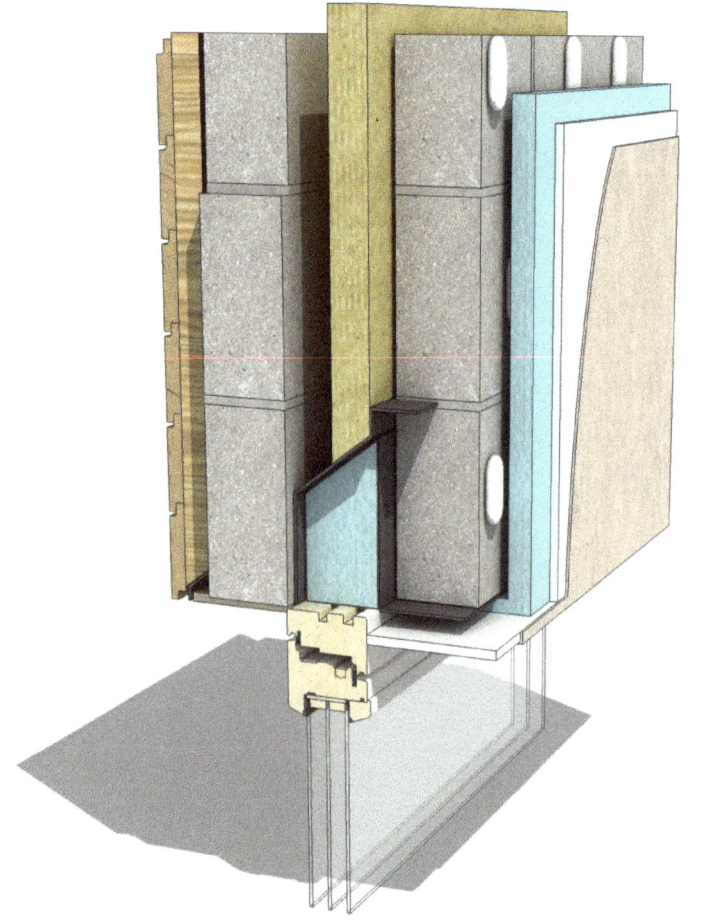

3D Detail M-W14 - External masonry cavity wall, horizontal timber cladding, window head

SECTION 5 - MASONRY CONSTRUCTION

M-W15

EXTERNAL MASONRY CAVITY WALL, HORIZONTAL TIMBER CLADDING, WINDOW SILL

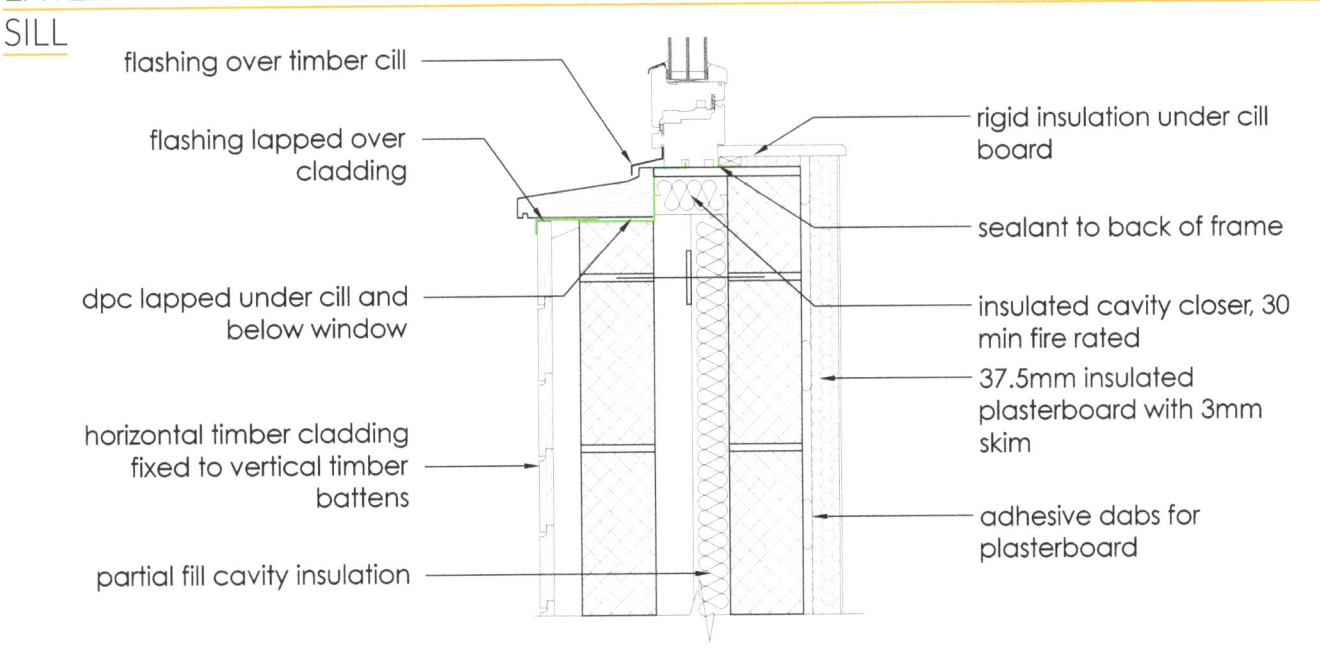

Labels (left side):
- flashing over timber cill
- flashing lapped over cladding
- dpc lapped under cill and below window
- horizontal timber cladding fixed to vertical timber battens
- partial fill cavity insulation

Labels (right side):
- rigid insulation under cill board
- sealant to back of frame
- insulated cavity closer, 30 min fire rated
- 37.5mm insulated plasterboard with 3mm skim
- adhesive dabs for plasterboard

Detail M-W15 - External masonry cavity wall, horizontal timber cladding, window sill

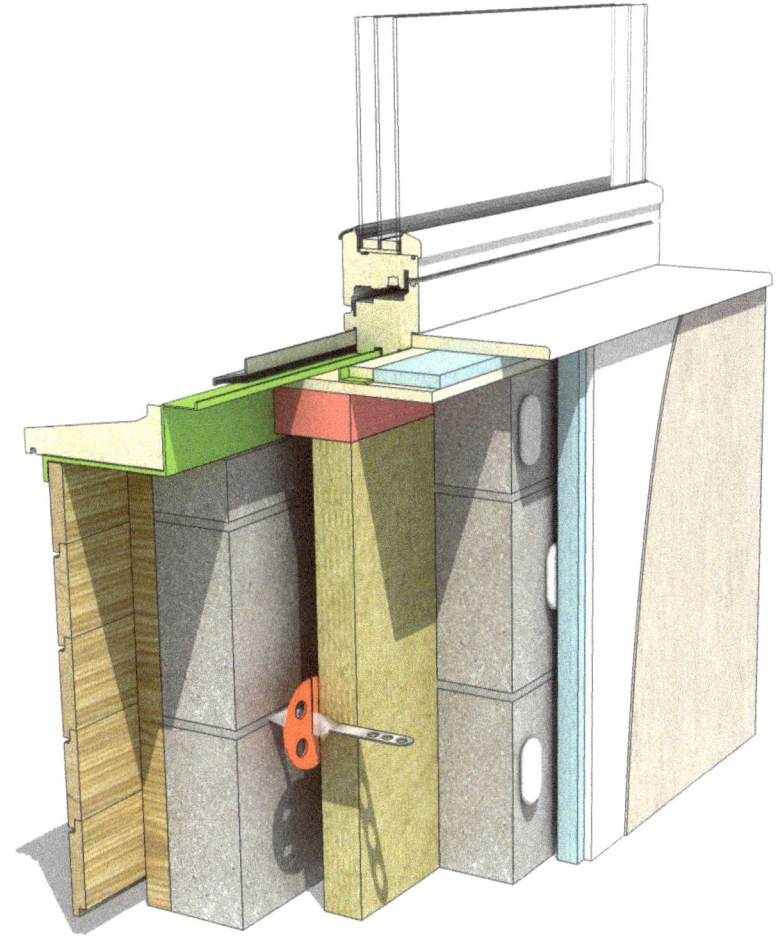

3D Detail M-W15 - External masonry cavity wall, horizontal timber cladding, window sill

M-W16

EXTERNAL MASONRY CAVITY WALL, HORIZONTAL TIMBER CLADDING, WINDOW JAMB (PLAN)

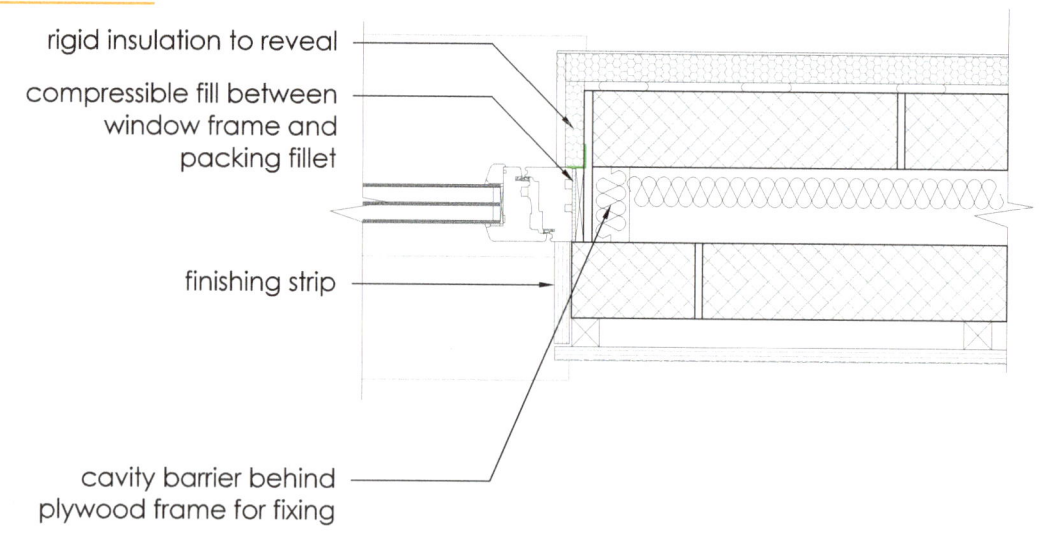

- rigid insulation to reveal
- compressible fill between window frame and packing fillet
- finishing strip
- cavity barrier behind plywood frame for fixing

Detail M-W16 - External masonry cavity wall, horizontal timber cladding, window jamb (plan)

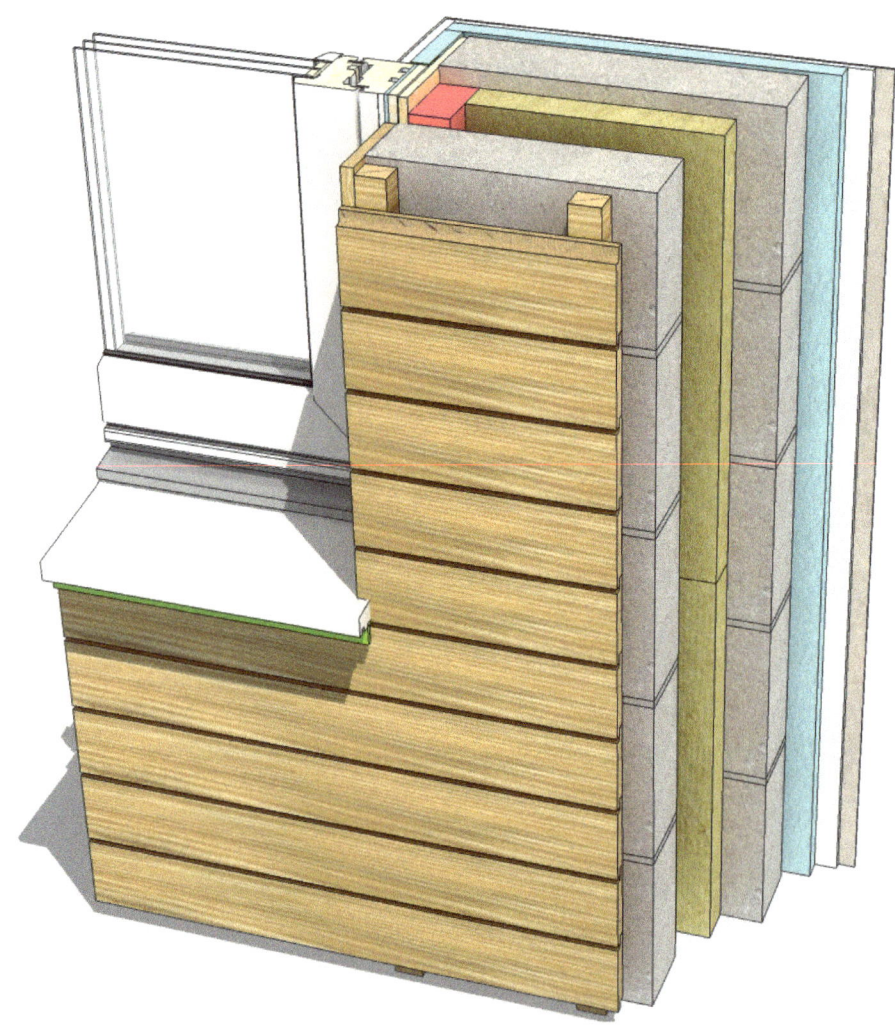

3D Detail M-W16 - External masonry cavity wall, horizontal timber cladding, window jamb

SECTION 5 - MASONRY CONSTRUCTION

M-W17

EXTERNAL MASONRY CAVITY WALL, VERTICAL TIMBER CLADDING, WINDOW HEAD

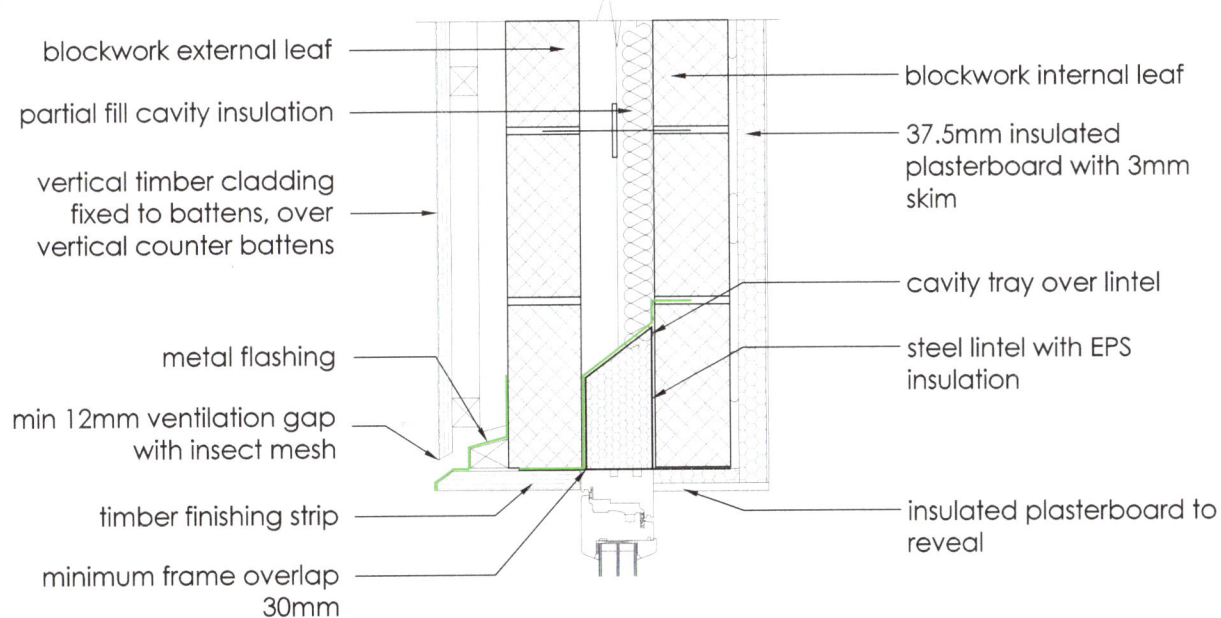

- blockwork external leaf
- partial fill cavity insulation
- vertical timber cladding fixed to battens, over vertical counter battens
- metal flashing
- min 12mm ventilation gap with insect mesh
- timber finishing strip
- minimum frame overlap 30mm
- blockwork internal leaf
- 37.5mm insulated plasterboard with 3mm skim
- cavity tray over lintel
- steel lintel with EPS insulation
- insulated plasterboard to reveal

Detail M-W17 - External masonry cavity wall, vertical timber cladding, window head

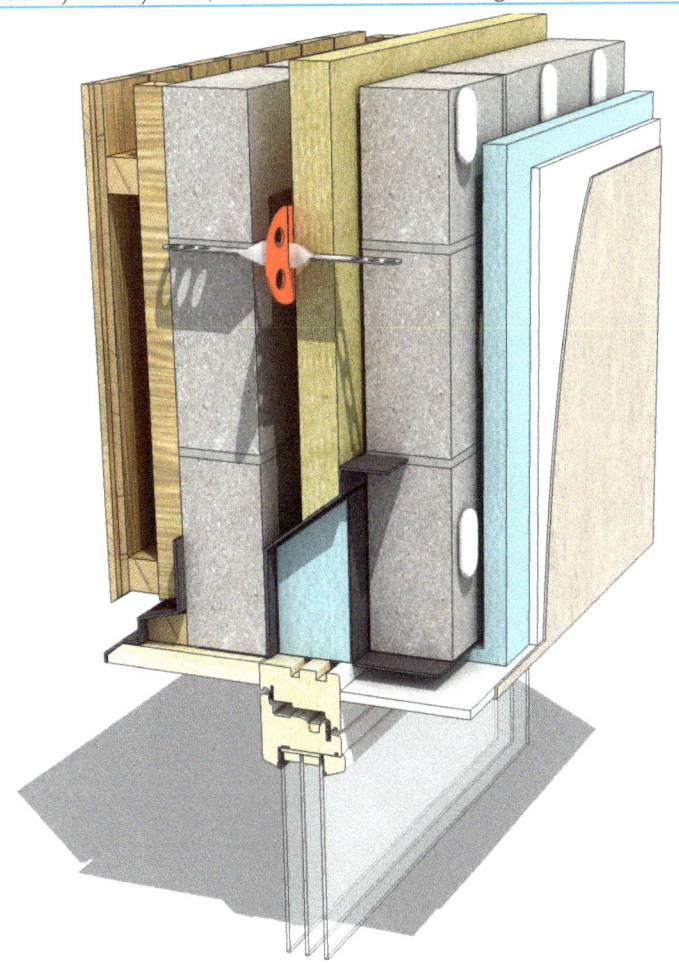

3D Detail M-W17 - External masonry cavity wall, vertical timber cladding, window head

M-W18

EXTERNAL MASONRY CAVITY WALL, VERTIAL TIMBER CLADDING, WINDOW SILL

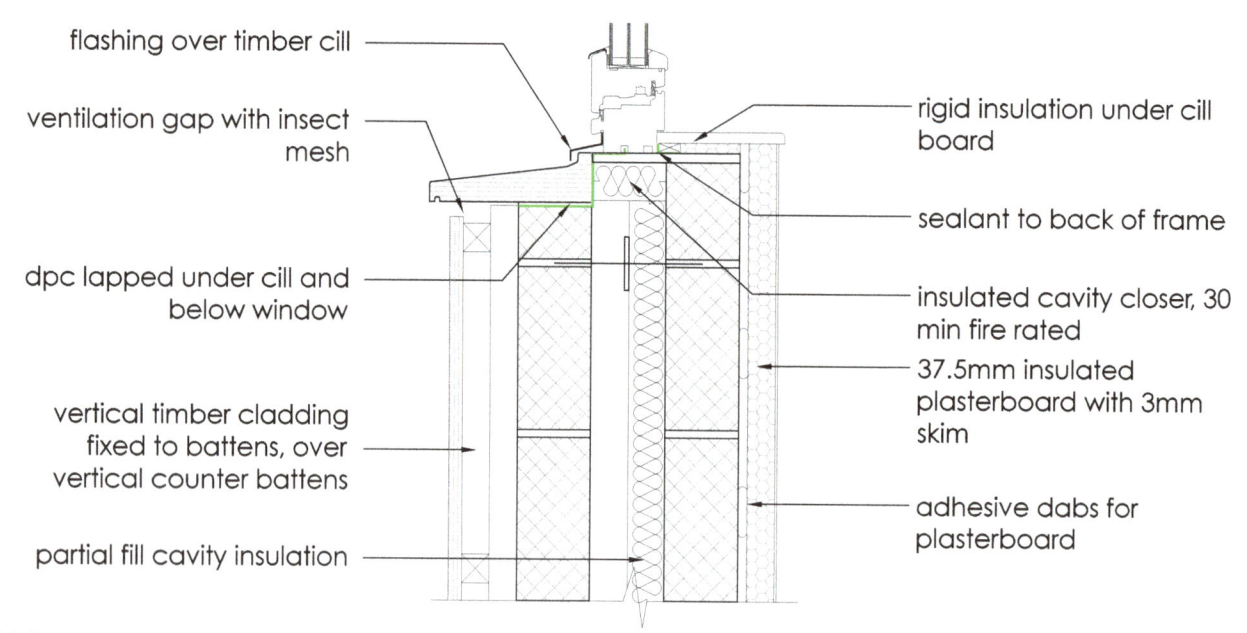

- flashing over timber cill
- ventilation gap with insect mesh
- dpc lapped under cill and below window
- vertical timber cladding fixed to battens, over vertical counter battens
- partial fill cavity insulation
- rigid insulation under cill board
- sealant to back of frame
- insulated cavity closer, 30 min fire rated
- 37.5mm insulated plasterboard with 3mm skim
- adhesive dabs for plasterboard

Detail M-W18- External masonry cavity wall, vertcal timber cladding, window sill

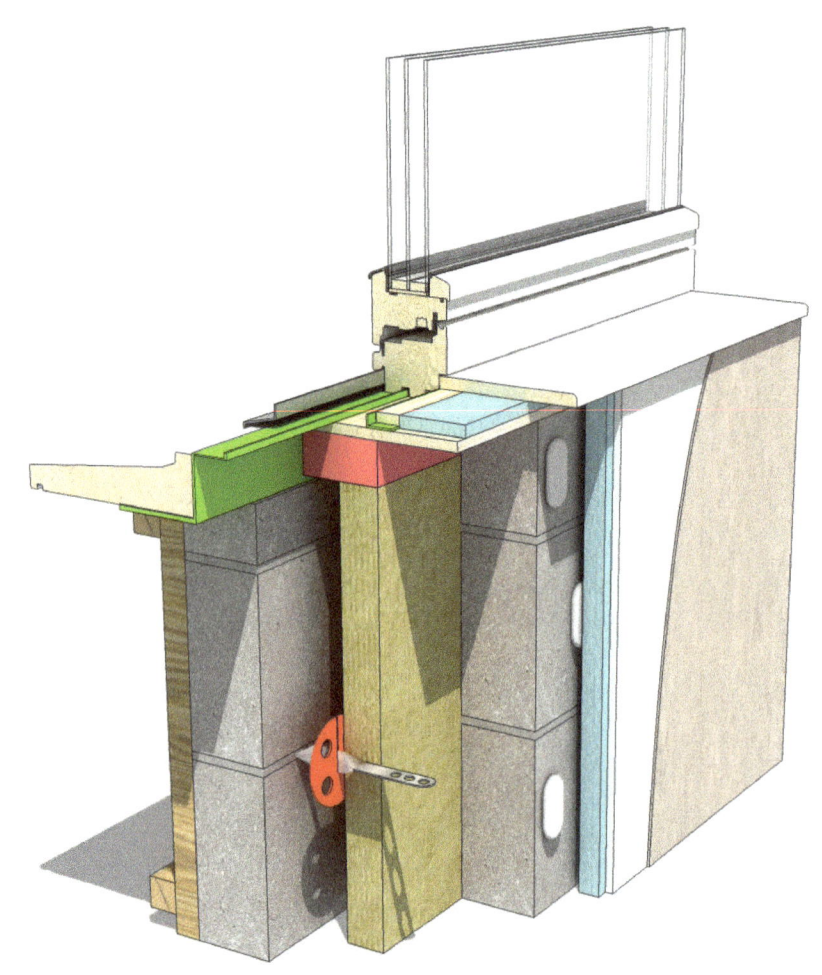

3D Detail M-W18 - External masonry cavity wall, vertical timber cladding, window sill

SECTION 5 - MASONRY CONSTRUCTION

M-W19

EXTERNAL MASONRY CAVITY WALL, VERTICAL TIMBER CLADDING, WINDOW JAMB (PLAN)

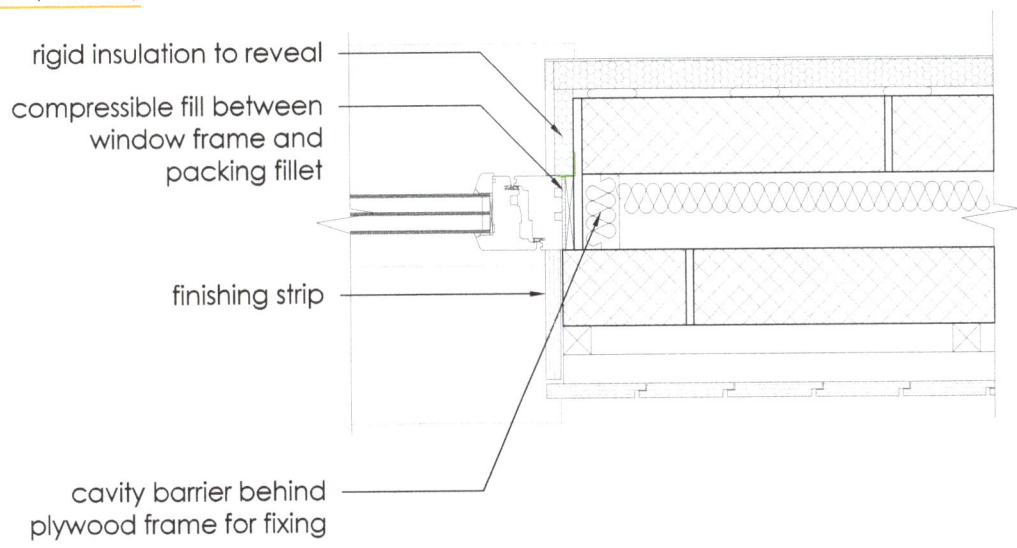

- rigid insulation to reveal
- compressible fill between window frame and packing fillet
- finishing strip
- cavity barrier behind plywood frame for fixing

Detail M-W19 - External masonry cavity wall, vertical timber cladding, window jamb (plan)

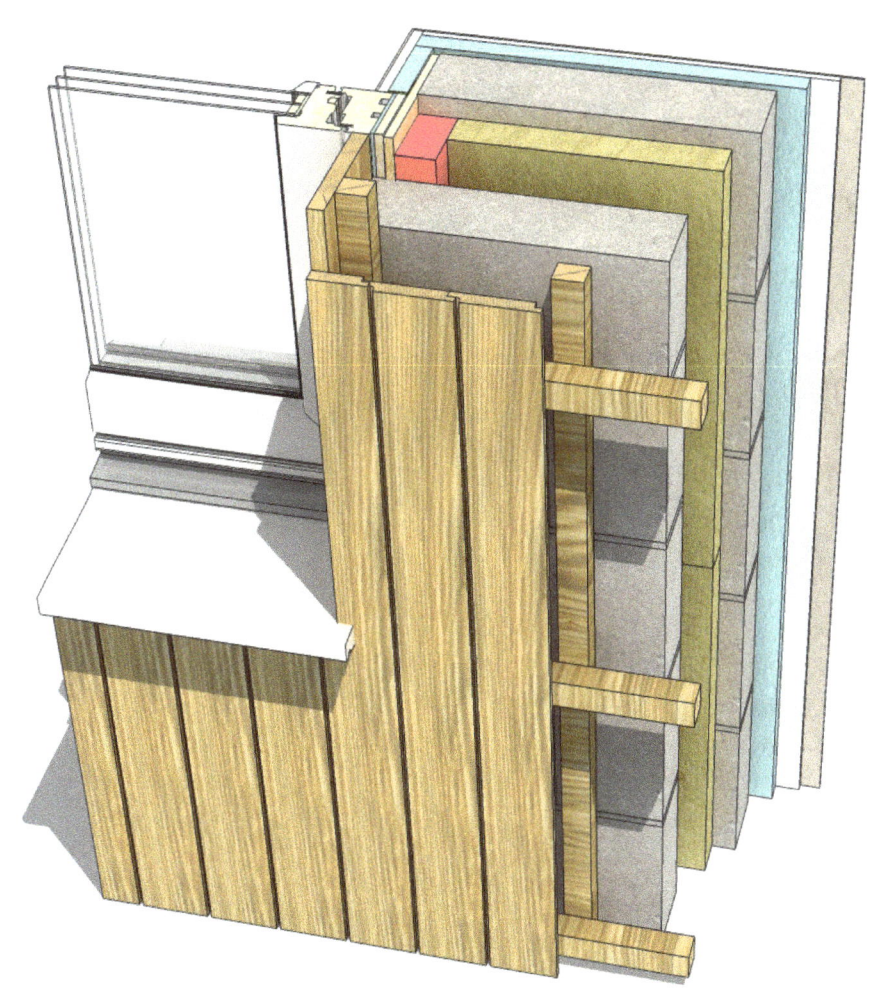

3D Detail M-W19 - External masonry cavity wall, vertical timber cladding, window jamb

M-W20

EXTERNAL MASONRY CAVITY WALL, INSULATION BELOW SLAB
DOOR THRESHOLD

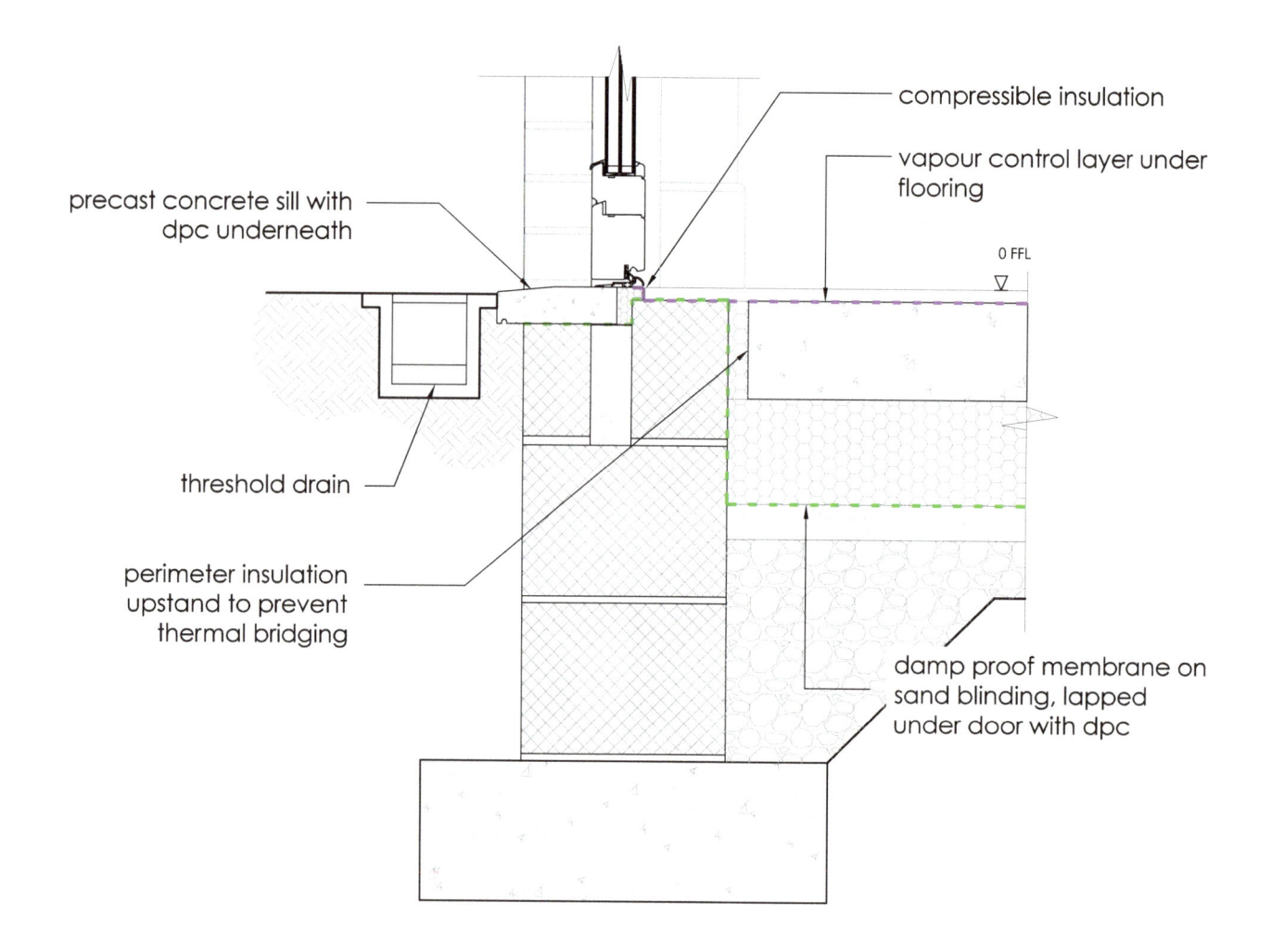

- precast concrete sill with dpc underneath
- threshold drain
- perimeter insulation upstand to prevent thermal bridging
- compressible insulation
- vapour control layer under flooring
- 0 FFL
- damp proof membrane on sand blinding, lapped under door with dpc

Detail M-W20 - External masonry cavity wall, insulation below slab, door threshold

SECTION 5 - MASONRY CONSTRUCTION

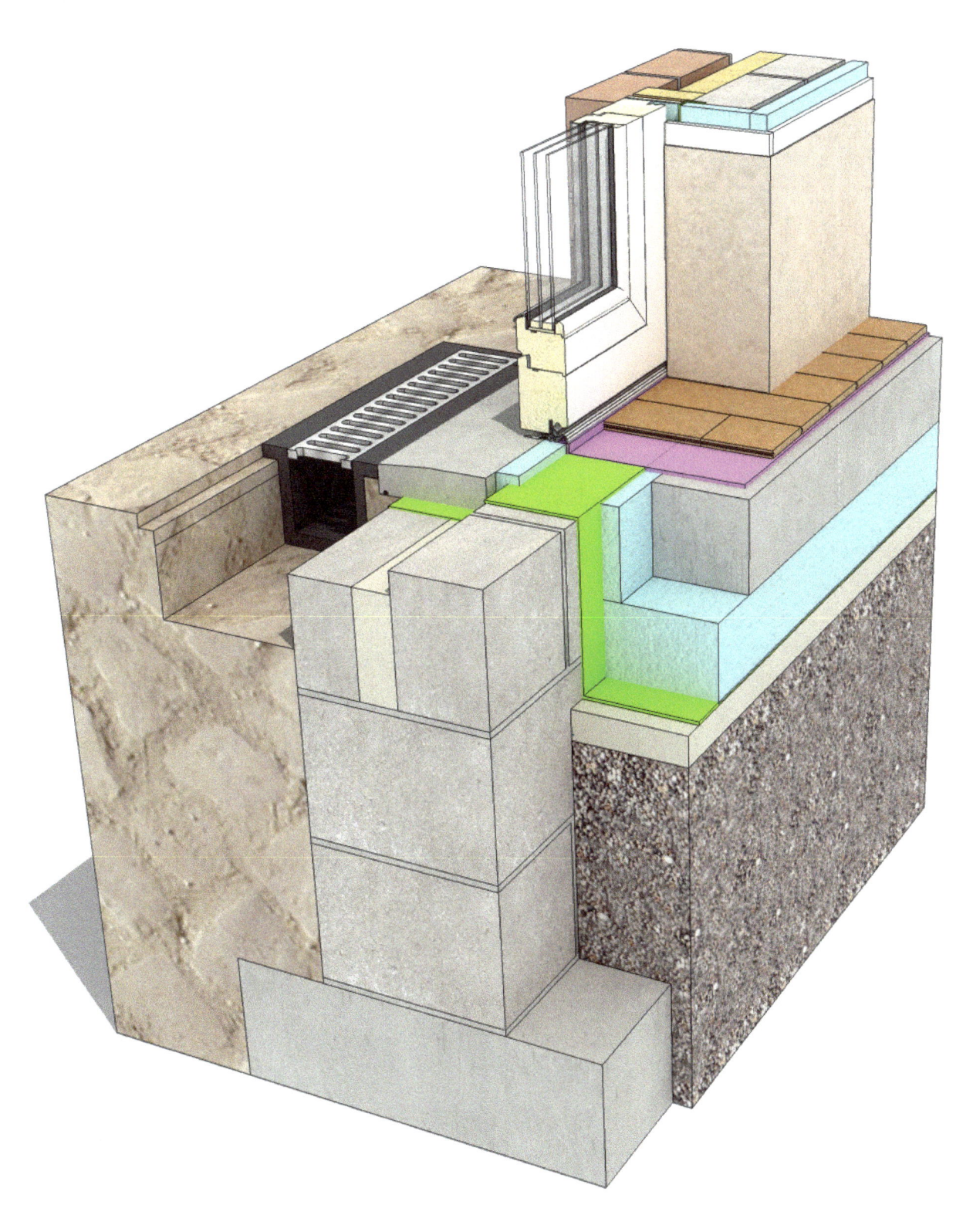

3D Detail M-W20 - External masonry cavity wall, insulation below slab, door threshold

M-W21

EXTERNAL MASONRY CAVITY WALL, INSULATION ABOVE SLAB
DOOR THRESHOLD

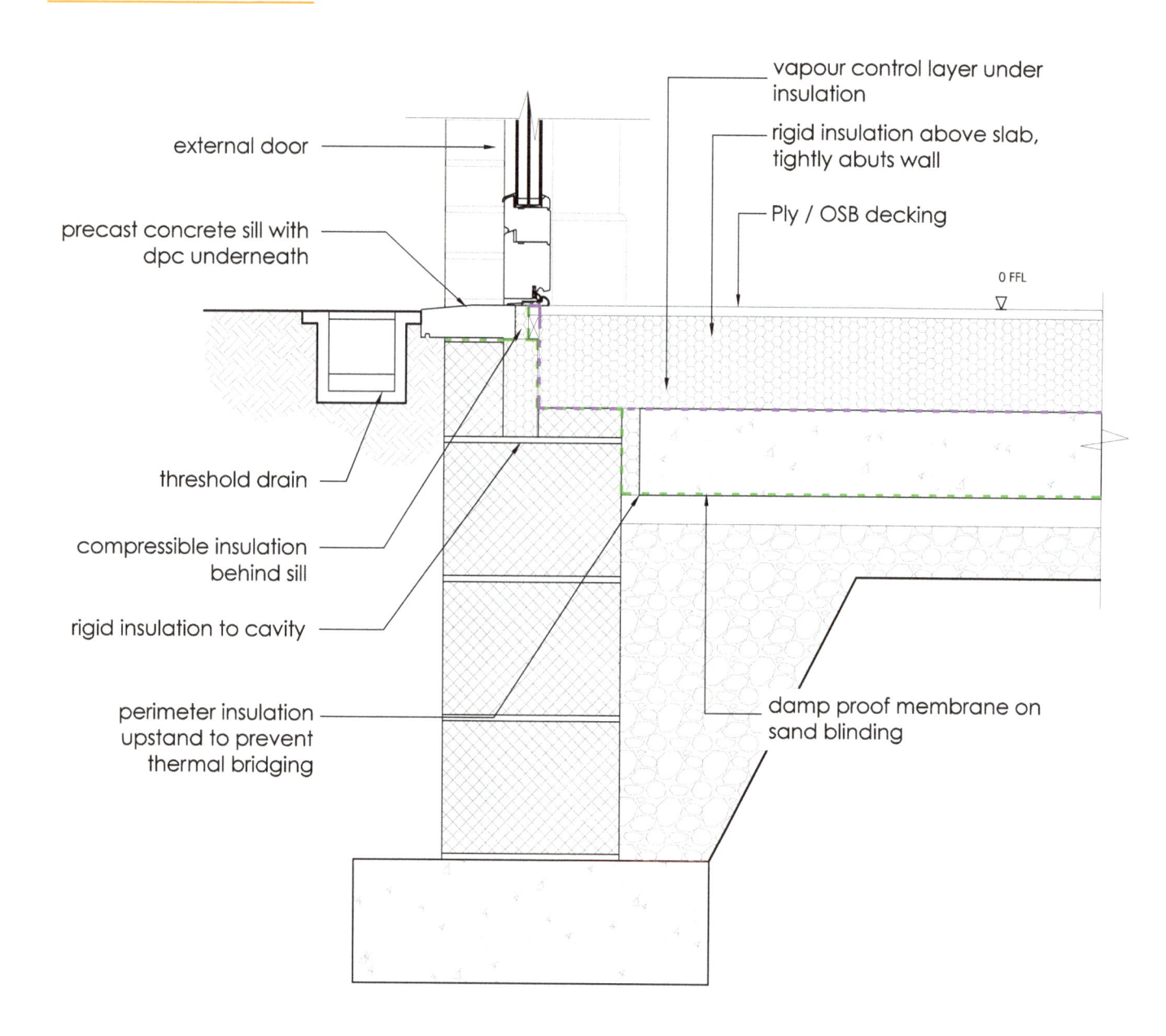

Labels (clockwise):
- external door
- precast concrete sill with dpc underneath
- threshold drain
- compressible insulation behind sill
- rigid insulation to cavity
- perimeter insulation upstand to prevent thermal bridging
- vapour control layer under insulation
- rigid insulation above slab, tightly abuts wall
- Ply / OSB decking
- 0 FFL
- damp proof membrane on sand blinding

Detail M-W21 - External masonry cavity wall, insulation above slab, door threshold

SECTION 5 - MASONRY CONSTRUCTION

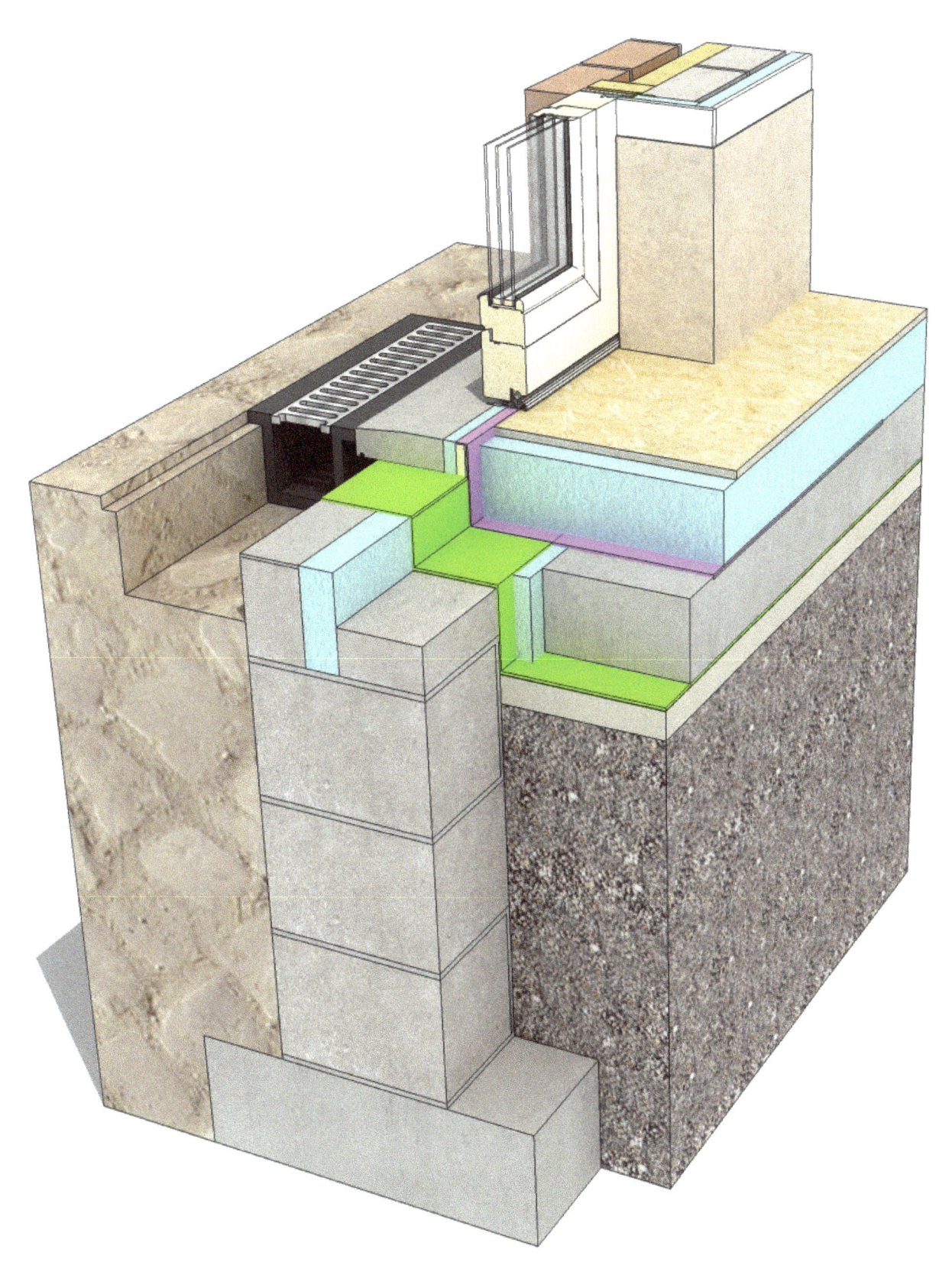

3D Detail M-W21 - External masonry cavity wall, insulation above slab, door threshold

M-W22

EXTERNAL MASONRY CAVITY WALL, SUSPENDED TIMBER FLOOR DOOR THRESHOLD

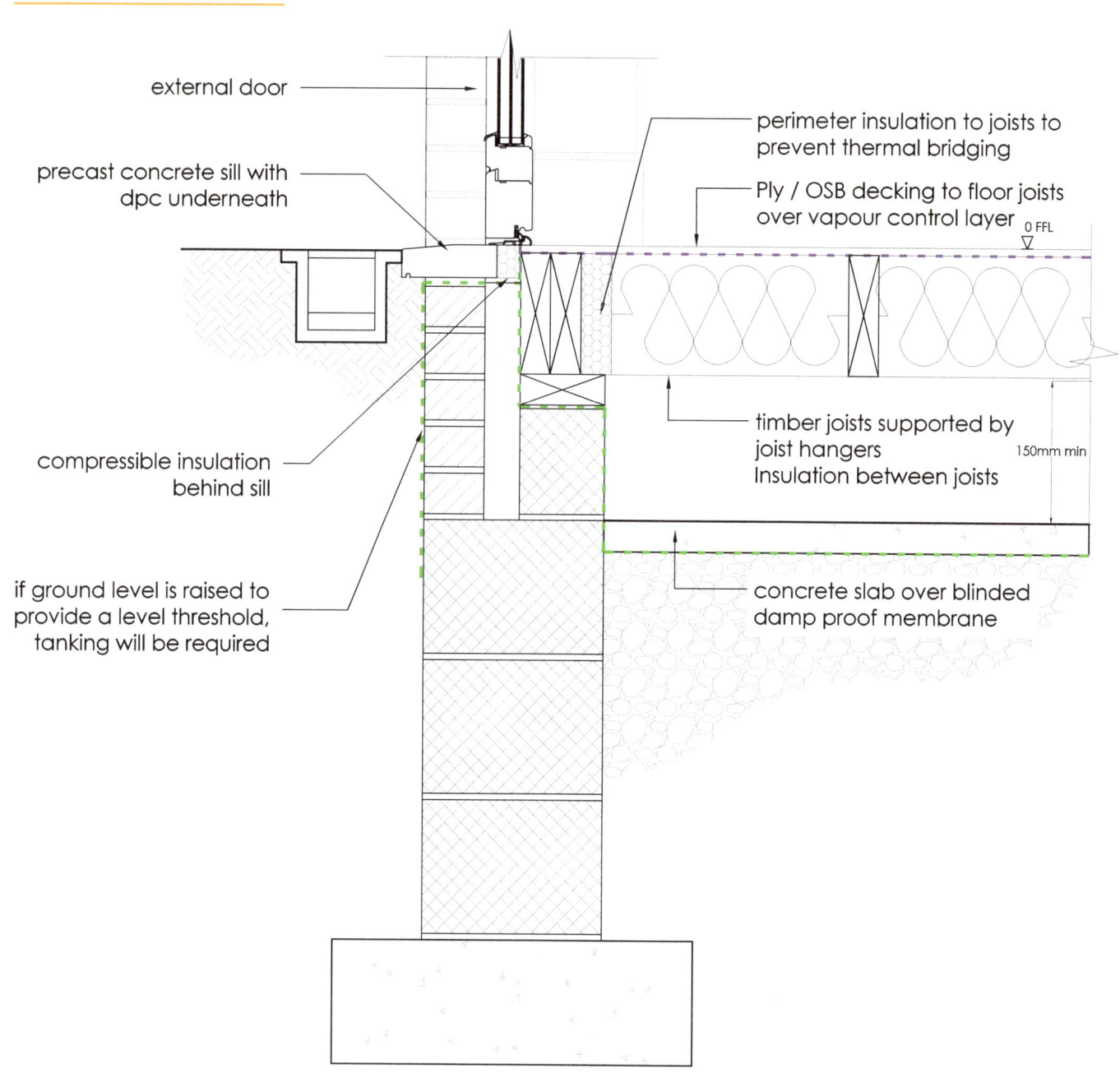

- external door
- precast concrete sill with dpc underneath
- compressible insulation behind sill
- if ground level is raised to provide a level threshold, tanking will be required
- perimeter insulation to joists to prevent thermal bridging
- Ply / OSB decking to floor joists over vapour control layer
- 0 FFL
- timber joists supported by joist hangers. Insulation between joists
- 150mm min
- concrete slab over blinded damp proof membrane

Detail M-W22 - External masonry cavity wall, suspended timber floor, door threshold

SECTION 5 - MASONRY CONSTRUCTION

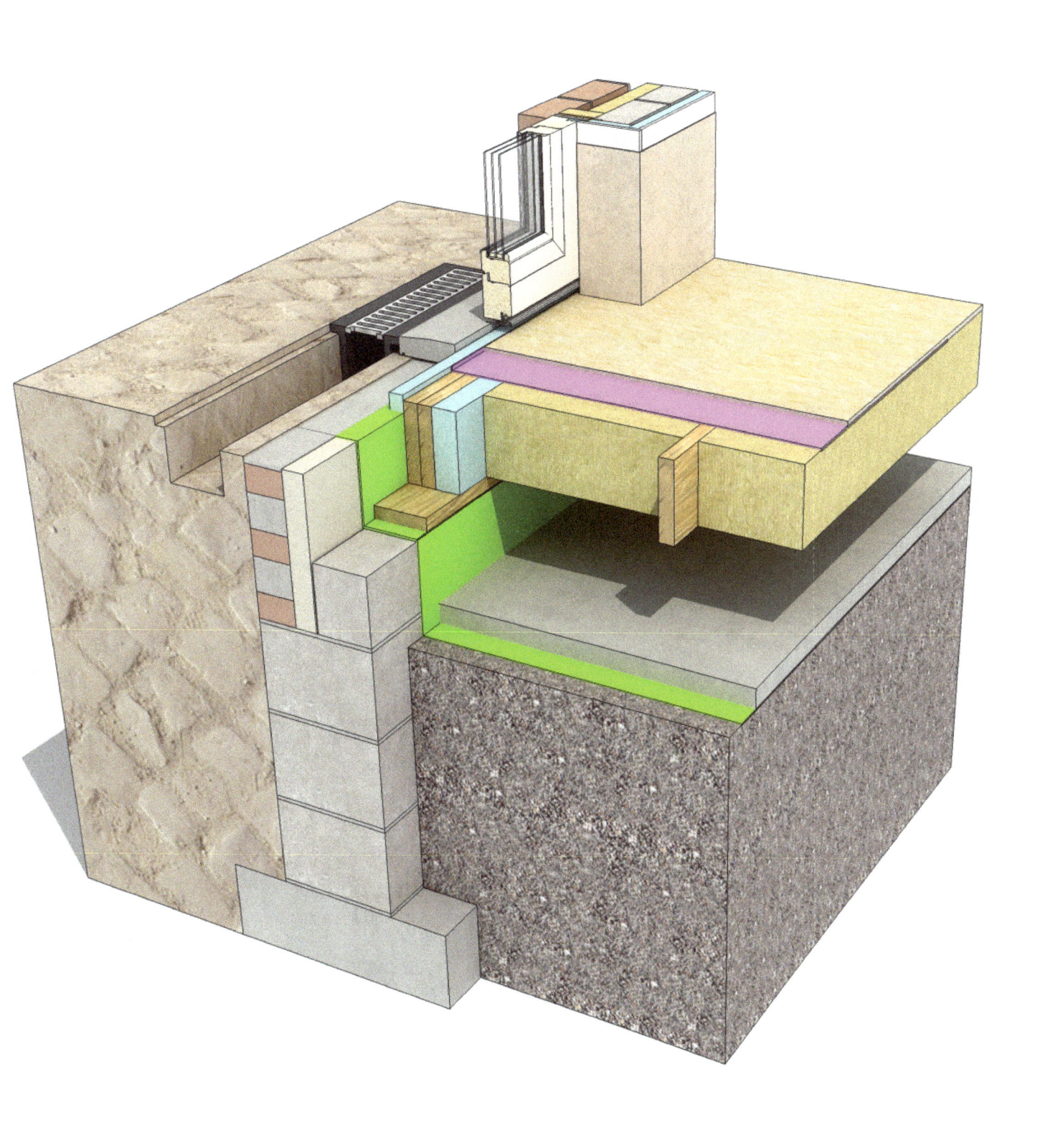

3D Detail M-W22 - External masonry cavity wall, suspended timber floor, door threshold

NOTES ON THE REGS

The following information is a partial list of requirements from the **Building Regulations Approved Documents** - for full and detailed explanations and requirements please consult the full publications.

GENERAL REQUIREMENTS

Moisture
The walls of the building shall adequately protect the building and people who use the building from harmful effects caused by:
- ground moisture
- precipitation and wind-driven spray
- interstitial and surface condensation
- spillage of water from or associated with sanitary fittings or fixed appliances

(Approved Doc C2)

Cavity Insulation
Fumes given off by insulating materials such as by urea formaldehyde foams should not be allowed to penetrate occupied parts of the building to an extent where it could become a health risks to persons in the building by becoming an irritant concentration.

(Approved Doc D)

Fire precautions
Materials and/or products used for the internal linings of walls shall restrict:
-the spread of flame;
-the amount of heat released.

Internal fire spread (structure)
A wall common to two or more buildings shall be designed and constructed so that it adequately resists the spread of fire between those buildings.

The building should be sub-divided by elements of fire resisting construction into compartments.

Any hidden voids in the construction shall be sealed and sub-divided to inhibit the unseen spread of fire and products of combustion, in order to reduce the risk of structural failure, and the spread of fire.

(Approved Doc B3)

External walls shall be constructed so as to have a low rate of heat release and thereby be capable of reducing the risk of ignition from an external source and the spread of fire over their surfaces.

The amount of unprotected area in the sides of the building shall be restricted so as to limit the amount of thermal radiation that can pass through the wall.

(Approved Doc B4)

Airborne and impact sound
Dwellings shall be designed so that the noise from domestic activity in an adjoining dwelling (or other parts of the building) is kept to a level that:

- does not affect the health of the occupants of the dwelling
- will allow them to sleep, rest and engage in their normal activities in satisfactory conditions.

(Approved Doc E1)

Dwellings shall be designed so that any domestic noise that is generated internally does not interfere with the occupants ability to sleep, rest and engage in their normal activities in satisfactory conditions.
(Approved Doc E2)

Domestic buildings shall be designed and constructed so as to restrict the transmission of echoes.
(Approved Doc E3)

Conservation of fuel and power
Reasonable provision shall be made for the conservation of fuel and power in buildings by:
- limiting heat gains and losses through thermal elements and other parts of the building fabric,
- from pipes ducts and vessels used for space heating, space cooling and hot water services.
- providing fixed building services which are energy efficient and have effective controls and are commissioned by testing and adjusting as necessary to ensure they use no more fuel and power than is reasonable in the circumstances.

(Approved Doc L)

SECTION 5 - MASONRY CONSTRUCTION

GENERAL NOTES:

Walls should comply with the relevant requirements of BS EN 1996-2:2006

For residential buildings, the maximum height of the building measured from the lowest finished ground level adjoining the building to the highest point of any wall or roof should not be greater than 15m.

Wall cladding
Wall cladding shall be capable of safely sustaining and transmitting all dead, imposed and wind loads. Provision shall be made where necessary, to accommodate differential movement of the cladding and the supporting structure of the building.
The cladding shall be securely fixed to and supported by the structure of the building using both vertical support and horizontal restraint.
The cladding and its fixings shall be of durable materials.

See approved documents for masonry unit and mortar requirements.

Strapping
Tension straps should be used to strap walls to floors above ground level, at intervals not exceeding 2m. Gable walls should be strapped to roofs.
The ends of every wall should be bonded or otherwise securely tied throughout their full height to a buttressing wall, pier or chimney.

Cavity barriers
Structure should be designed so that the unseen spread of fire and smoke within concealed spaces is prevented.

Cavity barriers should be provided:
- at the edge of cavities
- around window and door openings
- at the junction between an external cavity wall and a compartment wall
- at the junction between an external cavity wall and a compartment floor
- at the top of an external cavity wall
- at the junction between an internal cavity wall and any assembly which forms a fire resisting barrier
- above the enclosures to a protected stairway in a dwelling with a floor more than 4.5m above ground level.

Cavity walls
All cavity walls should have
- leaves at least 90mm thick and cavities at least 50mm wide
- wall ties with a horizontal spacing of 900mm and a vertical spacing of 450mm
- wall ties spaced not more than 300mm apart vertically within a distance of 225mm from the vertical edges of all openings, movement joints and roof verges.

Damp proof courses
Internal and external walls that are subject to moisture from the ground should have a damp-proof course to prevent the passage of moisture. The damp proof course should be continuous with any damp proof membrane in the floor.
If the wall is an external wall, the damp proof course should be at least 150mm above the level of the adjoining ground.

If the wall is an external cavity wall either:
- the cavity should be taken down at least 225mm below the level of the lowest damp-proof course or
- a damp proof tray should be provided so as to prevent precipitation passing into the inner leaf, with weep holes every 900mm to assist in the transfer of moisture through the external leaf.

ROOF DETAILS

M-R1

EXTERNAL MASONRY CAVITY WALL, EAVES DETAIL, VENTILATED ROOF SPACE INSULATION BETWEEN AND OVER CEILING JOISTS

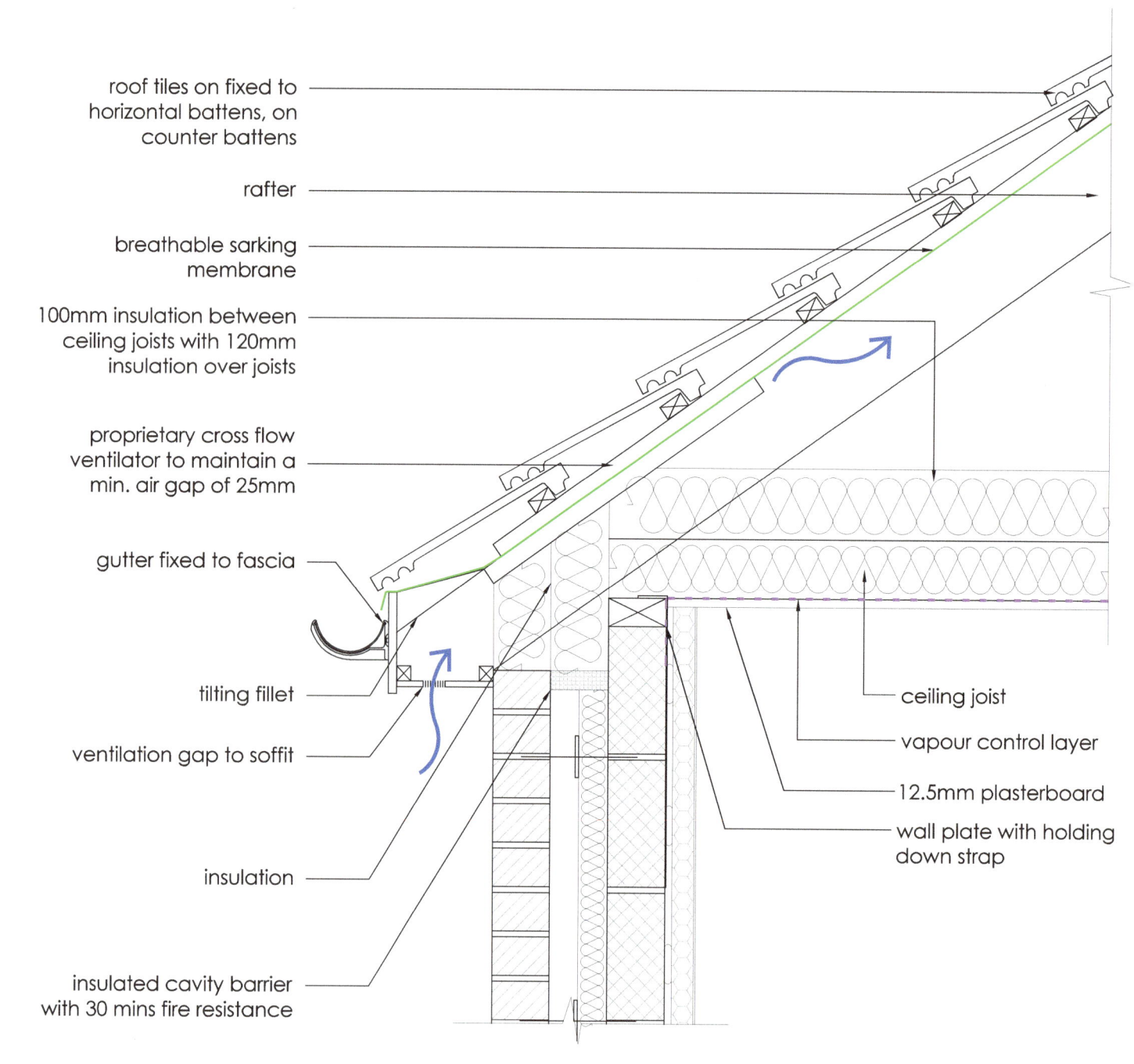

Labels (left side):
- roof tiles on fixed to horizontal battens, on counter battens
- rafter
- breathable sarking membrane
- 100mm insulation between ceiling joists with 120mm insulation over joists
- proprietary cross flow ventilator to maintain a min. air gap of 25mm
- gutter fixed to fascia
- tilting fillet
- ventilation gap to soffit
- insulation
- insulated cavity barrier with 30 mins fire resistance

Labels (right side):
- ceiling joist
- vapour control layer
- 12.5mm plasterboard
- wall plate with holding down strap

Detail M-R1 - External masonry cavity wall, eaves detail, ventilated roof space, insulation between and over ceiling joists

NOTES:

U-value 0.12 Wm²K or better

SECTION 5 - MASONRY CONSTRUCTION

3D Detail M-R1 - External masonry cavity wall, eaves detail, ventilated roof space, insulation between and over ceiling joists

M-R2

EXTERNAL MASONRY CAVITY WALL, GABLE DETAIL - VENTILATED ROOF SPACE INSULATION BETWEEN AND OVER CEILING JOISTS

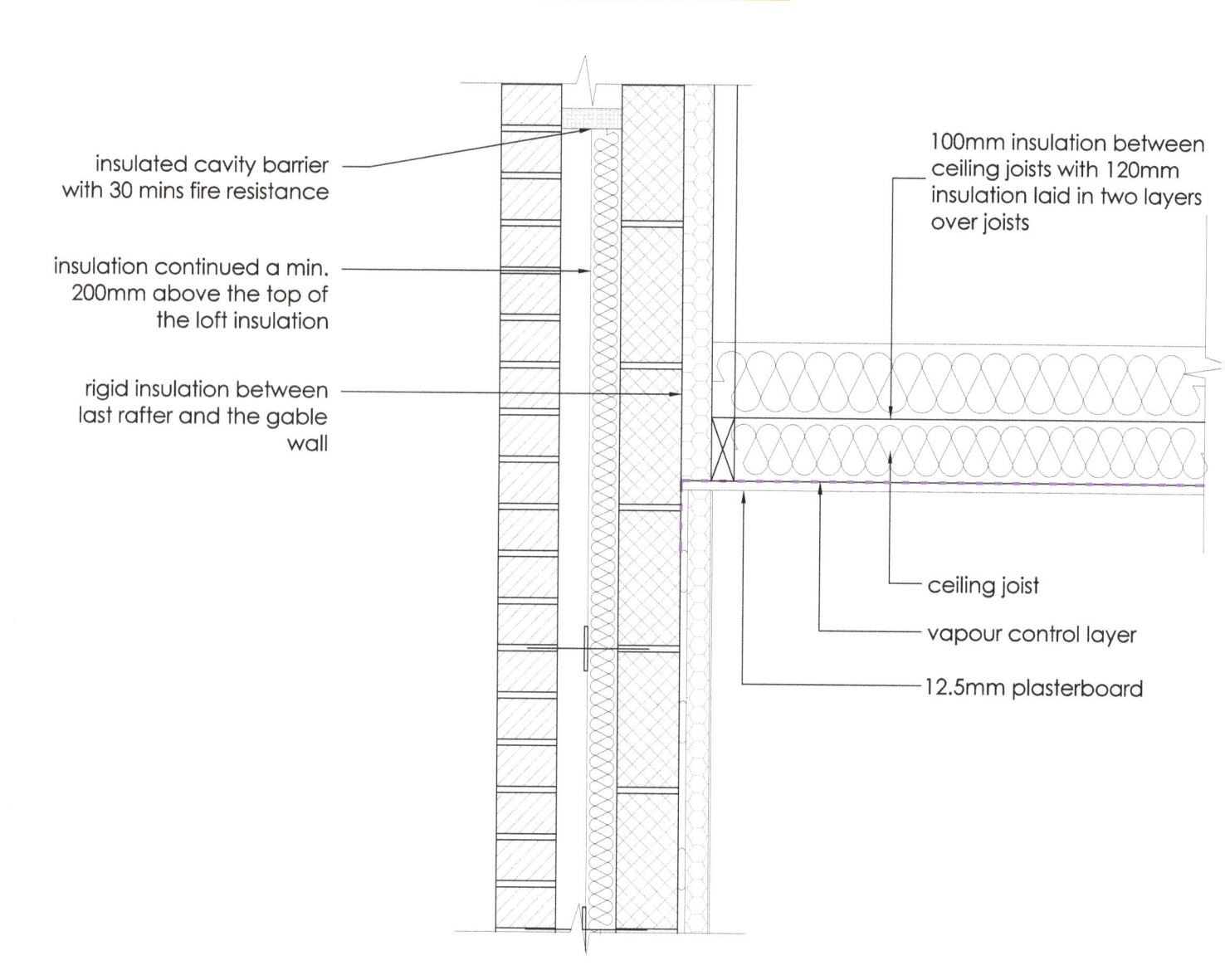

insulated cavity barrier with 30 mins fire resistance

insulation continued a min. 200mm above the top of the loft insulation

rigid insulation between last rafter and the gable wall

100mm insulation between ceiling joists with 120mm insulation laid in two layers over joists

ceiling joist

vapour control layer

12.5mm plasterboard

Detail M-R2 - External masonry cavity wall, gable detail, ventilated roof space, insulation between and over ceiling joists

NOTES:
U-value 0.12 Wm²K or better

SECTION 5 - MASONRY CONSTRUCTION

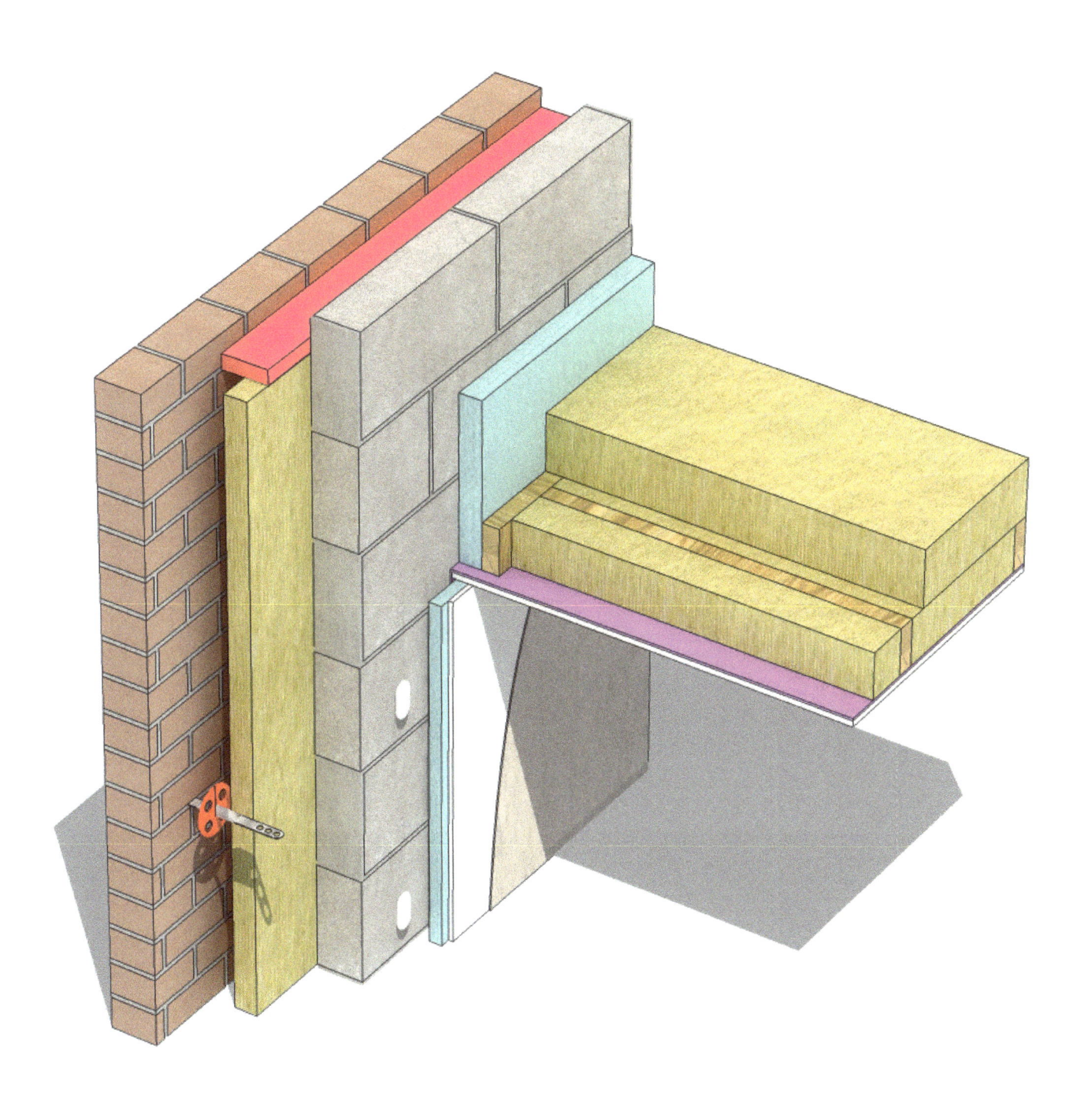

3D Detail M-R2 - External masonry cavity wall, gable detail, ventilated roof space, insulation between and over ceiling joists

M-R3

EXTERNAL MASONRY CAVITY WALL, EAVES DETAIL - INSULATION BETWEEN AND UNDER RAFTERS

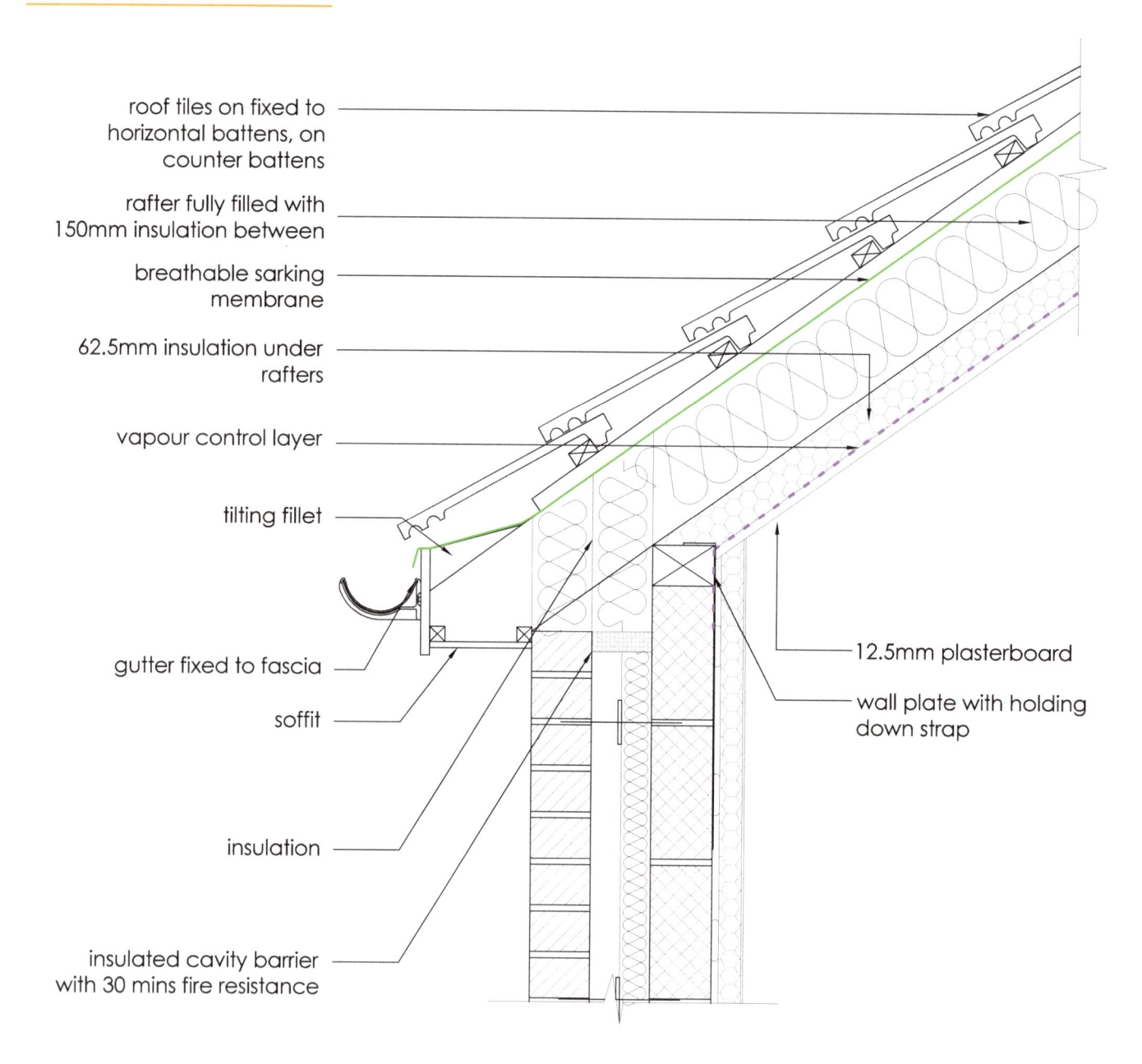

Labels on diagram:
- roof tiles on fixed to horizontal battens, on counter battens
- rafter fully filled with 150mm insulation between
- breathable sarking membrane
- 62.5mm insulation under rafters
- vapour control layer
- tilting fillet
- gutter fixed to fascia
- soffit
- insulation
- insulated cavity barrier with 30 mins fire resistance
- 12.5mm plasterboard
- wall plate with holding down strap

Detail M-R3 - External masonry cavity wall, eaves detail, insulation between and under rafters

NOTES:

U-value 0.12 Wm^{2}K or better
Any ventilation requirements according to manufacturers instructions

SECTION 5 - MASONRY CONSTRUCTION

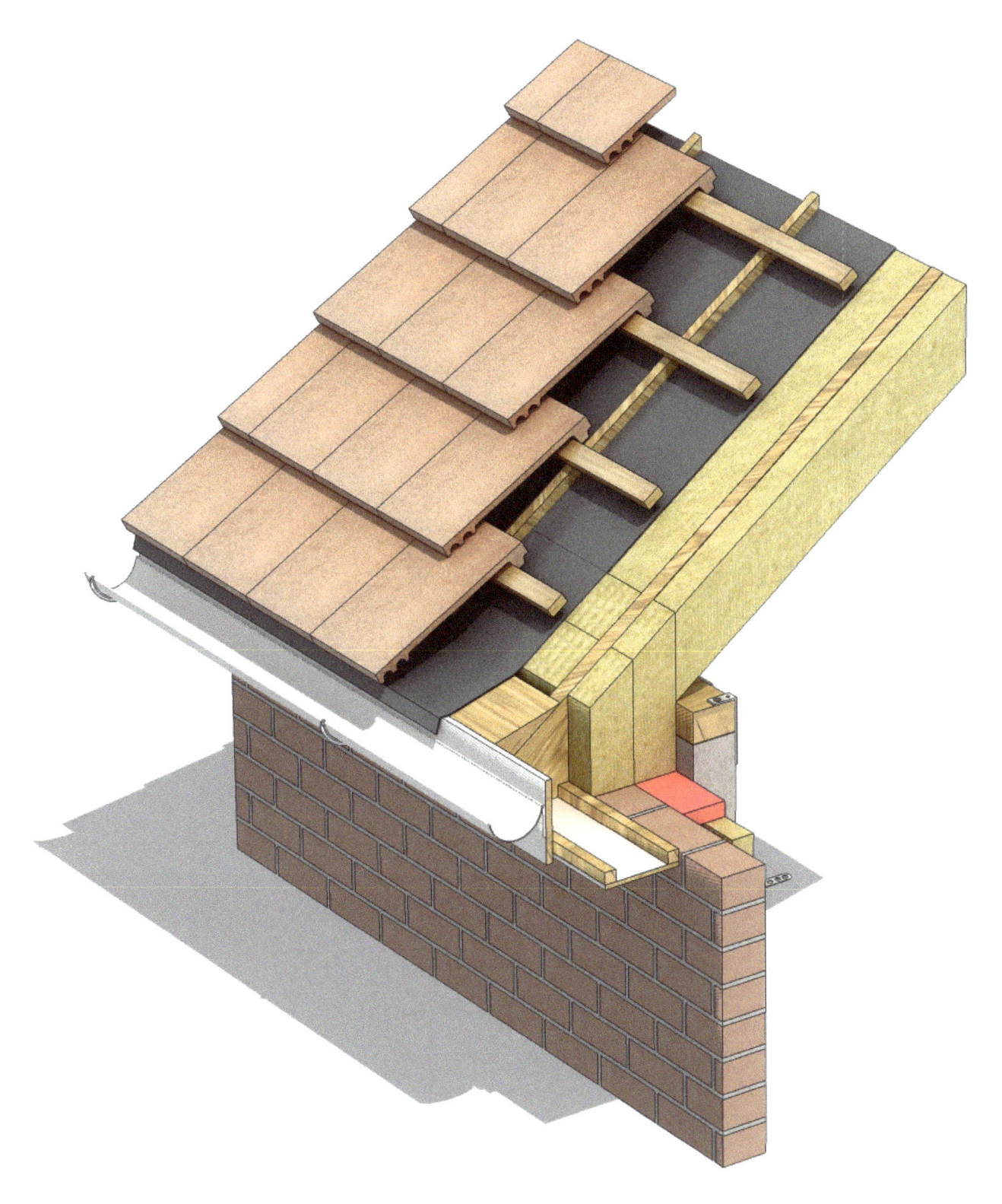

3D Detail M-R3 - External masonry cavity wall, eaves detail, insulation between and under rafters

M-R4

EXTERNAL MASONRY CAVITY WALL, GABLE DETAIL - INSULATION BETWEEN AND UNDER RAFTERS

- roof tiles on fixed to horizontal battens, on counter battens
- breathable sarking membrane
- rafter fully filled with 150mm insulation between
- edging tile or clip
- fascia
- soffit
- insulation between joists and over cavity insulation
- insulated cavity barrier with 30 mins fire resistance
- 12.5mm plasterboard
- vapour control layer
- 62.5mm rigid insulation under rafters

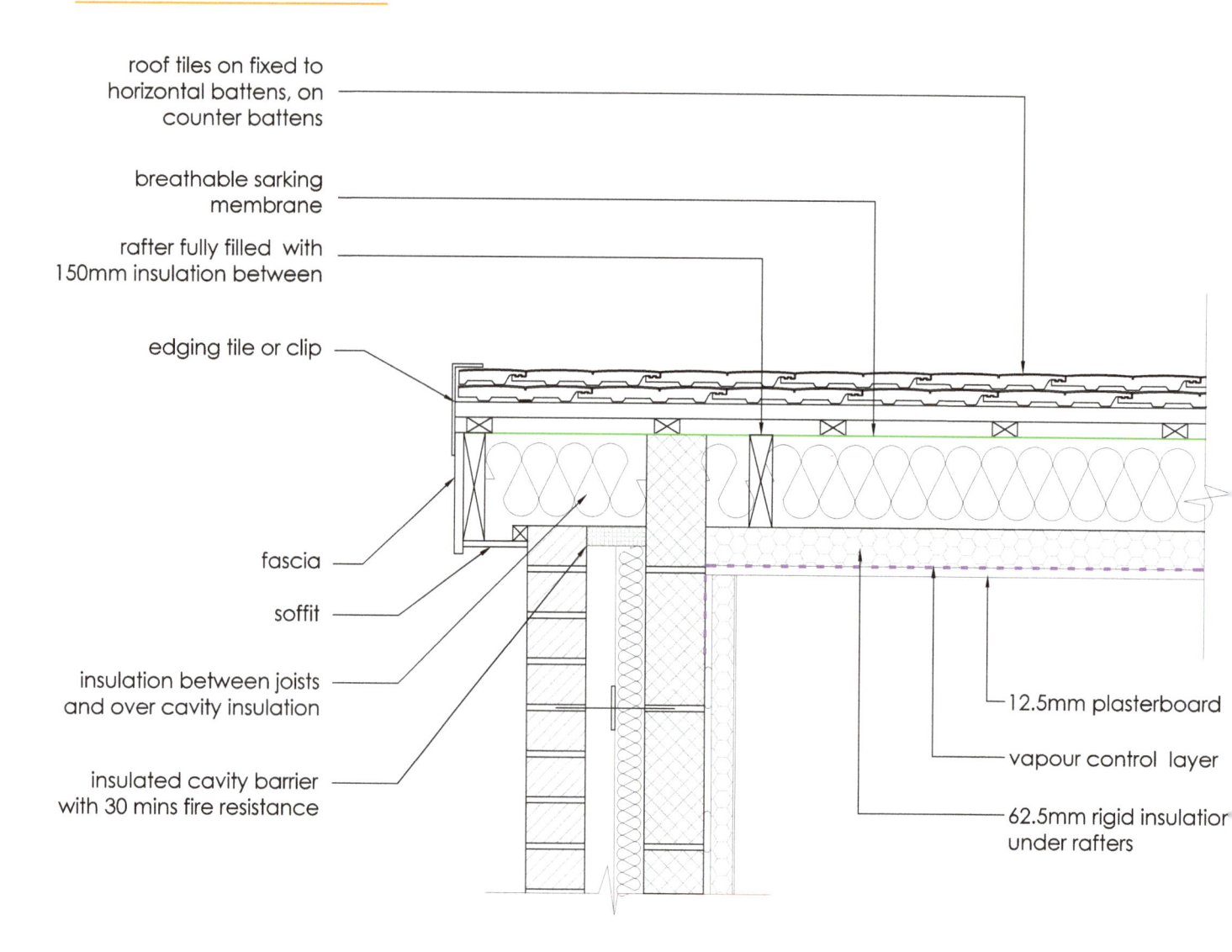

Detail M-R4 - External masonry cavity wall, gable detail, insulation between and under rafters

NOTES:

U-value 0.12 Wm²K or better
Any ventilation requirements according to manufacturers instructions

SECTION 5 - MASONRY CONSTRUCTION

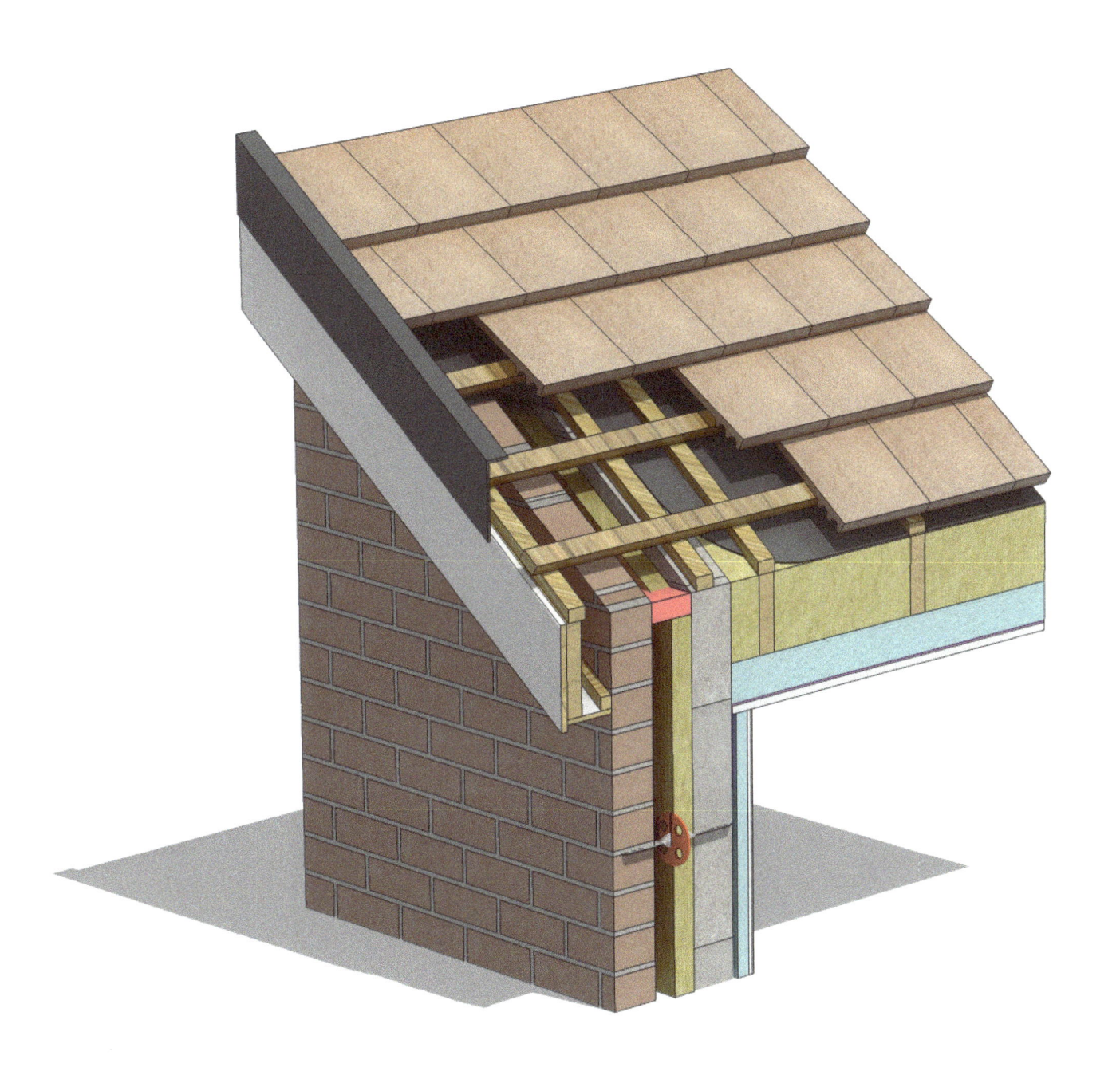

3D Detail M-R4 - External masonry cavity wall, gable detail, insulation between and under rafters

M-R5

EXTERNAL MASONRY CAVITY WALL, EAVES DETAIL - INSULATION BETWEEN AND OVER RAFTERS

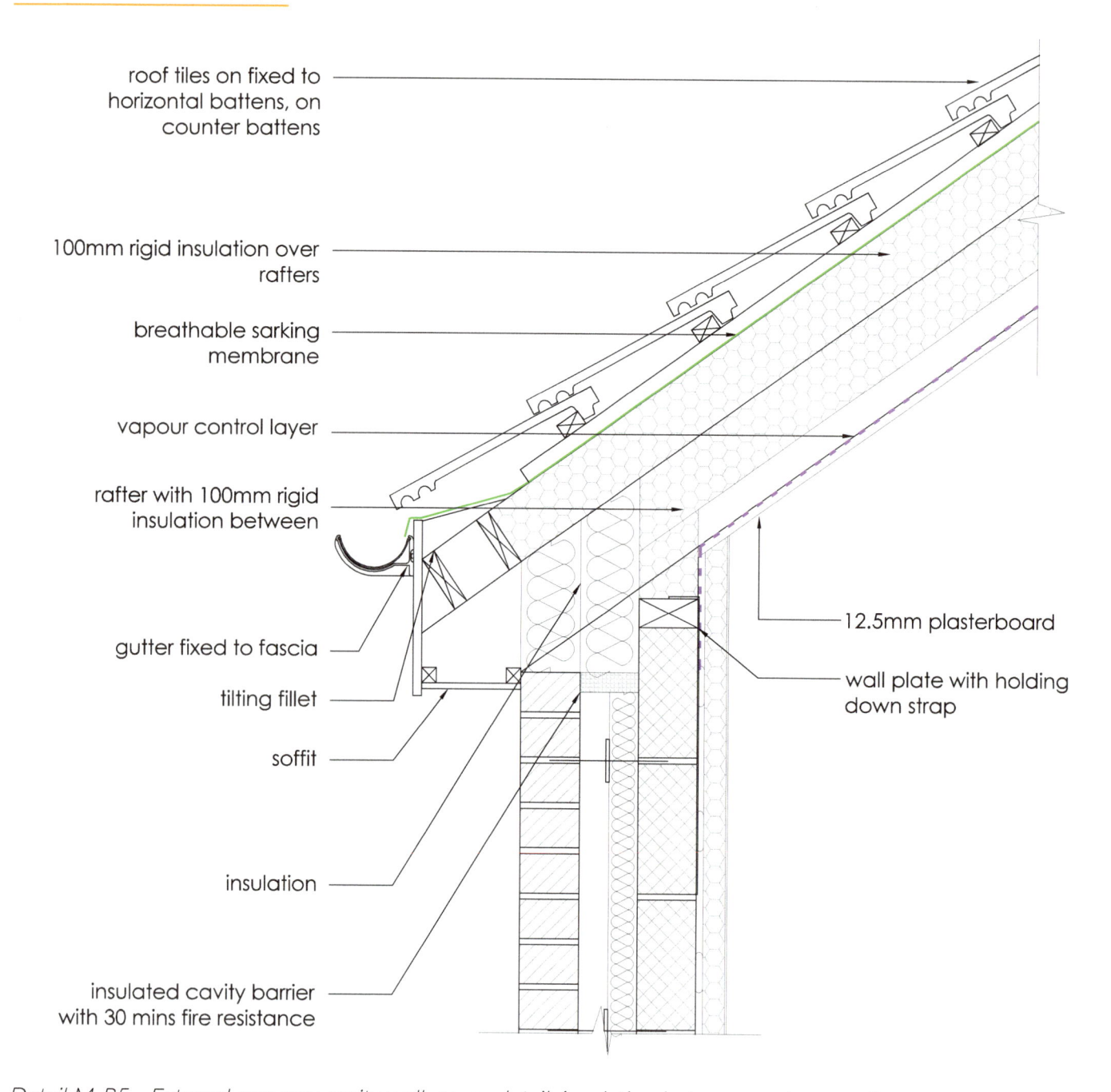

Labels (left side):
- roof tiles on fixed to horizontal battens, on counter battens
- 100mm rigid insulation over rafters
- breathable sarking membrane
- vapour control layer
- rafter with 100mm rigid insulation between
- gutter fixed to fascia
- tilting fillet
- soffit
- insulation
- insulated cavity barrier with 30 mins fire resistance

Labels (right side):
- 12.5mm plasterboard
- wall plate with holding down strap

Detail M-R5 - External masonry cavity wall, eaves detail, insulation between and over rafters

NOTES:

U-value 0.12 Wm²K or better
Any ventilation requirements according to manufacturers instructions

SECTION 5 - MASONRY CONSTRUCTION

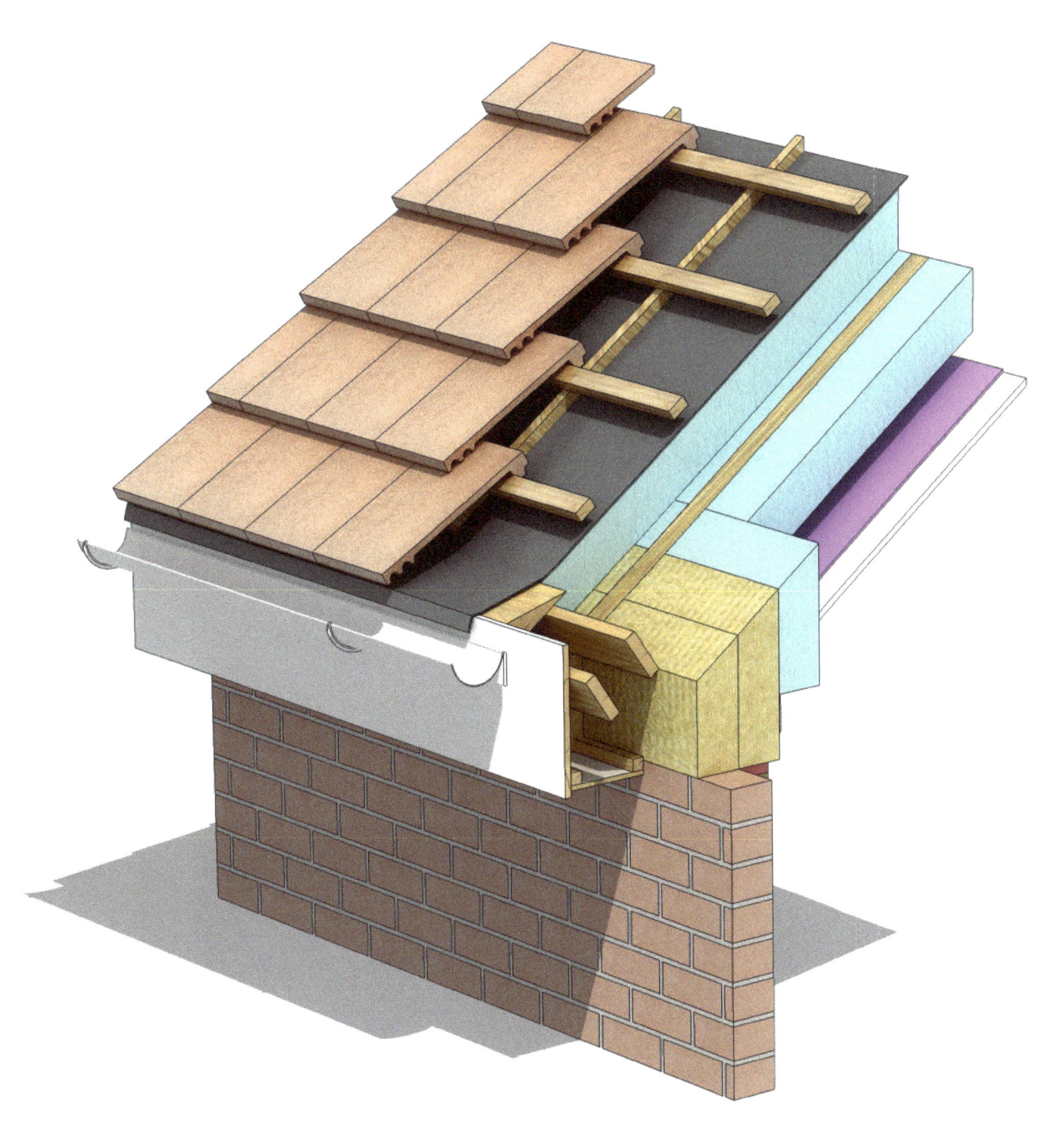

3D Detail M-R5 - External masonry cavity wall, eaves detail, insulation between and over rafters

M-R6A

EXTERNAL MASONRY CAVITY WALL, FLAT ROOF, INSULATION ABOVE ROOF DECK

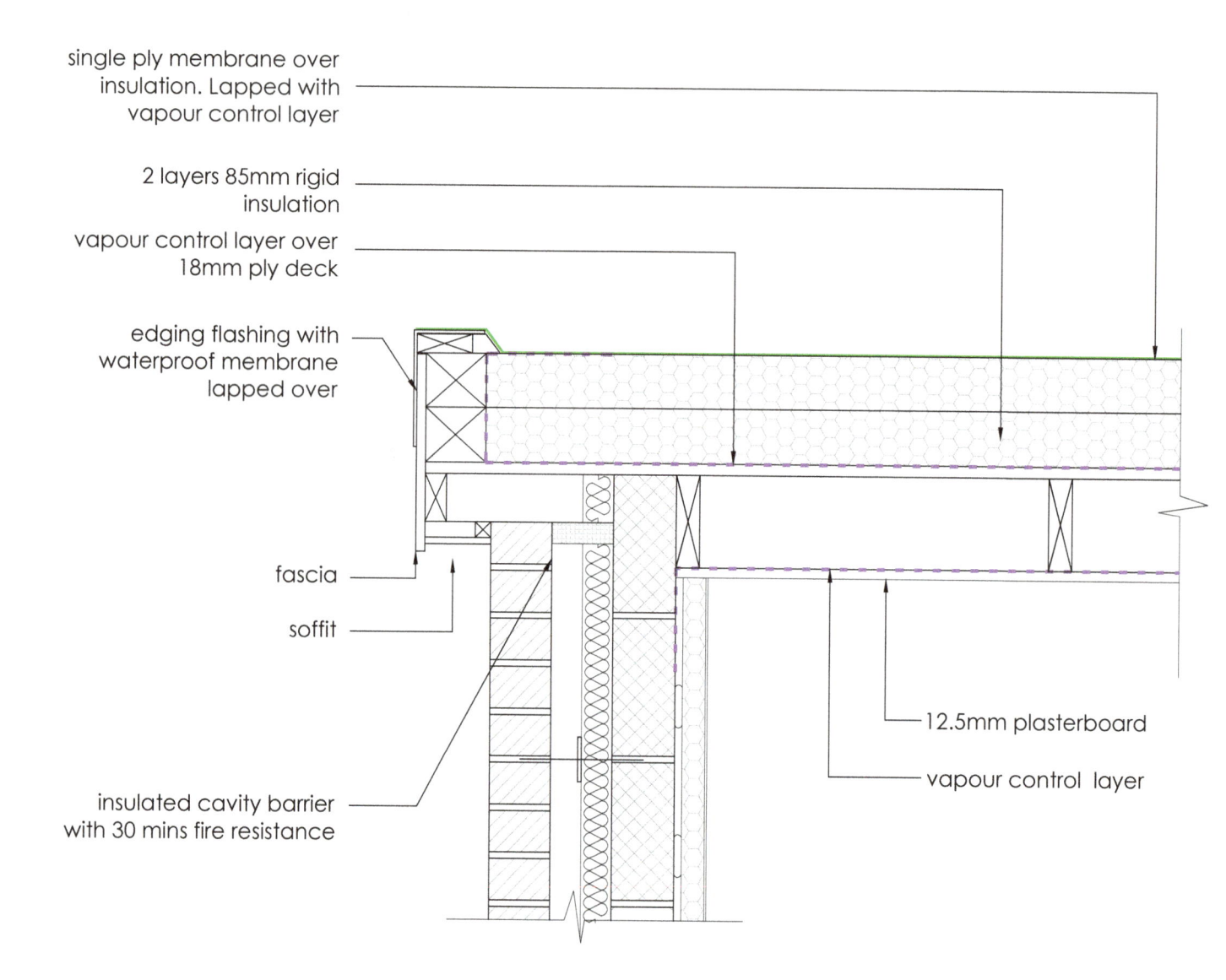

- single ply membrane over insulation. Lapped with vapour control layer
- 2 layers 85mm rigid insulation
- vapour control layer over 18mm ply deck
- edging flashing with waterproof membrane lapped over
- fascia
- soffit
- insulated cavity barrier with 30 mins fire resistance
- 12.5mm plasterboard
- vapour control layer

Detail M-R6A - External masonry cavity wall, flat roof, insulation above roof deck

NOTES:
U-value 0.12 Wm^{2}K or better

SECTION 5 - MASONRY CONSTRUCTION

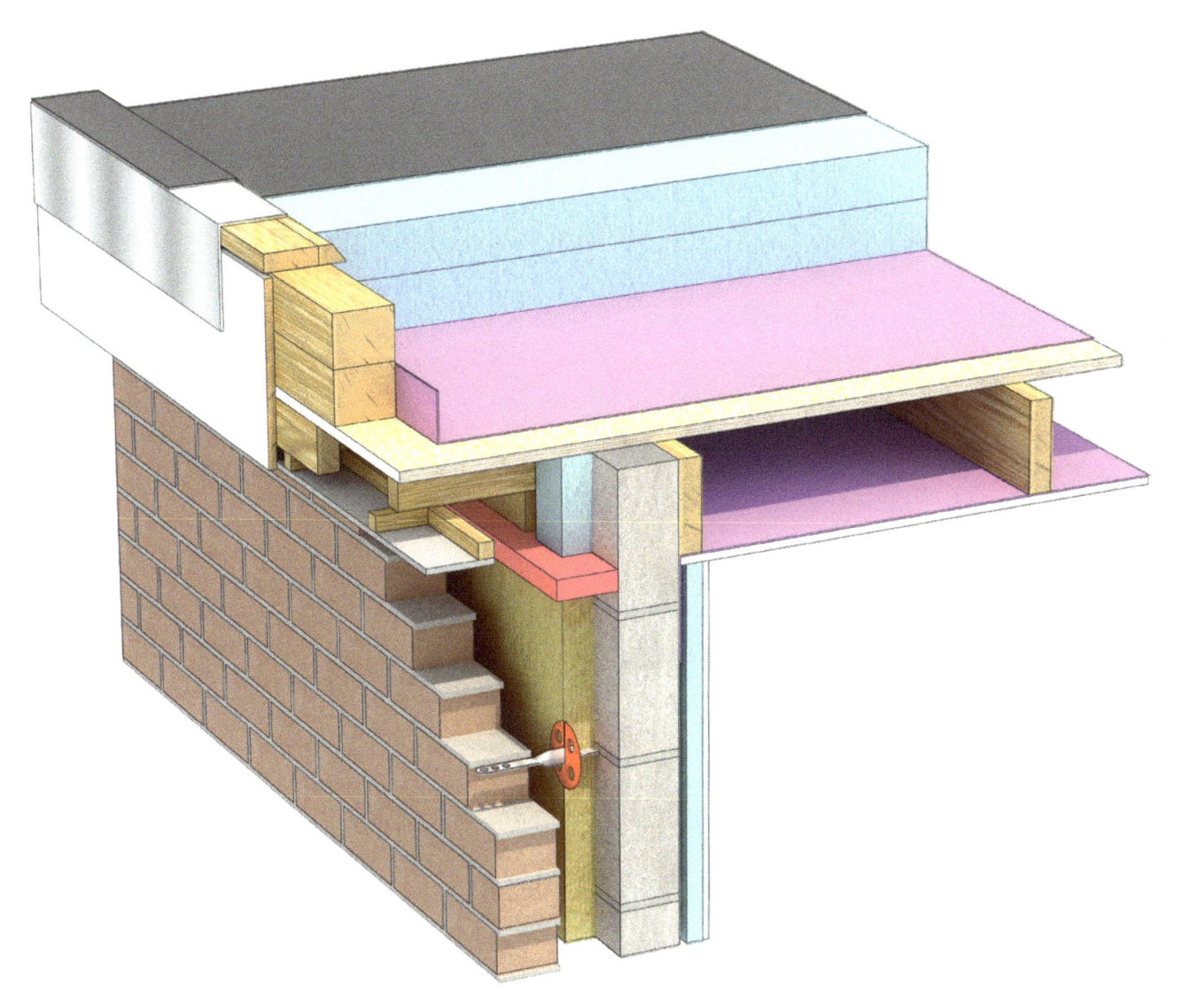

3D Detail M-R6A - External masonry cavity wall, flat roof, insulation above roof deck

M-R6B

EXTERNAL MASONRY CAVITY WALL, FLAT ROOF, WARM DECK, EAVES DETAIL

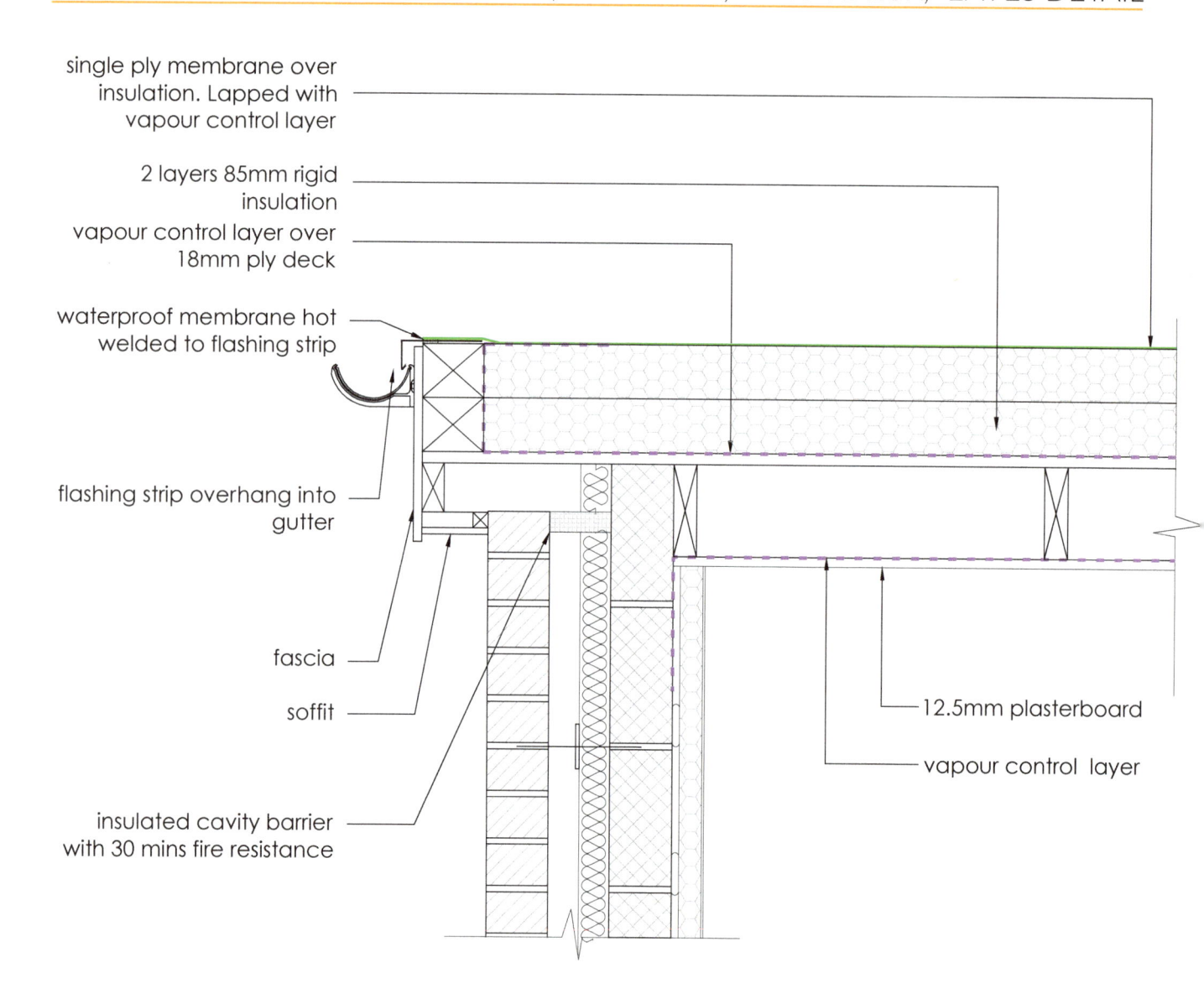

- single ply membrane over insulation. Lapped with vapour control layer
- 2 layers 85mm rigid insulation
- vapour control layer over 18mm ply deck
- waterproof membrane hot welded to flashing strip
- flashing strip overhang into gutter
- fascia
- soffit
- insulated cavity barrier with 30 mins fire resistance
- 12.5mm plasterboard
- vapour control layer

Detail M-R6B - External masonry cavity wall, flat roof, warm deck, eaves detail

NOTES:
U-value 0.12 Wm²K or better

SECTION 5 - MASONRY CONSTRUCTION

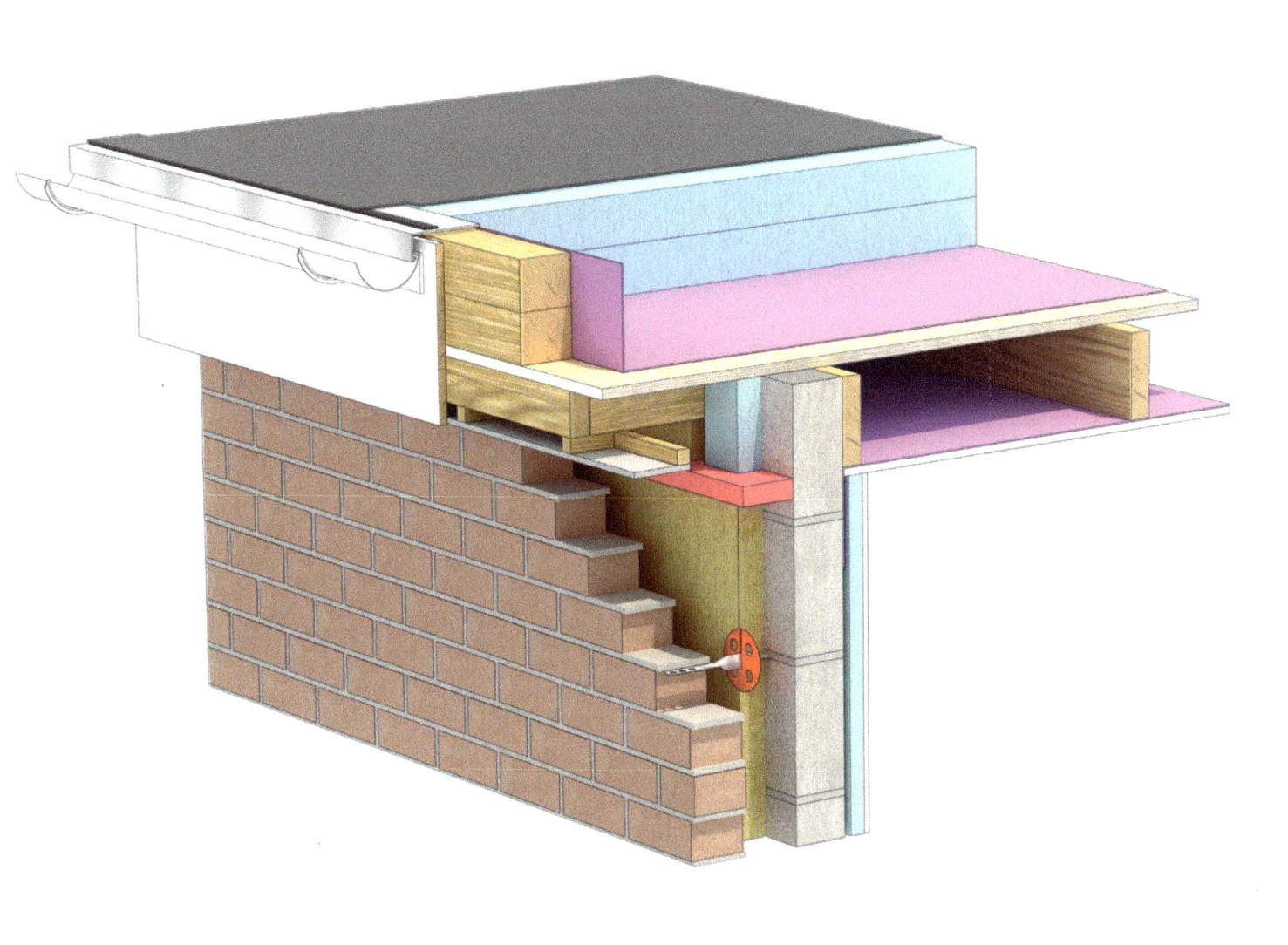

3D Detail M-R6B - External masonry cavity wall, flat roof, warm deck, eaves detail

M-R7

EXTERNAL MASONRY CAVITY WALL, FLAT ROOF WITH PARAPET INSULATION ABOVE JOISTS

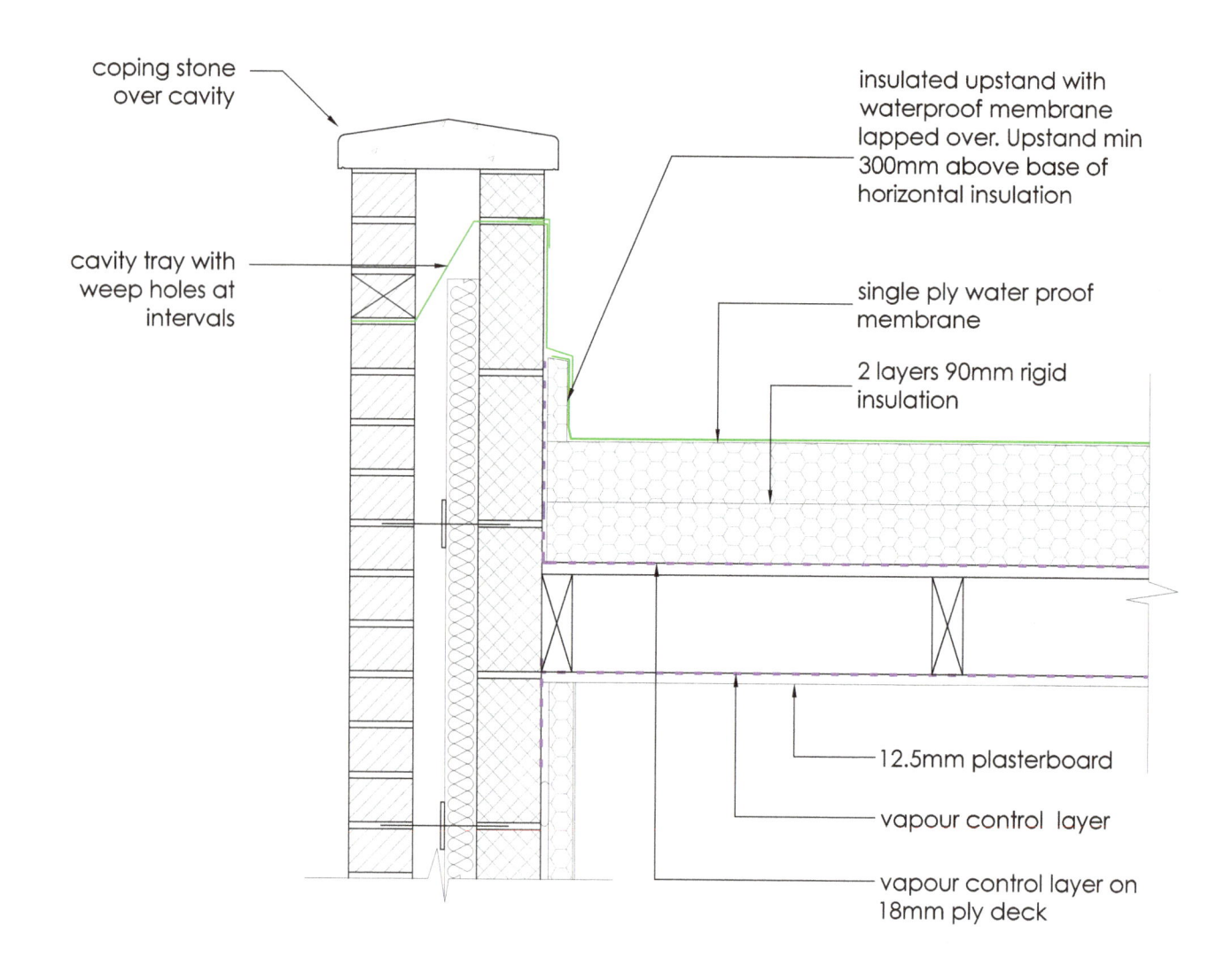

Labels (left):
- coping stone over cavity
- cavity tray with weep holes at intervals

Labels (right):
- insulated upstand with waterproof membrane lapped over. Upstand min 300mm above base of horizontal insulation
- single ply water proof membrane
- 2 layers 90mm rigid insulation
- 12.5mm plasterboard
- vapour control layer
- vapour control layer on 18mm ply deck

Detail M-R7 - External masonry cavity wall, flat roof with parapet, insulation above joists

NOTES:
U-value 0.12 Wm²K or better

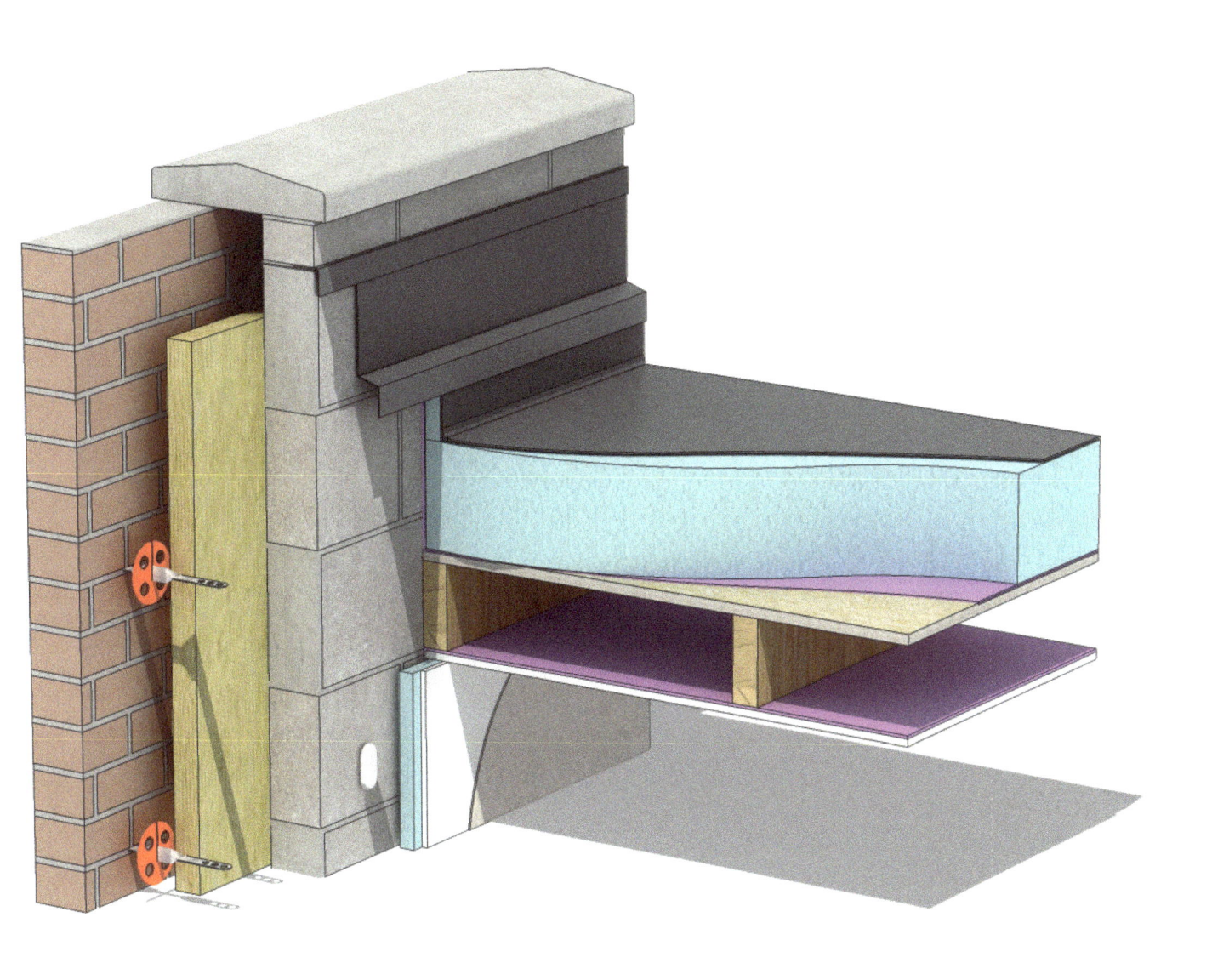

3D Detail M-R7 - External masonry cavity wall, flat roof with parapet, insulation above joists

M-R8

EXTERNAL MASONRY CAVITY WALL, FLAT ROOF WITH PARAPET INSULATION ABOVE JOISTS - ALTERNATIVE COPING DETAIL

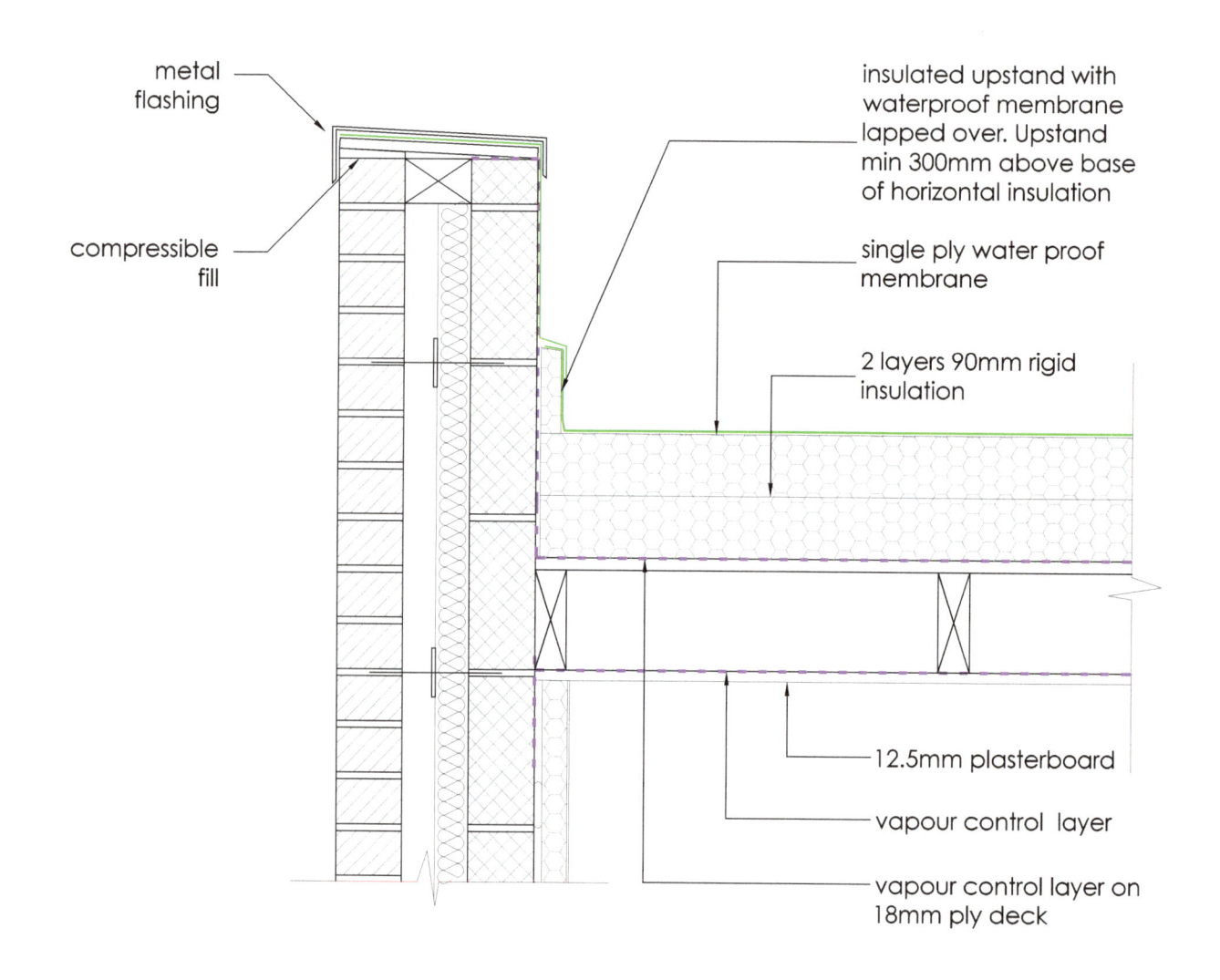

Labels on drawing:
- metal flashing
- compressible fill
- insulated upstand with waterproof membrane lapped over. Upstand min 300mm above base of horizontal insulation
- single ply water proof membrane
- 2 layers 90mm rigid insulation
- 12.5mm plasterboard
- vapour control layer
- vapour control layer on 18mm ply deck

Detail M-R8 - External masonry cavity wall, flat roof with parapet, insulation above joists - alternatvie coping detail

NOTES:
U-value 0.12 Wm²K or better

SECTION 5 - MASONRY CONSTRUCTION

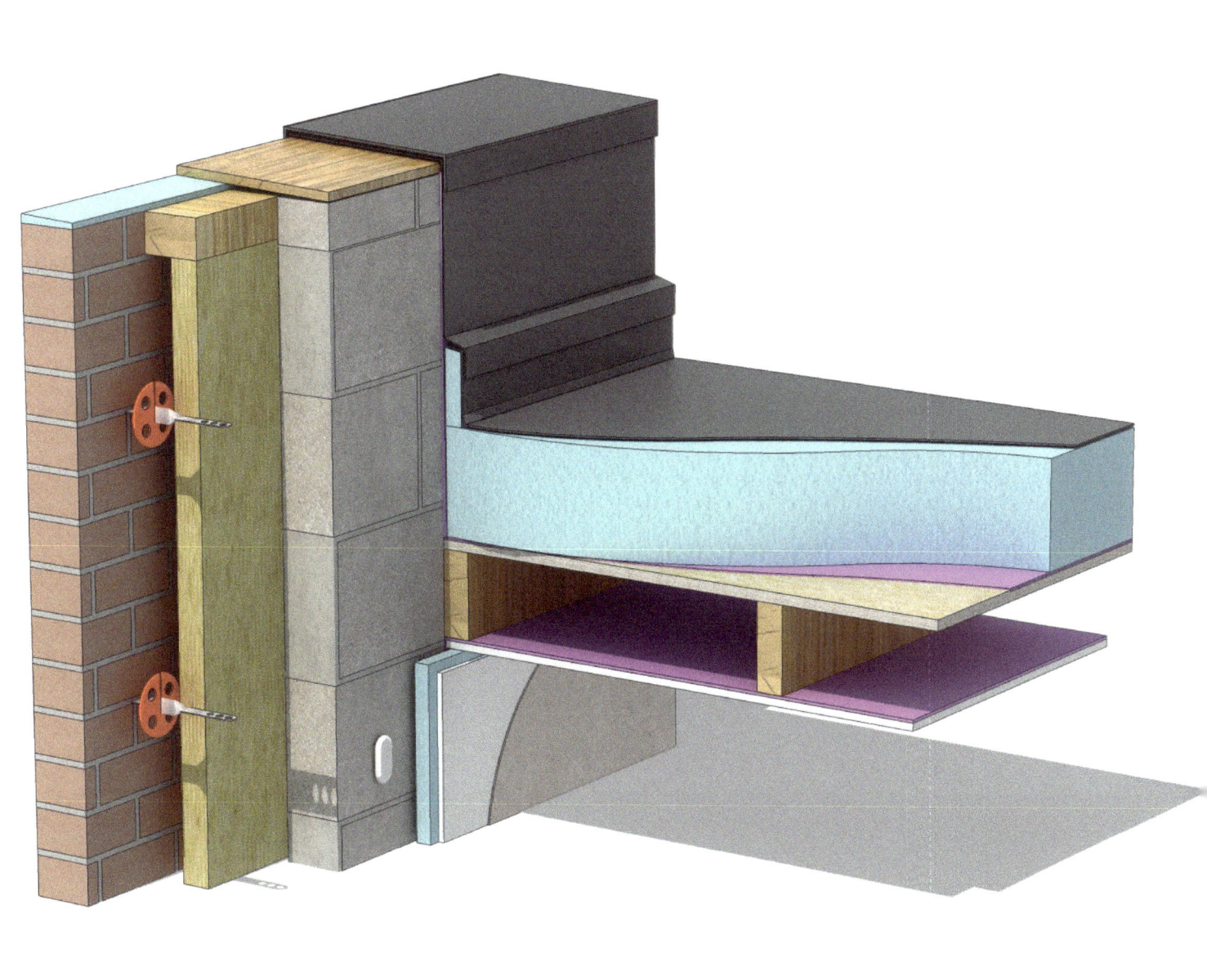

3D Detail M-R8 - External masonry cavity wall, flat roof with parapet, insulation above joists - alternative coping detail

M-R9

ROOF LIGHT DETAIL - WARM ROOF, INSULATION BETWEEN AND UNDER RAFTERS

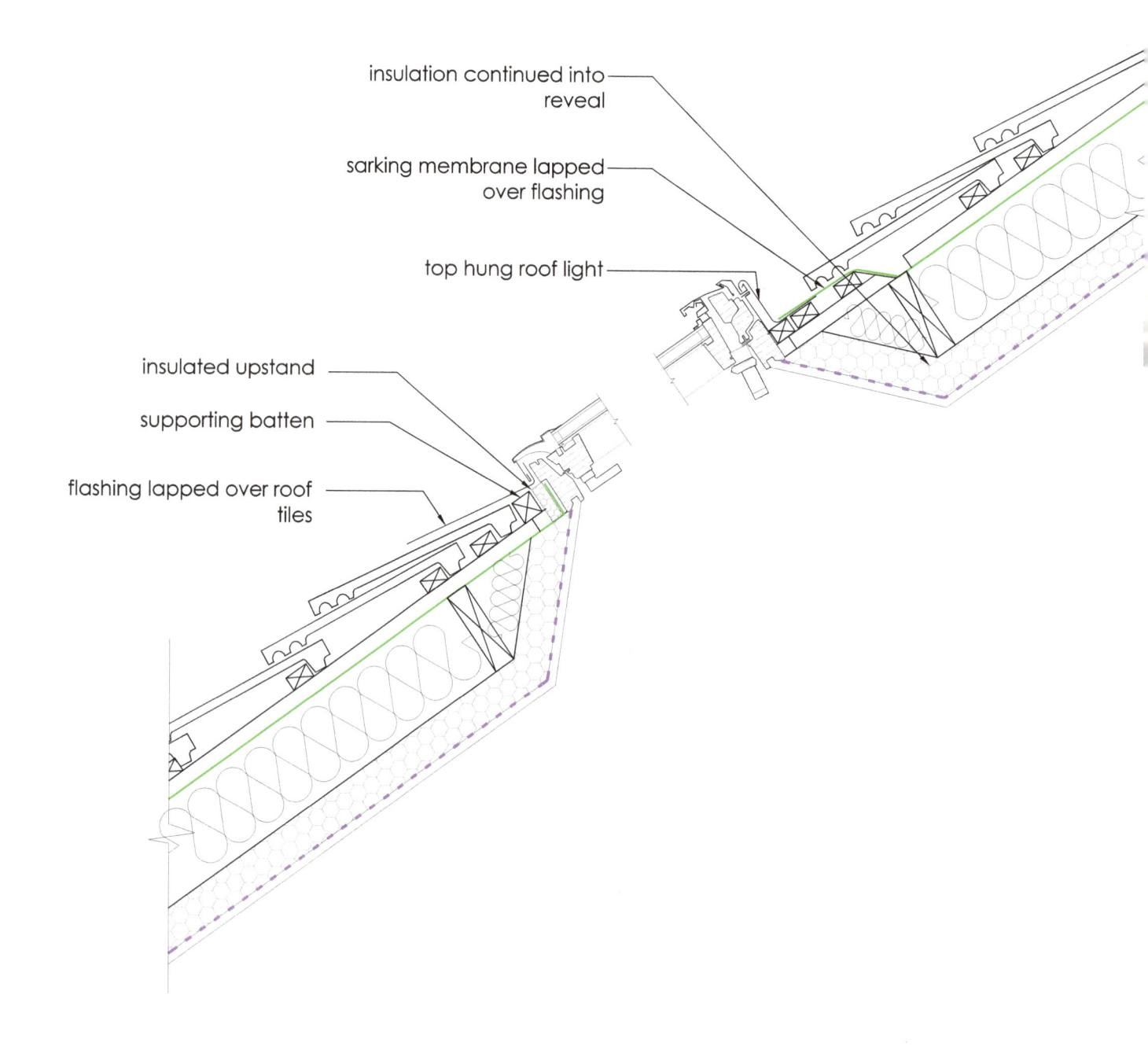

Labels:
- insulation continued into reveal
- sarking membrane lapped over flashing
- top hung roof light
- insulated upstand
- supporting batten
- flashing lapped over roof tiles

Detail M-R9 - Roof light detail, warm roof, insulation between and under rafters

NOTES:

U-value 0.12 Wm²K or better
Any ventilation according to manufacturers instructions

SECTION 5 - MASONRY CONSTRUCTION

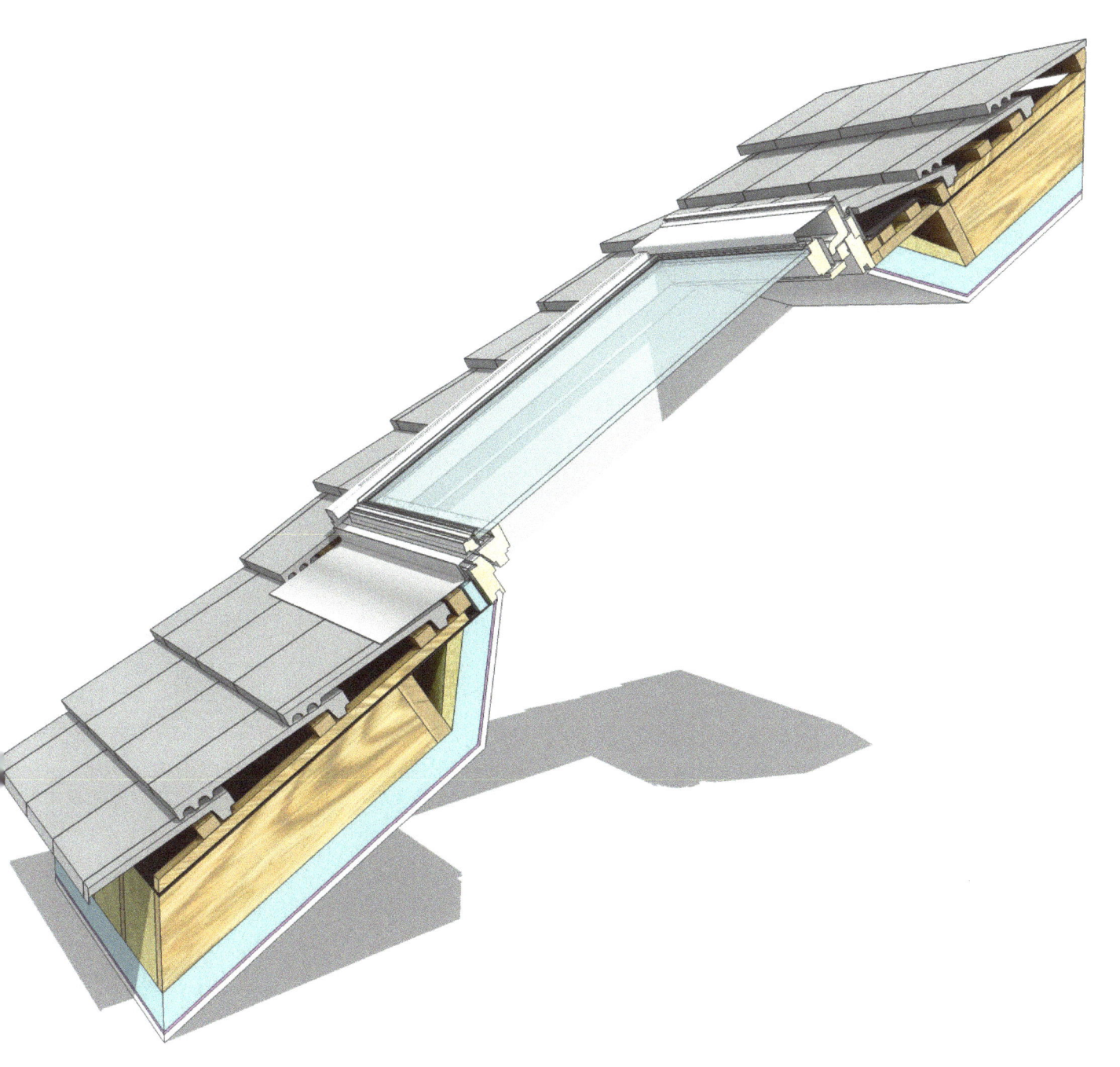

3D Detail M-R9 - Roof light detail, warm roof, insulation between and under rafters

M-R10

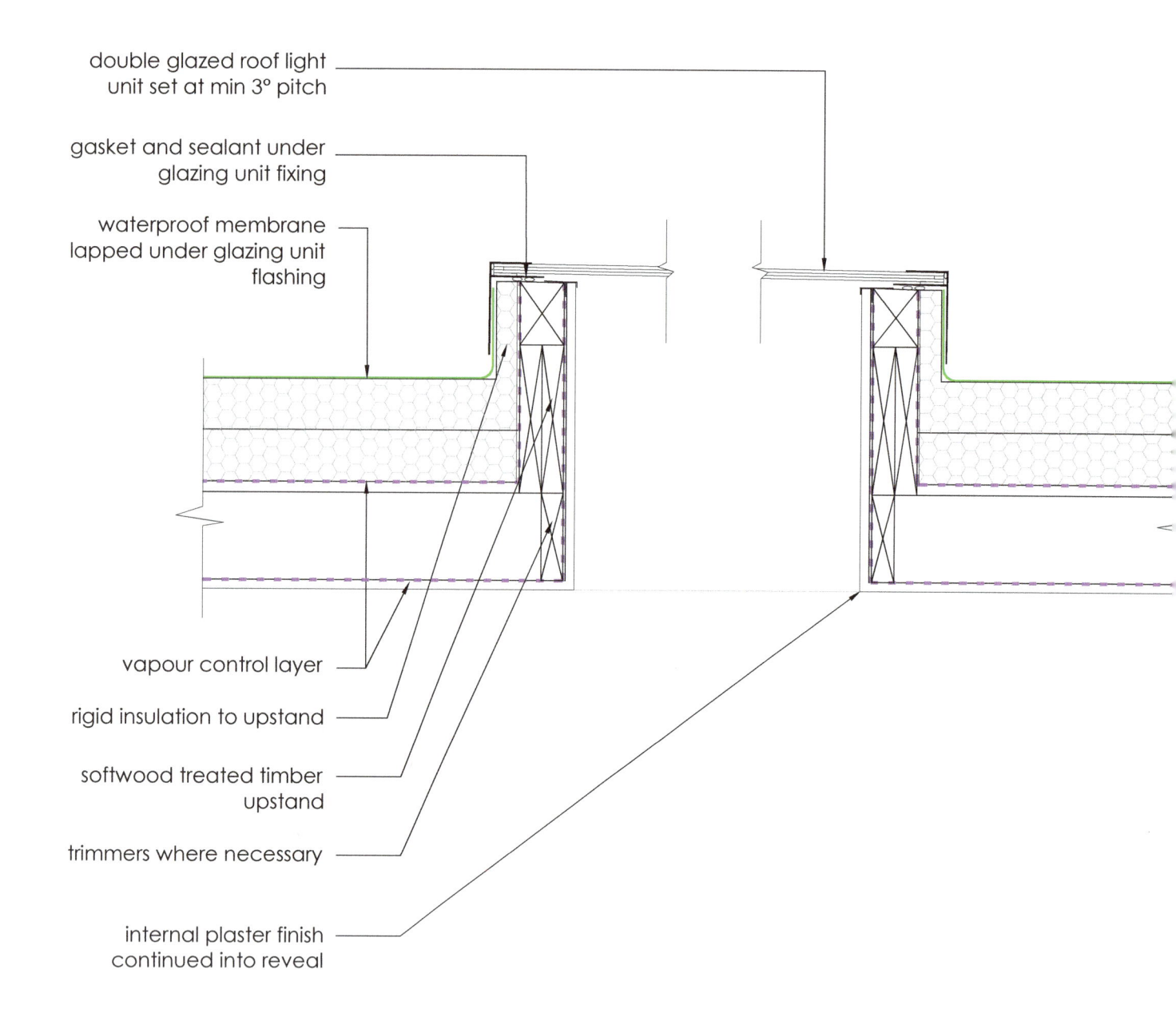

FLAT ROOF - ROOF LIGHT DETAIL, INSULATION ABOVE ROOF DECK

Labels:
- double glazed roof light unit set at min 3° pitch
- gasket and sealant under glazing unit fixing
- waterproof membrane lapped under glazing unit flashing
- vapour control layer
- rigid insulation to upstand
- softwood treated timber upstand
- trimmers where necessary
- internal plaster finish continued into reveal

Detail M-R10 - Flat roof, roof light detail, insulation above roof deck

NOTES:
U-value 0.12 Wm²K or better

SECTION 5 - MASONRY CONSTRUCTION

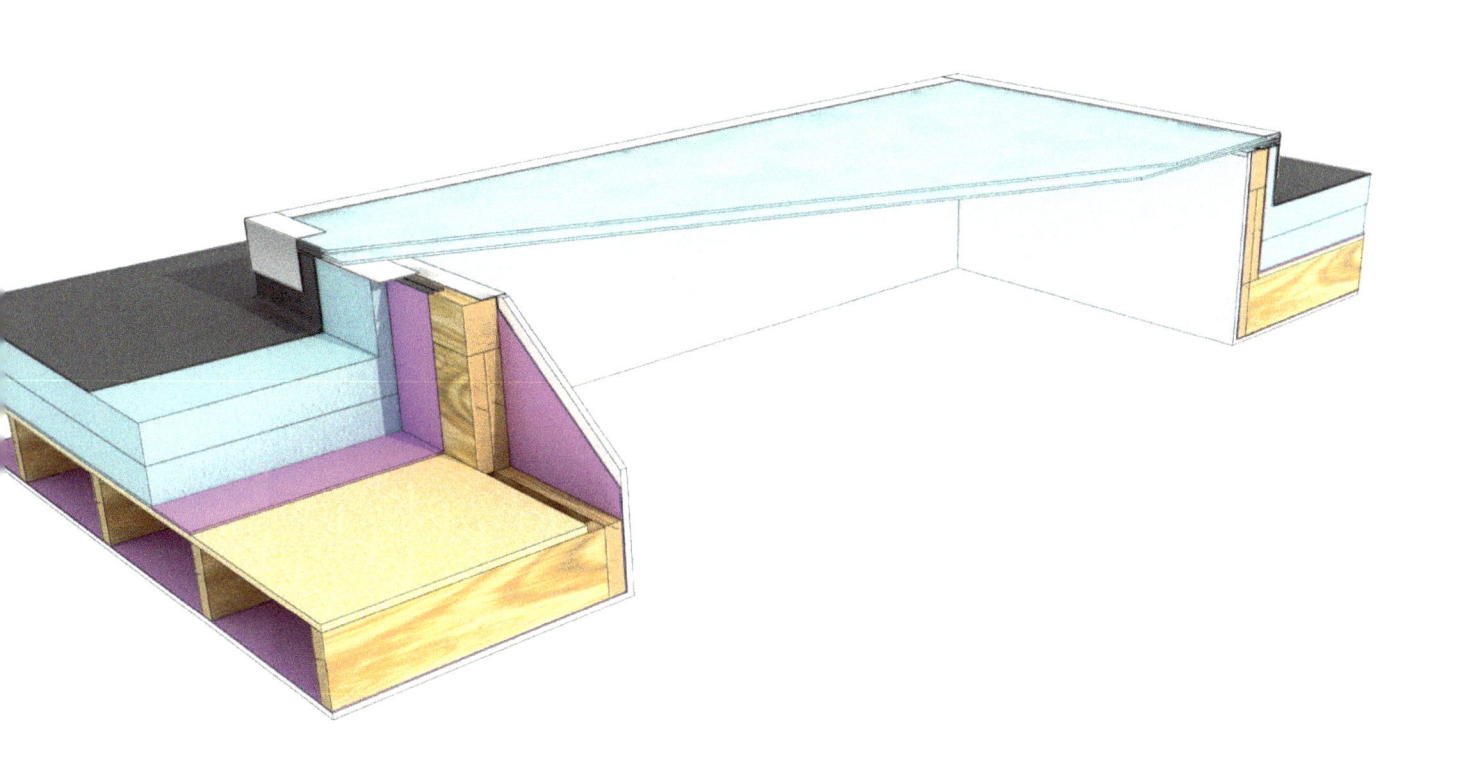

3D Detail M-R10 - Flat roof - Roof light detail, insulation above roof deck

M-R11

RIDGE DETAIL, BEDDED RIDGE, UNVENTED

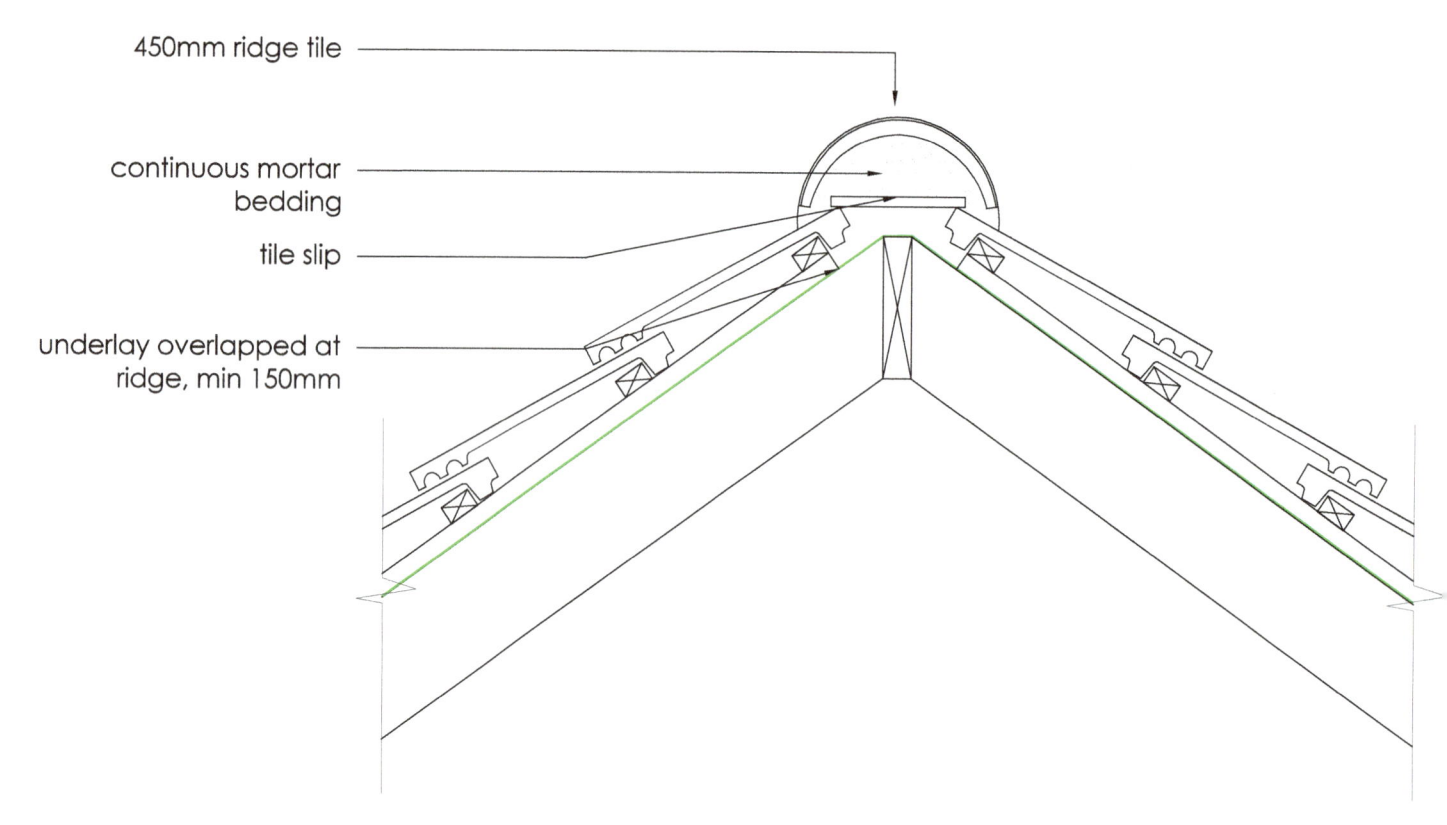

- 450mm ridge tile
- continuous mortar bedding
- tile slip
- underlay overlapped at ridge, min 150mm

Detail M-R11 - Ridge detail, bedded ridge, unvented

SECTION 5 - MASONRY CONSTRUCTION

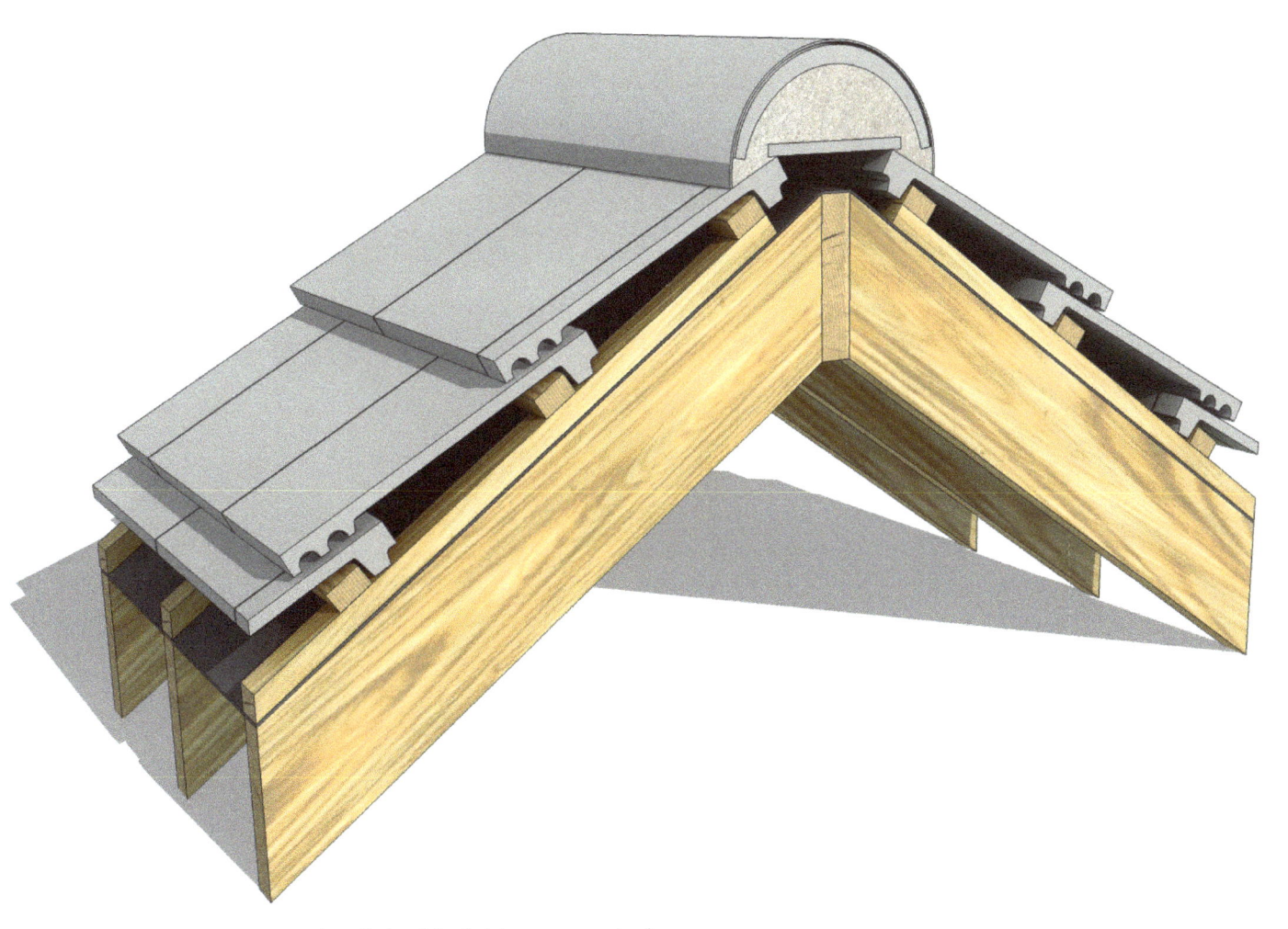

3D Detail M-R11 - Ridge detail, bedded ridge, unvented

M-R12
RIDGE DETAIL, VENTILATED

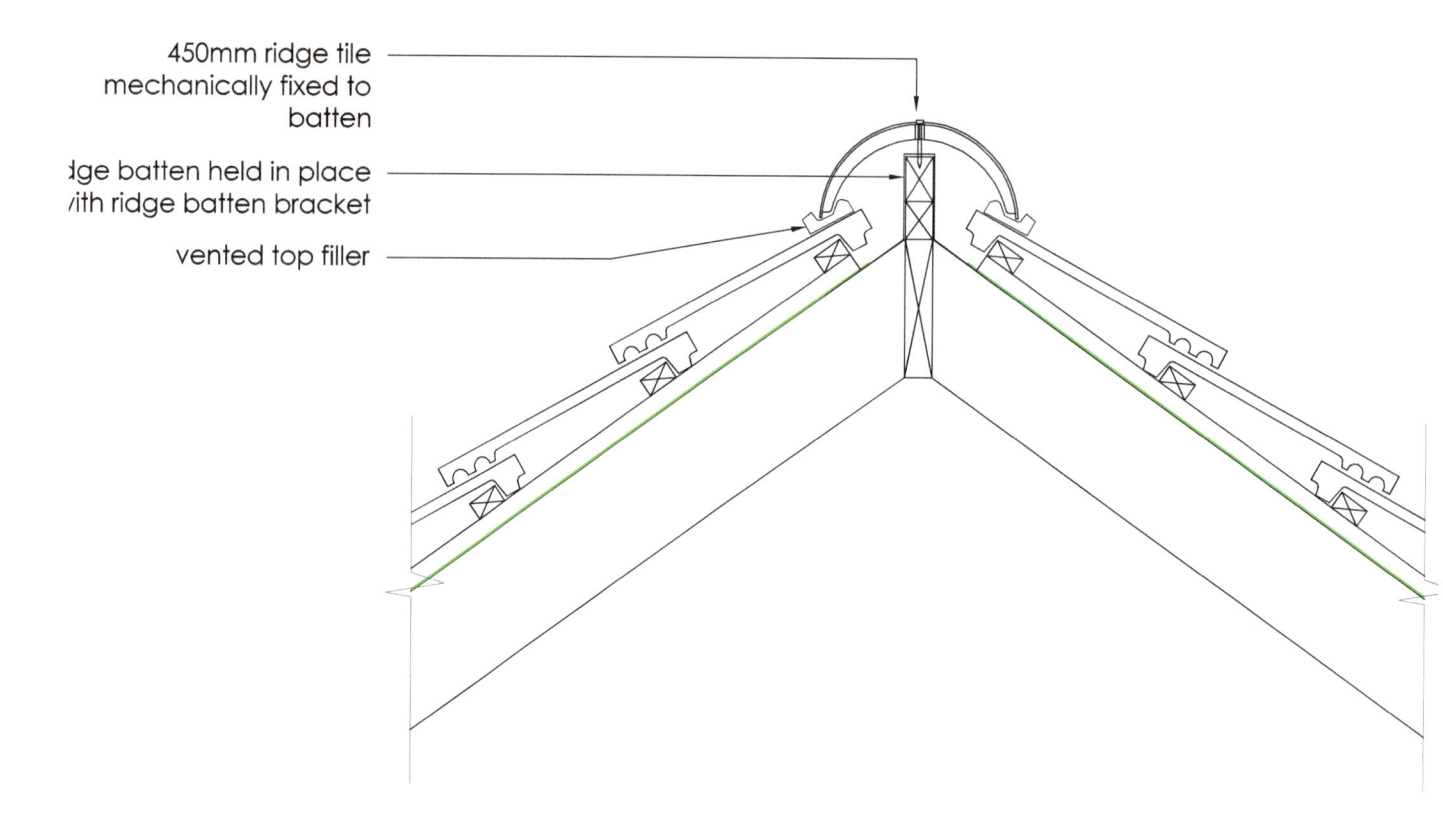

- 450mm ridge tile mechanically fixed to batten
- Ridge batten held in place with ridge batten bracket
- vented top filler

Detail M-R12 - Ridge detail, ventilated

SECTION 5 - MASONRY CONSTRUCTION

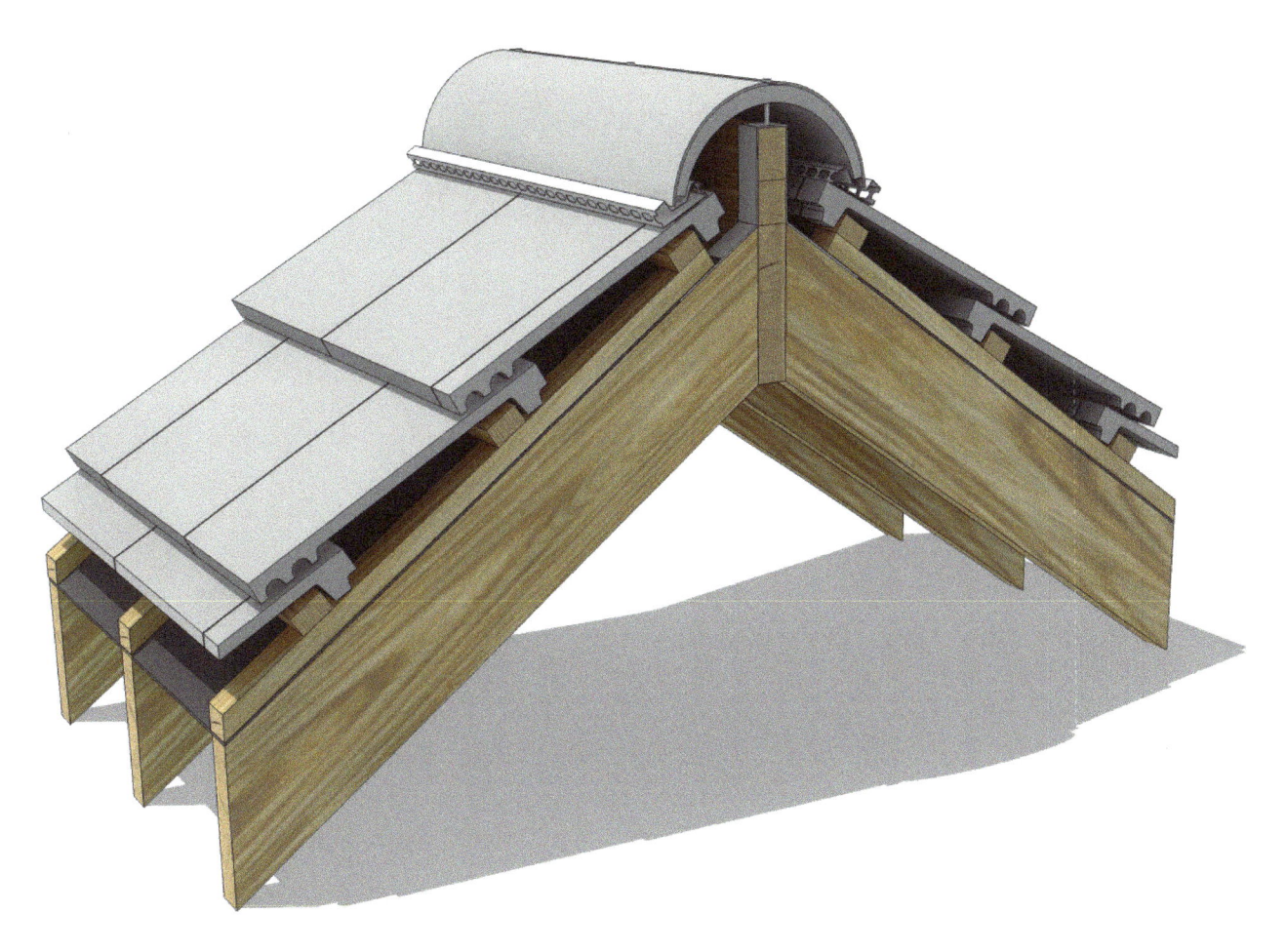

3D Detail M-R12 - Ridge detail, ventilated

M-R13
VALLEY DETAIL, VENTILATED ROOF SPACE

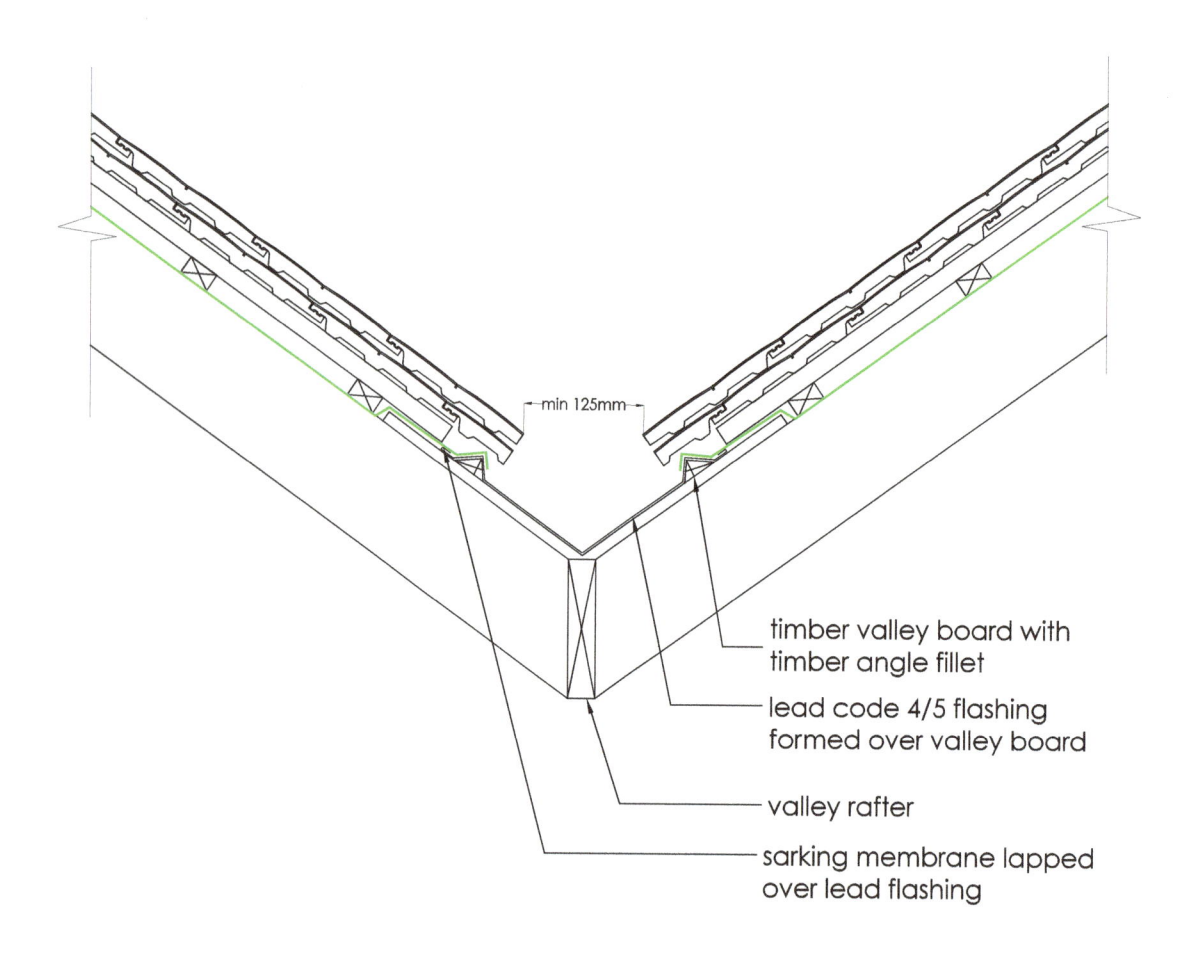

- min 125mm
- timber valley board with timber angle fillet
- lead code 4/5 flashing formed over valley board
- valley rafter
- sarking membrane lapped over lead flashing

Detail M-R13 - Valley detail, ventilated roof space

NOTES:
Alternative valley could consist of valley tiles instead of lead, or GRP (glass reinforced plastic) pre fabricated trough

SECTION 5 - MASONRY CONSTRUCTION

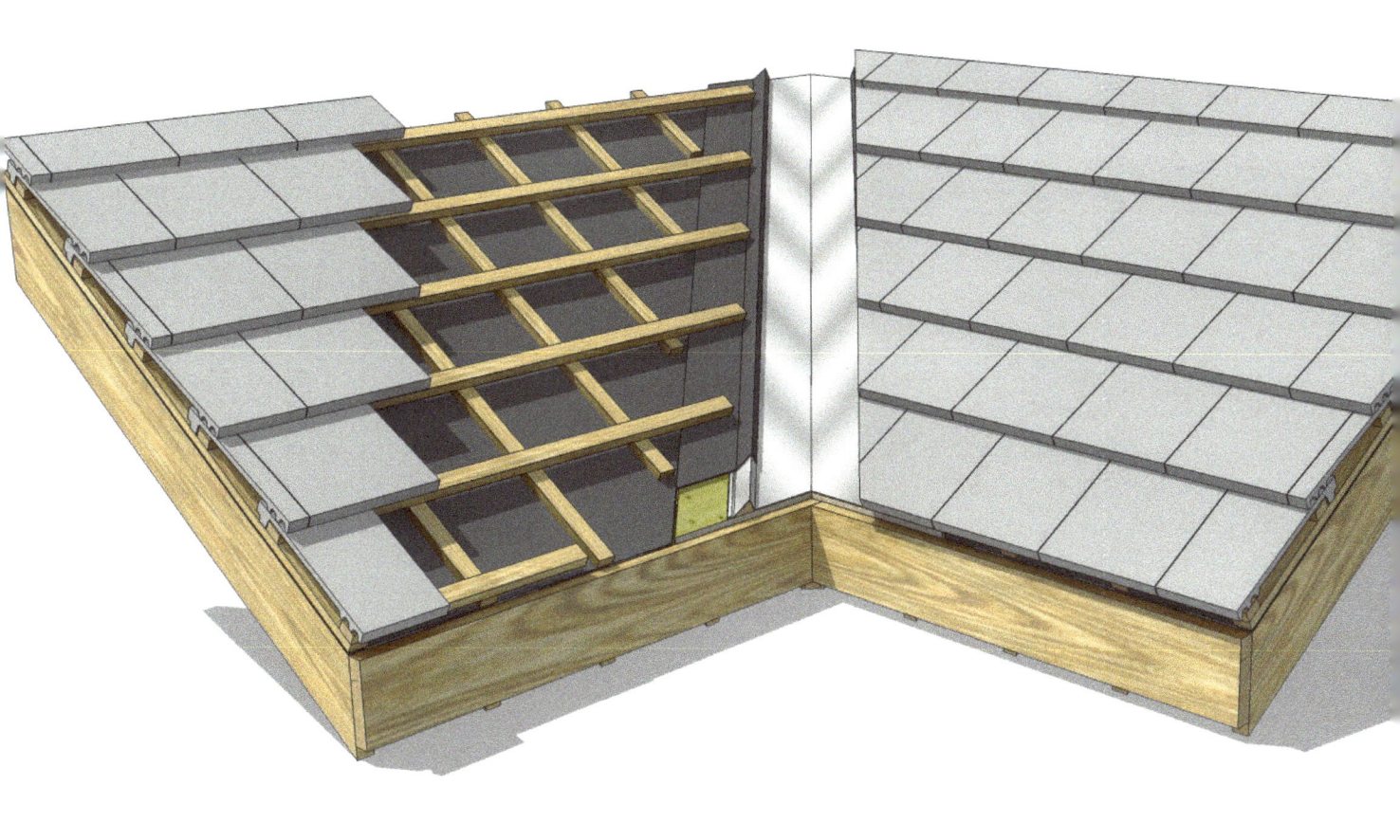

3D Detail M-R13 - Valley detail, ventilated roof space

NOTES ON THE REGS

The following information is a partial list of requirements from the **Building Regulations Approved Documents** - for full and detailed explanations and requirements please consult the full publications.

GENERAL REQUIREMENTS - ROOFS

The building shall be constructed so that the combined dead, imposed and wind loads are sustained and transmitted by it to the ground.

(Approved Doc A1)

Precautions against moisture
The roof of the building shall be resistant to the penetration of moisture from rain or snow to the inside of the building.
All floors next to the ground, walls and roof shall not be damaged by moisture from the ground, rain or snow and shall not carry that moisture to any part of the building that it would damage.

(Approved Doc C2)

Rainwater
Rainwater from roofs shall be carried away from the surface either by a drainage system or by other means.
The rainwater drainage system shall carry the flow of rainwater form the roof to an outfall.

(Approved Doc H3)

Fire precautions
As a fire precaution, all materials used for internal linings of a building should have a low rate of surface flame spread and (in some cases) a low rate of heat release.

(Approved Doc B2)

External fire spread
The roof shall be constructed so that the risk of spread of flame and fire penetration from an external fire source is restricted.
The risk of a fire spreading from the building to a building beyond the boundary should be limited.

Internal fire spread
Ideally the building should be subdivided by elements of fire resisting construction into compartments.

All openings in fire separating elements shall be suitably protected in order to maintain the integrity of the continuity of the fire separation.
Any hidden voids in the construction shall be sealed and sub-divided to inhibit the unseen spread of fire and products of combustion, in order to reduce the risk of structural failure, and the spread of fire.

(Approved Doc B3)

Ventilation
There shall be adequate means of ventilation provided for people in the building.

(Approved Doc F)

Conservation of fuel and power
Reasonable provision shall be made for the conservation of fuel and power in buildings by:
- limiting heat gains and losses through thermal elements and other parts of the building fabric,
- from pipes ducts and vessels used for space heating, space cooling and hot water services.
- providing fixed building services which are energy efficient and have effective controls and are commissioned by testing and adjusting as necessary to ensure they use no more fuel and power than is reasonable in the circumstances.

(Approved Doc L)

TIMBER FRAME
CONSTRUCTION

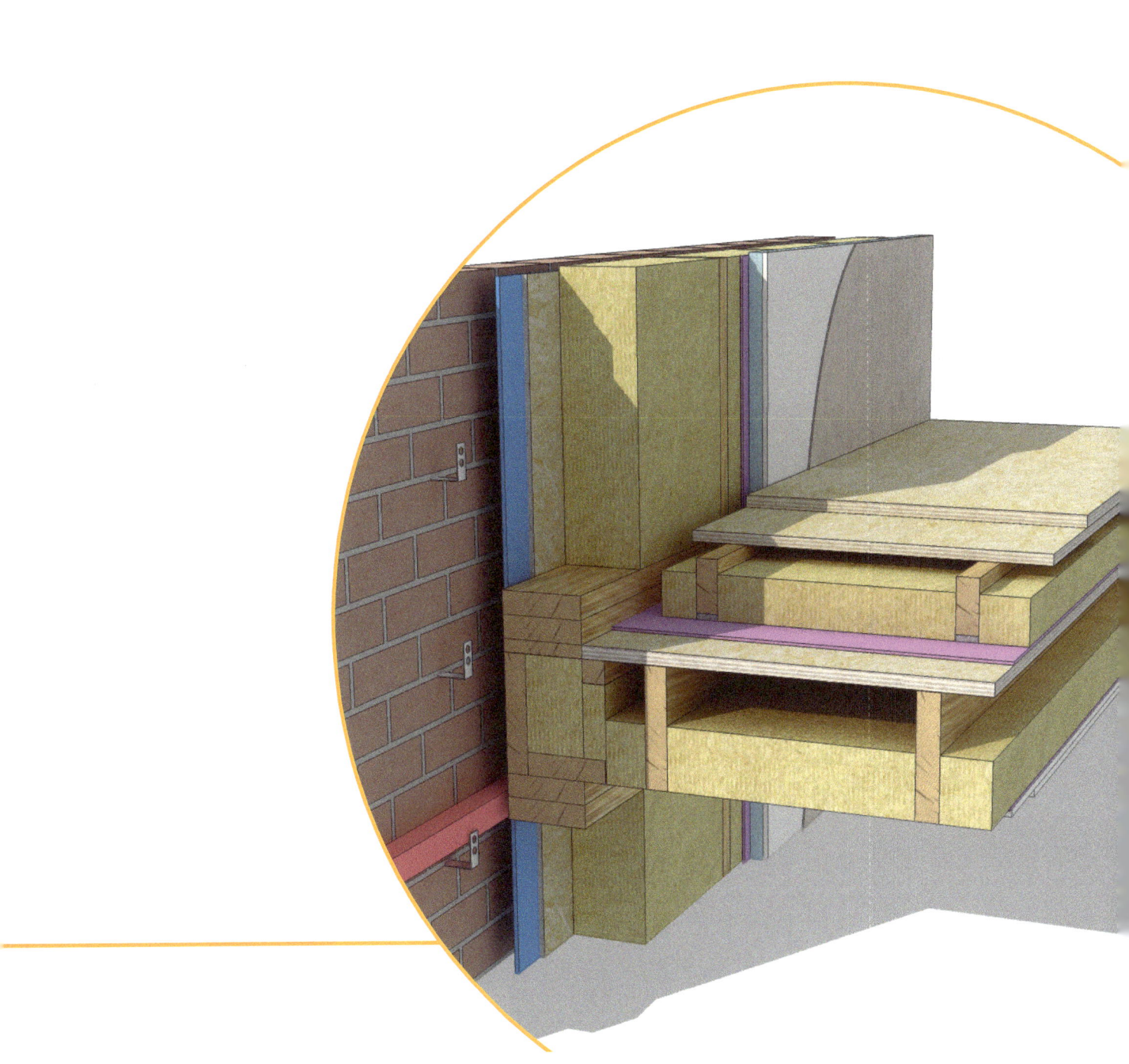

INTRODUCTION

Timber frame construction is fast, clean and dry. Timber frame construction has sufficient stability to support the floors and roof of small buildings and lends itself well to residential construction. Timber frame houses can be constructed quickly. Off site pre-fabrication methods allow for the erection of the majority of house in one day, with roof and finishes completed soon after. (Off site prefabrication will be explored in a future chapter.) Alternatively the timber frame can be built by carpenters on site.

The structure of a timber frame system must be designed by a structural engineer to ensure structural stability and compliance with the Building Regulations.

FOUNDATIONS

Foundations for a timber frame are designed as discussed in Section 2 - Foundations, and depend on site conditions, loading and compliance with the Building Regulations among other things.

The stability of the timber frame will depend on the foundation being a sound base onto which the frame can be built. The base of the frame, a preservative treated timber wall plate (sometimes referred to as sole plate), will be secured to the foundation or slab in order for the frame work to be constructed. The wall plate can be fixed by nailing through the timber and DPC into the structure below, however, more recently galvanised metal strips are used to fix the timber to the structure below, which avoids puncturing the DPC.

FLOORS

Both the ground and upper floors are similar in timber frame construction as they are in masonry construction.

The most common materials used for the construction of ground and upper floors tend to be concrete or timber. Required span, resistance to passage of sound, and fire resistance will often be factors to consider when deciding which material to use in floor design.

FUNCTIONAL REQUIREMENTS

The functional requirements of a floor are:
- Strength and stability
- Resistance to weather and ground moisture
- Durability
- Fire safety
- Resistance to passage of heat
- Resistance to passage of sound

TYPES OF GROUND FLOORS

Concrete Floors

There are two types of concrete floor system commonly used in residential construction; ground bearing and suspended. Ground bearing floors, where the concrete slab is supported by the ground below. Suspended concrete floors do not rely on the ground below, but instead are supported by the external walls and therefore the foundations below. In this section we will look at both types of concrete floor.

Ground Bearing Concrete Floor

The ground bearing concrete floor slab is supported by the load bearing strata below. The slab abuts but is not tied to the external foundation walls. The build up of this type of system can typically be:
- Hardcore fill to compacted to create suitable level (approx 200mm thick)
- Damp proof membrane (DPM), often laid over sand binding
- Rigid floor insulation (can be position above or below the concrete slab)
- Concrete floor cast in situ
- Floor screed if required, followed by floor finishes

There are many different options for positioning of damp proof membrane and insulation, which can be seen in the following details in this section.

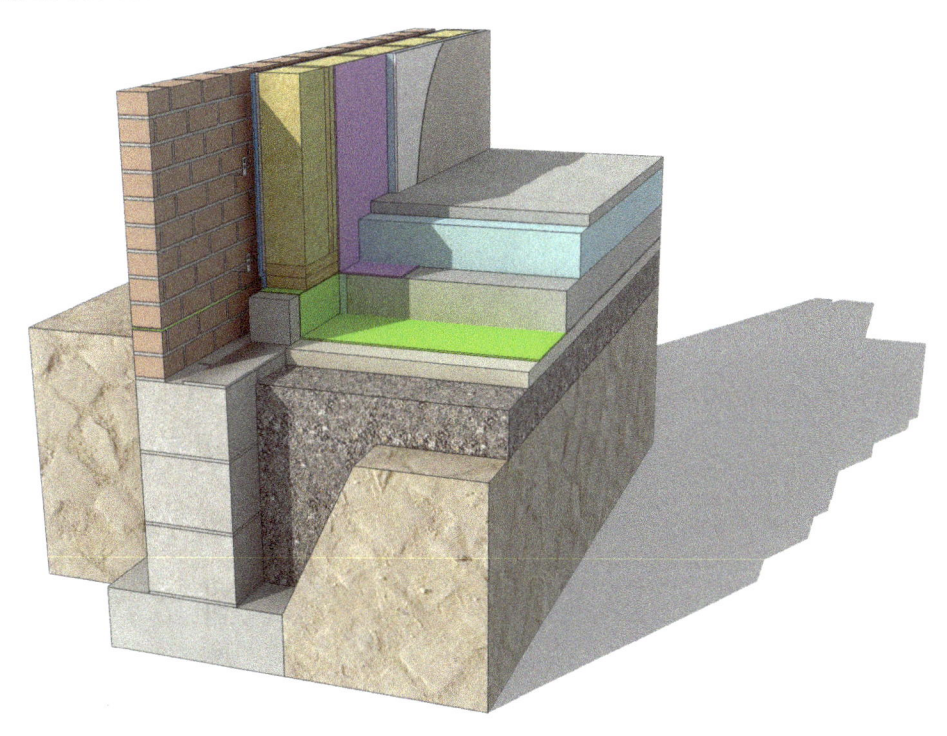

Figure 6.1 - Example of ground bearing concrete floor

Suspended Concrete Floor

Suspended concrete floors have become popular in UK house construction. They are typically used in situations such as sloping sites, the ground has poor bearing capacity, or there is likelihood of ground volume change. Suspended floors are also used when the water table is high, or when aggressive chemicals are present in the soil that may attack the concrete slab.

The ground floor is made up of suspended concrete slab or beam and block floor, supported by the external and internal load bearing walls, which transfer the loads to the foundations below. Both pre-cast concrete planks or slabs can be used, as well as cast in situ reinforced slabs along with beam and block systems.

Beam and block

These systems use concrete T beams that span between the walls, concrete infill blocks are then inserted between the beams to provide a solid base for the concrete topping or screed that is spread and levelled over the concrete units. Depth of the beams is between 130mm and 250mm and is determined by the span required, and the loads to be supported.

Timber Floors

Although timber ground floor construction used to be a popular method, today it is not as common as the concrete alternatives. A suspended timber floor is constructed as a timber platform of boards nailed across timber joists supported on sleeper walls, and the external and internal load bearing walls surrounding them.

Ventilation must be provided throughout the underfloor void and through any sleeper walls with cross ventilation. Due to airtightness, acoustic and sometimes structural requirements of the Building Regulations, joist ends tend to be supported by joist hangers rather than being built into external or sleeper walls.

The floor is insulated in the form of rigid insulation between joists, or quilt between joists supported by netting. Floorboards are fixed over the floor joists and insulation, usually in the form of plywood, chipboard or OSB to required structural performance. These boards are then applied with a floor finish, such as carpet, vinyl and so on.

UPPER FLOORS

Timber Upper Floors

In timber frame construction timber is the material of choice for upper floor construction.

Upper floor construction tends to consist of a series of timber joists or beams covered with timber floorboards, or more commonly sheets of chipboard. The size of the joists depend on the span and expected loading. The head of the ground floor wall frames provide support of the floor joists on top of which the upper floor wall frame is fixed.

In order to prevent twisting or warping in the joists, it is sometimes common to find a line of strutting fixed at right angles to the joists. This strutting can reduce bounce in the floor.

More recent additions to timber floor construction are the timber I beams or metal web joists. These engineered joists can span greater distances than traditional timber cut joists and reduce the requirement of internal load bearing walls. The web joists also have the added benefit of not requiring notching or drilling for pipes and cables as they already have voids within the joist.

The Building Regulations require a minimum performance standard of acoustic insulation for floors to bedrooms, bathrooms and other rooms containing a WC. Likewise, upper floors over an unheated area of the dwelling, such as a garage, require the same insulation standard as that of a ground floor.

Figure 6.2 - Examples of I beams and web joists

WALLS

The main function of an external wall is to provide shelter against the weather and fluctuations of outside temperature. The wall requires sufficient strength to support loads from upper floors and the roof.

FUNCTIONAL REQUIREMENTS

The functional requirements of the external wall are:
- Strength and stability
- Resistance to weather and ground moisture
- Durability
- Fire safety
- Resistance to the passage of heat
- Acoustic control
- Security
- Aesthetics

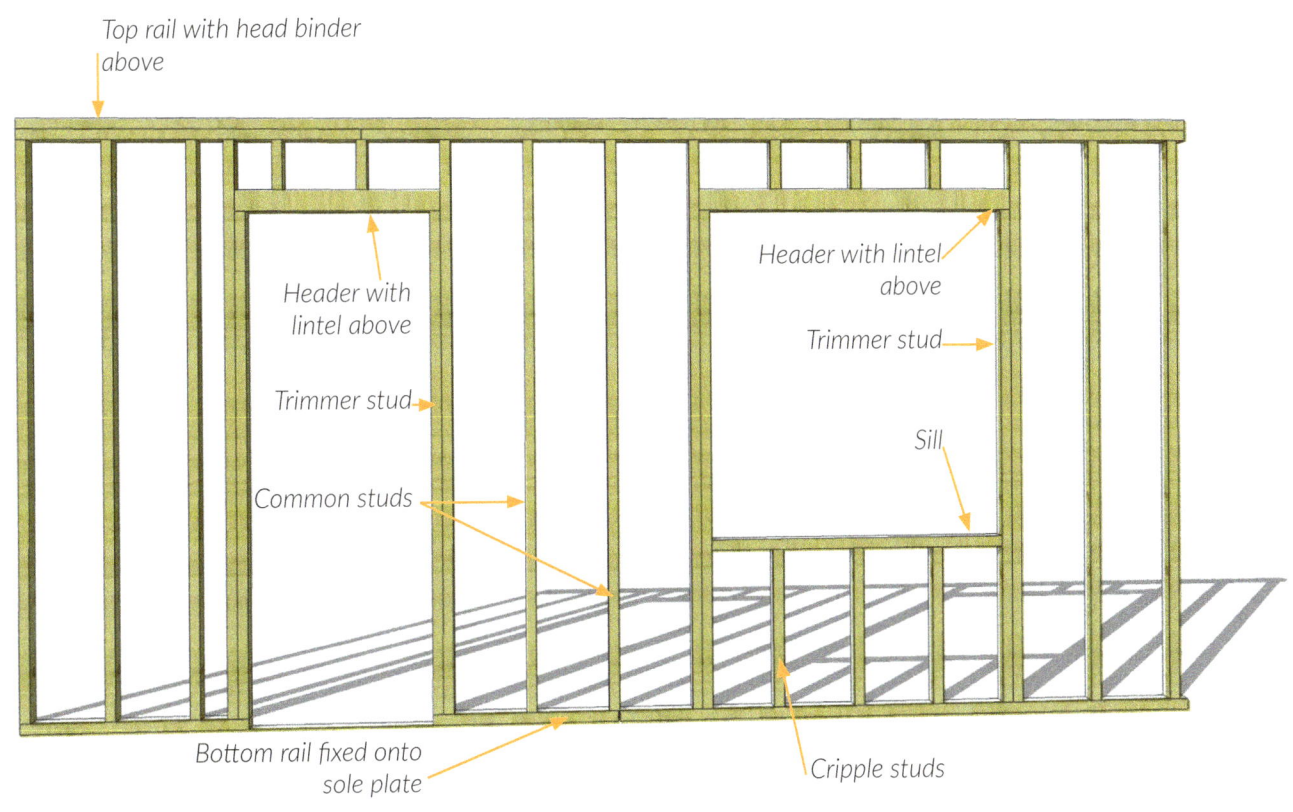

Figure 6.3 - Openings in a stud wall

A typical timber frame wall consists of the internal load bearing structure of vertical timber studwork, nailed to top and bottom timber plates. The outside of the studding is usually finished with OSB or plywood. This is known as sheathing which stiffens the frame.

The internal face of the studs are finished with a lining of plasterboard. Insulation is usually inserted between the studs, but additional insulation can be added to both the outside or inside faces of the studs. A cladding is then applied to the outer face of the timber frame, which can be timber boarding, tiles, brickwork and many other options.

Traditionally timber frame walls were clad with timber weatherboarding, nailed to the frame. Although we do still see this form of cladding, the variety and options for timber frame cladding systems has increased significantly.

BREATHER MEMBRANE

Cladding systems usually protect against some water penetration, however it is good practice to install a breather membrane onto the outer face of the sheathing, behind the cladding. This acts as a second line of defence against the weather, specifically driving rain, wind and so on. The breather membrane acts as a barrier to water and at the same time allows any moisture vapour to be released from inside the structure. The breather membrane contributes to air tightness, and reduces uncontrolled ventilation heat loss.

INSULATING THE WALL

Insulation can be fixed between the vertical studs of the wall, or on the inside or outside of the framing. The disadvantage of the fixing the insulation between the studs is that there will be a small degree of thermal bridging through the studs, and sometimes wasteful cutting to fit the insulation between the stud work.

Fixing the insulation to the outside of the frame removes the necessity to cut the insulation boards and reduces the thermal bridging. However, some cladding finishes need to be fixed to battens, with are nailed through the insulation into the studs beyond.

Internal insulation is usually in the form of an insulated plasterboard.

With increasing requirements for high insulation standards, we often see a combination of insulation positions to achieve the required U-value of the wall, as insulating between the studs alone can be insufficient.

FIRE SAFETY

The Building Regulations Approved Document Part B sets out the requirements for structural resistance to fire. A timber framed wall covered with plasterboard internally satisfies the requirement for houses of up to two storeys. It is important to study the requirements of the document in detail, to establish the needs of each specific project.

The passage of fire through connecting voids in timber frame construction is prevented by using cavity barriers between connecting external and party walls. The addition of edge seals will reduce the passage of heat and also improve air tightness. Cavity barriers are required around all external openings, on the party wall line and at the top of all external walls, i.e. eaves and verges.

RESISTANCE TO PASSAGE OF SOUND

Timber frames are generally of small mass and therefore offer little resistance to the passage of sound. The insulation that is required by the Building Regulations for the conservation of heat will provide some reduction to airborne sound. In addition, an external cladding of brickwork will also help with reducing external noise. Acoustic plasterboard can also be specified in areas where increase sound protection is required.

VAPOUR CONTROL LAYER

Moisture laden air on the inside of a building can pass through the structure by moisture vapour pressure and condense to water on the cold side of the insulation. This condensation can cause damage to the wall assembly, so it is important to install a vapour check, or vapour control layer on the warm side of the insulation. This layer stops vapour passing through into the wall assembly. Vapour control layers must be lapped and have a minimum number of perforations of sockets, pipes and switches.

Some insulation, particularly closed cell insulating materials such as XPS, in the form of rigid bards are impermeable to moisture vapour and can themselves act as a vapour barrier. However, installation is important, and must be carried out in accordance with manufacturers instructions.

OPENINGS

Openings in timber frame wall panels require a timber lintel directly below the top rail at the head of the opening. Softwood timber lintels are usually sufficient for the majority of domestic loads and spans. Additional framing is often required at an opening. Vertical cripple studs can be placed alongside the opening to provide additional support to the lintel above.

PARTY WALLS

If the house is part of a terrace or semi detached it will have a party wall. This party wall must provide fire protection, along with adequate resistance to airborne sound. The requirements of the Building Regulations can be achieved by using two independent timber frame panels, with a gap between them of 50mm. Two layers of plasterboard is then fixed to the outer face of the frames. Insulating quilt is fitted within the cavity or between the studs in one of the panels to provide the sound insulation.

ROOFS

There are no specific differences in the roof construction of a timber framed structure compared to other types of construction. However, it is important to ensure that any additional point loads from the roof are suitably supported by additional studs or posts in the timber frame below.

For general information on roof construction refer to the masonry section.

FOUNDATION & FLOOR DETAILS

T-G1

TIMBER FRAME WALL, GROUND BEARING CONCRETE SLAB, INSULATION BELOW SLAB

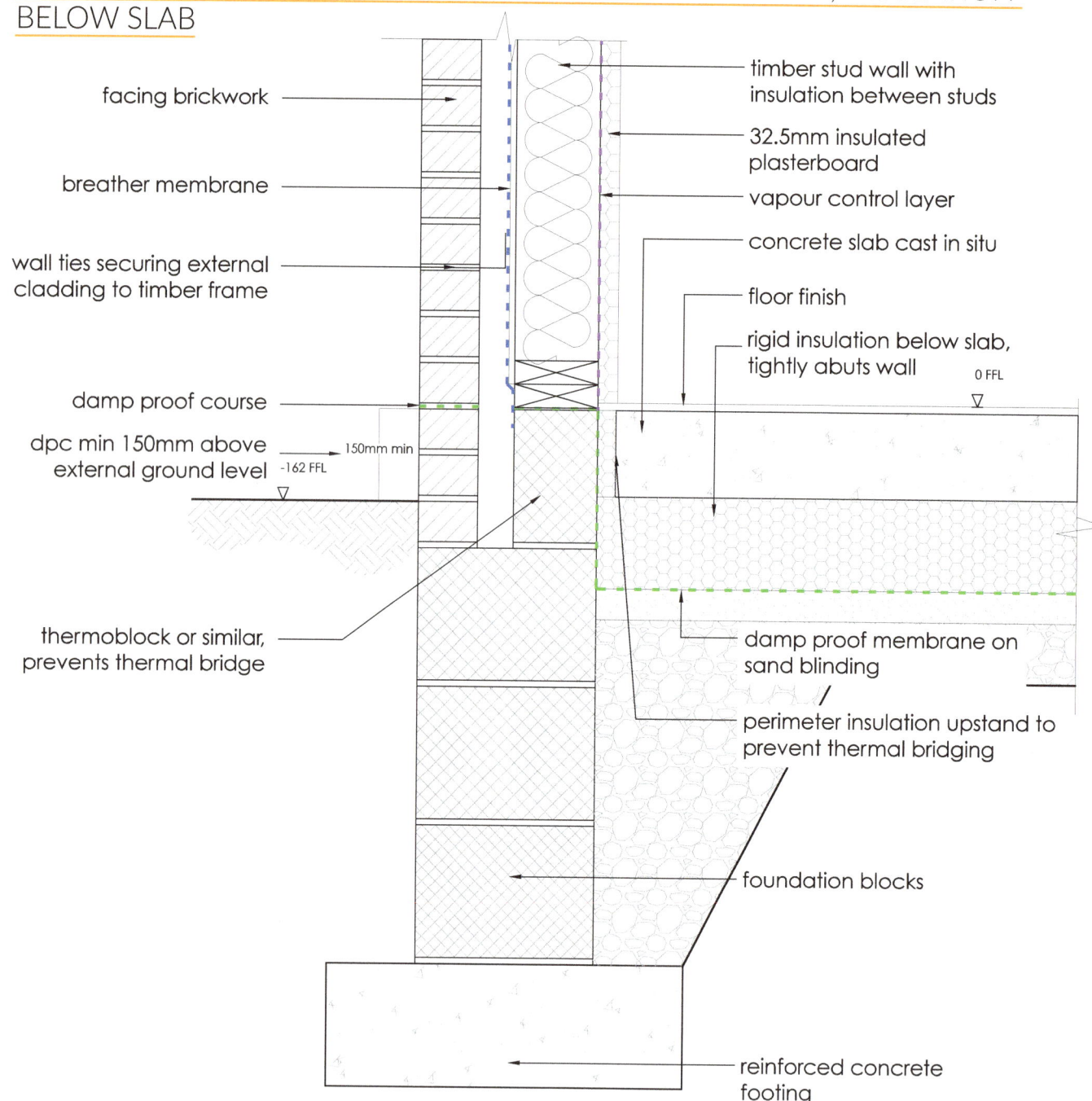

Labels (left side):
- facing brickwork
- breather membrane
- wall ties securing external cladding to timber frame
- damp proof course
- dpc min 150mm above external ground level — 150mm min, -162 FFL
- thermoblock or similar, prevents thermal bridge

Labels (right side):
- timber stud wall with insulation between studs
- 32.5mm insulated plasterboard
- vapour control layer
- concrete slab cast in situ
- floor finish
- rigid insulation below slab, tightly abuts wall — 0 FFL
- damp proof membrane on sand blinding
- perimeter insulation upstand to prevent thermal bridging
- foundation blocks
- reinforced concrete footing

Detail T-G1 - Timber frame wall, ground bearing concrete slab, insulation below slab

NOTES:

U-value 0.13 Wm²K or better

Perimeter strip of insulation abuts concrete slab and blockwork wall. Potential thermal bridge area at blockwork below timber frame - specify Thermoblock or similar. A thermoblock is a highly insulated load bearing block that helps to eliminate cold bridging at junctions.

Vapour control/separation layer over insulation to prevent interstitial condensation and seeping of concrete into insulation board cracks - check with insulation manufacturer.

SECTION 6 - TIMBER FRAME

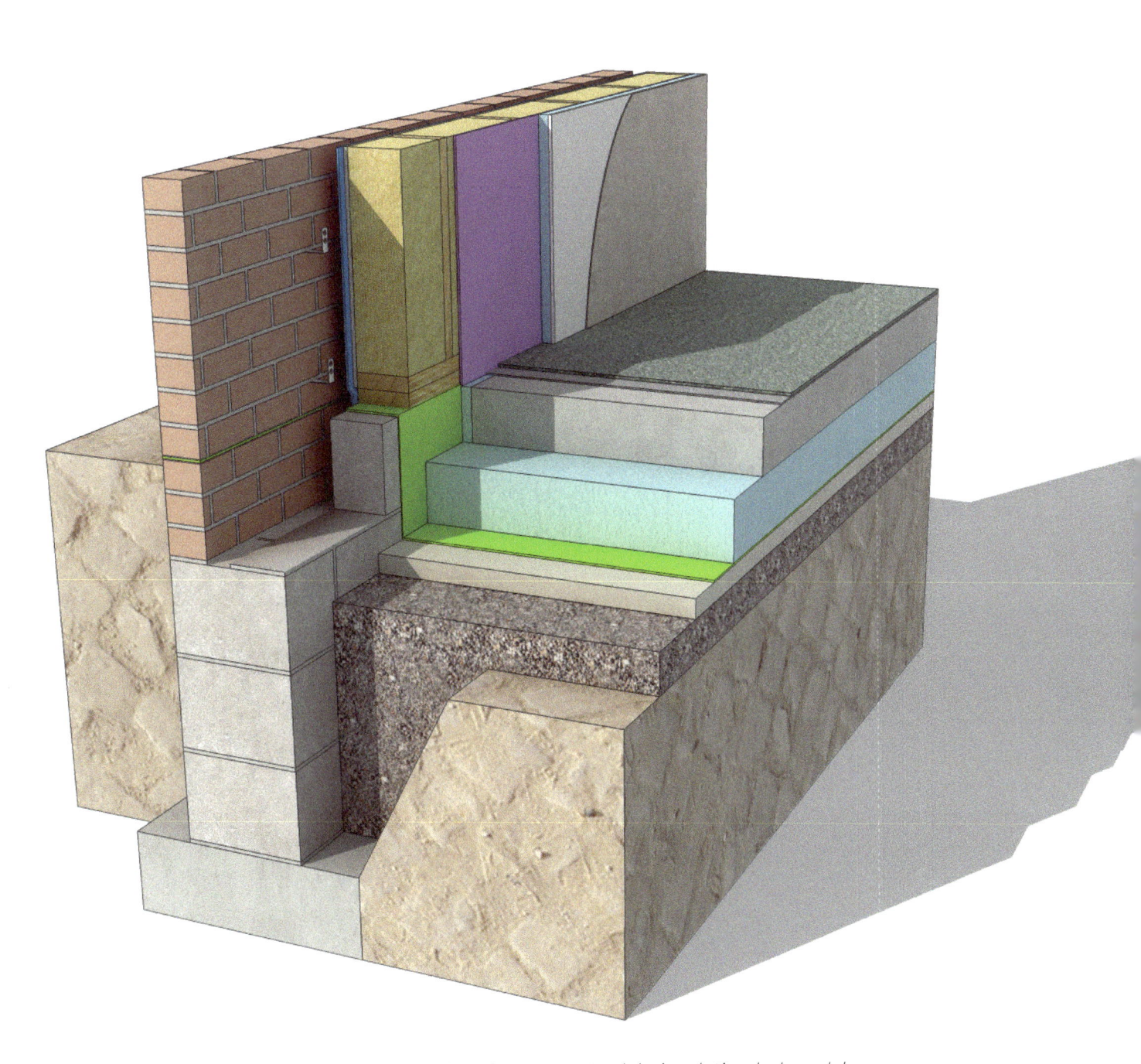

3D Detail T-G1 - Timber frame wall, ground bearing concrete slab, insulation below slab

T-G2

TIMBER FRAME WALL, GROUND BEARING CONCRETE SLAB, INSULATION ABOVE SLAB

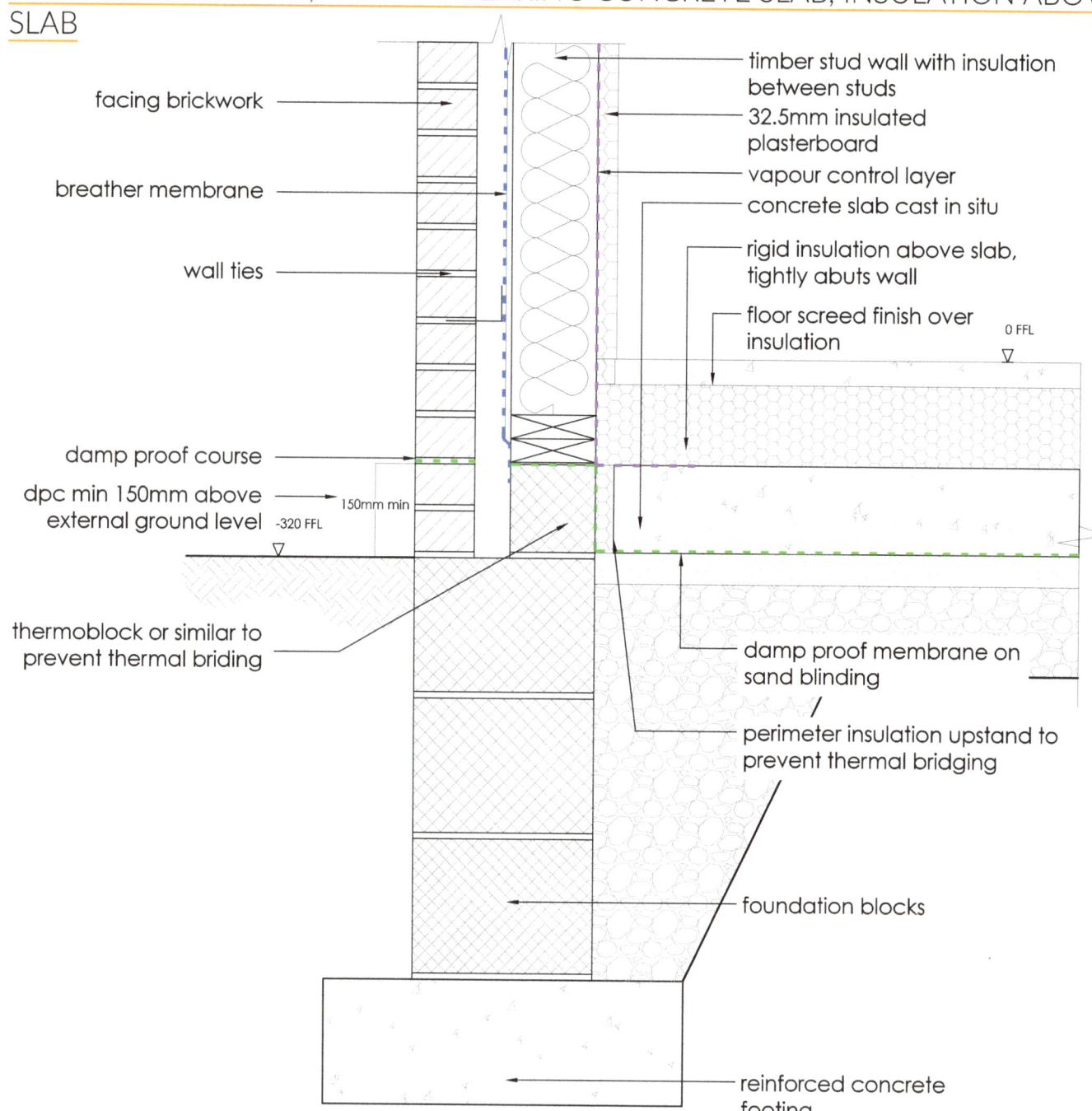

Labels (on drawing):
- facing brickwork
- breather membrane
- wall ties
- damp proof course
- dpc min 150mm above external ground level -320 FFL
- 150mm min
- thermoblock or similar to prevent thermal briding
- timber stud wall with insulation between studs
- 32.5mm insulated plasterboard
- vapour control layer
- concrete slab cast in situ
- rigid insulation above slab, tightly abuts wall
- floor screed finish over insulation
- 0 FFL
- damp proof membrane on sand blinding
- perimeter insulation upstand to prevent thermal bridging
- foundation blocks
- reinforced concrete footing

Detail T-G2 - Timber frame wall, ground bearing concrete slab, insulation above slab

NOTES:

U-value 0.13 Wm²K or better
Perimeter strip of insulation abuts concrete slab and blockwork wall. Floor screed over insulation, minimum 65mm thick, or proprietary screed min 35mm thick. Perimeter insulation to screen. Alternative floor finish over insulation of chipboard/OSB/ply, must be flooring grade and include a vapour control layer between the board and the insulation. Damp proof membrane can also be positioned over slab. Vapour control/separation layer over insulation to prevent interstitial condensation and seeping of screed into insulation board cracks - check with insulation manufacturer.

SECTION 6 - TIMBER FRAME

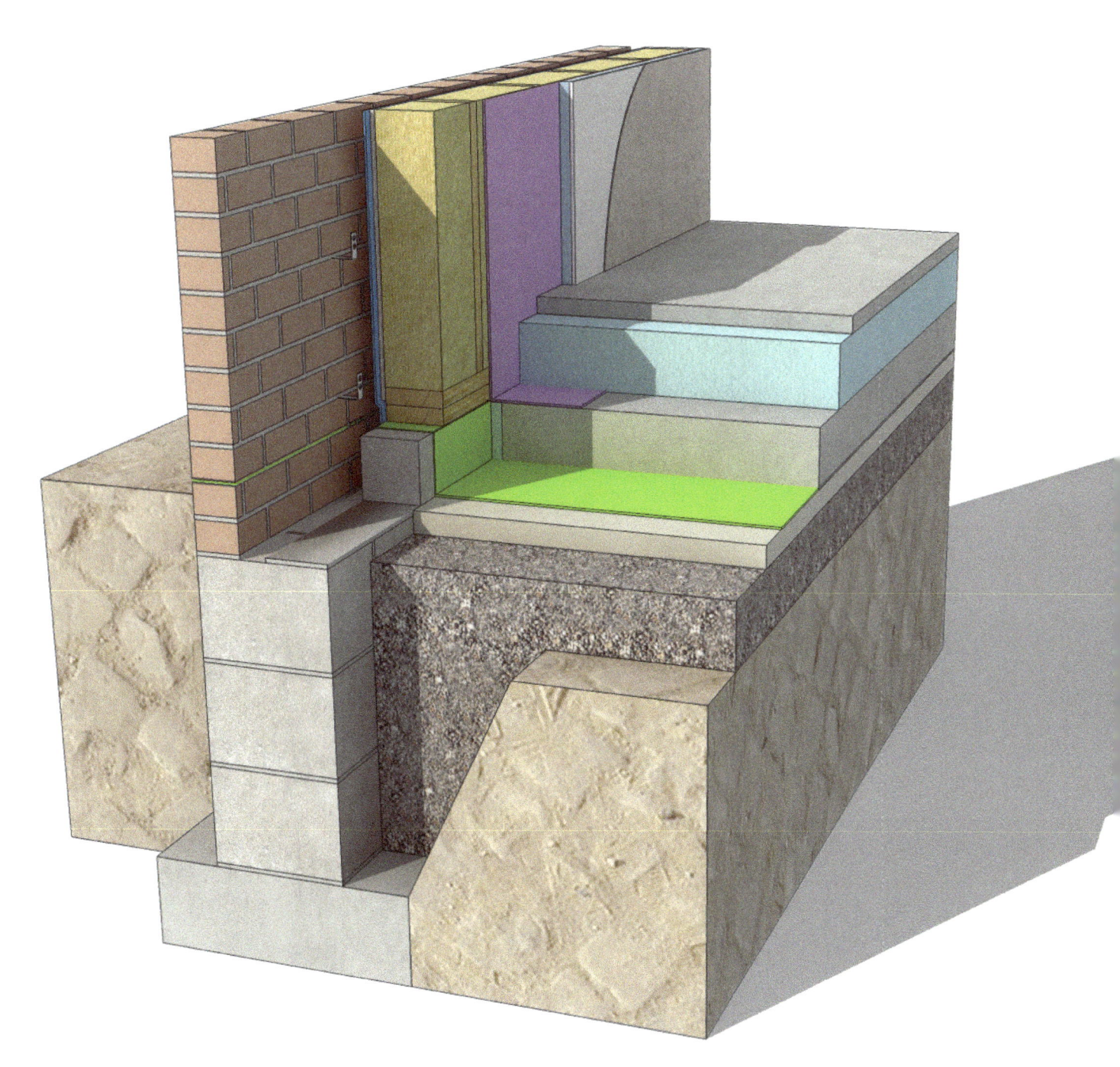

3D Detail T-G2 - Timber frame wall, ground bearing concrete slab, insulation above slab

T-G3

TIMBER FRAME WALL, SUSPENDED CONCRETE SLAB, INSULATION BELOW SLAB

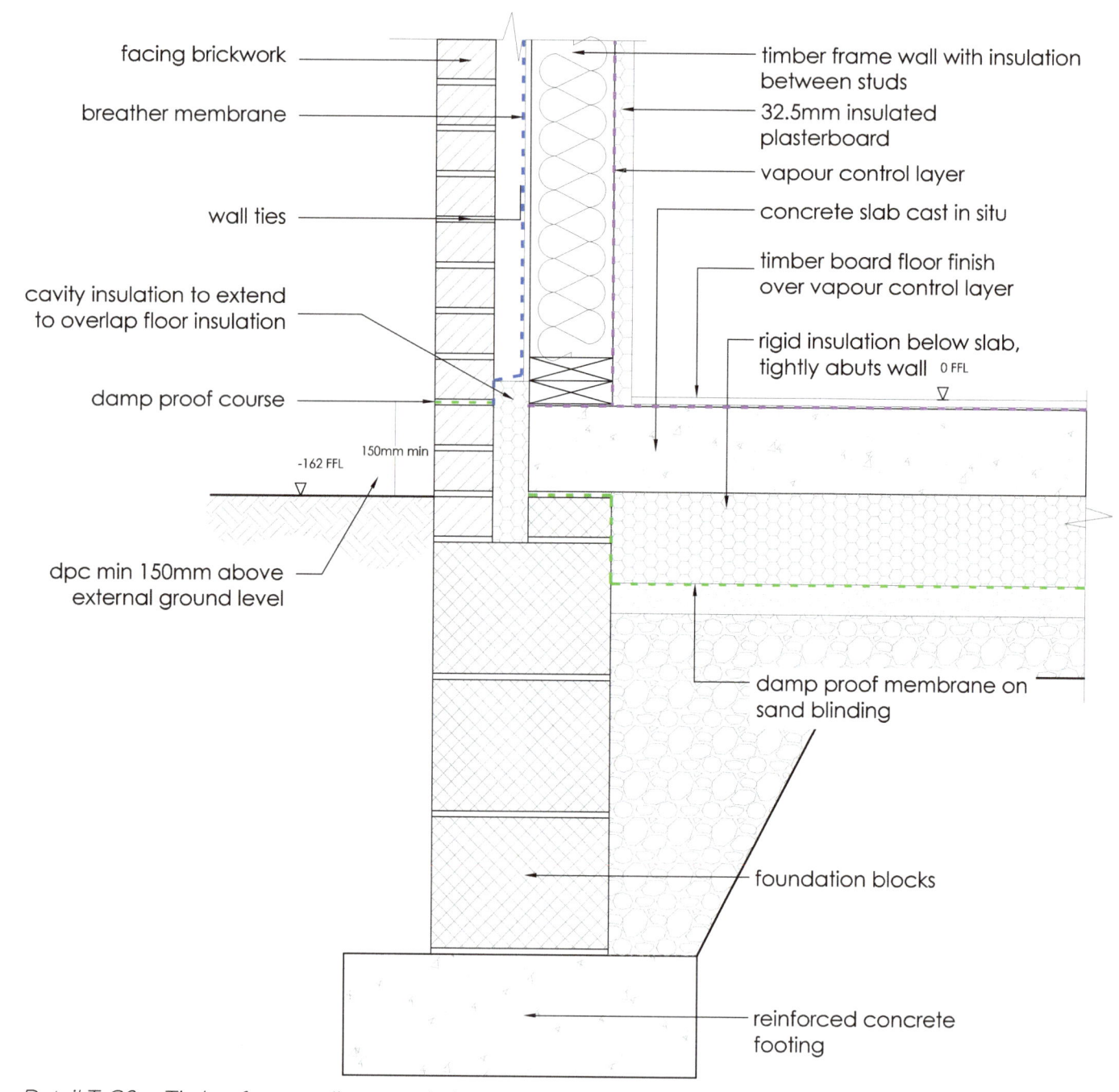

Labels (left side):
- facing brickwork
- breather membrane
- wall ties
- cavity insulation to extend to overlap floor insulation
- damp proof course
- 150mm min
- -162 FFL
- dpc min 150mm above external ground level

Labels (right side):
- timber frame wall with insulation between studs
- 32.5mm insulated plasterboard
- vapour control layer
- concrete slab cast in situ
- timber board floor finish over vapour control layer
- rigid insulation below slab, tightly abuts wall 0 FFL
- damp proof membrane on sand blinding
- foundation blocks
- reinforced concrete footing

Detail T-G3 - Timber frame wall, suspended concrete slab, insulation below slab

NOTES:

U-value 0.13 Wm²K or better

If using timber floor, vapour control layer required between concrete slab and timber floor. Additional structural insulation can be inserted between the cavity below floor level for increased thermal performance and to prevent thermal bridging.

Vapour control/separation layer over insulation to prevent interstitial condensation and seeping of concrete into insulation board cracks - check with insulation manufacturer.

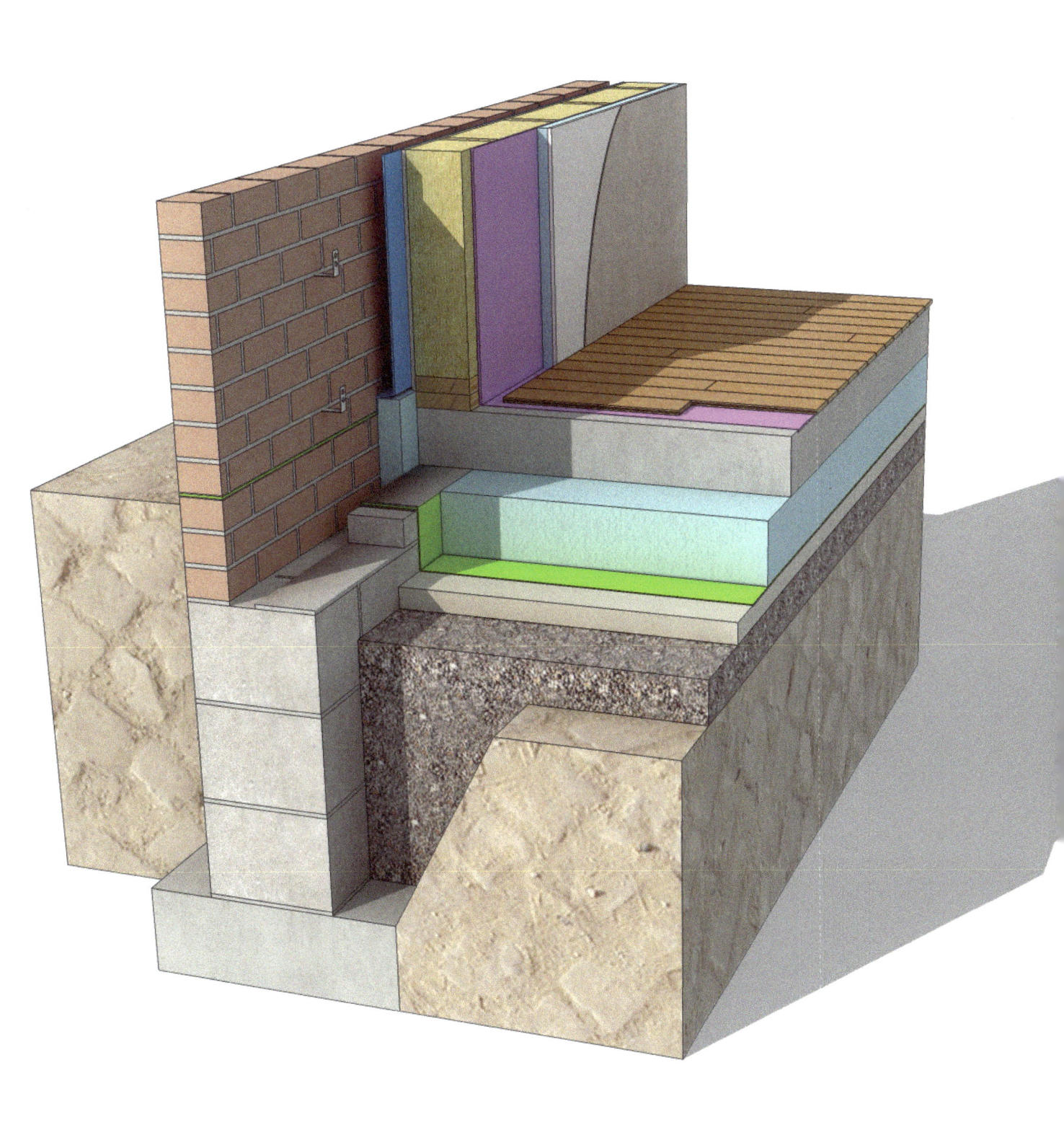

3D Detail T-G3 - Timber frame wall, suspended concrete slab, insulation below slab

T-G4

TIMBER FRAME WALL, BEAM AND BLOCK FLOOR

Labels (left side):
- facing brickwork
- wall ties
- breather membrane
- damp proof course
- dpc min 150mm above external ground level
- thermoblock or similar to prevent thermal bridging
- ventilation to void provided by ventilation sleeves at intervals connecting to air bricks
- reinforced concrete footing

Labels (right side):
- timber frame wall with insulation between studs
- 32.5mm insulated plasterboard
- vapour control layer
- perimeter insulation to screed to prevent thermal bridging
- floor screed finish over insulation
- precast beam and block floor with infill blocks
- damp proof membrane
- infill block built into wall
- foundation blocks

Dimensions: 150mm min; 0 FFL; -225 FFL

Detail T-G4 - Timber frame wall, beam and block floor

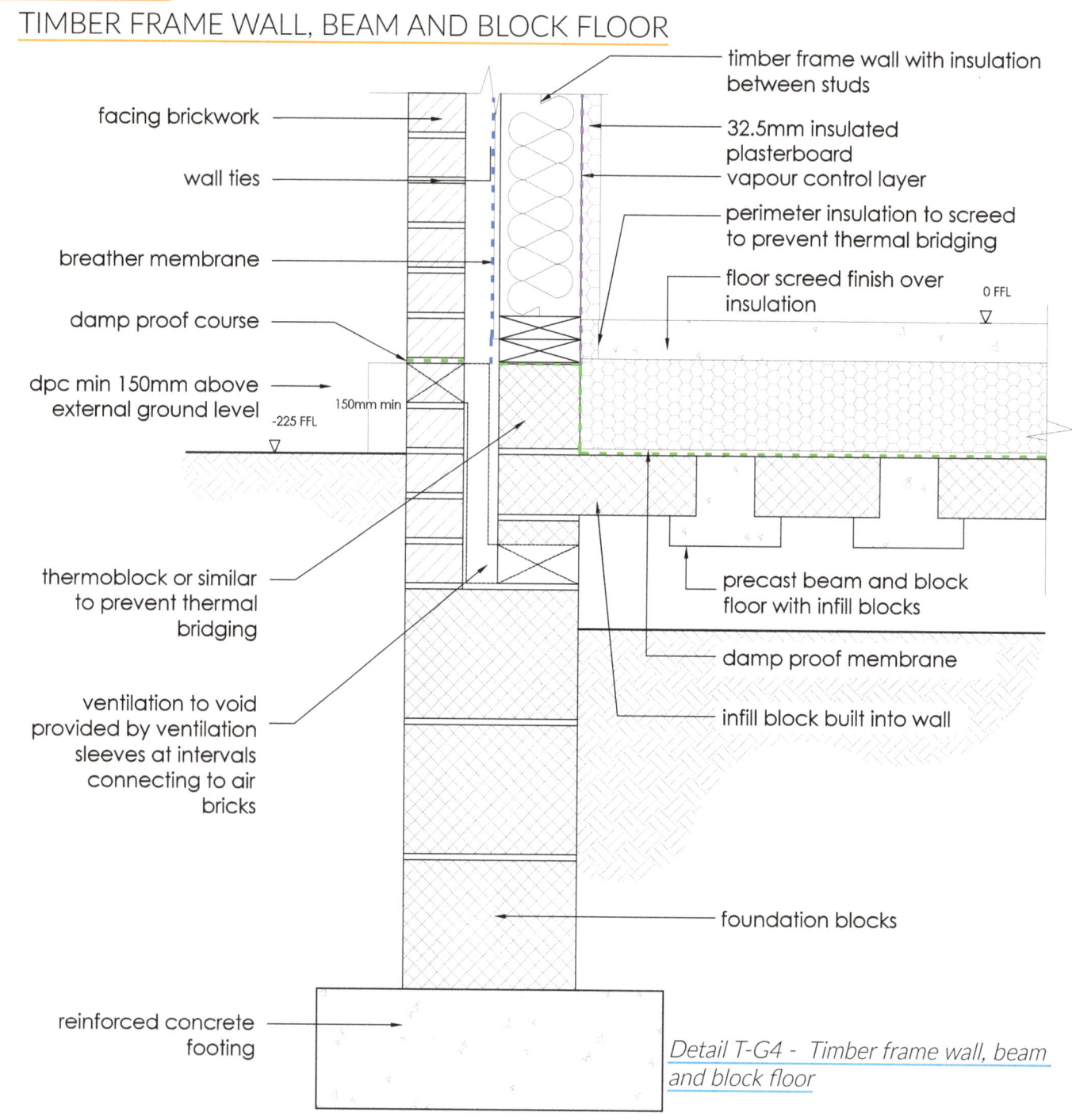

NOTES:

U-value 0.13 Wm²K or better

Perimeter strip of insulation abuts screed and blockwork wall. Floor screed over insulation, minimum 65mm thick, or proprietary screed min 35mm thick. Alternative floor finish over insulation of chipboard/OSB/ply to be flooring grade, must include a vapour control layer between the chipboard and the insulation. Void below beam and block floor is ventilated, using air bricks and connection sleeves at intervals. A thermoblock is a highly insulated load bearing block that helps to eliminate cold bridging at junctions. Vapour control/separation layer over insulation to prevent interstitial condensation and seeping of screed into insulation board cracks - check with insulation manufacturer.

SECTION 6 - TIMBER FRAME

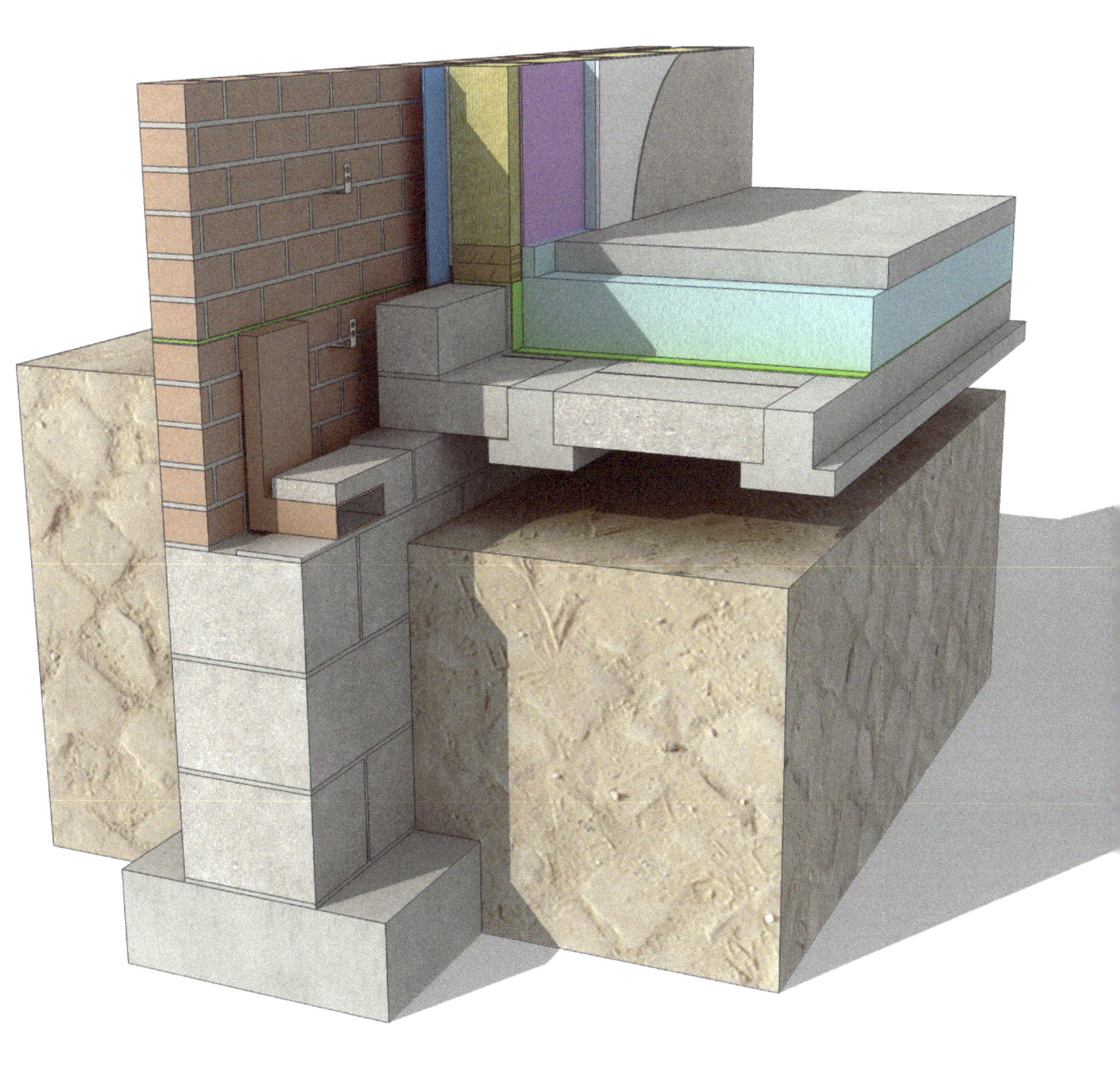

3D Detail T-G4 - Timber frame wall, beam and block floor

T-G5

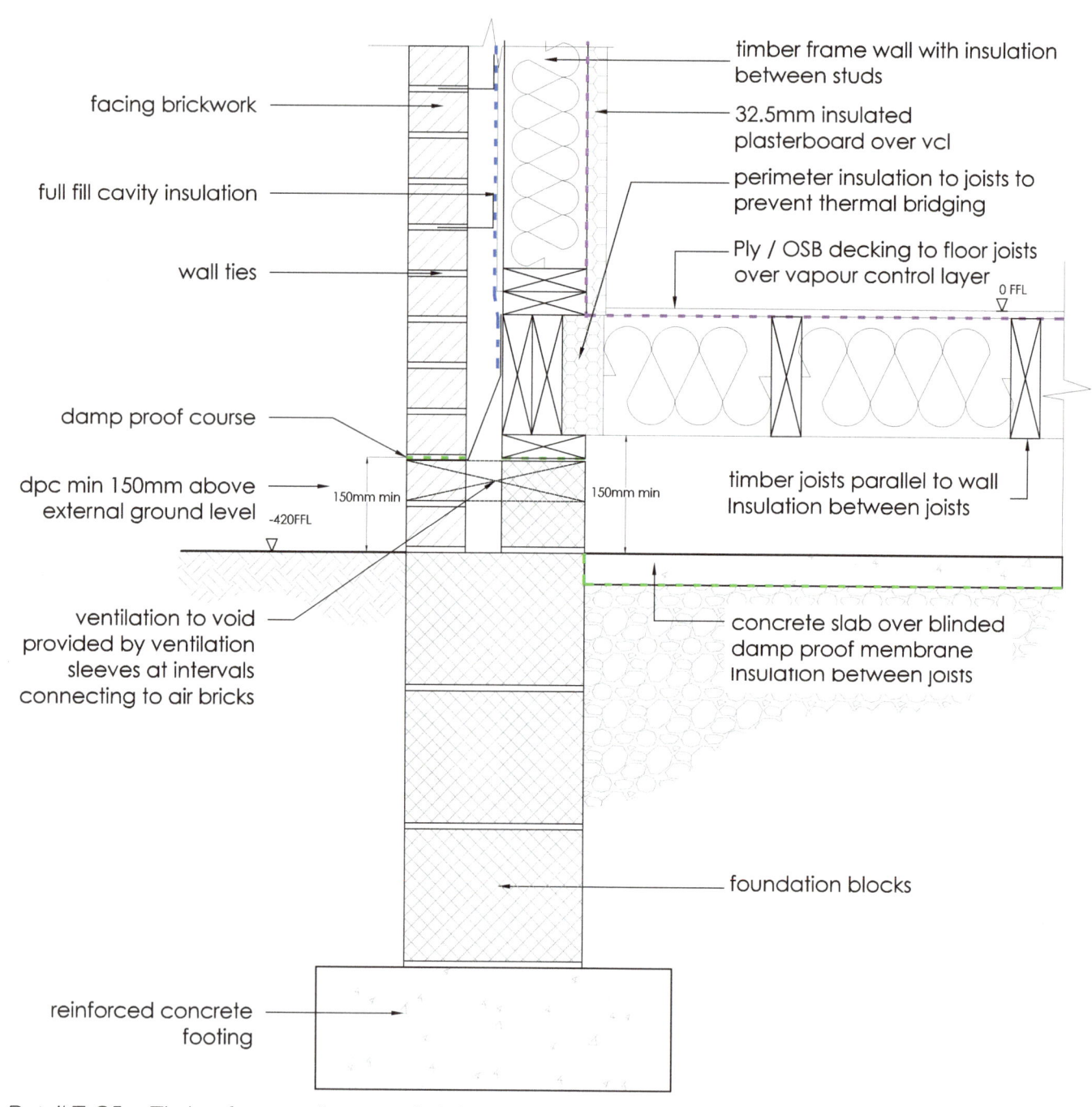

TIMBER FRAME WALL, SUSPENDED TIMBER FLOOR

- facing brickwork
- full fill cavity insulation
- wall ties
- damp proof course
- dpc min 150mm above external ground level
- ventilation to void provided by ventilation sleeves at intervals connecting to air bricks
- timber frame wall with insulation between studs
- 32.5mm insulated plasterboard over vcl
- perimeter insulation to joists to prevent thermal bridging
- Ply / OSB decking to floor joists over vapour control layer
- timber joists parallel to wall Insulation between joists
- concrete slab over blinded damp proof membrane Insulation between joists
- foundation blocks
- reinforced concrete footing

150mm min
-420FFL
0 FFL

Detail T-G5 - Timber frame wall, suspended timber floor

NOTES:

U-value 0.13 Wm²K or better
Perimeter strip of insulation abuts screed and blockwork wall. External wall insulation must extend min 215mm below top of floor insulation to avoid thermal bridging. Void below suspended floor is ventilated, using air bricks and connection sleeves at intervals. Min 150mm ventilation void area. Joists design according to individual project requirements and TRADA span tables.

3D Detail T-G5 - Timber frame wall, suspended timber floor

T-G6

TIMBER FRAME WALL, TIMBER INTERMEDIATE FLOOR, JOISTS PERPENDICULAR TO WALL

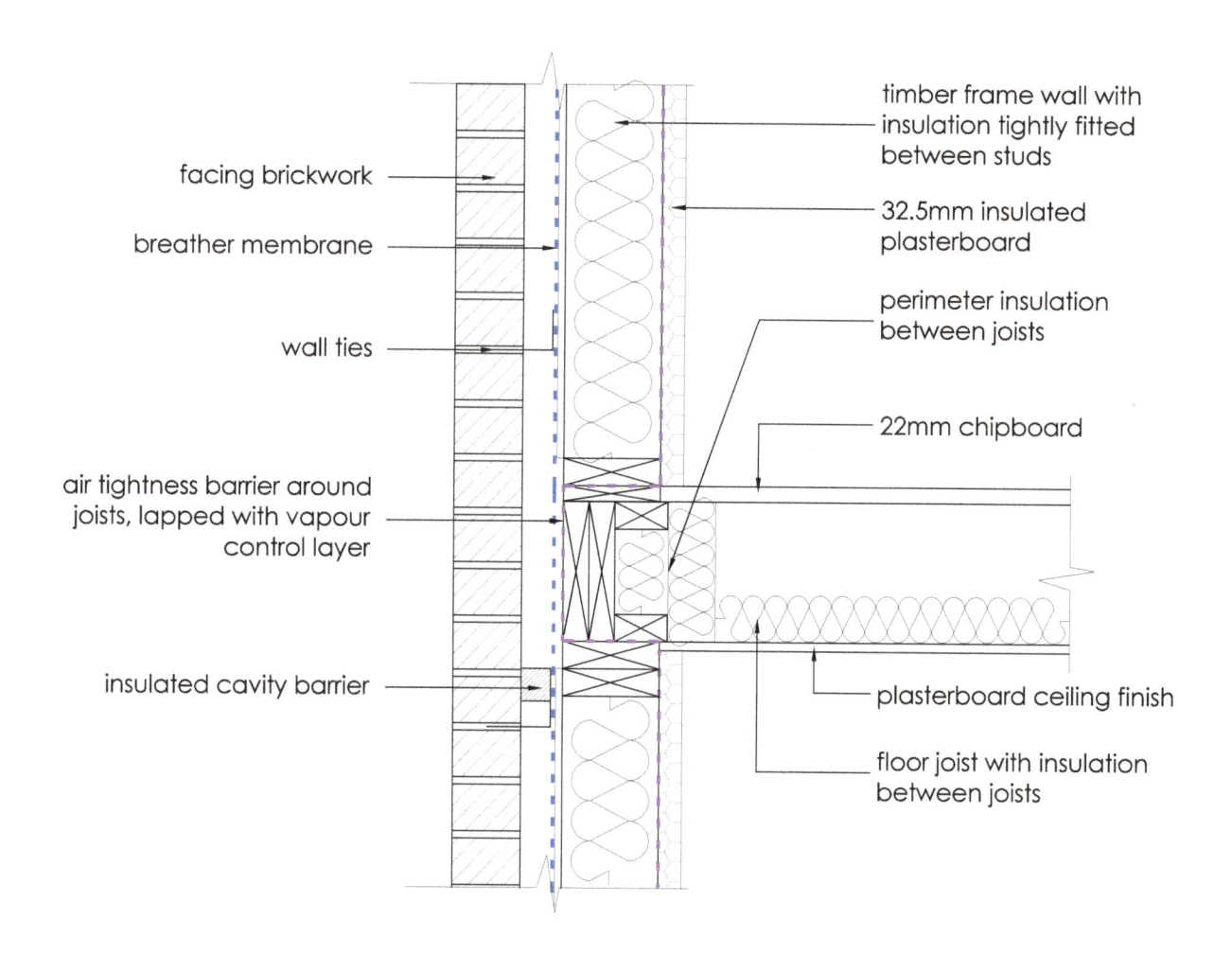

- facing brickwork
- breather membrane
- wall ties
- air tightness barrier around joists, lapped with vapour control layer
- insulated cavity barrier
- timber frame wall with insulation tightly fitted between studs
- 32.5mm insulated plasterboard
- perimeter insulation between joists
- 22mm chipboard
- plasterboard ceiling finish
- floor joist with insulation between joists

Detail T-G6 - Timber frame wall, timber intermediate floor, joists perpendicular to wall

SECTION 6 - TIMBER FRAME

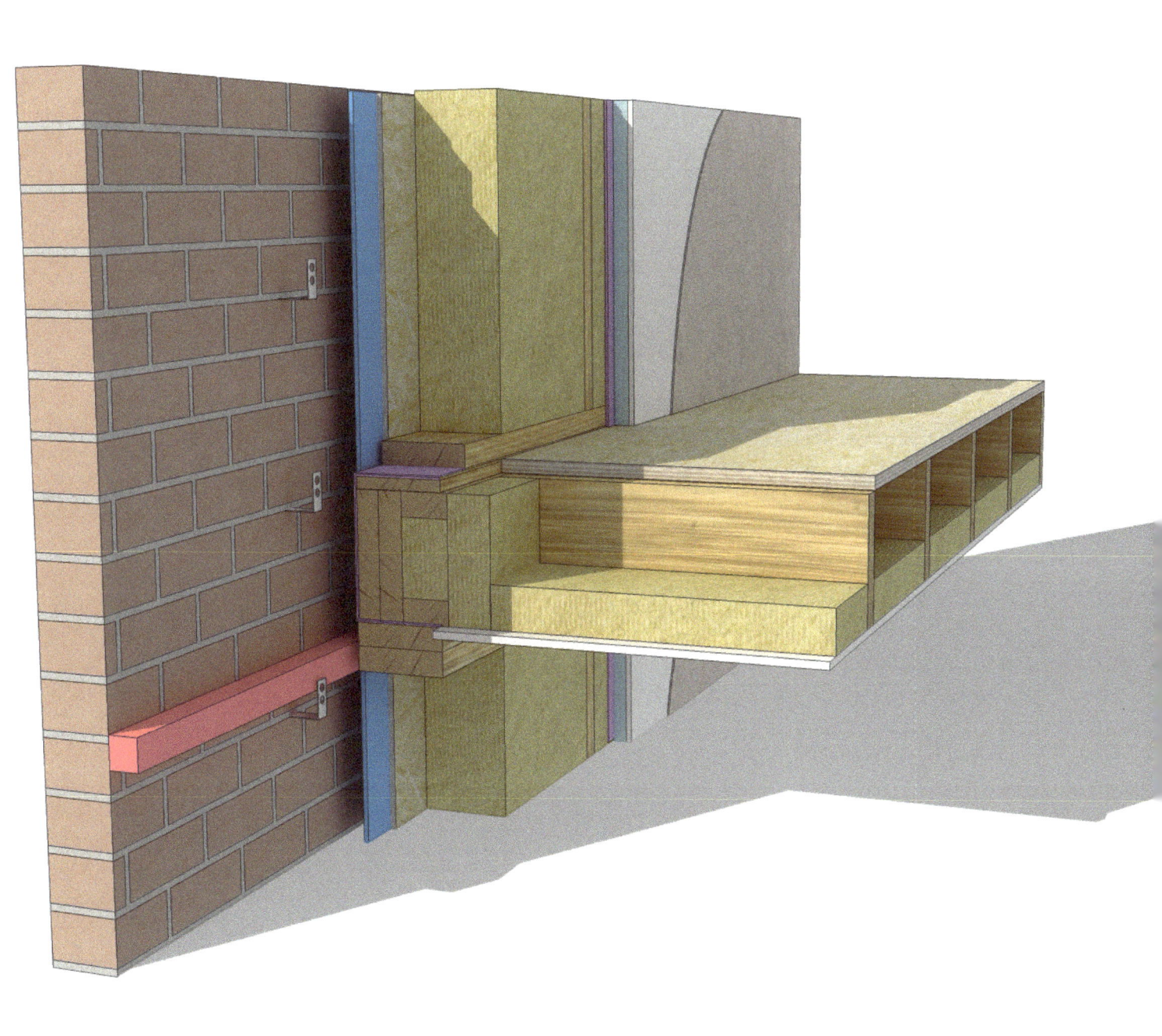

3D Detail T-G6 - Timber frame wall, timber intermediate floor, joists perpendicular to wall

T-G7

TIMBER FRAME WALL, TIMBER SEPARATING FLOOR, JOISTS PARALLEL TO WALL

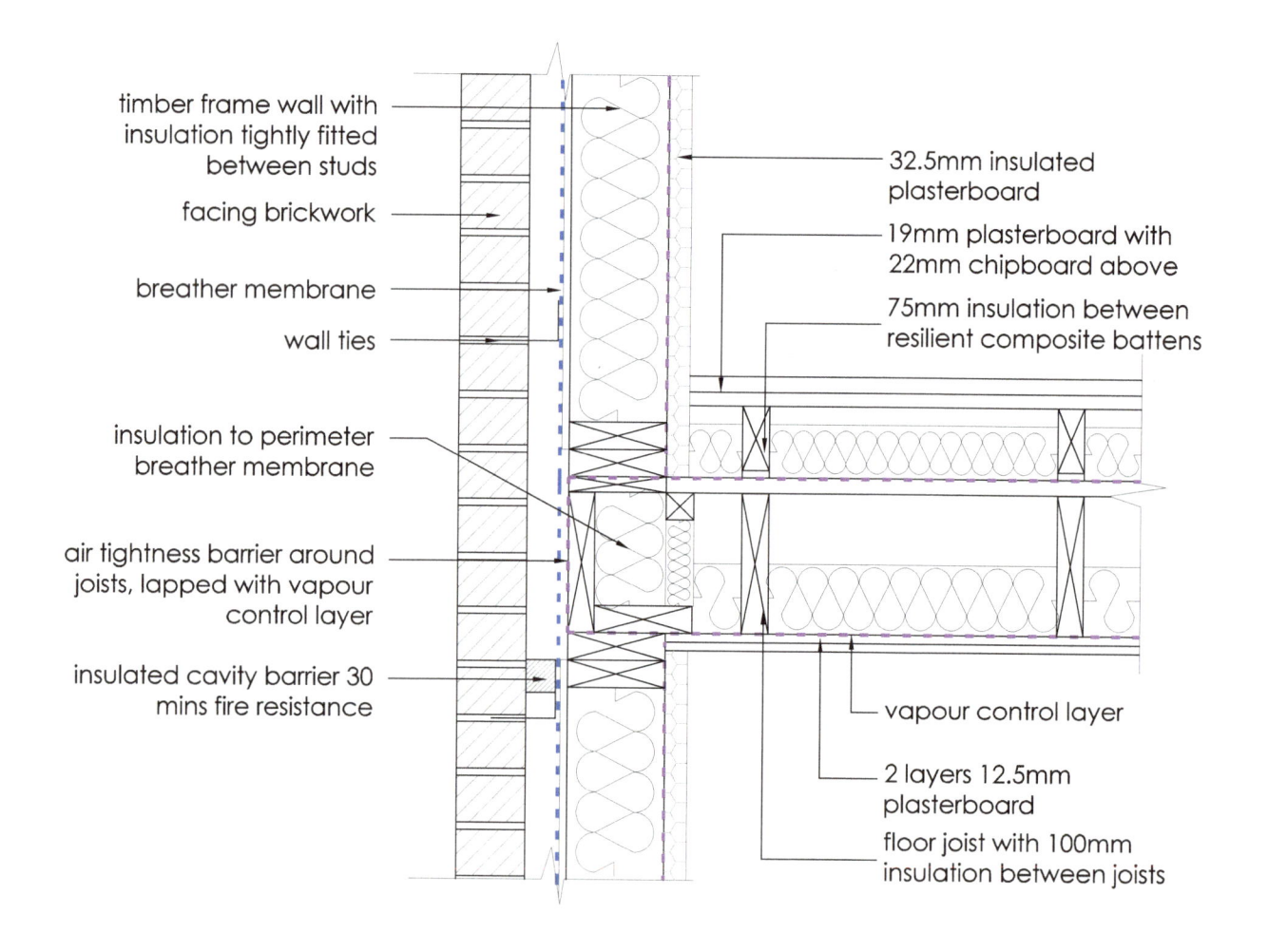

Labels (left side):
- timber frame wall with insulation tightly fitted between studs
- facing brickwork
- breather membrane
- wall ties
- insulation to perimeter breather membrane
- air tightness barrier around joists, lapped with vapour control layer
- insulated cavity barrier 30 mins fire resistance

Labels (right side):
- 32.5mm insulated plasterboard
- 19mm plasterboard with 22mm chipboard above
- 75mm insulation between resilient composite battens
- vapour control layer
- 2 layers 12.5mm plasterboard
- floor joist with 100mm insulation between joists

Detail T-G7 - Timber frame wall, timber separating floor, joists parallel to wall

NOTES:

There are many different arrangements for a separating floor, this is just one example

SECTION 6 - TIMBER FRAME

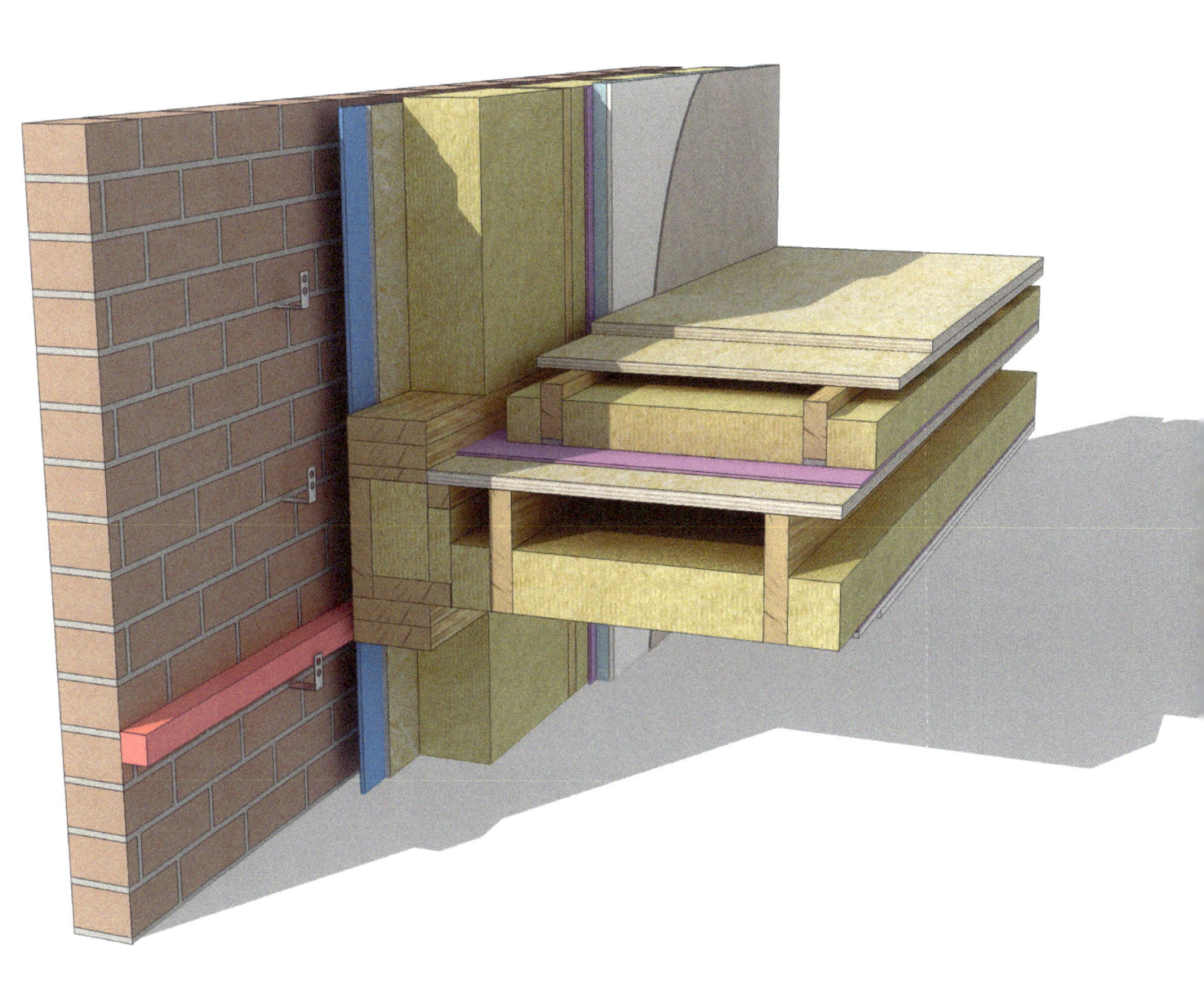

3D Detail T-G7 - Timber frame wall, timber separating floor, joists parallel to wall

NOTES ON THE REGS

The following information is a partial list of requirements from the **Building Regulations Approved Documents** - for full and detailed explanations and requirements please consult the full publications.

GENERAL REQUIREMENTS - FOUNDATIONS

The building shall be constructed so that:
- the combined dead, imposed and wind loads are sustained and transmitted by it to the ground, safely and without causing any building deflection/deformation or ground movement that will affect the stability of any part of the building.
- ground movement caused by swelling, shrinkage or freezing of the sub-soil, land slip or subsidence will not affect the stability of any part of the building.

(Approved Doc A)

The walls and floors of the building shall adequately protect the building and people who use the building from harmful effects caused by ground moisture, precipitation wind wind-driven spray, interstitial and surface condensation, and spillage of water from or associated with sanitary fittings or fixed appliances. All floors next to the ground, walls and roof shall not be damaged by moisture from the ground, rain or snow and shall not carry that moisture to any part of the building that it would damage.

(Approved Doc C2)

Site preparation and resistance to contaminants and water

- The ground to be covered by the building shall be reasonably free from any material that might damage the building or affect its stability, including vegetable matter, topsoil and pre-existing foundations.
- Reasonable precautions shall be taken to avoid danger to health and safety caused by contaminants on or in the ground covered, or to be covered, by the building and any land associated with the building.
- Adequate subsoil drainage shall be provided if it is needed to avoid: passage of ground moisture to the interior of the building; damage to the building, including damage through the transport of water-borne contaminants to the foundations of the building

(Approved Doc C1)

Rainwater drainage
Rainwater drainage systems shall ensure that rainwater soaking into the ground is distributed sufficiently so that it does not damage foundations of the proposed building or any adjacent structure.

(Approved Doc H3)

GENERAL NOTES:

Foundations - plain concrete
There should not be:
- non engineered fill or a wide variation in ground conditions within the loaded area
- weaker or more compressible ground at such a depth below the foundation as could impair the stability of the structure.

Foundations stepped on elevation should overlap by twice the height of the step, by the thickness of the foundation, or 300mm, whichever is greater.

Residential Buildings
The maximum height of the building measured from the lowest finished ground level to the highest point of any wall or roof should be less than 15m.
The height of the building should not exceed twice the least width of the building.

GENERAL REQUIREMENTS - FLOORS

Construction
The building shall be constructed so that the combined dead, imposed and wind loads area sustained and transmitted by it to the ground:
- safely
- without causing such deflection or deformation of any part of the building as will impair the

SECTION 6 - TIMBER FRAME

stability of any part of another building.

(Approved Doc A1)

The building shall be constructed so that ground movement caused by:
- swelling, shrinkage or freezing of the subsoil
- landslip or subsidence
- will not impair the stability of any part of the building

(Approved Doc A2)

Fire Precautions
As a fire precaution, the spread of flame over the internal linings of a building and the amount of heat released from internal linings shall be restricted;
- all load bearing elements of structure of the building shall be capable of withstanding the effects of fire for an appropriate period without loss of stability;
- ideally the building should be subdivided by elements of fire-resisting construction into compartments;
- all openings in fire-separating elements shall be suitably protected in order to maintain the integrity of the continuity of the fire separation;
- any hidden voids in the construction shall be sealed and subdivided to inhibit the unseens spread of fire and products of combustion, in order to reduce the risk of structural failure, and the spread of fire.

(Approved Doc B3)

Precautions against moisture
The floor son the building shall adequately protect the building and people who use the building from harmful effects caused by:
- ground moisture
- precipitation
- interstitial and surface condensation
- spillage of water from or associated with sanitary fittings or fixed appliances.

All floors next to the ground, walls and roof shall not be damaged by moisture from the ground, rain or snow and shall not carry that moisture to any part of the building that it would damage.

Airborne and Impact sound
Dwellings shall be designed so that the noise from domestic activity in an adjoining dwelling (or other parts of the building) is kept to a level that:
- does not affect the health of the occupants of the dwelling
- will allow them to sleep, rest and engage in their normal activities in satisfactory conditions

(Approved Doc E1)

Dwellings shall be designed so that any domestic noise that is generated internally does not interfere with the occupants ability to sleep, rest and engage in their normal activities in satisfactory conditions.
(Approved Doc E2)

Domestic buildings shall be designed and constructed so as to restrict the transmission of echoes.
(Approved Doc E3)

Ventilation
There shall be adequate means of ventilation provided for people in the building
(Approved Doc F)

Conservation of fuel and power
Reasonable provision shall be made for the conservation of fuel and power in buildings by:
- limiting heat gains and losses through thermal elements and other parts of the building fabric,
- from pipes ducts and vessels used for space heating, space cooling and hot water services.
-providing fixed building services which are energy efficient and have effective controls and are commissioned by testing and adjusting as necessary to ensure they use no more fuel and power than is reasonable in the circumstances.
(Approved Doc L)

GENERAL NOTES:
Suspended timber floors must:
- Ensure the ground is covered so as to resist moisture and prevent plant growth.
- Have a ventilated air space between he ground covering and the timber.
- Have a damp proof course between the timber and any material which can carry moisture from the ground

Floors that separate a dwelling from another dwelling shall resist the transmission of airborne sounds. Floors above a dwelling that separate it from another dwell shall resist:
- the transmission of impact sound (such as speech, music, loudspeakers and impact sources such as footsteps or furniture moving)
- the flow of sound energy through walls and floors
- the level of airborne sound

WALL DETAILS

T-W1

TIMBER FRAME WALL, BRICK CLADDING

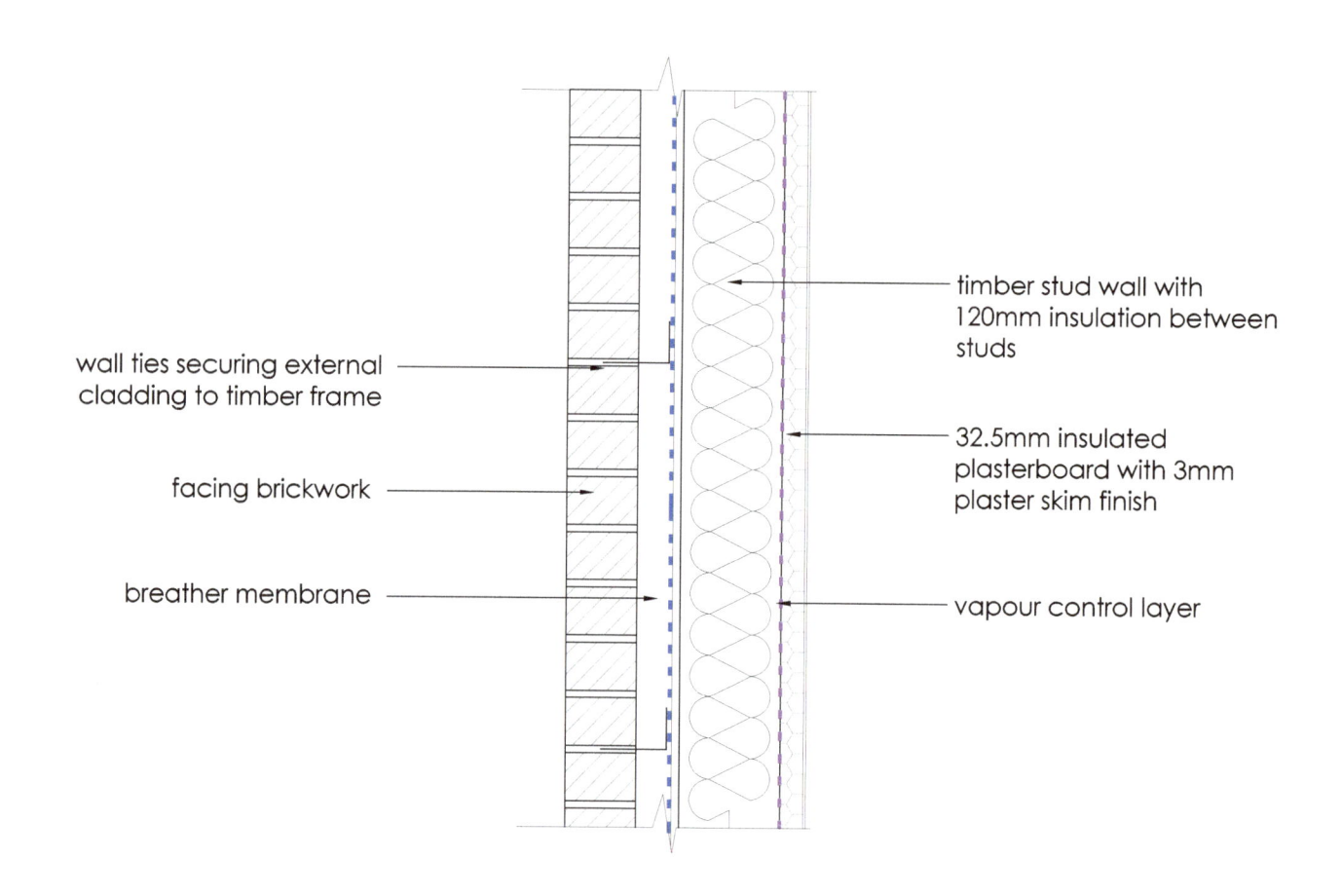

- wall ties securing external cladding to timber frame
- facing brickwork
- breather membrane
- timber stud wall with 120mm insulation between studs
- 32.5mm insulated plasterboard with 3mm plaster skim finish
- vapour control layer

Detail T-W1 - Timber frame wall, brick cladding

NOTES:
U Value 0.17W/m²K or better

SECTION 6 - TIMBER FRAME

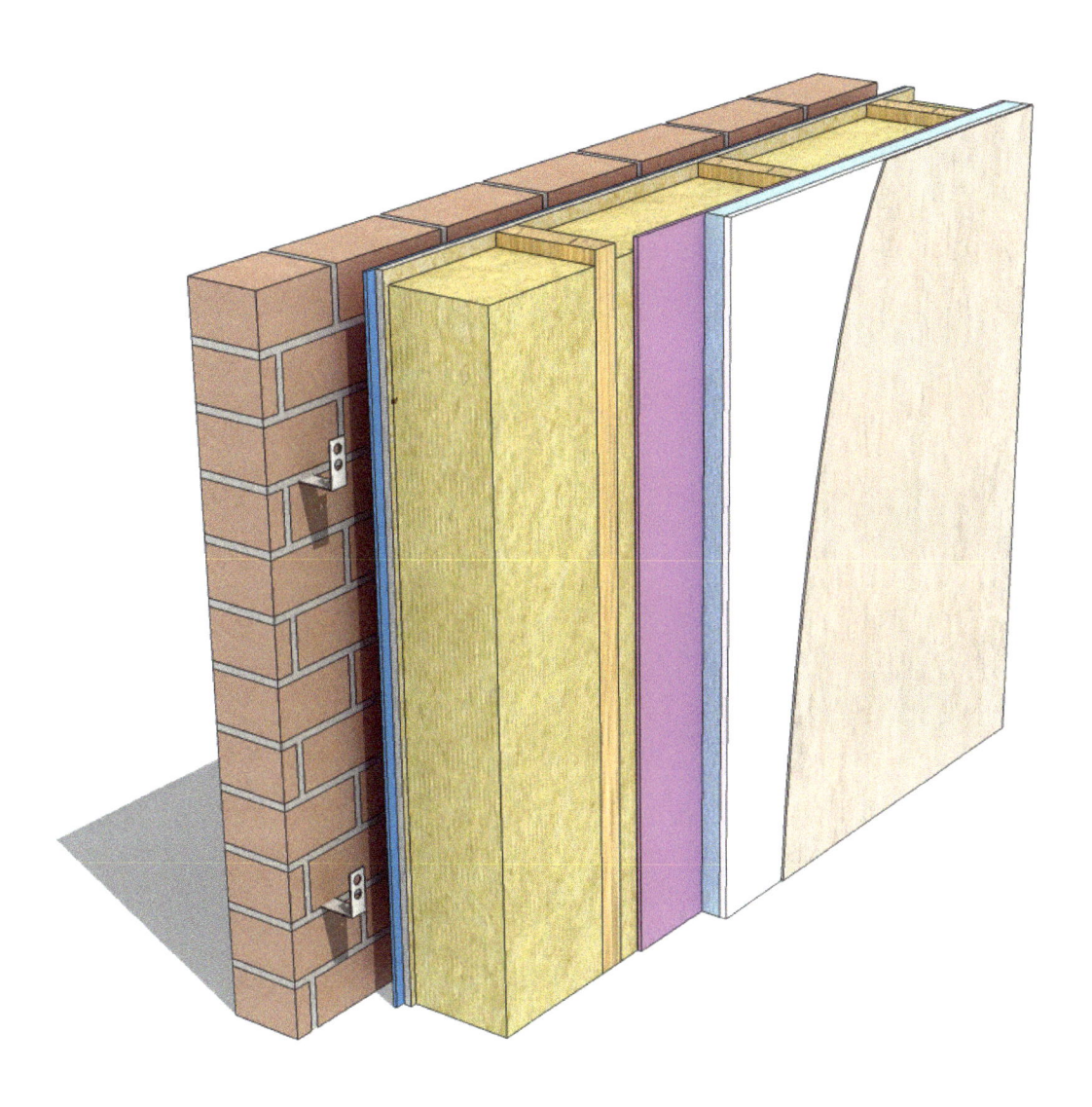

3D Detail T-W1- Timber frame wall, brick cladding

T-W2

TIMBER FRAME WALL, BRICK CLADDING, INSULATED SHEATHING BOARD

- facing brickwork
- wall ties securing external cladding to timber frame, with retaining clip to fix insulation in place
- breather membrane over OSB sheathing board
- 50mm rigid insulation
- timber stud wall with 50mm rigid insulation between studs
- 15mm plasterboard
- 3mm plaster skim
- vapour control layer

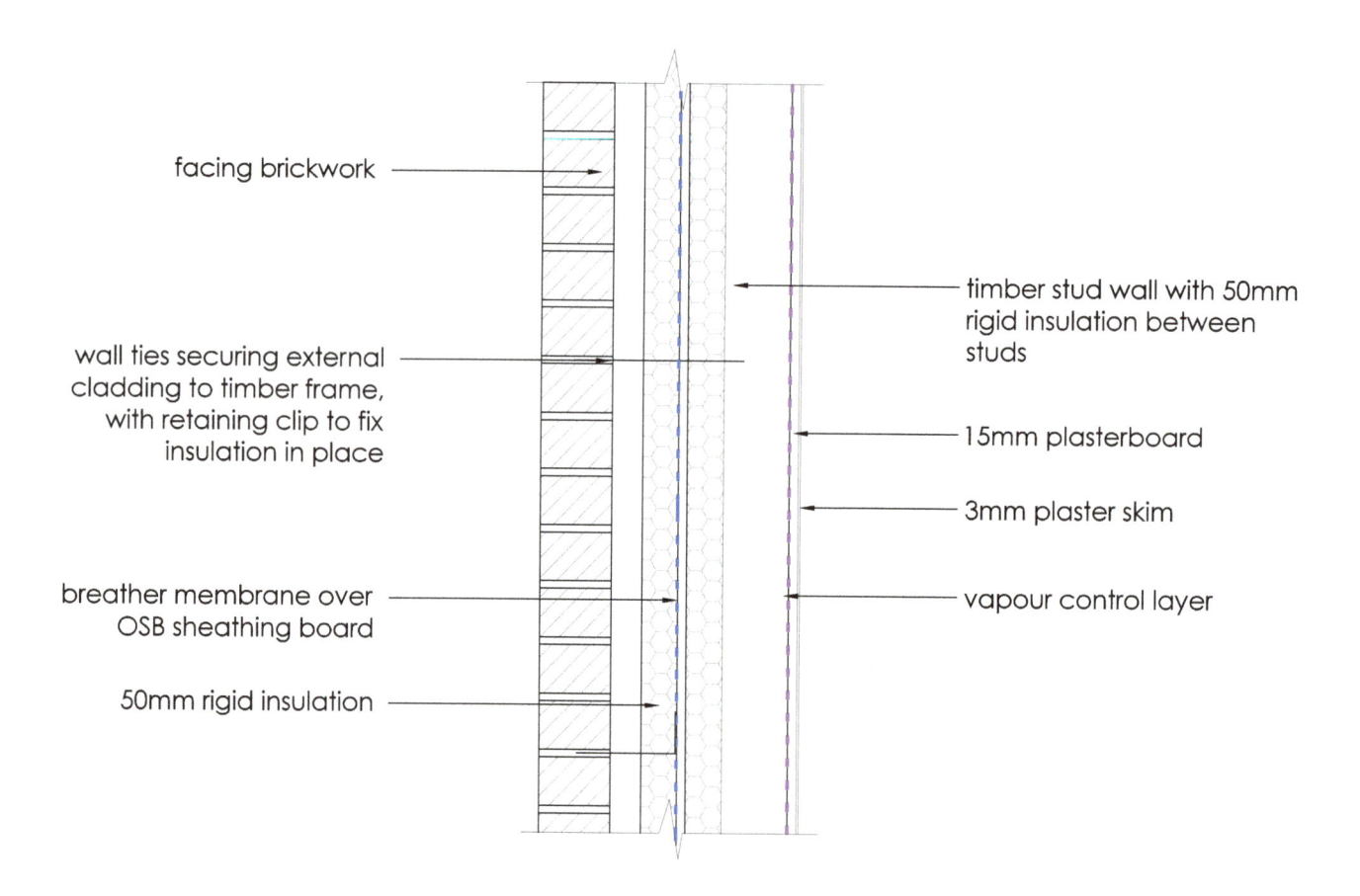

Detail T-W2 - Timber frame wall, brick cladding, insulated sheathing board

NOTES:

U Value 0.17W/m²K or better
Wall ties fix through insulation directly into the timber stud of the main frame.

SECTION 6 - TIMBER FRAME

3D Detail T-W2 - Timber frame wall, brick cladding, insulated sheathing board

T-W3

TIMBER FRAME WALL, RENDER FINISH, INSULATED PLASTERBOARD

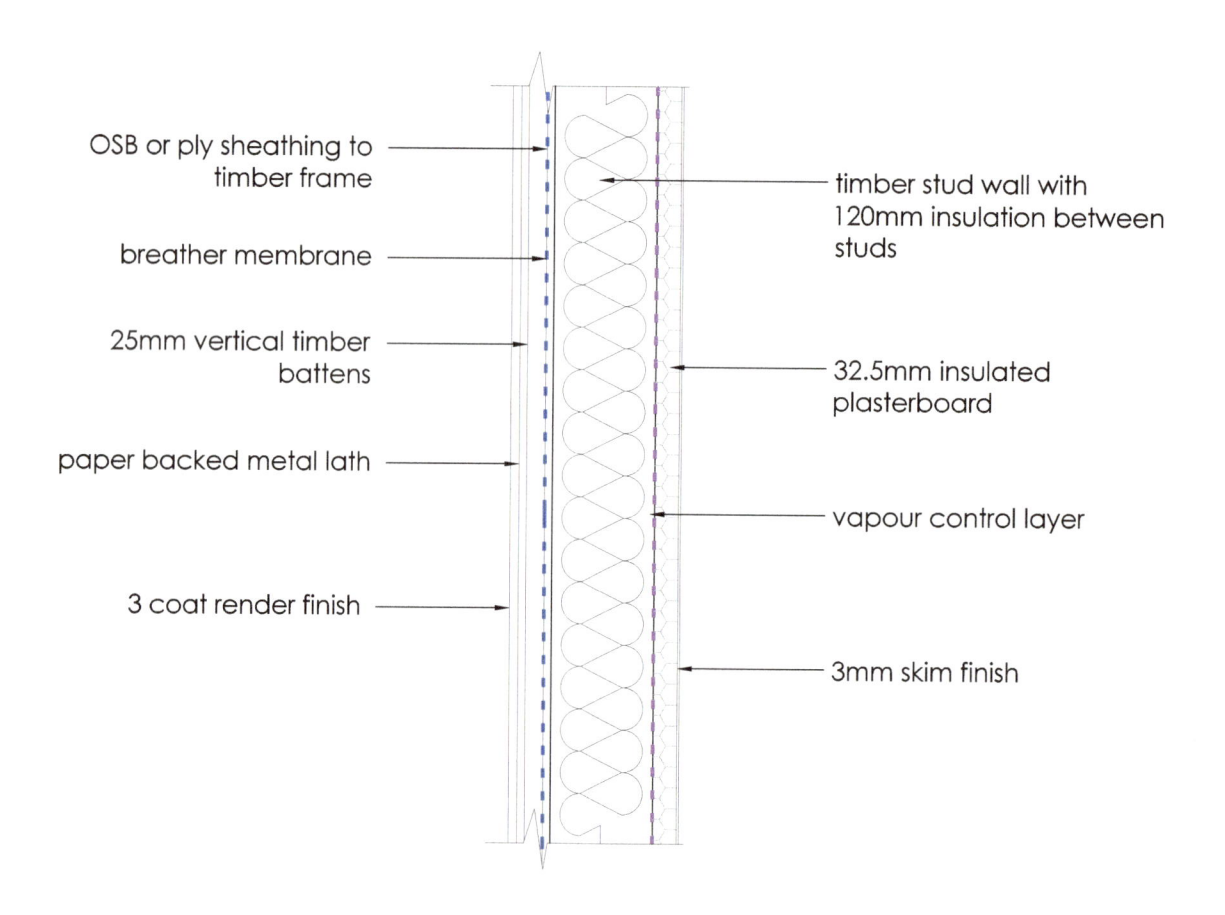

Labels (left side):
- OSB or ply sheathing to timber frame
- breather membrane
- 25mm vertical timber battens
- paper backed metal lath
- 3 coat render finish

Labels (right side):
- timber stud wall with 120mm insulation between studs
- 32.5mm insulated plasterboard
- vapour control layer
- 3mm skim finish

Detail T-W3 - Timber frame wall, render finish, insulated plasterboard

NOTES:
U Value 0.18W/m²K or better

SECTION 6 - TIMBER FRAME

3D Detail T-W3 - Timber frame wall, render finish, insulated plasterboard

T-W4

TIMBER FRAME WALL, HORIZONTAL TIMBER CLADDING, INSULATION OVER SHEATHING

- horizontal timber cladding fixed to vertical timber battens
- breather membrane over OSB sheathing board
- 60mm rigid insulation
- breathable sarking membrane
- timber stud wall with 60mm rigid insulation between studs
- 15mm plasterboard
- 3mm plaster skim
- vapour control layer

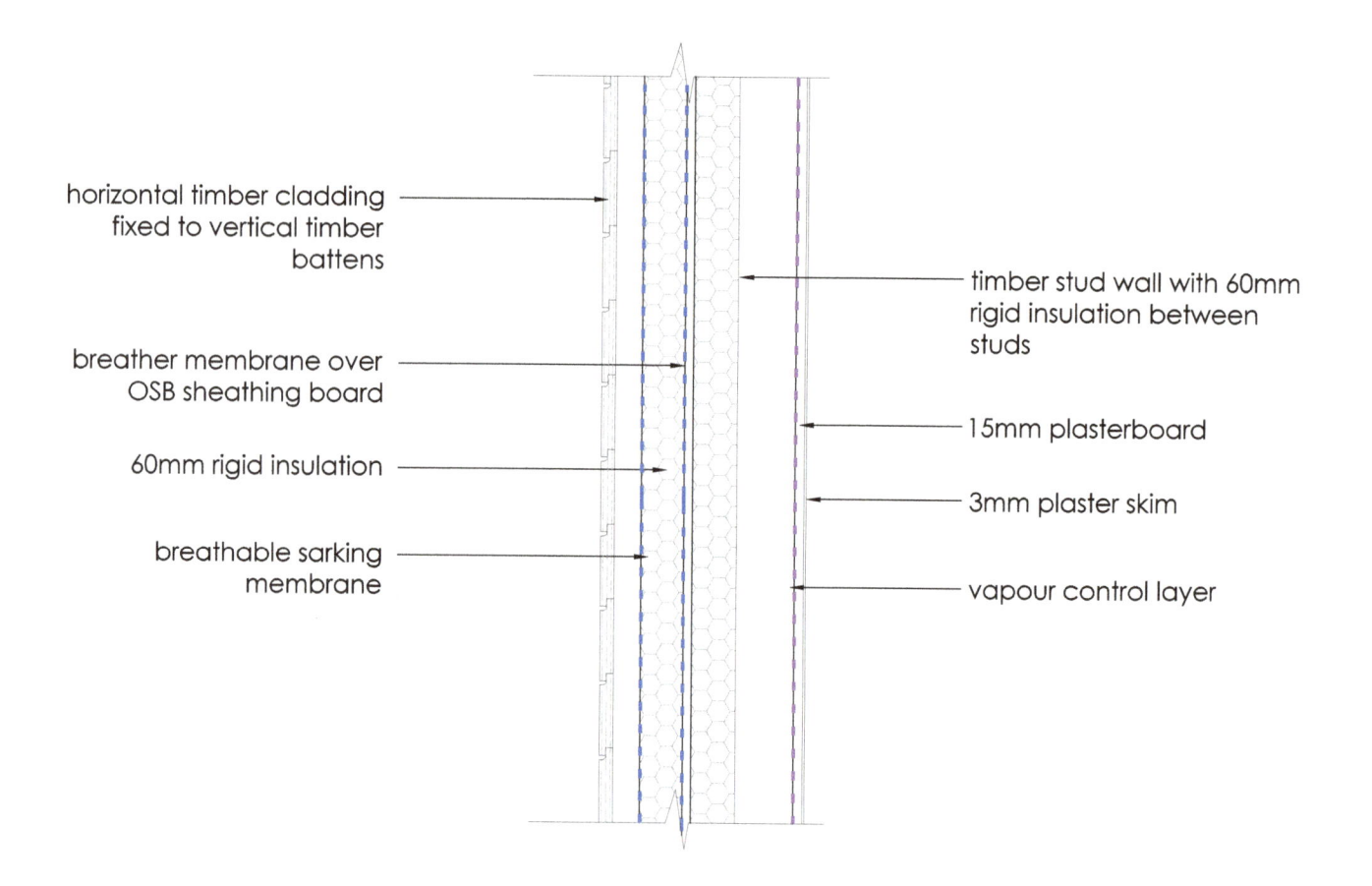

Detail T-W4 - Timber frame wall, horizontal timber cladding, insulation over sheathing

NOTES:

U Value 0.16W/m²K or better

SECTION 6 - TIMBER FRAME

3D Detail T-W4 - Timber frame wall, horizontal timber cladding, insulation over sheathing

T-W5

TIMBER FRAME WALL, VERTICAL TIMBER CLADDING, INSULATED PLASTERBOARD

- OSB or ply sheathing to timber frame
- horizontal timber battens
- breather membrane over OSB sheathing
- vertical timber cladding
- vertical timber counter battens
- timber stud wall with 120mm insulation between studs
- 32.5mm insulated plasterboard
- vapour control layer
- 3mm skim finish

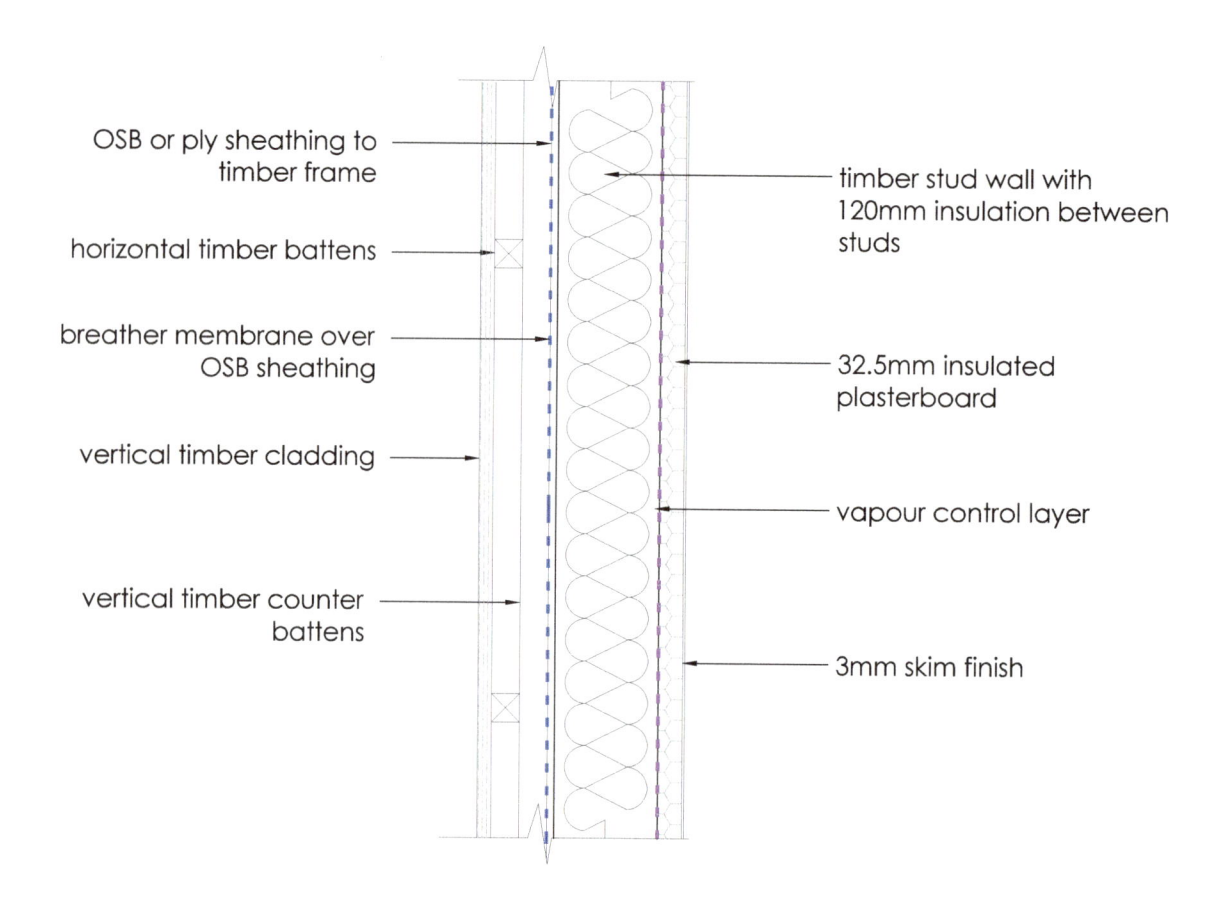

Detail T-W5 - Timber frame wall, vertical timber cladding, insulated plasterboard

NOTES:

U Value 0.18W/m²K or better

3D Detail T-W5 - Timber frame wall, vertical timber cladding, insulated plasterboard

T-W6

TIMBER FRAME PARTY WALL, TO ACHIEVE ZERO U VALUE

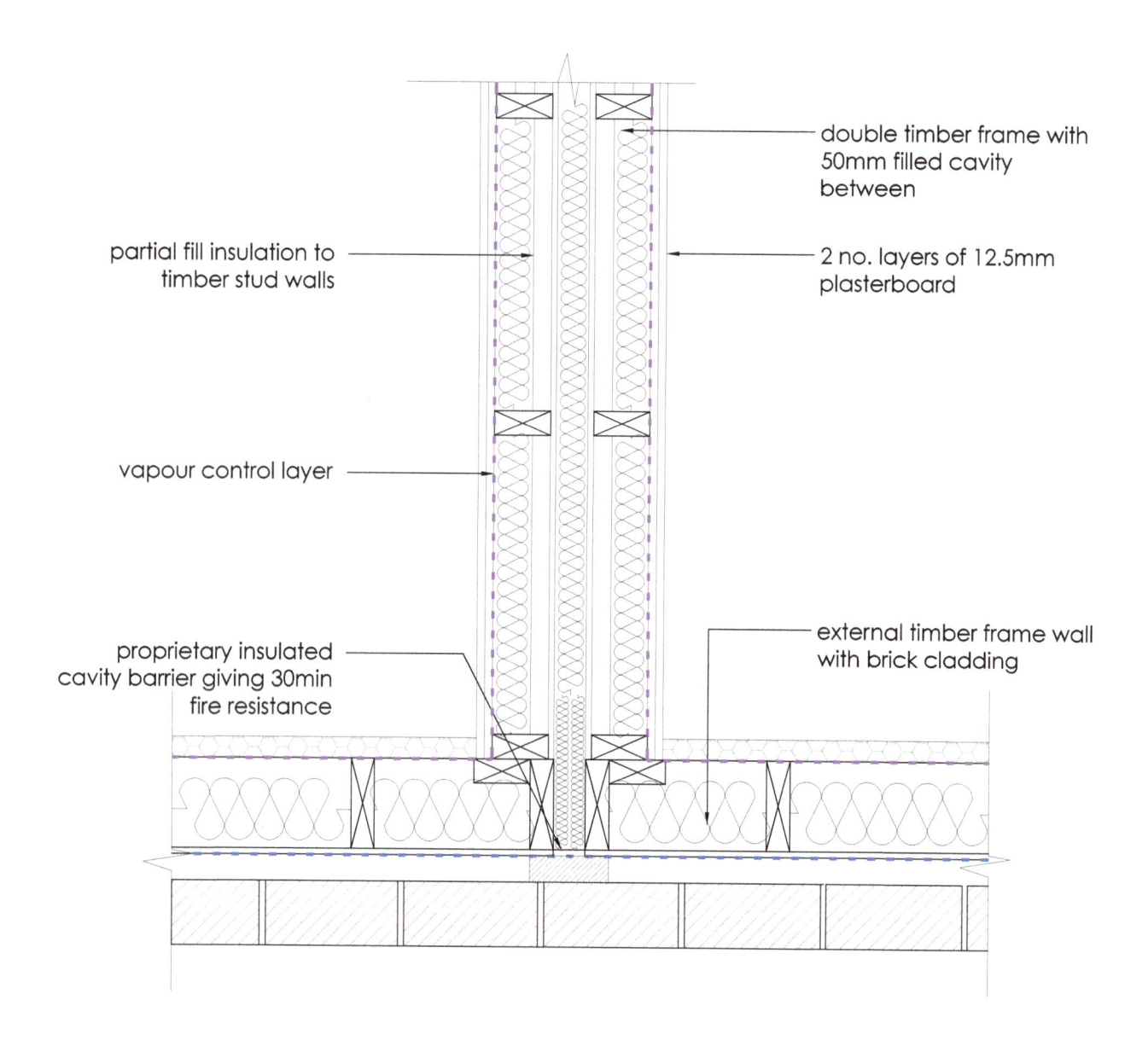

- double timber frame with 50mm filled cavity between
- 2 no. layers of 12.5mm plasterboard
- partial fill insulation to timber stud walls
- vapour control layer
- external timber frame wall with brick cladding
- proprietary insulated cavity barrier giving 30min fire resistance

Detail T-W6 - Timber frame party wall, to achieve zero u value

NOTES:
U Value 0.00W/m²K

SECTION 6 - TIMBER FRAME

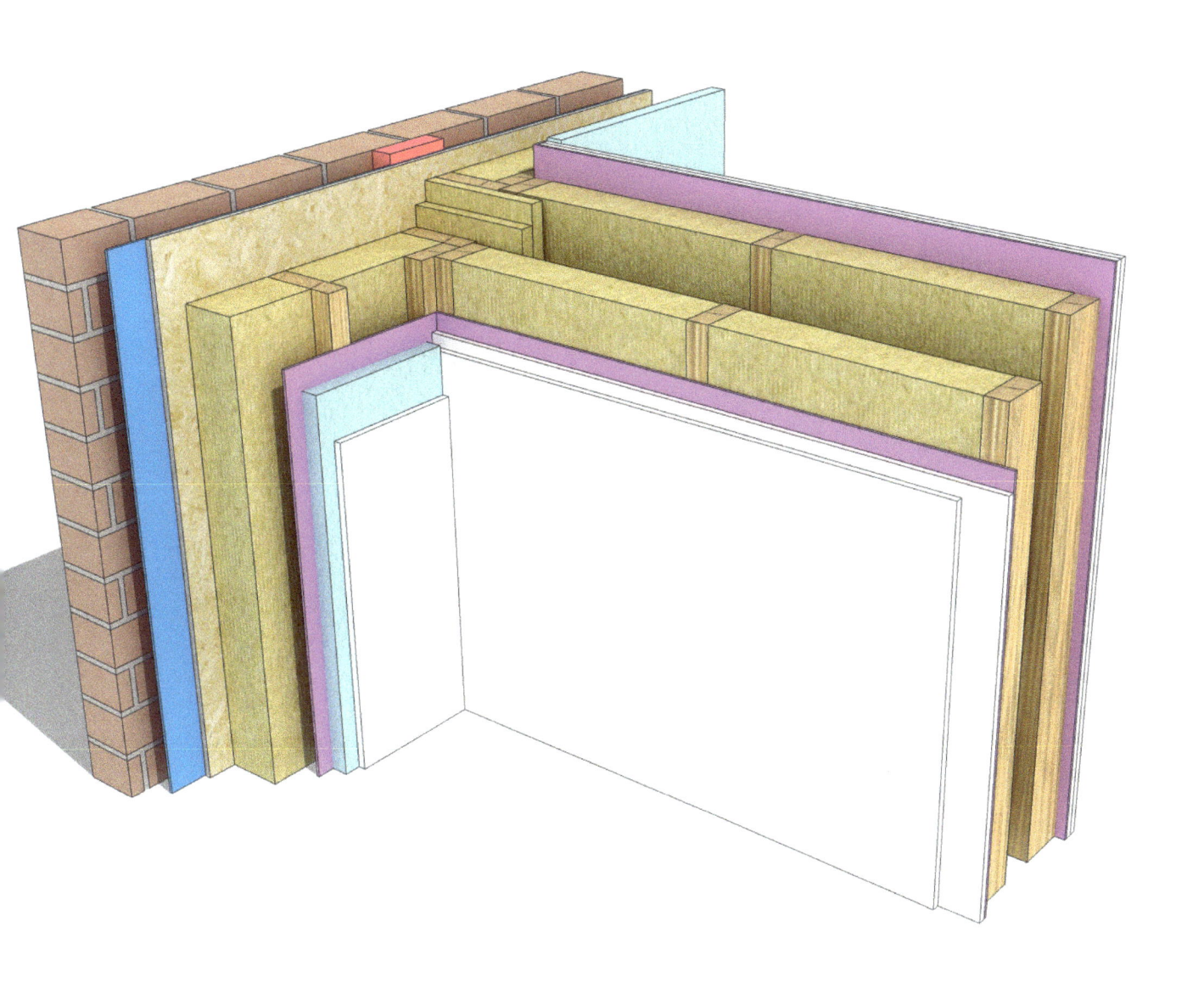

3D Detail T-W6 - Timber frame party wall, to achieve zero u value

T-W7

TIMBER FRAME WALL, BRICK CLADDING, WINDOW HEAD

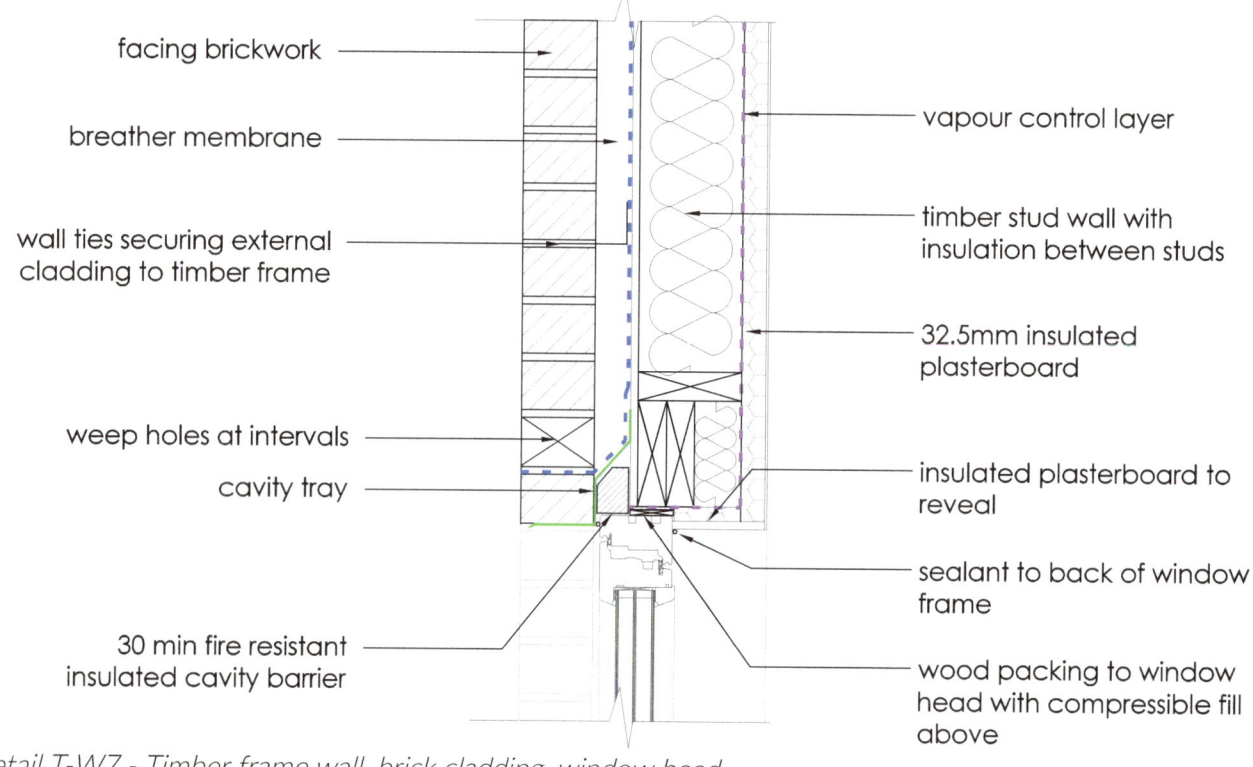

Labels (left side):
- facing brickwork
- breather membrane
- wall ties securing external cladding to timber frame
- weep holes at intervals
- cavity tray
- 30 min fire resistant insulated cavity barrier

Labels (right side):
- vapour control layer
- timber stud wall with insulation between studs
- 32.5mm insulated plasterboard
- insulated plasterboard to reveal
- sealant to back of window frame
- wood packing to window head with compressible fill above

Detail T-W7 - Timber frame wall, brick cladding, window head

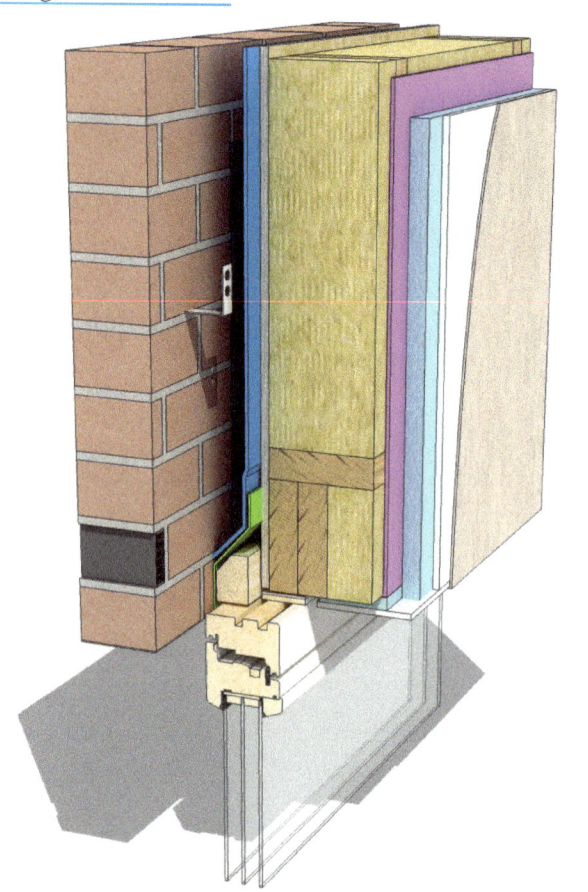

3D Detail T-W7 - Timber frame wall, brick cladding, window head

SECTION 6 - TIMBER FRAME

T-W8

TIMBER FRAME WALL, BRICK CLADDING, WINDOW SILL

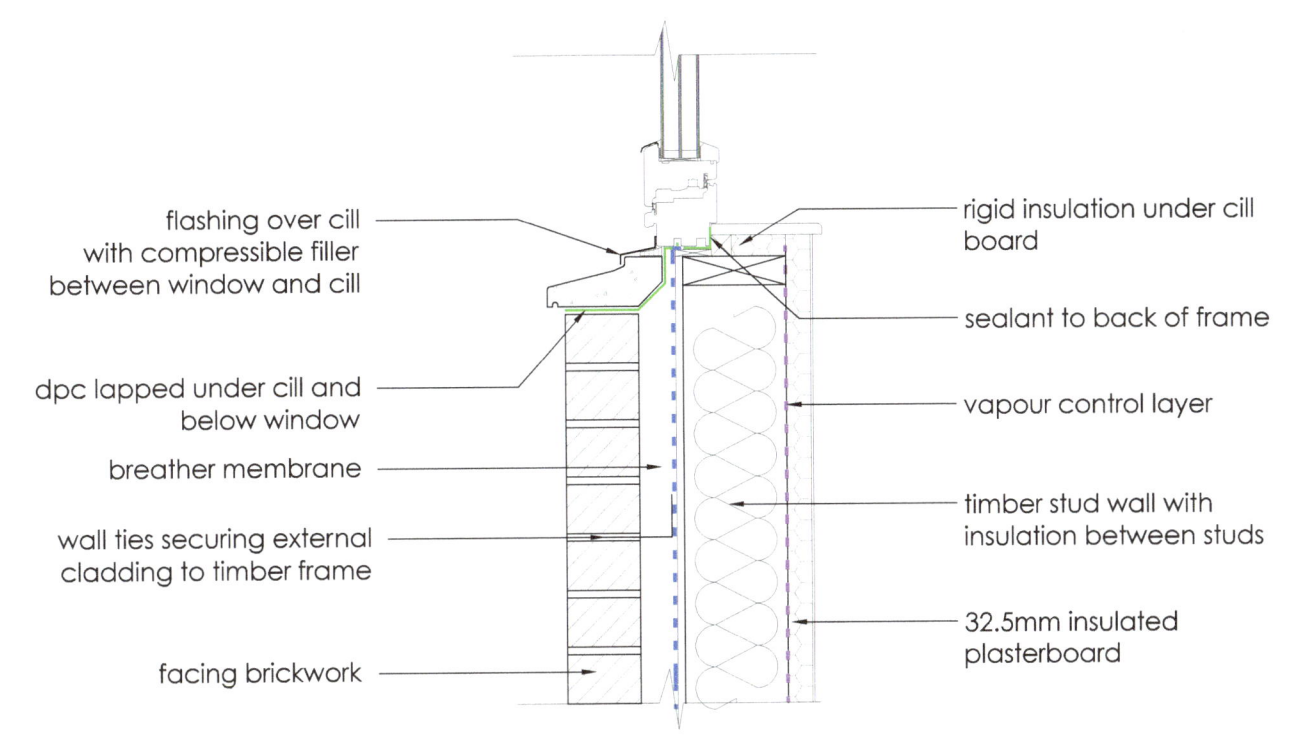

- flashing over cill with compressible filler between window and cill
- dpc lapped under cill and below window
- breather membrane
- wall ties securing external cladding to timber frame
- facing brickwork
- rigid insulation under cill board
- sealant to back of frame
- vapour control layer
- timber stud wall with insulation between studs
- 32.5mm insulated plasterboard

Detail T-W8 - Timber frame wall, brick cladding, window sill

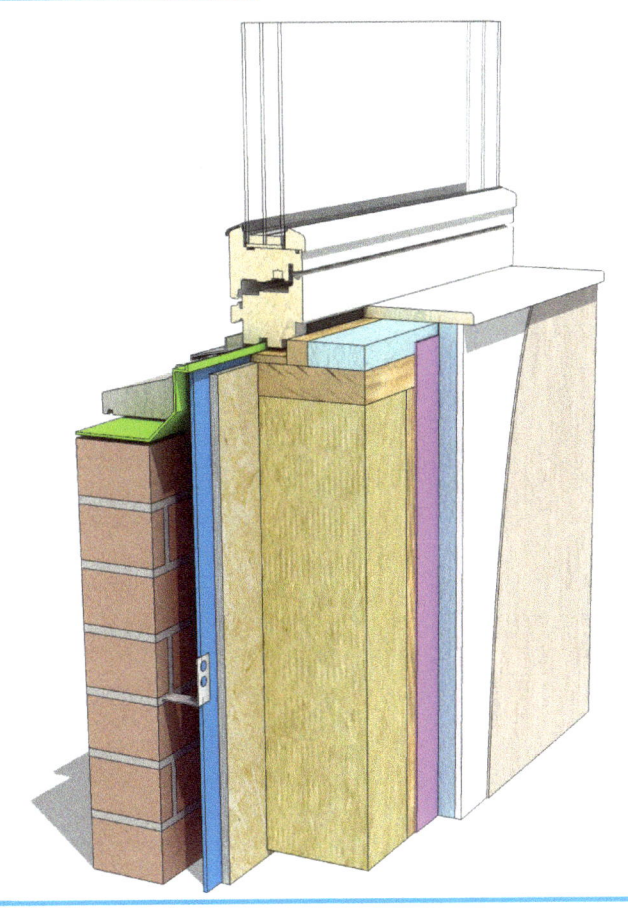

3D Detail T-W8 - Timber frame wall, brick cladding, window sill

208

T-W9

TIMBER FRAME WALL, BRICK CLADDING, WINDOW JAMB (PLAN)

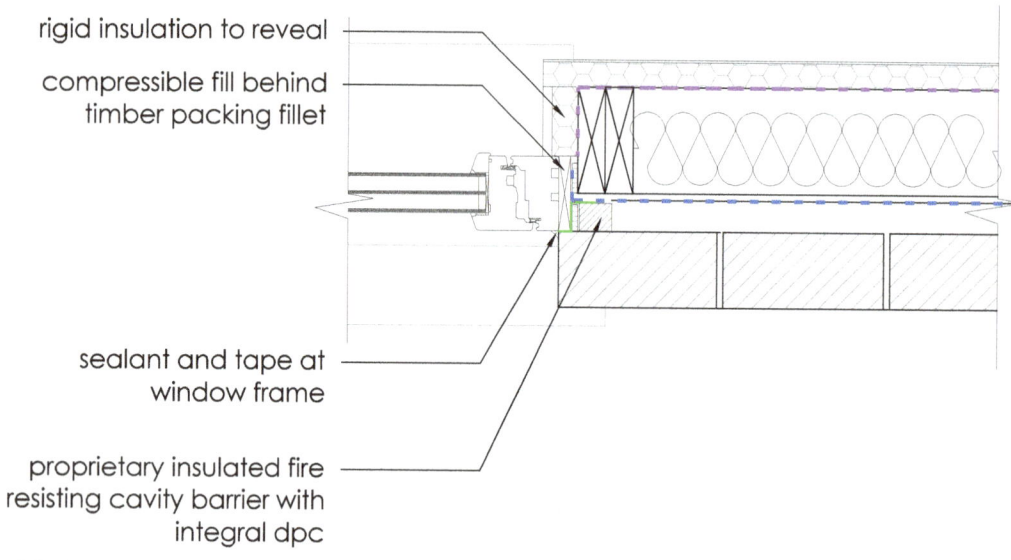

- rigid insulation to reveal
- compressible fill behind timber packing fillet
- sealant and tape at window frame
- proprietary insulated fire resisting cavity barrier with integral dpc

Detail T-W9 - Timber frame wall, brick cladding, window jamb (plan)

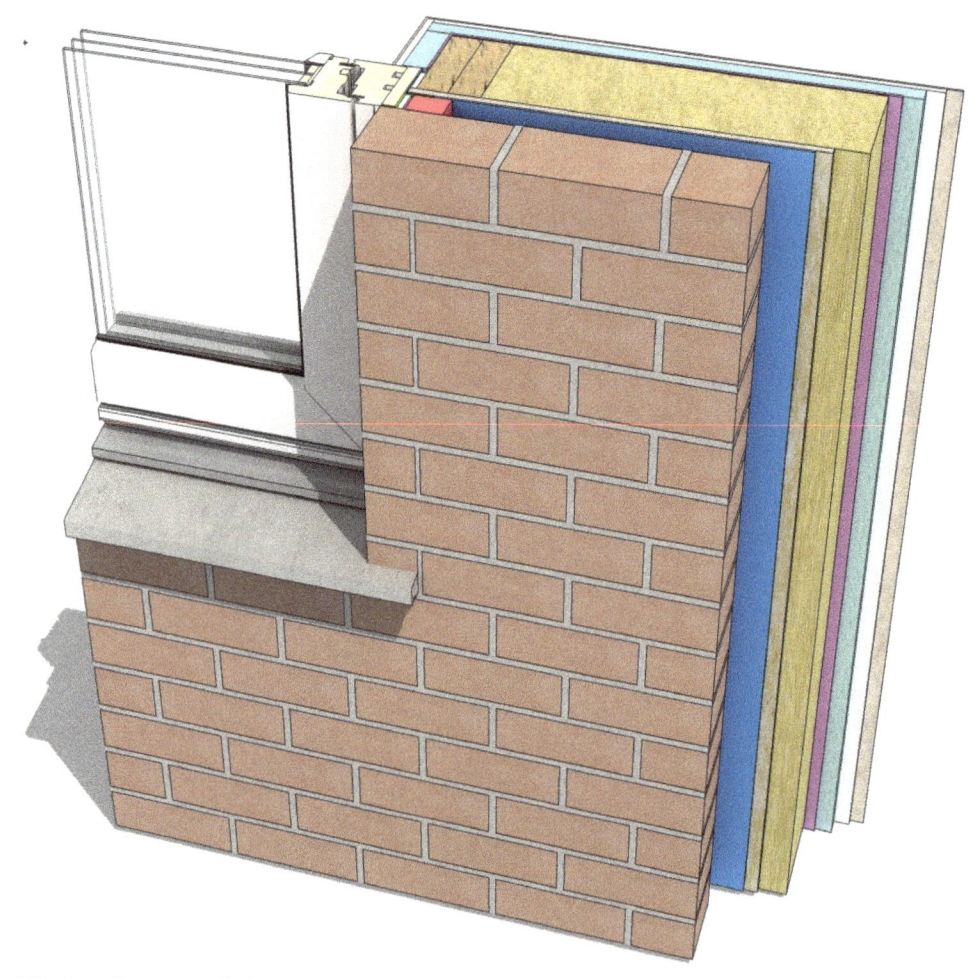

3D Detail T-W9 - Timber frame wall, brick cladding, window jamb

SECTION 6 - TIMBER FRAME

T-W10

TIMBER FRAME WALL, RENDER FINISH, WINDOW HEAD

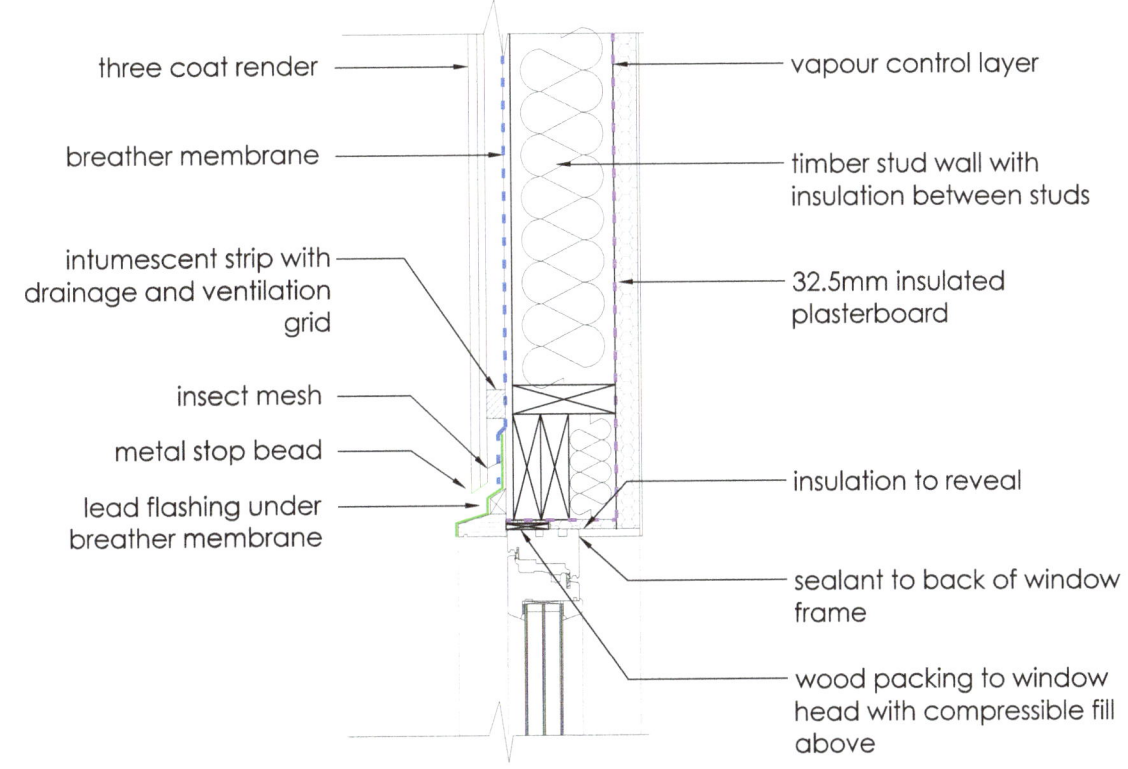

Labels (left side):
- three coat render
- breather membrane
- intumescent strip with drainage and ventilation grid
- insect mesh
- metal stop bead
- lead flashing under breather membrane

Labels (right side):
- vapour control layer
- timber stud wall with insulation between studs
- 32.5mm insulated plasterboard
- insulation to reveal
- sealant to back of window frame
- wood packing to window head with compressible fill above

Detail T-W10 - Timber frame wall, render finish, window head

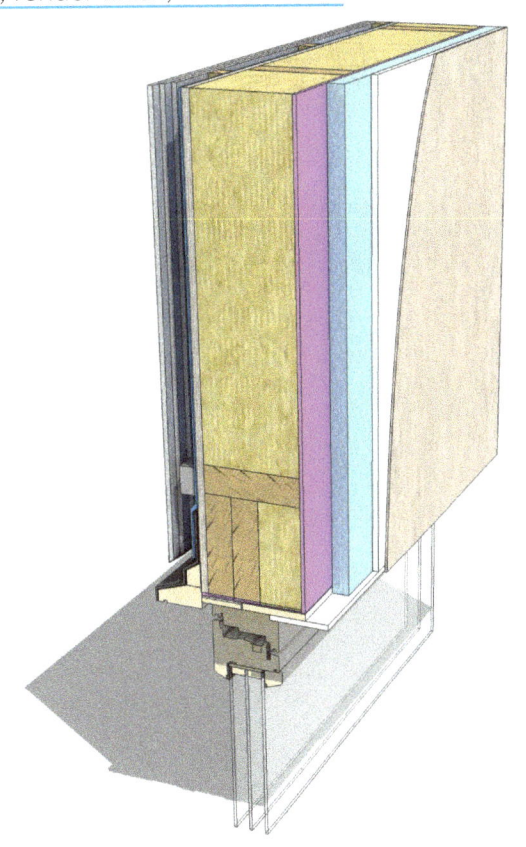

3D Detail T-W10 - Timber frame wall, render finish, window head

T-W11

TIMBER FRAME WALL, RENDER FINISH, WINDOW SILL

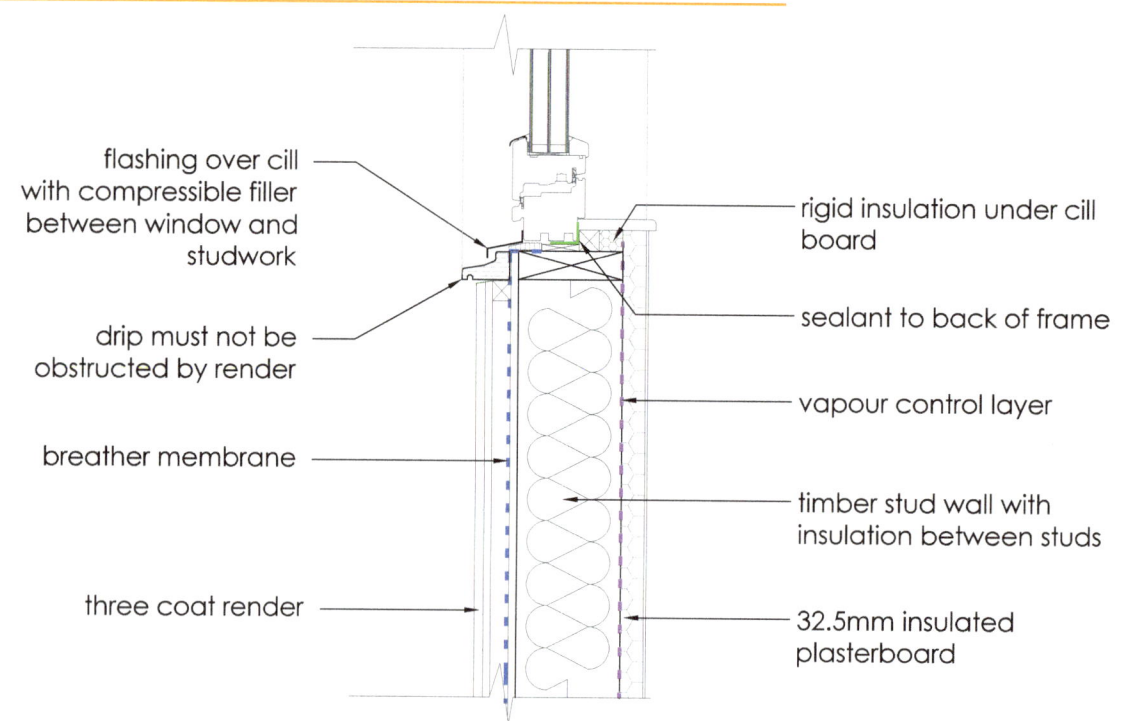

Labels (left side):
- flashing over cill with compressible filler between window and studwork
- drip must not be obstructed by render
- breather membrane
- three coat render

Labels (right side):
- rigid insulation under cill board
- sealant to back of frame
- vapour control layer
- timber stud wall with insulation between studs
- 32.5mm insulated plasterboard

Detail T-W11 - Timber frame wall, render finish, window sill

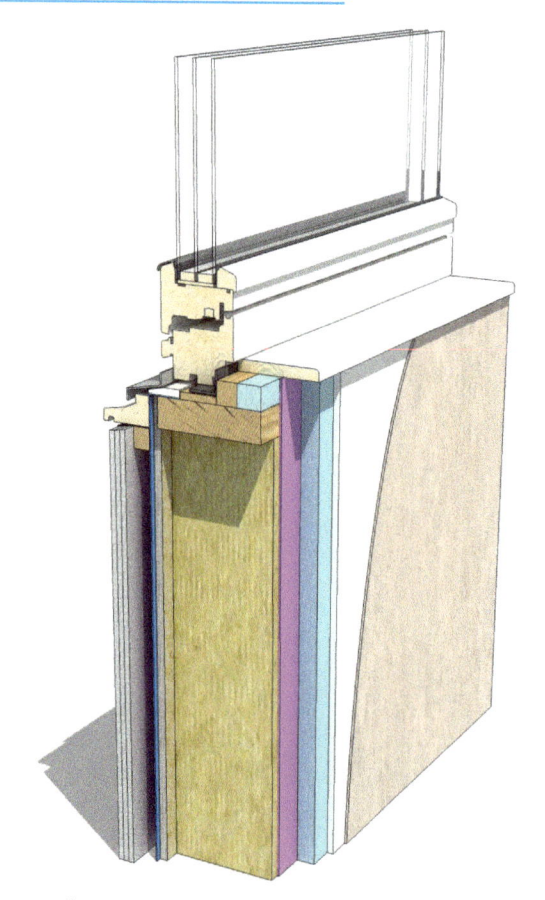

3D Detail T-W11 - Timber frame wall, render finish, window sill

SECTION 6 - TIMBER FRAME

T-W12

TIMBER FRAME WALL, RENDER FINISH, WINDOW JAMB

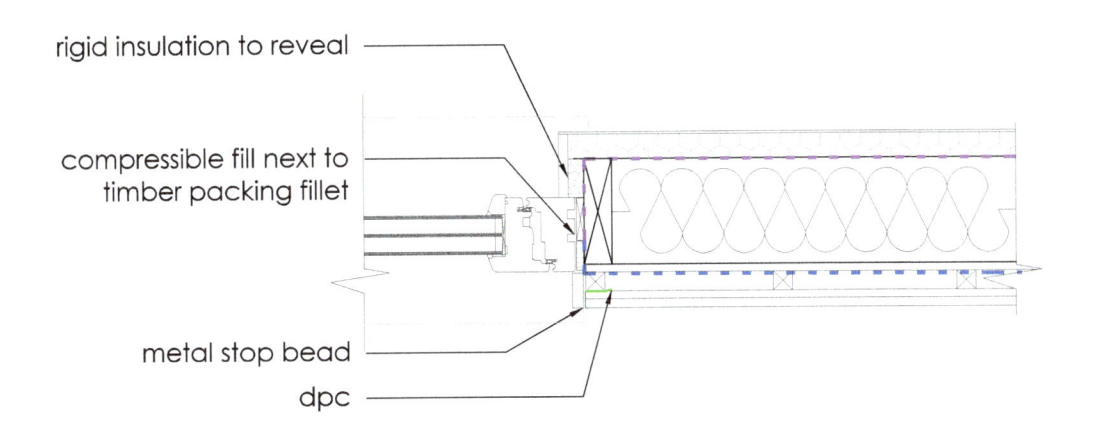

- rigid insulation to reveal
- compressible fill next to timber packing fillet
- metal stop bead
- dpc

Detail T-W12 - Timber frame wall, render finish, window jamb

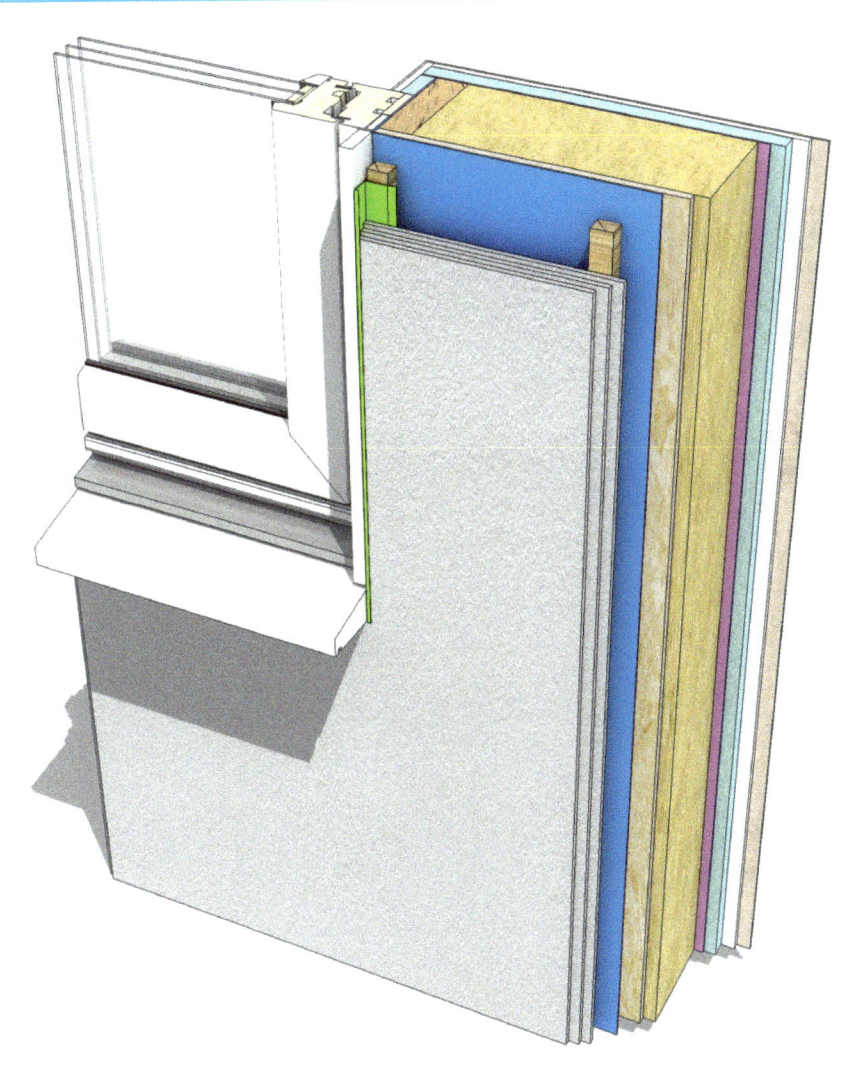

3D Detail T-W12 - Timber frame wall, render finish, window jamb

T-W13

TIMBER FRAME WALL, HORIZONTAL TIMBER CLADDING, WINDOW HEAD

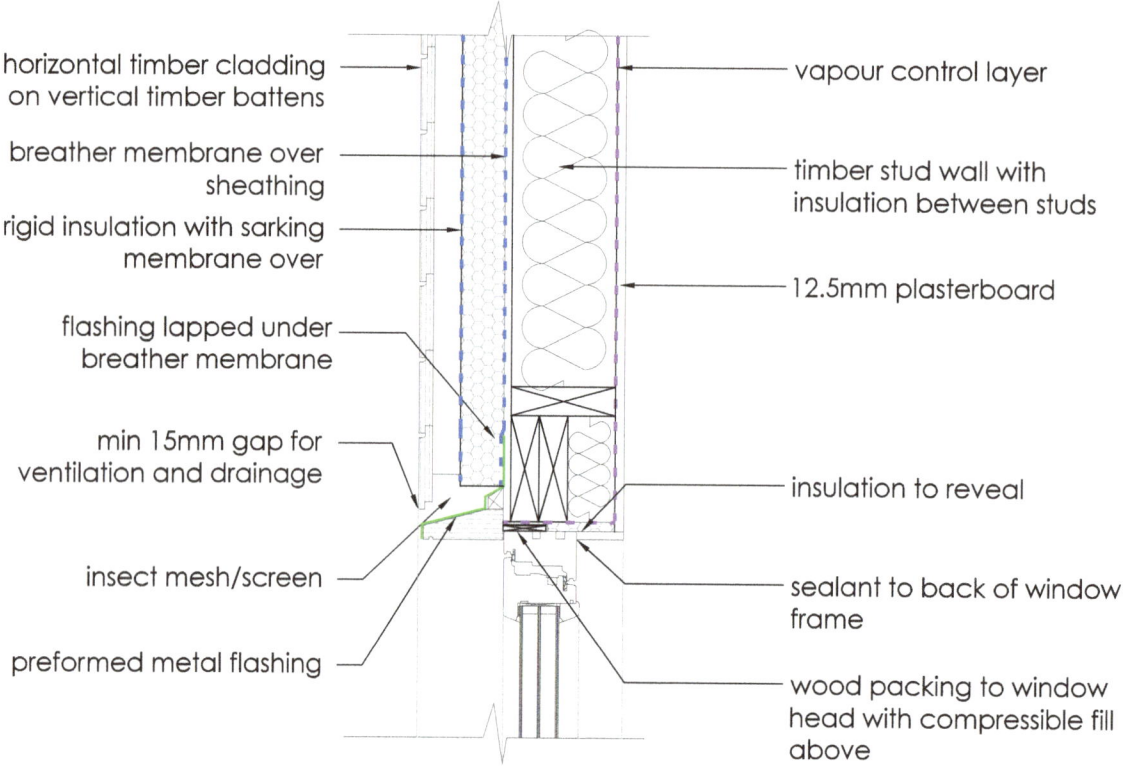

Labels (left):
- horizontal timber cladding on vertical timber battens
- breather membrane over sheathing
- rigid insulation with sarking membrane over
- flashing lapped under breather membrane
- min 15mm gap for ventilation and drainage
- insect mesh/screen
- preformed metal flashing

Labels (right):
- vapour control layer
- timber stud wall with insulation between studs
- 12.5mm plasterboard
- insulation to reveal
- sealant to back of window frame
- wood packing to window head with compressible fill above

Detail T-W13 - Timber frame wall, horizontal timber cladding, window head

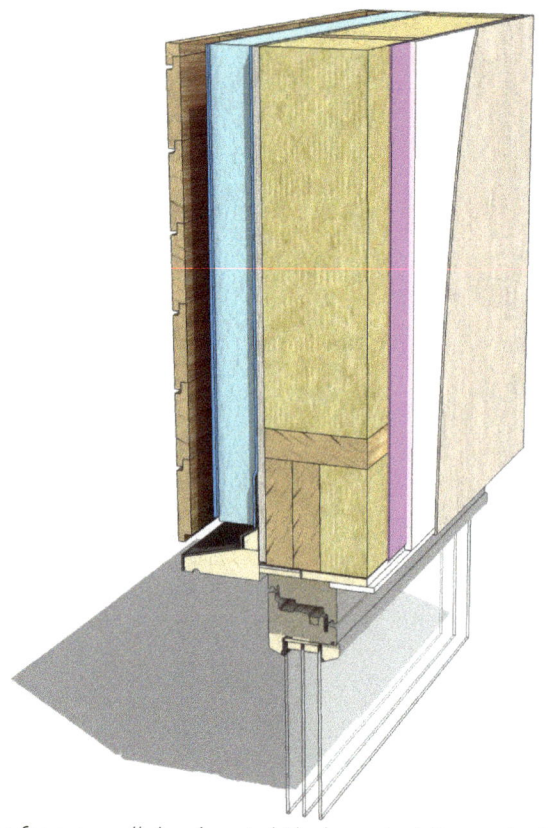

3D Detail T-W13 - Timber frame wall, horizontal timber cladding, window head

SECTION 6 - TIMBER FRAME

T-W14

TIMBER FRAME WALL, HORIZONTAL TIMBER CLADDING, WINDOW SILL

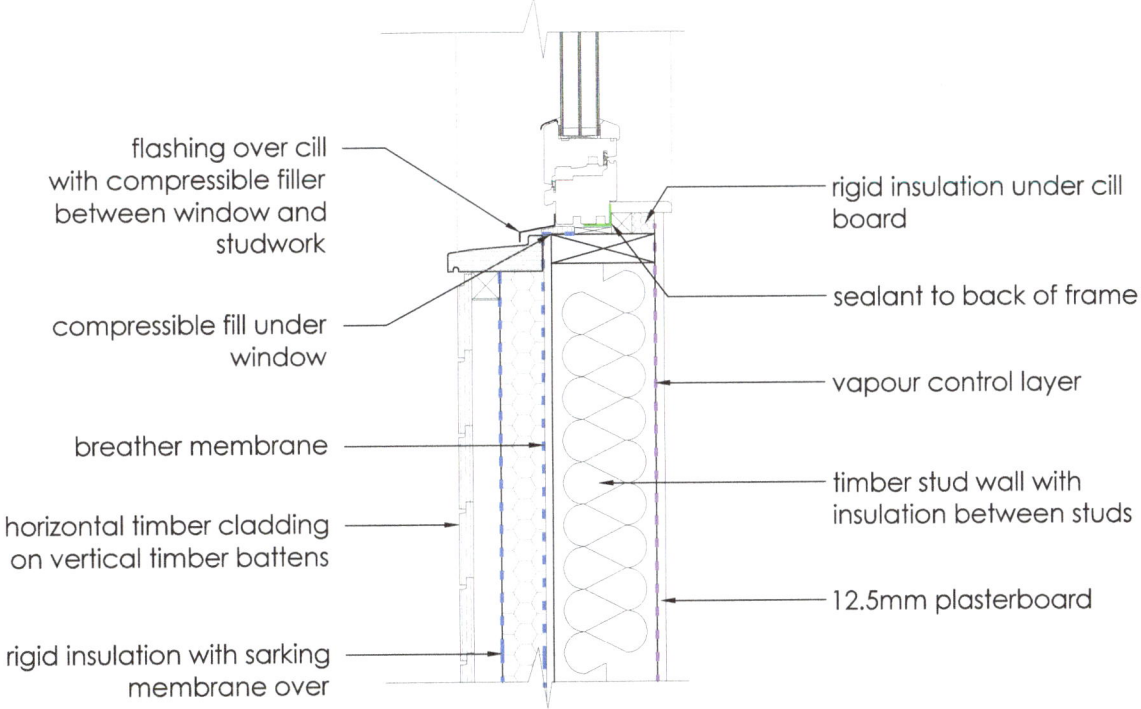

- flashing over cill with compressible filler between window and studwork
- compressible fill under window
- breather membrane
- horizontal timber cladding on vertical timber battens
- rigid insulation with sarking membrane over
- rigid insulation under cill board
- sealant to back of frame
- vapour control layer
- timber stud wall with insulation between studs
- 12.5mm plasterboard

Detail T-W14 - Timber frame wall, horizontal timber cladding, window sill

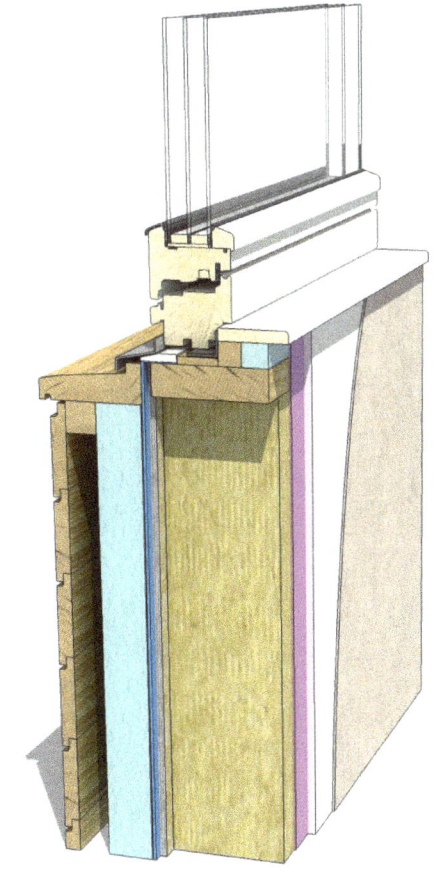

3D Detail T-W14 - Timber frame wall, horizontal timber cladding, window sill

T-W15

TIMBER FRAME WALL, HORIZONTAL TIMBER CLADDING, WINDOW JAMB

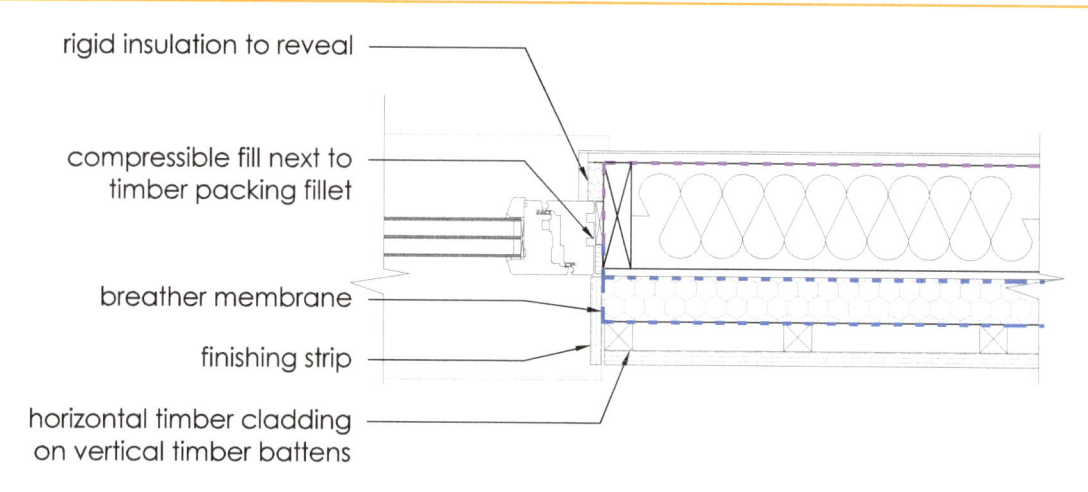

- rigid insulation to reveal
- compressible fill next to timber packing fillet
- breather membrane
- finishing strip
- horizontal timber cladding on vertical timber battens

Detail T-W15 - Timber frame wall, horizontal timber cladding, window jamb

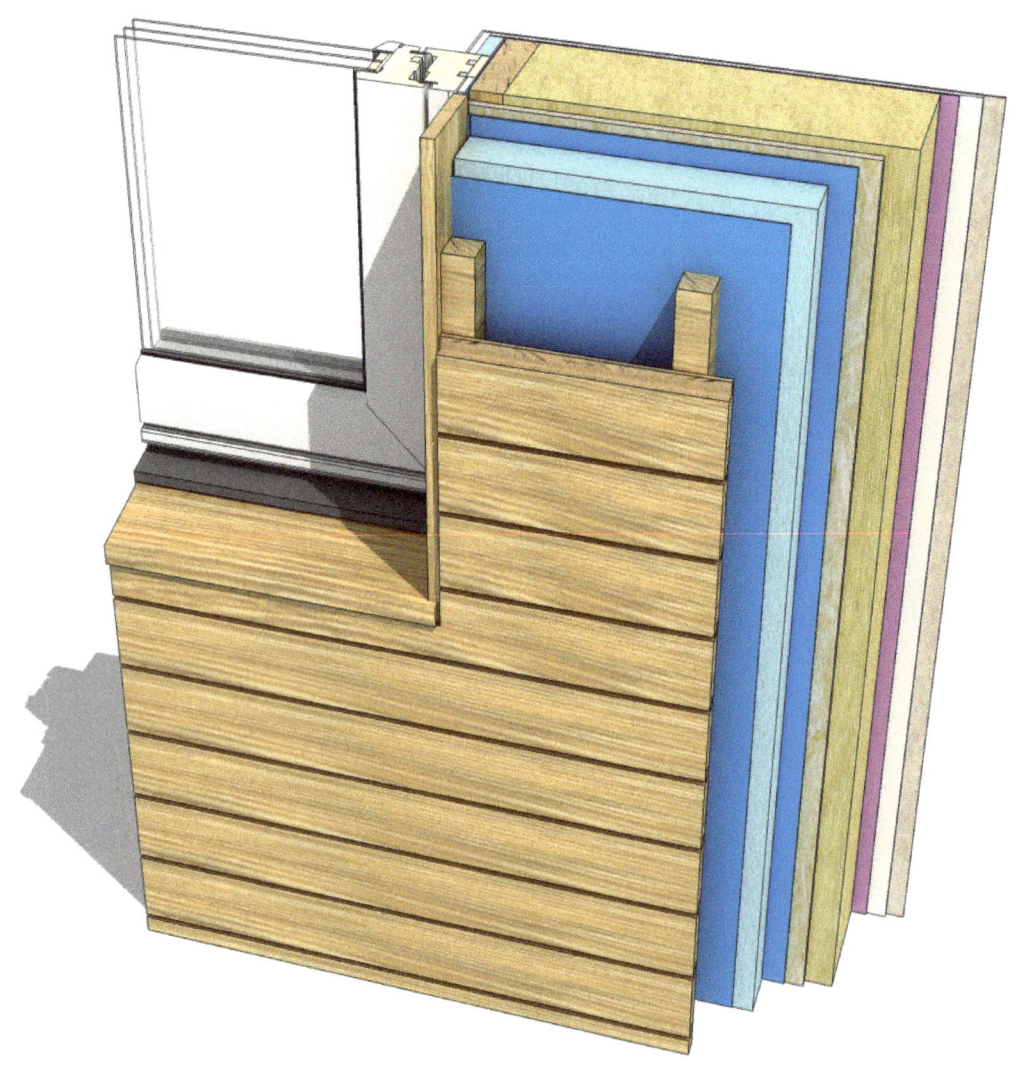

3D Detail T-W15 - Timber frame wall, horizontal timber cladding, window jamb

SECTION 6 - TIMBER FRAME

T-W16

TIMBER FRAME WALL, VERTICAL TIMBER CLADDING, WINDOW HEAD

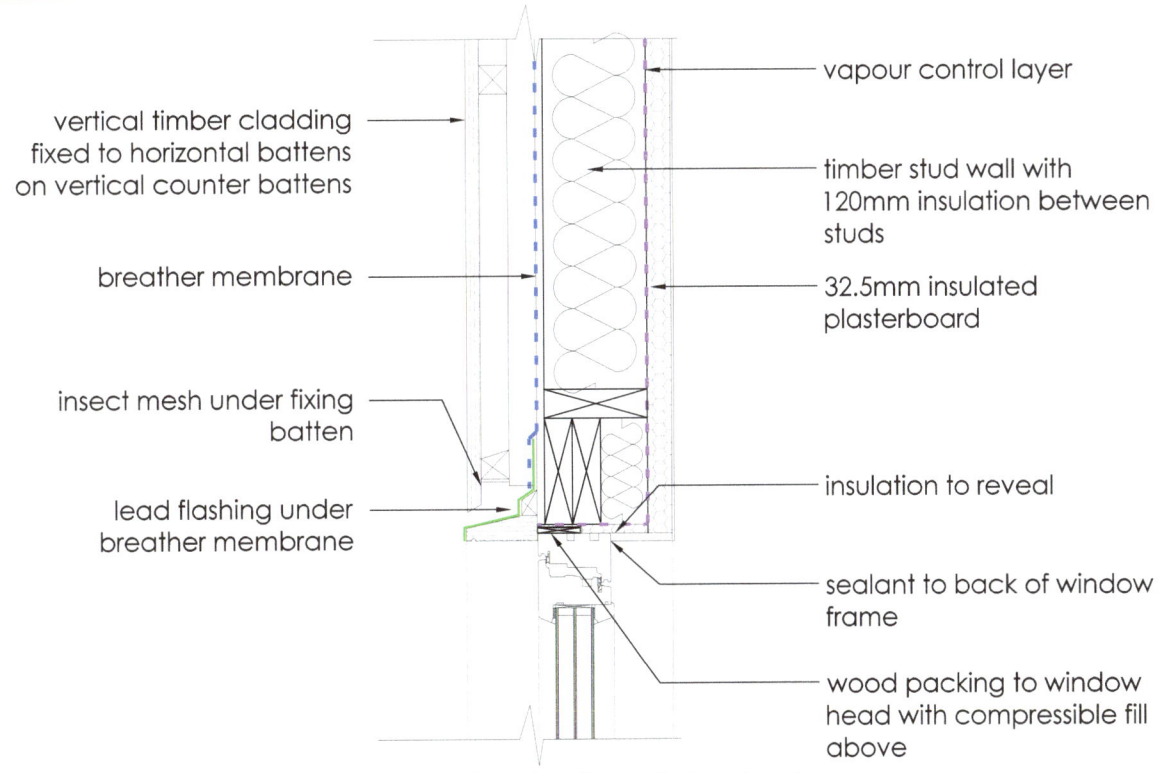

- vertical timber cladding fixed to horizontal battens on vertical counter battens
- breather membrane
- insect mesh under fixing batten
- lead flashing under breather membrane
- vapour control layer
- timber stud wall with 120mm insulation between studs
- 32.5mm insulated plasterboard
- insulation to reveal
- sealant to back of window frame
- wood packing to window head with compressible fill above

Detail T-W16 - Timber frame wall, vertical timber cladding, window head

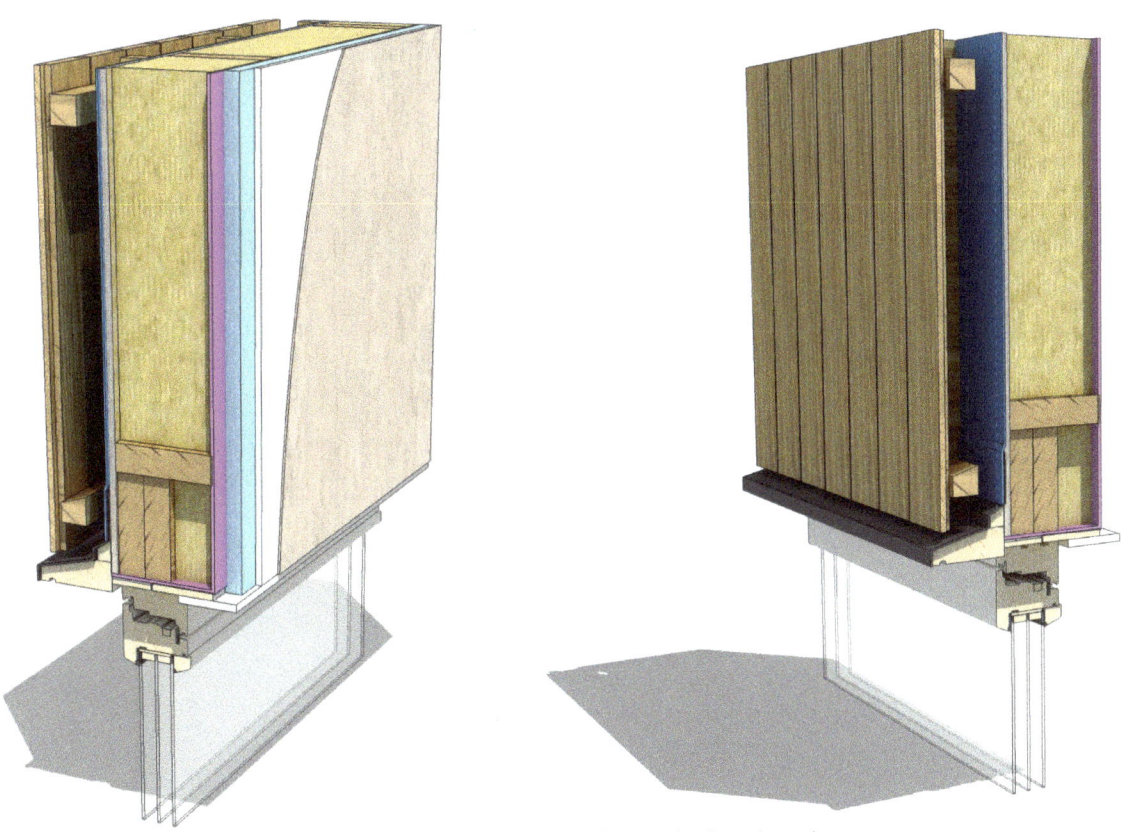

3D Detail T-W16 - Timber frame wall, vertical timber cladding, window head

T-W17

TIMBER FRAME WALL, VERTICAL TIMBER CLADDING, WINDOW SILL

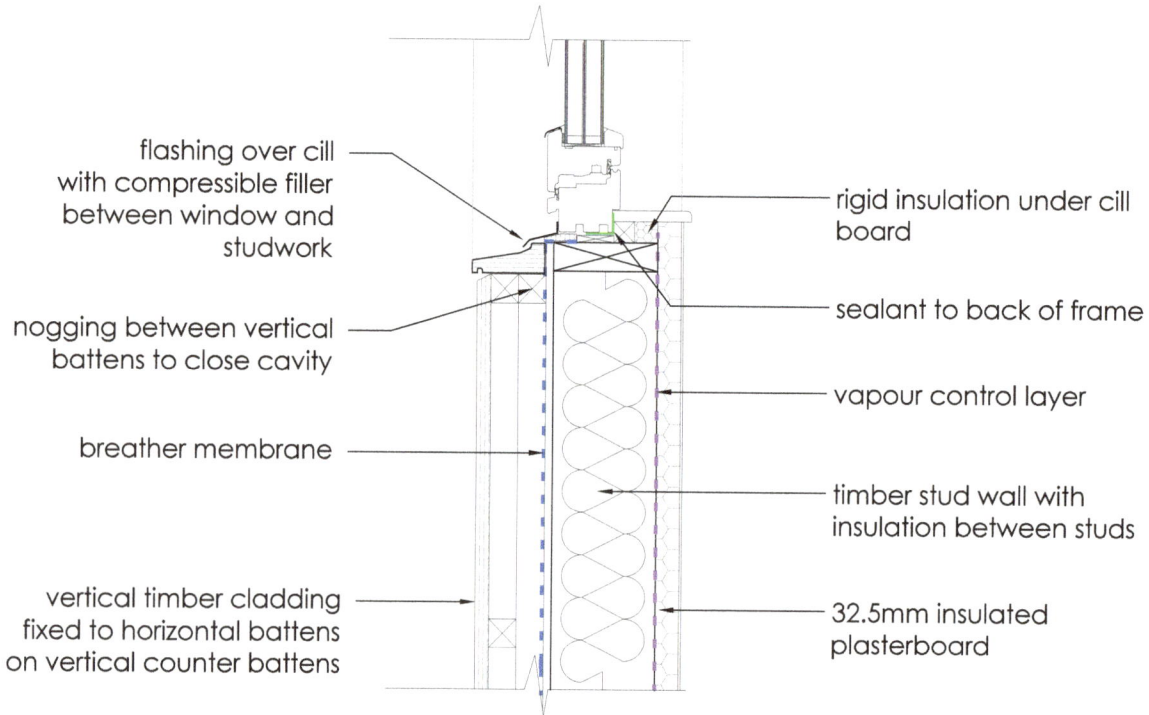

- flashing over cill with compressible filler between window and studwork
- nogging between vertical battens to close cavity
- breather membrane
- vertical timber cladding fixed to horizontal battens on vertical counter battens
- rigid insulation under cill board
- sealant to back of frame
- vapour control layer
- timber stud wall with insulation between studs
- 32.5mm insulated plasterboard

Detail T-W17 - Timber frame wall, vertical timber cladding, window sill

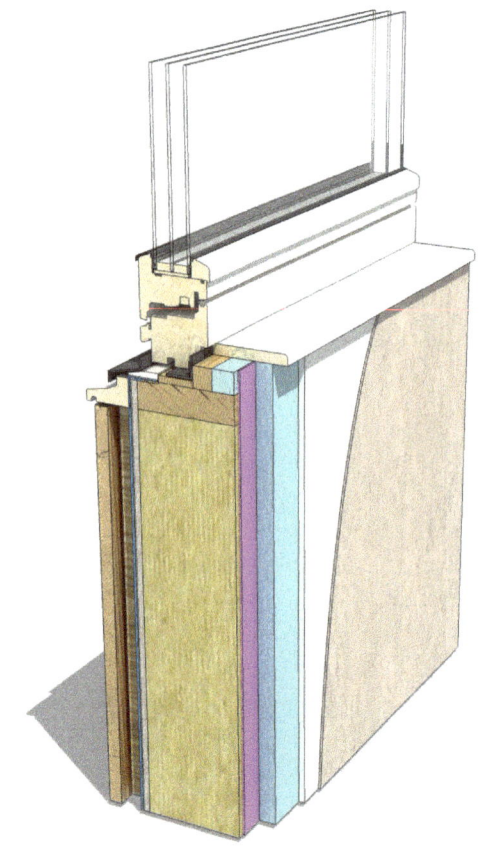

3D Detail T-W17 - Timber frame wall, vertical timber cladding, window sill

SECTION 6 - TIMBER FRAME

T-W18

TIMBER FRAME WALL, VERTICAL TIMBER CLADDING, WINDOW JAMB

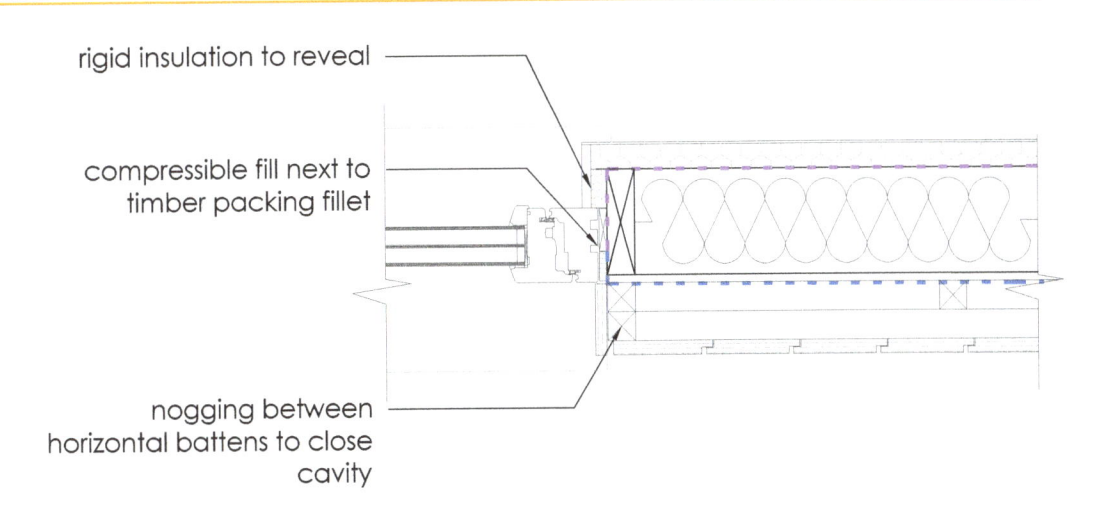

- rigid insulation to reveal
- compressible fill next to timber packing fillet
- nogging between horizontal battens to close cavity

Detail T-W18 - Timber frame wall, vertical timber cladding, window jamb (plan)

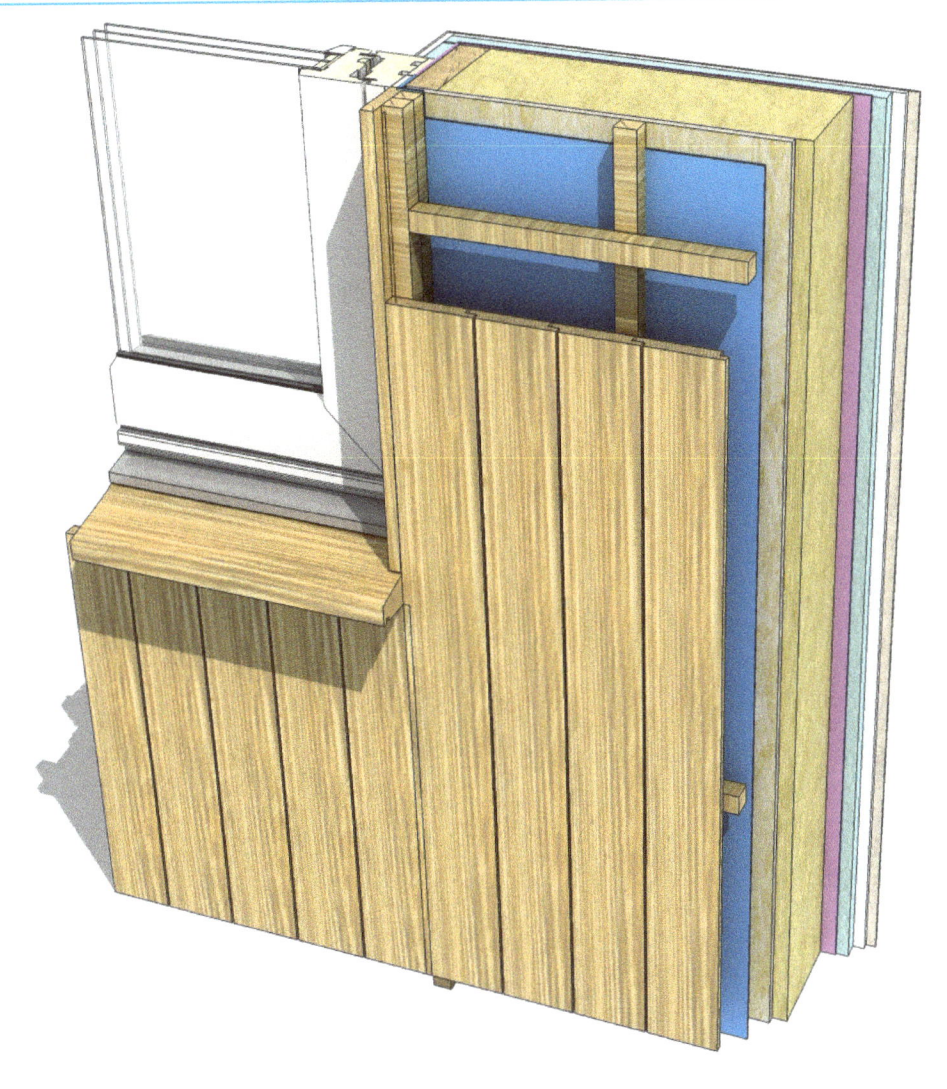

3D Detail T-W18 - Timber frame wall, vertical timber cladding, window jamb

NOTES ON THE REGS

The following information is a partial list of requirements from the **Building Regulations Approved Documents** - for full and detailed explanations and requirements please consult the full publications.

GENERAL REQUIREMENTS - WALLS

Moisture
The walls of the building shall adequately protect the building and people who use the building from harmful effects caused by:
- ground moisture
- precipitation and wind-driven spray
- interstitial and surface condensation
- spillage of water from or associated with sanitary fittings or fixed appliances

(Approved Doc C2)

Cavity Insulation
Fumes given off by insulating materials such as by urea formaldehyde foams should not be allowed to penetrate occupied parts of the building to an extent where it could become a health risks to persons in the building by becoming an irritant concentration.

(Approved Doc D)

Fire precautions
Materials and/or products used for the internal linings of walls shall restrict:
-the spread of flame;
-the amount of heat released.

Internal fire spread (structure)
A wall common to two or more buildings shall be designed and constructed so that it adequately resists the spread of fire between those buildings.

The building should be sub-divided by elements of fire resisting construction into compartments.

Any hidden voids in the construction shall be sealed and sub-divided to inhibit the unseen spread of fire and products of combustion, in order to reduce the risk of structural failure, and the spread of fire.

(Approved Doc B3)

External walls shall be constructed so as to have a low rate of heat release and thereby be capable of reducing the risk of ignition from an external source and the spread of fire over their surfaces.

The amount of unprotected area in the sides of the building shall be restricted so as to limit the amount of thermal radiation that can pass through the wall.

(Approved Doc B4)

Airborne and impact sound
Dwellings shall be designed so that the noise from domestic activity in an adjoining dwelling (or other parts of the building) is kept to a level that:

- does not affect the health of the occupants of the dwelling
- will allow them to sleep, rest and engage in their normal activities in satisfactory conditions.

(Approved Doc E1)

Dwellings shall be designed so that any domestic noise that is generated internally does not interfere with the occupants ability to sleep, rest and engage in their normal activities in satisfactory conditions.
(Approved Doc E2)

Domestic buildings shall be designed and constructed so as to restrict the transmission of echoes.
(Approved Doc E3)

Conservation of fuel and power
Reasonable provision shall be made for the conservation of fuel and power in buildings by:
- limiting heat gains and losses through thermal elements and other parts of the building fabric,
- from pipes ducts and vessels used for space heating, space cooling and hot water services.
- providing fixed building services which are energy efficient and have effective controls and are commissioned by testing and adjusting as necessary to ensure they use no more fuel and power than is reasonable in the circumstances.

(Approved Doc L)

SECTION 6 - TIMBER FRAME

GENERAL NOTES:

Walls should comply with the relevant requirements of BS EN 1996-2:2006

For residential buildings, the maximum height of the building measured from the lowest finished ground level adjoining the building to the highest point of any wall or roof should not be greater than 15m.

Wall cladding
Wall cladding shall be capable of safely sustaining and transmitting all dead, imposed and wind loads. Provision shall be made where necessary, to accommodate differential movement of the cladding and the supporting structure of the building.
The cladding shall be securely fixed to and supported by the structure of the building using both vertical support and horizontal restraint.
The cladding and its fixings shall be of durable materials.

See approved documents for masonry unit and mortar requirements.

Strapping
Tension straps should be used to strap walls to floors above ground level, at intervals not exceeding 2m.
Gable walls should be strapped to roofs.
The ends of every wall should be bonded or otherwise securely tied throughout their full height to a buttressing wall, pier or chimney.

Cavity barriers
Structure should be designed so that the unseen spread of fire and smoke within concealed spaces is prevented.

Cavity barriers should be provided:
- at the edge of cavities
- around window and door openings
- at the junction between an external cavity wall and a compartment wall
- at the junction between an external cavity wall and a compartment floor
- at the top of an external cavity wall
- at the junction between an internal cavity wall and any assembly which forms a fire resisting barrier
- above the enclosures to a protected stairway in a dwelling with a floor more than 4.5m above ground level.

Cavity walls
All cavity walls should have
- leaves at least 90mm thick and cavities at least 50mm wide
- wall ties with a horizontal spacing of 900mm and a vertical spacing of 450mm
- wall ties spaced not more than 300mm apart vertically within a distance of 225mm from the vertical edges of all openings, movement joints and roof verges.

Damp proof courses
Internal and external walls that are subject to moisture from the ground should have a damp-proof course to prevent the passage of moisture. The damp proof course should be continuous with any damp proof membrane in the floor.
If the wall is an external wall, the damp proof course should be at least 150mm above the level of the adjoining ground.

If the wall is an external cavity wall either:
- the cavity should be taken down at least 225mm below the level of the lowest damp-proof course or
- a damp proof tray should be provided so as to prevent precipitation passing into the inner leaf, with weep holes every 900mm to assist in the transfer of moisture through the external leaf.

ROOF DETAILS

T-R1

TIMBER FRAME WALL, EAVES DETAIL, INSULATION BETWEEN AND OVER CEILING JOISTS

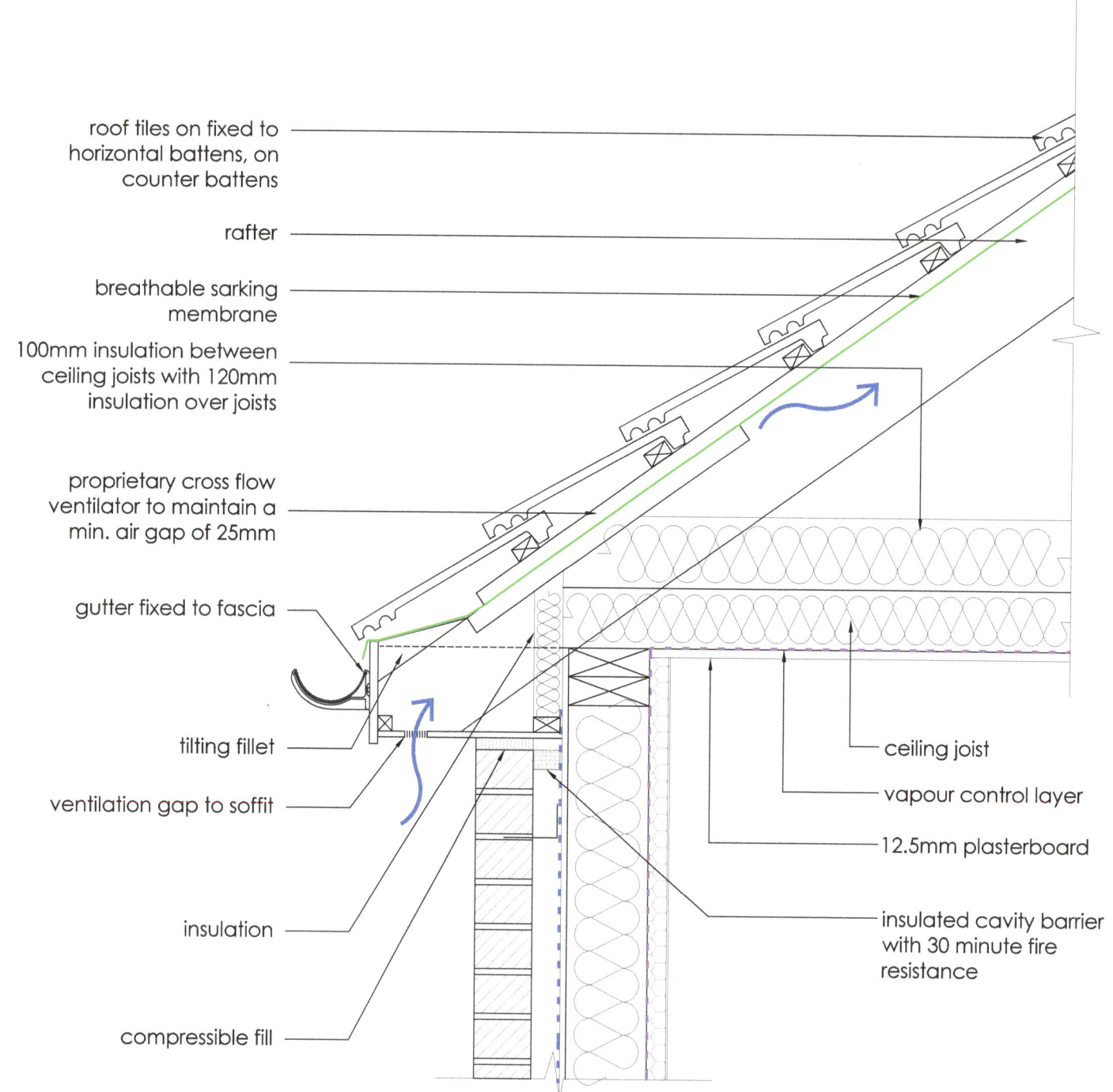

Labels (left side):
- roof tiles on fixed to horizontal battens, on counter battens
- rafter
- breathable sarking membrane
- 100mm insulation between ceiling joists with 120mm insulation over joists
- proprietary cross flow ventilator to maintain a min. air gap of 25mm
- gutter fixed to fascia
- tilting fillet
- ventilation gap to soffit
- insulation
- compressible fill

Labels (right side):
- ceiling joist
- vapour control layer
- 12.5mm plasterboard
- insulated cavity barrier with 30 minute fire resistance

Detail T-R1 - Timber frame wall, eaves detail, insulation between and over ceiling joists

NOTES:
U Value 0.12W/m²K or better

SECTION 6 - TIMBER FRAME

3D Detail T-R1- Timber frame wall, eaves detail, insulation between and over ceiling joists

T-R2

TIMBER FRAME WALL, GABLE DETAIL, INSULATION BETWEEN AND OVER CEILING JOISTS

100mm insulation between ceiling joists with 120mm insulation laid over joists

insulated cavity barrier with 30 mins fire resistance

ceiling joist

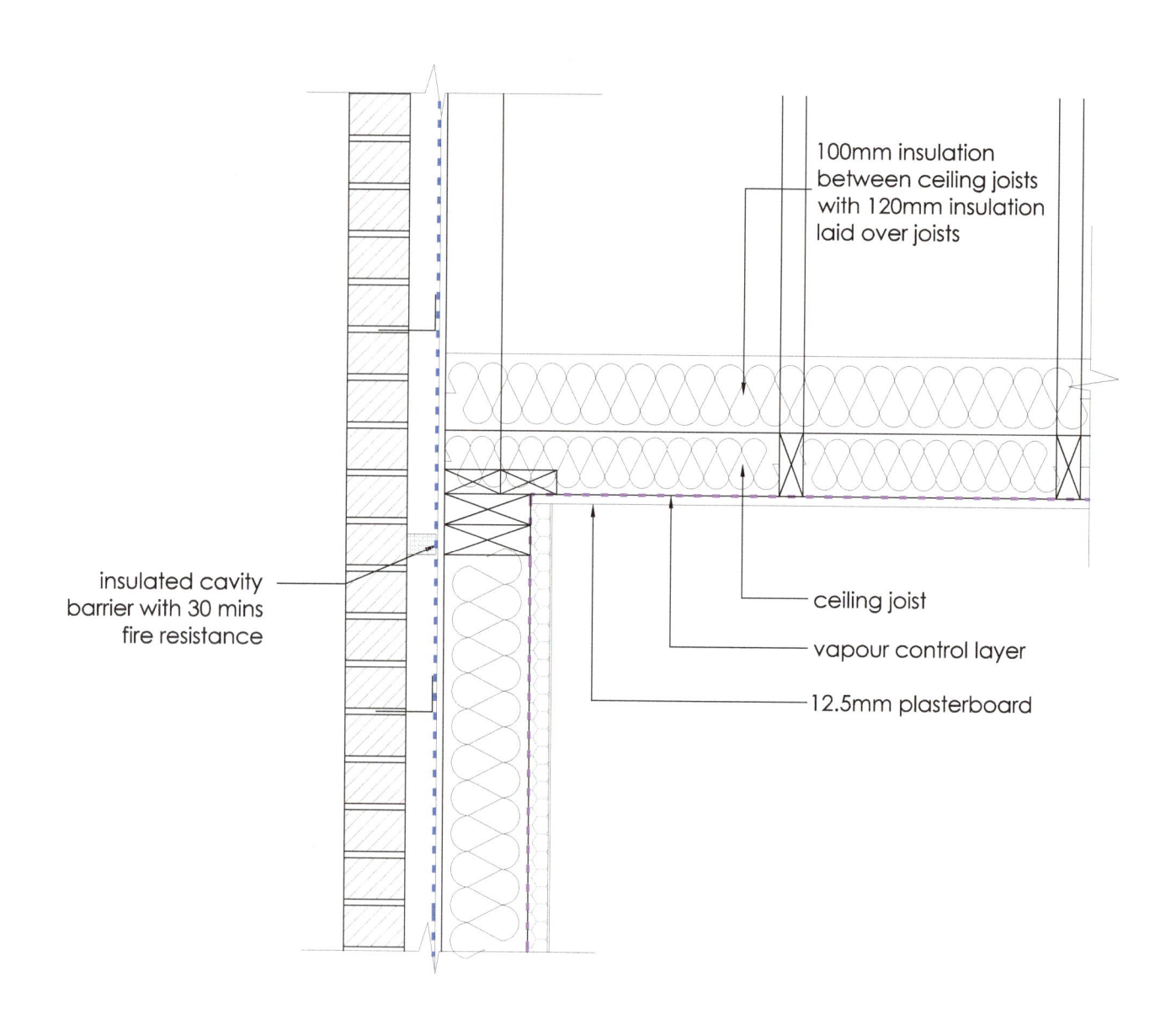

vapour control layer

12.5mm plasterboard

Detail T-R2- Timber frame wall, gable detail, insulation between and over ceiling joists

NOTES:
U Value 0.12W/m²K or better

SECTION 6 - TIMBER FRAME

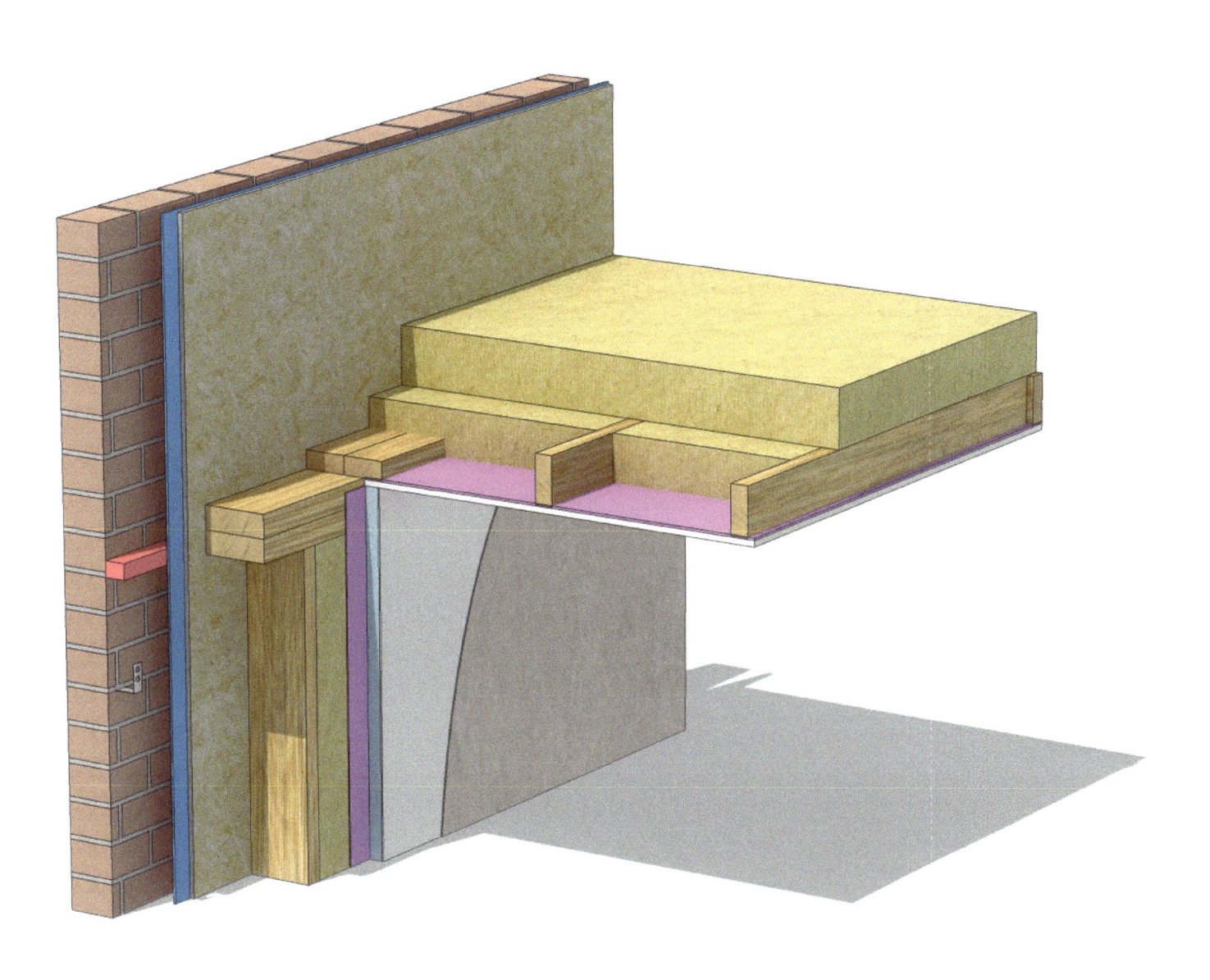

3D Detail T-R2- Timber frame wall, gable detail, insulation between and over ceiling joists

T-R3

TIMBER FRAME WALL, EAVES DETAIL, INSULATION BETWEEN AND UNDER RAFTERS

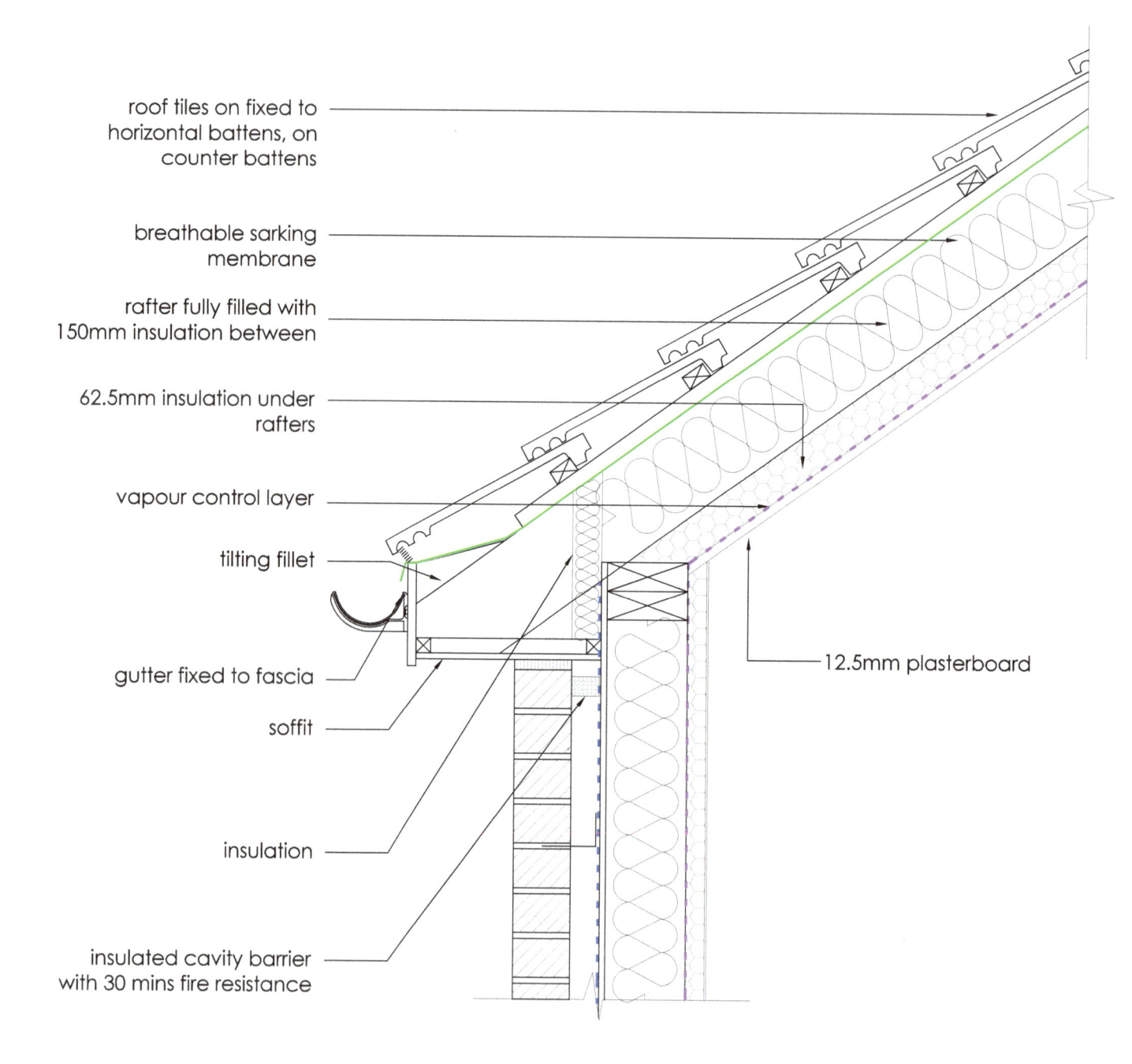

Labels on diagram:
- roof tiles on fixed to horizontal battens, on counter battens
- breathable sarking membrane
- rafter fully filled with 150mm insulation between
- 62.5mm insulation under rafters
- vapour control layer
- tilting fillet
- gutter fixed to fascia
- soffit
- insulation
- insulated cavity barrier with 30 mins fire resistance
- 12.5mm plasterboard

Detail T-R3- Timber frame wall, eaves detail, insulation between and under rafters

NOTES:

U Value 0.12W/m²K or better
Any ventilation requirements according to manufacturers instructions

SECTION 6 - TIMBER FRAME

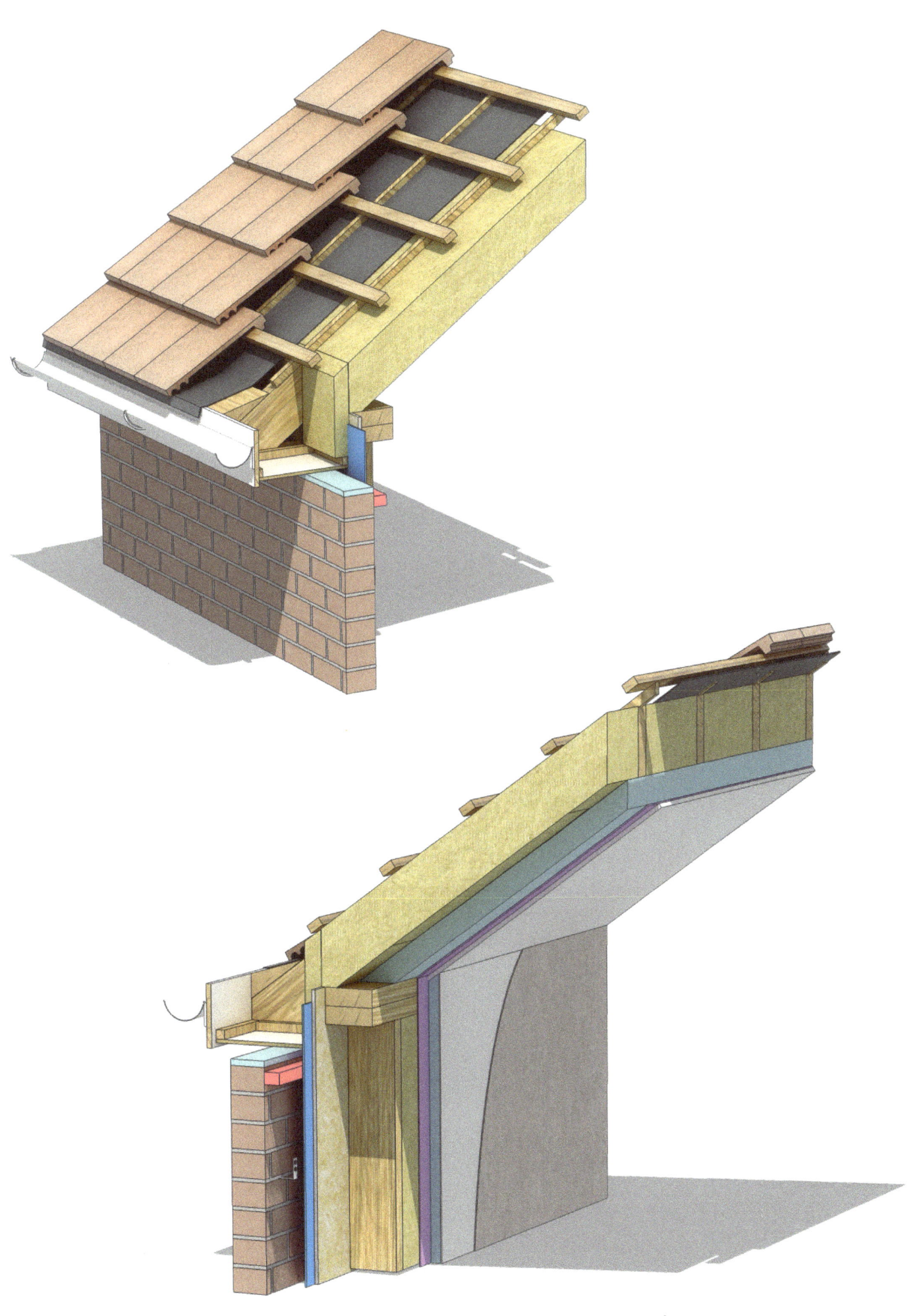

3D Detail T-R3- Timber frame wall, eaves detail, insulation between and under rafters

T-R4

TIMBER FRAME WALL, GABLE DETAIL, INSULATION BETWEEN AND UNDER RAFTERS

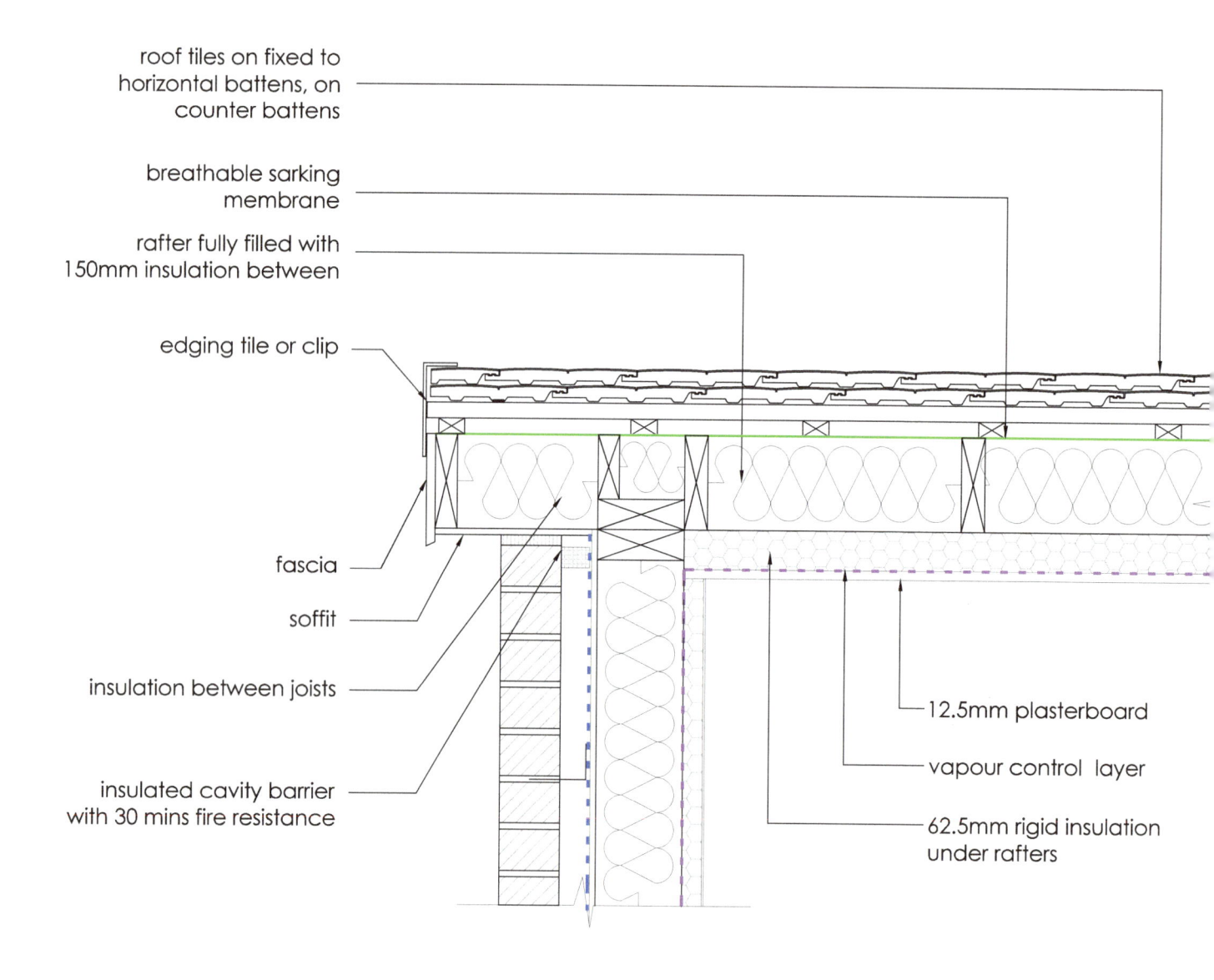

Labels on diagram:
- roof tiles on fixed to horizontal battens, on counter battens
- breathable sarking membrane
- rafter fully filled with 150mm insulation between
- edging tile or clip
- fascia
- soffit
- insulation between joists
- insulated cavity barrier with 30 mins fire resistance
- 12.5mm plasterboard
- vapour control layer
- 62.5mm rigid insulation under rafters

Detail T-R4- Timber frame wall, gable detail, insulation between and under rafters

NOTES:

U Value 0.12W/m²K or better
Any ventilation requirements according to manufacturers instructions

SECTION 6 - TIMBER FRAME

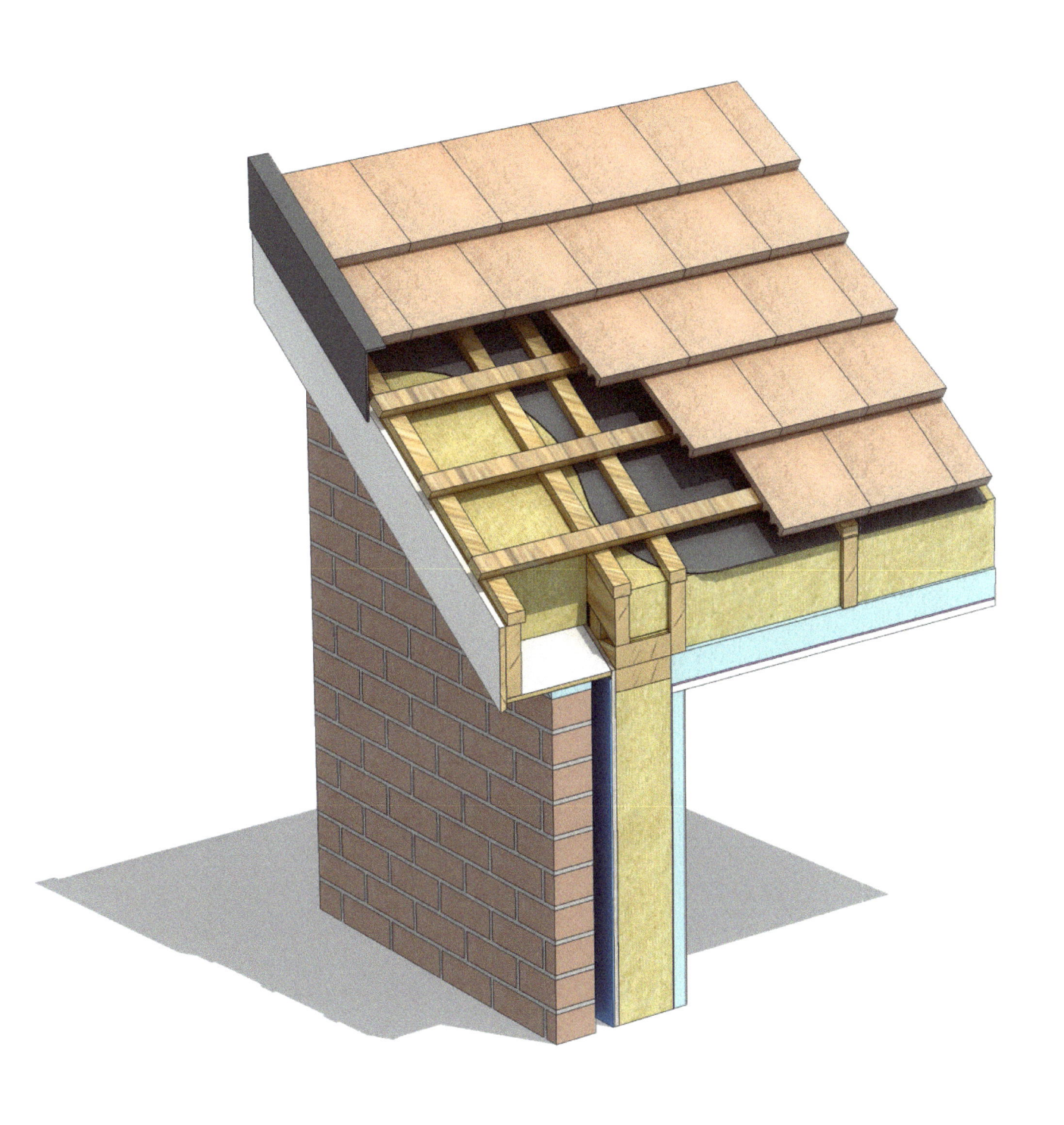

3D Detail T-R4- Timber frame wall, gable detail, insulation between and under rafters

T-R5

TIMBER FRAME WALL, EAVES DETAIL, INSULATION BETWEEN AND OVER RAFTERS

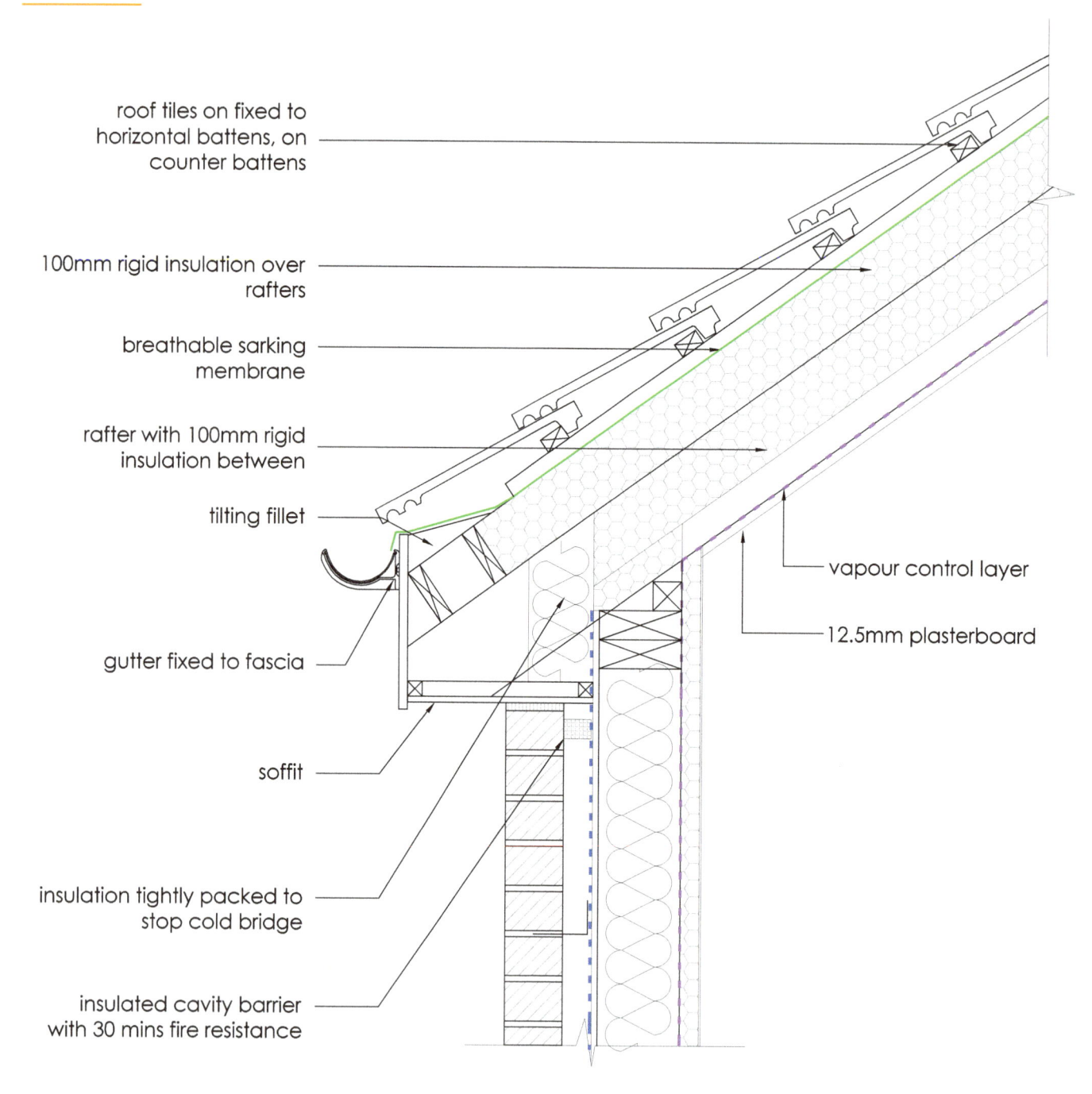

- roof tiles on fixed to horizontal battens, on counter battens
- 100mm rigid insulation over rafters
- breathable sarking membrane
- rafter with 100mm rigid insulation between
- tilting fillet
- gutter fixed to fascia
- soffit
- insulation tightly packed to stop cold bridge
- insulated cavity barrier with 30 mins fire resistance
- vapour control layer
- 12.5mm plasterboard

Detail T-R5- Timber frame wall, eaves detail, insulation between and over rafters

NOTES:

U Value 0.12W/m²K or better
Any ventilation requirements according to manufacturers instructions

SECTION 6 - TIMBER FRAME

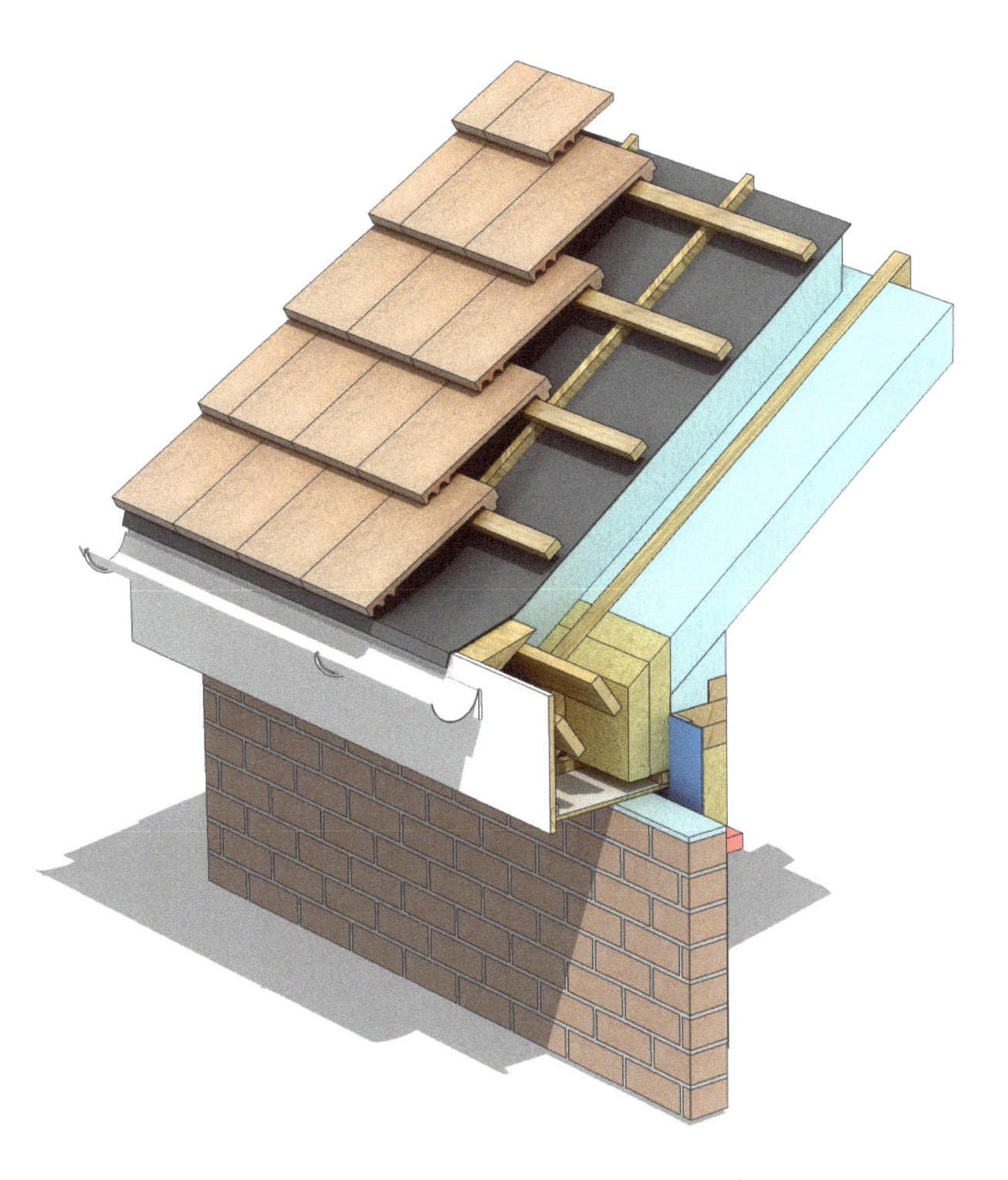

3D Detail T-R5 - Timber frame wall, eaves detail, insulation between and over rafters

T-R6

TIMBER FRAME WALL, FLAT ROOF, INSULATION ABOVE ROOF DECK

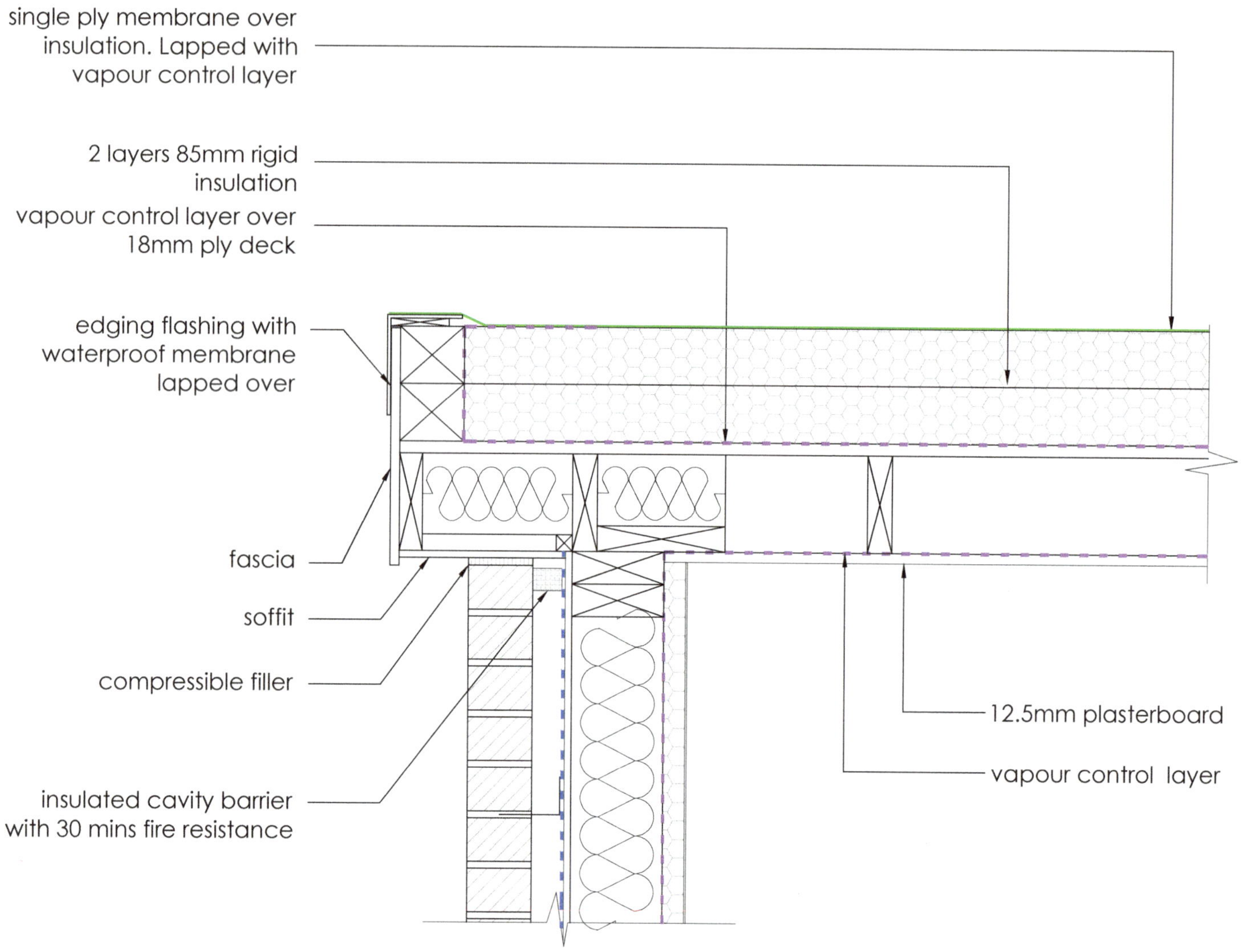

single ply membrane over insulation. Lapped with vapour control layer
2 layers 85mm rigid insulation
vapour control layer over 18mm ply deck
edging flashing with waterproof membrane lapped over
fascia
soffit
compressible filler
insulated cavity barrier with 30 mins fire resistance
12.5mm plasterboard
vapour control layer

Detail T-R6- Timber frame wall, flat roof, insulation above roof deck

NOTES:

U Value 0.12W/m²K or better

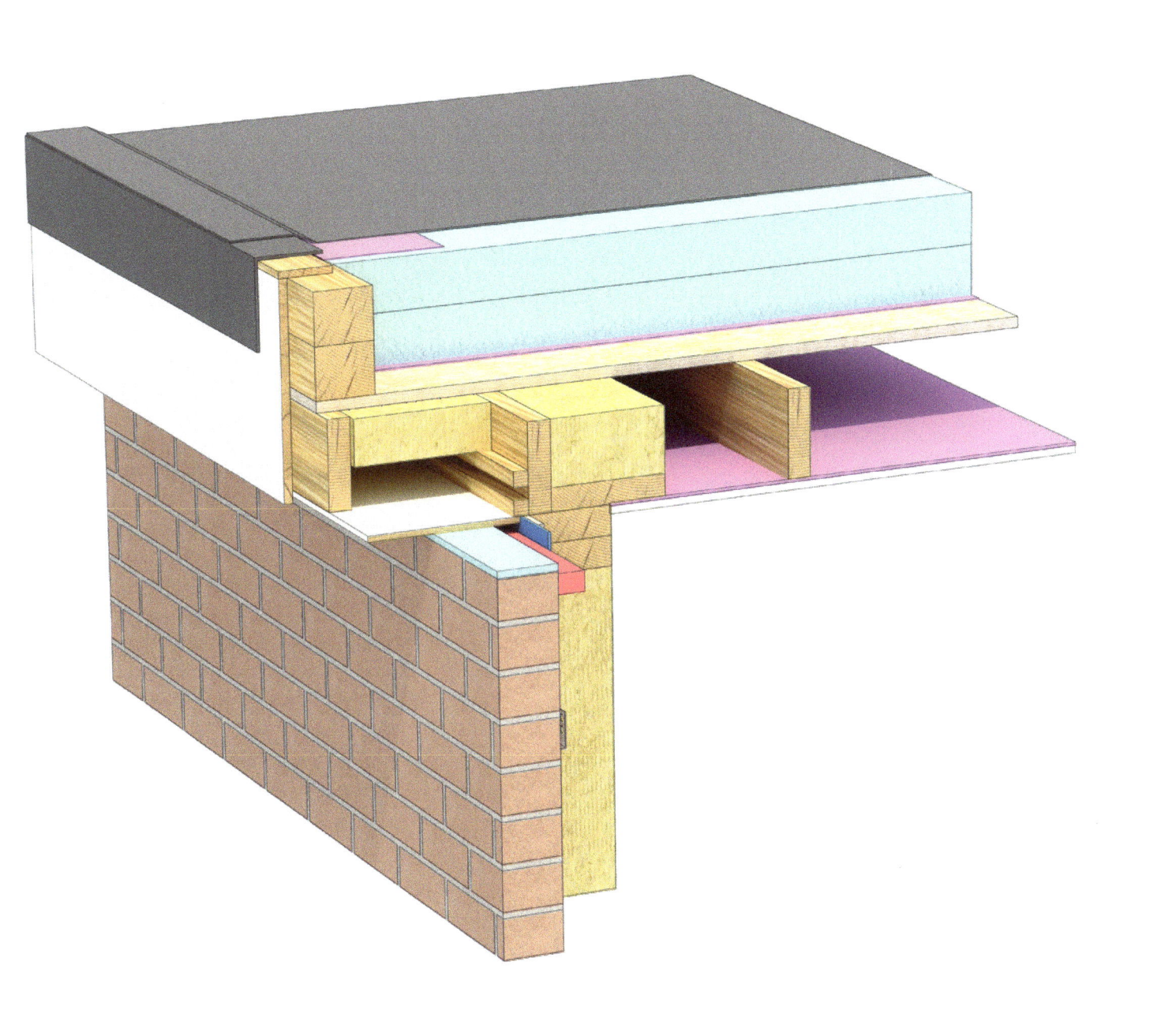

3D Detail T-R6- Timber frame wall, flat roof, insulation above roof deck

T-R7

TIMBER FRAME WALL, FLAT ROOF WITH PARAPET, INSULATION ABOVE JOISTS

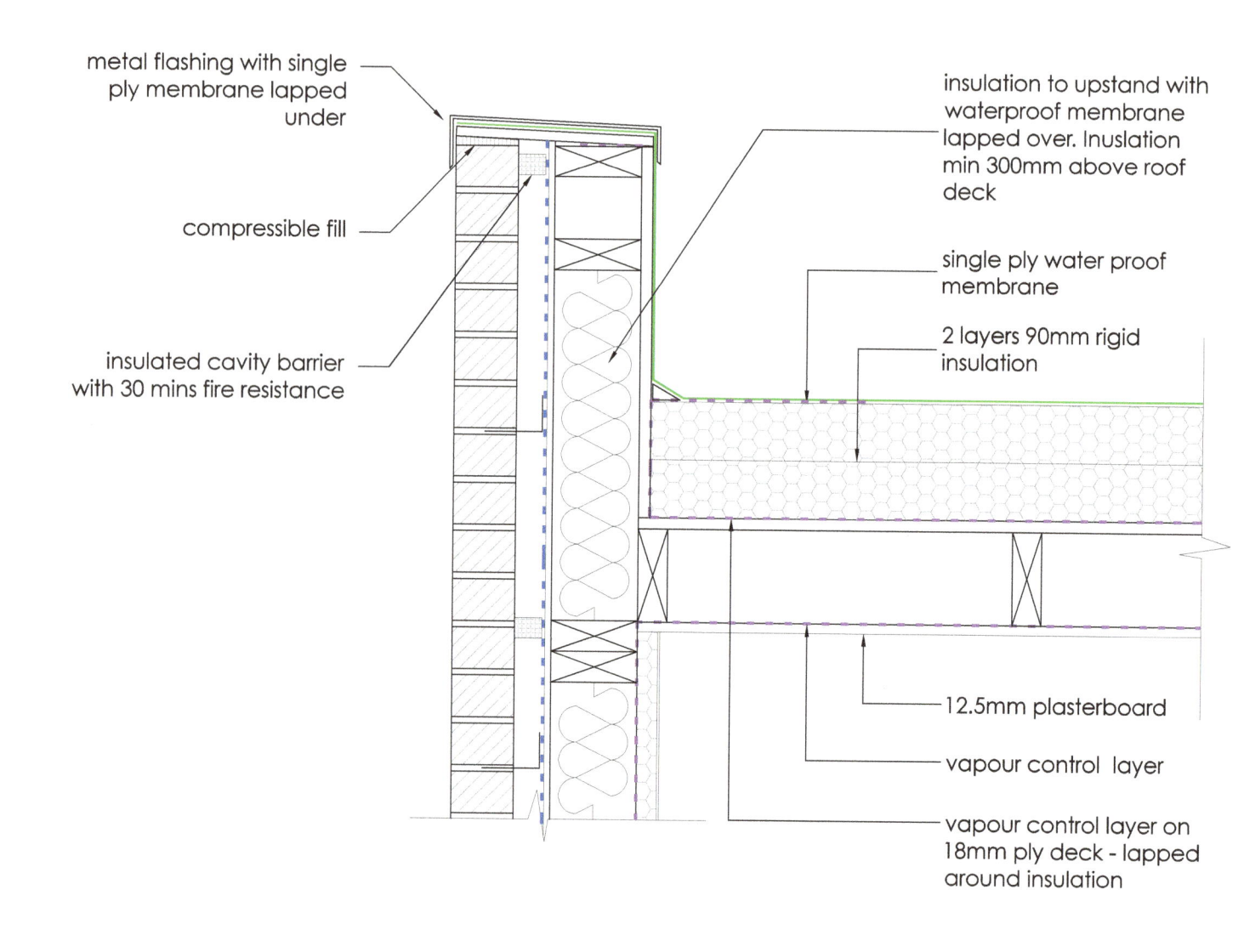

Labels (left side):
- metal flashing with single ply membrane lapped under
- compressible fill
- insulated cavity barrier with 30 mins fire resistance

Labels (right side):
- insulation to upstand with waterproof membrane lapped over. Inuslation min 300mm above roof deck
- single ply water proof membrane
- 2 layers 90mm rigid insulation
- 12.5mm plasterboard
- vapour control layer
- vapour control layer on 18mm ply deck - lapped around insulation

Detail T-R7- Timber frame wall, flat roof with parapet, insulation above joists

NOTES:
U Value 0.12W/m²K or better

SECTION 6 - TIMBER FRAME

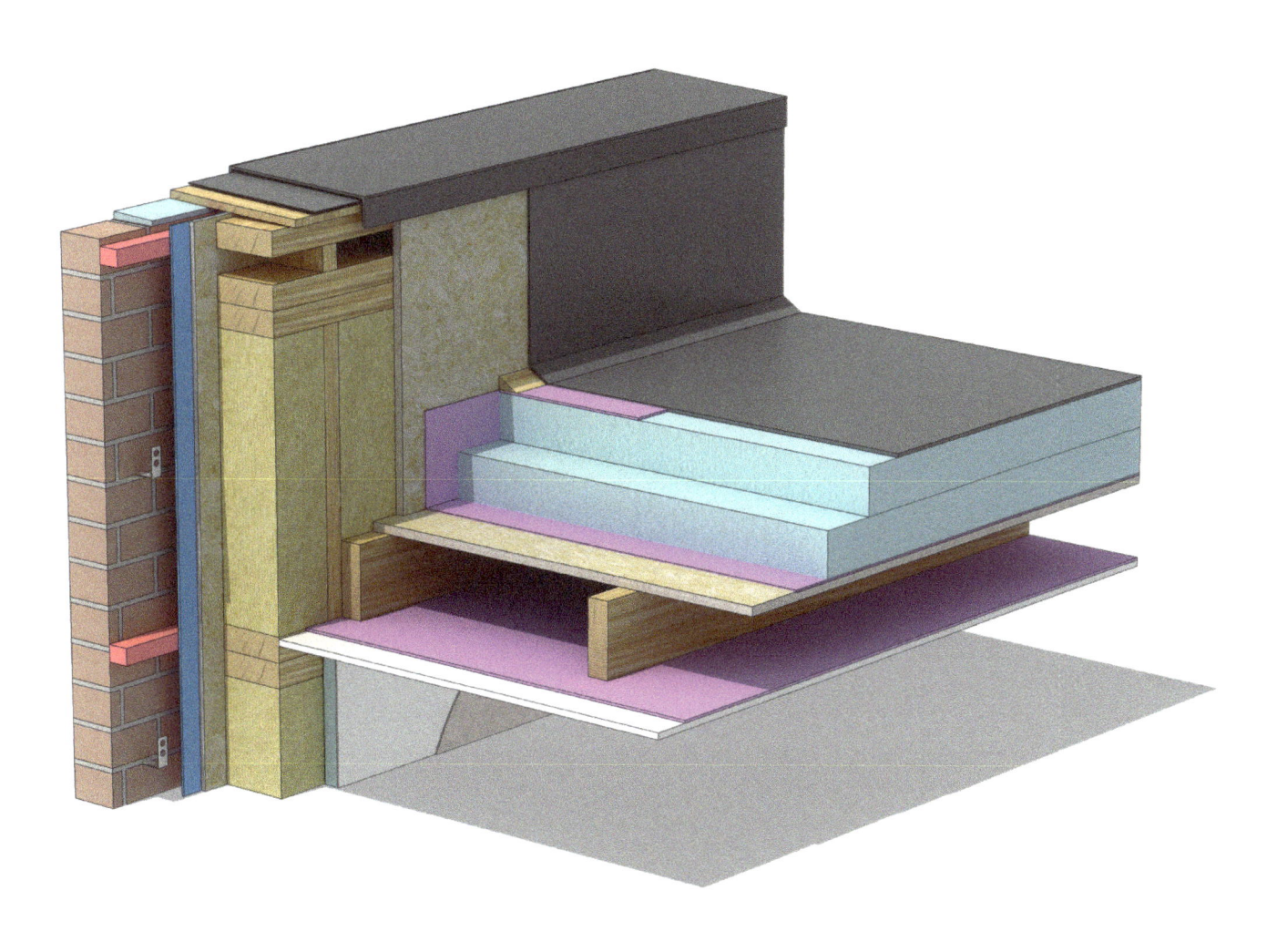

3D Detail T-R7- Timber frame wall, flat roof with parapet, insulation above joists

NOTES ON THE REGS

The following information is a partial list of requirements from the **Building Regulations Approved Documents** - for full and detailed explanations and requirements please consult the full publications.

GENERAL REQUIREMENTS - ROOFS

The building shall be constructed so that the combined dead, imposed and wind loads are sustained and transmitted by it to the ground.

(Approved Doc A1)

Precautions against moisture
The roof of the building shall be resistant to the penetration of moisture from rain or snow to the inside of the building.
All floors next to the ground, walls and roof shall not be damaged by moisture from the ground, rain or snow and shall not carry that moisture to any part of the building that it would damage.

(Approved Doc C2)

Rainwater
Rainwater from roofs shall be carried away from the surface either by a drainage system or by other means.
The rainwater drainage system shall carry the flow of rainwater form the roof to an outfall.

(Approved Doc H3)

Fire precautions
As a fire precaution, all materials used for internal linings of a building should have a low rate of surface flame spread and (in some cases) a low rate of heat release.

(Approved Doc B2)

External fire spread
The roof shall be constructed so that the risk of spread of flame and fire penetration from an external fire source is restricted.
The risk of a fire spreading from the building to a building beyond the boundary should be limited.

Internal fire spread
Ideally the building should be subdivided by elements of fire resisting construction into compartments.

All openings in fire separating elements shall be suitably protected in order to maintain the integrity of the continuity of the fire separation.
Any hidden voids in the construction shall be sealed and sub-divided to inhibit the unseen spread of fire and products of combustion, in order to reduce the risk of structural failure, and the spread of fire.

(Approved Doc B3)

Ventilation
There shall be adequate means of ventilation provided for people in the building.

(Approved Doc F)

Conservation of fuel and power
Reasonable provision shall be made for the conservation of fuel and power in buildings by:
limiting heat gains and losses through thermal elements and other parts of the building fabric,
- from pipes ducts and vessels used for space heating, space cooling and hot water services.
-providing fixed building services which are energy efficient and have effective controls and are commissioned by testing and adjusting as necessary to ensure they use no more fuel and power than is reasonable in the circumstances.

(Approved Doc L)

STEEL FRAME CONSTRUCTION

INTRODUCTION

Light steel frame systems are not too dissimilar to a timber frame construction. Rolled steel sections are constructed in a platform frame structure. The sections are delivered to site pre cut and pre punched, or in some cases are delivered in prefabricated panels. Where panels are not used the method of construction is fairly labour intensive, and as a result not widely used.

The steel frame forms the inner leaf of the cavity wall - with the outer leaf brick cladding or a rendered blockwork as the most common material used. The frame is usually fixed to the substructure using large expanding bolts. The steel frame carries the load of the floors and roof, the cladding is not load bearing. Insulation is usually fitted to the external face of the steel frame, with the plasterboard lining fixed to the internal face. Improved thermal performance can be achieved by placing additional insulation within the frame - but consideration must be taken to the thermal bridging issues that can arise with the steel studs. Given the position of insulation to the outer face of the steel frame, the steel stays warm, and therefore a vapour control layer is not normally required.

The ground floor of a steel frame construction can be either a suspended floor system or a cast in situ concrete slab system. First floor construction is often steel lattice joists fitted with plywood or OSB decking.

The roof of a steel frame system can be constructed using timber trussed rafters or lightweight steel trusses. If timber trusses are used a timber wall plate is bolted to the top of the steel panels. Roof coverings are no different from standard roof construction.

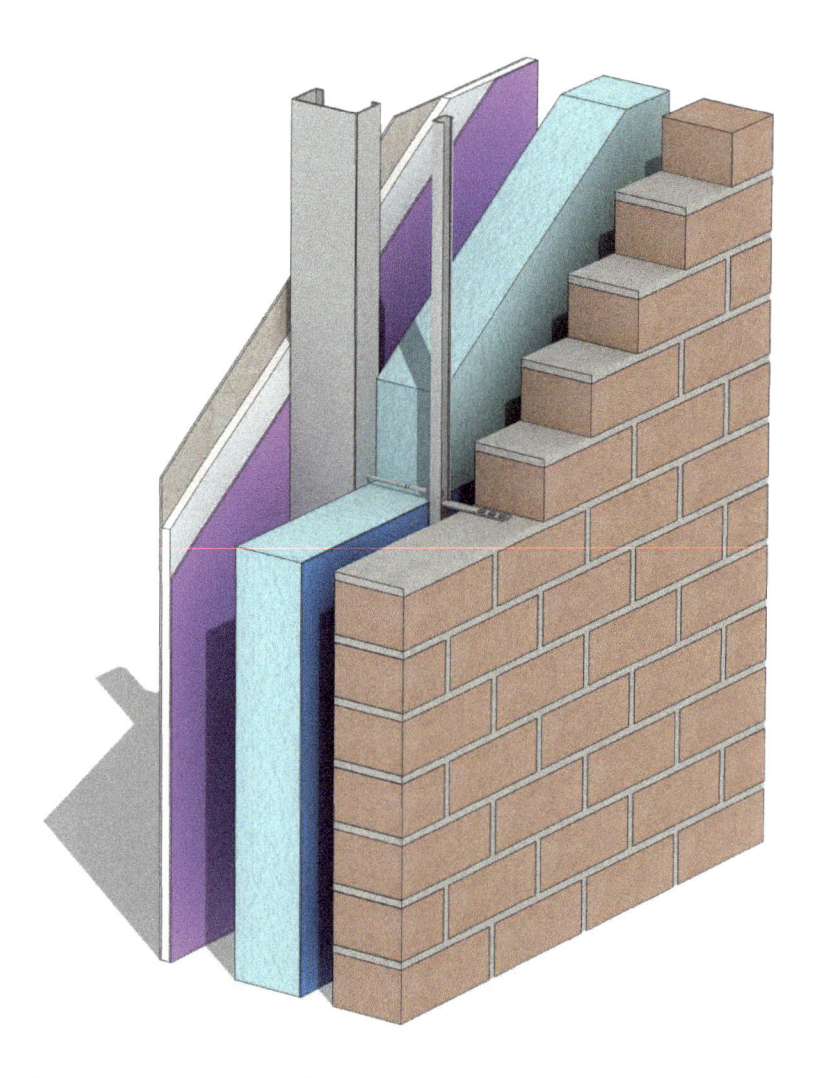

Figure 7.1 - Example of steel frame construction

238

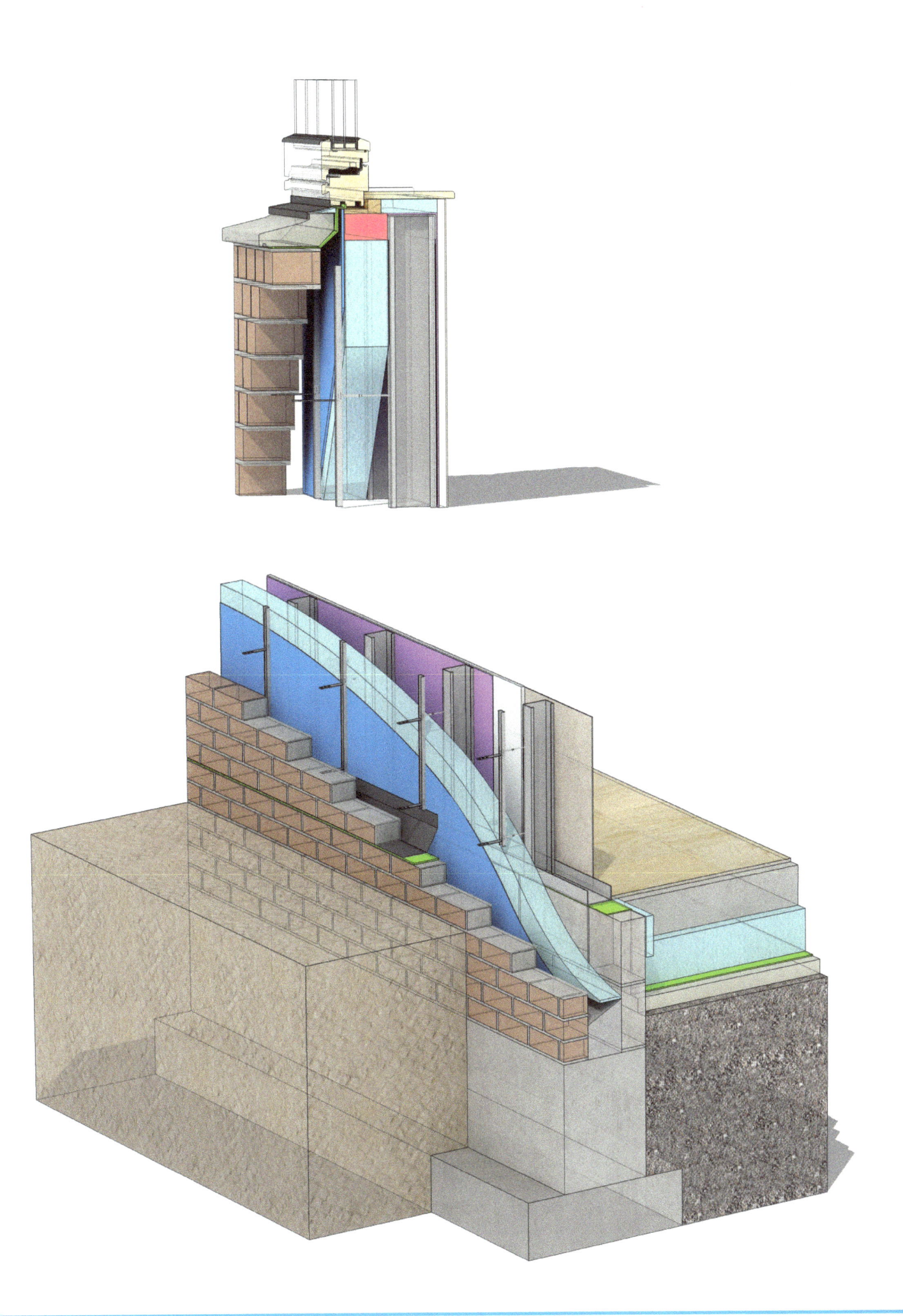

STEEL FRAME DETAILS

S-G1

STEEL FRAME WALL, GROUND BEARING CONCRETE SLAB, INSULATION BELOW

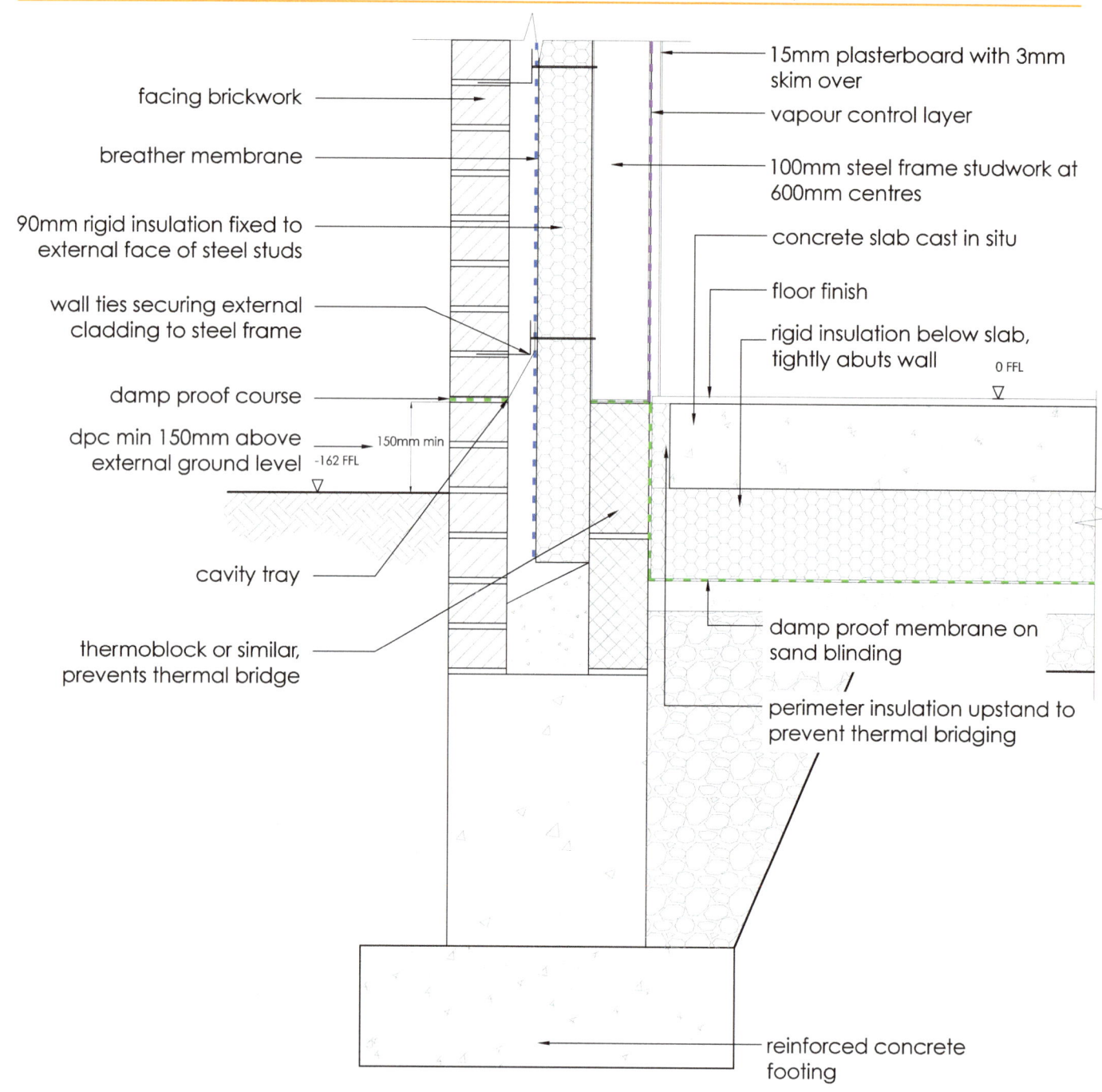

Labels (left side):
- facing brickwork
- breather membrane
- 90mm rigid insulation fixed to external face of steel studs
- wall ties securing external cladding to steel frame
- damp proof course
- dpc min 150mm above external ground level
- cavity tray
- thermoblock or similar, prevents thermal bridge

Labels (right side):
- 15mm plasterboard with 3mm skim over
- vapour control layer
- 100mm steel frame studwork at 600mm centres
- concrete slab cast in situ
- floor finish
- rigid insulation below slab, tightly abuts wall
- damp proof membrane on sand blinding
- perimeter insulation upstand to prevent thermal bridging
- reinforced concrete footing

Dimensions: 150mm min, -162 FFL, 0 FFL

Detail S-G1 - Steel frame wall, ground bearing concrete slab, insulation below slab

NOTES:

U Value 0.13W/m²K or better
Perimeter strip of insulation abuts concrete slab and blockwork wall.
Potential thermal bridge area at blockwork below steel frame, specify Thermoblock or similar. U-value dependent on perimter / area value.
Vapour control layer to steel frame if required.

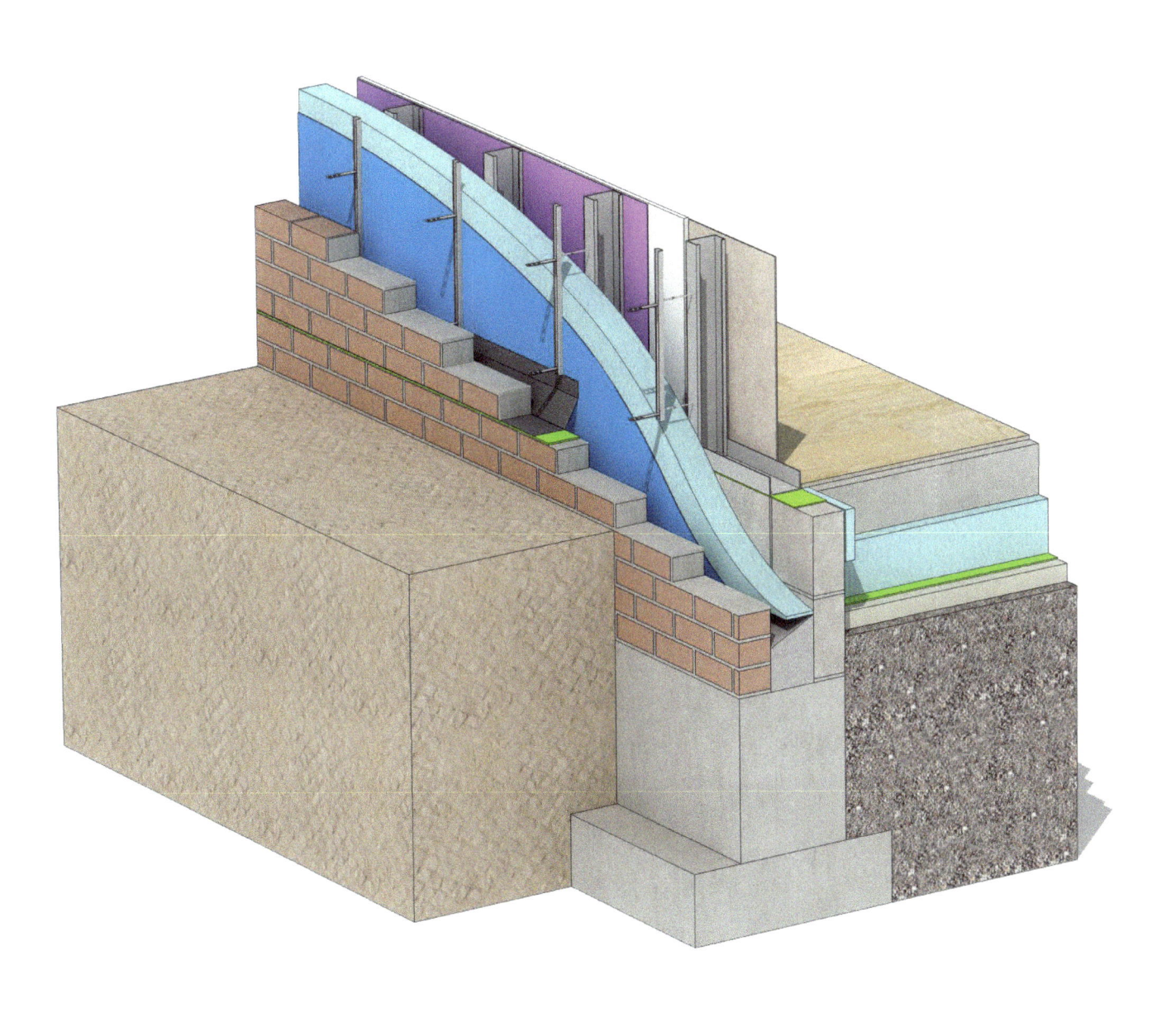

3D Detail S-G1- Steel frame wall, ground bearing concrete slab, insulation below slab

S-G2

STEEL FRAME WALL, GROUND BEARING CONCRETE SLAB, INSULATION ABOVE

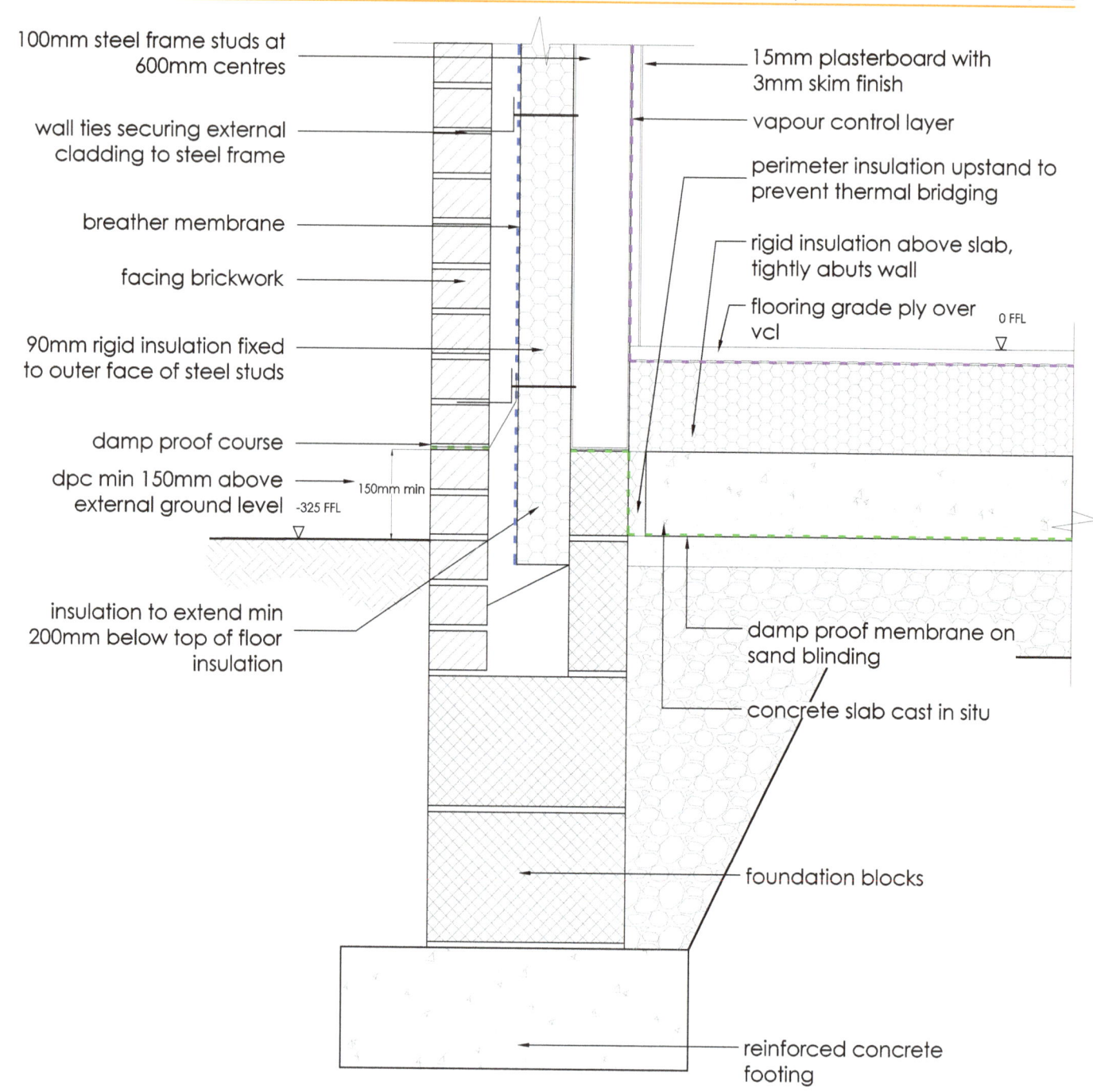

Labels (left side):
- 100mm steel frame studs at 600mm centres
- wall ties securing external cladding to steel frame
- breather membrane
- facing brickwork
- 90mm rigid insulation fixed to outer face of steel studs
- damp proof course
- dpc min 150mm above external ground level -325 FFL
- 150mm min
- insulation to extend min 200mm below top of floor insulation

Labels (right side):
- 15mm plasterboard with 3mm skim finish
- vapour control layer
- perimeter insulation upstand to prevent thermal bridging
- rigid insulation above slab, tightly abuts wall
- flooring grade ply over vcl
- 0 FFL
- damp proof membrane on sand blinding
- concrete slab cast in situ
- foundation blocks
- reinforced concrete footing

Detail S-G2 - Steel frame wall, ground bearing concrete slab, insulation above slab

NOTES:

U Value 0.13W/m²K or better
Perimeter strip of insulation abuts concrete slab and blockwork wall.
Perimeter insulation to screed. Alternative floor finish of chipboard/osb/ply must include vapour control layer between board and insulation. Damp proof membrane can also be positioned over slab. U-value dependent on perimeter/area value.
Vapour control layer to steel frame if required.

SECTION 7 - STEEL FRAME

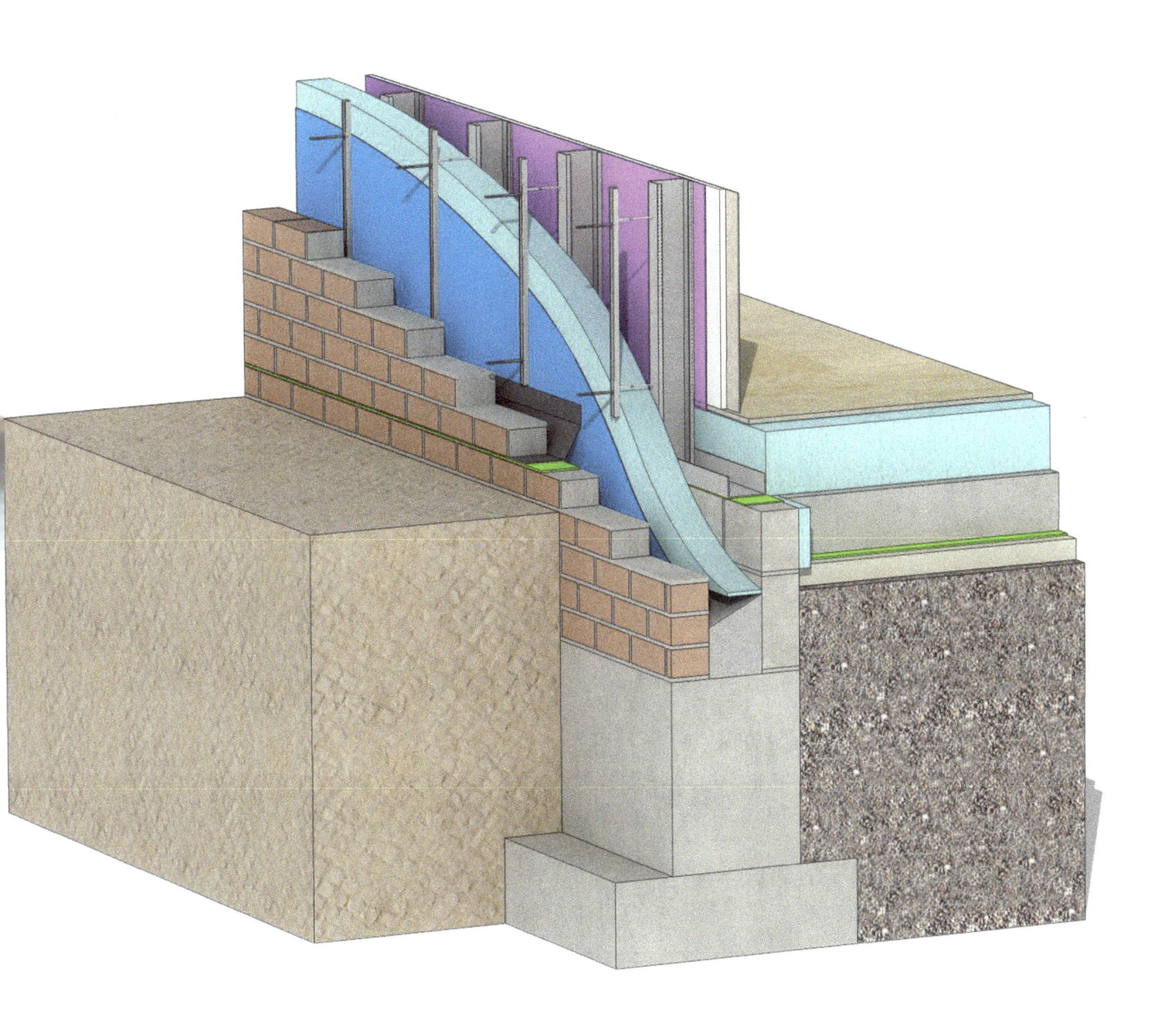

3D Detail S-G2 - Steel frame wall, ground bearing concrete slab, insulation above slab

S-G3

STEEL FRAME WALL, TIMBER INTERMEDIATE FLOOR

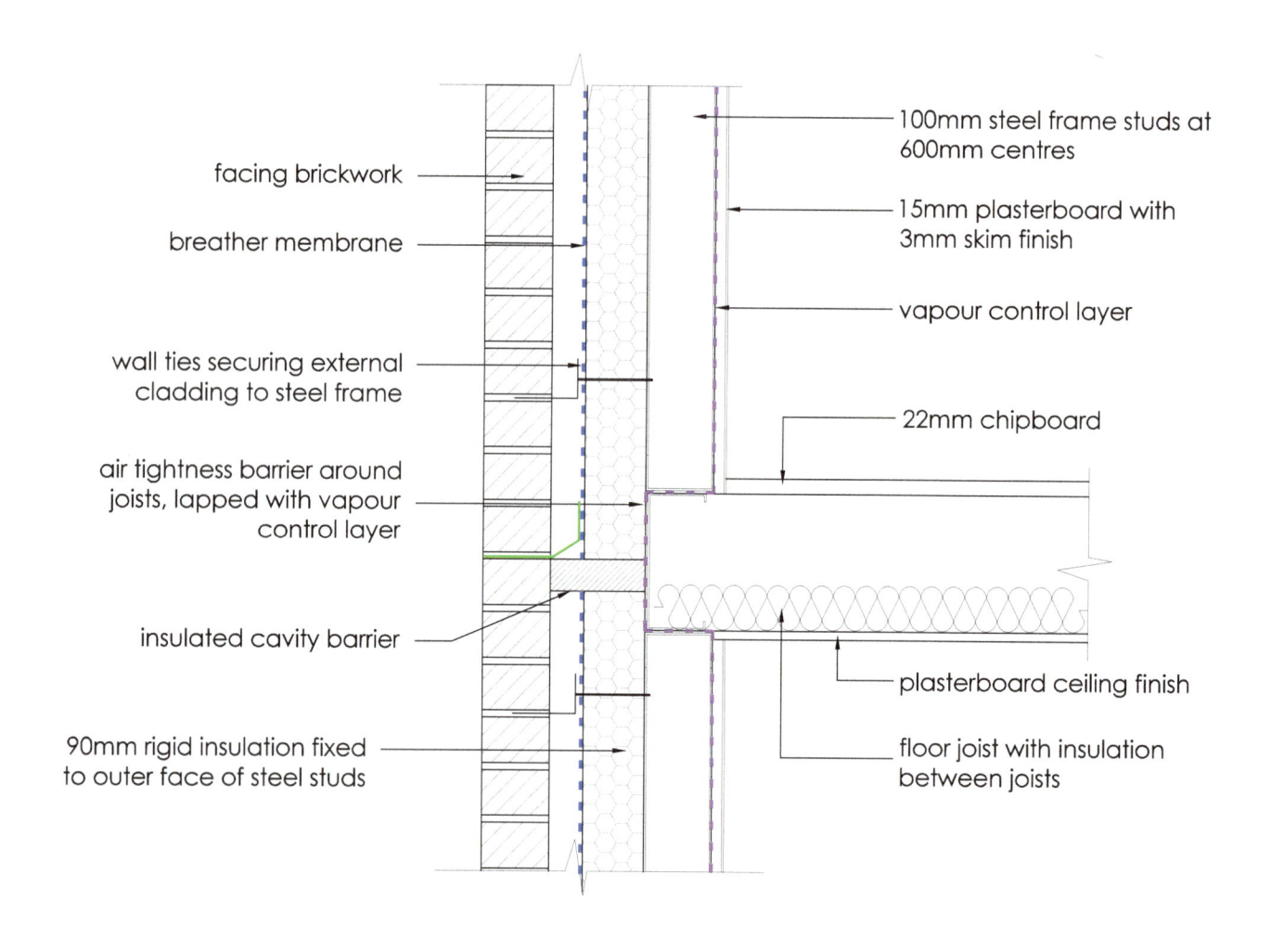

- facing brickwork
- breather membrane
- wall ties securing external cladding to steel frame
- air tightness barrier around joists, lapped with vapour control layer
- insulated cavity barrier
- 90mm rigid insulation fixed to outer face of steel studs
- 100mm steel frame studs at 600mm centres
- 15mm plasterboard with 3mm skim finish
- vapour control layer
- 22mm chipboard
- plasterboard ceiling finish
- floor joist with insulation between joists

Detail S-G3 - Steel frame wall, timber intermediate floor

NOTES:

Vapour control layer to steel frame if required.

SECTION 7 - STEEL FRAME

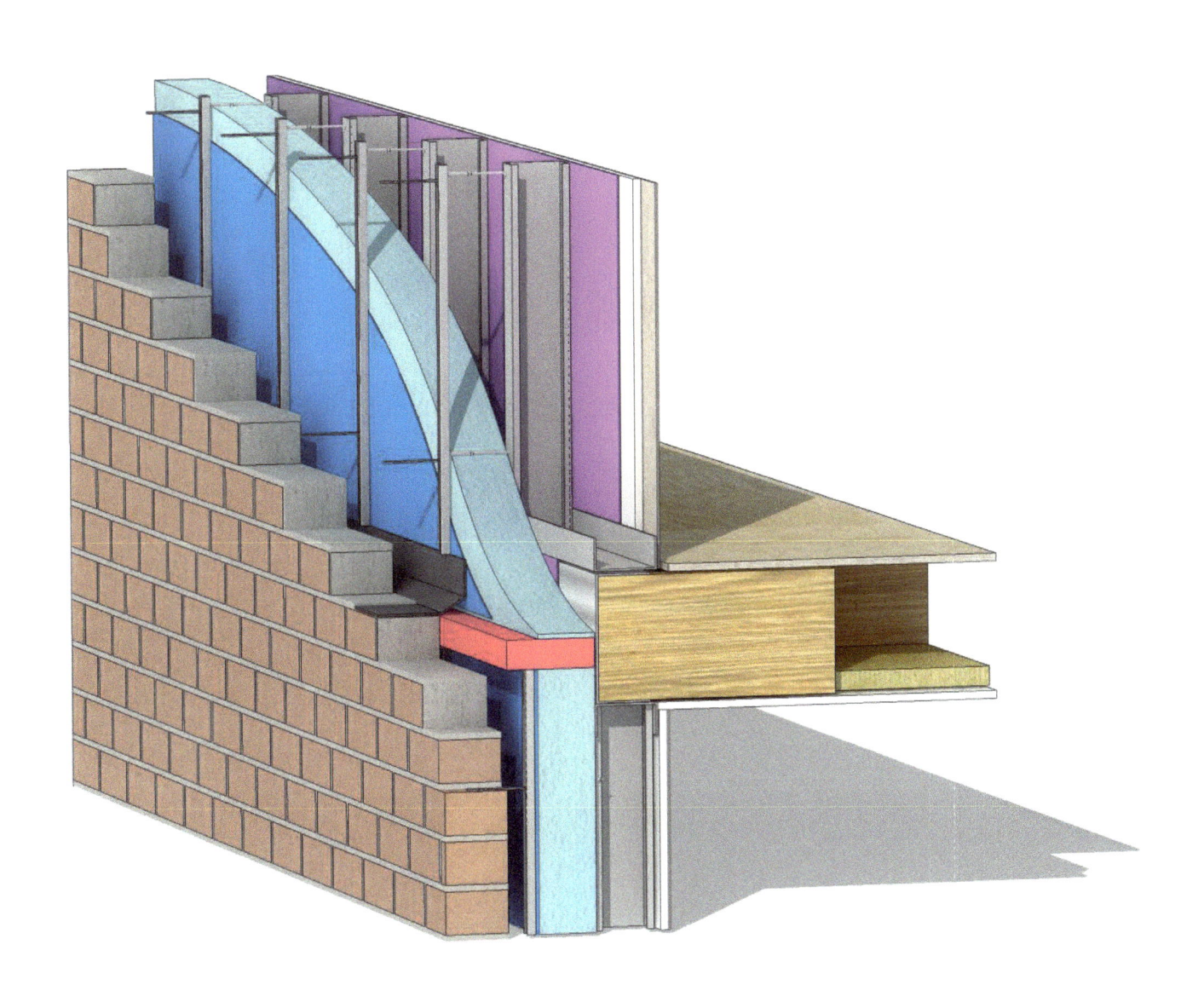

3D Detail S-G3- Steel frame wall, timber intermediate floor

S-G4
STEEL FRAME WALL, TIMBER SEPARATING FLOOR

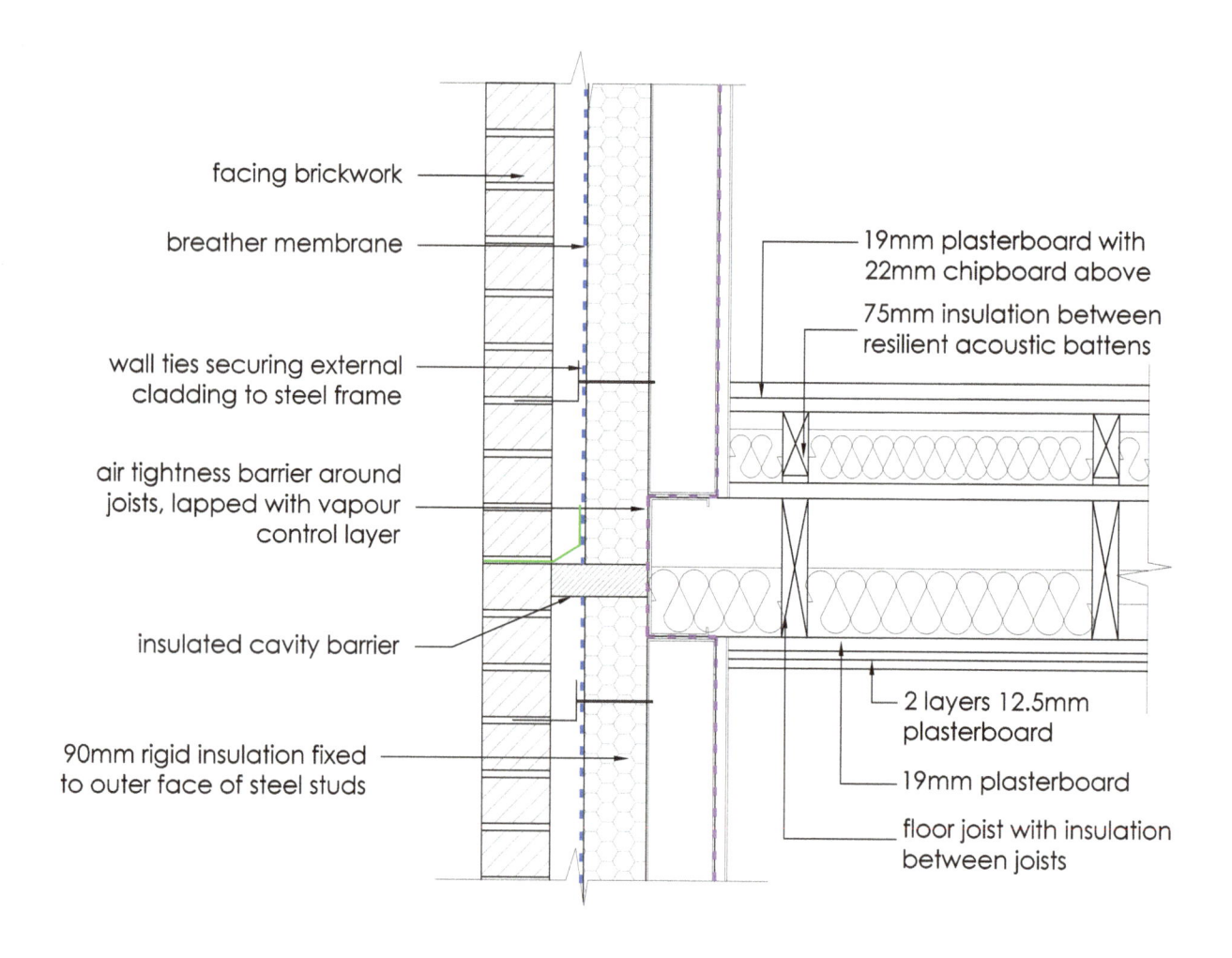

Labels on detail:
- facing brickwork
- breather membrane
- wall ties securing external cladding to steel frame
- air tightness barrier around joists, lapped with vapour control layer
- insulated cavity barrier
- 90mm rigid insulation fixed to outer face of steel studs
- 19mm plasterboard with 22mm chipboard above
- 75mm insulation between resilient acoustic battens
- 2 layers 12.5mm plasterboard
- 19mm plasterboard
- floor joist with insulation between joists

Detail S-G4 - Steel frame wall, timber separating floor

NOTES:

There are many different arrangements for a separating floor - this is just one example.
Further reading - Robust Details
Vapour control layer to steel frame if required.

SECTION 7 - STEEL FRAME

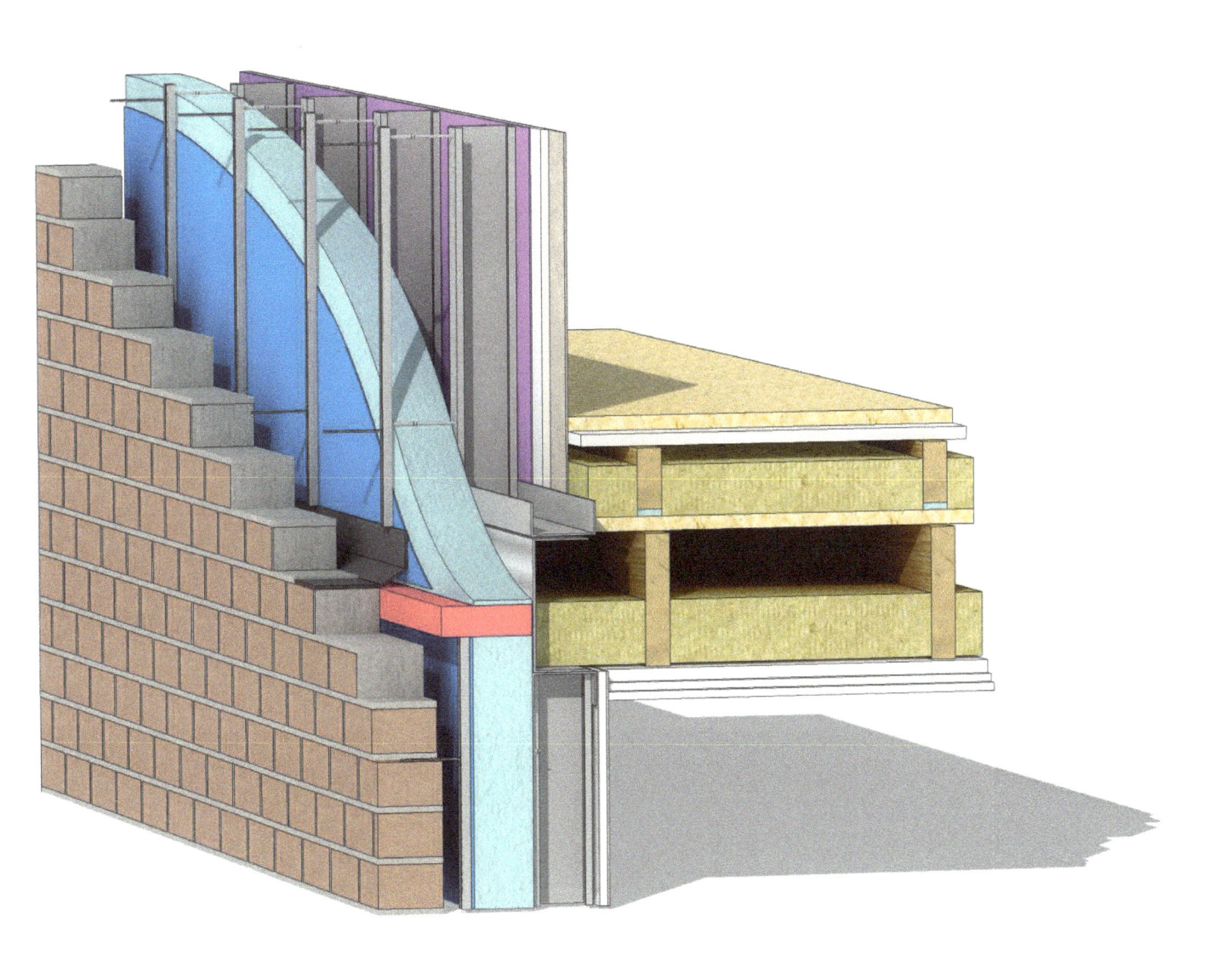

3D Detail S-G4- Steel frame wall, timber separating floor

S-W1

STEEL FRAME WALL, BRICK CLADDING

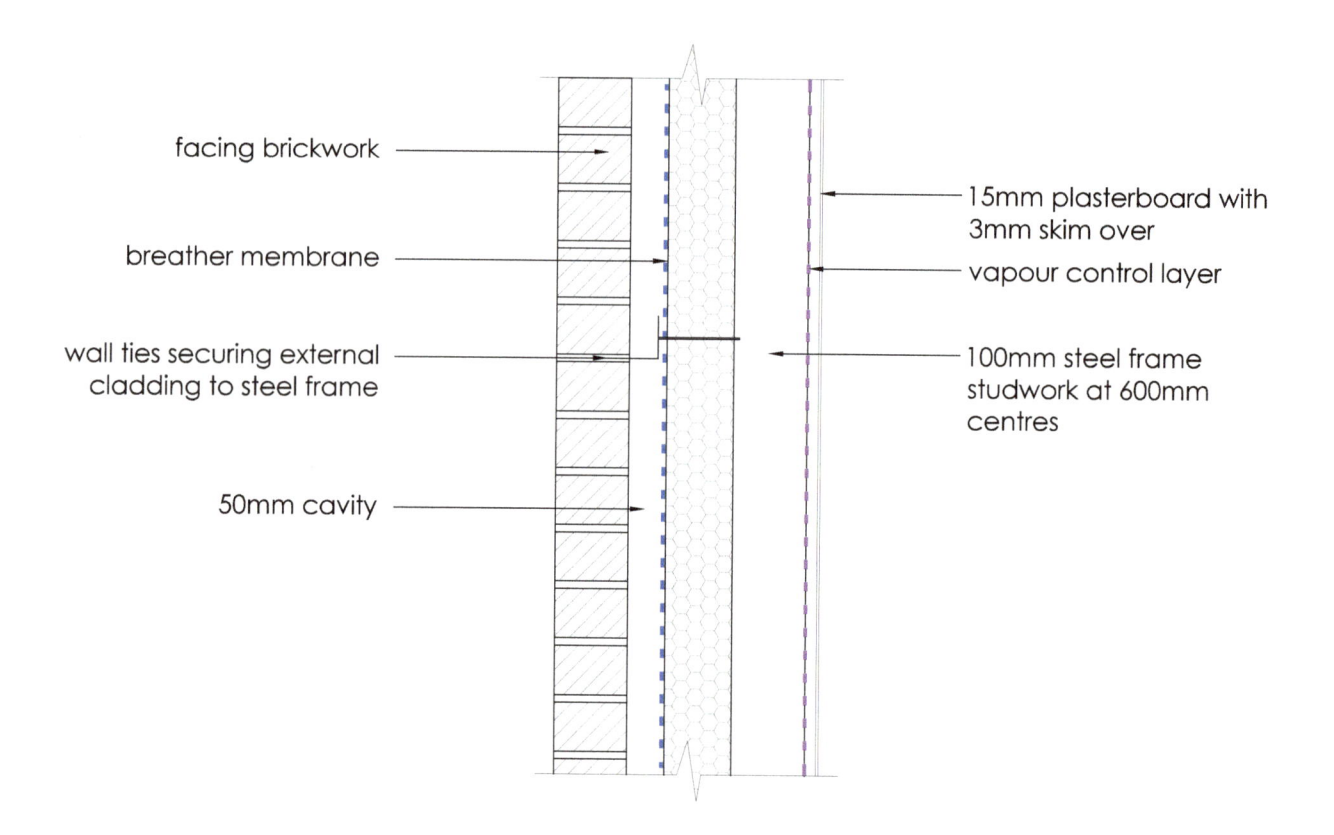

- facing brickwork
- breather membrane
- wall ties securing external cladding to steel frame
- 50mm cavity
- 15mm plasterboard with 3mm skim over
- vapour control layer
- 100mm steel frame studwork at 600mm centres

Detail S-W1 - Steel frame wall, brick cladding

NOTES:

U Value 0.18W/m²K or better
Vapour control layer to steel frame if required.

SECTION 7 - STEEL FRAME

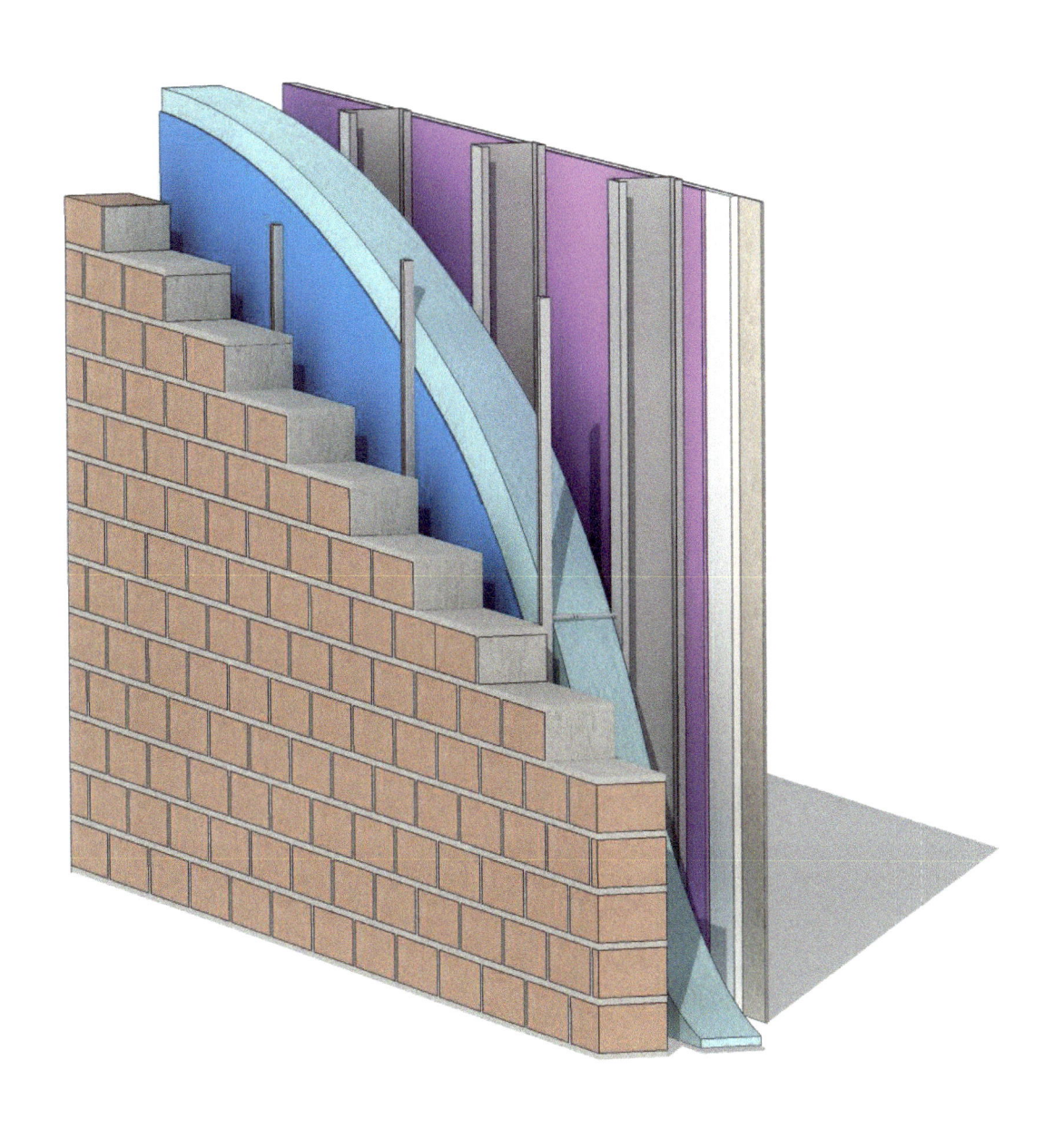

3D Detail S-W1 - Steel frame wall, brick cladding

S-W2

STEEL FRAME WALL, BRICK CLADDING (PLAN VIEW)

- 100mm steel studwork at 600mm centres
- wall tie fixes through insulation to steel stud
- wall tie min 55mm bearing on brickwork
- wall tie sits in vertical channel

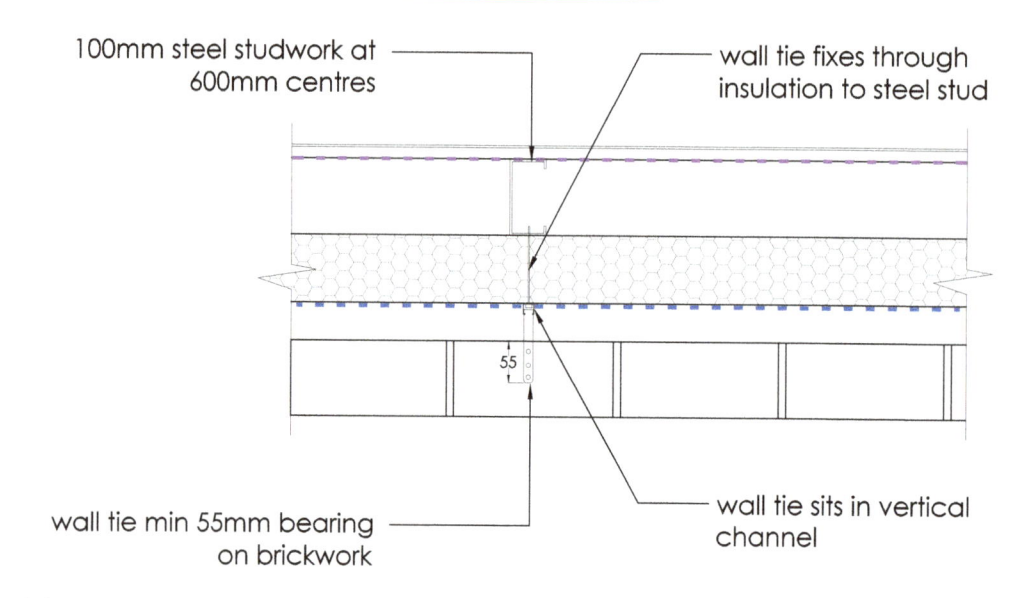

Detail S-W2 - Steel frame wall, brick cladding (plan view)

S-W3

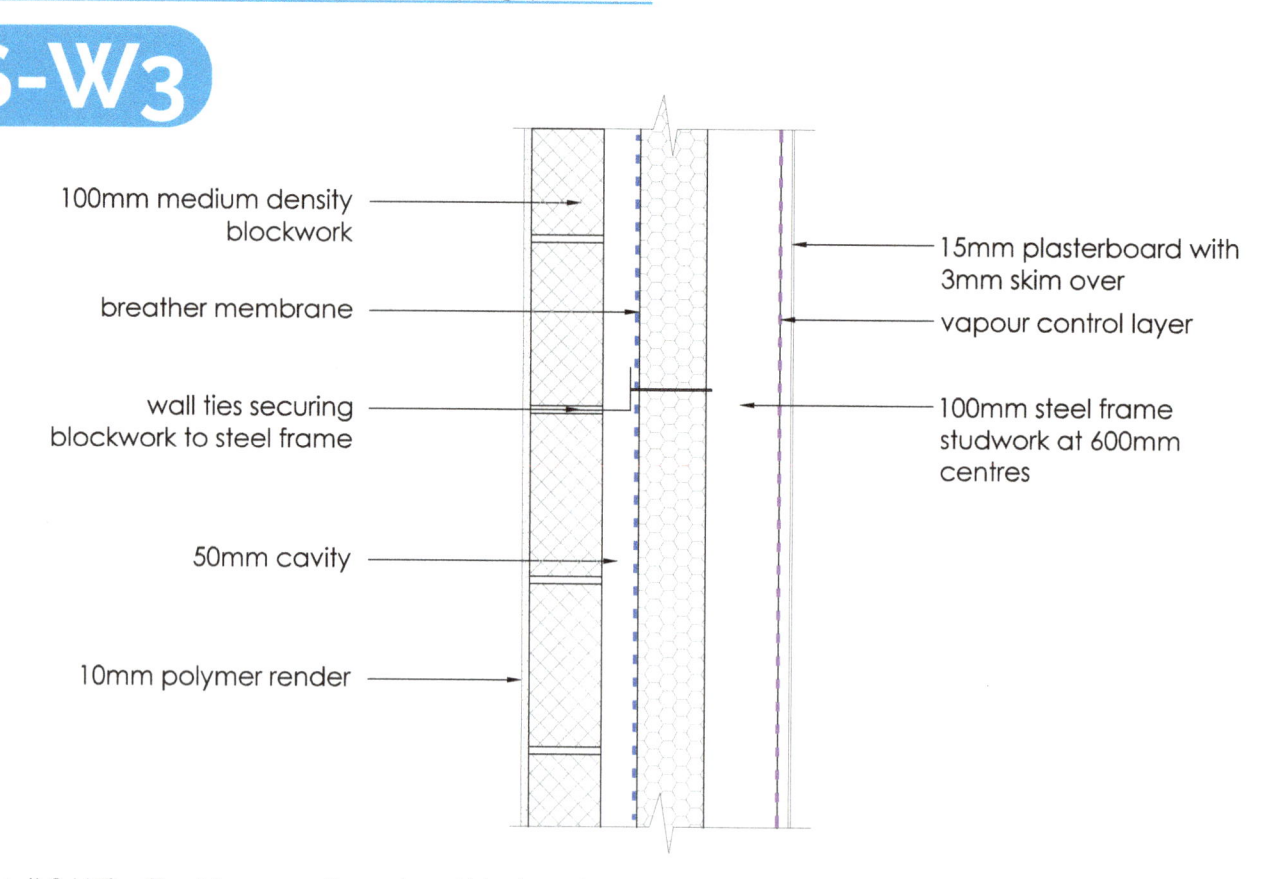

- 100mm medium density blockwork
- breather membrane
- wall ties securing blockwork to steel frame
- 50mm cavity
- 10mm polymer render
- 15mm plasterboard with 3mm skim over
- vapour control layer
- 100mm steel frame studwork at 600mm centres

Detail S-W3 - Steel frame wall, rendered blockwork

NOTES:

U Value 0.18W/m²K or better
Vapour control layer to steel frame if required.

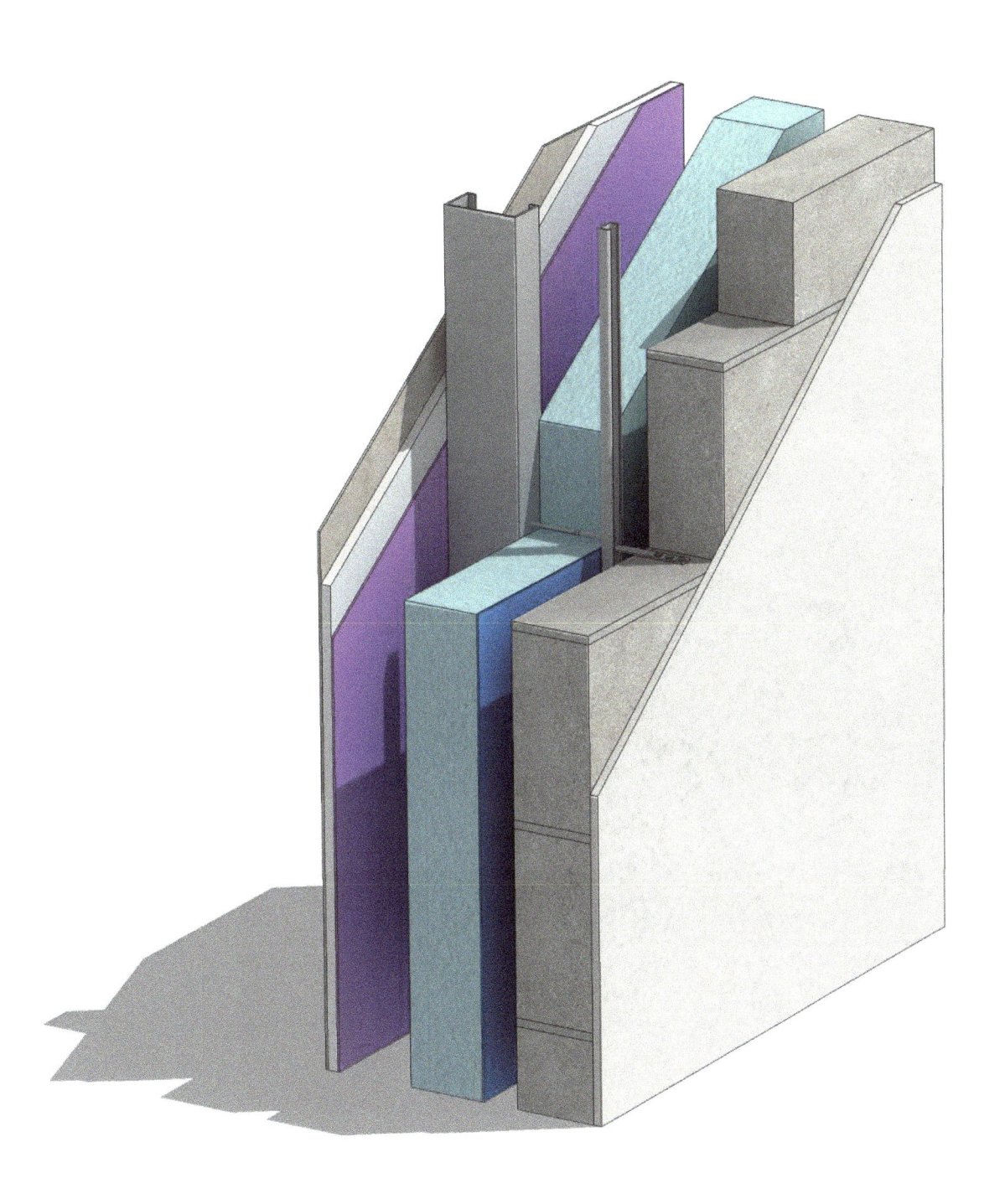

3D Detail S-W3 - Steel frame wall, rendered blockwork

S-W4

STEEL FRAME WALL, BRICK CLADDING, WINDOW HEAD AND CILL

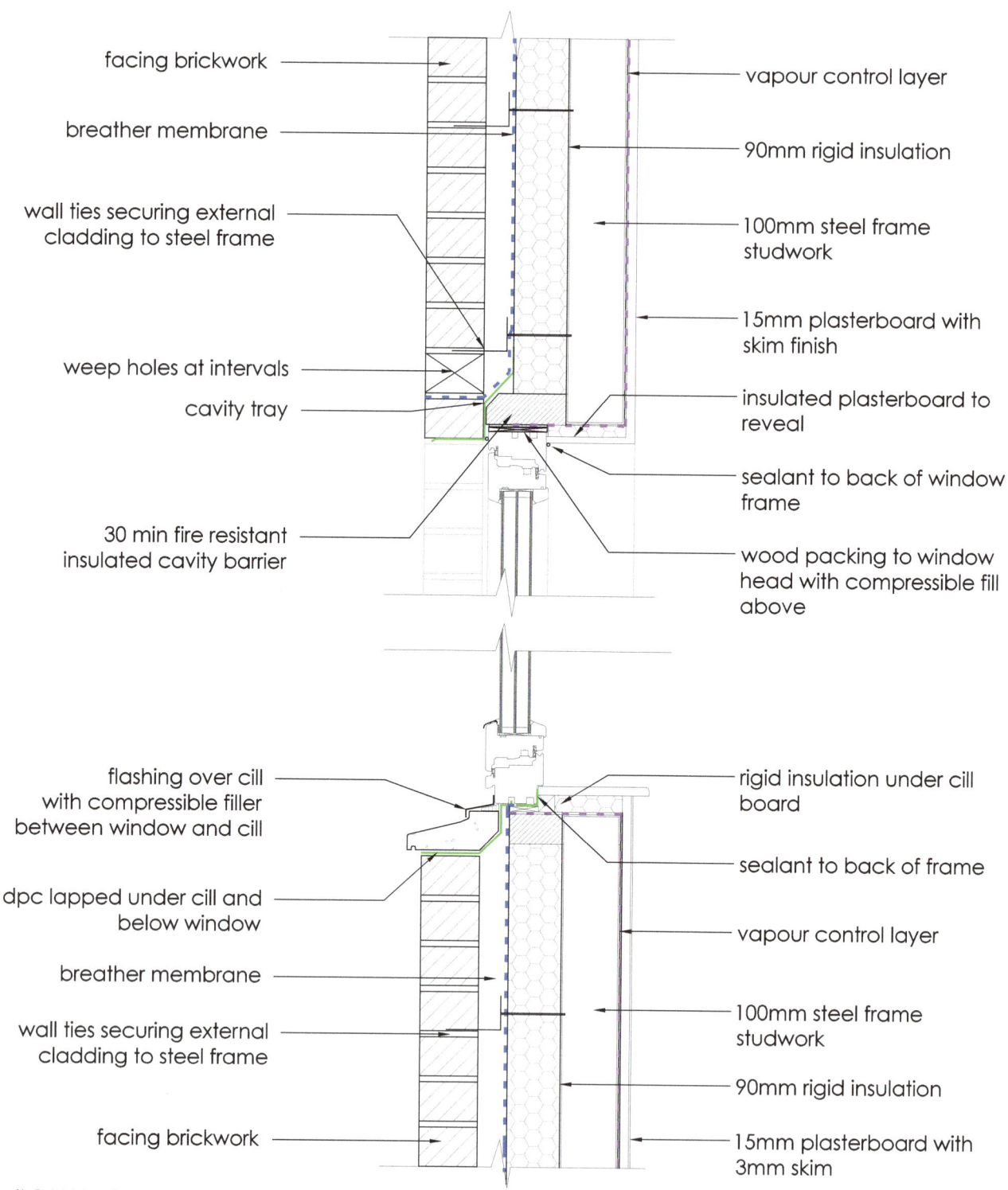

Labels (top detail - window head):
- facing brickwork
- breather membrane
- wall ties securing external cladding to steel frame
- weep holes at intervals
- cavity tray
- 30 min fire resistant insulated cavity barrier
- vapour control layer
- 90mm rigid insulation
- 100mm steel frame studwork
- 15mm plasterboard with skim finish
- insulated plasterboard to reveal
- sealant to back of window frame
- wood packing to window head with compressible fill above

Labels (bottom detail - window cill):
- flashing over cill with compressible filler between window and cill
- dpc lapped under cill and below window
- breather membrane
- wall ties securing external cladding to steel frame
- facing brickwork
- rigid insulation under cill board
- sealant to back of frame
- vapour control layer
- 100mm steel frame studwork
- 90mm rigid insulation
- 15mm plasterboard with 3mm skim

Detail S-W4 - Steel frame wall, brick cladding, window head and cill

NOTES:

Vapour control layer to steel frame if required.

SECTION 7 - STEEL FRAME

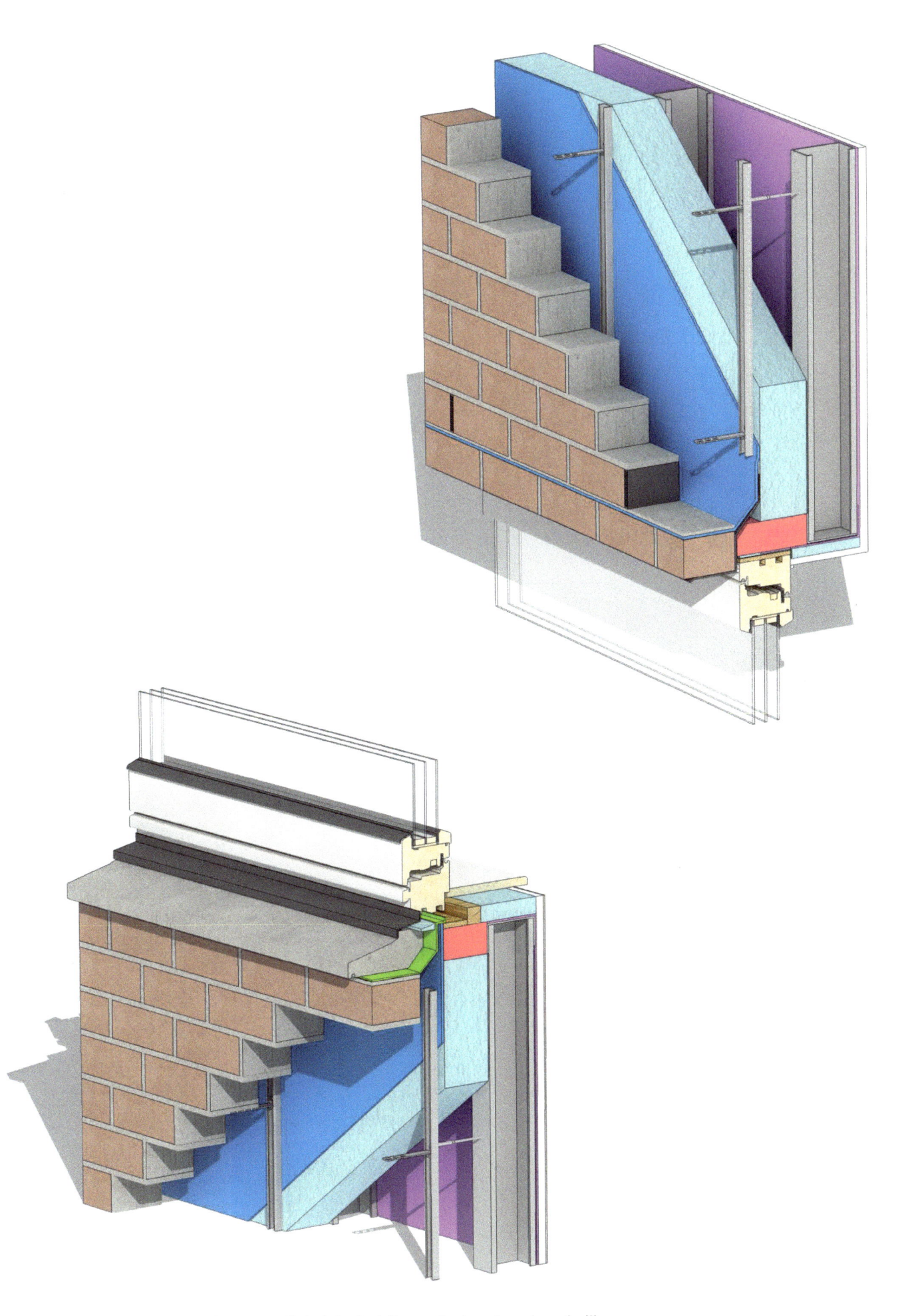

3D Detail S-W4 - Steel frame wall, brick cladding, window head and cill

S-R1

STEEL FRAME WALL, EAVES DETAIL, VENTILATED ROOF SPACE (COLD ROOF)

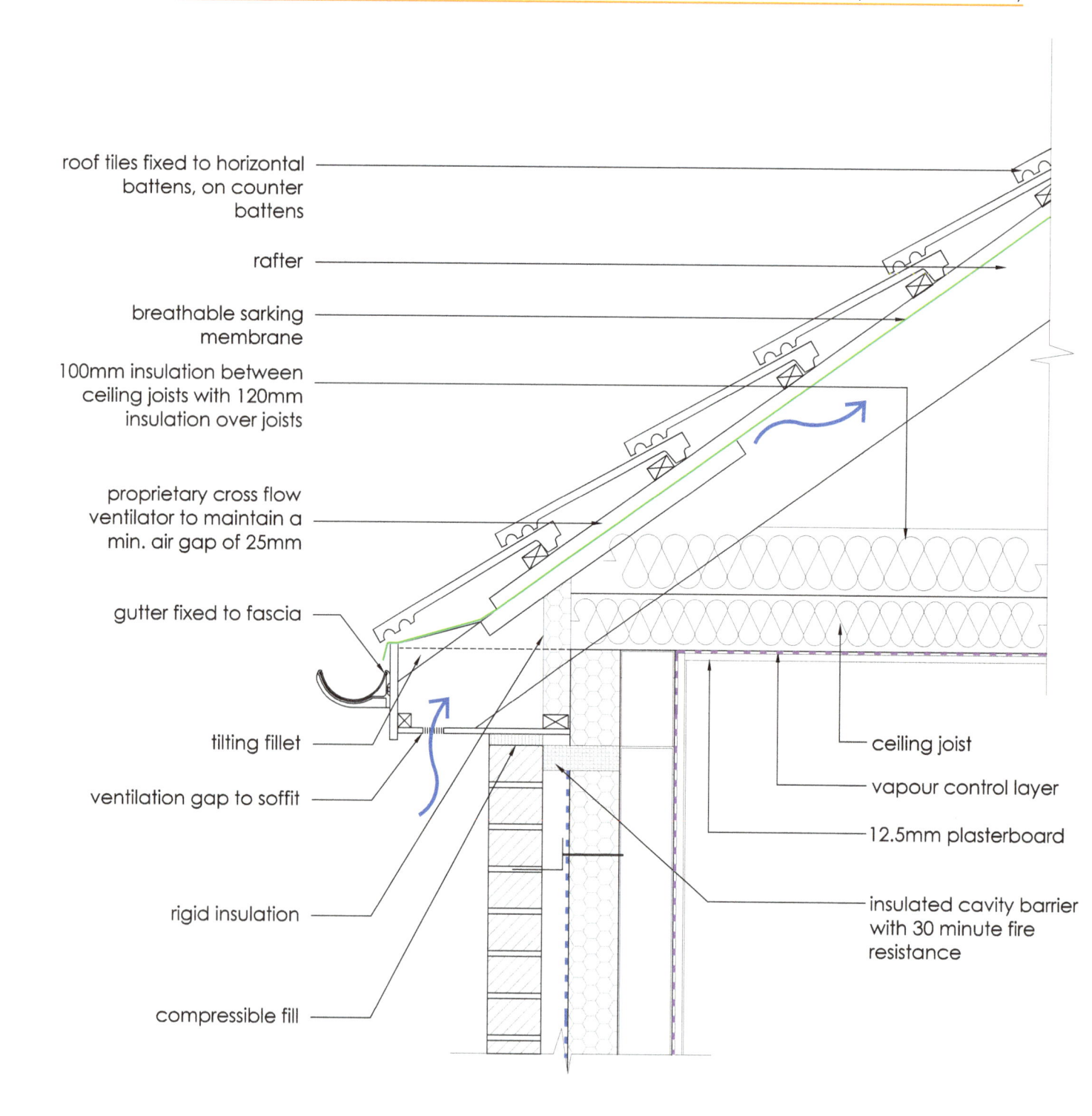

Labels (left side):
- roof tiles fixed to horizontal battens, on counter battens
- rafter
- breathable sarking membrane
- 100mm insulation between ceiling joists with 120mm insulation over joists
- proprietary cross flow ventilator to maintain a min. air gap of 25mm
- gutter fixed to fascia
- tilting fillet
- ventilation gap to soffit
- rigid insulation
- compressible fill

Labels (right side):
- ceiling joist
- vapour control layer
- 12.5mm plasterboard
- insulated cavity barrier with 30 minute fire resistance

Detail S-R1 - Steel frame wall, eaves detail, ventilated roof space (cold roof)

NOTES:

U Value 0.12W/m²K or better

SECTION 7 - STEEL FRAME

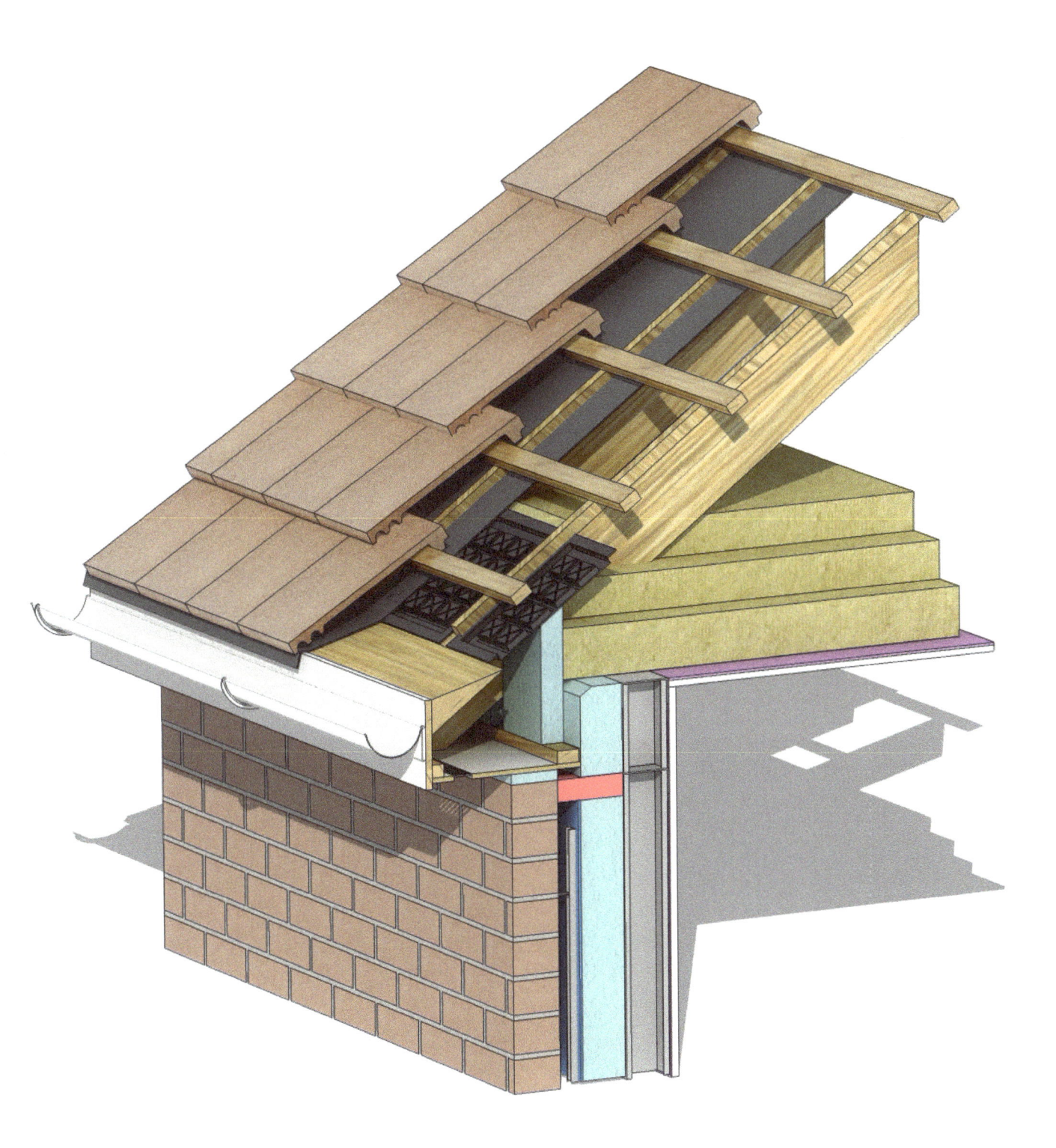

3D Detail S-R1 - Steel frame wall, eaves detail, ventilated roof space (cold roof)

S-R2

STEEL FRAME WALL, EAVES DETAIL, UNVENTILATED ROOF SPACE

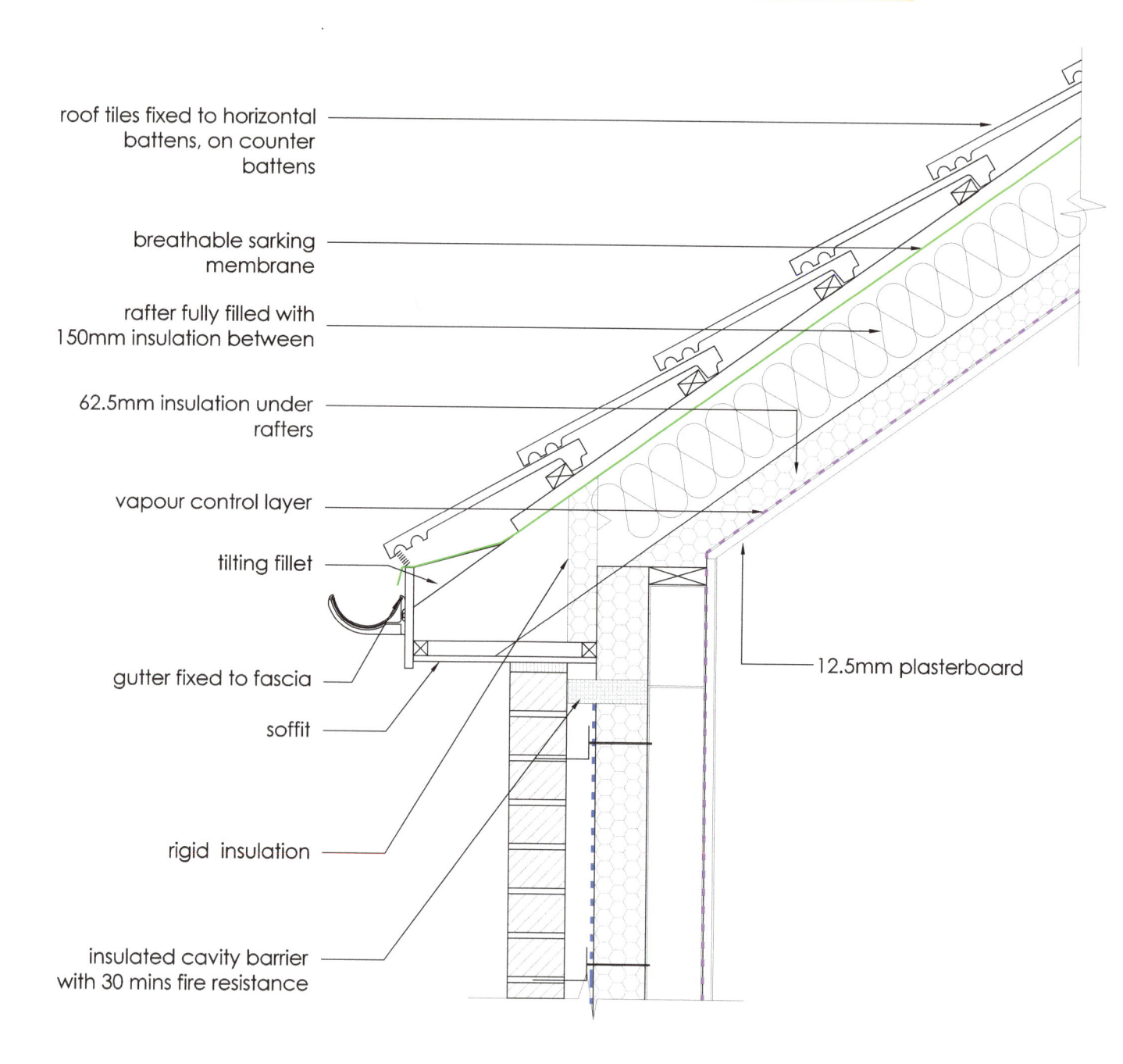

- roof tiles fixed to horizontal battens, on counter battens
- breathable sarking membrane
- rafter fully filled with 150mm insulation between
- 62.5mm insulation under rafters
- vapour control layer
- tilting fillet
- gutter fixed to fascia
- soffit
- rigid insulation
- insulated cavity barrier with 30 mins fire resistance
- 12.5mm plasterboard

Detail S-R2 - Steel frame wall, eaves detail, unventilated roof space, insulation between and under rafters

NOTES:

U Value 0.12W/m²K or better
Any ventilation requirements according to manufacturer

SECTION 7 - STEEL FRAME

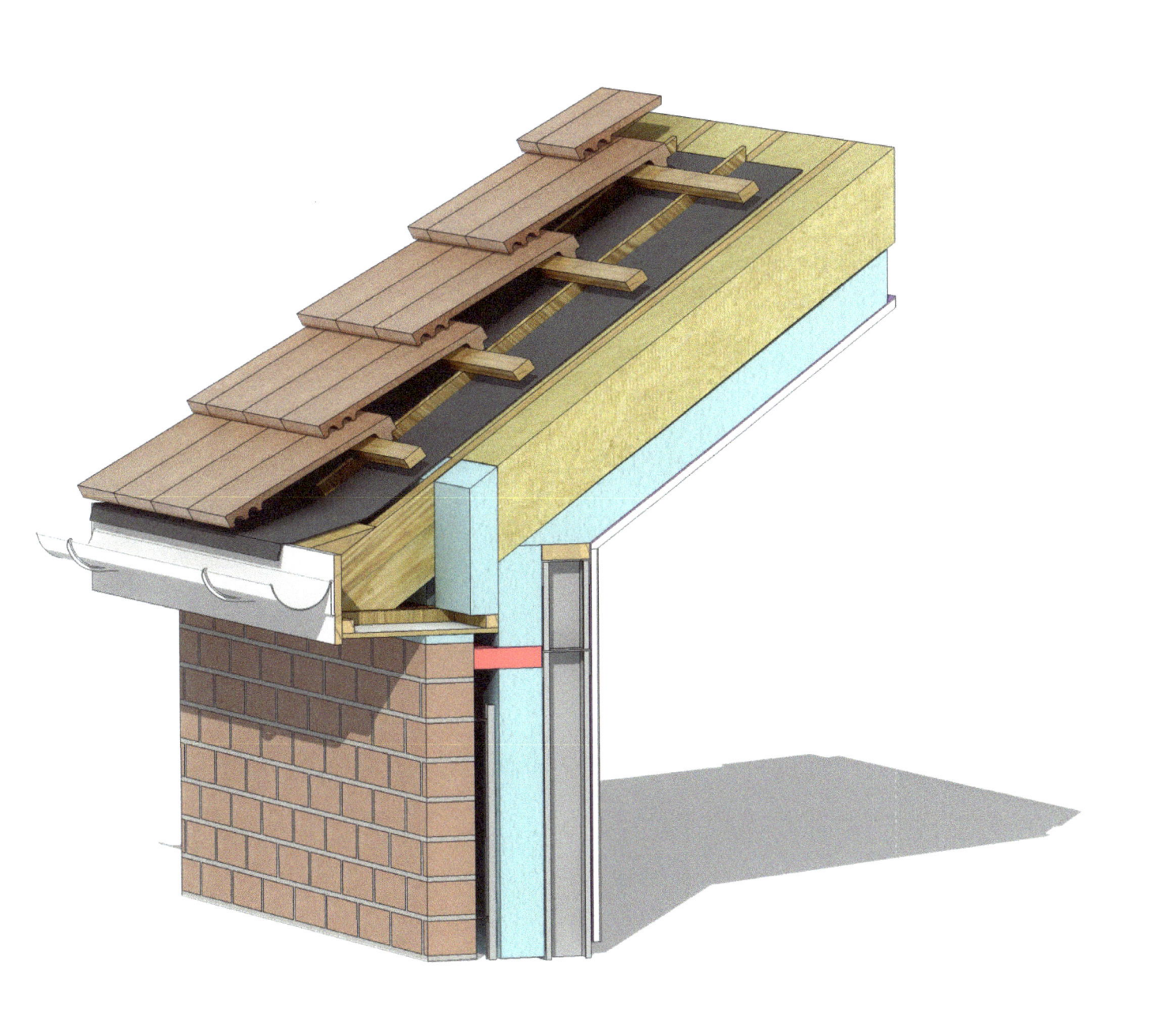

3D Detail S-R2 - Steel frame wall, eaves detail, unventilated roof space, insulation between and under rafters

SECTION 7 - STEEL FRAME

STRUCTURAL INSULATED PANELS (SIPS)

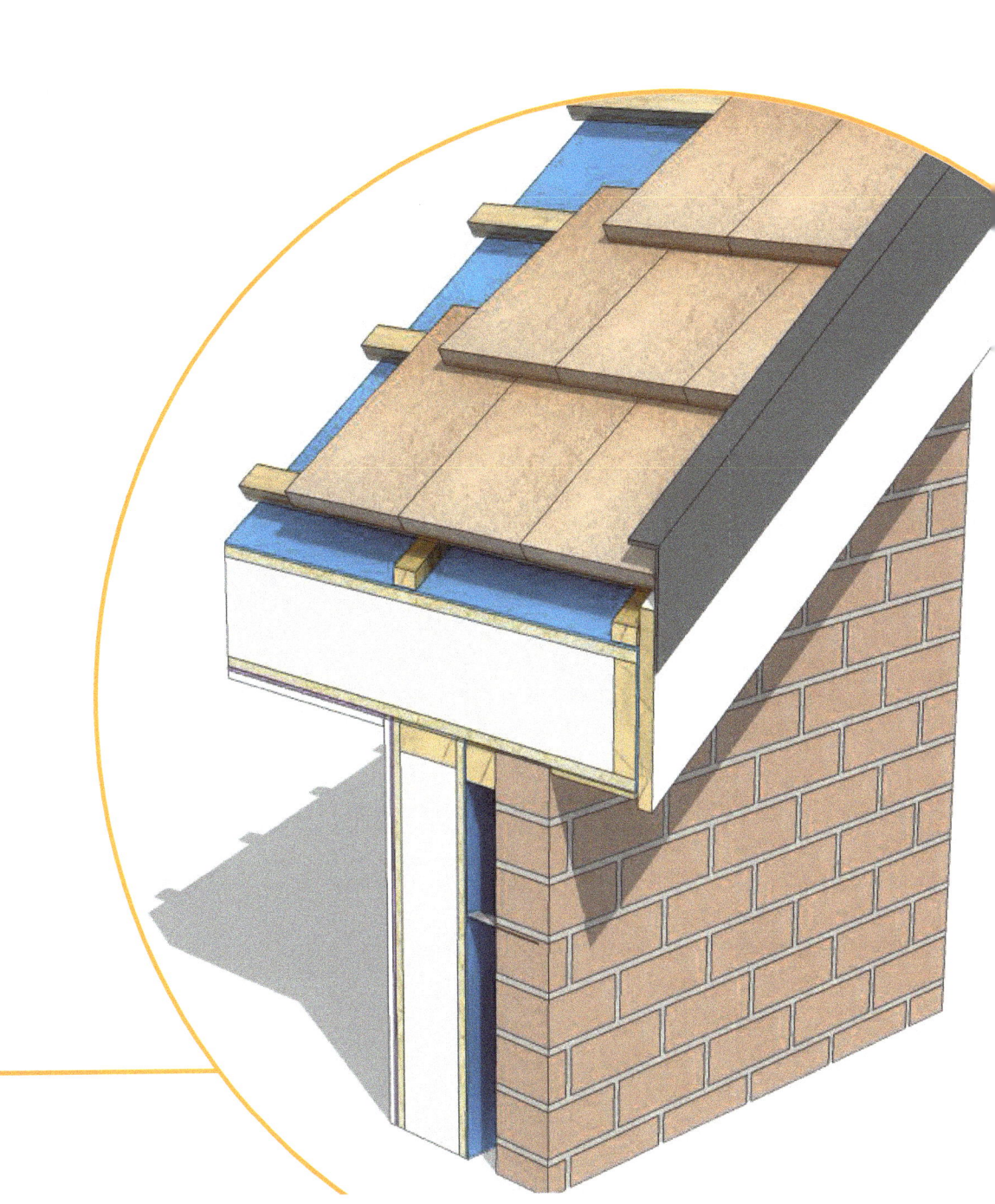

INTRODUCTION

SIPS are a high performance building system for both residential and light commercial construction. Structural Insulated Panels (SIPS) are structural frames made from a sandwich of two layers of structure, and one layer of insulation. The outer layers tend to be OSB, with the insulation layer being premium carbon treated expanded polystyrene (EPS). The edges of the panels are formed so that they can be easily fitted together over a connection plate. The wall panels vary in thickness from 100mm to around 172mm and are usually around 1200mm wide and 3000mm high. Roof panels are much larger, at around 6500mm, and are self-supporting, which means there is no need for trusses, making the roof space a useable area.

The panels are manufactured under factory conditions, and can be prefabricated to almost any design.

The panels are strong, and highly insulated, with no need for a cavity. The walls can achieve U-values as low as 0.14 W/Km2, using just a standard panel without extra insulation. They allow for extremely fast and efficient construction times on site, whilst being a cost effective option.

The SIPS can be finished with external claddings such as brick, render, timber cladding and so on. The roofing panels can be finished with slates, tiles and metal roofing.

Typical construction consists of a standard foundation system, with a sole plate installed above dpc level to provide a suitable base for the panel to be fitted to with angle brackets to secure in place. Openings are factory formed, with the door or window installed on site. Joist hangers are secured to the panels to support the first floor joists. Roof panels can be fixed to a wall plate on top of the first floor panels, or roof trusses can also be used.

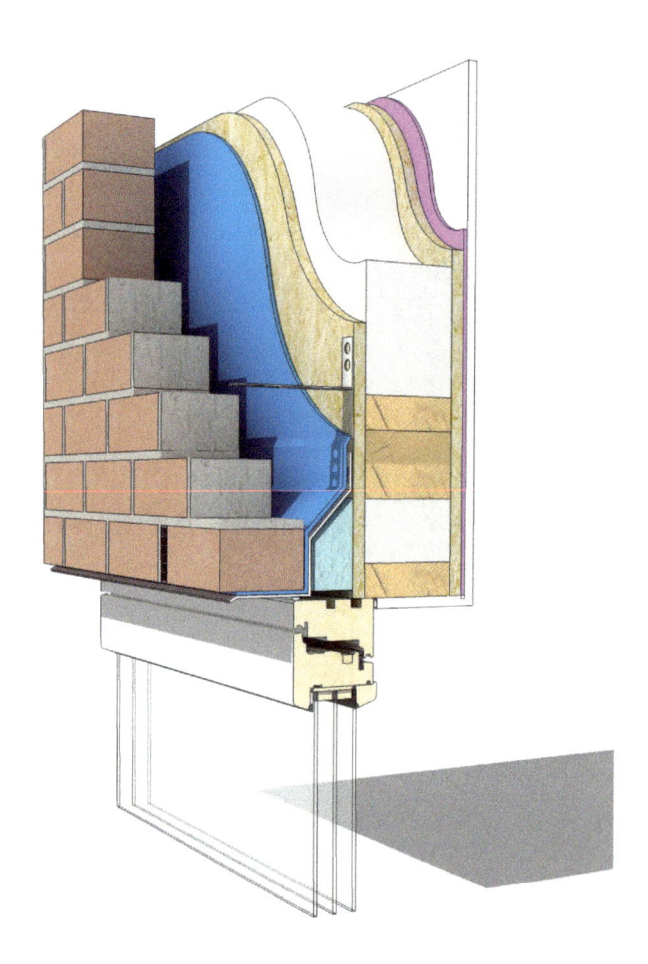

Figure 6.1 - Example of SIP construction

260

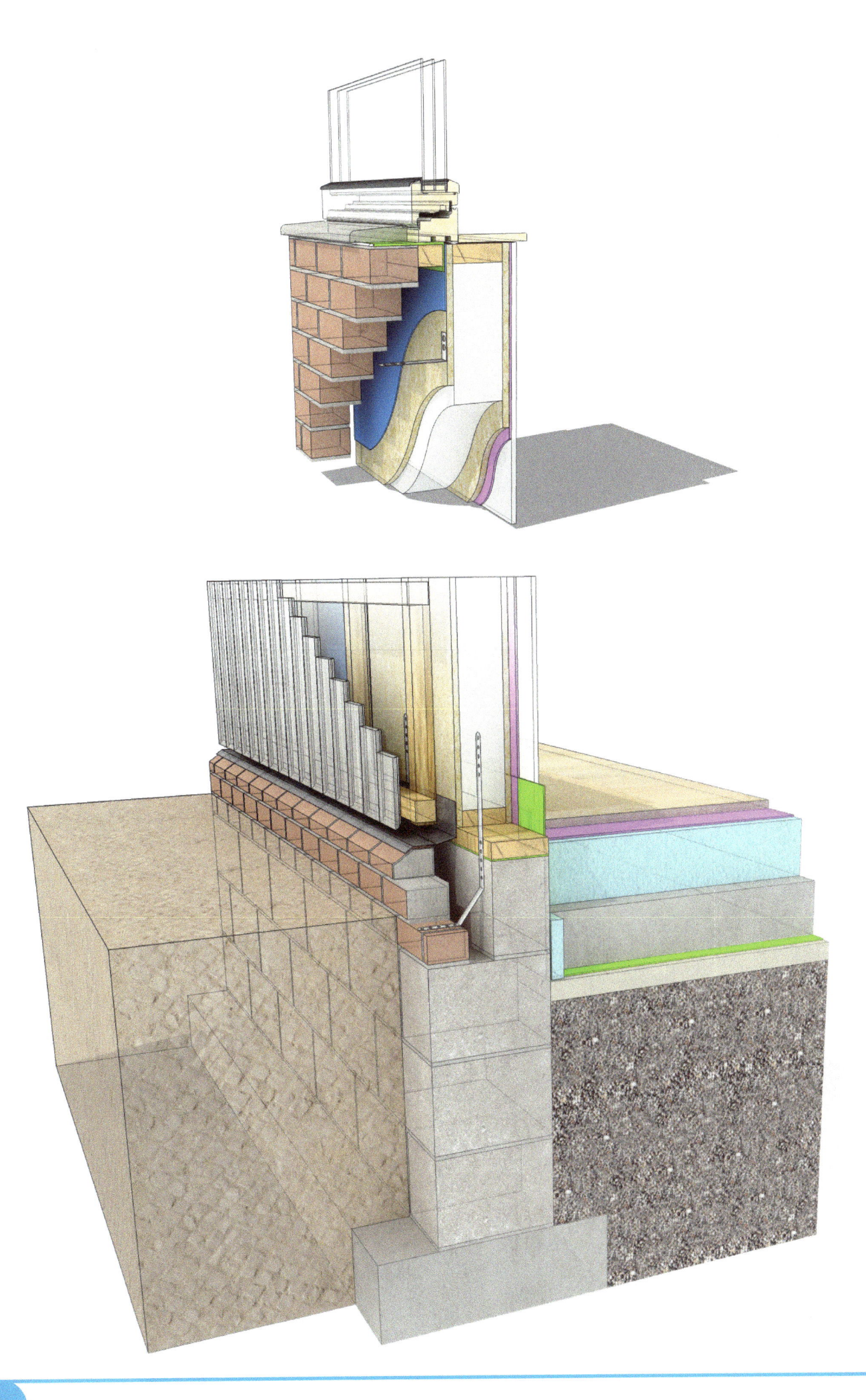

SIP DETAILS

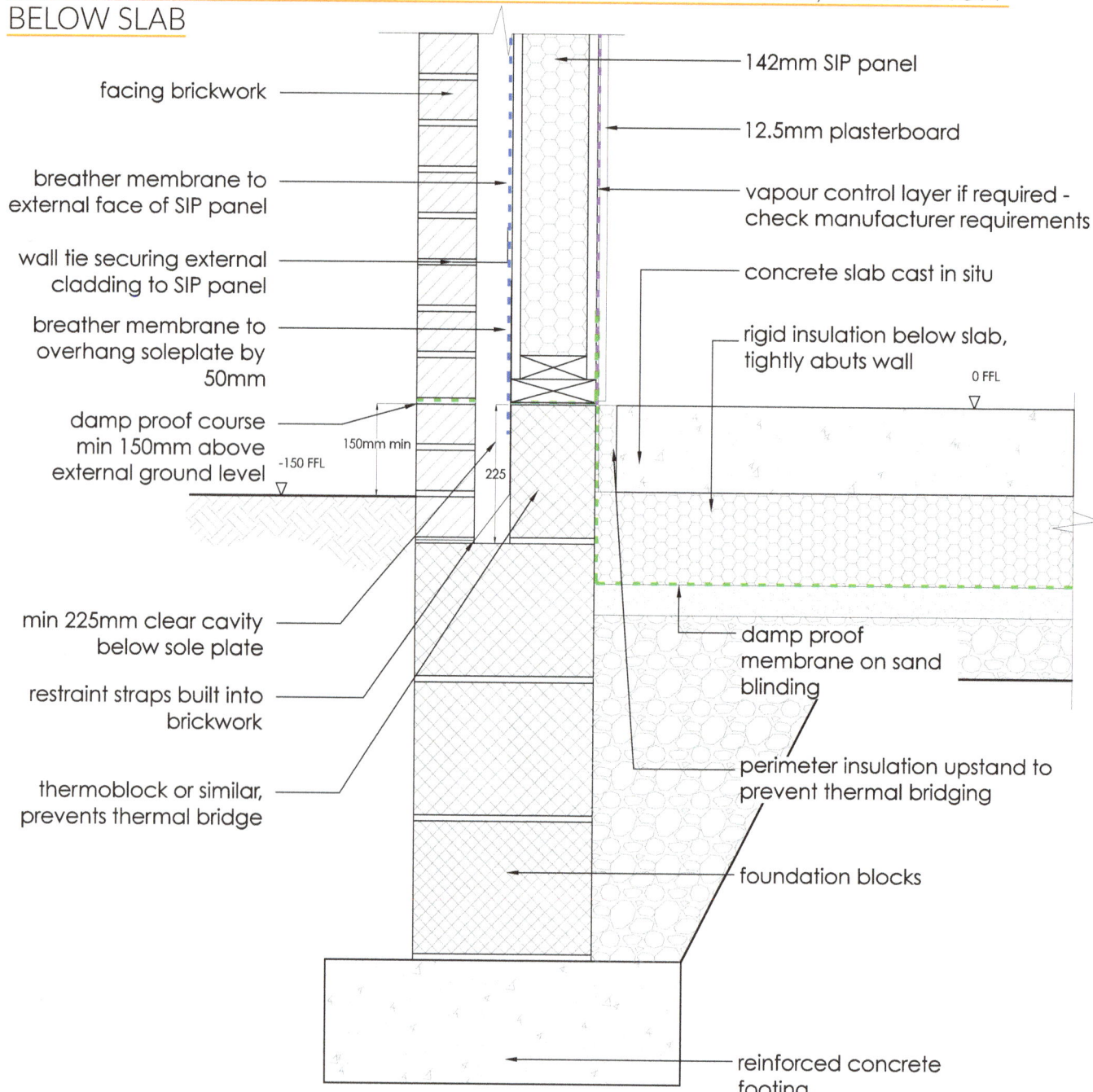

SIP1

SIP, BRICK CLADDING, GROUND BEARING CONCRETE SLAB, INSULATION BELOW SLAB

Labels (left side):
- facing brickwork
- breather membrane to external face of SIP panel
- wall tie securing external cladding to SIP panel
- breather membrane to overhang soleplate by 50mm
- damp proof course min 150mm above external ground level
- min 225mm clear cavity below sole plate
- restraint straps built into brickwork
- thermoblock or similar, prevents thermal bridge

Labels (right side):
- 142mm SIP panel
- 12.5mm plasterboard
- vapour control layer if required - check manufacturer requirements
- concrete slab cast in situ
- rigid insulation below slab, tightly abuts wall
- damp proof membrane on sand blinding
- perimeter insulation upstand to prevent thermal bridging
- foundation blocks
- reinforced concrete footing

Dimensions: -150 FFL, 150mm min, 225, 0 FFL

Detail SIP1 - SIP - Brick cladding, ground bearing concrete slab, insulation below slab

NOTES:

U Value 0.13W/m²K or better
Perimeter strip of insulation abuts concrete slab and blockwork wall. Potential thermal bridge area at blockwork below SIP, specify thermoblock or similar. A thermoblock is a highly insulated load bearing block that helps to eliminate cold bridging at junctions.
This drawing shows one foundation option, and is not site specific. 50mm cavity must be maintained between brick cladding and SIP panel.
Plasterboard could be fitted to counter battens for service void.

SECTION 8 - SIPS

breather membrane to overhang soleplate by 50mm

vapour control layer if required - check manufacturer requirements

damp proof course min 150mm above external ground level

dpm

dpc

Detail SIP1A - SIP - Brick cladding, ground bearing concrete slab. Enhanced DPC DPM detail

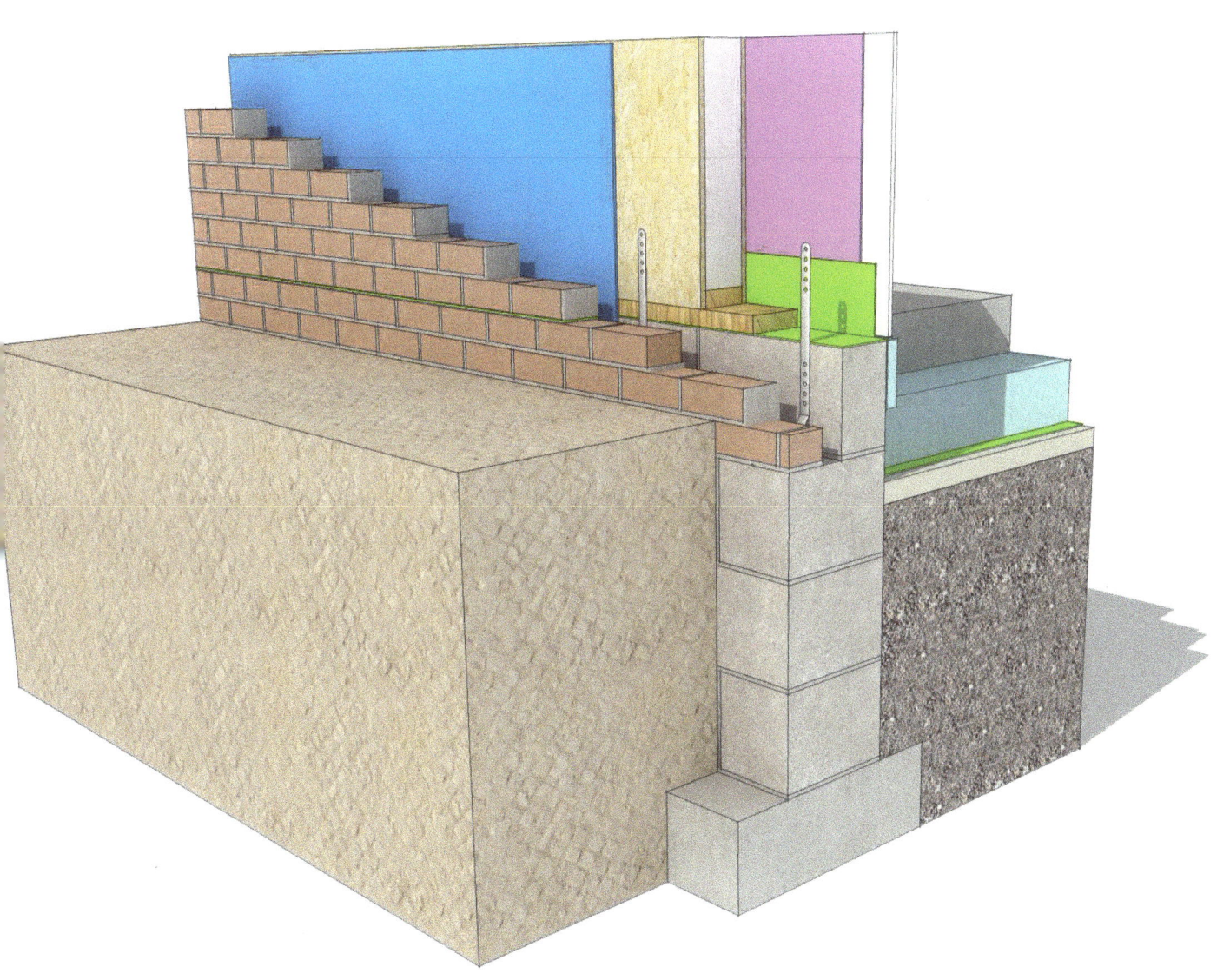

3D Detail SIP1 - SIP - Brick cladding, ground bearing concrete slab, insulation below slab

262

SIP2

SIP, TIMBER CLADDING, GROUND BEARING CONCRETE SLAB, INSULATION ABOVE SLAB

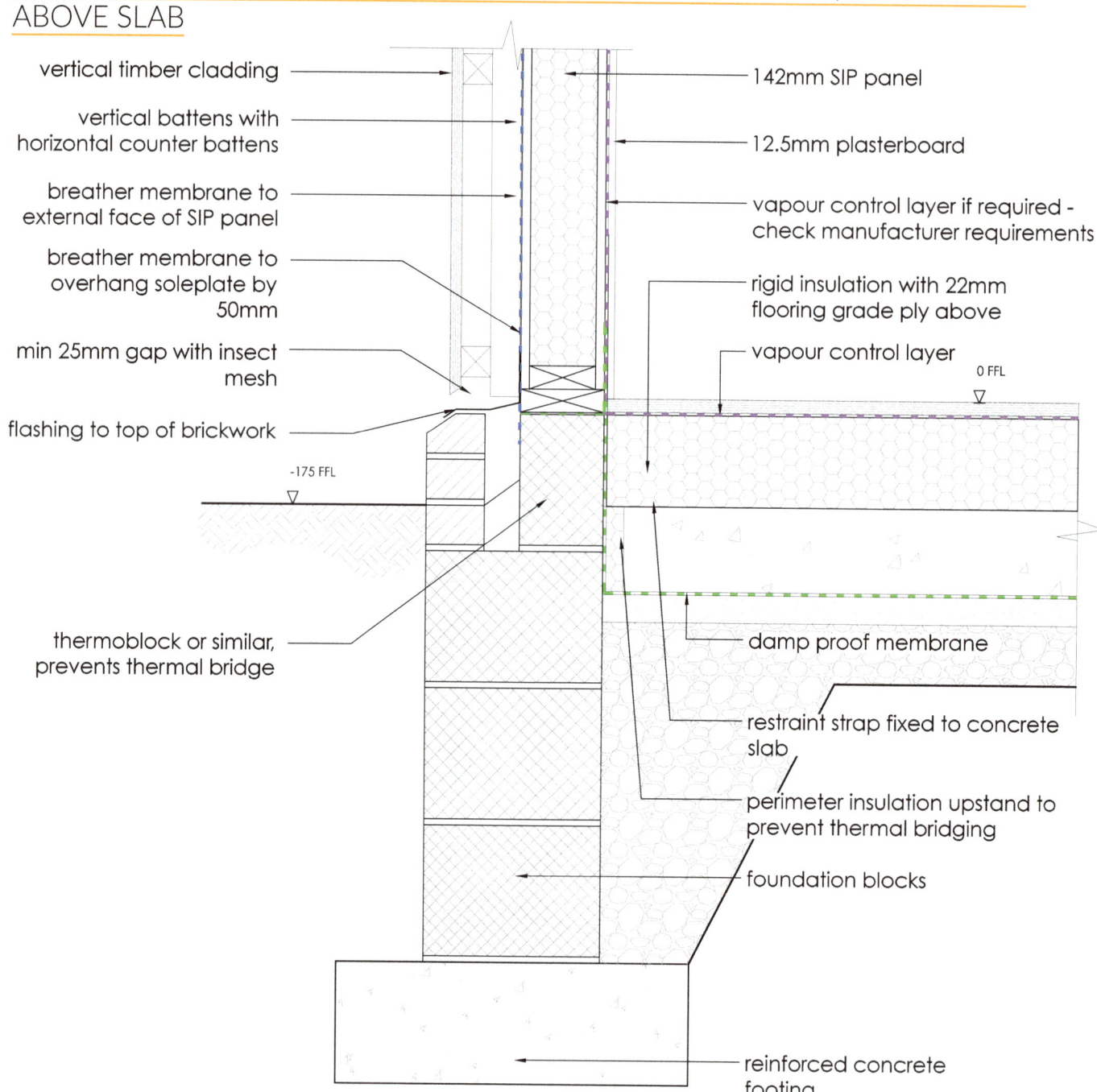

Labels (left side):
- vertical timber cladding
- vertical battens with horizontal counter battens
- breather membrane to external face of SIP panel
- breather membrane to overhang soleplate by 50mm
- min 25mm gap with insect mesh
- flashing to top of brickwork
- thermoblock or similar, prevents thermal bridge

Labels (right side):
- 142mm SIP panel
- 12.5mm plasterboard
- vapour control layer if required - check manufacturer requirements
- rigid insulation with 22mm flooring grade ply above
- vapour control layer
- damp proof membrane
- restraint strap fixed to concrete slab
- perimeter insulation upstand to prevent thermal bridging
- foundation blocks
- reinforced concrete footing

Levels: 0 FFL, -175 FFL

Detail SIP2 - SIP - Timber cladding, ground bearing concrete slab, insulation above slab

NOTES:

U Value 0.13W/m²K or better
Perimeter strip of insulation abuts concrete slab and blockwork wall. Potential thermal bridge area at blockwork below SIP, specify thermoblock or similar. A thermoblock is a highly insulated load bearing block that helps to eliminate cold bridging at junctions.
This drawing shows one foundation option, and is not site specific. 50mm cavity must be maintained between brick cladding and SIP panel.
Plasterboard could be fitted to counter battens for service void.

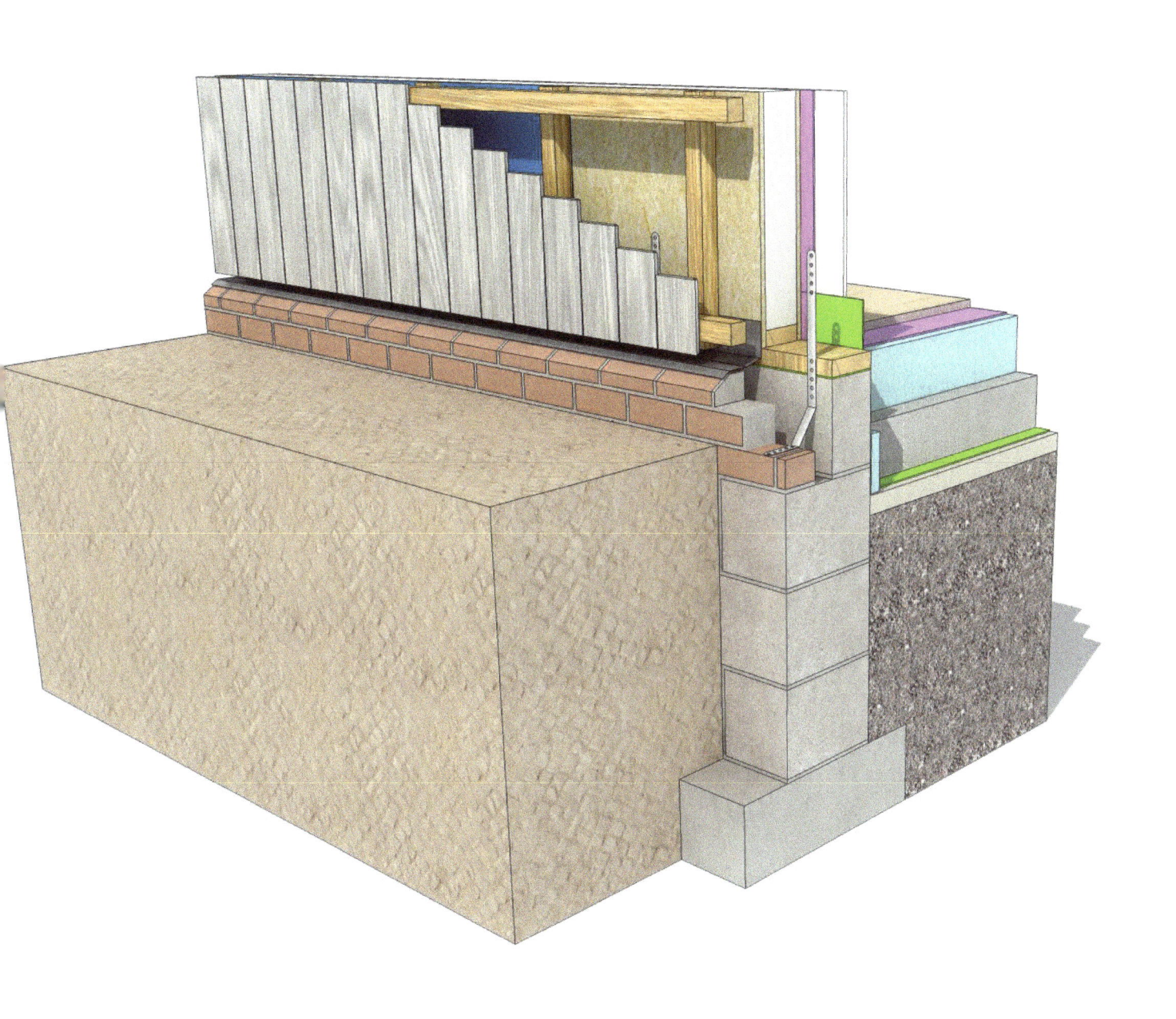

3D Detail SIP2 - SIP - Timber cladding, insulation above slab

SIP3

SIP, TIMBER CLADDING, GROUND BEARING CONCRETE SLAB, INSULATION ABOVE SLAB - ALTERNATIVE DETAIL

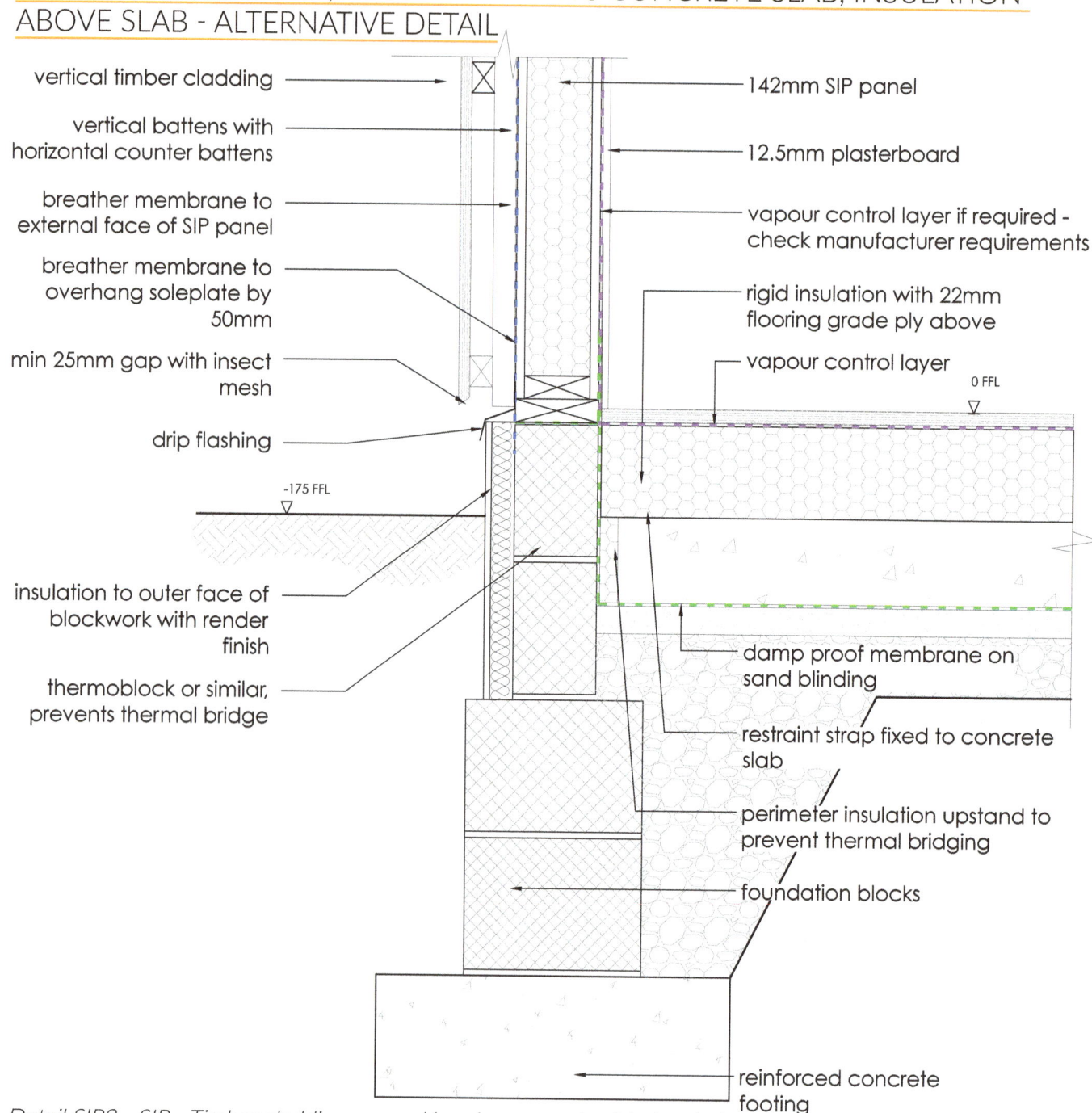

Labels (left side):
- vertical timber cladding
- vertical battens with horizontal counter battens
- breather membrane to external face of SIP panel
- breather membrane to overhang soleplate by 50mm
- min 25mm gap with insect mesh
- drip flashing
- -175 FFL
- insulation to outer face of blockwork with render finish
- thermoblock or similar, prevents thermal bridge

Labels (right side):
- 142mm SIP panel
- 12.5mm plasterboard
- vapour control layer if required - check manufacturer requirements
- rigid insulation with 22mm flooring grade ply above
- vapour control layer
- 0 FFL
- damp proof membrane on sand blinding
- restraint strap fixed to concrete slab
- perimeter insulation upstand to prevent thermal bridging
- foundation blocks
- reinforced concrete footing

Detail SIP3 - SIP - Timber cladding, ground bearing concrete slab, insulation above slab - alternative detail

NOTES:

U Value 0.13W/m²K or better
Perimeter strip of insulation abuts concrete slab and blockwork wall. Potential thermal bridge area at blockwork below SIP, specify thermoblock or similar. A thermoblock is a highly insulated load bearing block that helps to eliminate cold bridging at junctions.
This drawing shows one foundation option, and is not site specific. 50mm cavity must be maintained between brick cladding and SIP panel.
Plasterboard could be fitted to counter battens for service void.

SECTION 8 - SIPS

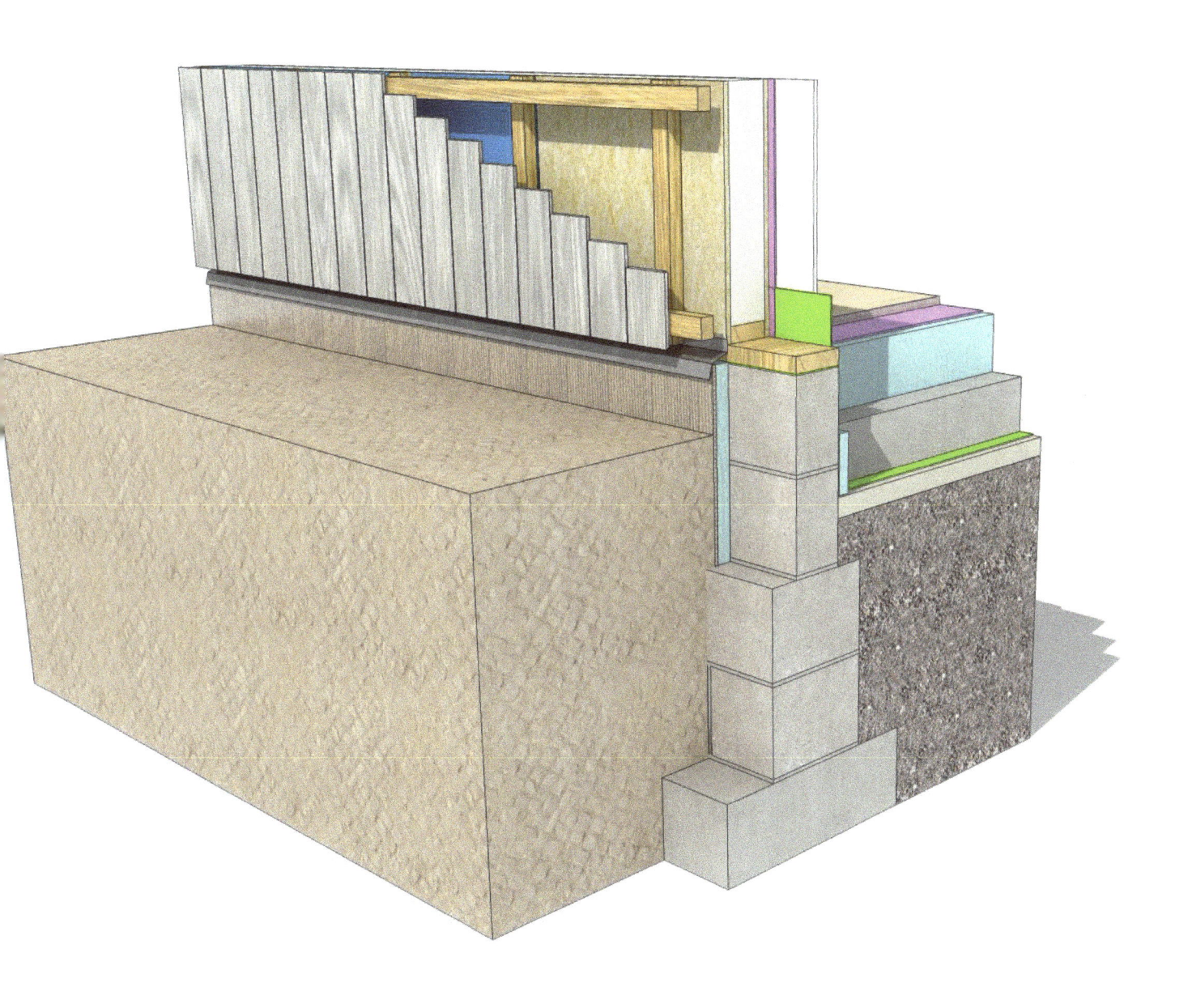

3D Detail SIP3 - SIP - Timber cladding, insulation above slab - alternative detail

SIP4

SIP, HORIZONTAL TIMBER CLADDING

- horizontal timber cladding
- vertical battens
- breather membrane
- 142mm SIP panel
- 12.5mm plasterboard
- vapour control layer

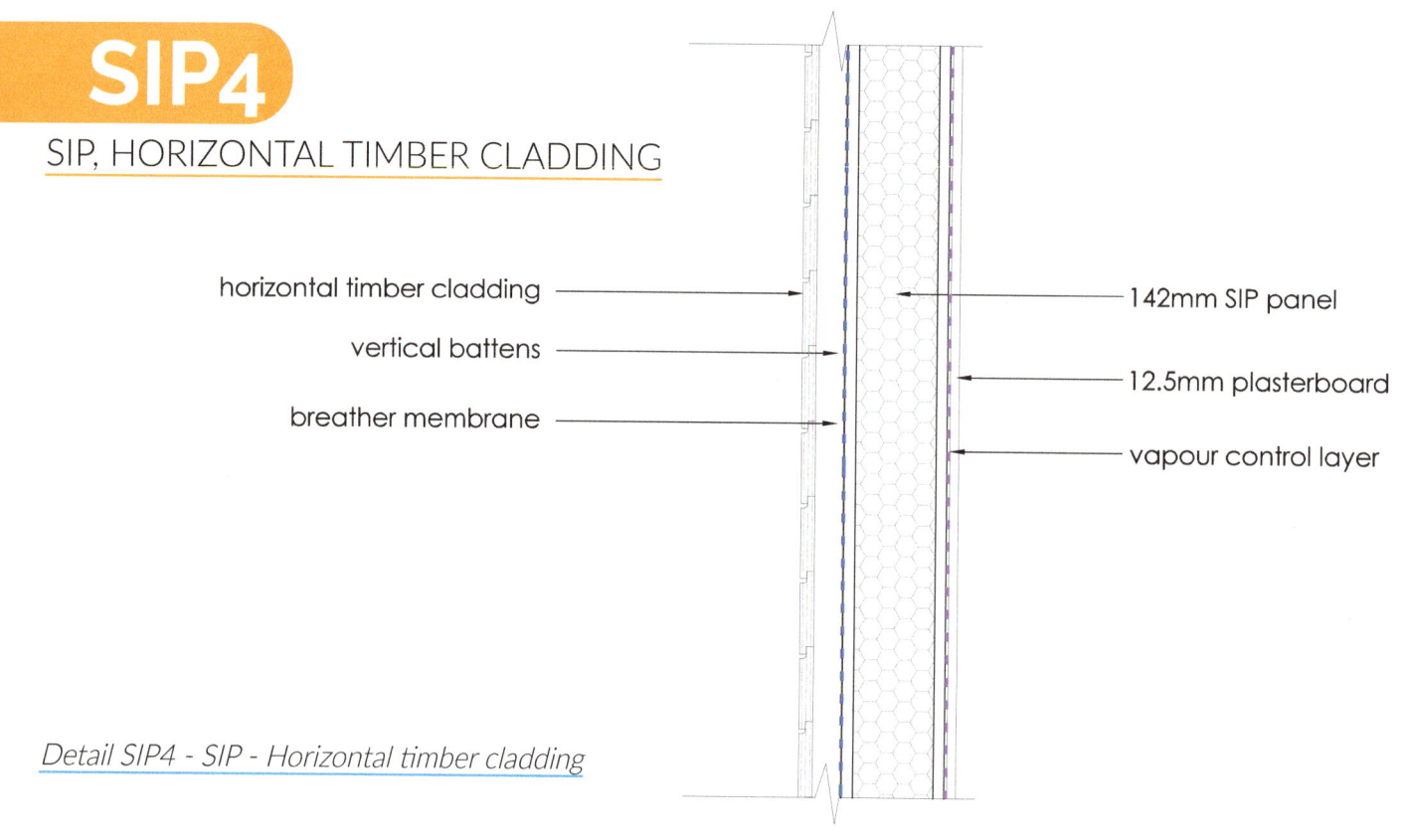

Detail SIP4 - SIP - Horizontal timber cladding

NOTES:

U Value 0.20W/m²K or better (See SIP5 for improved U-Value)
Plasterboard could be fixed to counter battens for service void
Improved U-Value can also be achieved with thicker SIP panel

SIP5

SIP, HORIZONTAL TIMBER CLADDING, IMPROVED THERMAL PERFORMANCE

- horizontal timber cladding
- vertical battens
- breather membrane
- 142mm SIP panel
- 12.5mm plasterboard
- vapour control layer
- 30mm rigid insulation

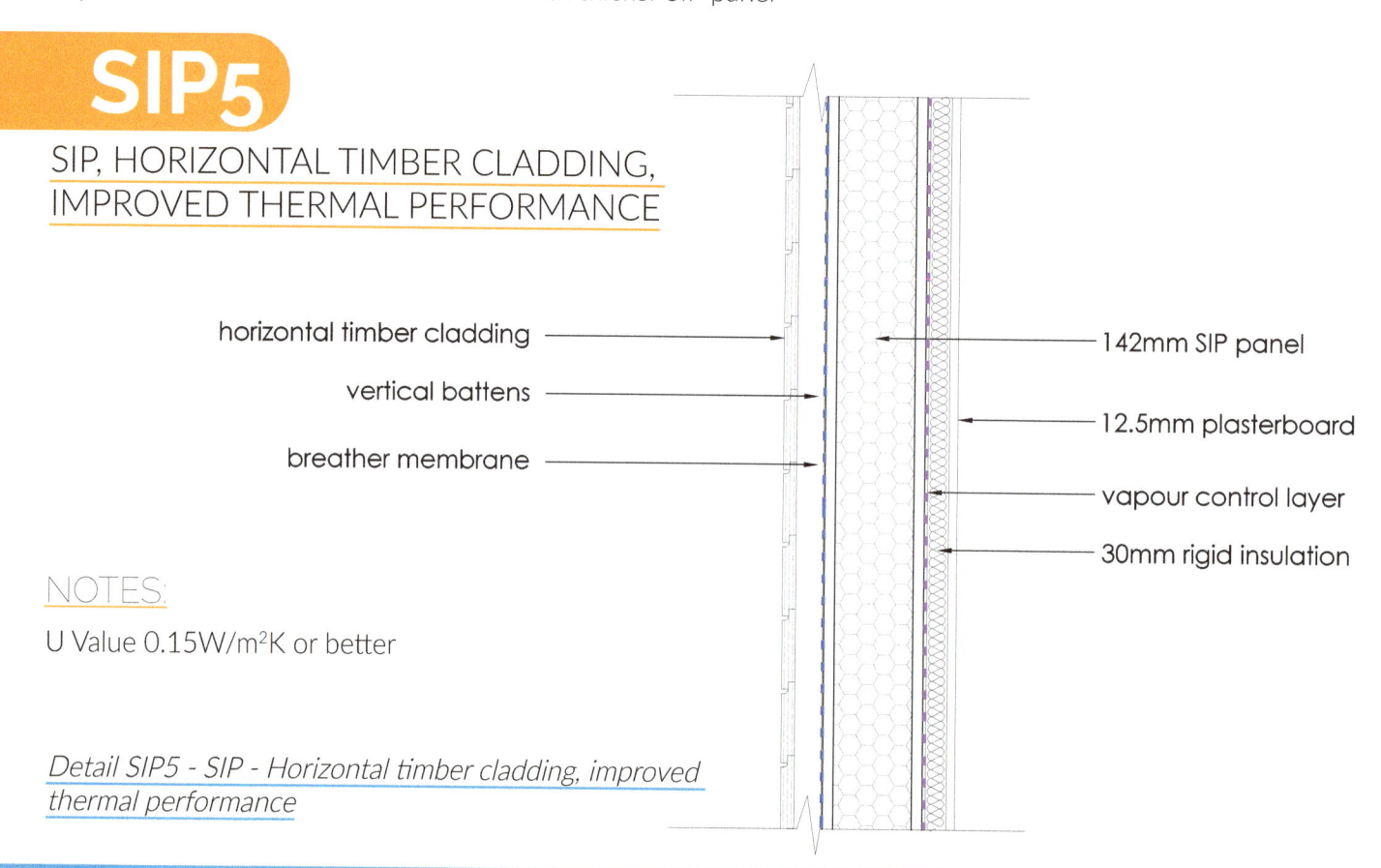

NOTES:

U Value 0.15W/m²K or better

Detail SIP5 - SIP - Horizontal timber cladding, improved thermal performance

SECTION 8 - SIPS

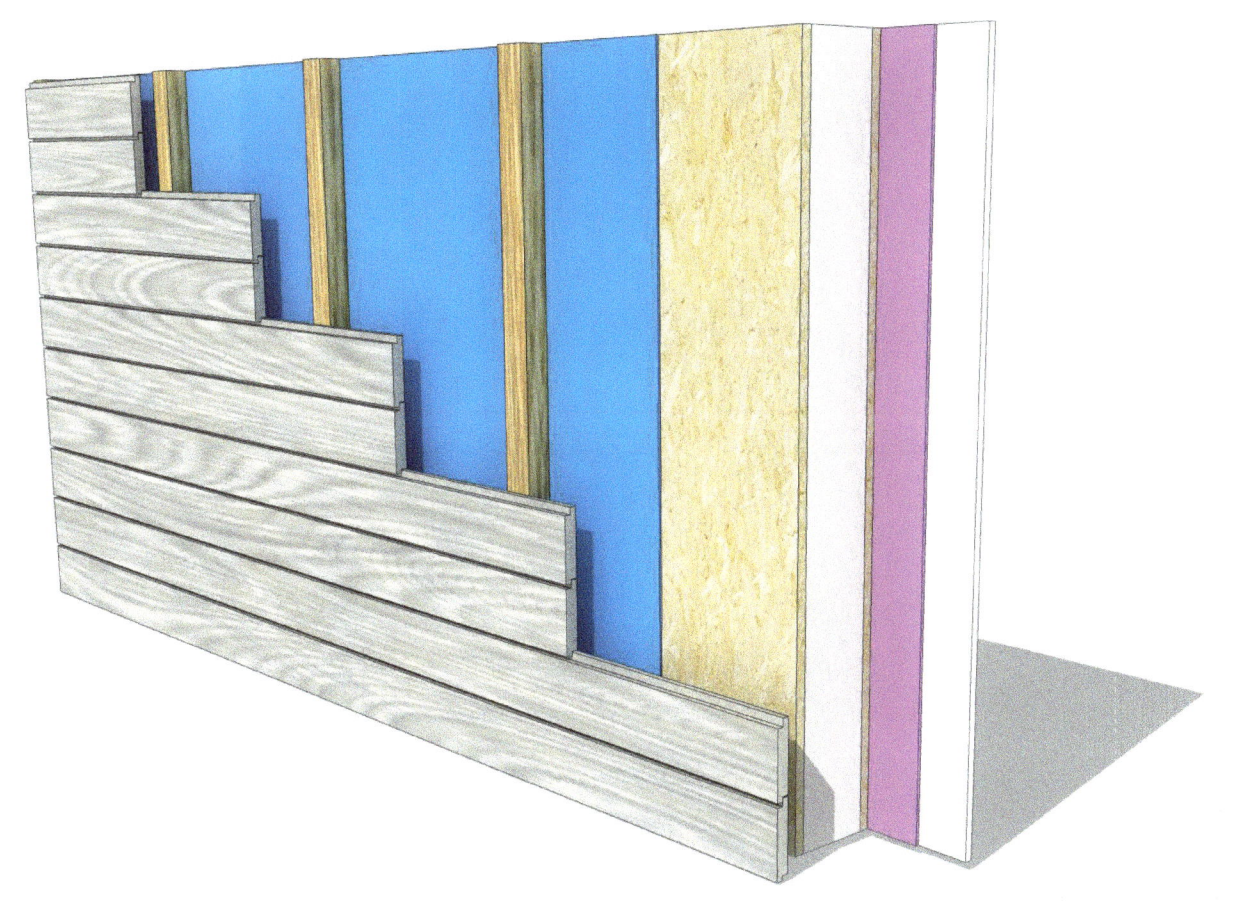

3D Detail SIP4 - SIP - Horizontal timber cladding

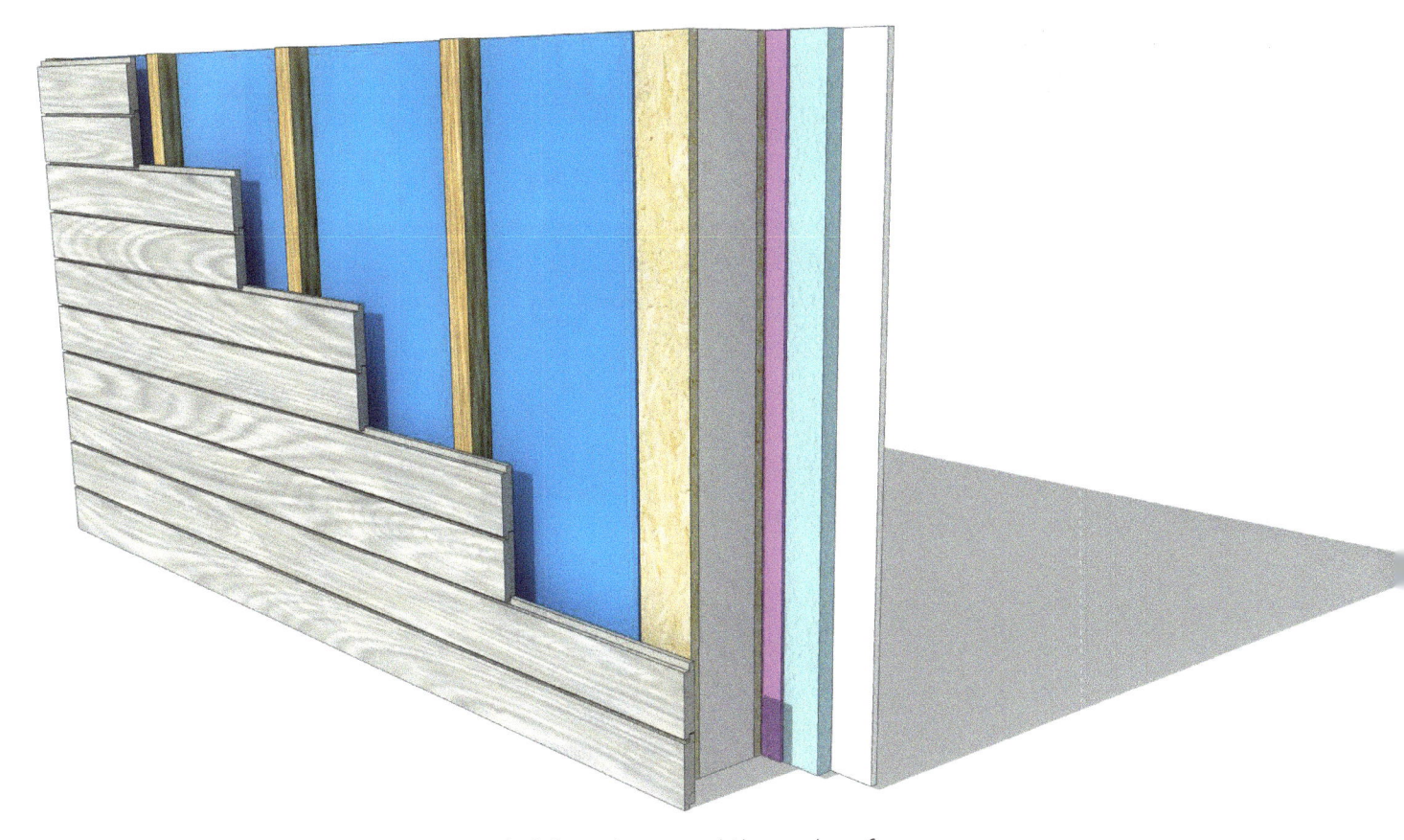

3D Detail SIP5 - SIP - Horizontal timber cladding - improved thermal performance

SIP6

SIP, RENDER FINISH

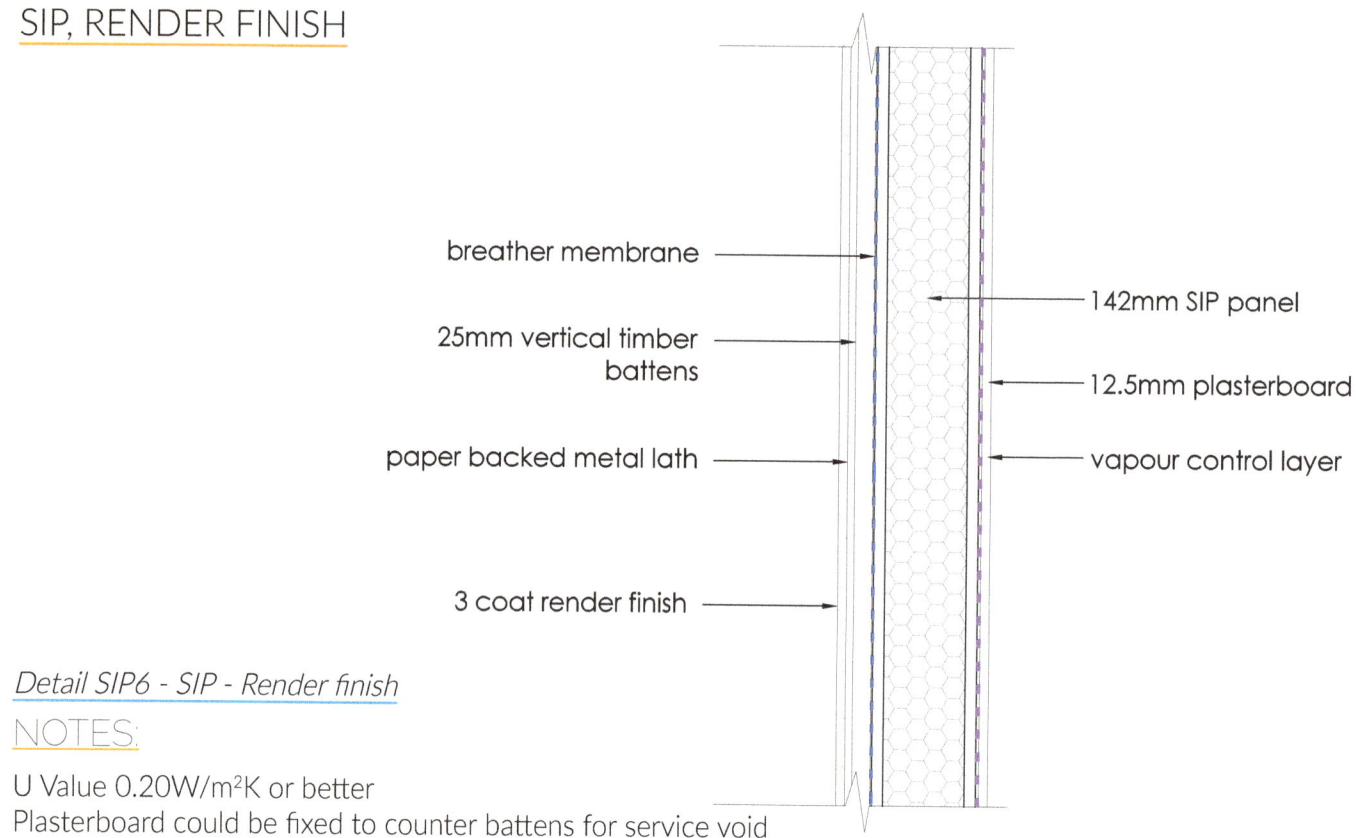

- breather membrane
- 25mm vertical timber battens
- paper backed metal lath
- 3 coat render finish
- 142mm SIP panel
- 12.5mm plasterboard
- vapour control layer

Detail SIP6 - SIP - Render finish

NOTES:

U Value 0.20W/m²K or better
Plasterboard could be fixed to counter battens for service void

SIP7

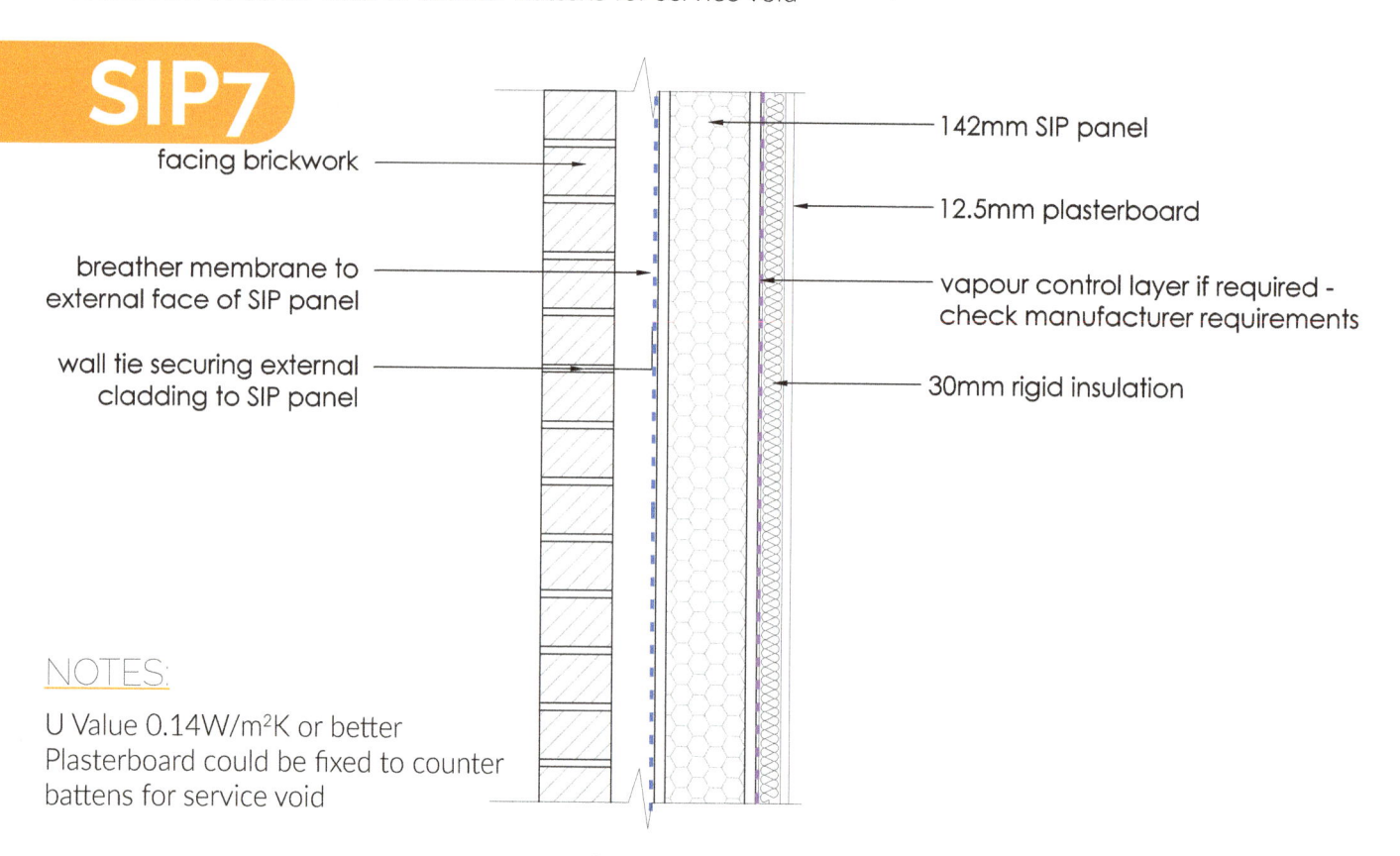

- facing brickwork
- breather membrane to external face of SIP panel
- wall tie securing external cladding to SIP panel
- 142mm SIP panel
- 12.5mm plasterboard
- vapour control layer if required - check manufacturer requirements
- 30mm rigid insulation

NOTES:

U Value 0.14W/m²K or better
Plasterboard could be fixed to counter battens for service void

Detail SIP7 - SIP - Brick cladding - improved thermal performance

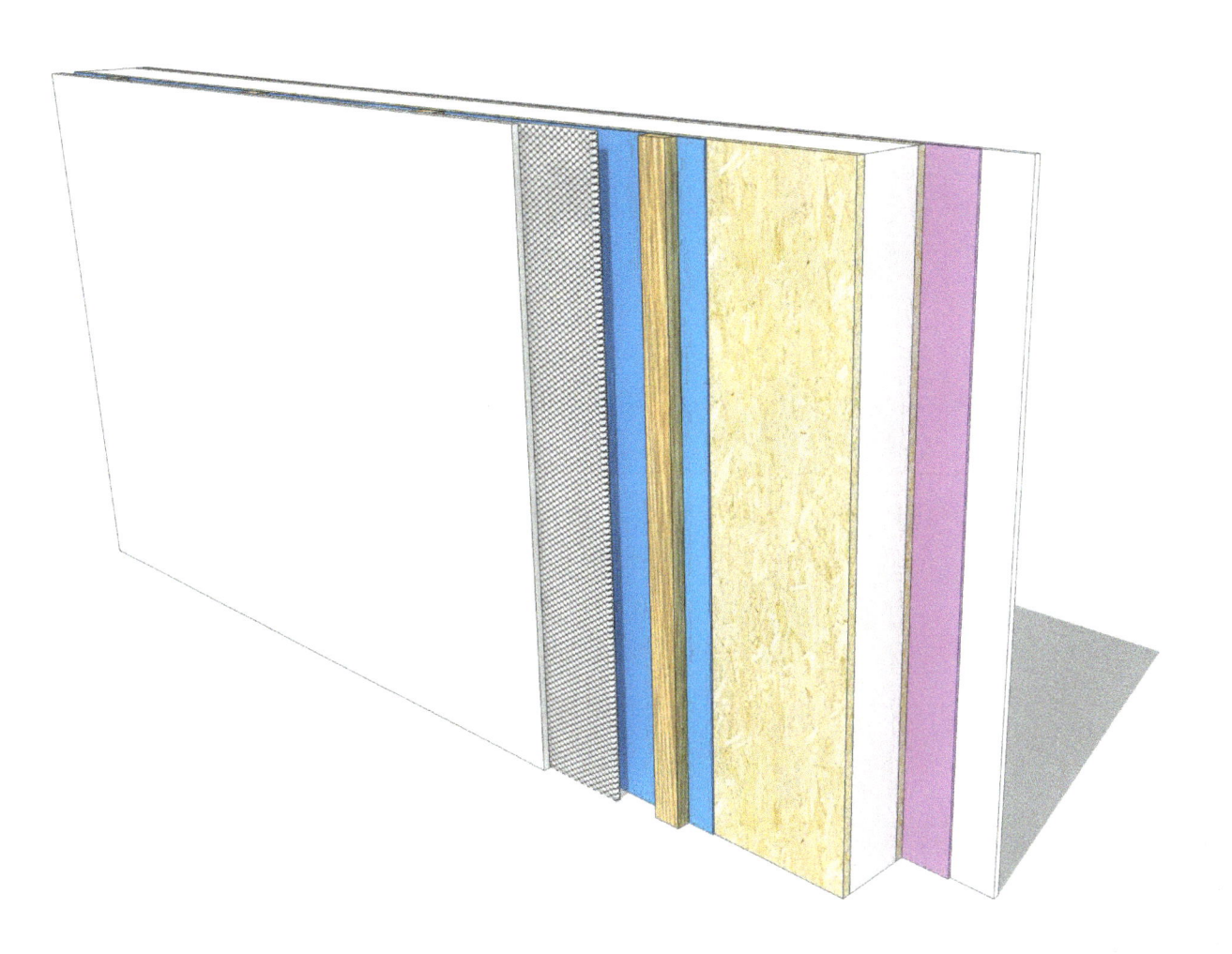

3D Detail SIP6 - SIP - Render finish

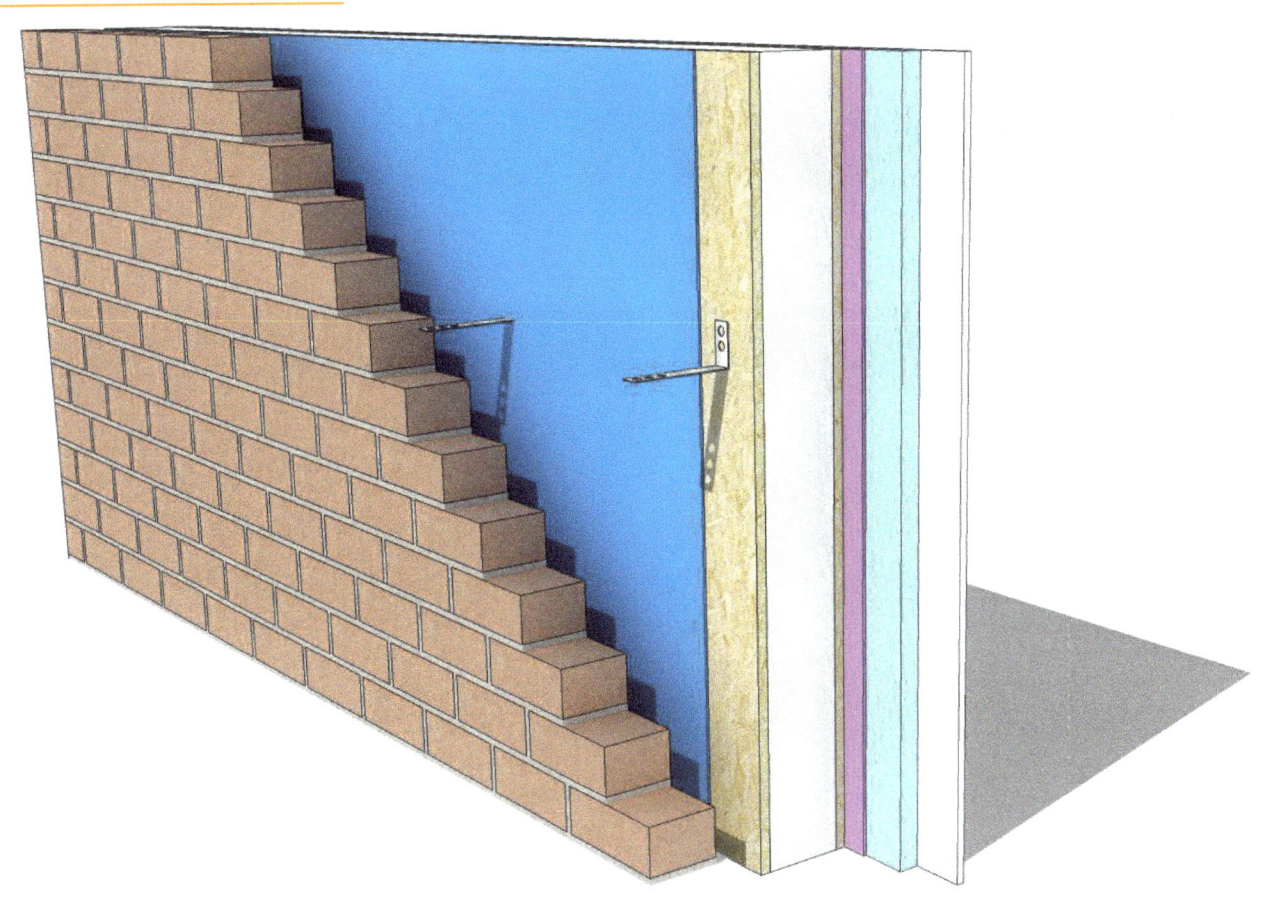

3D Detail SIP7 - SIP - Brick cladding - improved thermal performance

SIP8

SIP, BRICK CLADDING, DOOR THRESHOLD

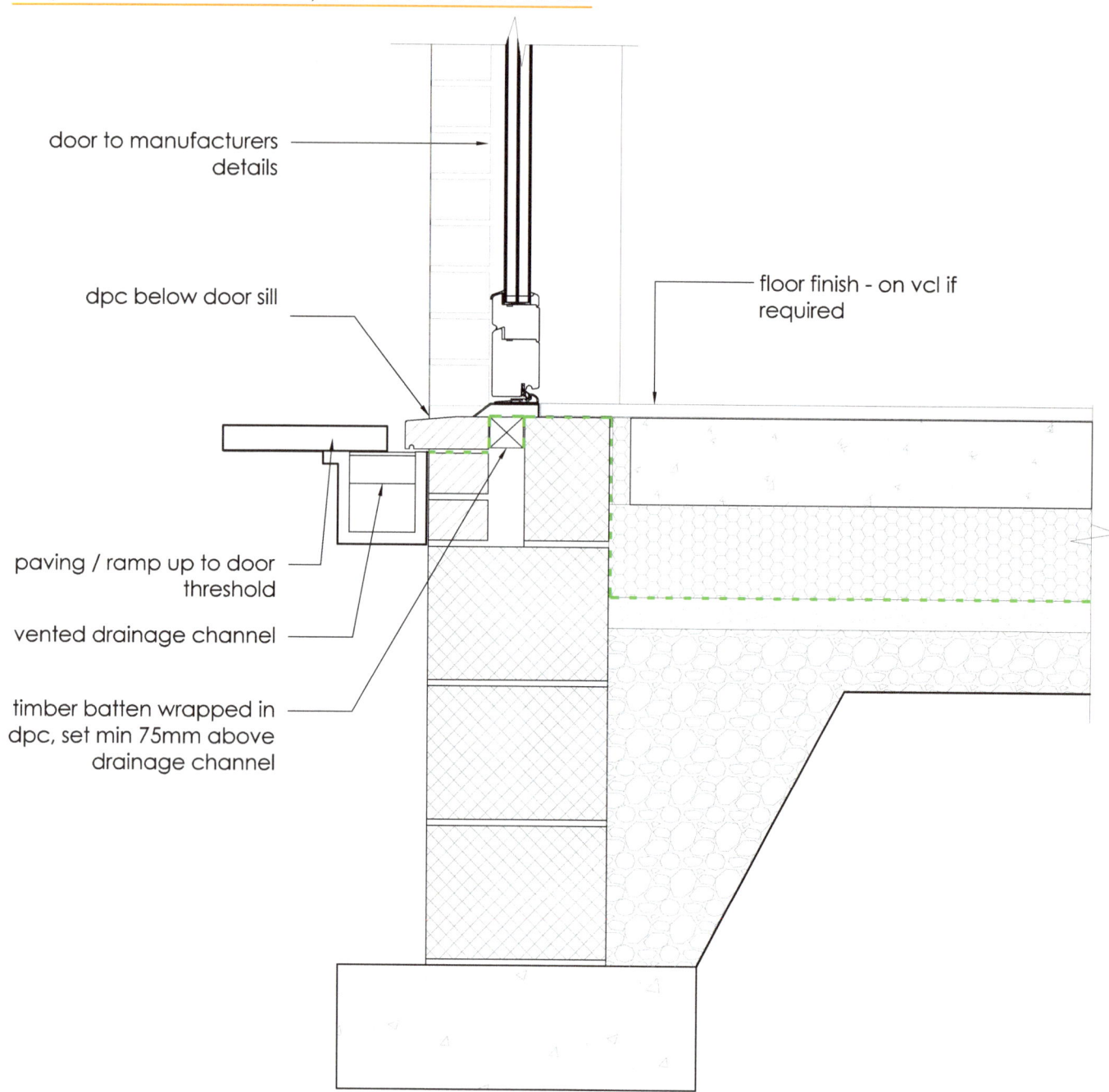

- door to manufacturers details
- dpc below door sill
- floor finish - on vcl if required
- paving / ramp up to door threshold
- vented drainage channel
- timber batten wrapped in dpc, set min 75mm above drainage channel

Detail SIP8 - SIP - Brick cladding, door threshold

NOTES:
U Value 0.13W/m²K or better

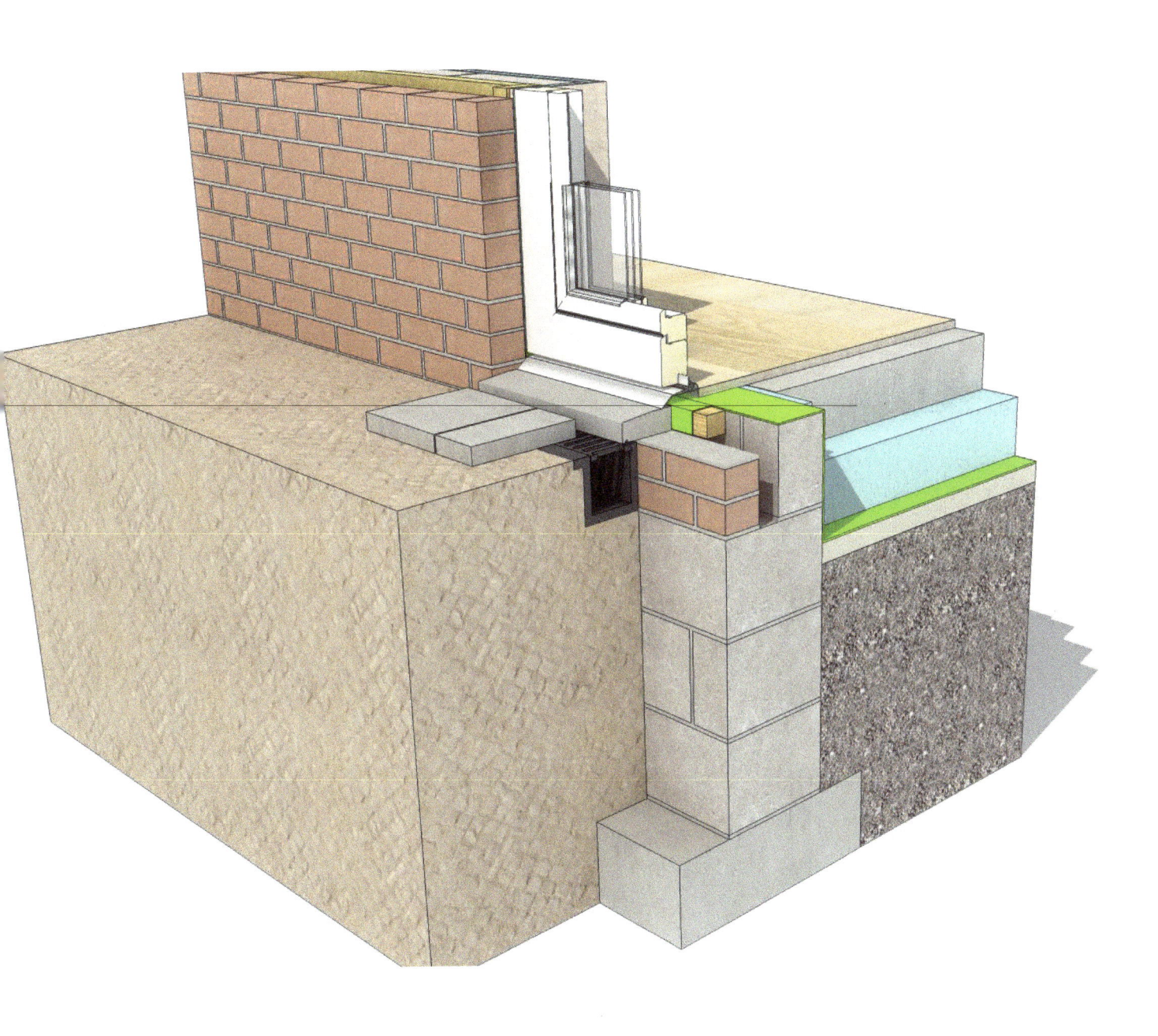

3D Detail SIP8 - SIP - Brick cladding, door threshold

SIP9
SIP, BRICK CLADDING, WINDOW HEAD AND CILL

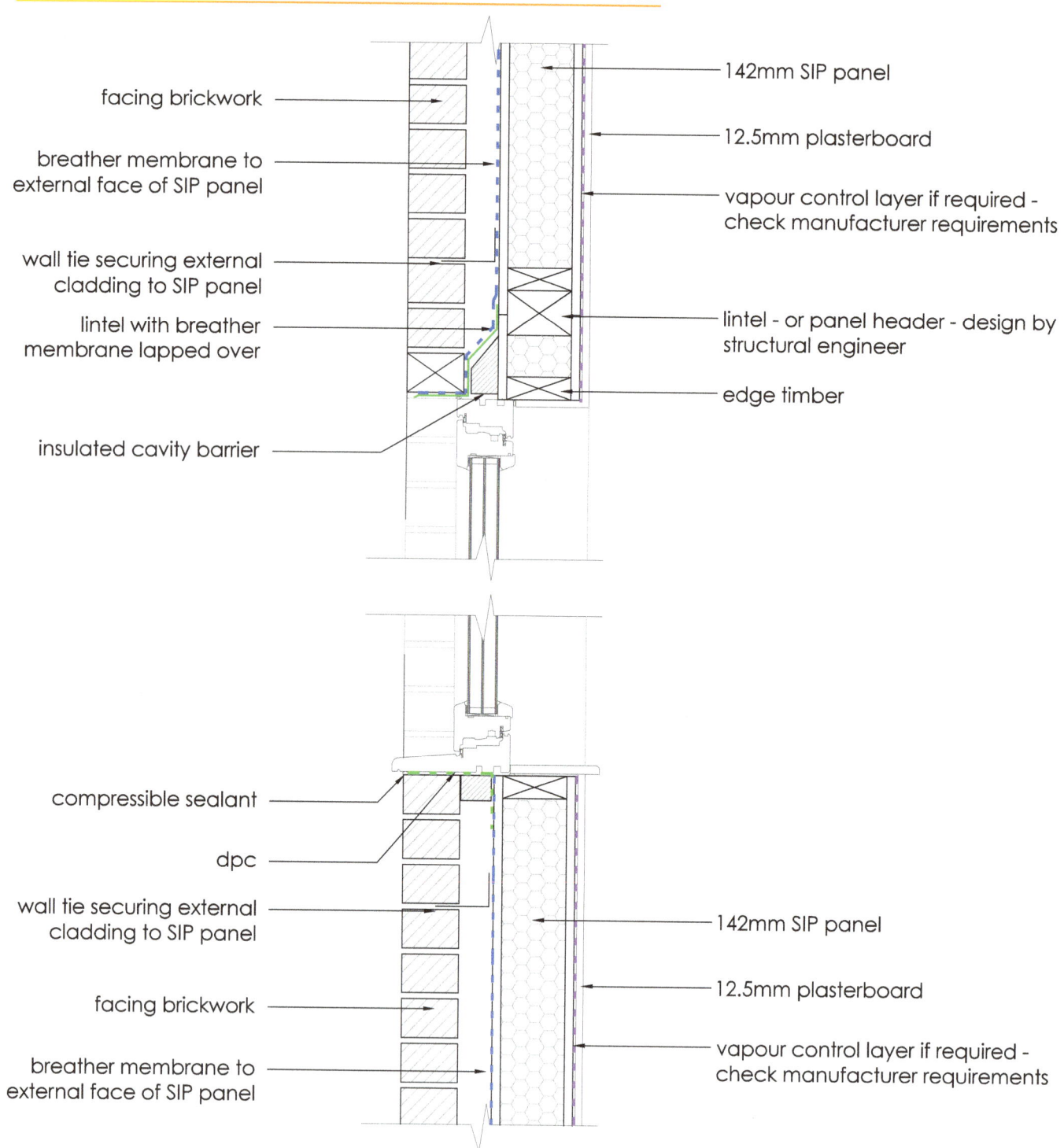

- facing brickwork
- breather membrane to external face of SIP panel
- wall tie securing external cladding to SIP panel
- lintel with breather membrane lapped over
- insulated cavity barrier
- 142mm SIP panel
- 12.5mm plasterboard
- vapour control layer if required - check manufacturer requirements
- lintel - or panel header - design by structural engineer
- edge timber
- compressible sealant
- dpc
- wall tie securing external cladding to SIP panel
- facing brickwork
- breather membrane to external face of SIP panel
- 142mm SIP panel
- 12.5mm plasterboard
- vapour control layer if required - check manufacturer requirements

Detail SIP9 - SIP - Brick cladding, window head and cill

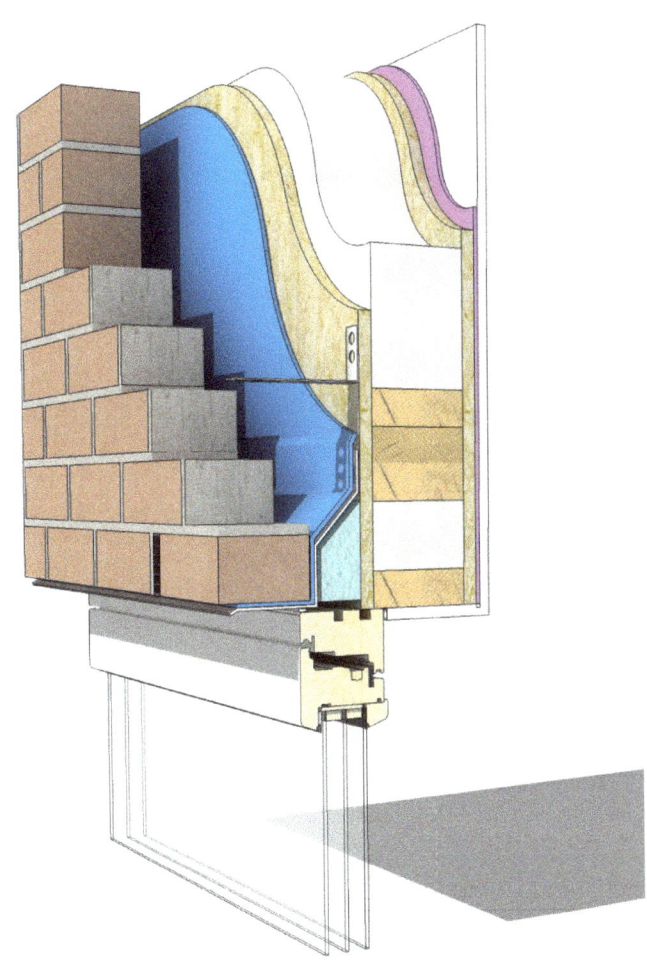

3D Detail SIP9 - SIP - Brick cladding, window head and cill

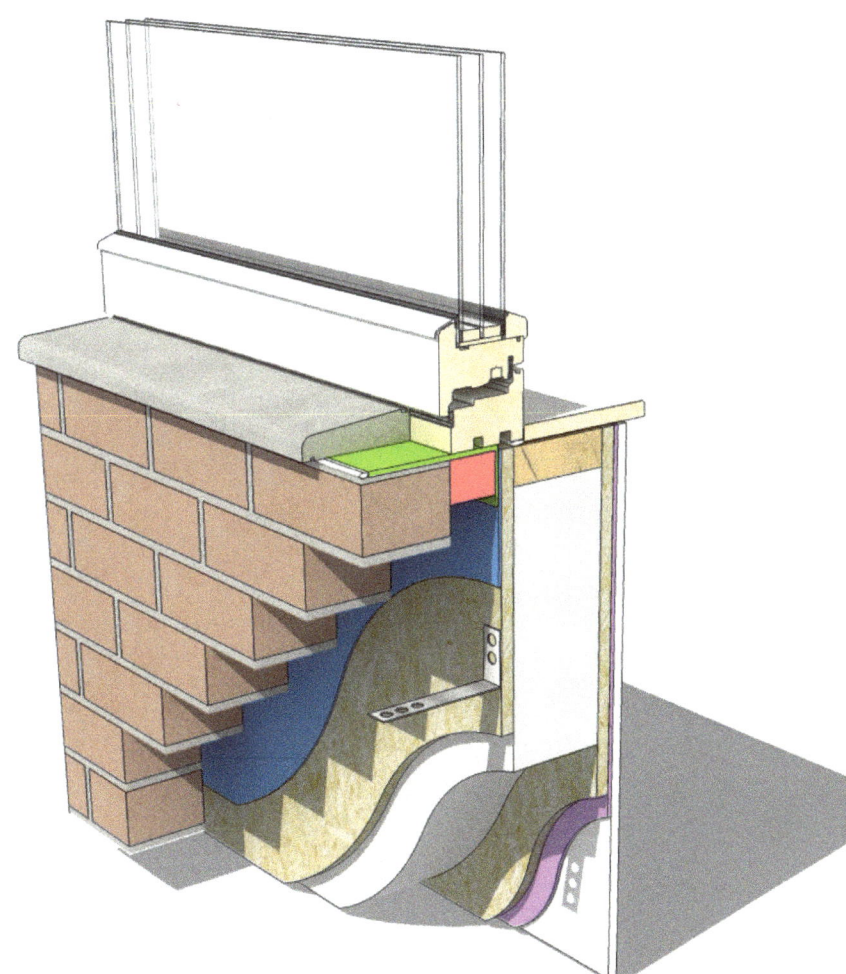

SIP10

SIP, BRICK CLADDING, FIRST FLOOR DETAIL

Labels (left side):
- facing brickwork
- breather membrane to external face of SIP panel
- wall tie securing external cladding to SIP panel
- insulated cavity barrier and fire stop
- wall tie securing external cladding to SIP panel

Labels (right side):
- 142mm SIP panel
- 12.5mm plasterboard
- vapour control layer if required - check manufacturer requirements
- 18mm OSB deck taken through between header and bottom plate
- engineered wood I-joist or softwood floor joist
- joist hanger fixed to SIP panel

Detail SIP10 - SIP - Brick cladding, first floor detail

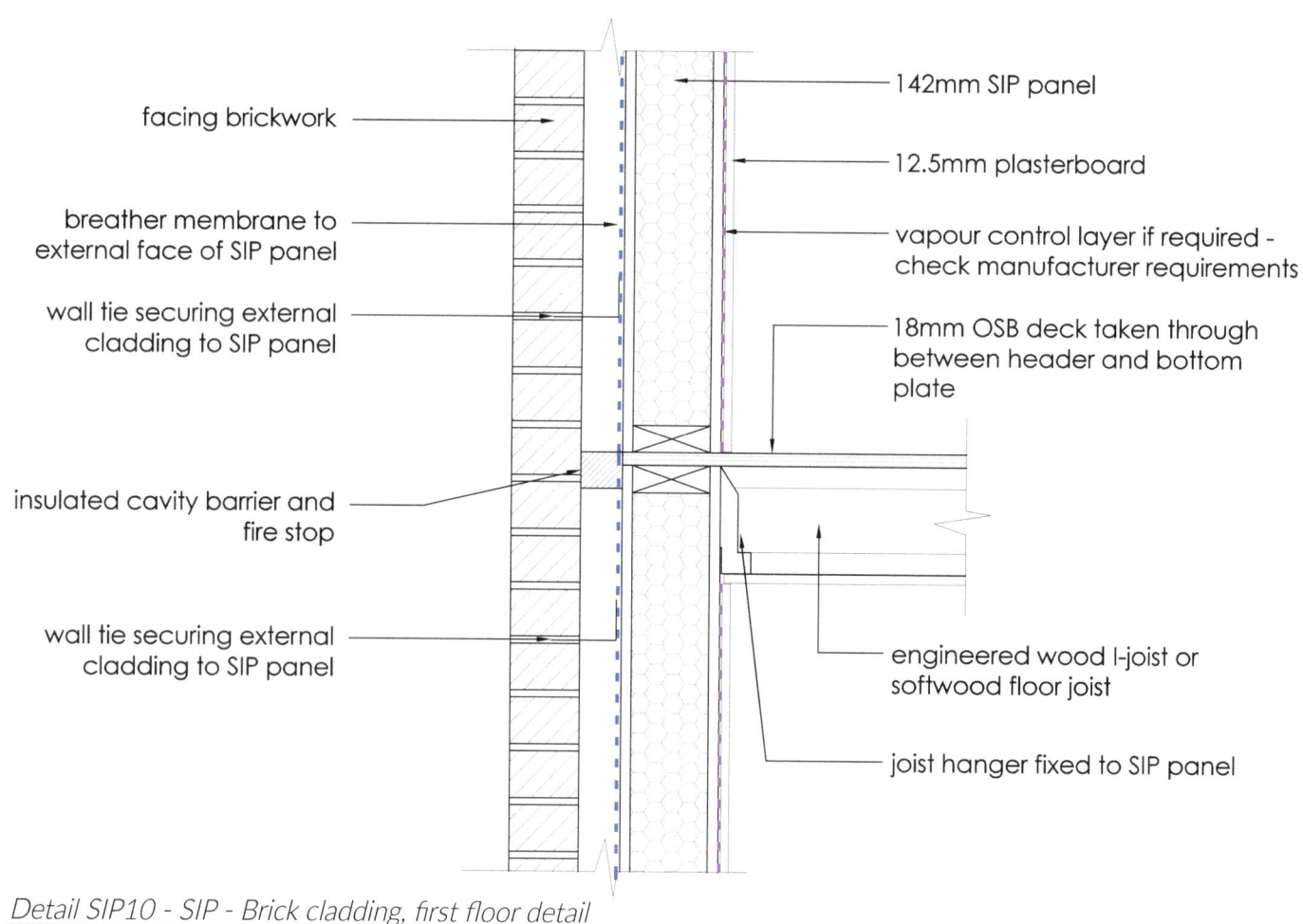

NOTES:
U Value 0.19W/m²K or better
Floor joist according to structural requirements
Web joist, I joist or softwood joist could be used

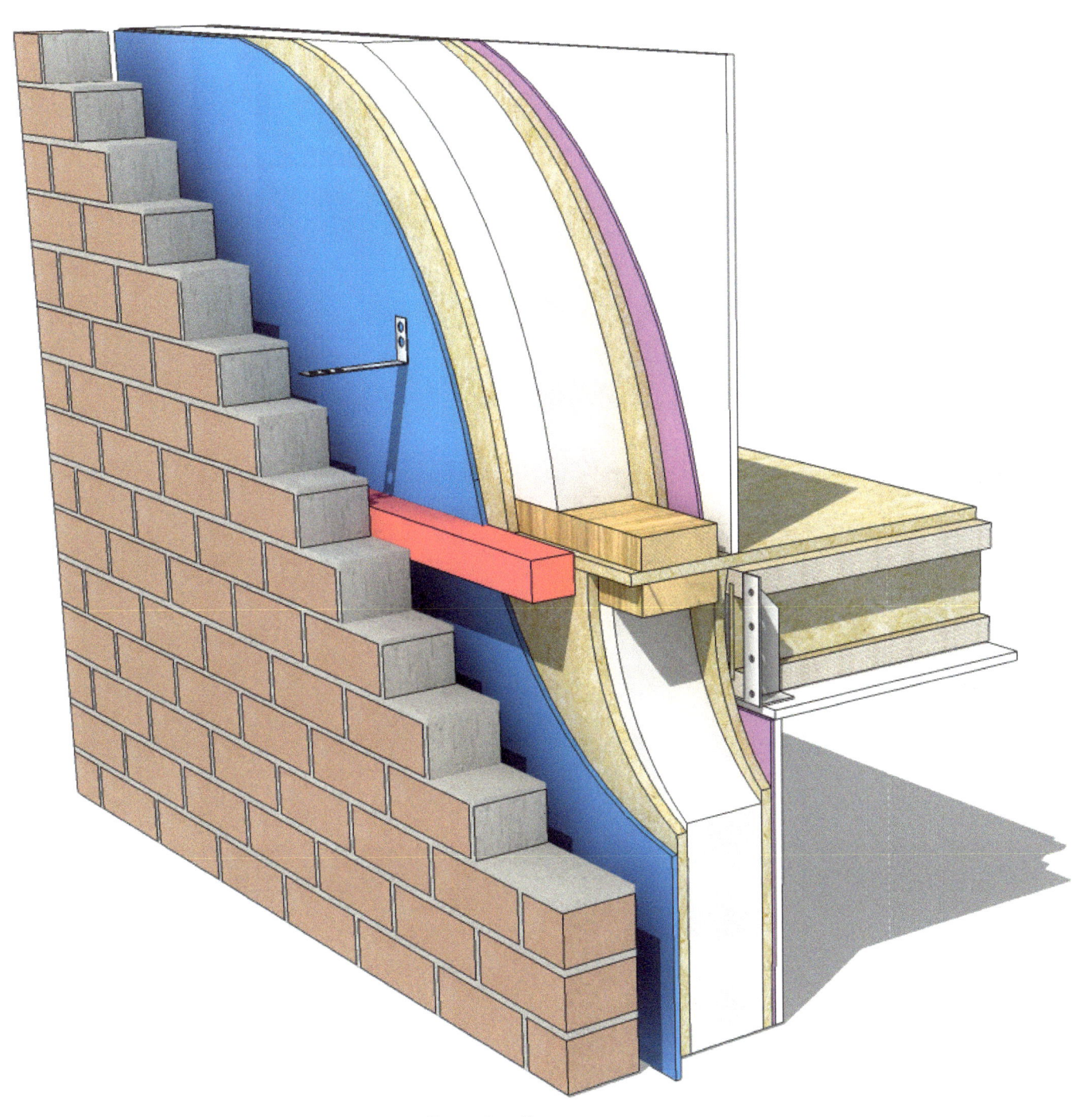

3D Detail SIP10 - SIP - Brick cladding, first floor detail

SIP11

SIP, BRICK CLADDING, EAVES DETAIL, ATTIC AS USABLE SPACE

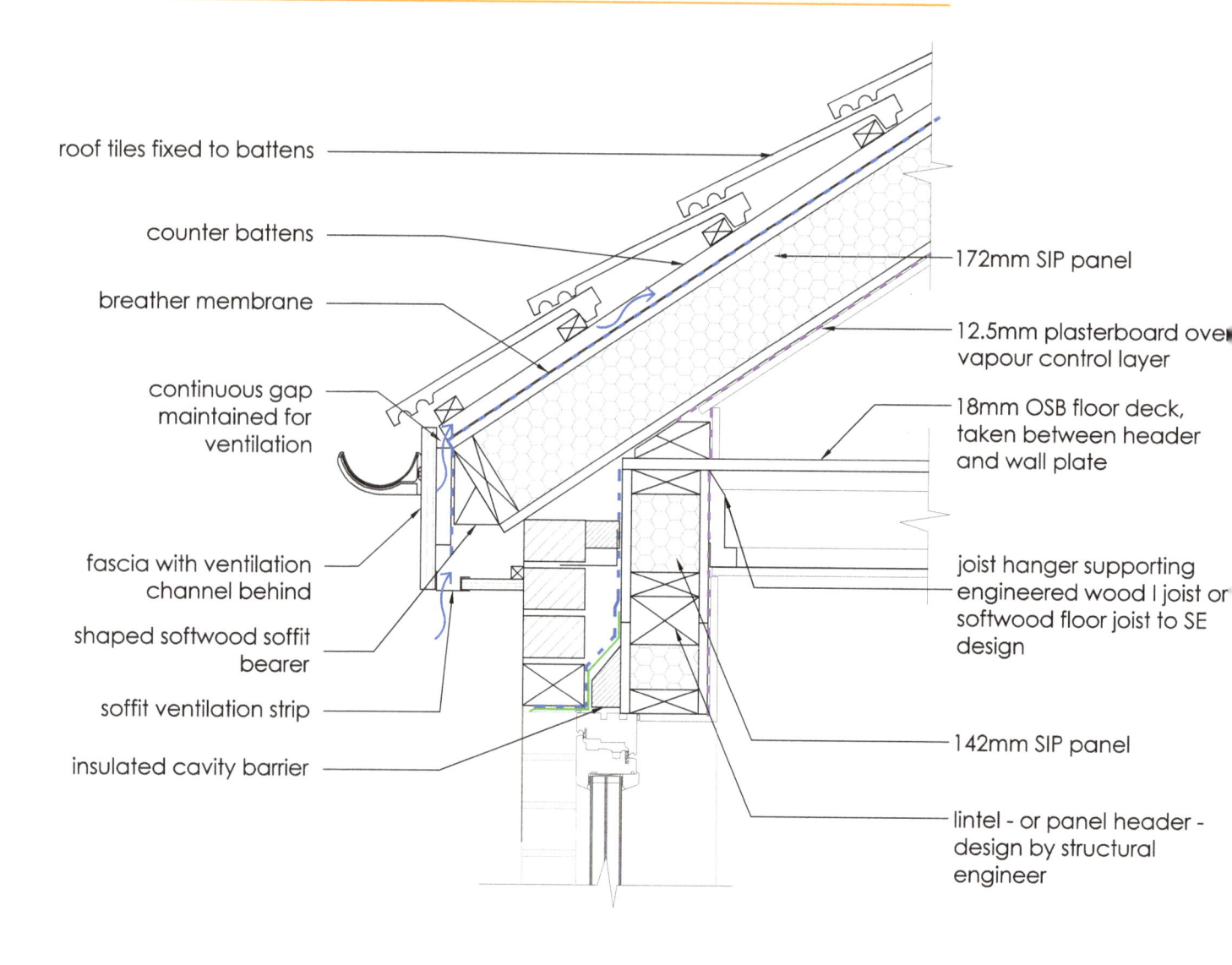

Labels (left side):
- roof tiles fixed to battens
- counter battens
- breather membrane
- continuous gap maintained for ventilation
- fascia with ventilation channel behind
- shaped softwood soffit bearer
- soffit ventilation strip
- insulated cavity barrier

Labels (right side):
- 172mm SIP panel
- 12.5mm plasterboard over vapour control layer
- 18mm OSB floor deck, taken between header and wall plate
- joist hanger supporting engineered wood I joist or softwood floor joist to SE design
- 142mm SIP panel
- lintel - or panel header - design by structural engineer

Detail SIP11 - SIP - Brick cladding, eaves detail, attic as usable space

NOTES:
U Value 0.15W/m²K or better
Joist according to structural requirements
Web joist, I joist or softwood joist could be used

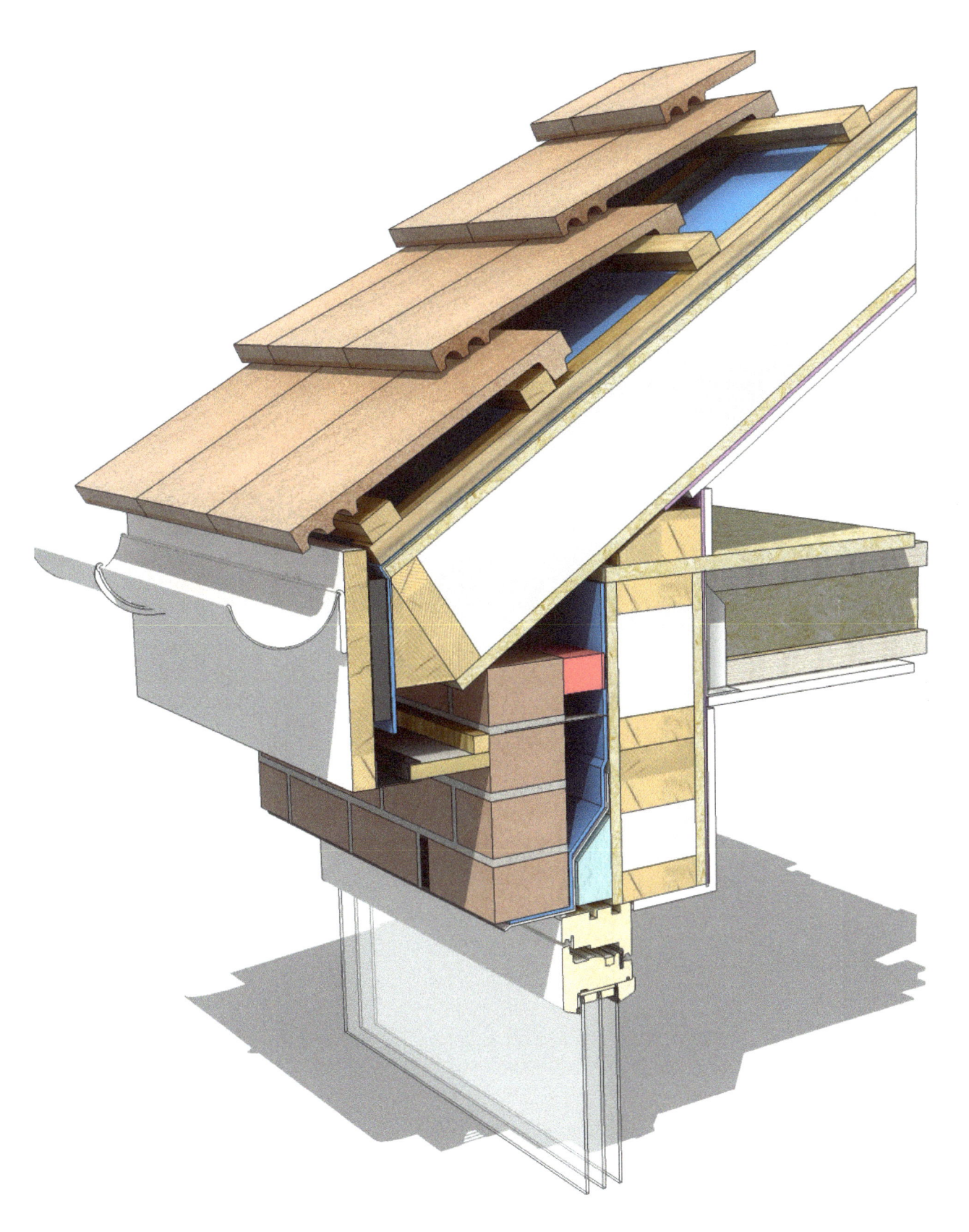

3D Detail SIP11 - SIP - Brick cladding, eaves detail, attic as usable space

SIP12

SIP, BRICK CLADDING, VERGE AND SOFFIT DETAIL (GABLE)

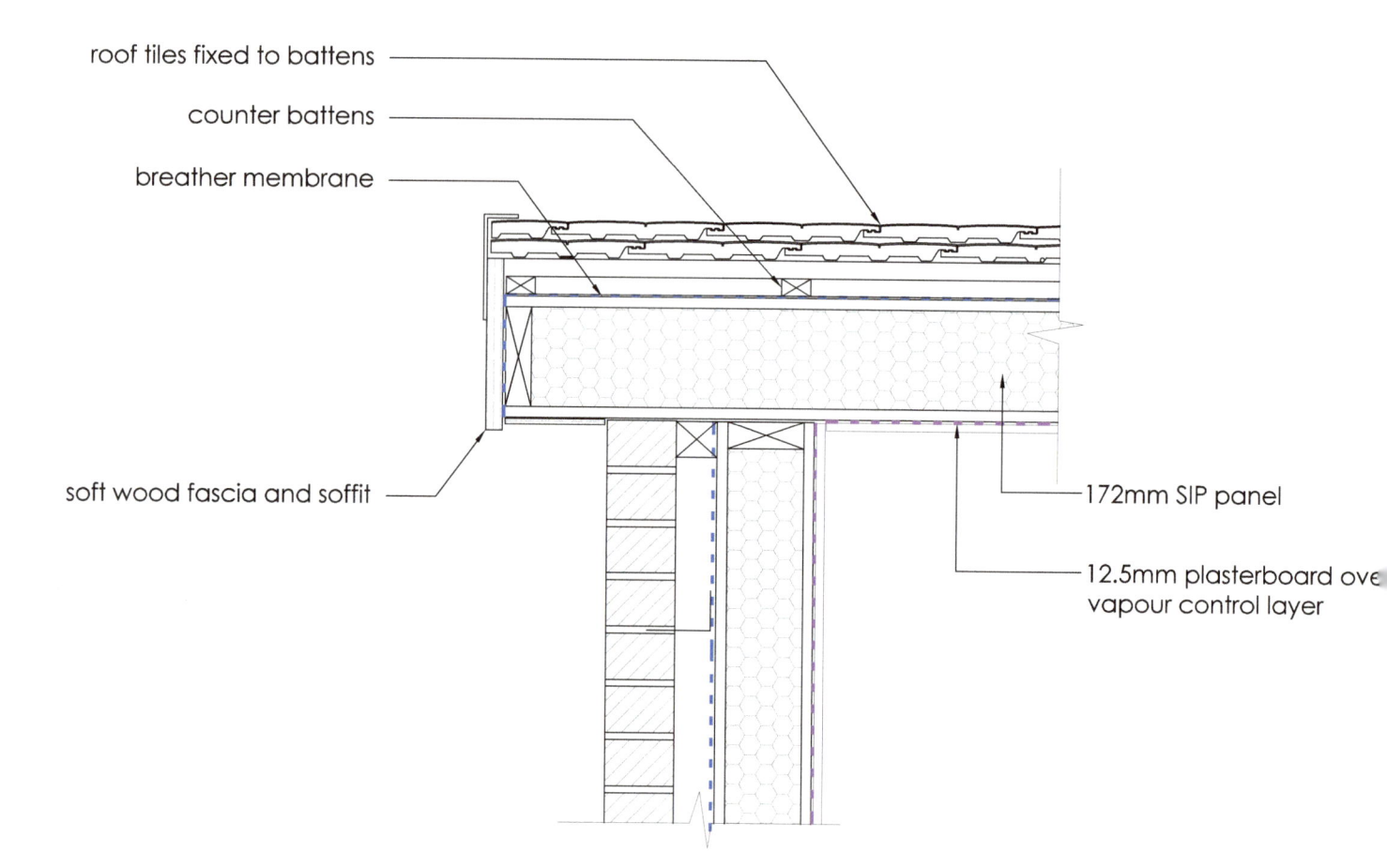

- roof tiles fixed to battens
- counter battens
- breather membrane
- soft wood fascia and soffit
- 172mm SIP panel
- 12.5mm plasterboard over vapour control layer

Detail SIP12 - SIP - Brick cladding, verge and soffit detail (gable)

NOTES:
Joist according to structural requirements
Web joist, I joist or softwood joist could be used

SECTION 8 - SIPS

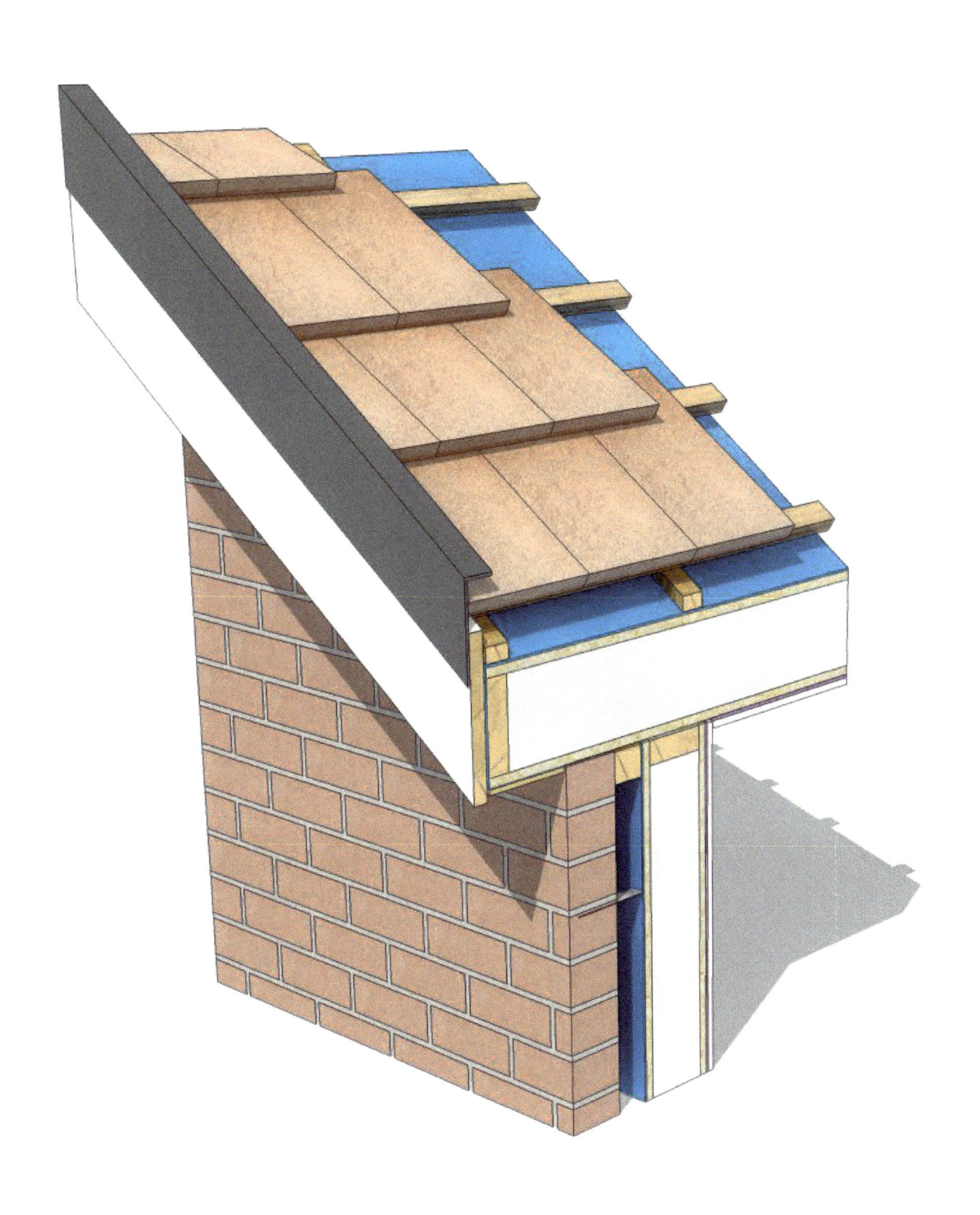

3D Detail SIP12 - SIP - Brick cladding, verge and soffit detail (gable)

SIP13

SIP, BRICK CLADDING, EAVES DETAIL - IMPROVED THERMAL PERFORMANCE

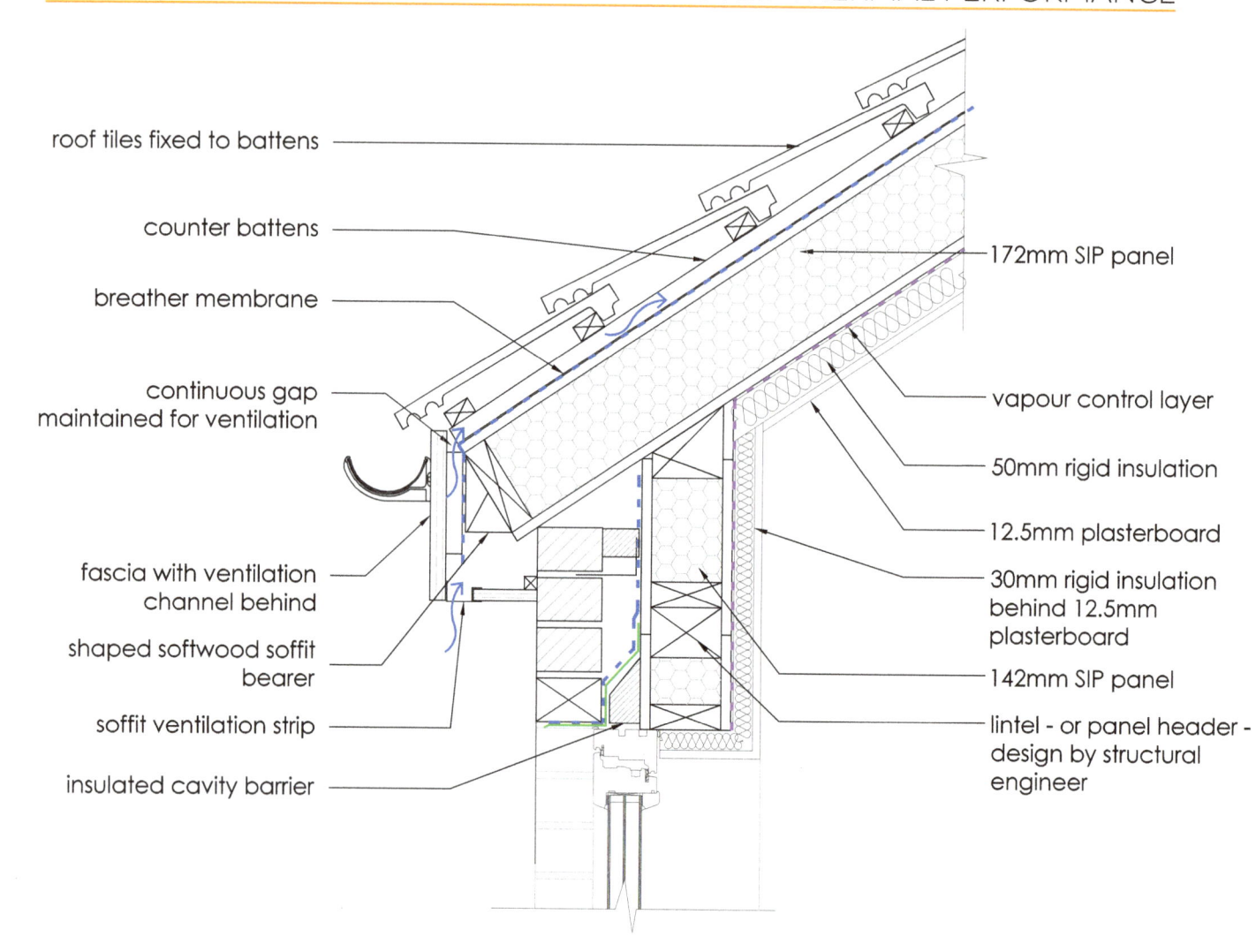

Labels (left side):
- roof tiles fixed to battens
- counter battens
- breather membrane
- continuous gap maintained for ventilation
- fascia with ventilation channel behind
- shaped softwood soffit bearer
- soffit ventilation strip
- insulated cavity barrier

Labels (right side):
- 172mm SIP panel
- vapour control layer
- 50mm rigid insulation
- 12.5mm plasterboard
- 30mm rigid insulation behind 12.5mm plasterboard
- 142mm SIP panel
- lintel - or panel header - design by structural engineer

Detail SIP13 - SIP - Brick cladding, eaves detail - improved thermal performance

NOTES:
U Value 0.11W/m²K or better
Joist according to structural requirements
Web joist, I joist or softwood joist could be used

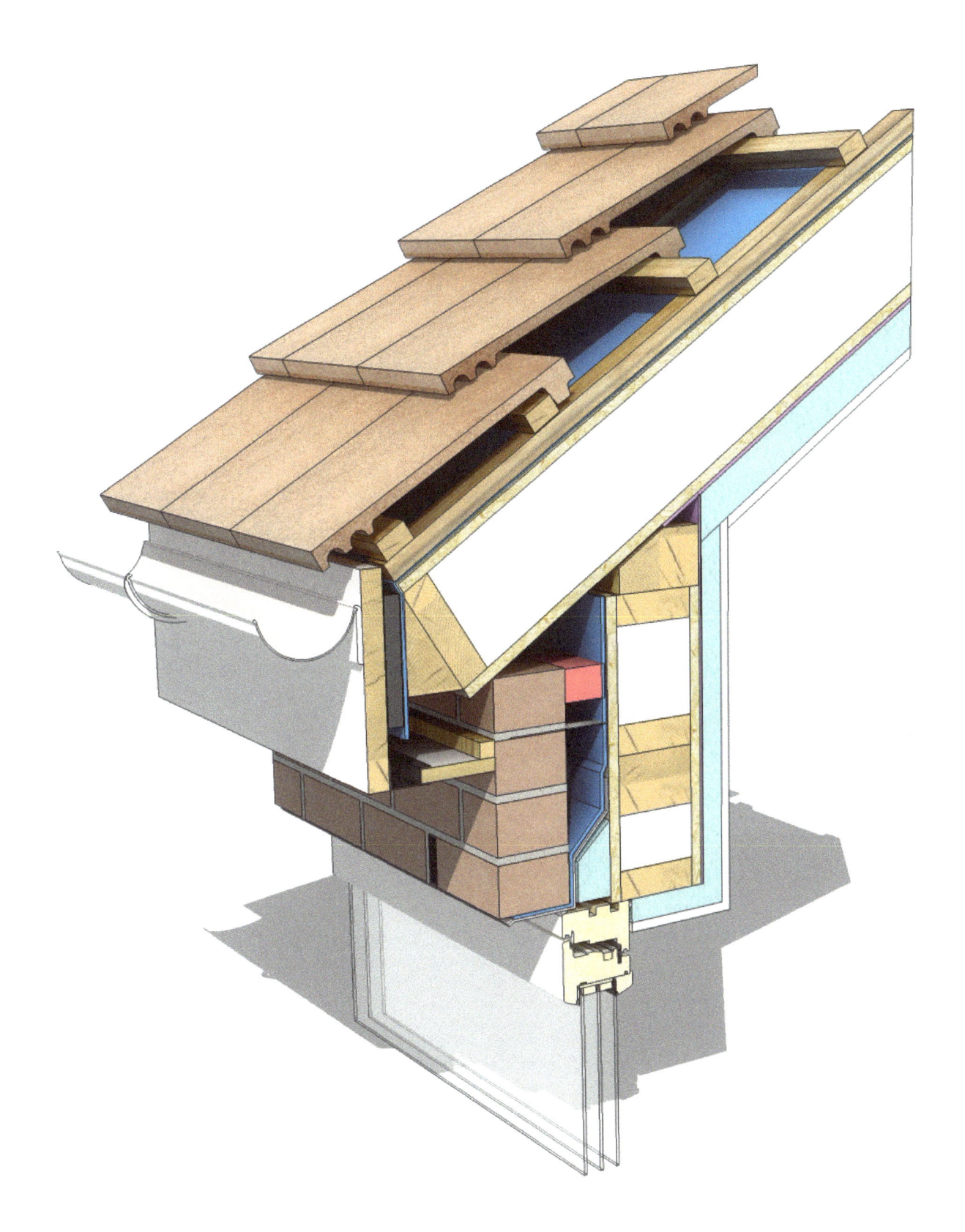

3D Detail SIP13 - SIP - Brick cladding, eaves detail - improved thermal performance

INSULATED CONCRETE FORMWORK (ICF)

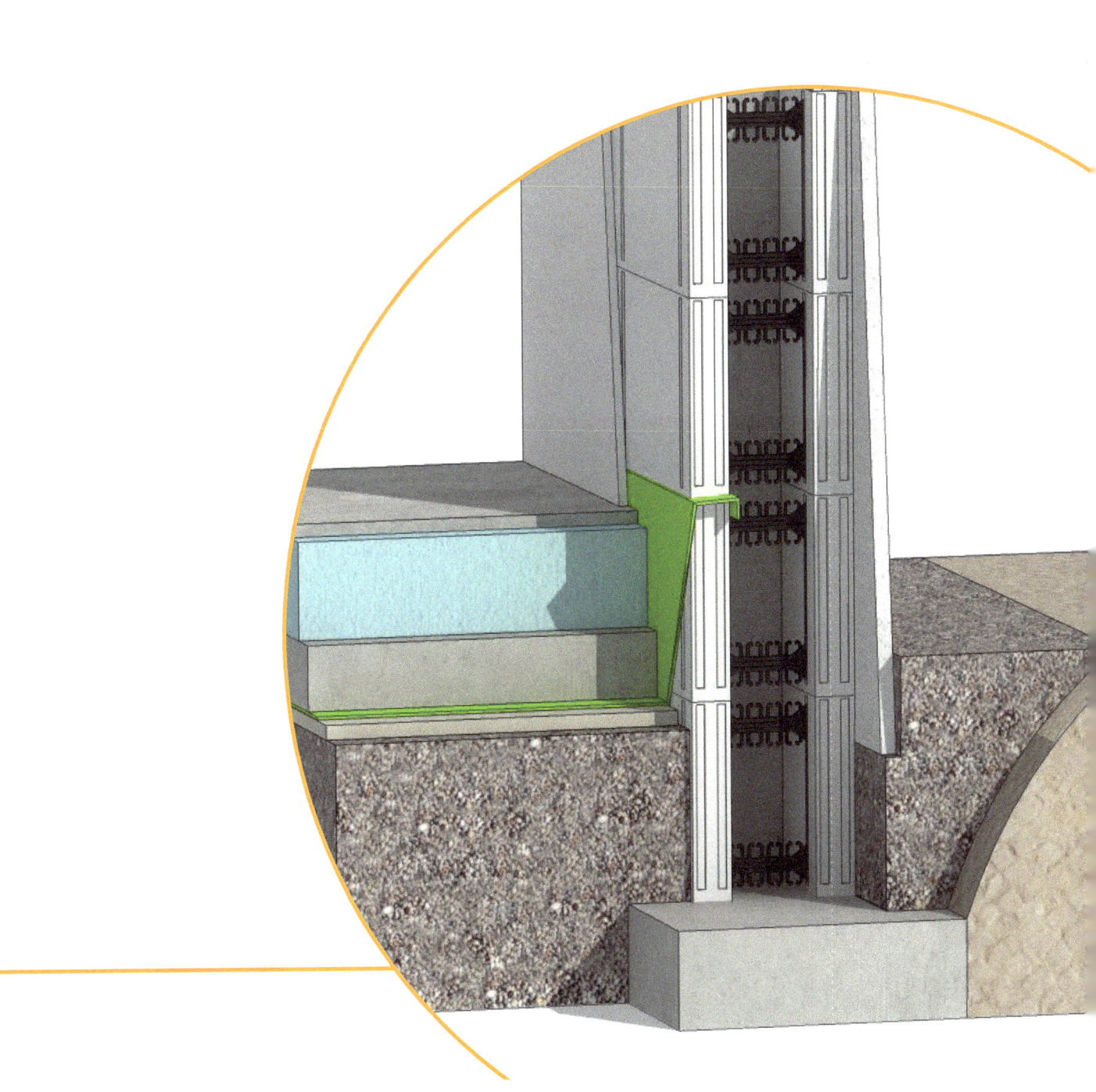

Insulating concrete formwork is a concrete based construction system whereby hollow blocks made from expanded polystyrene insulation (EPS) are stacked to form the shape of the building creating a cavity for the structural walls. The cavity is then filled with concrete to form the structural element of the wall. Sometimes, reinforcing steel is added before concrete placement to give additional strength to the wall. The forms are then left in place to provide an airtight well insulated building. External and internal finishes can then be applied to the formwork.

The ICFs use prefabricated components that are easy to assemble. There are many manufacturers and different systems available, each boasting its own advantages. I have decided to include just one example of a set of details for this type of construction in this book, purely because I think it is worth considering as a newer form of construction. I would urge you to explore the subject beyond this book.

ICF1

ICF, STRIP AND BLOCK FOUNDATION WITH GROUND BEARING SLAB

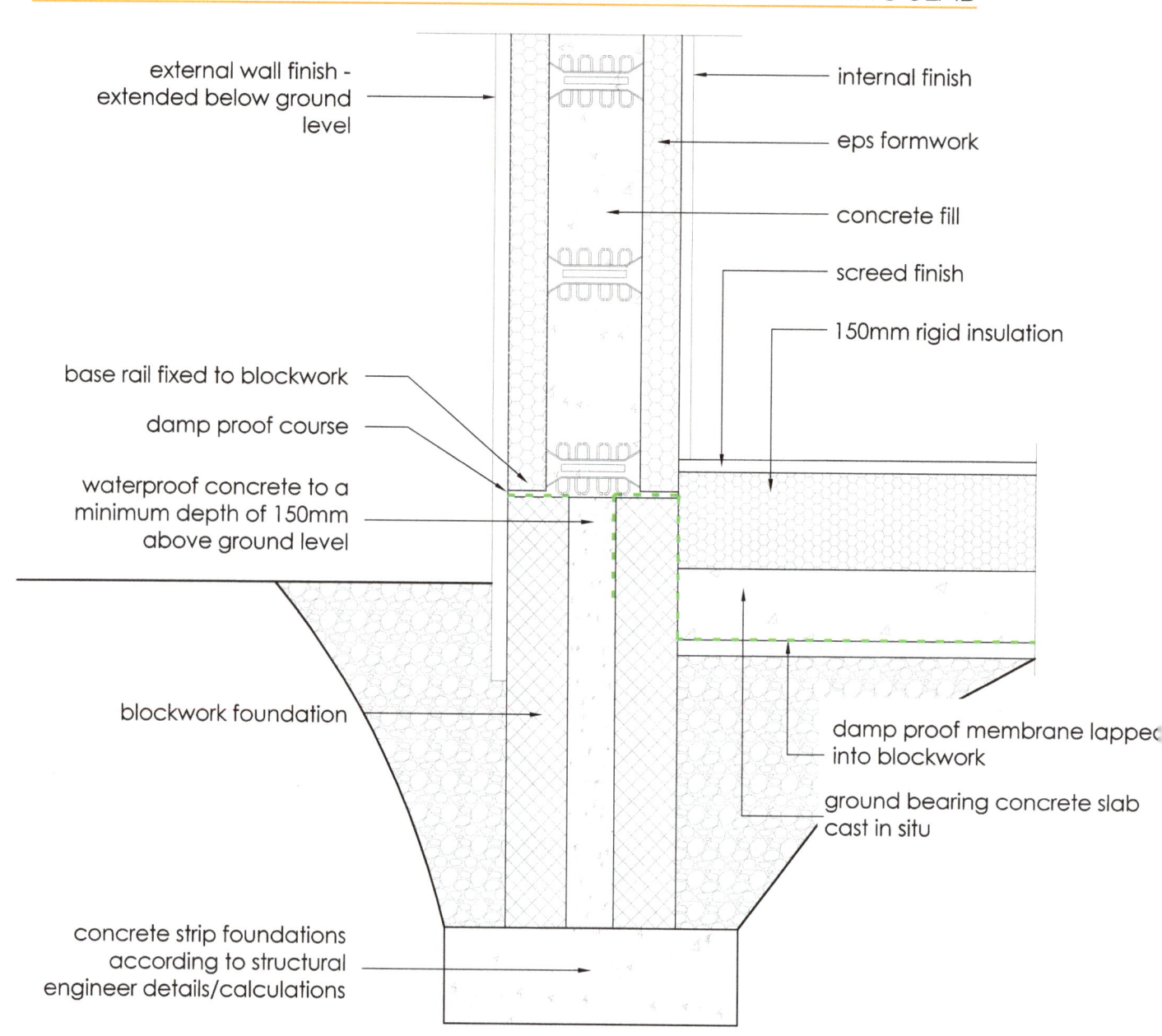

Labels (left side):
- external wall finish - extended below ground level
- base rail fixed to blockwork
- damp proof course
- waterproof concrete to a minimum depth of 150mm above ground level
- blockwork foundation
- concrete strip foundations according to structural engineer details/calculations

Labels (right side):
- internal finish
- eps formwork
- concrete fill
- screed finish
- 150mm rigid insulation
- damp proof membrane lapped into blockwork
- ground bearing concrete slab cast in situ

Detail ICF1 - ICF - Strip and block foundation with ground bearing slab

NOTES:
U Value 0.13W/m²K or better

SECTION 9 - ICF

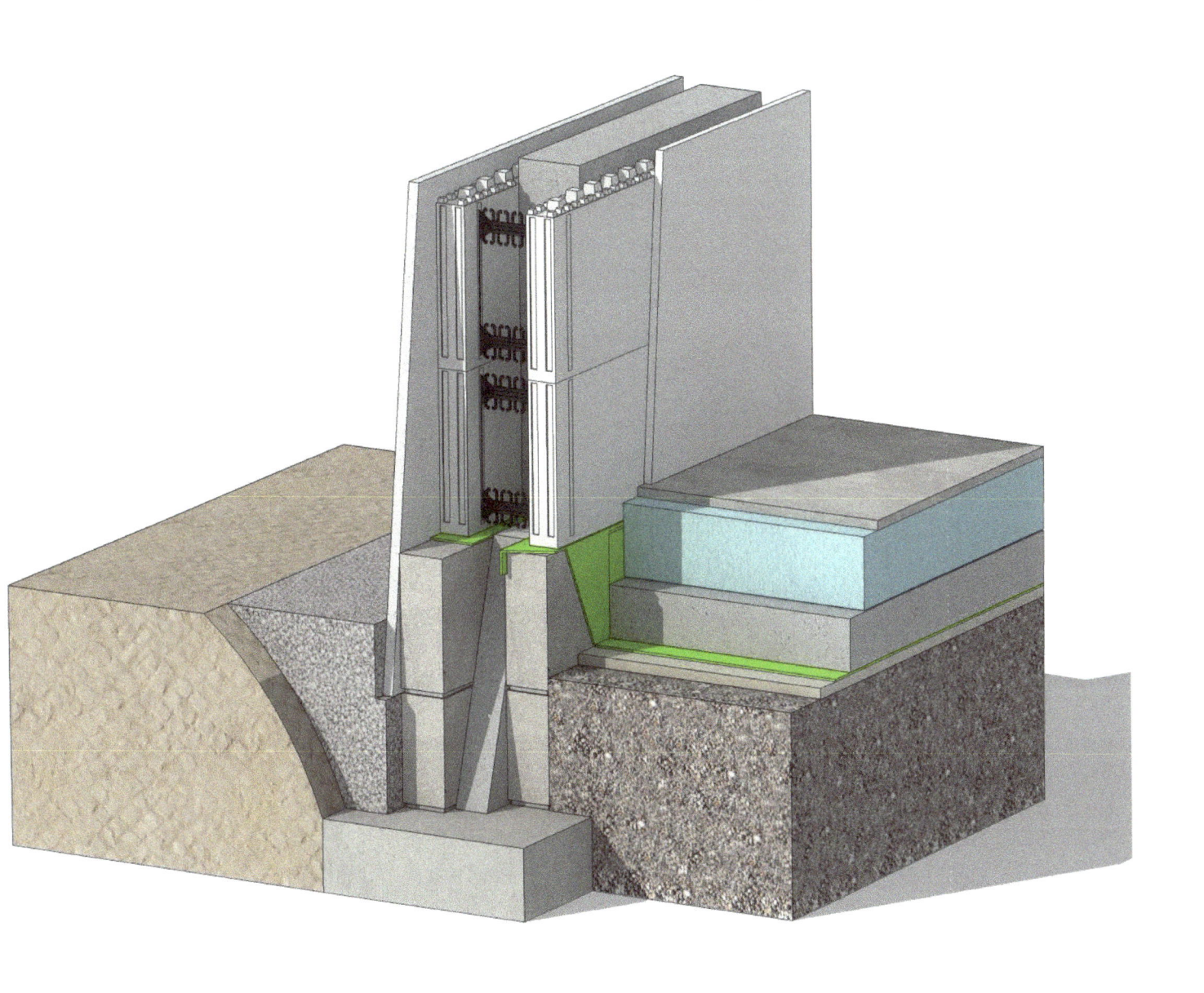

3D Detail ICF1 - ICF - Strip and block foundation with ground bearing slab

ICF2

ICF - STRIP FOUNDATION WITH GROUND BEARING SLAB

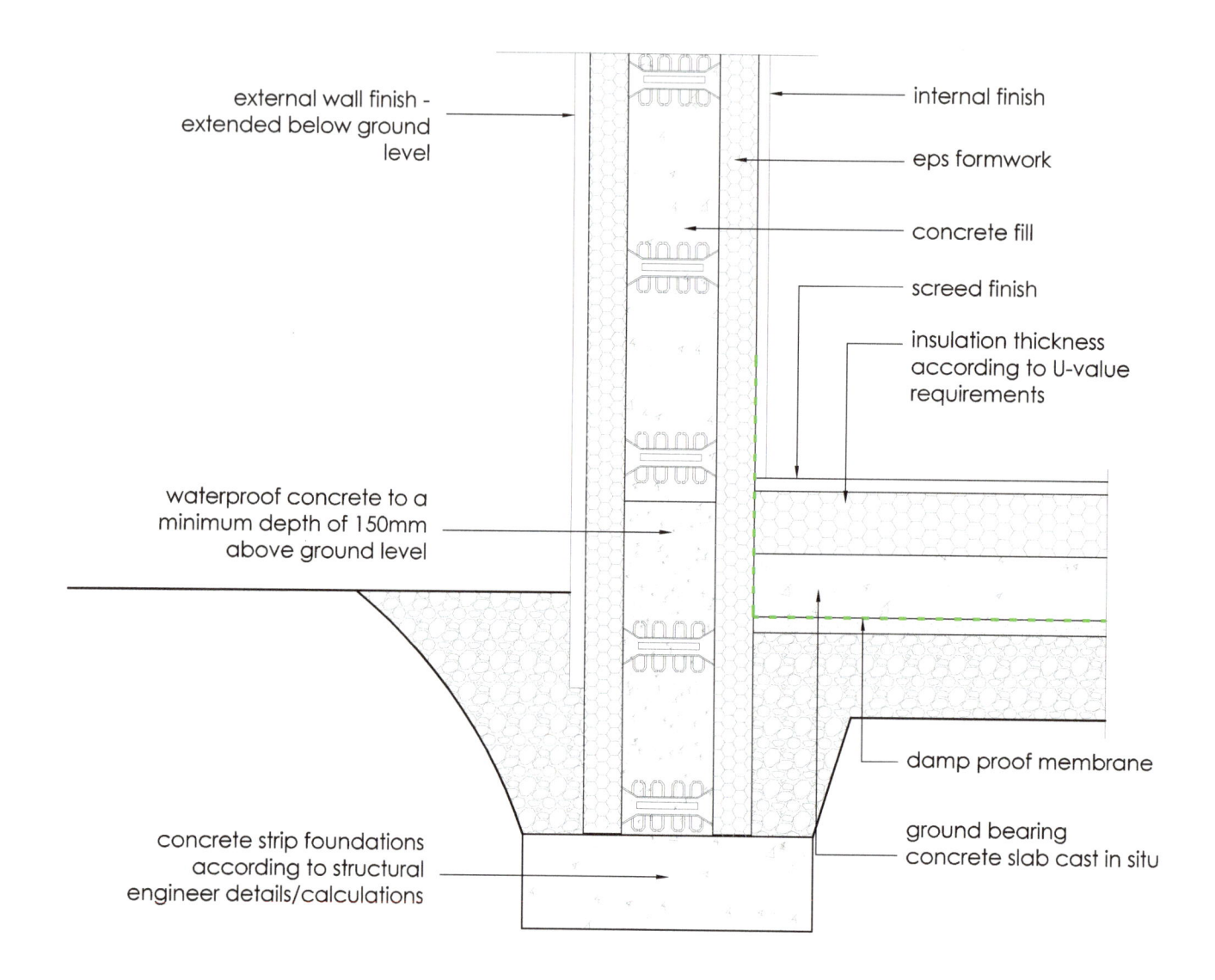

- external wall finish - extended below ground level
- internal finish
- eps formwork
- concrete fill
- screed finish
- insulation thickness according to U-value requirements
- waterproof concrete to a minimum depth of 150mm above ground level
- damp proof membrane
- concrete strip foundations according to structural engineer details/calculations
- ground bearing concrete slab cast in situ

Detail ICF2 - ICF - strip foundation with ground bearing slab

NOTES:
U Value 0.13W/m²K or better

SECTION 9 - ICF

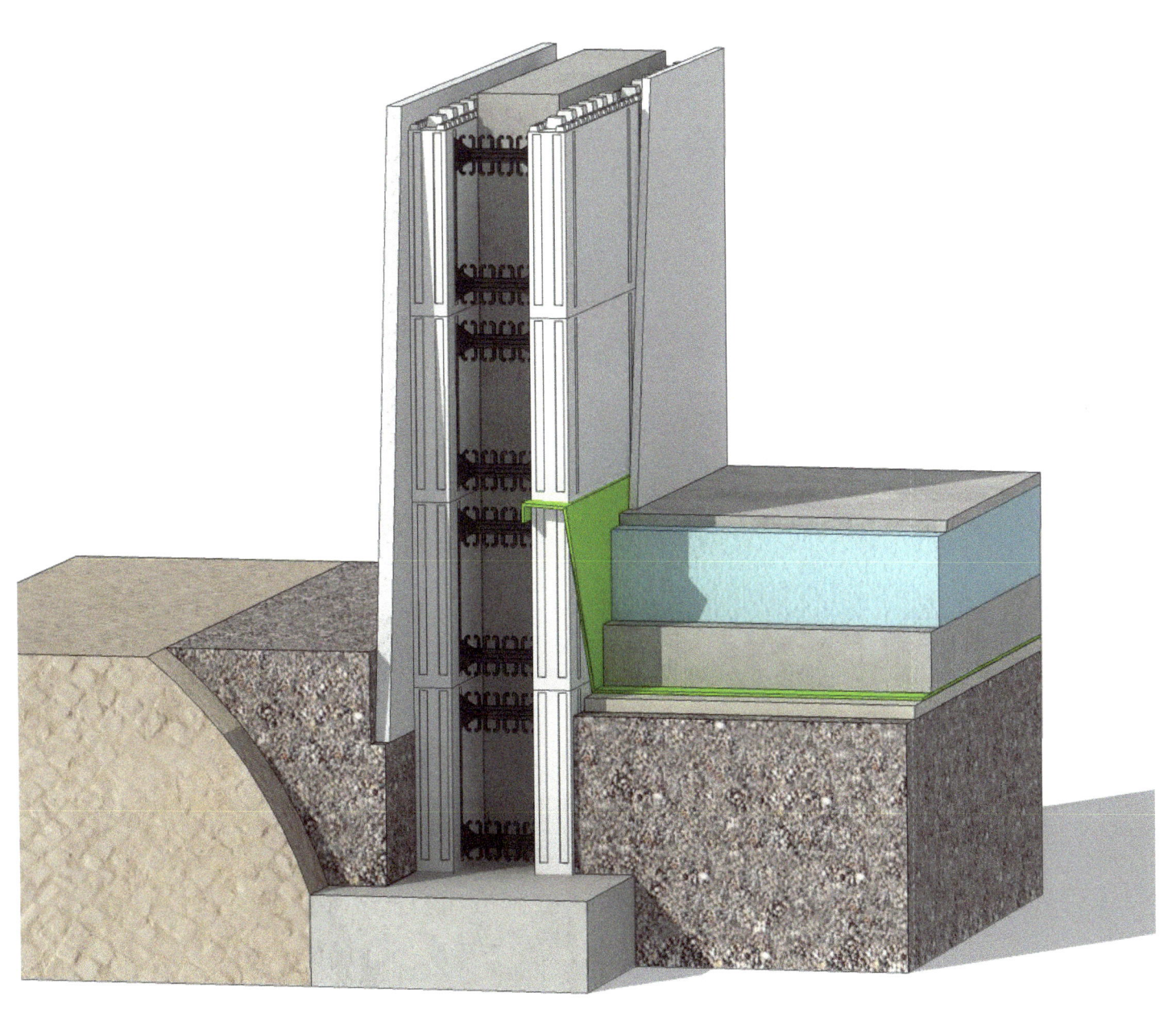

3D Detail ICF2 - ICF - strip foundation with ground bearing slab

ICF3
ICF - PRECAST CONCRETE INTERMEDIATE FLOOR DETAIL

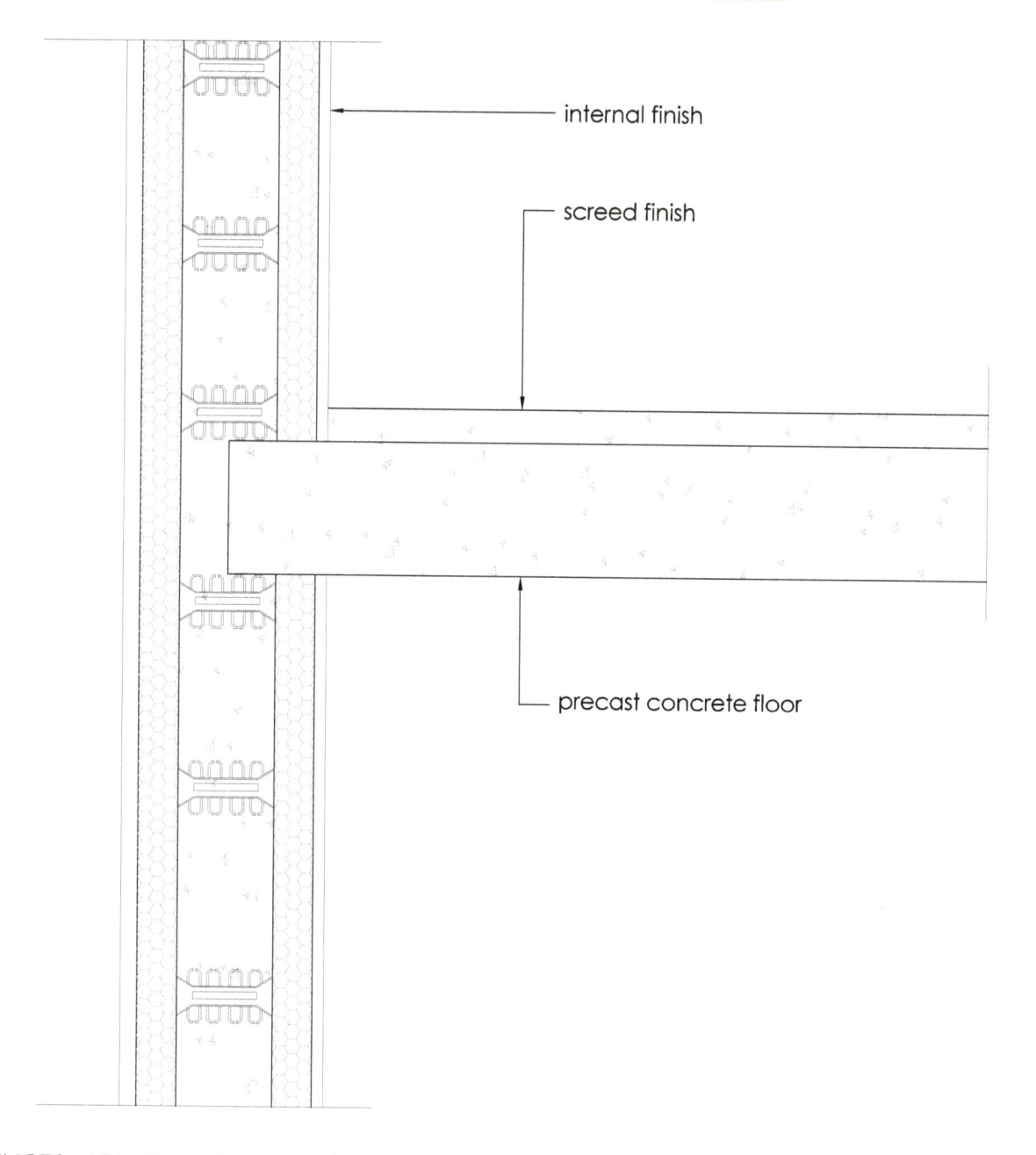

- internal finish
- screed finish
- precast concrete floor

Detail ICF3 - ICF - Precast concrete intermediate floor

NOTES:

Gaps between underside of floor and icf should be filled
Airtightness is provided by continuous horizontal and vertical concrete

SECTION 9 - ICF

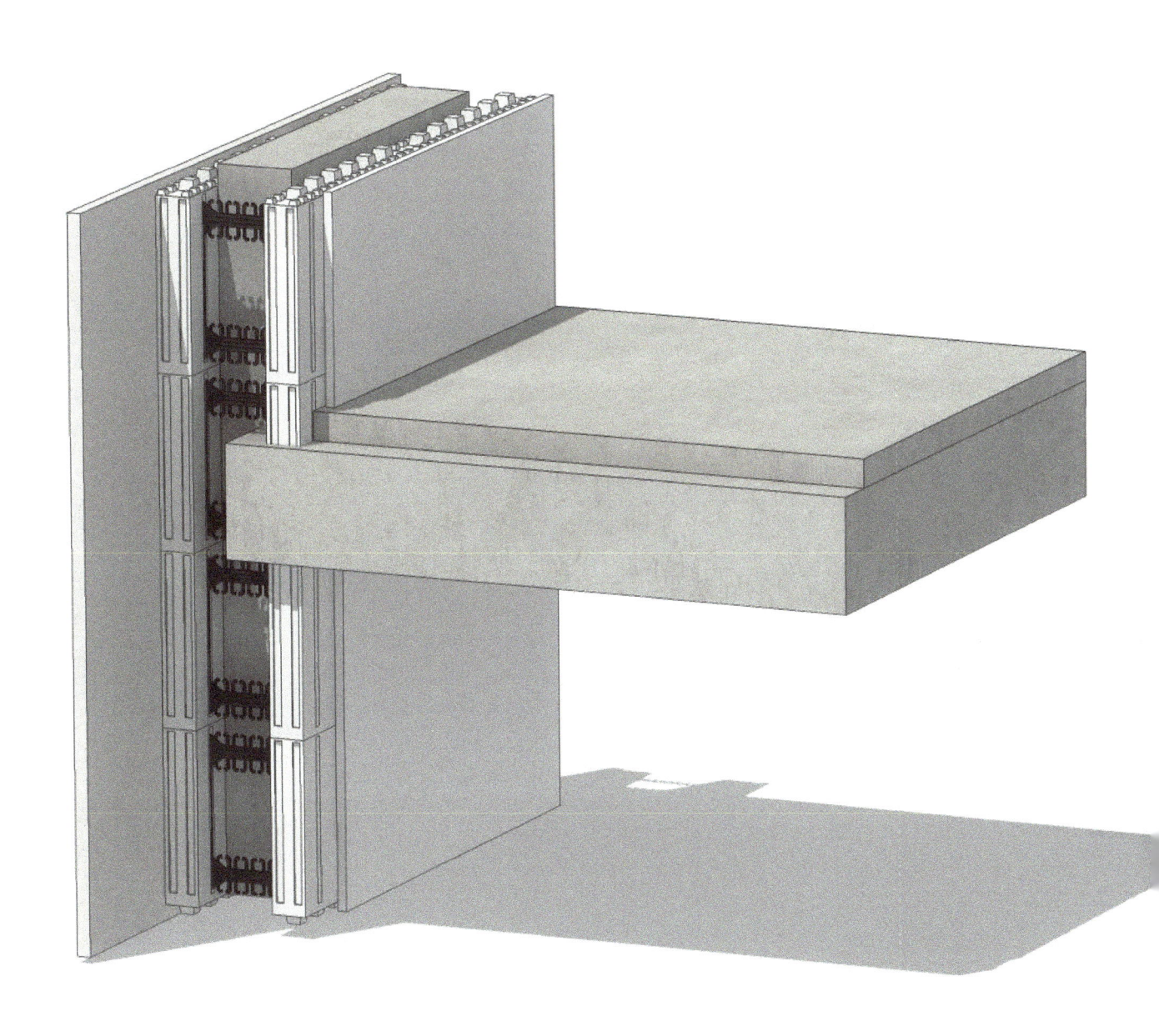

3D Detail ICF3 - ICF - Precast concrete intermediate floor

ICF4
ICF - WINDOW HEAD AND CILL

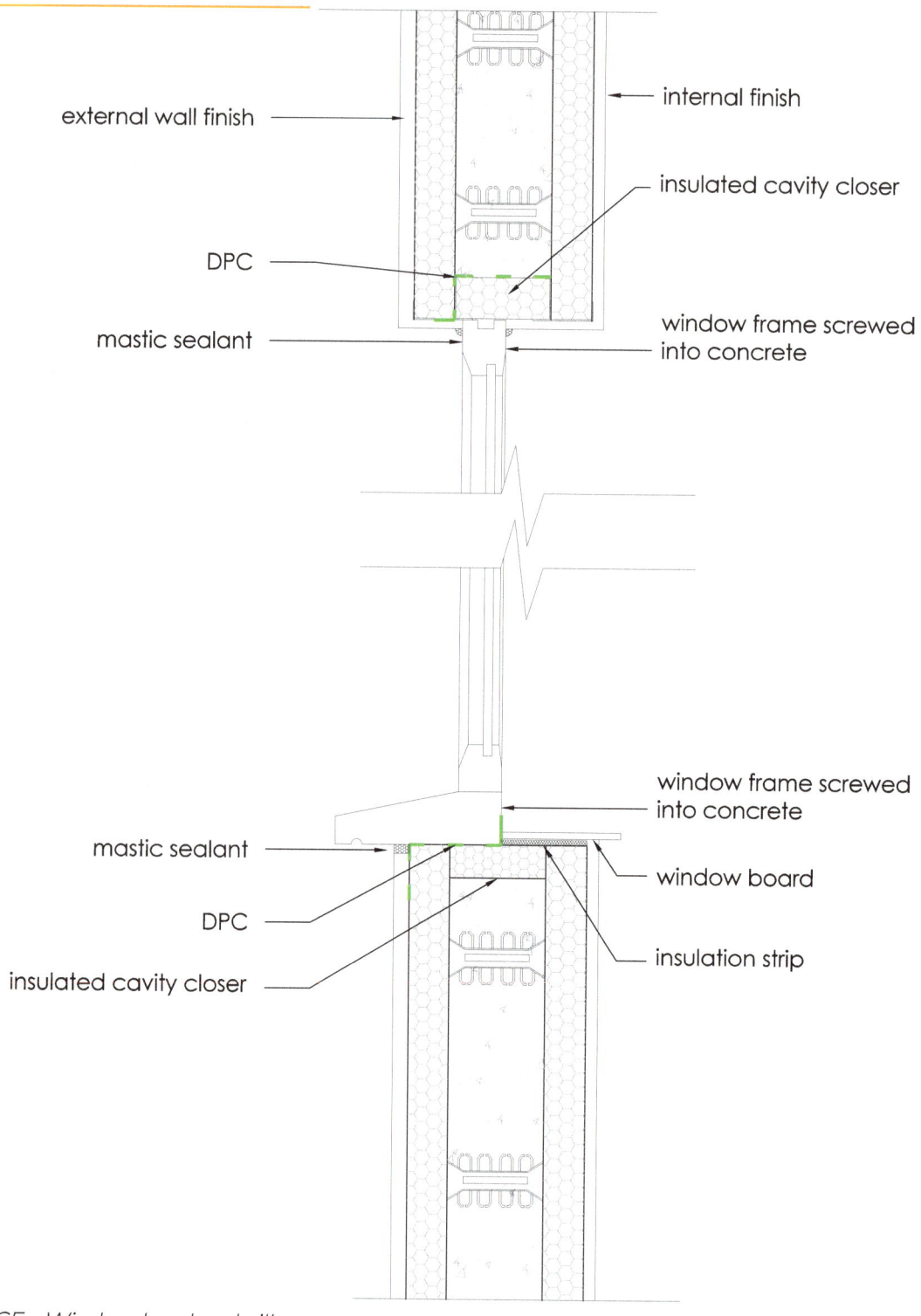

- external wall finish
- internal finish
- insulated cavity closer
- DPC
- mastic sealant
- window frame screwed into concrete
- window frame screwed into concrete
- window board
- mastic sealant
- DPC
- insulation strip
- insulated cavity closer

Detail ICF4 - ICF - Window head and cill

NOTES:
Insulated cavity closers to prevent thermal bridging

SECTION 9 - ICF

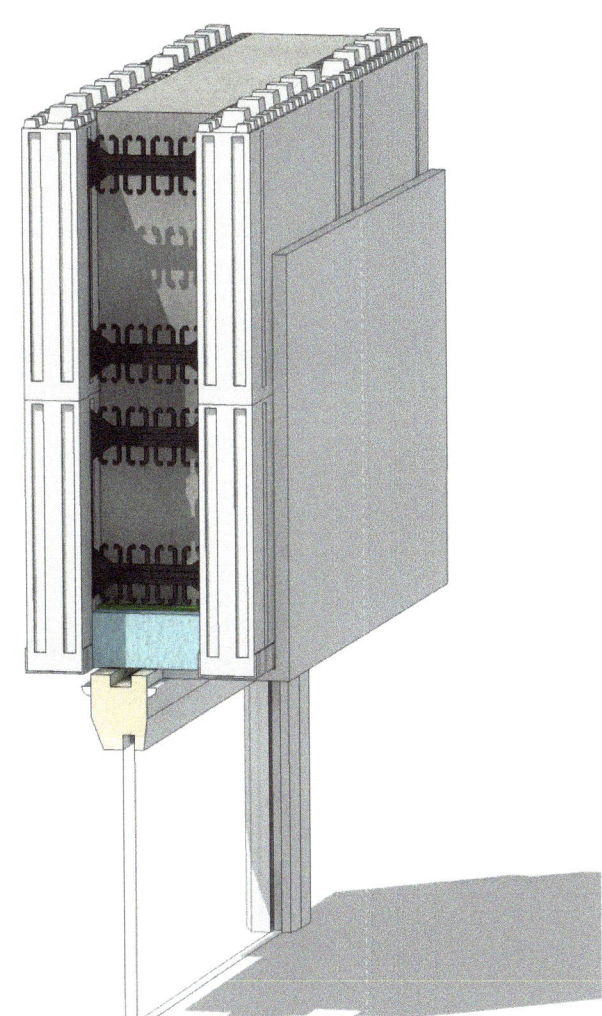

3D Detail ICF4 - ICF - Window head and cill

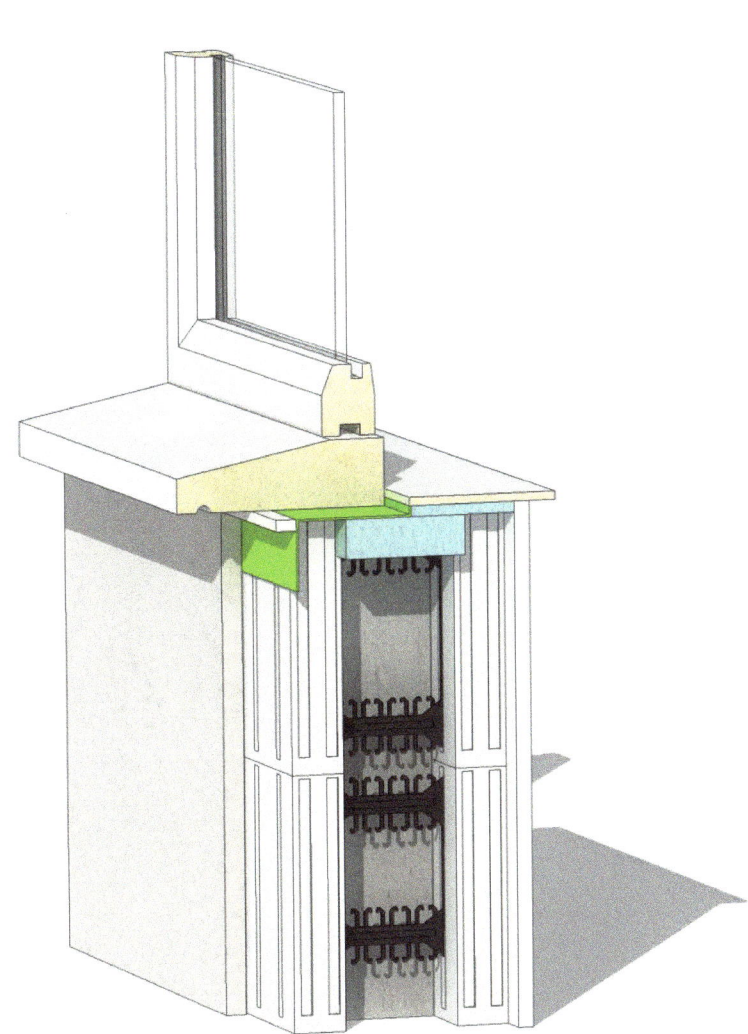

ICF5

ICF - FLAT ROOF DETAIL

- coping stone
- single ply waterproof membrane lapped and taped
- 2 layers of rigid insulation 80mm and 95mm
- vapour control layer over 50mm screed to falls
- structural roof

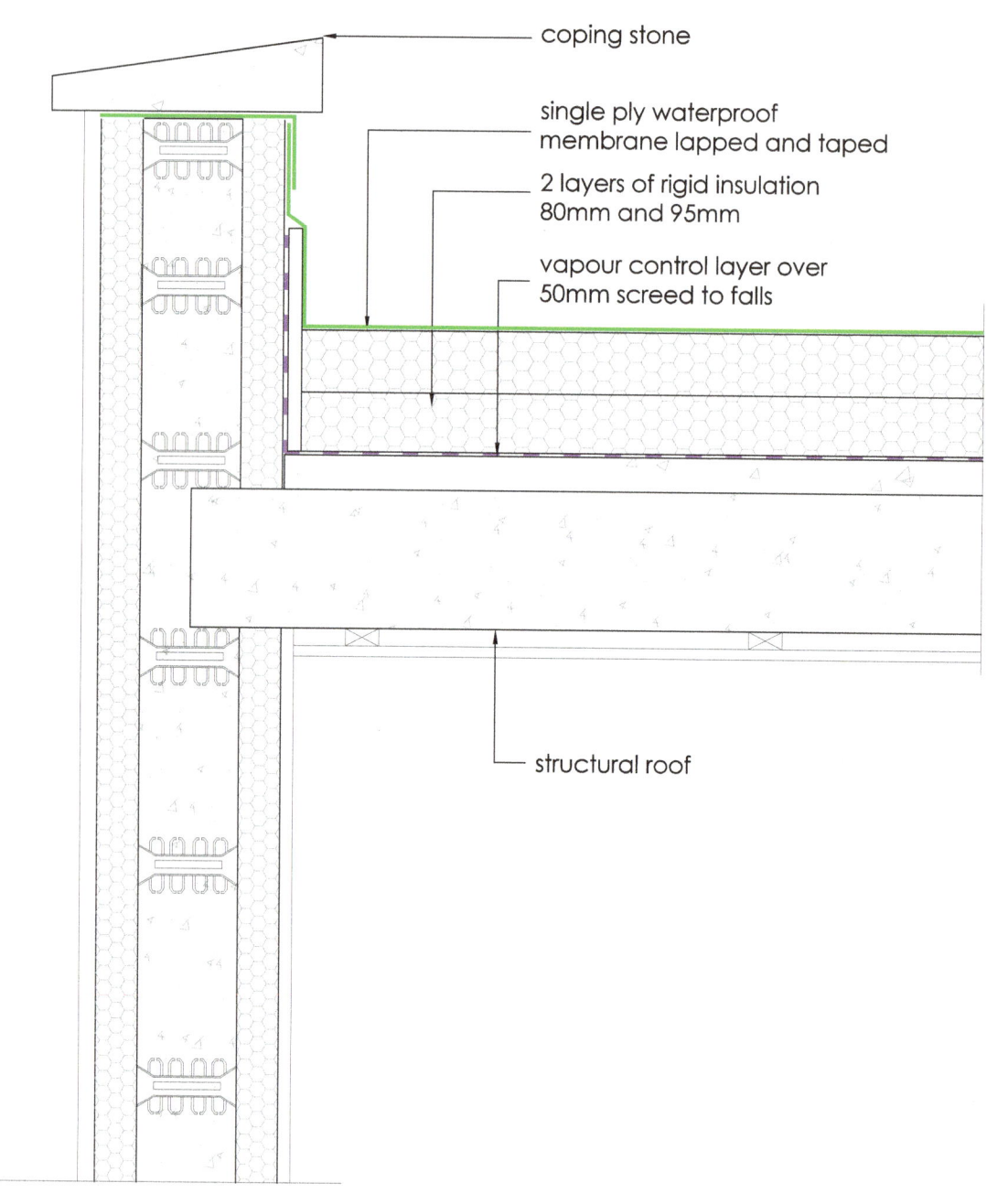

Detail ICF5 - ICF - Flat roof detail

NOTES:

U Value 0.13W/m²K or better
Continuous insualtion on both sides of parapet minimises thermal bridging

SECTION 9 - ICF

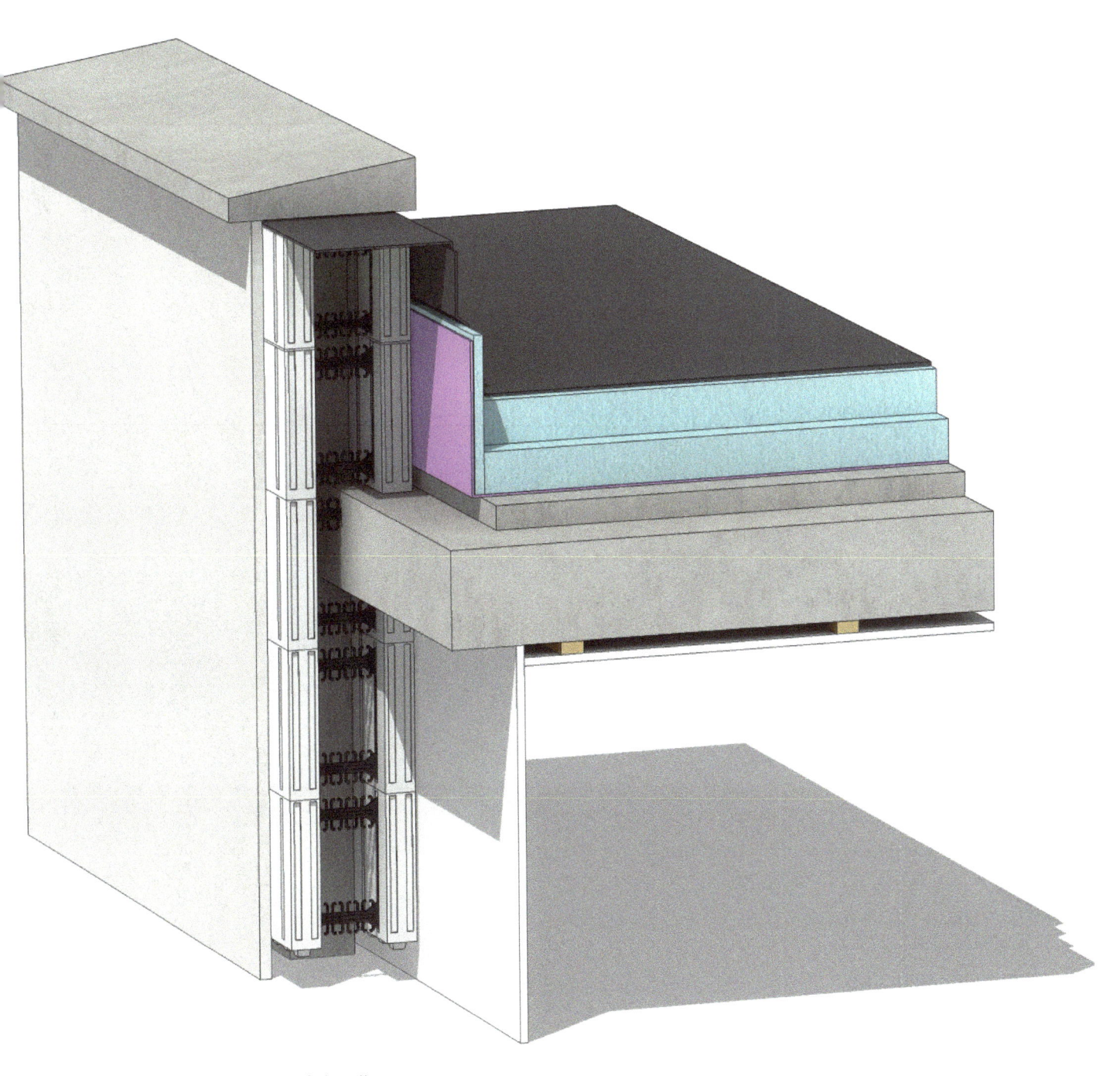

3D Detail ICF5 - ICF - Flat roof detail

ICF6

ICF - PITCHED ROOF DETAIL

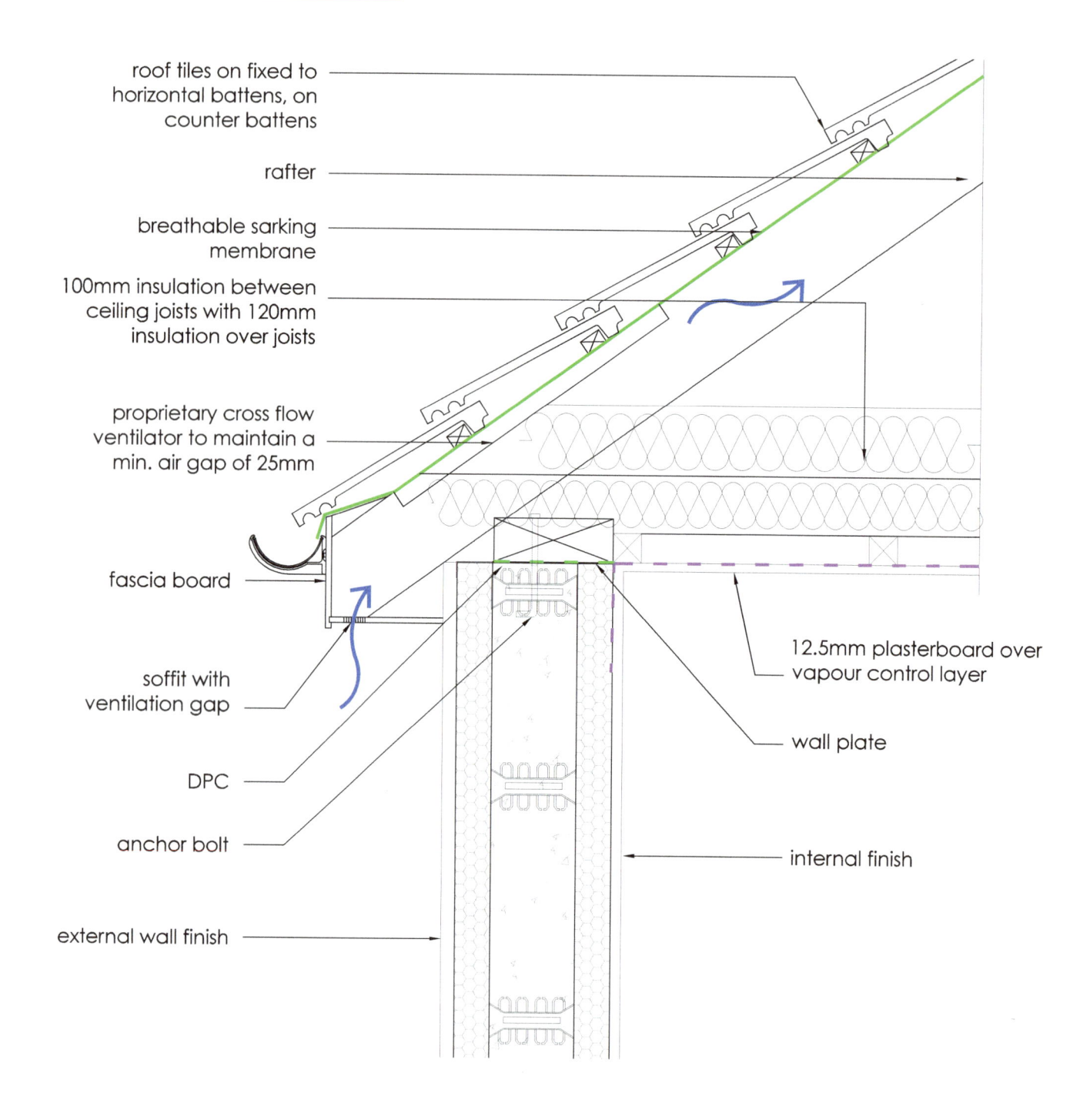

- roof tiles on fixed to horizontal battens, on counter battens
- rafter
- breathable sarking membrane
- 100mm insulation between ceiling joists with 120mm insulation over joists
- proprietary cross flow ventilator to maintain a min. air gap of 25mm
- fascia board
- soffit with ventilation gap
- DPC
- anchor bolt
- external wall finish
- 12.5mm plasterboard over vapour control layer
- wall plate
- internal finish

Detail ICF6 - ICF - Pitched roof detail

NOTES:

U Value 0.12W/m²K or better

SECTION 9 - ICF

3D Detail ICF6 - ICF - Pitched roof detail

GREEN ROOF

INTRODUCTION

A green or living roof is a flat or low pitched roof with a layer of planting over the waterproofing membrane. The layers of soil and planting provide insulation to the roof along with protection to the waterproofing layer, not to mention its environmental credentials. Green roofs are largely associated with urban sites as a means to provide habitats for insects, birds and other small animals to improve biodiversity. Green roofs retain water and lower run off which in turn will reduce the drainage and water storage requirements on site. Up to 75% of rainwater can be absorbed in green roofs.

There are two main types of green roof, Extensive and Intensive.

EXTENSIVE

The extensive roof has a shallow soil, typically up to 100mm, and is planted with sedum, moss and grasses. It is used where access is not required to the roof, other than for maintenance, watering and so on. The extensive roof is lightweight, relatively cost effective and requires very little maintenance. These roofs can be constructed on timber, steel or concrete decks. A low pitch (up to 30) or flat roof can be used with an extensive green roof design, although on a slope greater than 20 the planting layer must be strapped horizontally to the structure to prevent the material slipping when saturated.

INTENSIVE

The intensive green roof has a deeper soil layer, typically 200150mm upwards, and allows for a wide variety of plant types to grow. The intensive roof can feature lawns, mature trees along with paved areas for recreational use, sometimes even water features can be seen on an intensive green roof. The intensive roof requires

Figure 8.1 - Example of green roof

regular watering, usually by dedicated irrigation systems. These roofs are constructed on a flat deck, typically reinforced concrete due to the increased weight.

TYPICAL BUILD UP

A green roof build up usually includes:

- Planting layer (grasses, sedum, etc)
- Soil, compost, growing medium
- Filter fleece(allows water through but prevents growing medium blocking the drainage system)
- Moisture retention layer and drainage system
- Protection layer (to prevent damage to waterproof membrane and root barrier)
- Waterproof membrane (with root barrier and metal foil between layers to prevent root damage)
- Insulation layer
- Vapour control layer if required
- Structural deck

DESIGN AND DETAIL

Domestic and residential applications generally adopt an extensive green roof approach which will be the focus of this section.

It is possible to design the green roof with a warm roof construction or inverted construction. The build up of the green roof elements will remain the same for both types, but the position of the insulation and waterproof membrane will change.

The insulation must be capable of resisting the dead load of the green roof, along with any additional live loads such as access for maintenance if required. Although the soil does offer a little insulation to the roof it is not taken into consideration when calculating U-value.

The waterproof membrane specified must be high performance, with a good life expectancy - this is due to the difficulty in renewing or repairing green roofs. The membrane can contain its own root protection, or alternatively a root barrier must be used.

Detailing of perimeters, outlets and protrusions through the roof should be carefully detailed. A minimum 150mm upstand of waterproofing layer above the soil level should always be used, along with a 300mm to 500mm wide layer of gravel to any junctions with up stands or roof lights.

The green roof should be designed with a minimum fall of 1:60 to avoid ponding.

Advantages
- Benefits include:
- Reduce stormwater runoff
- Protection of waterproof membrane
- Improved sound insulation
- Improve air quality
- Improve environmental benefits
- Create habitat and biodiversity
- Aesthetic benefits

Disadvantages
- Initial cost - increased load = increased structure
- Fire resistance
- Maintenance

GR1

GREEN ROOF, EXTERNAL MASONRY CAVITY WALL, UPSTAND TO WALL DETAIL

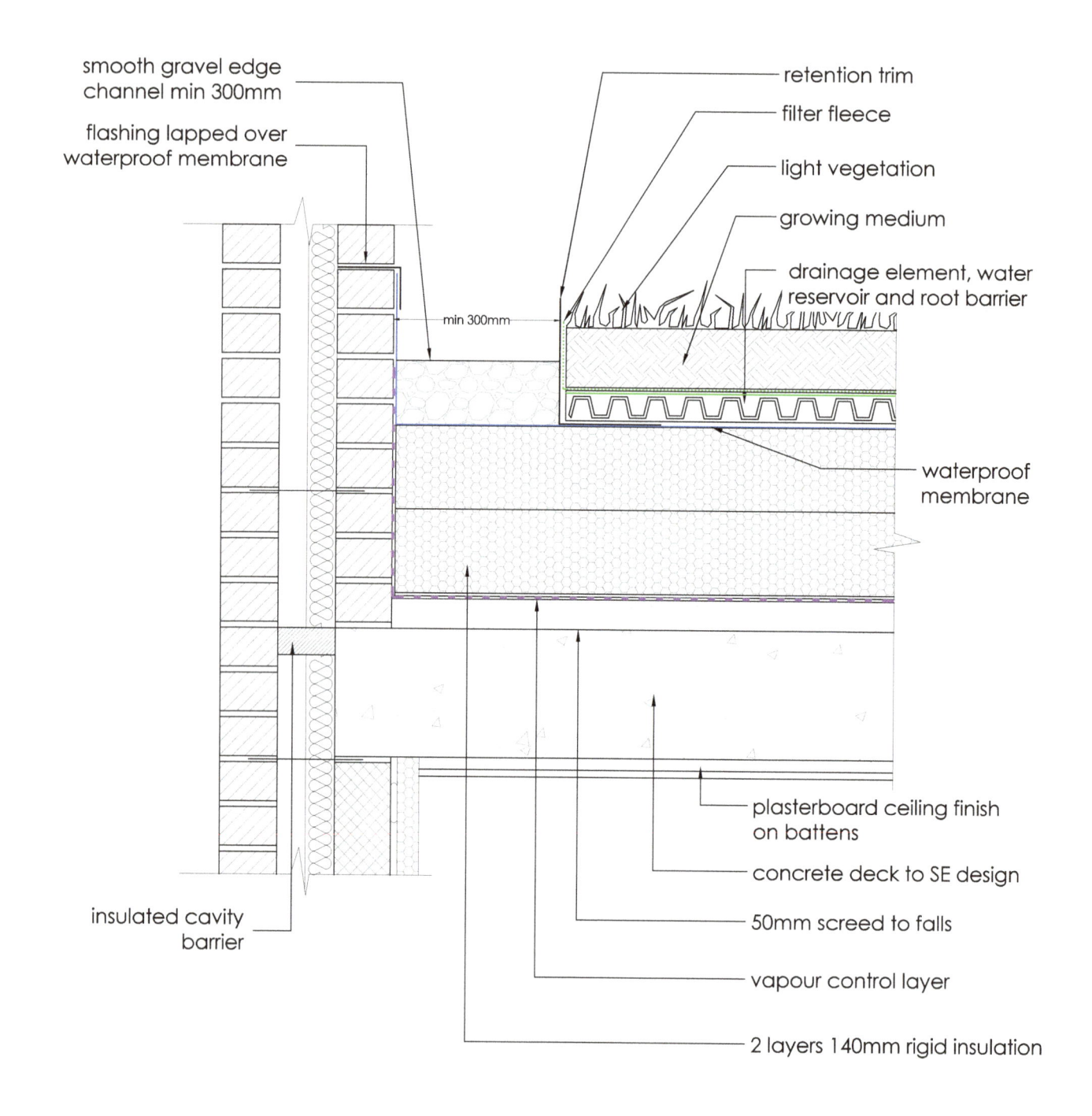

Labels (clockwise from top left):
- smooth gravel edge channel min 300mm
- flashing lapped over waterproof membrane
- min 300mm
- retention trim
- filter fleece
- light vegetation
- growing medium
- drainage element, water reservoir and root barrier
- waterproof membrane
- plasterboard ceiling finish on battens
- concrete deck to SE design
- 50mm screed to falls
- vapour control layer
- 2 layers 140mm rigid insulation
- insulated cavity barrier

Detail GR1 - Green roof, external masonry cavity wall, upstand to wall detail

NOTES:
U Value 0.13W/m²K or better

SECTION 10 - GREEN ROOF

3D Detail GR1 - Green roof, external masonry cavity wall, upstand to wall detail

GR2

GREEN ROOF, EXTERNAL MASONRY CAVITY WALL, PARAPET WALL DETAIL

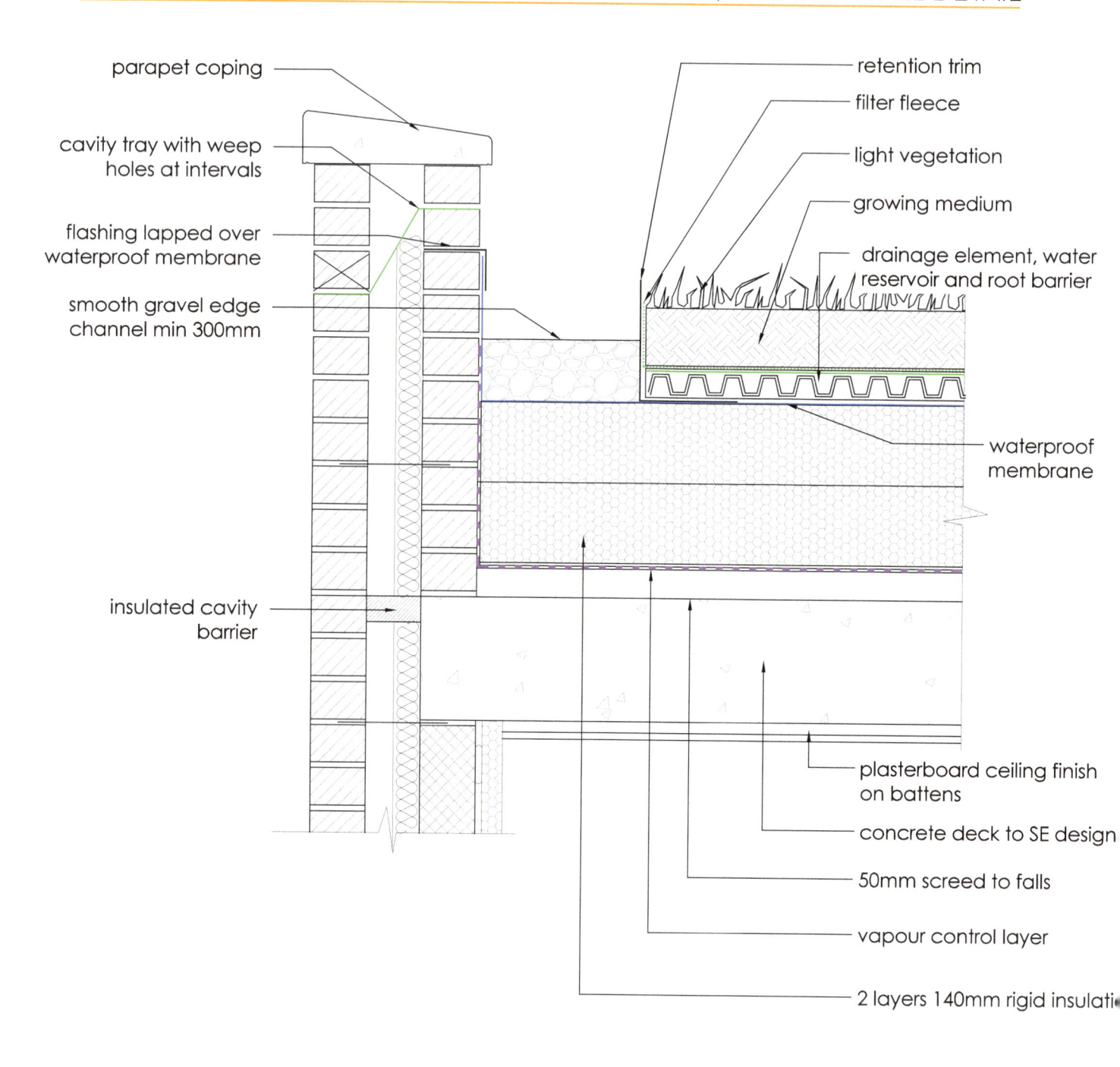

Labels (left side):
- parapet coping
- cavity tray with weep holes at intervals
- flashing lapped over waterproof membrane
- smooth gravel edge channel min 300mm
- insulated cavity barrier

Labels (right side):
- retention trim
- filter fleece
- light vegetation
- growing medium
- drainage element, water reservoir and root barrier
- waterproof membrane
- plasterboard ceiling finish on battens
- concrete deck to SE design
- 50mm screed to falls
- vapour control layer
- 2 layers 140mm rigid insulation

Detail GR2 - Green roof, external masonry cavity wall, parapet wall detail

NOTES:

U Value 0.13W/m²K or better

303

SECTION 10 - GREEN ROOF

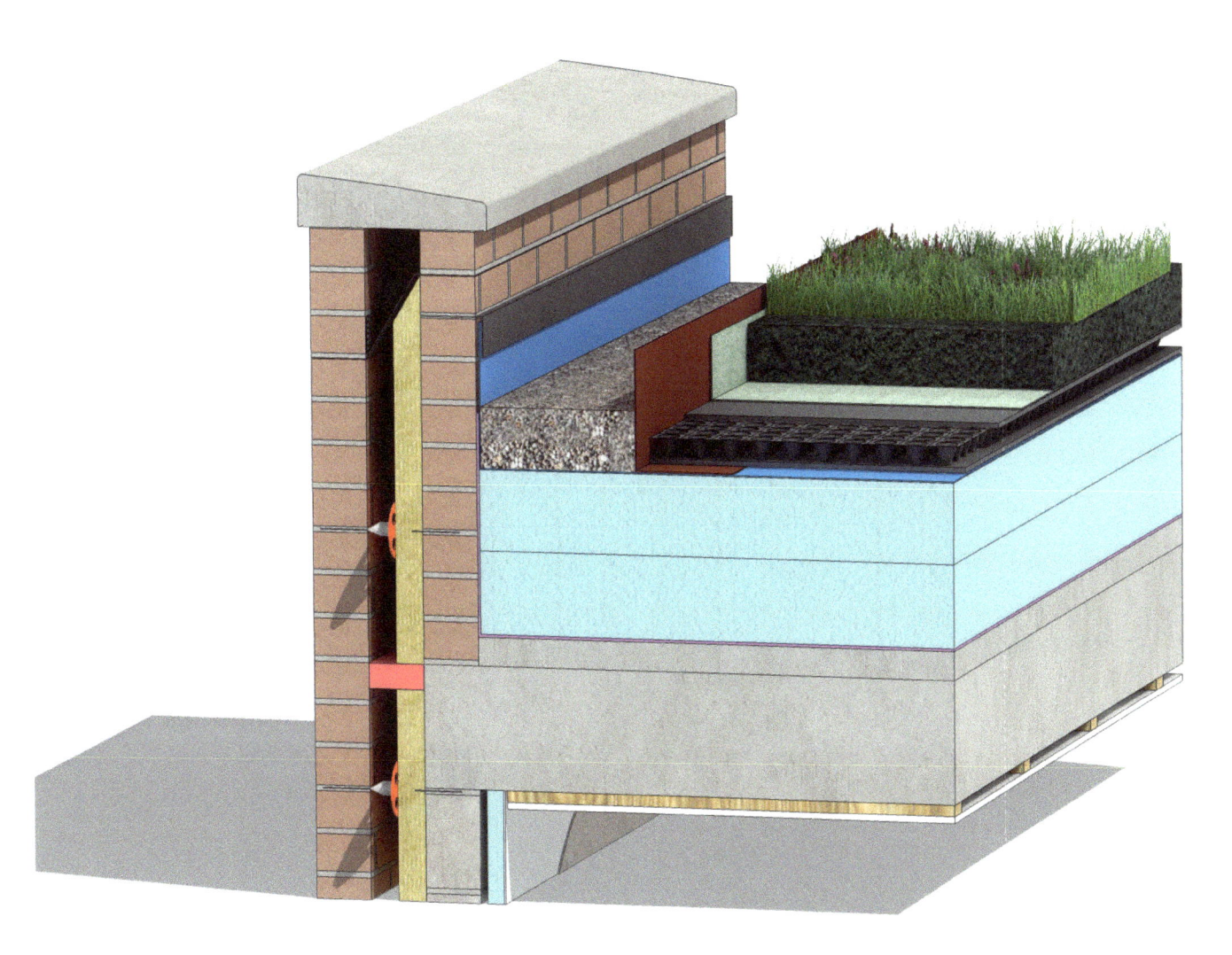

3D Detail GR2 - Green roof, external masonry cavity wall, parapet wall detail

GR3

GREEN ROOF, EXTERNAL MASONRY CAVITY WALL, KERB DETAIL

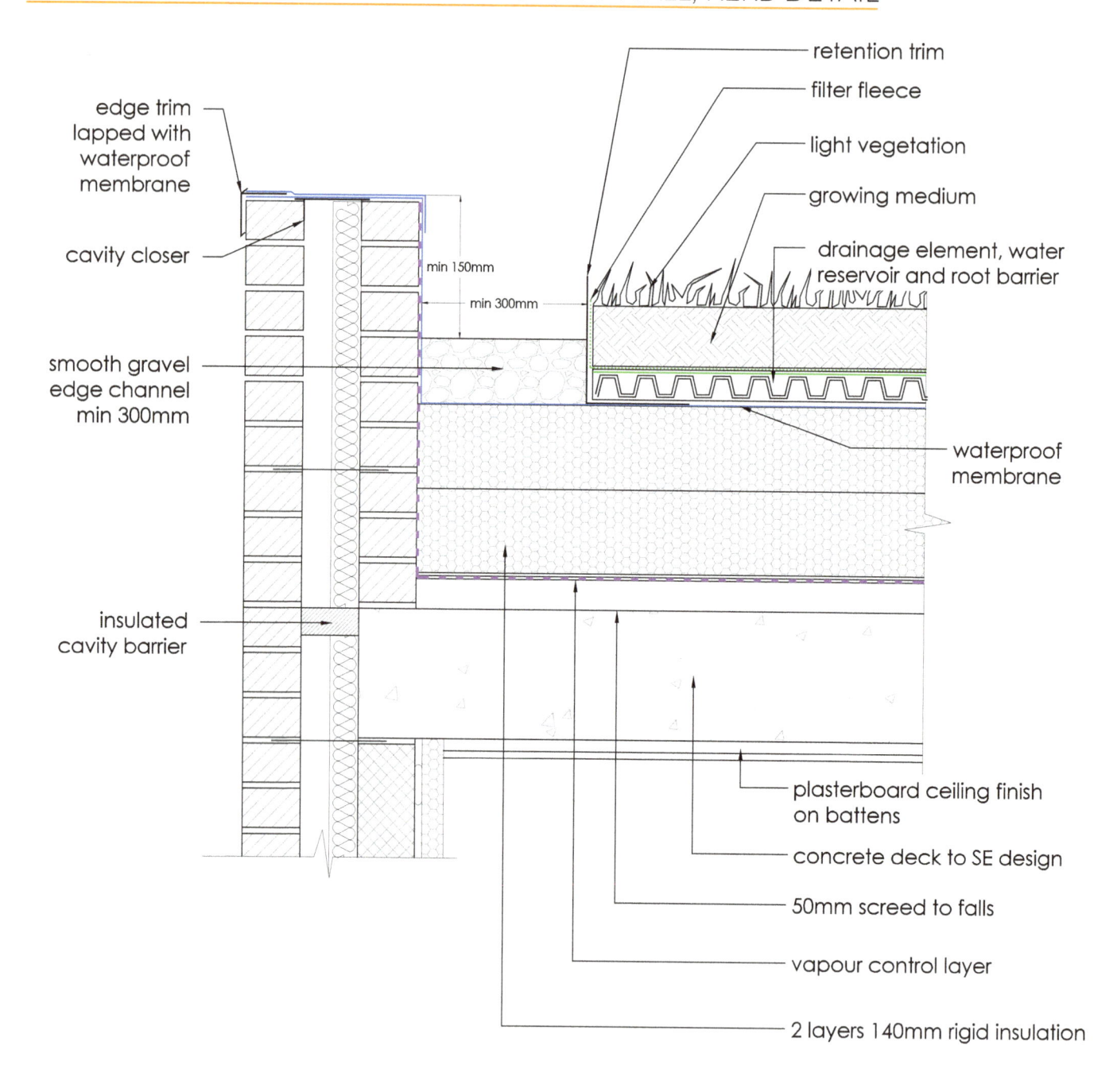

Labels (left side):
- edge trim lapped with waterproof membrane
- cavity closer
- smooth gravel edge channel min 300mm
- insulated cavity barrier

Labels (right side):
- retention trim
- filter fleece
- light vegetation
- growing medium
- drainage element, water reservoir and root barrier
- waterproof membrane
- plasterboard ceiling finish on battens
- concrete deck to SE design
- 50mm screed to falls
- vapour control layer
- 2 layers 140mm rigid insulation

Dimensions: min 150mm, min 300mm

Detail GR3 - Green roof, external masonry cavity wall, kerb detail

NOTES:
U Value 0.13W/m²K or better

3D Detail GR3 - Green roof, external masonry cavity wall, kerb detail

GR4

GREEN ROOF, EXTERNAL MASONRY CAVITY WALL, DRAINAGE DETAIL

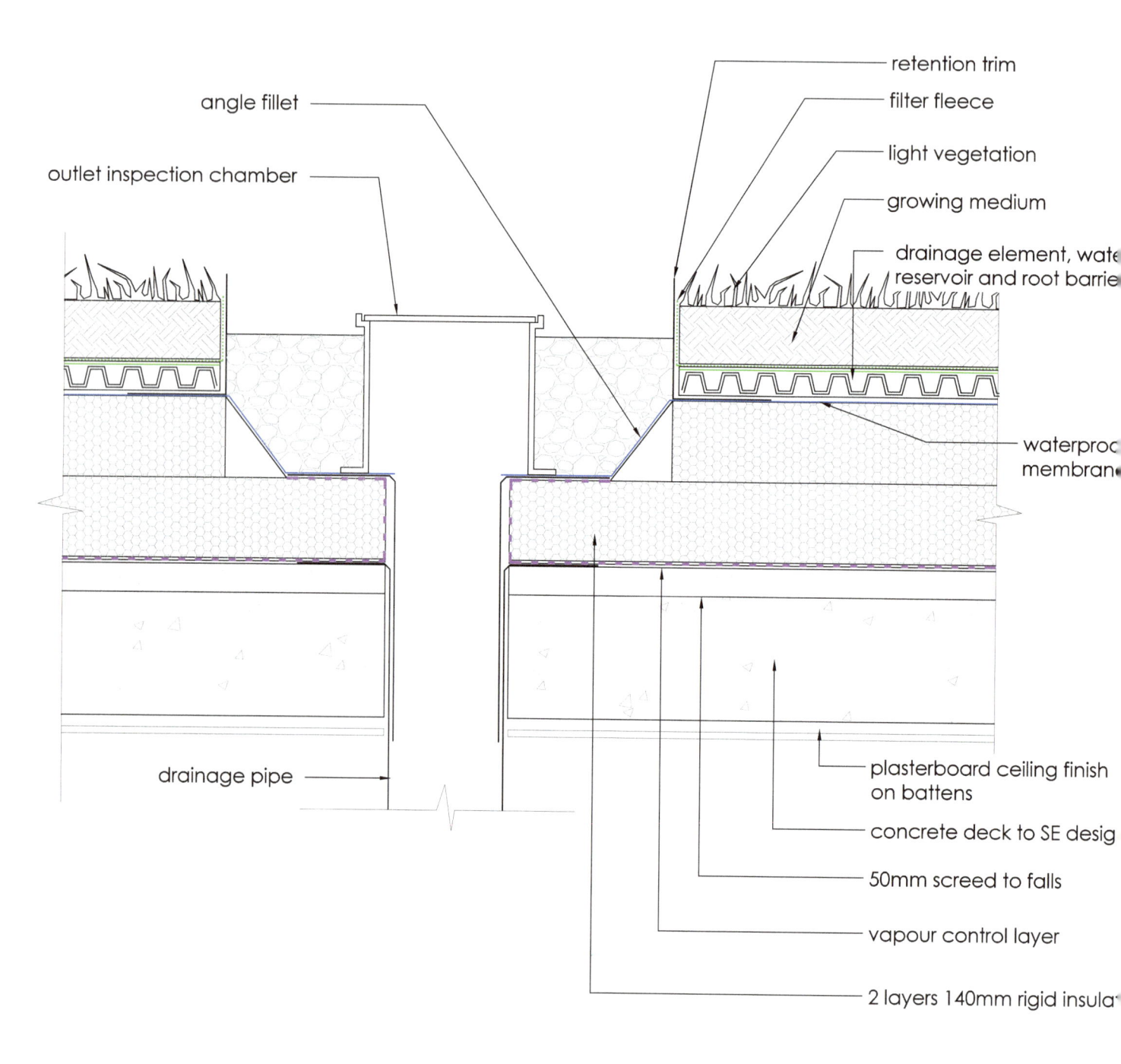

Labels (clockwise):
- outlet inspection chamber
- angle fillet
- retention trim
- filter fleece
- light vegetation
- growing medium
- drainage element, water reservoir and root barrier
- waterproof membrane
- plasterboard ceiling finish on battens
- concrete deck to SE design
- 50mm screed to falls
- vapour control layer
- 2 layers 140mm rigid insulation
- drainage pipe

Detail GR4 - Green roof, external masonry cavity wall, drainage detail

NOTES:

U Value 0.13W/m²K or better

SECTION 10 - GREEN ROOF

3D Detail GR4 - Green roof, external masonry cavity wall, drainage detail

SECTION 10 - GREEN ROOF

BIBLIOGRAPHY / FURTHER READING

BOOKS

Architects Pocket Book (Third Edition, 2008) - Charlotte Baden-Powell, Jonathan Hetreed, Ann Ross

Architecture in Detail II - Graham Bizley

Architectural Details 2003 - by Detail, Review of Architecture

Architectural Detailing; Function, Constructibility, Aesthetics; Edward Allen, Patrick Rand

Building Construction Handbook (Sixth Edition) - Roy Chudley, Roger Greeno

Building Regulations in Brief (Eighth Edition) - Ray Tricker, Samantha Alford

Barry's Introduction to Construction of Buildings (Third Edition) - Stephen Emmitt, Christopher A Gorse

Building Regulations in Brief - Ray Tricker, Samantha Alford

Construction Technology - Eric Fleming

Construction of Houses (Fifth Edition) - Duncan Marshall, Derek Worthing

Environmental Science in Building (Seventh Edition) - McMullan

Fundamental Building Technology - Andrew J Charlett, Craig Mayberry-Thomas

Materials for Architects & Builders (Fourth Edition) - Arthur Lyons

Robust Details Part E - Robust Details

Timber Frame Construction Manual (Fourth Edition) - TRADA

Consider well known manufactures who have a wide range of explanatory documentation relating to their products and systems.

INDEX

Figure Index

Figure 1.1 - Factors influencing the impact of the external environment ... 9
Figure 1.2 - Forces leading to moisture ingress ... 10
Figure 1.3 - Neutralising moisture ingress ... 10
Figure 1.4 - Deflection of airflow with a pitched roof overhang ... 11
Figure 1.5 - Table of U-values ... 13
Figure 1.6 - Table of thermal conductivity of common construction materials ... 14
Figure 1.7 - Forces driving airflow through the building enclosure ... 18
Figure 1.8 - Typical leakage paths ... 18
Figure 1.9 - Wind pressure effects ... 19
Figure 1.10 - Stack effect pressures ... 19
Figure 1.11 - Table A2 from Approved Document Part B, Fire Safety, Volume 1 Dwellinghouses ... 23
Figure 1.12 - Table A1 from Approved Document Part B, Fire Safety, Volume 1 Dwellinghouses ... 24
Figure 1.13 - Table A8 from Approved Document Part B, Fire Safety, Volume 1 Dwellinghouses ... 25
Figure 2.1 - Forces leading to moisture ingress ... 28
Figure 2.2 - Wash of a parapet coping stone ... 29
Figure 2.3 - Wash of a flat roof with insulation cut to falls ... 29
Figure 2.4 - Wash of a window sill ... 29
Figure 2.5 - Overlap of ridge tile ... 30
Figure 2.6 - Overlap flashing to roof light ... 30
Figure 2.7 - Overlap of roof tiles ... 30
Figure 2.8 - Overhang and drip of roof eaves ... 31
Figure 2.9 - Overhang and drip of window sill ... 31
Figure 2.10 - Overhang and drip of parapet coping stone ... 31
Figure 2.11 - Capillary break of a window flashing ... 32
Figure 2.13 - Drain and weep of a cavity wall ... 32
Figure 2.12 - Capillary break in a vertical panel joint ... 32
Figure 2.14 - Labyrinth in both vertical and horzontal joints between panels ... 33
Figure 2.15 - Vapour control layer ... 34
Figure 2.16 - Breather membrane ... 34
Figure 2.17- Insulated plasterboard ... 37
reveal to window head ... 37
Figure 2.18- Insulated plasterboard reveal and ... 37
PU/PIR insulated cavity closer to window jamb ... 37
Figure 2.19- Cavity closer with PU/PIR insulation core, insulation under internal window sill ... 37
Figure 2.20- Increased eaves insulation ... 38
Figure 2.21- Perimeter insulation to concrete slab and lightweight blockwork to innerleaf ... 38
Figure 2.22- Additional insulation on inside face of a timber frame and steel frame construction ... 38
Figure 3.1 - Typical hardwoods and softwoods ... 46
Figure 3.2- Typical thermal conductivity of insulation materials ... 57
Figure 4.1 - Soil types and suitability ... 59
Figure 4.2 - Minimum width of concrete strip foundations ... 61
Figure 4.3 - Examples of strip foundation ... 61
Figure 4.4 - Examples of pile, pad and raft foundations ... 62
Figure 5.1 - Ground bearing concrete floor ... 65
Figure 5.2 - Beam and block floor ... 66
Figure 5.3 - I beams and web joists ... 67

Figure 5.4 - Insulated lintel ... 70
Figure 5.5 - Parts of a roof ... 71
Figure 5.6 - Couple roof and close couple roof ... 72
Figure 5.7 - Collar roof and purlin roof ... 73
Figure 5.8 - Eaves example ... 74
Figure 5.9 - Cold roof example ... 75
Figure 5.10 - Warm roof example ... 75
Figure 5.11 - Ventilation through the roof using cross flow ventilator ... 76
Figure 5.12 - Parapet wall example ... 78
Figure 6.1 - Example of ground bearing concrete floor ... 174
Figure 6.2 - Examples of I beams and web joists ... 175
Figure 6.3 - Openings in a stud wall ... 176
Figure 7.1 - Example of steel frame construction ... 237
Figure 6.1 - Example of SIP construction ... 259
Figure 8.1 - Example of green roof ... 299

2D Details Index

Detail M-G1 - External masonry cavity wall, ground bearing concrete slab, insulation below slab 79
Detail M-G1A- External masonry cavity wall, ground bearing concrete slab, insulation below slab, cavity foundation wall option 81
Detail M-G2 - External masonry cavity wall, ground bearing concrete slab, insulation above slab 83
Detail M-G2A - External masonry cavity wall, ground bearing concrete raft, insulation above slab 85
Detail M-G3 - External masonry cavity wall, suspended concrete slab, insulation below slab 87
Detail M-G4 - External masonry cavity wall, beam and block floor 89
Detail M-G5 - External masonry cavity wall, suspended timber floor 91
Detail M-G6 - Ground floor build up option - timber floor on battens 93
Detail M-G7 - Ground floor build up option - timber floating floor 94
Detail M-G8 - Ground floor build up option - screed finish, insulation under slab 95
Detail M-G9 - Ground floor build up option - screed finish, insulation over slab 96
Detail M-G10 - Underfloor heating - suspended timber floor 97
Detail M-G11 - Underfloor heating - timber floor on battens 98
Detail M-G12 - Underfloor heating - screed finish, insulation over slab 99
Detail M-G13 - External masonry cavity wall, timber intermediate floor 101
Detail M-G14 - External masonry cavity wall, timber intermediate floor with sound insulation 103
Detail M-G15 - External masonry cavity wall, concrete separating floor 105
Detail M-W1 - External masonry cavity wall, render finish 109
Detail M-W2 - External masonry cavity wall, insulated render finish 111
Detail M-W3 - External masonry cavity wall, horiztonal timber cladding 113
Detail M-W4 - External masonry cavity wall, vertical timber cladding 115
Detail M-W5 - External masonry cavity wall, patial fill, insulated plasterboard 117
Detail M-W6 - Solid masonry wall, external render, insulated plasterboard 119
Detail M-W7 - Party wall to achieve zero U-value (plan) 121
Detail M-W8 - External masonry cavity wall, window head, solid timber window 123
Detail M-W9 - External masonry cavity wall, window sill, solid timber window 124
Detail M-W10 - External masonry cavity wall, window jamb (plan) 125
Detail M-W11 - External masonry cavity wall, render finish, window head 126
Detail M-W12 - External masonry cavity wall, render finish, window sill 127
Detail M-W13 - External masonry cavity wall, render finish, window jamb (plan) 128
Detail M-W14- External masonry cavity wall, horizontal timber cladding, window head 129
Detail M-W15 - External masonry cavity wall, horizontal timber cladding, window sill 130
Detail M-W16- External masonry cavity wall, horizontal timber cladding, window jamb (plan) 131
Detail M-W17 - External masonry cavity wall, vertical timber cladding, window head 132
Detail M-W18- External masonry cavity wall, vertcal timber cladding, window sill 133
Detail M-W19 - External masonry cavity wall, vertical timber cladding, window jamb (plan) 134
Detail M-W20 - External masonry cavity wall, insulation below slab, door threshold 135
Detail M-W21 - External masonry cavity wall, insulation above slab, door threshold 137
Detail M-W22 - External masonry cavity wall, suspended timber floor, door threshold 139
Detail M-R1 - External masonry cavity wall, eaves detail, ventilated roof space, insulation between and over ceiling joists 143
Detail M-R2 - External masonry cavity wall, gable detail, ventilated roof space, insulation between and over ceiling joists 145
Detail M-R3 - External masonry cavity wall, eaves detail, insulation between and under rafters 147
Detail M-R4 - External masonry cavity wall, gable detail, insulation between and under rafters 149
Detail M-R5 - External masonry cavity wall, eaves detail, insulation between and over rafters 151
Detail M-R6A - External masonry cavity wall, flat roof, insulation above roof deck 153
Detail M-R6B - External masonry cavity wall, flat roof, warm deck, eaves detail 155

Detail	Page
Detail M-R7 - External masonry cavity wall, flat roof with parapet, insulation above joists	157
Detail M-R8 - External masonry cavity wall, flat roof with parapet, insulation above joists - alternatvie coping detail	159
Detail M-R9 - Roof light detail, warm roof, insulation between and under rafters	161
Detail M-R10 - Flat roof, roof light detail, insulation above roof deck	163
Detail M-R11 - Ridge detail, bedded ridge, unvented	165
Detail M-R12 - Ridge detail, ventilated	167
Detail M-R13 - Valley detail, ventilated roof space	169
Detail T-G1 - Timber frame wall, ground bearing concrete slab, insulation below slab	179
Detail T-G2 - Timber frame wall, ground bearing concrete slab, insulation above slab	181
Detail T-G3 - Timber frame wall, suspended concrete slab, insulation below slab	183
Detail T-G4 - Timber frame wall, beam and block floor	185
Detail T-G5 - Timber frame wall, suspended timber floor	187
Detail T-G6 - Timber frame wall, timber intermediate floor, joists perpendicular to wall	189
Detail T-G7 - Timber frame wall, timber separating floor, joists parallel to wall	191
Detail T-W1 - Timber frame wall, brick cladding	195
Detail T-W2 - Timber frame wall, brick cladding, insulated sheathing board	197
Detail T-W3 - Timber frame wall, render finish, insulated plasterboard	199
Detail T-W4 - Timber frame wall, horizontal timber cladding, insulation over sheathing	201
Detail T-W5 - Timber frame wall, vertical timber cladding, insulated plasterboard	203
Detail T-W6 - Timber frame party wall, to achieve zero u value	205
Detail T-W7 - Timber frame wall, brick cladding, window head	207
Detail T-W8 - Timber frame wall, brick cladding, window sill	208
Detail T-W9 - Timber frame wall, brick cladding, window jamb (plan)	209
Detail T-W10 - Timber frame wall, render finish, window head	210
Detail T-W11 - Timber frame wall, render finish, window sill	211
Detail T-W12 - Timber frame wall, render finish, window jamb	212
Detail T-W13 - Timber frame wall, horizontal timber cladding, window head	213
Detail T-W14 - Timber frame wall, horizontal timber cladding, window sill	214
Detail T-W15 - Timber frame wall, horizontal timber cladding, window jamb	215
Detail T-W16 - Timber frame wall, vertical timber cladding, window head	216
Detail T-W17 - Timber frame wall, vertical timber cladding, window sill	217
Detail T-W18 - Timber frame wall, vertical timber cladding, window jamb (plan)	218
Detail T-R1- Timber frame wall, eaves detail, insulation between and over ceiling joists	221
Detail T-R2- Timber frame wall, gable detail, insulation between and over ceiling joists	223
Detail T-R3- Timber frame wall, eaves detail, insulation between and under rafters	225
Detail T-R4- Timber frame wall, gable detail, insulation between and under rafters	227
Detail T-R5- Timber frame wall, eaves detail, insulation between and over rafters	229
Detail T-R6- Timber frame wall, flat roof, insulation above roof deck	231
Detail T-R7- Timber frame wall, flat roof with parapet, insulation above joists	233
Detail S-G1 - Steel frame wall, ground bearing concrete slab, insulation below slab	239
Detail S-G2 - Steel frame wall, ground bearing concrete slab, insulation above slab	241
Detail S-G3 - Steel frame wall, timber intermediate floor	243
Detail S-G4 - Steel frame wall, timber separating floor	245
Detail S-W1 - Steel frame wall, brick cladding	247
Detail S-W2 - Steel frame wall, brick cladding (plan view)	249
Detail S-W3 - Steel frame wall, rendered blockwork	249
Detail S-W4 - Steel frame wall, brick cladding, window head and cill	251
Detail S-R1 - Steel frame wall, eaves detail, ventilated roof space (cold roof)	253
Detail S-R2 - Steel frame wall, eaves detail, unventilated roof space, insulation between and under rafters	255
Detail SIP1 - SIP - Brick cladding, ground bearing concrete slab, insulation below slab	261

Detail SIP1A - SIP - Brick cladding, ground bearing concrete slab, Enhanced DPC DPM detail   262
Detail SIP2 - SIP - Timber cladding, ground bearing concrete slab, insulation above slab   263
Detail SIP3 - SIP - Timber cladding, ground bearing concrete slab, insulation above slab - alternative detail   265
Detail SIP4 - SIP - Horizontal timber cladding   267
Detail SIP5 - SIP - Horizontal timber cladding, improved thermal performance   267
Detail SIP6 - SIP - Render finish   269
Detail SIP7 - SIP - Brick cladding - improved thermal performance   269
Detail SIP8 - SIP - Brick cladding, door threshold   271
Detail SIP9 - SIP - Brick cladding, window head and cill   273
Detail SIP10 - SIP - Brick cladding, first floor detail   275
Detail SIP11 - SIP - Brick cladding, eaves detail, attic as usable space   277
Detail SIP12 - SIP - Brick cladding, verge and soffit detail (gable)   279
Detail SIP13 - SIP - Brick cladding, eaves detail - improved thermal performance   281
Detail ICF1 - ICF - Strip and block foundation with ground bearing slab   285
Detail ICF2 - ICF - strip foundation with ground bearing slab   287
Detail ICF3 - ICF - Precast concrete intermediate floor   289
Detail ICF4 - ICF - Window head and cill   291
Detail ICF5 - ICF - Flat roof detail   293
Detail ICF6 - ICF - Pitched roof detail   295
Detail GR1 - Green roof, external masonry cavity wall, upstand to wall detail   301
Detail GR2 - Green roof, external masonry cavity wall, parapet wall detail   303
Detail GR3 - Green roof, external masonry cavity wall, kerb detail   305
Detail GR4 - Green roof, external masonry cavity wall, drainage detail   307

3D Details Index

3D Detail M-G1 - External masonry cavity wall, ground bearing concrete slab, insulation below slab 80

3D Detail M-G1A - External masonry cavity wall, ground bearing concrete slab, insulation below slab, cavity foundation wall option 82

3D Detail M-G2 - External masonry cavity wall, ground bearing concrete slab, insulation above slab 84

3D Detail M-G2A - External masonry cavity wall, ground bearing concrete raft, insulation above slab 86

3D Detail M-G3 - External masonry cavity wall, suspended concrete slab, insulation below slab 88

3D Detail M-G4 - External masonry cavity wall, beam and block floor 90

3D Detail M-G5 - External masonry cavity wall, suspended timber floor 92

3D Detail M-G6 - Ground floor build up option - timber floor on battens 93

3D Detail M-G7 - Ground floor build up option - timber floating floor 94

3D Detail M-G8 - Ground floor build up option - screed finish, insulation under slab 95

3D Detail M-G9 - Ground floor build up option - screed finish, insulation over slab 96

3D Detail M-G10 - Underfloor heating - suspended timber floor 97

3D Detail M-G11 - Underfloor heating - timber floor on battens 98

3D Detail M-G12 - Underfloor heating - screed finish, insulation over slab 99

3D Detail M-G13 - External masonry cavity wall, timber intermediate floor 102

3D Detail M-G14 - External masonry cavity wall, timber intermediate floor with sound insulation 104

3D Detail M-G15 - External masonry cavity wall, concrete separating floor 106

3D Detail M-W1 - External masonry cavity wall, render finish 110

3D Detail M-W2 - External masonry cavity wall, insulated render finish 112

3D Detail M-W3 - External masonry cavity wall, horizontal timber cladding 114

3D Detail M-W4 - External masonry cavity wall, vertical timber cladding 116

3D Detail M-W5 - External masonry cavity wall, partial fill, insulated plasterboard 118

3D Detail M-W6 - Sold masonry wall, external render, insulated plasterboard 120

3D Detail M-W7 - Party wall to achieve zero U-value 122

3D Detail M-W8 - External masonry cavity wall, window head solid timber window 123

3D Detail M-W9 - External masonry cavity wall, window sill, solid timber window 124

3D Detail M-W10 - External masonry cavity wall, window jamb 125

3D Detail M-W11 - External masonry cavity wall, render finish, window head 126

3D Detail M-W12 - External masonry cavity wall, render finish, window sill 127

3D Detail M-W13 - External masonry cavity wall, render finish, window jamb 128

3D Detail M-W14 - External masonry cavity wall, horizontal timber cladding, window head 129

3D Detail M-W15 - External masonry cavity wall, horizontal timber cladding, window sill 130

3D Detail M-W16 - External masonry cavity wall, horizontal timber cladding, window jamb 131

3D Detail M-W17 - External masonry cavity wall, vertical timber cladding, window head 132

3D Detail M-W18 - External masonry cavity wall, vertical timber cladding, window sill 133

3D Detail M-W19 - External masonry cavity wall, vertical timber cladding, window jamb 134

3D Detail M-W20 - External masonry cavity wall, insulation below slab, door threshold 136

3D Detail M-W21 - External masonry cavity wall, insulation above slab, door threshold 138

3D Detail M-W22 - External masonry cavity wall, suspended timber floor, door threshold 140

3D Detail M-R1 - External masonry cavity wall, eaves detail, ventilated roof space, insulation between and over ceiling joists 144

3D Detail M-R2 - External masonry cavity wall, gable detail, ventilated roof space, insulation between and over ceiling joists 146

3D Detail M-R3 - External masonry cavity wall, eaves detail, insulation between and under rafters 148

3D Detail M-R4 - External masonry cavity wall, gable detail, insulation between and under rafters 150
3D Detail M-R5 - External masonry cavity wall, eaves detail, insulation between and over rafters 152
3D Detail M-R6A - External masonry cavity wall, flat roof, insulation above roof deck 154
3D Detail M-R6B - External masonry cavity wall, flat roof, warm deck, eaves detail 156
3D Detail M-R7 - External masonry cavity wall, flat roof with parapet, insulation above joists 158
3D Detail M-R8 - External masonry cavity wall, flat roof with parapet, insulation above joists - alternative coping detail 160
3D Detail M-R9 - Roof light detail, warm roof, insulation between and under rafters 162
3D Detail M-R10 - Flat roof - Roof light detail, insulation above roof deck 164
3D Detail M-R11 - Ridge detail, bedded ridge, unvented 166
3D Detail M-R12 - Ridge detail, ventilated 168
3D Detail M-R13 - Valley detail, ventilated roof space 170
3D Detail T-G1 - Timber frame wall, ground bearing concrete slab, insulation below slab 180
3D Detail T-G2 - Timber frame wall, ground bearing concrete slab, insulation above slab 182
3D Detail T-G3 - Timber frame wall, suspended concrete slab, insulation below slab 184
3D Detail T-G4 - Timber frame wall, beam and block floor 186
3D Detail T-G5 - Timber frame wall, suspended timber floor 188
3D Detail T-G6 - Timber frame wall, timber intermediate floor, joists perpendicular to wall 190
3D Detail T-G7 - Timber frame wall, timber separating floor, joists parallel to wall 192
3D Detail T-W1- Timber frame wall, brick cladding 196
3D Detail T-W2 - Timber frame wall, brick cladding, insulated sheathing board 198
3D Detail T-W3 - Timber frame wall, render finish, insulated plasterboard 200
3D Detail T-W4 - Timber frame wall, horizontal timber cladding, insulation over sheathing 202
3D Detail T-W5 - Timber frame wall, vertical timber cladding, insulated plasterboard 204
3D Detail T-W6 - Timber frame party wall, to achieve zero u value 206
3D Detail T-W7 - Timber frame wall, brick cladding, window head 207
3D Detail T-W8 - Timber frame wall, brick cladding, window sill 208
3D Detail T-W9 - Timber frame wall, brick cladding, window jamb 209
3D Detail T-W10 - Timber frame wall, render finish, window head 210
3D Detail T-W11 - Timber frame wall, render finish, window sill 211
3D Detail T-W12 - Timber frame wall, render finish, window jamb 212
3D Detail T-W13 - Timber frame wall, horizontal timber cladding, window head 213
3D Detail T-W14 - Timber frame wall, horizontal timber cladding, window sill 214
3D Detail T-W15 - Timber frame wall, horizontal timber cladding, window jamb 215
3D Detail T-W16 - Timber frame wall, vertical timber cladding, window head 216
3D Detail T-W17 - Timber frame wall, vertical timber cladding, window sill 217
3D Detail T-W18 - Timber frame wall, vertical timber cladding, window jamb 218
3D Detail T-R1- Timber frame wall, eaves detail, insulation between and over ceiling joists 222
3D Detail T-R2- Timber frame wall, gable detail, insulation between and over ceiling joists 224
3D Detail T-R3- Timber frame wall, eaves detail, insulation between and under rafters 226
3D Detail T-R4- Timber frame wall, gable detail, insulation between and under rafters 228
3D Detail T-R5- Timber frame wall, eaves detail, insulation between and over rafters 230
3D Detail T-R6- Timber frame wall, flat roof, insulation above roof deck 232
3D Detail T-R7- Timber frame wall, flat roof with parapet, insulation above joists 234
3D Detail S-G1- Steel frame wall, ground bearing concrete slab, insulation below slab 240
3D Detail S-G2- Steel frame wall, ground bearing concrete slab, insulation above slab 242
3D Detail S-G3- Steel frame wall, timber intermediate floor 244
3D Detail S-G4- Steel frame wall, timber separating floor 246
3D Detail S-W1 - Steel frame wall, brick cladding 248
3D Detail S-W3 - Steel frame wall, rendered blockwork 250

3D Detail S-W4 - Steel frame wall, brick cladding, window head and cill	252
3D Detail S-R1 - Steel frame wall, eaves detail, ventilated roof space (cold roof)	254
3D Detail S-R2 - Steel frame wall, eaves detail, unventilated roof space, insulation between and under rafters	256
3D Detail SIP1 - SIP - Brick cladding, ground bearing concrete slab, insulation below slab	262
3D Detail SIP2 - SIP - Timber cladding, insulation above slab	264
3D Detail SIP3 - SIP - Timber cladding, insulation above slab - alternative detail	266
3D Detail SIP4 - SIP - Horizontal timber cladding	268
3D Detail SIP5 - SIP - Horizontal timber cladding - improved thermal performance	268
3D Detail SIP6 - SIP - Render finish	270
3D Detail SIP7 - SIP - Brick cladding - improved thermal performance	270
3D Detail SIP8 - SIP - Brick cladding, door threshold	272
3D Detail SIP9 - SIP - Brick cladding, window head and cill	274
3D Detail SIP10 - SIP - Brick cladding, first floor detail	276
3D Detail SIP11 - SIP - Brick cladding, eaves detail, attic as usable space	278
3D Detail SIP12 - SIP - Brick cladding, verge and soffit detail (gable)	280
3D Detail SIP13 - SIP - Brick cladding, eaves detail - improved thermal performance	282
3D Detail ICF1 - ICF - Strip and block foundation with ground bearing slab	286
3D Detail ICF2 - ICF - strip foundation with ground bearing slab	288
3D Detail ICF3 - ICF - Precast concrete intermediate floor	290
3D Detail ICF4 - ICF - Window head and cill	292
3D Detail ICF5 - ICF - Flat roof detail	294
3D Detail ICF6 - ICF - Pitched roof detail	296
3D Detail GR1 - Green roof, external masonry cavity wall, upstand to wall detail	302
3D Detail GR2 - Green roof, external masonry cavity wall, parapet wall detail	304
3D Detail GR3 - Green roof, external masonry cavity wall, kerb detail	306
3D Detail GR4 - Green roof, external masonry cavity wall, drainage detail	308

End

Note all insulation thicknesses should be calculated in order to achieve required u-values, according to building regulation standards.
All structural members should be calculated and assessed by a structural engineer.
These drawings MUST NOT be used as construction drawings, and are purely an educational resource.
These drawings are not finished or complete construction drawings and should not be used as such.
To read the full terms of use follow this link: http://www.firstinarchitecture.co.uk/about/terms-of-use/

All details can be purchased in dwg and skp format from
www.firstinarchitecture.co.uk
Email: emma@firstinarchitecture.co.uk

All images copyright to 'Understanding Architectural Details', Emma Walshaw. First In Architecture

Lightning Source UK Ltd.
Milton Keynes UK
UKHW051852140721
387163UK00004B/62

9 781916 334304